Mass Media and Society

Third Edition

Edited by
James Curran
Professor of Communications, Goldsmiths College,
University of London
and
Michael Gurevitch
Professor, College of Journalism, University of Maryland

ARNOLD

A member of the Hodder Headline Group
LONDON
Co-published in the United States of America by
Oxford University Press Inc., New York

First published in Great Britain in 1991
Second edition published in 1996
Third edition published in 2000 by
Arnold, a member of the Hodder Headline Group
338 Euston Road, London NW1 3BH

http: //www.arnoldpublishers.com

Co-published in the United States of America by
Oxford University Press Inc.,
198 Madison Avenue, New York NY10016

The advice and information in this book are believed to be true
and accurate at the date of going to press, but neither the authors
nor the publisher can accept any legal responsibility or liability
for any errors or omissions.

British Library Cataloguing in Publication Data
A catalogue record for this book is available from the British Library

Library of Congress Cataloging-in-Publication Data
A catalog record for this book is available from the Library of Congress

ISBN 0 340 73201 6 (pb)

1 2 3 4 5 6 7 8 9 10

Production Editor: Wendy Rooke
Production Controller: Iain McWilliams

Typeset in 10pt Times by J&L Composition Ltd, Filey
Printed and bound in Great Britain by MPG Books Ltd, Bodmin

What do you think about this book? Or any other Arnold title?
Please send your comments to feedback.arnold@hodder.co.uk

Contents

Section III: Mediation of Meaning

List of Contributors

Jay G. Blumler, Professor Emeritus, University of Leeds and University of Maryland

Joseph Man Chan, Professor, Department of Journalism and Communication, Chinese University of Hong Kong

John Corner, Professor of Communication, University of Liverpool

James Curran, Professor of Communications, Goldsmiths College, University of London

Peter Dahlgren, Professor of Media and Communication, Lund University

Simon Frith, Professor of Film and Media, University of Stirling

Oscar H. Gandy Jr, Professor of Communication, Annenberg School, University of Pennsylvania

Christine Geraghty, Head of the Department of Media and Communications Studies, Goldsmiths College, University of London

Peter Golding, Professor of Sociology, University of Loughborough

Michael Gurevitch, Professor, College of Journalism, University of Maryland

Daniel C. Hallin, Professor of Communication, University of California, San Diego

Chin-Chuan Lee, Professor of Journalism and Mass Communication, University of Minnesota

Judith Lichtenberg, Associate Professor, Department of Philosophy and Institute for Philosophy and Public Policy, University of Maryland

Angela McRobbie, Professor of Communications, Goldsmiths College, University of London

Graham Murdock, Reader in Sociology of Culture, University of Loughborough

Keith Negus, Lecturer in Media and Communications, Goldsmiths College, University of London

Zhongdang Pan, Associate Professor of Journalism and Communication, Chinese University of Hong Kong

Andrea L. Press, Associate Professor, Institute of Communication Research, University of Illinois

Patria Román-Velázquez, Lecturer in Communications and Media Studies, Department of Sociology, City University, London

David Rowe, Associate Professor in Media and Cultural Studies, Department of Leisure and Tourism Studies, University of Newcastle, Australia

Michael Schudson, Professor of Communication, University of California, San Diego

Clement Y.K. So, Associate Professor of Journalism and Communication, Chinese University of Hong Kong

Colin Sparks, Professor of Media Studies, University of Westminster

Annabelle Sreberny, Professor, Centre for Mass Communication Research, University of Leicester

Acknowledgements

The editors and publishers would like to thank the following for permission to use copyright material in this book:

The World Bank for Table 5.1 from *UNESCO Statistical Yearbook*, 1993; The UNESCO Press for Table 5.2 from *UNESCO Statistical Yearbook*, © UNESCO, 1989 and for Table 5.3 from *World Communication Report*, © UNESCO, 1989; Oxford University Press for data for Table 5.4 from *Human Development Report 1994*; KGTV, San Diego for Figure 10.1.

Introduction

This third edition of *Mass Media and Society* continues what by now might be regarded as a mini-tradition – that of offering, every five years or so, a revised and updated version of a book exploring the finest current thinking in the field of media and society. When the first edition was published under this title in 1990 we saw it as a continuation of the earlier reader, of the same title, produced in 1977 to accompany the Open University's course on 'Mass Communication and Society'. When the second, revised edition was issued in 1995 it began to exhibit the makings of a 'mini-series' with a life of its own, unrelated to its original Open University origins. This third edition betrays little genetic relationship to its ancient great-grandparent.

The co-conspirators involved in this enterprise may have had different reasons for returning every few years to the task of preparing yet another edition. The publishers may have considered the prospect of building on the previous editions' proven track record. Indeed, the reception accorded to the first and the second editions of this book has been gratifying. The book has been reprinted several times and translated into Chinese, Korean, Greek and Japanese. As editors, we too were pleased by the range and diversity of the readers and users of this collection, be they instructors, students or others who apparently found it useful. As editors we also had other, more academic motives. Cognizant of the fluid and fast-developing nature of the field we thought it appropriate to update this collection in order to capture, with every new edition, the changing contours of the field. We regarded each new edition as a snapshot of the preoccupations of scholars working on issues of media and society, and sought not only to identify the current state of the field but also to establish, cumulatively, a picture of its historical development.

The first edition was published in the heyday of the debate in media studies between a liberal pluralist and a critical marxist/neo-marxist perspective. This debate was foregrounded in the first edition and also served as background for many of the essays presented therein. The second, follow-up edition took on board changes resulting from the rise of the 'new revisionism' in media studies. This third edition has a major transfusion of new blood – new contributors with fresh perspectives, and different concerns and preoccupations. It presents eleven new essays; in addition, almost all of the chapters published in the earlier editions and reappearing here have been revised and updated, in major or minor ways.

Does this collection of essays merely reflect changes in the field or does it contribute, perhaps in a small way, to defining the terrain of the field and nudging it in a certain direction? Our hope, of course, is that it does both, but especially the latter. It could be argued that media studies forever risk becoming imprisoned inside their own specialized and somewhat narrow concerns, focusing primarily on the mass media. It hardly needs saying that such a focus seems rather quaint and dated in an era engulfed by the entry of new communication technologies into our lives, with their myriad consequences for the conduct of social, political and economic, as well as inter-personal, communication. Media studies are therefore in need of constant, vigilant updating, lest the field be isolated not only from the realities of the turbulent changes in the 'real world' but also from the new ideas and perspectives bubbling up in cognate areas.

While the structure of the book conforms to that of the earlier editions, we open this new edition with three essays that link the study of the media to the analysis of three primary axes of media and social research: class, gender and race. These concerns are not new, of course, but (in varying degrees) each of these essays, by Murdock, Press and Gandy draws upon and introduces ideas and frameworks developed outside media research but potentially capable of enriching it. We also included in this first section two essays inherited from the earlier edition – Golding and Murdock's update of their overview of the political economy perspective on the media and Sreberny's discussion of the counterpulls, the global and the local, in international communication. Curran's revision of his essay on democracy and the media illustrates how rapidly ideas and thinking have shifted, requiring a significant reconstruction of his central arguments. Likewise, the new chapter by Blumler and Gurevitch explores the need for rethinking the conceptual frameworks for the study of political communication in view of the profound changes in the social, political and technological environment in which political communication processes take place.

Another strand developed in the second edition and further continued here is the significance of the link between media and cultural studies. Curiously (but perhaps not surprisingly) journalism and literary fiction have historically been regarded as separate, almost oppositional genres, obeying different guidelines and aiming at different goals. Consequently, the study of these different genres was also guided by different paradigms. Recognition of the common roots of these two forms of story-telling came fairly late to journalism studies (and may still not be universally acknowledged even today by journalism's practitioners and researchers). Hence the importance of continuing to build and strengthen the connections between media research and cultural studies. But an even more obvious reason for exploring the family relationship between journalistic and non-journalistic forms of story-telling is the increasing blurring of the lines in the media themselves between the notionally factual and the apparently fictive. The convergence of the two is apparent not only in the proliferation of media genres that straddle the conventional separation of fact and fiction, but also in the structures of media organizations in which old divisions between news and entertainment are increasingly ignored. The production, and hence study of journalism and popular culture are now fully intertwined. A number of chapters speak to these issues, most directly the contributions by McRobbie, Hallin and Geraghty.

A third theme, already present in the second edition but more pronounced here, has to do with the ramifications of the rapid transformations brought about by new communication technologies. The globalization of television news, (the topic of one of the chapters in the previous edition) appears to be a stone-age issue compared to the impact of the internet. This is addressed directly by Sparks who argues that, contrary to popular belief, the internet may well reproduce and exacerbate the limitations of the press. More generally, the influence of new technology in transforming the production of entertainment, and modifying political communication and cultural identity, is featured in other essays (such as those by Frith, Blumler and Gurevitch, and Negus and Román-Velázquez).

However, the central theme that runs like a recurring refrain throughout this entire edition is globalization. We have rerun Sreberny's essay on globalization debates because it still provides a clear and cogent starting point. Her claim is that globalization amounts to a 'paradigm shift . . . in which notions of national sociologies, national cultures and national media models don't work as simply any longer'. While few would dissent from this, the extent of this paradigm shift is still open to debate. Chin-Chuan Lee *et al.* show the continuing importance of 'national prisms' in reporting the same global event; Rowe points to the way in which the globalization of sport has fuelled nationalism; and Dahlgren emphasizes the continuing relevance of the nation in contemporary definitions of citizenship and civic culture. Still more contentious are contrasting evaluations of the implications of globalization. Contributors to this book can be divided between those, like Frith and Dahlgren, who see globalization in mainly positive terms, and those like Negus and Román-Velázquez who see it in more negative terms as reproducing the unequal power geometry of the globe.

While responding to new and emergent trends, we have not neglected some of the traditional core issues of media research, such as Schudson's revisiting of different sociological approaches to news production, Hallin's discussion of commercialism and professionalism in the media, Lichtenberg's defence of objectivity and Corner's return to the perennial issue of media influence.

We are grateful to the authors of the new essays who accepted our invitation to contribute to this book, and to those authors already familiar to readers of the previous editions who succumbed to our requests and pleas to revise and update their earlier contributions. Above all we owe a debt of gratitude to Lesley Riddle, our editor at Arnold, without whose faith in the worthiness of these collections and her persistence and determination to bring it to fruition this third edition would have never been born.

SECTION I

Mass Media and Society: General Perspectives

1

Reconstructing the Ruined Tower: Contemporary Communications and Questions of Class

Graham Murdock

Picking over the rubble

There was a time, not so long ago, before the present boundary fences were erected, when cultural and communications studies was common land. Scholars from far-flung settlements converged on this open space to gather data and graze new conceptual strains produced by cross-breeding. The few structures that dotted the landscape were mostly makeshift affairs, temporary shelters erected to service immediate needs. The one major building was a dark, forbidding, stone tower. Wherever you stood, your eye was drawn to it. Its visibility made it an object of endless speculation. Some set out to trace its origins and transformations over the years. Some tried to describe its organization and workings. And some recorded the stories of those who lived and worked there, crafting melancholy narratives of dashed hopes and blighted lives or recounting stirring tales of heroic resistance and dogged refusal. Over the years, however, progressively larger and larger cracks appeared in the tower's foundations until it was eventually declared unsound and demolished. It was replaced by a stylish new housing development in which each dwelling was built to a unique design reflecting the owners' particular personality and preferences. The stark vertical contours of class had given way to the open horizons of difference.

In conversations and arguments about these changes, attention quickly moved from structural constraint to self-expression, from blocked mobility to fluidity, from necessity to desire. Many commentators welcomed these shifts, arguing that the tower's looming presence had held back new thinking on stratification for far too long, returning observers again and again to the same narrow agenda of investigation and debate. They gleefully declared 'the death of class' and revelled in their role as gravediggers (Pakulski and Waters, 1996). Others felt that reports of the death may have been exaggerated. They saw people picking over the rubble and imagined the spectre of class still haunting their conceptual dreams, like a zombie in a horror film, blinding them to the new 'realities of our lives' in a fast-changing world (Beck, 1999: 25). This argument is upside down. It is the refusal to acknowledge that class remains a fundamental structuring principle of every aspect of life in late capitalism, including communications, that blocks a comprehensive view of contemporary conditions.

One of the most resonant slogans that appeared on walls and posters across Paris in the spring of 1968 was: 'under the paving stones, the beach'. This deeply romantic promise could stand as the *leitmotif* for the great wave of recent research devoted to uncovering the possibilities for personal liberation and self-expression concealed within the mundane and the circumscribed. It is time to reverse this perception and insist that under the beach lie the paving stones. This is particularly important in media and cultural studies, where too many commentators have spent too much of the last decade or so detailing the pleasures of everyday consumption. As Zigmunt Bauman points out, 'there is life after and beyond television' and for many people 'reality remains what it always used to be: tough, solid, resistant and harsh' (Bauman, 1992: 155). Class may have been abolished rhetorically in many texts but an impressive amount of empirical evidence confirms that it remains a pivotal force in shaping the ways we live now. It is supremely ironic that the postmodern theoretical 'turn', which has propelled questions of identity, consumption and difference to the centre of academic attention, has coincided almost exactly with the neo-liberal revolution in economic and social policy. But then, it is easy to 'think that class does not matter' if you remain relatively 'unaffected by the deprivations and exclusions it produces' (Skeggs, 1997: 7).

'The retreat from class' is the perfect academic expression 'of the new individualism' (Crompton, 1998: 9), a convenient loss of memory that has evaded the relentless erosion of hard-fought-for welfare provisions and public resources, and ignored the steadily widening gap between the top and bottom of the income scale. This chasm is particularly stark in Britain where the Conservative governments of Thatcher and Major succeeded in restoring it to a condition not seen since the late nineteenth century. We therefore find ourselves in the paradoxical situation where 'class has . . . been re-declared dead . . . at a time . . . when its economic configuration has become even sharper' (Westergaard, 1995: 113–4). To ignore this brute reality is to collude with the destruction of dignity and hope and to embrace, however unwittingly, the marketeer's deceitful celebration of an undifferentiated expansion in choice and opportunity.

A critical approach, worthy of the name, must look beneath this promotional rhetoric. It must recover the underlying mechanisms that reproduce structural inequality and trace their ripples through everyday life. For myself, and many others, this is a personal epiphany as well as an intellectual project, a way of relating biographies to histories, of trying to make connections and 'generate theory which can speak across the void, to make class matter' (Skeggs, 1997: 15). Reconstructing the ruined tower of class analysis is central to this project. This is not an exercise in nostalgia, salvage or restoration. We 'have to rethink what class means in the era of late modernism and global capitalism' (Dahlgren, 1998: 302), and ruthlessly rework the materials and techniques handed down by successive architects, deciding what to keep, what to modify and what to throw away.

Manufacturing inequality

The process is not novel. Before the nineteenth century was two decades old, it was clear that the established vocabulary of 'ranks' and 'estates' had been over-taken by events. It was altogether too rigid to catch capitalism's creative destruction of the old social order. A new, more flexible, term was needed to describe the emerging pattern of economic divisions. That term was 'class'. But as John Stuart Mill noted in 1834, the classification of society into 'landlords, capitalists and labourers' rapidly became as ossified and ahistorical as the feudal vision it had displaced. Too many commentators, he complained:

> . . . seem to think of the distinction of society into those three classes as if it were one of God's ordinances not man's, and . . . scarcely any one of them seems to have proposed to himself as a subject of inquiry, what changes the relations of those classes to one another are likely to undergo in the progress of society.
> (Quoted in Briggs, 1985: 3)

Of the various writers who took up the challenge of mapping shifts in class relations, Marx has been by far and away the most enduringly influential. Unfortunately, he died conceptually intestate. Although he saw class as the axial principle of social division, and class struggle as the principle engine of historical change, he never provided a concise definition of what exactly he meant by a class. As he notes on the final page of the last, and unfinished, volume of his magnum opus, *Capital*, 'What constitutes a class' is the obvious 'first question to be answered' in any class analysis (Marx, 1863–7) but, tantalizingly, the manuscript breaks off a few lines later before he offers an answer. Looking across the range of his work, however, we can identify five basic dimensions to his analysis of class:

- class structure
- class formation
- class culture
- class consciousness, and
- class action.

Even his fiercest critics have tended to accept this list as a serviceable agenda for research and debate.

Class structure

Like most of his contemporaries and successors, Marx identified classes with economic position. The key division for him was between those who owned the tangible forms of property – land, real estate, factories, shares – that could be used to generate profits, and those whose livelihood depended on selling their labour power for a weekly wage or monthly salary. In a much-quoted sentence towards the beginning of *The Manifesto of the Communist Party*, written in 1848 when he was thirty, he argued that capitalist society was 'more and more split-ting' along this central fault line, producing 'two great classes directly facing each other: Bourgeoisie and Proletariat' (Marx and Engels, 1846: 36). Many commentators have misread this remark. It was intended to characterize a long-term tendency, not to describe the situation at the time he was writing. Although

Marx saw increasing polarization as an inevitable consequence of more and more productive resources being concentrated in the hands of large corporations and of workers increasingly labouring for a wage rather than for themselves, in his journalism and polemical commentaries on contemporary events, he was always careful to point up the complexities of contemporary class divisions. His blind spot was the middle classes.

He readily conceded that there was a proliferating group of 'middle and intermediate' strata produced by the growth of the professions, the rise of managerial occupations and the expansion of state bureaucracies, that stood between capital and labour, softening – or as he put it, 'obliterating' – this central division, but he persisted in arguing that, in the end, 'this is immaterial for our analysis' (Marx, 1863–7: 885). This cavalier dismissal, particularly of the swelling ranks of experts and professionals with no managerial role within capitalist enterprises, has posed continual problems for analysts wanting to formulate 'a coherent Marxist concept of the class structure' (Wright, 1997b: 64). The middle classes appear in their models as a permanent awkward squad.

Class formation

For Marx, command over capital was not simply the Bourgeoisie's defining possession, it was 'the means to the exploitation of the proletariat' (Crompton, 1998: 27). Its deployment in production consolidated the central division between capital and labour. Along with most of his contemporaries, Marx assumed that the value added to raw materials during their conversion into saleable goods depended on the labour expended on them. He then went on to argue that the wages employers paid covered only part of this value, leaving a surplus that they appropriated for themselves. The appearance of equal exchange – 'a fair day's pay for a fair day's work' – concealed a perpetual-motion machine of exploitation that continually manufactured structural inequality. But, there was a time-bomb ticking away in capitalism's basement. Concentrating workers in large factories and high-density housing might maximize industrial efficiency but it also created the conditions for pooled ideas and communal action in a way that was not true of peasants, scattered across the nation in isolated settlements. For Marx, peasants might be defined as a class analytically, by virtue of their common position in the system of production, but they could not become a class 'for themselves', pursuing their interests collectively. They were destined to remain like potatoes in a sack: in a shared location but inert (see Marx, 1852: 106). At the same time, the culture of industrial workers was not an automatic guarantee of militancy.

Class cultures

There was no question in Marx's mind that every class generates a 'distinct and peculiarly formed' set of 'sentiments, modes of thought and views of life' out of its collective experience, which members continually draw on in their attempts to make sense of their situation. Individuals enter these class-based cultures at birth, and through continual immersion in 'tradition and upbringing' they come to provide the taken-for-granted 'starting point' for views, judgements and actions (Marx, 1852: 37). Ironically, Marx's own cultural tastes, formed by growing up in a respectable middle-class German family with a strong Rabbinical tradition, demonstrated this process very well, as he wryly recognized. When a sympathizer's wife teased him, pointing out that she couldn't imagine a man of such aristocratic tastes fitting very well into the egalitarian society he predicted in his writings, he was honest enough to reply: 'Neither can I', adding that though he was sure that 'These times will come . . . we must be away by then' (quoted in Wheen, 1999: 296). In the meantime, he had to explain how his contemporaries came to recognize themselves as members of a particular class.

Class consciousness

As Michael Mann has pointed out (1973: 13) class consciousness operates at several levels that are easily uncoupled. To become a class 'for themselves', workers needed access to a language that supported opposition. The cultures of working-class neighbourhoods and occupations generated strong class *identities*, encouraging people to see themselves as members of a distinctive class, but they did not always cast capitalists as the principal enemy or see the struggle against them as the major means of achieving personal liberation and an alternative society. On the contrary, as Frank Parkin argued in an influential formulation, these 'subordinate' meaning systems tended to emphasize 'various modes of adaptation, rather than full . . . opposition to, the status quo' (Parkin, 1972: 88).

Class action

Translating class identity into class struggle has been the principle mission of socialist parties. Deflecting this movement has been one of the major effects of a commercialized media culture anchored around consumerism. As Marx famously argued in the opening chapter of the first volume of *Capital*, capitalism presents itself as a cornucopia of commodities whose origins are forgotten in the anticipation of pleasure. Promotional culture depends on projecting attention forward, to the moment of possession, repressing uncomfortable images of the exploitation involved in production. Consumer goods present themselves as compensation for alienating work, not as an echo of its miseries; they promise a sphere of freedom to set against the dictates of necessity.

The central institutions of promotional culture (advertising agencies, department stores, public relations), the first modern commercial mass media (tabloid newspapers, consumer magazines, movies), and mass socialist and labour parties, were all products of capitalist modernity. They emerged at more or less the same time and their competing visions of the good society have been locked together like wrestlers ever since.

Marx died before promotional culture or commercialized media assumed their contemporary forms, but he was in no doubt that control 'over the means of mental production' lay, in the end, with the capitalist class (Marx and Engels, 1846: 64). In this conception, intellectuals and cultural workers are cast as a subordinate fraction of this class: loyal lieutenants, crafting ideas and representations that promote the system's benefits. He did concede that this convenient division of labour might, on occasion 'develop into a certain opposition and hostility', but he quickly added that wherever this collision endangers the survival of the class, it 'automatically comes to nothing' (1846: 65).

At the same time, he remained too much of a Romantic not to believe that true 'art' and key ideas could transcend place and time. He had no difficulty applauding Milton for producing *Paradise Lost* 'for the same reason that a silk-worm produces silk. It was an activity of his nature', even though he later sold the manuscript for £5, while condemning 'the literary proletarian of Leipzig, who fabricates books under the direction of his publisher' (Marx, 1969: 401). He forgets to mention that whereas Milton was already a celebrated poet with a substantial readership at the time he wrote *Paradise Lost,* the hack of Leipzig was an unknown foot soldier in the reserve army of fictional ephemera. This raises the possibility that class positions may also be determined by the resources that actors bring to the market-place.

Coins of exchange

This idea was pursued by the German sociologist Max Weber, writing in the decades after Marx's death, against the background of a further rapid expansion in the middle and intermediate classes, including the burgeoning ranks of cultural professionals – journalists, teachers, librarians, scientists, musicians, visual artists – employed in the rapidly expanding commercial cultural industries and the growing ensemble of publicly funded cultural institutions. Weber made sense of the new cleavages in the class structure by arguing that Marx's 'basic distinction between the propertied and the propertyless can be further differentiated by the kinds of property or services' people bring to their bargaining over jobs and rewards (Hall, 1997: 18). He saw acquired skills and formal education as particularly important coins of exchange. In a widely influential book, Anthony Giddens stretched this definition of market capacity still further to include 'all forms of relevant attributes which individuals may bring to the bargaining encounter' (Giddens, 1981: 103). As we shall see, this general idea has been most fruitfully developed by Pierre Bourdieu, in his model of competing forms of capital.

Extensions and refurbishments

Disciplining the awkward squad

By the early 1970s, commentators were increasingly talking about a fundamental shift in the economic organization of capitalism: away from the classic industrial order addressed by Marx, towards a system centred on services, and command over strategic information and knowledge. Some writers described it as a 'post-industrial society' (Bell, 1979), others as an 'information society', but there was widespread agreement that 'clerks, teachers, lawyers and entertainers' were beginning to 'outnumber coalminers, steelworkers, dockers and builders' (Webster, 1995: 13). This shift forced Marxist writers to revisit Marx's 'awkward squad' the middle classes.

The most consistent attempt to rethink Marx's analysis has come from Eric Olin Wright. He began by arguing that, although experts and professionals differ from industrial workers in being able to exercise a degree of self-direction and autonomy within work, they remain proletarians by virtue of the fact that they still have to sell their labour power in order to earn a living. Consequently, they find themselves in a contradictory position with one foot in one camp and one foot in the other. However, as he conceded, this model did not fit professionals working for publicly funded institutions. Universities presented a particular problem. The leading theorist of 'post-industrialism', Daniel Bell, argued that because they played a pivotal role in codifying and testing knowledge in key areas of emerging economic activity such as information processing, biotechnology and new materials, they were the pivotal institutions in the emerging economic order (Bell, 1979: 198). Academic wishful thinking aside, there is clearly a case to answer here. Like Marx before him, Wright, himself a university professor, had managed to explain the social position of everyone except himself. This led him to revise his position and suggest that the top end of the class structure is organized around the distribution of three kinds of assets: capital assets, organizational assets (which managers command), and skill and knowledge assets (which professionals and experts possess), with each group trying to monopolize and exploit their holdings to the full in struggles over the distribution of the surplus. As he notes, this very Weberian solution cuts through the 'conceptual knots' generated by Marxian models (Wright, 1997a: 60) and suggests a way of combining them which sees 'exploitation as defining the central cleavages within a class structure and differential market capacities as defining *strata within* classes' (Wright 1997b: 36).

Pierre Bourdieu also arrives at a synthesis between Marx and Weber but by a different route. He takes Weber's notion of market capacities and converts it into Marx's rhetoric of capital, arguing that there are three basic forms of capital circulating in capitalist societies: economic capital, social capital ('which consists of resources based on connections and group membership') and cultural capital (Bourdieu, 1987: 4). In this model the class structure appears as a multi-dimensional space in which classes are defined, first by the amount or volume of capital they possess, second by its composition and, third, by the changing weight and make-up of their holdings over time as they try to maximize their advantages, struggling to convert the initial hand they have been dealt into three aces (1987: 4).

Not surprisingly, it is the idea of cultural capital that has attracted most interest among scholars working in communications and cultural studies. However, it has proved to be a particularly slippery concept. At some points in his work, Bourdieu offers a relatively narrow definition, equating it with 'informational capital'. Elsewhere he identifies it with the knowledge underwritten by academic or professional qualifications. But more often he defines it in terms of familiarity with a particular range of cultural artefacts and practices, especially those that have acquired what he calls 'symbolic capital' by virtue of being classified by central cultural institutions, such as schools and museums, as worthy of being sought and possessed (Bourdieu, 1973). This highly selective conversion of cultural capital into symbolic capital is, he argues, one of the central ways that class inequalities are reproduced and legitimated.

Picking up on Marx's account of class cultures, he argues that the communal experiences generated by particular class locations produce shared sets 'of generalized schemes of thought, perception, appreciation and action' which are handed on to the next generation through the everyday talk and rituals of family

and neighbourhood (Bourdieu, 1968). However, these class-based meaning systems – or 'habituses' as he prefers to calls them – do not carry equal weight
within schools and other major cultural institutions. On the contrary, he argues,
the education system identifies 'real' culture with the forms of knowledge and
expression possessed by the middle and upper classes and stigmatizes the ver-
nacular knowledge and popular tastes of working-class cultures as inferior and
unworthy of serious attention. This places children from subordinate-class locations at a permanent disadvantage. Since they have not been socialized into the
legitimate habitus within the family they have to run harder to catch up. Many
fail, or give up, exiting from full-time education with only a glancing acquain-
tance with Culture with a capital 'C' and often with an antagonism towards it.
As a consequence they count themselves out of the audiences for 'high' culture,
confirming the symbolic advantage that middle-class groups already enjoy. Even
those who successfully use the education system as a route to upward mobility
often feel that they have only squatter's rights. As Annette Kuhn has noted:

> You can so easily internalize the judgements of a different culture and believe – no,
> *know*- – that there is something shameful and wrong about you. . . . You know that if
> you . . . act as if you were one of the entitled, you risk exposure and humiliation. And
> you learn that these feelings may return to haunt you for the rest of your life.
>
> (Kuhn, 1995: 97–80; original emphasis)

'This fear of being summoned before some hidden bar of judgement and being
found inadequate infects the lives of' many people who appear to be 'coping
perfectly well from day to day'. It is one of the 'hidden injuries' of class, no less
real for being mostly unspoken (Sennett and Cobb, 1972: 33).

   This argument, and Bourdieu's general model, has major implications for the
study of consumption and media audiences since it suggests that we need to
explore the symbolic as well as the economic barriers to participation. While
conceding that Bourdieu's schema may help to account for the marked class and
educational differences in attendance at legitimated cultural sites such as public
art galleries, a number of commentators have argued that it doesn't help much
in explaining current patterns of media consumption, particularly television
viewing, where the evidence points to 'a significant breaking down of the class-
based distinctions among types of cultural consumption and their related hierarchy of values' (Garnham, 1993: 188). Bourdieu would reply that class-based
habituses structure not only *what* people consume but *how* they consume. As he
points out, 'any cultural asset, from cookery to dodecaphonic music by way of
the Wild West film can be a subject for apprehension ranging from simple actual
sensation to scholarly appreciation' (Bourdieu, 1968: 593). If this wasn't the
case, it would very difficult to explain how so many people working in cultural
and media studies can spend so much time demonstrating that even the most
ephemeral products of the communication industries can be read at multiple
levels and in relation to myriad theories. This labour of decoding is not an academic monopoly however. As recent interpretative work on media audiences has
shown, people constantly read between the lines and locate particular television
programmes, films or records on mental and emotional maps criss-crossed by
multiple lines of knowledge, resonance and judgement. Some of these lines will
have been drawn by socialization within the family and by educational career,
but others will have been added later. As Bourdieu notes, habituses are 'durable

but not eternal'. They are 'constantly subjected to experiences, and are therefore constantly affected by them in a way that either reinforces or modifies' their structure (Bourdieu and Wacquant, 1992: 133).

Bourdieu's refurbishment of class analysis suggests three important lessons for research on everyday consumption and media audiences. First, though we need to start with the constraints imposed by the unequal distribution of material assets, we must go on to uncover the symbolic and social dynamics of participation and choice. Second, we need to explore how the unequal recognition, respect and legitimacy accorded to different forms of culture, and the 'hidden injuries' and resistances they generate, structure people's deep relations to artefacts and experiences. Third, we need to examine the interplay between class-based meaning systems and other discourses that provide resources for identity, interpretation and action.

This last point was developed in a particularly fertile way by David Morley in his influential study of audience responses to the British television current affairs programme *Nationwide*. He begins by arguing that he set out to show 'how members of different groups and classes, sharing different "cultural codes", will interpret a given message differently ... in a way "systematically related" to their socio-economic position' (Morley, 1980: 15). But he goes on to suggest that 'any adequate schema' will also need to 'address itself to the multiplicity of discourses at play within the social formation' (1980: 21). Some of these – like the rhetorics of socialism or militant trade unionism (which his group of shop stewards mobilized in their responses) – may derive from discourses of class and support class identities, but others, like discourses of feminism or nationalism, sustain other ways of looking and other identities.

These other discourses have become a major focus of study within cultural studies, leading many writers to ignore class. As a result, the field has become increasingly dominated by 'discourse about gender, race, ethnicity, sexuality, in short, about almost all differences *other than* those of class' (Milner, 1999: 145; original emphasis). In many accounts, class has become a category that no longer speaks its name, dismissed as yesterday's issue.

Beneath the beach

'The strange death of class' (Milner, 1999: 173) in much writing in contemporary cultural studies represents a fundamental break with the field's founding concern with debunking the comfortable assumption that rising affluence was washing away the old class lines and producing a more open society. As Stuart Hall put it, 'all the evidence leads us to say that it is false to describe this increasing fluidity as tending to the condition of "classlessness". It would be more accurate to say that ... we are dissolving one way of experiencing class situations and making another' (1967: 94). This argument was explored empirically through a wave of work on youth subcultures. This was a highly strategic choice, since an increasing number of writers at the time were arguing that the new mass media, particularly rock and pop music, had created a universal youth culture that transcended class. In this enticing vision, 'teenagers appeared as the harbingers of the coming society of spectacular consumption, announcing the imminent arrival of a capitalist society without classes' (Murdock and McCron, 1976: 17). Against this, the new research set out to demonstrate the resilience of class by showing how subcultural tastes and styles were fundamentally structured by the class-based distribution of experiences and meanings (see Hall and Jefferson, 1976; Murdock, 1974). This work was rightly taken to task by later writers for its masculine and ethnocentric biases. But learning to forget about class did scant justice to the complexities thrown up by continuing shifts in the stratification system.

Intellectual irresponsibilities

As well as raising issues for research on audiences, Bourdieu's writings also pose questions for work on the cultural industries. He includes in the dominant class anyone who holds a high volume of any kind of capital. This leads him to endorse Marx's argument that intellectual workers are 'best considered as a subordinate fraction of the same class as the bourgeoisie itself' because they are able to exploit their very sizeable holdings of cultural capital to secure significant economic and social advantages, but cannot command the levels of economic or social capital enjoyed by capitalists (Milner, 1999: 140). Other writers, notably John Frow (1995), have questioned this conclusion, arguing that intellectuals often enjoy rather greater independence from the bourgeoisie than either Bourdieu or Marx allow, and that they are more usefully seen as a separate but weakly formed class, dealing in education-generated knowledge (a position that comes close to Daniel Bell's view). Even if we accept this as a plausible characterization of intellectuals, extending the argument to cultural workers more generally, immediately presents problems since a number of major areas of cultural enterprise – advertising, public relations, market research – are rather more obviously tied to the business of servicing capital. We might want to address this problem by distinguishing between cultural workers operating in the private and public sectors, on the grounds that public institutions are less directly governed by market imperatives and ideologies, though given the rapid marketization of universities and public broadcasting organizations in recent years, this is now debatable.

Identifying the class position of various groups of cultural workers and mapping their degrees of relative autonomy is not just an academic exercise, it has real political consequences. Viable democratic politics depends on a shared commitment to renegotiate not simply individual entitlements but what we mean by the 'common good'. This requires debate and dialogue across class boundaries and class interests. The cultural industries provide the major areas where these encounters now take place. The relative openness of this space and its hospitality to dissent is therefore crucial to sustaining democratic life. There is little point in arguing for one way of organizing cultural production rather than another unless we can demonstrate that particular structures and forms of financing are more likely to create the conditions that secure the expressive diversity, informed critique and open debate required by a complex democracy. The academic flight from class analysis has largely left this issue behind, displaying a studied disinterest in the social responsibilities owed by intellectuals.

Demolitions

By the time Bourdieu's monumental study of class and culture in contemporary France, *Distinction*, appeared in English in 1984, the demolition of class analysis was in full swing. It was propelled by several interlinked movements.

First, the general turn from social structure to cultural life within sociology progressively removed questions of economic process from the research agenda. The newly fashionable 'conception of "culture" as a series of discourses, endlessly renegotiated . . . by all those who participated in them' had the effect of rendering 'invisible the fact that cultural products such as books, films, "science" or advertisements' were also the 'products of human . . . labour' undertaken within particular work and market conditions which fundamentally shaped their direction, form and overall diversity (Huws, 1999: 32). Far from being 'weightless' and free floating as some commentators imagined, cultural production remained inextricably bound up with capitalist dynamics and market relations. Indeed, the further concentration of key productive resources in the hands of the new mega-media corporations, with interests spanning every major field of communications (which Peter Golding and I outline in Chapter 4 of this volume) has tightened these connections still further.

In much writing on media and culture, however, the changing conditions of production came a poor second if they were mentioned at all. Attention was fixed firmly on the dynamics of consumption conceived primarily as a system of signs which generated new symbolic spaces for experiments in identity. This in turn directed attention away from the possible links between consumption and class position to questions around the relations between commodities and self-expression – a shift mirrored by the parallel movement within commercial market research, from identifying market segments by class and other demographic variables to mapping personal traits and dispositions. In the process, 'the language of class warfare' was 'ousted by the language of psychographics' (Fletcher, 1999: 22) burying Marx's proletariat under a welter of consumer types: 'Emulators', 'Sustainers', 'Experientials' and 'I-am-Me's'.

These parallel shifts reproduced the fetishism of commodities which Marx had argued was the basic plot device in capitalism's grand narrative of steadily increasing choice and betterment. The active audiences and nomadic consumers celebrated in the new wave of cultural and media studies looked more and more like the sovereign individuals of Adam Smith's capitalism, breaking the bonds of origin and place and achieving self-realization through market choices. This comforting story of personal fulfilment could only be sustained by conveniently forgetting the exploitations involved in commodity production and ignoring the deep structural inequalities the system reproduced.

This emphasis on individual choice was reinforced by a new stress on the fluidity and plurality of social identities. As one British sociologist put it: 'Are we seriously to believe that in their everyday lives people think of themselves as members of a class rather than say . . . drinkers, smokers, football supporters?' (Saunders, 1989: 4–5).

This is a classic 'Lego' model, in which divisions with very different weights and consequences are simply joined together, like the coloured building blocks in the children's game, and pulled along in a line. In this conception class has been reduced to just another difference among many (Coole, 1996). There is no sense that it may be more fundamental, more enduring and more far-reaching in its effects on the ways we live and think of ourselves.

In fact, there was a great deal of empirical evidence that class remained a difference that made more of a difference than many others. As two other British sociologists concluded, available research suggested that there 'was no reason to suppose that over recent decades, classes in Britain – the working class included – have shown any weakening in either their social cohesion or their ideological distinctiveness' (Goldthorpe and Marshall, 1992: 391).

Even if we accept the general argument that working-class cultures and consciousness have remained surprisingly resilient in the face of change, we are still confronted with the decline of trade unionism, the evaporating commitment to class-based politics, and the rise of new social movements, particularly feminism and ecology. These certainly offer new foci for campaigning and new political identities but, as Andrew Milner has argued, these are best understood 'as the substitute, not so much for class as for individuality' (Milner, 1999: 168). They offer nodes of solidarity and communality in an increasingly unstable and heartless world. To call for extended rights of consumption and personal choice, though laudable in themselves, does little to challenge 'the fundamentally class-divided nature of late-capitalist society' (Milner, 1999: 166). Not only can major corporations live quite comfortably with many of the demands being made by representing themselves as more 'caring' and customer-friendly, they can also capitalize on them by creating new markets to replace those under attack or, if needed, moving offshore to emerging markets in economies where civil society is less well mobilized and less effective in making its demands felt.

Recently, however, there have been signs that the long retreat from class analysis in cultural and communications theory may be ending; as the country & western song puts it, more and more people are forgetting to remember to forget. A new series on 'core cultural concepts' from a major publishing house in the field includes a volume on 'class' (Milner, 1999), while a new collection urges 'cultural studies to return to the question of social class as a primary focus of study' (Munt, 1999). These may be straws in the wind, but then straw is indispensable in making bricks.

Reconstructions

What is it then that we want to build? By way of illustration, let me suggest three general areas where class analysis remains pivotal to a proper understanding of currents shifts in the organization of communications and culture.

Cultural labour under 'flexible' capitalism

Is not surprising that commentators from Marx onwards have had so much trouble locating cultural workers on their maps of the class structure. This general category conceals a wide range of different relations to capitalist production and market relations. A few have been supported by a private income or, in Marx's case, by funds donated by Engels, topped up with an unexpected legacy. Engels earned the money working for the family firm but gave it with no strings attached, which allowed the great sage a rare degree of freedom in organizing

his intellectual labour. This is comparatively rare, however. Most cultural workers have to earn a living by selling their skills. Some work for themselves as free-
lances. Others launch small businesses employing a few other people. These
'semi-autonomous' workers, or 'independents' as they are often called nowadays, either produce material on spec and hawk it around or try to secure a commission from a patron. But historically, under capitalism, more and more
cultural workers have been employed (on contracts of varying duration) by one
of the major commercial cultural producers. This situation has prompted a
lively and long-running debate about the relative degrees of creative autonomy
they enjoy.

Discussion has focused particularly on the tensions between the commercial
and political interests of owners on the one side and the professional integrity
and creative ambitions of journalists, television dramatists, film-makers and
musicians, on the other. Concern that owners will exploit their economic and
organizational power and place their private interests before the public good
underpins objections to further concentrations of corporate ownership, while a
steady stream of evidence of actual abuses reinforces arguments that capital's
domination of cultural production produces 'Rich Media' but 'Poor Democracy'
(McChesney, 1999). This issue remains highly relevant. Indeed, the recent rise of
mega-media corporations makes it more pertinent than ever.

In tackling it, however, we need to take account of the accelerating movement
towards a more 'flexible' cultural labour force, which is replacing life-long
careers, or even relatively long-term contracts, with a system of payment by
results. The increasing parcelling-out of programme production to 'independent' companies within British television is a good example. A recent survey of
employment conditions in the industry found less than a third of those questioned (31 per cent) on the payroll of the major broadcasting organizations, as
against 38 per cent who were working freelance (defined as 'on contracts of less
than a year'), 11 per cent who were working for an 'independent' producers and
15 per cent who owned their own production company (British Film Institute,
1997: 8). This shift to 'outsourcing' will be given a further push by the transition
to digital technologies which will concentrate programme production in 'small
teams of computer-literate newcomers' (Ursell, 1998: 151). British universities,
once a bastion of security, have gone through a parallel move towards greater
'flexibility' with a substantial shift towards casualization and short-term contracts, and the abolition of the traditional tenure arrangements.

These developments raise interesting questions about the class position and
affiliations of intellectual and cultural workers within contemporary capitalism.
They suggest that a major cleavage may be opening up between groups with relatively secure conditions of employment or their own successful businesses and
those operating in conditions of permanent insecurity and dependence. The
implications of 'flexibility' for the overall diversity of cultural expression
deserves urgent investigation. As Angela McRobbie's recent work on fashion
designers (see Chapter 12 of this volume) suggests, however, the connections are
unlikely to be straightforward. On the one hand her respondents' relatively low
earnings, coupled with their high degree of financial insecurity and instability of
employment, suggested a process of 'proletarianization'. On the other hand,
their occupational identities, as university graduates with a quasi-professional
status meant that they consistently 'disregarded or disavowed those skills

associated with the more menial side of fashion manufacture' and thereby reproduced 'some of the most traditional of class divides in their own working practice. They wanted to believe that they were above manual labour' (McRobbie, 1998: 187).

The onward march of 'flexibility' also returns us to Pierre Bourdieu's multi-dimensional model of class formation. In order to use it productively, however, we need to look again at the shifting relations between skills possession, formal accreditation and cultural competence concealed in his portmanteau conception of cultural capital. The rapid growth of courses in cultural and communications studies within higher education and the growing professionalization of skills training suggests that formal accreditation may come to play a more important role in regulating entry to cultural labour markets than it has in the past. At the same time, emerging evidence suggests that social capital continues to play a central role, confirming the old adage that 'it's not so much what you know as who you know'. The BFI survey found that personal contacts were easily the most important channel used by respondents to seek and obtain work in television (British Film Institute, 1997: i). And as Angela McRobbie notes, the fickleness of fortune in fashion markets increases the importance of contingency and serendipity in providing 'unexpected windfalls and opportunities' through chance meetings and unexpected encounters (McRobbie, 1998: 179).

Classing difference

McRobbie's fashion designers were almost all women and, as she points out, the insecurities of their market situation imposed heavy costs on their personal choices. The interplay between gender and class has been a central theme in feminist writing, with many commentators arguing that 'patriarchy' – the subordination of women's lives to men's interests – is as important, if not more important, than class in reproducing structural inequality. Some class analysts have responded by uncoupling class from gender. Eric Wright, for example, regretfully accepts that his model of class 'probably does not – and perhaps cannot – provide adequate tools for understanding many of the important issues bound up with gender oppression' (Wright, 1997a: 60). Fortunately, some feminist researchers have not been so easily dissuaded from exploring the interplay between class and gender. As Carolyn Steedman notes, approaching 'the felt injuries of a social system through the experiences of women and girls suggests that beneath the voices of class-consciousness may perhaps lie another language, that might be heard to express the feelings of those outside the gate', but 'there is no language that does not' also 'let the literal accents of class show' (Steedman, 1986: 113–14).

After extensive ethnographic work with a group of working-class women in the north of England, Beverley Skeggs concludes that 'class was completely central to' their lives (Skeggs, 1997: 161). She is particularly interested in the way that the unequal distribution of capital (in Bourdieu's extended sense) combines with the circulation of competing discourses of identity to lower their ambitions. For them the hidden injuries of class were very forcefully gendered: 'They were never able to feel comfortable with themselves, always convinced that others will find something about them wanting and undesirable' (Skeggs, 1997: 162). The dominant image of working-class women as disreputable, dangerous and sexually voracious was a particular source of anxiety. In response they rejected the models of individualism offered by feminism and opted for a 'respectable' femininity. However, as Skeggs argues, this choice should not be read as a sign of passive resignation but as the outcome of an active 'emotional politics of class'. They had entered a system where 'access to positive valuations [was] limited or closed' and were 'forever trying to make the best out of limited resources' (Skeggs, 1997: 161–62).

Class boundaries are not completely fixed, however. Individuals manage to get 'out' and 'away' though education or marriage. The pains and pleasures of leaving and the difficulties of moving between grounded and erudite cultures were major themes in early British work in cultural studies. Richard Hoggart and Raymond Williams, and many of the younger generation who followed in their wake, were working-class 'scholarship boys' who had fought their way through the education system and had gone on to become university teachers and researchers. As Derek Wynne's recent research (1998) shows, the strategic deployment of cultural capital is typical of those who have moved into the middle class by way of higher education. It is their trump card in the game of distinction, a visible marker of their arrival in their new location. In contrast, those who have made their way up through the school of hard knocks or have launched their own businesses are more inclined to display their command of economic capital through conspicuous consumption; they are constantly looking over their shoulders, seeking to prove their success to those left behind.

Despite this flurry of research, in most tales of mobility the protagonists are almost always male. Steph Lawler's recent work with upwardly mobile working-class women is an exception. She notes how the pathologizing of working-class sexuality, intersected with 'the lack of a history of being middle class' among the women she talked to compounded the hidden injuries produced by the moments when they 'were shamed by the (real or imagined) judgements of others – judgements which hinged on the women's lack of the "right" judgement, the "right" knowledge, the "right" taste' (Lawler, 1999: 13). They felt that the habitus they laid claim to could never be fully inhabited and the dispositions it required never completely possessed (1999: 17). They were condemned to be perpetual visitors in other people's houses, continually on their best behaviour.

This emerging work suggests that while feminists are right to insist that class is always gendered, gender is equally always classed. Consequently, it is not a matter of choosing to focus on class *or* difference but of exploring the ways in which the two intersect. Much recent work on media audiences has used variants of focus group methodology to explore people's interpretations and responses to films and television programmes. The problem is that these relatively short, usually one-off, occasions cannot produce the depth of evidence that the arguments developed by Skeggs and others require. If we are going to relate biographies to histories, we need biographies which will allow us to uncover the subtler connections between subjectivities, social discourses and cultural practices. For this, life histories of the kind Bourdieu collects in his recent book, *The Weight of the World* (1999), are essential. If we are to do justice to the complexity of everyday media practices we need to show how they are formed by personal journeys as well as by social locations and public discourses.

Global shifts

As C. Wright Mills pointed out some time ago, however, a truly comprehensive analysis must also move continually backwards and forwards, from the particular to the general, reconnecting the 'the most intimate features of the human self' with 'the most remote and impersonal transformation' (Mills, 1970: 14). Because most work to date has been 'based on the convenient assumption that class structure and nation state coincide' (Breen and Rottman, 1998: 16), class analysis is not as well equipped to make these links as it should be. In the era of globalizing capitalism this is a serious limitation.

The last two decades have seen a sustained romance with neo-liberalism's promotion of private ownership, market dynamics and minimal public regulation, among government of very different political complexions. Over this time, the world's three largest nations – Russia, China and India – which for most of the post-war period were relatively (though differentially) isolated from the capitalist world system, have re-entered it, albeit by different routes and for different reasons. This movement has major implications for the role of class analysis in communications and cultural research.

As many writers have observed, the erosion and removal of regulatory barriers, coupled with the rise of transnational satellite and computer networks, has massively extended the global reach of major corporations. This raises the possibility that we may be witnessing the formation of a new 'transnational capitalist class' made up of the executives of the leading transnational corporations, politicians, state bureaucrats who support greater inward investment and 'borderless' economic flows, and, last but not least, the captains of the leading media companies. The allegiance of this class is not to the nation-state but to the new global corporate playing field (see Sklair, 1995: 133–37). Within this formation, communications companies play a pivotal double role.

First, they provide the essential communications infrastructure that enables this new, geographically dispersed, class to develop internal networks of exchange and solidarity. Mapping these emerging transnational flows and connections is an urgent research task. Second, they seek to reorganize public communications around consumerism in the interests of market extension, promoting it as an identity and way of life that transcends national borders and excludes no one.

As Marx saw very clearly, capitalism's never-ending search for new markets would propel it 'over the whole surface of the globe'. It must, he argued, 'nestle everywhere, settle everywhere, establish connections everywhere', not simply as an economic system but as a map of desire, compelling all countries 'to introduce what it calls civilization into their midst' (Marx and Engels, 1948: 38–39). Written in the late 1840s, a century and a half before the full conditions for this global *putsch* have finally been met, this has proved to be a startlingly prescient analysis. In communications and cultural studies, however, this movement has mostly been approached through the rhetorics of 'postcolonialism' or 'globalization'. Both present problems.

Postcolonial theory has been constructed by the privileged nomads of the intellectual diaspora whose movement across borders is propelled by foundation grants and prestigious university chairs. As a consequence their writings are filled with 'talk about cultural difference, but not – or not much – about economic exploitation' (Eagleton, 1994: 13). They dissect the problems of choice and identity in great detail but say little about the new forms of bondage, dispossession and forced migration imposed by capitalism's global restructuring. Nor are these processes made any more visible within the dominant rhetoric of 'globalization'. On the contrary, its convenient conceptual fuzziness 'has the effect . . . of making transnational relationships of power appear as a natural necessity', an inevitability to be managed or, better still, employed to advantage (Bourdieu and Wacquant, 1999: 42). Critical scholarship must break with these evasions. Interrogating emerging patterns of global immiseration and tracing their consequences for subjectivities and solidarities is an indispensable first step to compiling a new transnational map of class; but it only a first step. As well as generating huge wins and catastrophic losses, contemporary global capitalism also delivers modest gains to regular players.

The rapid rise of marketization and liberalization in China, India and South-East Asia has led to a notable expansion in both business ownership and in occupations linked to the management and servicing of commercial enterprise. This emerging stratum is often called the 'new' middle class or the 'new rich' (Buckley, 1999: 218) to distinguish it from the traditional middle class comprised of independent professionals and state bureaucrats. Some commentators, though, prefer a wider definition which includes clerical workers, public administrators and professionals, as well as corporate owners and managers (see Stivens 1998: 15). Analysts agree, however, that the expanded middle classes (however defined and subdivided) are the pioneers of the new consumer system in marketizing societies.

In both India and China, consumption is emerging as both 'a profound basis for group identity' (Appadurai and Breckenridge, 1995: 6) and a central site for social display and competition. The 'new middle-class lifestyle' celebrated in advertising and popular television, pulls lower-class aspirations towards it (McCarthy, 1994: 45) offering visible markers of the 'new' and modern to set against the old and outmoded (Stivens, 1998: 5). Whilst the constant flows of people and goods returning 'home' from travel and diasporic settlement reinforce strong contrasts between the transnational and the parochial, openness and limitation (Lakha, 1999: 269), the new marketeers beckon people to join a placeless community of cosmopolitan consumers. If we look at the lives of women, however, we see once again how relations between this meta-ideology and the new class formation are also profoundly gendered and how the identities they support are continually cross-cut by other discourses.

In her ethnography of women viewers in New Delhi, Purima Mankekar argues that the Indian state television system of the early 1990s addressed female members of the upwardly mobile classes as the prime market for the consumer goods promoted by the programmes' commercial sponsors while simultaneously seeking to enlist them in 'the project of constructing a national culture' through their involvement in serializations of the great Indian mythological cycles, and in patriotic serials dramatizing women's central role in knitting together home and homeland (Mankekar, 1993: 547). As a consequence, she argues, the imagined liberties of consumerism were in permanent tension with the presented duties of nationalism and commercial images of women's self-actualization continually 'circumscribed by metanarratives of nation and family' (1993: 553). Dulali Nag has shown how this central tension is reproduced in the advertising material used to promote the saris worn by Bengali middle-class women. Some texts reinforce the sari's position as the central signifier of continuity and nation by using quotations from early twentieth-century modernist Bengali literature, others evoke associations of consumer modernity by mobilizing material from a popular film magazine (Nag, 1991).

As this developing work shows, it is precisely because they are positioned in the vanguard of the movement towards consumer modernity that the new middle classes in general, and middle-class women in particular, are at the epicentre of the unfolding struggle over the terms of this transition.

If the body of recent work emerging from India and other marketizing societies confirms that class analysis remains central to understanding contemporary change, it also demonstrates once again the urgent need to refurbish it.

Conclusion

What then can we take away from this discussion? I would suggest five main conclusions.

- First, that the fashionable injunction to examine the shifting links between the national, the local, and the global applies with particular force to the analysis of class.
- Second, that the most promising approach to mapping present-day class formations is to build on Pierre Bourdieu's provocative suggestions and work towards a new synthesis of Marxian analyses of production and exploitation and Weberian discussions of market capacities.
- Third, that rather than opposing class to difference, we need to explore how differences are classed and how, at the same time, they continually cut across the organization of class experience.
- Fourth, in examining the role of class-based meaning systems in providing resources for interpretation and action, we must always look for the ways they intersect with other discourses.
- And fifth, in exploring class identities we must always go beyond overt statements of loyalty and affiliation to examine how class subjectivities are shaped and bent by the unequal distribution of recognition and respect, and by the hidden injuries this generates.

References

APPADURAI, A. and BRECKENRIDGE, C.A., 1995: 'Public modernity in India' in Breckenridge, C.A. (ed.), *Consuming Modernity: Public Culture in a South Asian World*, London: University of Minnesota Press, 1–20.

BAUMAN, Z., 1992: *Intimations of Postmodernity*, London: Routledge.

BECK, U., 1999: 'Goodbye to all that wage slavery', *New Statesman*, 5 March, 25–27.

BELL, D., 1979: *The Cultural Contradictions of Capitalism*, London: Heinemann Educational Books.

BOURDIEU, P. and WACQUANT, L., 1992: *An Invitation to Reflexive Sociology*, Cambridge: Polity Press.

BOURDIEU, P. and WACQUANT, L., 1999: 'On the cunning of imperialist reason', *Theory, Culture and Society* Vol. 16, No. 1 (February), 41–58.

BOURDIEU, P., 1968: 'Outline of a sociological theory of art perception', *International Social Science Journal* Vol. 20, No. 4, 589–612.

——, 1973: 'Cultural reproduction and social reproduction' in Richard Brown (ed.), *Knowledge, Education and Cultural Change*, London: Tavistock, 71–112.

——, 1987: 'What makes a social class? On the theoretical and practical existence of groups', *Berkeley Journal of Sociology* 22, 1–17.

——, *et al* (1999) *The Weight of the World: Social Suffering in Contemporary Society*, Cambridge: Polity Press.

BREEN, R. and ROTTMAN, D.B., 1998: 'Is the national state the appropriate geographical unit for class analysis?', *Sociology* Vol. 32, No. 1 (February), 1–21.

BRIGGS, A., 1985: 'The language of "class" in early nineteenth-century England' in Briggs, A., The *Collected Essays of Asa Briggs Volume 1: Words, Numbers, Places, People*, Brighton: The Harvester Press, 3–33.

BRITISH FILM INSTITUTE, 1997: *Television Tracking Study: Second Interim Report*, London: The British Film Institute.

BUCKLEY, C., 1999: 'How a revolution becomes a dinner party: stratification, mobility and the new rich in urban China' in Michael P. (ed.), *Culture and Privilege in Capitalist Asia*, London: Routledge, 208–29.

COOLE, D., 1996: 'Is class a difference that makes a difference?', *Radical Philosophy* 77, 17–25.

CROMPTON, R., 1998: *Class and Stratification: An Introduction to Current Debates* (2nd edn), Cambridge: Polity Press.

DAHLGREN, P., 1998: 'Critique: elusive audiences' in Dickinson, R., Harindranath, R. and Linne, O. (eds) *Approaches to Audiences: A Reader*, London: Arnold, 298–310.

EAGLETON, T., 1994: 'Goodbye to the Enlightenment', *The Guardian*, 2 August, London, 12–13.

FLETCHER, W., 1999: 'Class is out. Personality is what counts', *The Guardian*, 16 July, London, 22.

FROW, J., 1995: *Cultural Studies and Cultural Value*, Oxford: Oxford University Press.

GARNHAM, N., 1993: 'Bourdieu, the cultural arbitrary, and television' in Calhoun, C., LiPuma, E. and Postone, M. (eds), *Bourdieu: Critical Perspectives*, Cambridge: Polity Press, 178–92.

GIDDENS, A., 1981: *The Class Structure of Advanced Societies*, London: Hutchinson.

GOLDTHORPE, J.H. and MARSHALL, G., 1992: 'The promising future of class analysis: a response to recent critiques', *Sociology* 26, 381–400.

HALL, J.R., 1997: 'Introduction: the reworking of class analysis' in Hall, J.R. (ed.), *Reworking Class*, London: Cornell University Press, 1–37.

HALL, S. and JEFFERSON, T., 1976: *Resistance Through Rituals: Youth Subcultures in Post-War Britain*, London: Hutchinson University Library.

HALL, S., 1967: 'Class and the Mass Media' in Mabey, R. (ed.), *Class: A Symposium*, London: Anthony Blond, 93–114.

HUWS, U., 1999: 'Material world: the myth of the weightless economy' in Panitch, L. and Leys, C. (eds), *Global Capitalism Versus Democracy*, London: Merlin Press, 29–55.

KUHN, A., 1995: *Family Secrets: Acts of Memory and Imagination*, London: Verso.

LAKHA, S., 1999: 'The state, globalisation and Indian middle-class identity' in Pinches, M. (ed.) *Culture and Privilege in Capitalist Asia*, London: Routledge, 251–74.

LAWLER, S., 1999: '"Getting out and getting away": women's narratives of class mobility', *Feminist Review* 63, autumn, 3–24.

MCCARTHY, P., 1994: *Postmodern Desire: Learning From India*, New Delhi: Promilla and Co Publishers.

MCCHESNEY, R.W., 1999: *Rich Media, Poor Democracy: Communication Politics in Dubious Times*, Urbana: University of Illinois Press.

26   *Graham Murdock*

MCROBBIE, A., 1998: *British Fashion Design: Rag Trade or Image Industry?*, London: Routledge.

MANKEKAR, P., 1993: 'National texts and gendered lives: an ethnography of television viewers in a North Indian city', *American Ethnologist* Vol. 20, No. 3, 543–63.

MANN, M., 1973: *Consciousness and Action Among the Western Working Class*, London: Macmillan.

MARX, K., 1852: *The Eighteenth Brumaire of Louis Bonaparte*, Moscow: Progress Publishers [1967].

——, 1863–7: *Capital: Volume Three*, London: Lawrence and Wishart [1974].

——, 1969: *Theories of Surplus Value: Part One*, London: Lawrence and Wishart.

MARX, K., and ENGELS, F., 1846: *The German Ideology: Part One*, edited and with an introduction by Arthur, C.J., London: Lawrence and Wishart [1974].

——, 1848: *The Communist Manifesto*, Harmondsworth: Penguin Books [1967].

MILLS, C.W., 1970: *The Sociological Imagination*, Harmondsworth: Penguin Books.

MILNER, A., 1999: *Class*, London: Routledge.

MORLEY, D., 1980: *The 'Nationwide' Audience: Structure and Decoding*, London: British Film Institute.

MUNT, S.R. (ed.), 1999: *Cultural Studies and the Working Class: Subject to Change*, London: Cassell.

MURDOCK, G. and MCCRON, R., 1976: 'Youth and class: the career of a confusion' in Mungham, G. and Pearson, G. (eds), *Working Class Youth Culture*, London: Routledge and Kegan Paul, 10–26.

MURDOCK, G., 1974: 'Mass communication and the construction of meaning' in Armistead, N. (ed.), *Reconstructing Social Psychology*, Harmondsworth: Penguin Books, 205–20.

NAG, D., 1991: 'Fashion, gender and the Bengali middle class', *Public Culture* Vol. 3, No. 2, 93–112.

PAKULSKI, J. and WATERS, M., 1996: *The Death of Class*, London: Sage Publications.

PARKIN, F., 1972: *Class Inequality and Political Order*, London: Paladin.

SAUNDERS, P., 1989: 'Left write in sociology', *Network*, May, 4–5.

SENNETT, R. and COBB, J., 1972: *The Hidden Injuries of Class*, Cambridge: Cambridge University Press.

SKEGGS, B., 1997: *Formations of Class and Gender: Becoming Respectable*, London: Sage Publications.

SKLAIR, L., 1995: *Sociology of the Global System* (second edn), London: Prentice Hall Harvester Wheatsheaf.

STEEDMAN, C., 1986: *Landscape for a Good Woman: a Story of Two Lives*, London: Virago.

STIVENS, M., 1998: 'Theorising gender, power and modernity in affluent Asia' in Sen, K. and Stivens, M. (eds), *Gender and Power in Affluent Asia*, London: Routledge, 1–34.

URSELL, G., 1998: 'Labour flexibility in the UK commercial television sector', *Media, Culture and Society* Vol. 20, No. 1, 129–53.

WEBSTER, F., 1995: *Theories of the Information Society*, London: Routledge.

WESTERGAARD, J., 1995: *Who Gets What?: The Hardening of Class Inequality in the Late Twentieth Century*, Cambridge: Polity Press.

WHEEN, F., 1999: *Karl Marx*, London: Fourth Estate.

WRIGHT, E.O., 1997a: 'Rethinking once again, the concept of class structure' in Hall, J.R. (ed.), *Reworking Class*, London: Cornell University Press, 41–72.

WRIGHT, E.O., 1997b: *Class Counts: Comparative Studies in Class Analysis*, Cambridge: Cambridge University Press.

WYNNE, D., 1998: *Leisure, Lifestyle and the New Middle Class: A Case Study*, London: Routledge.

2

Recent Developments in Feminist Communication Theory: Difference, Public Sphere, Body and Technology

Andrea L. Press

Thinking about women has expanded beyond the categories that once marked the emergence of feminist communication theory. While several seminal articles (Rakow, 1986; Steeves, 1987) well mapped the dimensions of feminist communication work in its early stages, and van Zoonen (1984) comprehensively summarized its growth and spread in its adulthood, feminist communication studies have now developed beyond even these imaginative characterizations. In fact, the main difficulty of writing an essay like this at the present moment is one of definition: feminist communication theory has grown so rapidly over the past two decades that, as a body of work, it has transcended its earlier identity. It is now essential to pose the question 'What is feminist communication theory?'; more specifically, 'What is "feminist" about feminist theory in communication at present?'; and, finally, 'What lessons can communication theory generally learn from this more specific body of work?'

The issue of identity in this field is newly problematic for a number of reasons. First, the notion of identity itself has been interrogated in communication studies, largely under the aegis of postmodernist and poststructuralist influences. While once Rakow could define the components of media study by differentiating work centred on producers, texts and audiences, in the era following postmodernism's critique of representation it is no longer possible to neatly differentiate these arenas.[1] To offer just one example, Grossberg and Radway in several postmodernist-inspired works (Grossberg, 1988; Radway, 1988) criticized audience study which gave false coherence to the subjectivity of audience members. Ang (1996) builds on this criticism in her recent work which criticizes those (including myself) who use categories (such as class, race and gender) too neatly in performing audience analyses. Feminist theorist Judith Butler's much-quoted works (1990, 1993) on gender as performance inform these and other recent critiques in communication studies which seek to discuss communication processes while eschewing fixed categories of identity.

At the heart of this 'revolution' in the definition and identity of the categories of feminist communication study is the implosion of gender itself as a concept. While early feminist work in most disciplines focused on filling in the female equivalent to the highly masculinized categories which characterized almost all academic study in western universities, new discussions question the dichotomization of gender categories from several directions. While anthropologist Sherry Ortner once wrote a seminal essay entitled 'Is Female to Male as Nature is to Culture?' (1979), recent work avoids such bilateral – indeed, such structural – thinking, seeking to escape its self-conscious adherence to categorical boundaries. Feminist essays in our field today, influenced by the sweeping power of Foucault and poststructuralist theory, are more likely to focus on how these categories are deployed to impose order on a chaotic reality rather than to flesh out their dichotomous meanings, as was Ortner's goal. Some employ a postmodernist critique of language and its categories, and have been central to much current feminist theory which has gone about the business of re-seeing and reconceptualizing traditional feminist topics through new theoretical lenses. These theorize – or attempt to theorize – various ways in which power is deployed, and infuses our language and communicative processes.

Another set of critiques which has turned feminist theory on its head, and in some cases has set the stage for postmodernist categorical challenges, is that which has challenged the essentialism, and accompanying biases, that have informed the definition of 'women' in much feminist research. Early feminist research has now been widely criticized for the white, western, middle-class and heterosexist biases that have informed its research samples and theoretical categories. These criticisms have proceeded from multicultural, postcolonial and other theoretical traditions that seek to decentre research agendas that use the category of 'woman' in a manner that foregrounds problems and issues of concern primarily to white, middle-class, western and heterosexual women.

Changes in feminist media theory are not only connected to changes in feminism – but also to changes in media theory, some of which have been prompted by these same developments in the theoretical terrains of the humanities and the social sciences. Media studies in most national contexts lies poised between the two and affected by changes in each – and, as an interdisciplinary endeavour, is also affected by changes in the various disciplines in which media research occurs, specifically history, sociology, women's studies (itself an interdisciplinary location), English, political science and others. So there is a great deal to cover in a discussion of feminist media studies today.

Since I cannot map the entire terrain of this field in a brief article, let me begin by carving out three specific arenas for my focus here, each of which foregrounds a particular set of theoretical insights drawn from the central theoretical debates that characterize the field.

- **Feminism, difference and identity** – Work which highlights the experiences of those who have remained unheard, and gives voice to that which has remained unspoken. This also includes theoretical debates about difference, their impact on the terms of feminist research, and the implications of these debates for representing women, and differences among them.
- **Feminism and the public sphere** – In this section, I look at the rise of the importance of historical work on media. Specifically, I examine the impact of this work on debates about the role of media in facilitating – or hindering – public debate, both historically and currently. Feminist work in this area tends to focus on giving voice to those previously unheard, such as

women, members of under-represented groups, and others whose ideas have not previously entered public debate. This category also includes much work that traditionally, in the communication field, has previously come under the heading of 'audience' research, which I argue now is considerably broader in scope than it was originally, partly because of the influence of public sphere theory.

- **New technologies and the body: feminism at the postmodernist margins** – Work which incorporates the traditional dimensions of feminist research into broader questions about media, technology and the relationship of both to the body. This body of work has challenged traditional dichotomies between the 'natural' and the 'technological', and has uncovered some of the underlying connections between these two seemingly exclusive categories, potentially transforming the study of technology which is so central to our field.

Of course, these three categories are not entirely exclusive, neat divisors of a field which is messy, crowded and full of overlapping and contradictory perspectives. Much feminist research falls into more than one of these categories, so they should be read as dominant impulses guiding different feminist theoretical products rather than inclusive descriptions of discrete categories. Nevertheless, for each of these categories, I will discuss one or two exemplars of research in this new tradition, by which I seek to illustrate the most salient features of each mode of research and its main contributions to media theory generally.

Feminism, difference and identity

The notion of difference – in feminist theorist Rita Felski's terms, the 'doxa' of difference (1997: 1) – is perhaps the single most important development in feminist theory over the last ten years. Very simply, what this means is that a focus on differences of various sorts – differences among women, in particular – has challenged the focus on the category of 'woman' which had come to dominate feminist theory. As Felski recounts, the ascendance of difference over identity has a particular history and meaning in feminism:

> The origins of feminist thought are usually attributed to such figures as Mary Wollstonecraft, who drew on Enlightenment ideals to protest against the subordination of women. Yet such ideals, it soon transpired, were not congenial friends of feminism but merely masks for a phallocentric logic based on the tyranny of identity. Second-wave feminists sought instead to reclaim the feminine; women's liberation lay in the affirmation of their irreducible difference rather than in the pursuit of an illusory goal of equality. This gynocentric ideal in turn has lost much of its power, thanks to the ascent of poststructuralism as well as to extensive criticisms of its political exclusions and biases. As a result, we are now in a postmodern condition, where female difference has fragmented into multiple differences and any appeal to general ideals or norms can only be considered politically questionable and theoretically naive.
>
> (Felski, 1997: 1)

So in feminism, difference is seen as dethroning an essentialist notion of 'woman', which dominated much of the feminist theory of the 1970s and 1980s. As Felski notes, female difference, in the age of postmodernism, has 'fragmented'; the era of seeking female 'essence' has passed.

The impact of this doxa on feminist media theory has been extensive. Born in the era of equality, maturing in the period of the second wave, feminist media theory has gone through several stages and embraced varying perspectives. Initially a project of the search for women's equality, and demonstrating its absence, in the 1980s feminist media theory was largely preoccupied with reclaiming the feminine, a concept it at the same time sought to define. Extensive work on soap operas (Livingstone and Liebes, 1995; Modleski, 1982; Seiter *et al.*, 1989; Brown, 1990, 1994), romances (Radway, 1984; Douglas, 1983; Snitow, 1983), melodrama (Gledhill, 1987; Mulvey, 1975), and other media genres specifically of interest to women dominated feminist work in this era. Articles such as Modleski's (1977) attempt to investigate the relationship between 'Soap Opera and Women's Time', with its naive reference to 'women's' as a collective entity, peppered our literature, which above all was characterized by a faith in 'the feminine', and a faith in what the analysis of feminine forms would reveal.[2]

The rise of difference theory has shaken permanently our faith in such grand narrative investigations, revealing the biases such naive uses of terms like 'woman', and 'the feminine', concealed. Feminist media studies is now neither a search for the sources of inequality between men and women *vis-à-vis* representation in media, nor its effects; nor is it affirmation of the value of the feminine, as it is represented in media or in different forms of reception. Instead, feminist media studies, influenced by the strength of feminist theories of difference, focuses on incorporating the acknowledgement of difference – of various sorts. Studies of both representation and reception now incorporate this knowledge of the power of difference – though what this means can vary dramatically, depending on the way difference and its meaning is interpreted by particular scholars.

In theoretical terms, the focus on difference has meant a vacillation in feminist media theory between very abstract discussions of the meaning and importance of difference, and very particularistic, often personal, discussions describing specific 'differences'. So, for example, in a debate between Ien Ang and Rita Felski in a recent issue of the leading feminist journal *Signs* (autumn 1997), Felski challenges Ang's claim that differences between women lead to incommensurable interpretations and theoretical perspectives. The example used to illustrate this debate is the set of competing readings of the pop singer Madonna allegedly offered by those coming from different racially determined perspectives. Many white feminists, according to Ang, have celebrated Madonna as a postmodern symbol of resistive femininity, a 'postmodern protofeminist heroine' (Ang, 1995: 63). They cite her daring satirization of female sexuality: many white commentators, such as those collected in Schwichtenberg (1993), see her as 'a woman who manages to create a cultural space where she can invent and play with daring representations of feminine sexuality while remaining in control and in charge' (Ang, 1995: 63).

Ang juxtaposes these interpretations to the perspective offered by the black feminist theorist bell hooks, arguing that Madonna is a feminist figure only from a specifically white perspective:

> In part, many black women who are disgusted by Madonna's flaunting of sexual experience are enraged because the very image of sexual agency that she is able to project and affirm with material gain has been the stick this society has used to justify its continued beating and assault on the black female body.
>
> (hooks 1992: 159–60; quoted in Ang, 1995: 63)

Ang contrasts these two positions as evidence of the incommensurability of white and black feminist perspectives:

> What we see exemplified here is a fundamental *incommensurability* between two competing feminist knowledges, dramatically exposing an irreparable chasm between a white and a black feminist truth. No harmonious compromise or negotiated consensus is possible here.
>
> (Ang, 1995: 64)

Felski critiques Ang's notion of incommensurability, claiming that even Ang's example of divergent interpretations of Madonna does not warrant such an extreme conclusion. Both readings, Felski argues, 'are shaped by overlapping conceptual frameworks and discursive regimes', enabling each to use terms such as *identity*, *the self*, and *oppression* (1997: 13). In addition, Felski claims that in summarizing the white position at least (and possibly the black feminist position as well), Ang has created a false unity, a straw [wo]man:

> I remain unconvinced . . . that race is necessarily the primary or most salient issue in disagreements over Madonna, which are also heavily shaped by generational and disciplinary divisions. . . . [W]hite feminists . . . are often very critical of Madonna, whom they perceive as buying into, rather than subverting, patriarchal notions of feminine beauty.
>
> (1997: 13, n. 5)

At issue for feminist media theory in this debate is the possibility of critical dialogue across racial and other divides. Given the chance to respond to Felski's critique in the *Signs* forum, while Ang grants some credit to Felski's criticism of incommensurability as an unproductive strategy, she also holds fast to her – and feminism's – need for recourse to such a term. Her primary evidence is her own experience as a woman of colour, and its incommensurability with the experiences of white feminists (or, more specifically, white feminists' lack of comparable experiences of discrimination, invisibility and cruelty). While claiming she does 'not intend to claim the authority of "experience" here' (1997: 59), Ang proceeds to do exactly that. In this, she parallels a trend in recent feminist media studies work, which elaborates and draws on experiences of difference, and by focusing thus, often implies an incommensurability of theoretical dialogue with others in the feminist community.

This debate echoes a broader set of issues plaguing the ascendance of difference theory within feminism. There is a clash between the political utility of retaining a category of 'woman' which implies some level of identity or similarity between women of different class, racial, ethnic and sexual groups, and the recognition that often the unified category of 'woman' has meant primarily, white, middle-class, heterosexual women only, to the exclusion of issues and interests pertaining to other women occupying identities more marginally located in western culture. Most feminist theorists addressing this issue argue not for the incommensurability of analysis between the dominant and others that Ang advocates, but put forth a more tempered version of the recognition of difference and its importance, involving, as Flax offers, the recommendation that:

> Feminist theories, like other forms of postmodernism, should encourage us to tolerate and interpret ambivalence, ambiguity, and multiplicity as well as expose the roots of our needs for imposing order and structure no matter how arbitrary and oppressive

these needs may be. If we do our work well, reality will appear even more unstable, complex and disorderly than it does now.

(Flax, 1990: 56–7; quoted in Ang, 1995: 67)

The upshot of this debate for feminist media studies has been ultimately productive for the field. It has turned our attention from an almost exclusive preoccupation with the representation, production and reception issues of white, middle-class, western, heterosexual women, to a more inclusive concern with issues pertinent to a variety of other women as well. Works such as Valdivia's *Feminism, Multiculturalism, and the Media: Global Diversities* (1995) focus on including a range of identity perspectives – Latina, Asian American, African American, Native American/First Nation, Jewish American and Portuguese (Lugo) American – in works focusing on media production and representation. It has also made us sensitive to the interrelationships between these perspectives, and those of the dominant culture. These insights have informed the growing body of postcolonial theory, which has been highly influential in feminist perspectives on difference (Gandhi, 1998; Spivak, 1999). This perspective has decentred western liberal feminism, calling into question the ways in which the latter has silenced voices other than its own. It is the question of suppressed voices which we take up in the next section, focusing on the public sphere and the communicative exchanges enabled by it.

Feminism and the public sphere

In this category, I include new research that looks at the way media – both historical developments in media, and contemporary media formations – enable and facilitate a public sphere for women's democratic participation. Most of this work draws from Habermas's vast body of work, particularly the historical and theoretical conceptualization of the public sphere embodied in his 1989 work, *The Structural Transformation of the Public Sphere: An Inquiry into a Category of Bourgeois Society*.[3] In this work, Habermas sets out a very idealistic version of the way in which public debate took place in certain settings, among certain groups, as bourgeois society developed. The work has been widely criticized both from an historical perspective,[4] and also, particularly important for our purposes, for the particular lines drawn in its assumptions between the public and private spheres of society, and the implications these have for women's role in society, for the possibility of women's participation in the public sphere and for the possibility that issues pertaining to women will be defined as discussable there. In this respect, Nancy Fraser's seminal article, 'What's Feminist About Critical Theory? The Case of Habermas and Gender' served a critical role in generating, and concretizing, this line of argument.[5]

Fraser's work (1989, 1990 and 1992) has inspired a plethora of more recent feminist work which is indebted to public sphere theory, but wary of many of its assumptions and particularly of its implications for women. Much of this work has been influential in current communication theory and current feminist theory. For example, Fraser herself has analysed the Anita Hill/Clarence Thomas televised debates from the perspective of what they mean for the existence of a public sphere in our society; of the role television plays in facilitating, and limiting, debate; and the place women, and what are defined as 'private' issues, do – or, in this case, do not – play in that debate (1992). According to her argument, Thomas was successful in the televised hearings at limiting public inquiry into what he defined as his 'private' life, and in so doing he limited the ability of feminists seeking to lift sexual harassment from the realm of the 'private', and put it instead on the agenda of public debate. Ironically, Hill was unable to limit similarly inquiry into her private life, inquiry that only served to delegitimate further the sexual harassment issue.

McLaughlin (1995) deftly summarizes the impact, and importance, of the public sphere literature for feminist communication theory. While pointing to the incisiveness of Fraser's (and others') critiques of the Habermasian formulation, she notes that certain major questions remain unsolved in the feminist debates over these issues. In particular, the role of the media remain undertheorized in most of the feminist critiques. Why is it, she asks, that public debate about feminism in the mainstream media rests so heavily on 'postfeminist' figures and celebrities like Camille Paglia and Katie Roiphie, while less commercialized figures and media products remain inaccessible to the majority of women (1995: 45)? Also, and perhaps most unfortunate, feminist theorists of the public sphere have remained unable to incorporate theories of difference into their discussions of 'women's' role in the public sphere, the overall importance of allowing previously defined 'private' issues in public debate 'for women', and the need for contestation within public debate about women and what 'their' issues are. Perhaps this level of disjuncture between much-publicized media discussions of feminism, and current widespread rifts and dissensions within the feminist movement, is the area which requires most discussion by feminist and difference theorists at present.

However, the legacy of work on the public sphere, despite these difficulties, has been and continues to be enormous in the influence it exerts on feminist work about mass media, their impact and their audiences. In what follows, I discuss several examples of work influenced by this body of theory. These include Miriam Hansen's (1991) master work on film entitled *Babel and Babylon: Spectatorship in American Silent Film*; Ellen Seiter's (1999) book, *Television and New Media Audiences*; Julie D'Acci's (1994) work on the production, crafting, and reception of the popular feminist television show *Cagney and Lacey* in *Defining Women*; and my own recent book, co-authored with Elizabeth Cole, entitled *Speaking of Abortion: Television and Authority in the Lives of Women* (Press and Cole, 1999).

Babel and Babylon is a tour de force. In a book that is not normally identified with feminist theory, Hansen ambitiously sets out to re-think and re-integrate the entire universe of feminist film theory as we know it. First challenging historical studies of film reception that falsely universalize the role of 'working-class' and immigrant women in developing modes of film reception, Hansen, drawing from current theories of the public sphere as elaborated in Habermas, Negt and Kluge,[6] operationalizes current feminist theoretical insights into the importance of race, ethnicity and class, as well as gender, in establishing the forms and boundaries of film spectatorship. A scholar of Valentino – and much of the book is devoted to a discussion of the contradiction between his mass of female fans and the patriarchal ways in which they were 'positioned' by his film image – Hansen addresses communication theory at many levels, in many arenas, including the following: historical theories of the public sphere; psychoanalytic modes of feminist film theory; queer theory and the analysis of film representation. In a unique work Hansen employs the insights of feminist theory to challenge and develop each of these areas.

Challenging theories of the public sphere which falsely locate early cinema as an almost entirely working-class amusement, Hansen argues that in fact early cinema was distinctive particularly for the mixing of class, ethnic and gender boundaries[7] which took place in the arenas of its reception. In this argument, Hansen confronts the work of other feminist theorists of the public sphere, but transcends it as well, using the critiques of theorists like Fraser to go beyond an argument that is often strictly about gender. Unlike so many other feminist public sphere theorists, she is able to incorporate categories of difference meaningfully into her theorization of the operation of the public sphere.

Confronting psychoanalytic feminist film theory, Hansen does what for two decades has eluded that body of work: she effectively historicizes its claims, contextualizing them in terms of time and place. Painstakingly, Hansen details the rise of what has become known as 'classical' Hollywood cinema, and the gendered spectator positions that have been detailed in feminist psychoanalytic film literature – more specifically, as Hansen herself states, she is concerned with elucidating 'the conception of spectatorship in general, with the relationship between textually constructed positions of gendered subjectivity and historically available possibilities of reception, and with the role of the critical reader in constructing and mediating both of these terms' (1991: 251). In particular, Hansen calls attention to the ambiguous nature of female spectatorship as both cult of consumption and manifestation of an alternative public sphere. In this way she ties the psychoanalytic literature, a normally self-referential body of work referencing only research written in its own terms,[8] to broader feminist debates about the nature of a tie between the mass media and a peculiarly feminist public sphere.

Hansen's work foreshadowed a proliferation of works about the role of the media, from a feminist perspective, in the public sphere at present. Many of these focused on particular public incidents, and detailed the angles of interest to feminists. For example, the Clarence Thomas/Anita Hill public hearings sparked much interest and debate (Flax, 1998; Morrison, 1992; Fraser, 1992). Fraser analyses the public rhetoric surrounding the trial from a feminist perspective which illustrates how Anita Hill's rhetoric was systematically delegitimized by those conducting the hearing and determining the rules by which it would proceed, in press coverage of it, and in reports of public response to it, while when Clarence Thomas made essentially similar claims, he was believed and even exalted in the popular reaction to the hearings (1992).

Similarly provocative was the very public trial of O.J. Simpson, the black sports and media star accused of murdering his wife and her boyfriend (McLaughlin, 1995). This trial was of particular interest for feminist interpreters in that, in public discourses about it, feminist discourses about domestic violence clashed with other discourses concerning racial discrimination in the American criminal justice system. Feminist accounts have analysed the respective hearings given to each, and the relationship between them, various media and other arenas of public debate.

A feminist book like Julie D'Acci's *Defining Women: Television and the Case of Cagney and Lacey* is an example of the new, contextualized research about media, its audience and the public discourses it generates. The book focuses on all of the influences that dialogically combined and struggled to produce the text of the *Cagney and Lacey* show as it emerged. In this case, the audience was one of the important influences, though by no means the only factor, contributing to the final product. D'Acci cleverly illustrates, using a combination of methods including archival research, ethnographic interviewing and textual analysis, the careful policing of the boundaries of the representation of femininity, both as regards appearance and action, by those holding the power in prime-time commercial television production in the United States.

Painstakingly, D'Acci illustrates how, even when feminists are centrally involved as writers, actresses and producers – as was true in the case of the *Cagney and Lacey* prime-time television drama – their contributions are subtly (and not so subtly) modified to bring their sometimes groundbreaking qualities more in line with the reproduction of dominant modes of femininity. Particularly striking was the reaction of network executives to the screen presence of Meg Foster, the first actress cast as policewoman Christine Cagney. Deemed too masculine and aggressive – and too 'dykey' by some studio executives – she was replaced by Sharon Gless, whom one reviewer described as 'blonde, single, [and] gorgeous in the imposing manner of Linda Evans on *Dynasty*' (cited in D'Acci, 1994: 35). D'Acci succinctly illustrates how such attributes of characters as clothes, make-up, hairstyles and speech become the battlegrounds on which the wars of femininity (and heterosexuality) are fought in the arena of television. Deviations from the norm are strongly – and effectively – policed, as D'Acci's in-depth illustration of this one case clearly shows. D'Acci's book is extremely effective for illustrating the way political, economic and other factors structure the public sphere for women. Her work serves as a warning against the tendency to idealize the mass-mediated public sphere as a place in which dialogue operates relatively free of such constraints. We see through her work both that these constraints are many, and that women in the media audience – as well as those involved in the creative process at the other end – struggle to break through them.

Current feminist work on audience reception of media is conducted under the shadow of feminist and other theorizations of the public sphere. The new trends in audience research consist of examining specific segments of the audience, in cultural context, posing the kinds of questions that have come to characterize research driven by the paradigm of the public sphere. So, for example, Ellen Seiter's book *Television and New Media Audiences* (1999) consists of a series of small-scale ethnographic studies of media consumption in different cultural contexts (in various preschools; in families whose parents attend a parenting discussion group; in fundamentalist families). Seiter uses each of these settings to probe questions about the consonance between public debate about social and political issues, and the consumption, interpretation and use of mass media, particularly television. What is distinctively feminist about her book is the minute attention she pays to the cultural assumptions about mothering, teaching and children, and their relationship to mass media – television in particular – and the way she uses close ethnographic data to expose many of these assumptions as ideological. In short, Seiter articulates the public dimension of much activity previously relegated to the 'private' realm.

My own recent book with Elizabeth Cole, *Speaking of Abortion: Television and Authority in the Lives of Women*, examines women's reception of television in the context of broader political, social and moral debates about the abortion issue, as these take place in what we argue are the normal public or semi-public arenas in which many women discuss such issues. Drawing both from British feminist cultural studies work, and from feminist theories of the public sphere as embodied in the work of Nancy Fraser and others, we seek to investigate the locales of public discussion and debate among women when they examine an issue which has both important public and private dimensions. In order to locate women's political talk, we argue, it must be sought in non-conventional settings. Traditionally defined political venues have often been male-dominated; but this does not mean that women's opinions are formed and expressed only in the private realm. Customary divisions between these spheres – which characterize much of the non-feminist political and public opinion literature – must be broken down if women's political opinions and discussions are to be investigated effectively. And it is in these opinions that the true influence of the mass media is to be found. Our work illustrated that reception study can no longer take place in isolation from the social, political and moral questions that give it scholarly weight and importance: the new face of audience study connects it inherently with these broader questions and contextualizes reception culturally and politically.

The dependence of the operation of the public sphere on mass-media channels has highlighted, in this literature and in feminist literature at large, the importance of new technological developments to all of these discussions about the way public debate operates, and the factors that limit it, in our society. This introduces a third major area of feminist debate, and the last we will discuss here: the literature about new technologies, their impact on women and feminism and the nature of technology itself.

New technologies and the body: feminism at the postmodernist margins

The issue of new technologies, in communication and elsewhere, has been approached by feminist theorists in our field from a variety of perspectives. Paradoxically perhaps, the subject of technology has led to a variety of philosophical works connecting this issue to the dichotomy between the technological and the natural, and the way our dichotomous thinking has been constructed culturally. There have been several seminal works in feminist theory which have encouraged this line of argument. In particular, the work of Judith Butler (1990, 1993) has been extremely influential in problematizing the link between 'sex' and 'gender'. In her most famous work, *Gender Trouble: Feminism and the Subversion of Identity* (1990), Butler writes about the relation of discourse to the construction of subjectivity, arguing (with Foucault) that there is no subject prior to the discursive.[9] In this work, Butler introduces what has become known as a 'performance theory' of gender. Essentially, Butler believes that sexual and gender identities, rather than being natural attributes of human beings, are constructed through the cultural performance of identities. As Hausman notes, 'Butler's purpose in writing *Gender Trouble* is to unsettle the premises of both feminist politics and theory insofar as each relies on the idea of an identity that precedes the subject of feminism' (1995: 177). These arguments clearly contradict the orthodoxies of the cultural feminism that was influential in the 1970s and 1980s, which held as self-evident the existence of two genders, and based its feminist arguments on this assumption. Hausman explains Butler's polemical goal by noting that her 'argument against "gender" is one whose real target is the politics of identity that have supported feminist theorizing and political action in recent years' (1995: 177).

Inspired by Foucault, Butler and others writing in this vein – many of whom have been enormously influential in feminist theory generally – the feminist theorist (and former biologist) Donna Haraway has produced an elaborate set of writings which challenge our most basic assumptions about the nature of technology and its role in society. These writings begin from Butler's assumption that the relationship between sex and gender must be problematized. In fact, Haraway insists that 'the ongoing tactical usefulness of the sex/gender distinction in life and social sciences has had dire consequences for much of feminist theory, tying it to a literal and functionalist paradigm despite repeated efforts to transcend those limits in a fully politicized and historicized concept of gender' (1991: 38).[10]

Perhaps the most famous metaphor Haraway constructs is the notion of the cyborg, which pervades her most famous work, *Simians, Cyborgs, and Women: The Reinvention of Nature* (1991). The cyborg is a figure which breaks down the boundaries between the technological and the human. As Haraway describes it on the first page of her book:

> A cyborg is a hybrid creature, composed of organism and machine. But, cyborgs are compounded of special kinds of machines and special kinds of organisms and appropriate to the late twentieth century. Cyborgs are . . . made of, first, ourselves and other organic creatures in our unchosen 'high-technological' guise as information systems, texts, and ergonomically controlled labouring, desiring, and reproducing systems. The second essential ingredient in cyborgs is machines in their guise, also, as communication systems, texts, and self-acting, ergonomically designed apparatuses.
>
> (Haraway, 1991: 1)

What Haraway seeks to demonstrate, in part through the metaphor of the cyborg, is the artificiality of the boundaries that constitute our customary categories of gender, infused as they are with notions that some parts of human life are natural and others cultural. Haraway seeks to deconstruct these boundaries, exposing them as fluid, the products of history and ideology.

Haraway and others writing in this general tradition have thrown open new possibilities for the role of gender in establishing 'identity'; in fact, the very notion of 'identity' has been substantively transformed in their paradigm, from a phenomenon which was previously understood to be fixed, immutable and largely determined, to one that is fluid, shifting and always in the process of creating new understandings of itself. These ideas have been quite central for a great deal of feminist theory, which has undergone a major paradigmatic shift in their wake. We are only just beginning to understand the consequences of these transformative notions for feminist theory in general, and feminist communication theory in particular.

This transformation occurs not without struggle, of course. Dissenting voices object to the discursive turn. Stabile (1994) takes on Haraway in a major polemical diatribe, in which she accuses her of focusing too facilely on the discursive in a postmodernist vein, at the expense of more concrete, political considerations. In an extended discussion of Haraway's major works, in particular her theory of the cyborg, Stabile charges that Haraway, along with other postmodernist thinkers, shifts attention away from a focus on why texts become popular, which would examine the political impact of these texts in specific historical contexts. Instead, Stabile charges that Haraway 'relies on the illusion that discourse can be wrenched free of its historical resonances and, thus purged, filled with counter-hegemonic interests' (1994: 143). This misguided focus serves to obscure the operations of power that a more materialist feminism would give us.

To make her point more broadly, Stabile points out how Haraway is indebted to Foucault, and shares his views that power is diffuse, non-specific and invisible, 'everywhere and nowhere' (Stabile, 1994: 147). But according to Stabile this leads Haraway to embody one of the central contradictions of postmodernism, which is that capitalism's power as a system is accepted as an overriding reality, while at the same time, postmodernism as a theory of knowledge claims that only local, and partial, knowledges can be sought (1994: 147–8).

The importance of this for feminism, and the reason this position is untenable for Stabile, is that once we accept these premises, no real political connections can be made between postmodernist feminist theory and the world outside it. Stabile cites Hall's critique of Foucault to express this: 'Hall says of Foucault that he "saves for himself 'the political' with his insistence on power, but he denies himself *a politics* because he has no idea of the 'relations of force'" (Hall, 1986: 49)'.

The same might be said with respect to Haraway's work, where the denial of a politics appears most vividly in the ideological underpinnings of the oppositional subject posited by Haraway and her proper sphere of activity (Stabile, 1994: 149). She continues elsewhere, 'For technomanic feminists [like Haraway], apathy is manifested in a blinkered immersion in the delights of postmodernism' (1994: 154), or, to put it more simply, Haraway ignores the social and economic conditions which make popular the technomanic metaphors she writes about, and which might make it possible to formulate a political strategy and position.

Of course, not all feminist theory about technology – not even all critical theory – has been guided by postmodernist theoretical perspectives. Others writing about new communication technologies employ different perspectives from which to analyse these phenomena, often in a much less metaphorical and/or discursive fashion than do Haraway and her followers. For example, there is a growing body of feminist work about computers and internet use which uses ethnographic and other more social class-grounded methods to document the differences between the way women and men use these technologies. Turkle (1995), and many of the essays in Cherny and Weise (1996) and Harcourt (1999), for example, illustrate that there are continuing gender differences in facility with computers, and with using the internet as a source of information. These books tackle topics like e-mail courtships, women's first experiences with computer technologies, media fandom online and the impact of the web on global networking. They are a first step toward the integration of feminist theory into empirical work on the web.

These works leave many questions unanswered as to the relevance of what has been called 'feminist methodology' to new frontiers of empirical work. My own forthcoming work (with Sonia Livingstone), an examination of the ways in which children and adolescents use the internet in the context of their families,[11] is conceived partly as an attempt to answer this question. Using a combination of ethnographic and interviewing methods, we seek to illustrate how computer use at home is beginning to restructure the organization of leisure time and, concomitantly, the relationships between children and children, and children and adults, in American and British families. Exploring gender differences, as well as class, ethnic and racial differences, will be an important component of this work. Central to the tenets of feminist methodology, we seek to examine computer use contextually, holistically and using dialogical methods of investigation. With these methods (which we combine with more traditional empirical methodologies), we seek to flesh out new theoretical perspectives about the embeddedness of technology in the everyday life of families with a discursive, ethnographic component. We therefore see our work as breaking new theoretical ground, but also as empirical in an ethnographic sense. Perhaps the difficulty I am having fitting this and other new feminist work into established categories and grids is indicative of the way paradigms in our field are in the process of a major transformation, partly brought on by the insights of new critical, feminist paradigms that re-map the boundaries between theoretical and empirical work.

Conclusion

I was asked to write in this essay about how recent developments in feminist theory can inform current communication theory generally. Each of the three areas of theoretical development I have detailed articulates in a unique way with more general theoretical developments in our field. Difference theory has sensitized communication scholars – feminist and others – to the blindnesses in our choice of research subjects and topics. It has challenged the way we have centralized white, middle-class, heterosexual experience, in reflection of what is rhetorically normalized in our conventional academic, and everyday, categories and language. Certainly, in the wake of difference debates, many of which have taken place between feminist theorists in women's studies contexts, many disciplines – not just communication – have become sensitized to this issue.

Public sphere debates have been significant for our field as well. In fact, this is a sub-field that has been central both for communication theory and feminist theory simultaneously. The concept of the public sphere has opened up new frameworks facilitating the discussion of political and communicative participation, or the lack of it, in our society at present and historically. The transformation in our concepts of audience has also been significant for both feminist studies, which have spawned a great deal of audience literature, and for our field more generally.

Postmodernist theory has been similarly far-ranging. Not just a feminist concept, it has nevertheless been formulated and developed widely by feminist theory. Feminist discussions of technology have been crucial to whatever detailed articulations of postmodernism have taken place over the last decade. These discussions have been particularly transformative of the way studies of new technological developments, many of which have been carried out outside the boundaries of feminist theory, have been framed. Few can make sense of new technologies without some level of reference to Haraway and others writing in her tradition.

The debate between Haraway and Stabile illustrates what has come to be a crucial divide in feminist theory today. Some might call the current situation a war between those who demand a direct political programme as a criterion of 'feminist'-ness, and others who put their faith in the more linguistic work of building – or, perhaps, deconstructing – critical knowledge. In many cases, what this actually means is tearing down edifices of knowledge that can be seen as too facile, or as serving the purposes of discipline, structure and control – rather than critique – in their method of construction. I have argued elsewhere (Press, 1989 and 1991) that feminist knowledge is inherently a critical mode of knowing, and that this is feminism's essential contribution to the disciplines it engages. Now, ten years later, the impact of feminist theory in this regard has become so widespread that in some ways, feminist theory as a distinct body of knowledge is difficult to define. Although I have tried to do so in this essay, I believe that the range of this discussion illustrates the almost impossibly diffuse nature of feminist theory, and feminist theoretical issues, today.

Certainly feminist communication theory, in the several decades since its inception, has mirrored the diffuse impact of feminist theory more generally in the humanities and social sciences. In our field, feminist theory has challenged many of our most trusted assumptions. More critically, the political and epistemological insights of this body of work have made it impossible for us to proceed comfortably with business as usual, as we go about our typical academic and political activities and pursuits. In many arenas, and certainly in the communication field, feminism in the academy has at long last achieved its goal of challenging the biases and exclusions that have long characterized the pursuit of knowledge in many disciplines. It remains for us, however, to transform these epistemological breakthroughs into ones with actual political impact and effects, not only within the academy, but in the many real-world venues existing outside it as well. The discursive turn in many ways has appeared to move us further from this goal; yet I do not agree with Stabile that this is the inevitable outcome of the powerful theoretical developments we have witnessed over the past 10–15 years. Perhaps their real value will become evident when discursive theories of power begin to affect us politically as well as linguistically in a progressive fashion. But we await the next ten years of feminist theorizing to usher us into that era.

Notes

1.   I am extremely indebted to Lisa McLaughlin for putting this point precisely this way, and citing Rakow in doing so, in personal correspondence. My entire discussion here owes much to my communications with her about the topic of this essay.

2.   Reprinted in Modleski (1982). Modleski's current work (1998) is extremely sophisticated about difference and overcomes this early bias.

3.   Of course, this major work can hardly be adequately summarized in this short chapter.

4.   See particularly Eley (1992) and Landes (1988).

5.   Reprinted in Fraser (1989).

6.   See Habermas (1974, 1989, 1992), and Negt and Kluge (1988).

7.   Not race, however; there was very little inter-racial spectatorship in early cinema.

8.   For an overview of psychoanalytic film literature, see Mayne (1993), Hansen (1991) and Penley (1988). This literature has – as has psychoanalytic literature more generally – been accused of falsely universalizing the experience of white middle-class women.

9.   I am indebted on this point to Hausman (1995). In this section generally, I am extremely indebted to conversations with Craig Robertson.

10.   This passage is cited in Hausman (1995: 8).

11.   This work is an offshoot of a broader comparative project which Livingstone *et al.* (1999) have been conducting for the past several years.

References

ANG, I., 1995: 'I'm a feminist but . . . "Other" women and postnational feminism' in Caine B. and Pringle, R. (eds), *Transitions: New Australian Feminisms,* New York: St Martin's Press, 57–73.

ANG, I., 1996: *Living Room Wars: Rethinking Media Audiences for a Postmodern World,* London and New York: Routledge.

BROWN, M.E. (ed.), 1990: *Television and Women's Culture: The Politics of the Popular,* London, Newbury Park, New Delhi: Sage.

BROWN, M.E., 1994: *Soap Opera and Women's Talk: The Pleasure of Resistance,* Thousand Oaks, California: Sage.

BUTLER, J., 1990: *Gender Trouble: Feminism and the Subversion of Identity,* New York: Routledge.

——, 1993: *Bodies That Matter: On the Discursive Limits of Sex,* New York: Routledge.

CALHOUN, C. (ed.), 1992: *Habermas and the Public Sphere,* Cambridge, MA: MIT Press.

CHERNY, L. and WEISE, E.R. (eds), 1996: *Gender and new Realities in Cyberspace,* Seattle: Seal Press.

D'ACCI, J., 1994: *Defining Women: The Case of Cagney and Lacey,* Chapel Hill: University of North Carolina Press.

DOUGLAS, A., 1983: 'Soft-Porn Culture', *The New Republic* 183(9), 25–29.

ELEY, G., 1992: 'Nations, Publics, and Political Cultures: Placing Habermas in the Nineteenth Century' in Calhoun, C. (ed.), *Habermas and the Public Sphere,* Cambridge, MA: MIT Press, 289–339.

FELSKI, R., 1997: 'The Doxa of Difference', *Signs* 23(1), 1–21.

FLAX, J., 1990: *Thinking Fragments: Psychoanalysis, Feminism, and Postmodernism in the Contemporary West,* Berkeley: University of California.

——, 1998: *The American Dream in Black and White: the Clarence Thomas Hearings,* Ithaca, New York: Cornell University.

FRASER, N., 1989: *Unruly Practices: Power, Discourse and Gender in Contemporary Social Theory,* Minneapolis: University of Minnesota Press.

——, 1990: 'Rethinking the Public Sphere: A Contribution to the Critique of Actually Existing Democracies', *Social Text* 25/26, 56–80.

——, 1992: 'Sex, Lies, and the Public Sphere: Some Reflections on the Confirmation of Clarence Thomas', *Critical Inquiry* 18(3), 595–612.

GANDHI, L., 1998: *Postcolonial Theory: A Critical Introduction,* New York: Columbia University Press.

GLEDHILL, C. (ed.), 1987: *Home Is Where the Heart Is: Studies in Melodrama and the Women's Film,* London: British Film Institute.

GROSSBERG, L., 1988: 'Wandering Audiences, Nomadic Critics', *Cultural Studies* 2(3), 377–92.

HABERMAS, J., 1974: 'The Public Sphere: An Encyclopaedic Article', *New German Critique* 1(3), 49–55.

——, 1989: *The Structural Transformation of the Public Sphere: An Inquiry into a Category of Bourgeois Society,* Cambridge, MA: MIT Press.

——, 1992: 'Further Reflections on the Public Sphere' in Calhoun, C. (ed.), *Habermas and the Public Sphere,* Cambridge: MIT Press, 421–79.

HANSEN, M., 1991: *Babel and Babylon: Spectatorship in American Silent Film*, Cambridge: Harvard University.

HARAWAY, D.J., 1991: *Simians, Cyborgs, and Women: The Reinvention of Nature*, New York: Routledge.

HARCOURT, W. (ed.), 1999: *Women @ Internet: Creating New Cultures in Cyberspace*, London and New York: Zed Books.

HAUSMAN, B., 1995: *Changing Sex: Transsexualism, Technology, and the Idea of Gender*, Chapel Hill: Duke.

LANDES, J., 1988: *Women and the Public Sphere in the Age of the French Revolution*, Ithaca, NY: Cornell University.

LIVINGSTONE, S.M. and LIEBES, T., 1995: 'Where Have all the Mothers Gone? Soap Opera's Replaying of the Oedipal Story', *Critical Studies in Mass Communication* 12, 155–75.

LIVINGSTONE, S.M., HOLDEN, K. and BOVILL, M., 1999: 'Children's Changing Media Environment: Overview of a European Comparative Study' in Carlsson, U. and von Feilitzen, C. (eds), *Children and Media: Participation and Education – Yearbook from the UNESCO International Clearinghouse on Children and Violence on the Screen*, Goteborg, Sweden: Nordicom/Unesco.

MCLAUGHLIN, L., 1995: 'From Excess to Access: Feminist Political Agency in the Public Sphere', *Javnost* (The Public) 2(4), 37–50.

MAYNE, J., 1993: *Cinema and Spectatorship*, New York and London: Routledge.

MODLESKI, T., 1977: ' The Search for Tomorrow in Today's Soap Operas', *Film Quarterly* 33(1): 12–21.

——, 1982: 'Soap Opera and Women's Time' in *Loving with a Vengeance: Mass-Produced Fantasies for Women*, New York: Methuen.

——, 1998: *Old Wives Tales, and other Women's Stories*, Ny: Nyu Press.

MORRISON, T. (ed.), 1992: *Race-ing Justice, En-gendering Power*, New York: Pantheon.

MULVEY, L., 1975: 'Visual Pleasure and Narrative Cinema', *Screen* 16(3), 6–18.

NEGT, O. and KLUGE, A., 1988: *The Public Sphere and Experience*, Minneapolis: University of Minnesota.

ORTNER, S., 1979: 'Is Female to Male as Nature is to Culture?' in Rosaldo, M. and Lamphere, L. (eds), *Woman, Culture, and Society*, Palo Alto: Stanford University Press, 67–87.

PENLEY, C. (ed.), 1988: *Feminism and Film Theory*, New York: Routledge.

PRESS, A.L., 1989: 'The Ongoing Feminist Revolution', *Critical Studies in Mass Communication* 6(2), 196–202.

——, 1991: *Women Watching Television: Gender, Class and Generation in the American Television Experience*, Philadelphia: University of Pennsylvania.

PRESS, A.L., and COLE, E.R., 1999: *Speaking of Abortion: Television and Authority in the Lives of Women*, Chicago: University of Chicago.

RADWAY, J., 1984: *Reading the Romance*, Chapel Hill: University of North Carolina.

——, 1988: 'Reception Study: Ethnography and the Problems of Dispersed Audiences and Nomadic Subjects', *Cultural Studies* 2(3), 359–76.

RAKOW, L., 1986: 'Rethinking Gender Research in Communication', *Journal of Communication*, winter, 11–26.

SCHWICHTENBERG, C. (ed.), 1993: *The Madonna Connection: Representational Politics, Subcultural Identities, and Cultural Theory*, Boulder: Westview.

SEITER, E., 1999: *Television and New Media Audiences*, Oxford: Clarendon Press.

SEITER, E., BORCHERS, H., KREUTZNER, G. and WARTH, E.-M. (eds), 1989: *Remote Control: Television, Audiences and Cultural Power*, London and New York: Routledge.

SNITOW, A.B. 1983: 'Mass Market Romance: Pornography for Women is Different' in Snitow, A.B., Stansell, C. and Thompson, S. (eds), *Powers of Desire: The Politics of Sexuality*, New York: Monthly Review Press, 245–63.

SPIVAK, G.C., 1999: *A Critique of Postcolonial Reason: Toward a History of the Vanishing Present*, Cambridge: Harvard University.

STABILE, C.A., 1994: *Feminism and the Technological Fix*, Manchester and New York: Manchester University Press.

STEEVES, L., 1987: 'Feminist Theories and Media Studies', *Critical Studies in Mass Communication* 4(2), 95–135.

TURKLE, S., 1995: *Life on the Screen: Identity in the Age of the Internet*, New York: Simon and Schuster.

VALDIVIA, A.N. (ed.), 1995: *Feminism, Multiculturalism, and the Media: Global Diversities*, Thousand Oaks, California, London and New Delhi: Sage.

ZOONEN, L. VAN, 1984: *Feminist Media Studies*, London, Thousand Oaks and New Delhi: Sage.

3

Race, Ethnicity and the Segmentation of Media Markets

Oscar H. Gandy, Jr[1]

Introduction

Audience segmentation is a social practice readily identified with a variety of modernist projects marked by a planned intervention in the lives of individuals. Segmentation is both the product and the source of strategic information about individuals who share an identifiable status based on any number of attributes. The focus of this chapter is the segmentation of media audiences on the basis of ascriptive, or claimed, membership in groups defined by race or ethnicity. Segments based on language (Hispanics) and race (African-American) are most clearly defined, but other constructions will be considered along the way.

Audience segmentation is a specific case of a more general process of social construction. It is part of a complex process through which the great variety that sets us apart as individuals is cast off, or ignored, in order to emphasize the similarities that help to shape and define us as members of groups.

The discourses of a variety of social actors – advertisers, government regulators, writers and programme producers, as well as political activists – are implicated in the construction of segments that become the focus of targeted communications. It is for this reason that we refer to these segments as audiences.

While segmentation is usually explored from the perspective of powerful actors whose discursive actions define categories and make distinctions, individuals also recognize themselves in these texts, and then behave in ways that tighten the link between the description and the experience of membership within groups defined as segments (Turow, 1997). Over time, these links may serve to reproduce, and make the boundaries between segments less permeable and more stable (Dervin, 1989).

Constructing the audience

James Anderson (1996) provides a well-developed approach to understanding an audience as a theoretical construct. Anderson's *formal* audiences can be understood as being encoded within the texts created by authors, as well as being constructed theoretically as analytical audiences for more strategic actors. The *analytical* audiences are especially relevant to the construction of audiences that Anderson defines as *empirical*. The audiences that are created through a process we refer to as 'segmentation' can be differentiated further when viewed from the perspective of different social agents with particular interests in the behaviour of audience segments. We can locate these agents in a variety of settings that range from corporate boards to college classrooms, and we can distinguish between them by means of the linkage between their interests and the interests of segment members.

As developed in relation to the governing paradigms thought to distinguish among broadcasters, four relatively distinct perspectives are worthy of our consideration for audience segmentation more generally. Ien Ang identifies two perspectives that at one time may have been seen as unalterably opposed. Where the first sees the audience as a potential consumer, the latter constructs the audience as composed of 'citizens who must be reformed, educated, informed as well as entertained – in short – "served" – presumably to enable them to better perform their democratic rights and duties' (Ang, 1991: 28–29). Webster and Phalen (1994) suggest that the audience can also be understood as a commodity that has been 'produced' for the market. Thus, from within the commercial sphere, important distinctions can be made between audiences that are the object, rather than the subject, of marketing efforts. Media critics and policy-oriented activists have historically constructed the audience, or segments of it, as victims who are likely to be harmed by repeated exposure to dangerous content, or by contact with others who have consumed such fare (Webster and Phalen, 1997: 126). Let us begin our exploration of audience segmentation with an introduction to audiences as publics, markets, commodities and victims.

Audience as public

Common to each of the primary constructions of audience is the assumption that audiences have interests and, in some formulations, those interests can be understood as rising to the level of rights. The rights, interests and reasonable expectations of publics are often used as the basis for evaluating the performance of mass media systems and organizations (McQuail, 1992). Both public and commercial broadcasters may be assigned specific social responsibilities under a 'public trustee' model (Polic and Gandy, 1991). Public media are often assigned a specific responsibility for the maintenance of an active public sphere. At the same time, struggles over the definition of this ideal have increasingly turned on an uncertainty regarding the need for a multiplicity of public spheres that would reflect and accommodate the substantial inequality that exists between groups in society (Fraser, 1993).

The functions served by targeted media, or audiences constructed as publics, differ substantially from those common to other constructions. For immigrant communities, these media often serve as a vital link to the country of origin. As a conduit between the homeland and exiles, or those who maintain an active interest in the politics of the homeland, these media are often used as a means of mobilizing support or opposition. They also serve as a focal point for the development of a local consensus, and a means of expression of the community's demands upon the wider host community. The heritage of Blacks in the UK is primarily that of immigrants from Africa and the Caribbean; this critical distinction is reflected in the differences in the number and variety of targeted media that have emerged in the UK (Benjamin, 1995).

The specification of a political role for media varies as a function of the size, character and social position of minority groups. This specification varies between nations as a function of their different histories of immigration, as well as in response to different constructions of an idealized nation. Germany has been identified as a nation with a very 'narrow ethnic definition of citizenship': while large populations of ethnic minorities are denied the benefits of citizenship in Germany, the state still supports ethnic targeting under the assumption that such programming will facilitate a return home at some time in the future (Husband, 1994: 5).

Even where there are similar constructions of the nation and its heritage (Karim, 1997), there are differences in the strategies that are believed to best serve the interests of the more powerful groups (Riggins, 1992). While not always distinct, one can identify integrationist approaches that may be seen to differ from multiculturalist strategies that place a higher value on the preservation and celebration of difference. One need not be cynical in order to find examples of policies that are designed to lessen the force of minority claims by dividing one group against the other. Such efforts at social control may also involve the state, or other dominant institutions in the planning of pre-emptive strikes. Most involve establishing a manageable communications entity before oppositional enterprises can be developed.

Targeted media may be seen as serving a pacification function. This may be especially effective in those communities in which immigrant groups are in competition for limited resources with each other, or perhaps with resident minorities at the bottom of the racial hierarchy. An emphasis on popular music programming is one way in which local broadcasters can be presented as being responsive to local communities while, at the same time, they are actively avoiding sensitive issues that might otherwise emerge in print or in discussion (Husband and Chouhan, 1985).

Other instrumentalist goals may lead to the development of minority-targeted media by governments in the belief that education and training, or other desirable social transformation would be produced more efficiently in this way. Similar motivations govern the investments made in ethnic media by religious organizations.

Simon Cottle describes the responsibility of the British Broadcasting Corporation (BBC) toward Britain's ethnic minorities as primarily being one of enhancing their representation (Cottle, 1998). In discussing the history of the BBC's efforts in this regard, Cottle notes that what is now referred to as 'multicultural programming' has gone through a complex, and often contentious, process of evolution. We might understand the nature of continuing struggles within Britain and other nations that have assigned these responsibilities primarily to the public broadcasting organization in terms of the conflict between the need to speak *to* persons of colour, and the need to speak *about* them to others.

More generally, however, when racial and ethnic minority audiences are framed as publics, they can readily be seen as being under-served by mainstream media (Husband and Chouhan, 1985). A variety of responses to criticism, including expanded programmes of research, have emerged. In the United States, the Corporation for Public Broadcasting initiated a programme of research that it hoped would improve its ability to serve 'the needs and interests of minority audiences' (Myrick and Keegan, 1981). It seems likely, however, that the rapidly spreading efforts to 'reinvent the welfare state' will help to shrink the size of government budgets allocated to the provision of specialized services to groups justified on the basis of some loosely articulated social need (Calabrese, 1997). Increasingly, the commercial market is presented as not only capable, but ultimately more efficient than state-run media in responding to a host of concerns subsumed under a public interest umbrella.

Audience as market

Those who produce and distribute media content see the audience of actual and potential consumers as a market. The behaviour of consumers in the market is governed by tastes and preferences that vary between individuals, but are assumed to be more similar within than between definable groups, or population segments. Audience research seeks to identify and describe the relationships between the characteristics of audience segments and the attributes of the content they prefer. Membership in racial and ethnic groups has increasingly come to be considered along with other demographic indicators as a predictor of media choice. Of course, racial and ethnic identity can never be a completely reliable basis for defining a market for media content. Racial and ethnic identity is only part of the complex of influences that shapes the decision to consume (Davis and Gandy, 1999). As Mahan (1995: 28) suggests, 'it is far from certain that an identity created through consumption of media or other popular culture products weakens, obliterates, or is even separable from other identities that operate in the same individual at other times'. In addition, as Ang (1991: 41) reminds us, the pursuit of knowledge regarding audience segments, actually produces *greater* ignorance over time because the 'institutionally-produced discursive constructions . . . are under constant pressure of reconstruction, whenever they turn out to be imperfect weapons in the quest for control'. Competition among those who see audiences as markets leads to the production of alternative, presumably more reliable, bases for segmentation. There are other problems inherent in the nature of markets.

Consumers are assumed to be rational actors and, in the context of efficient markets, the price they are willing to pay reflects the value they derive from consumption of media products. Yet, even from the perspective of mainstream economists, it is possible that some segments of the population can be seen as being 'under-supplied' by the market (Siegelman and Waldfogel, 1998; Wildman and Karamanis, 1998). It is in the nature of the logic of capital that if there is more money to be earned by supplying programmes desired by a large majority of the population, producers will supply more content than is actually required by this majority. The largest segments will thus be 'over-supplied', and resources will be 'wasted'. On the other hand, content of interest to smaller, or minority, audiences will not be produced in amounts that will satisfy the preferences of that minority. The tendency to supply less content than minority consumers would be willing to buy is complicated further by the fact that, in some media markets, advertisers rather than consumers pay for the creation and distribution of content to audiences.

Where the interests of advertisers and minority segments diverge, the under-supply of content is bound to be severe. To the extent that advertisers place a lower value on gaining access to particular minority audiences, those who would produce content for that segment will be punished by the market. As rational actors, they must ultimately withdraw from this particular market, and if they are to remain in the media business, they must turn their attention to producing for other audiences.

If having a preference for content preferred by few others is correlated with being relatively poor, both direct and advertiser-financed markets are almost certain to supply less of minority interest content than is desired (Wildman and Karamanis, 1998).

Audience as commodity

The audience conceived as a market is fundamentally different from that same audience when it is thought of as a commodity – a product created for sale within the market. Dallas Smythe is credited with introducing the notion of the 'commodity audience' into the often heated debates among critical scholars who were, from his perspective, needlessly fixated on ideological concerns (Jhally and Livant, 1986; Meehan, 1993). Although Smythe's arguments failed to take root within cultural studies, mainstream media scholars continue to emphasize his essential point:

> The first and most serious mistake that an analyst of the television industry can make is to assume that advertising-supported television broadcasters are in the business to broadcast programmes. They are not. Broadcasters are in the business of producing *audiences*. These audiences, or means of access to them, are sold to advertisers. The product of a television station is measured in dimensions of people and time. The price of the product is quoted in dollars per thousand viewers per unit of commercial time, typically 20 or 30 seconds.
>
> (Owen and Wildman, 1992: 3)

The production of audiences for the market can be understood as an industrial process through which different combinations of inputs (such as scripts, music, talented acting and special effects) can produce audiences with varying degrees of efficiency. The relative importance of particular inputs can be estimated through linear regression where output is measured by ratings or sales, and inputs can be measured in units as precise as the number of acts of violence (Gandy and Signorielli, 1981). The same approach can be applied to the production of audience segments by estimating unique models for each segment. We assume that audience attention is captured by content and that it is attractive to audience members. It is reasonable to expect that different music, settings, actors and outcomes will be more attractive to some types of viewer than others. These types can be thought of as taste segments.

What is crucial to understanding a media system governed by a capitalist logic, is that not all audiences are equally valued in the market. If particular audience segments that are attracted (produced) by particular content are undervalued in the market, advertisers will be unwilling the pay the same 'cost per thousand' they would be willing to pay for more 'desirable' audiences. Rational participants in such markets cannot survive by producing audiences that no one will buy, nor can they survive by producing those audiences if the costs of production exceed the income that can be derived from their sale.

As with all goods sold in the market, producers and distributors of audiences have an incentive to try and increase the perceived value of their commodities. Producers of minority audiences have the same incentive to represent their wares as being of high quality; however, unlike the vendors of other commodities, the need to overcome racial and ethnic prejudice and stereotypes represents an additional burden. Ironically, the use of stereotypes in the effort to sell these 'problematic' audiences, may serve to reinforce negative or extremely limited impressions of the populations from which the segments are derived.

Audience as victim

Historically, media critics have charged the industry with bringing harm to individuals and to society at large. The harm can be direct or indirect (indirect harm being caused by misrepresentation or marginalization). Critics are most often successful in bringing about the desired public response when they frame their critique in terms that define the victims as being incapable of defending themselves. While cultural criticism can no longer characterize the entire audience as naive innocents, unable to resist temptation, or see through the bald misrepresentation of people and relationships, few hesitate to claim that children represent a population at risk.

Less frequently, critics will suggest that there are adult populations that may be incapable of defending their members against subtle communicative appeals. The paternalism that is inherent in these appeals is especially troublesome because the population groups are assumed to have a large proportion of their adult members at risk. Groups defined by ethnicity and race are believed to be particularly vulnerable to appeals inviting the consumption or abuse of dangerous commodities (Smith and Cooper-Martin, 1997). This criticism has been particularly sharp with regard to the targeted marketing of alcohol and tobacco products to African-Americans, Indians and Hispanics.

There is a particular irony to be examined in this regard. Minority-owned media are more likely to be struggling financially because they serve an undervalued market. As a result they are more likely to be dependent upon income from the purveyors of suspect goods and services. The Black press, for example, has long been criticized for its publication of ads for 'aphrodisiacs, patent medicines, clairvoyants' services, lucky charms and other appeals to superstition, and skin lighteners' (Wolseley, 1990: 330).

Audience segmentation

While segmentation became the dominant approach to constructing the audience as consumer at the end of the twenty-first century, the concept of segmentation actually emerged quite early in the development of consumer culture (Ewan, 1976). While early segmentation was based on gender, rather than race or ethnicity, marketers quickly developed specialized appeals that were designed to capture the attention and loyalty of women as a segment of the reading and listening audience.

Language use was, and continues to be, a primary basis for segmenting ethnic audiences. The size and stability of linguistically defined audience segments varies widely among nations and communities, and across historical periods. This variability reflects the differential rates at which loyalty to one's linguistic heritage is eroded by adoption of the language of the majority community. Differences in reliance and use of the mother tongue among members of French, German and Italian communities in the United States help to explain differences in the survival of the associated ethnic press that once served these immigrant groups (Haller, 1988). The decision to maintain and reproduce linguistic competence in the face of fierce pressure to conform to an 'English only' standard, reflects a high level of group identification.

Group identification

Racial and ethnic identity varies as a reflection of the influence of a complex of factors that push and pull individuals towards diffusion and assimilation, or the maintenance of socio-cultural distinctiveness within the dominant society (Cornell and Hartmann, 1998; Subervi-Velez, 1986).

Important work published in recent years has helped us to understand the ways in which racial and ethnic identities are formed and transformed (Gandy, 1998). A critical distinction is made between identity and identification: identity is understood as a reflection of individual and collective agency, while identification is understood as a result of the exercise of power by others. Among the more sophisticated analyses of identity formation that engage both power and agency are those which describe the ways in which social structures help to determine the *salience* of particular identities (Cornell and Hartmann, 1998). Unfortunately, there has been only scant attention paid to those factors that determine the role that racial and ethnic identity, rather than identification, play in the construction of audience segments. Identity is thought to reflect, as well as shape, the response of individuals to particular media content. Audience segments may differ to the extent that racial and ethnic identity has a central core that is political and collectivist.

Anderson (1996) distinguishes between 'strategic' and 'engaged' audiences on the basis of the extent to which these audiences are formally organized, and engage with each other in mutually dependent relationships. Strategic audiences may be understood in relation to associated concepts of interpretative communities, social locations and cultural capital. Theorists assume that a high degree of common understanding and appreciation of cultural artefacts has been derived from similar experiences. A critical response to media content is assumed to reflect a common ideological perspective. An acknowledged group identity of this type is revealed when a particular group, such as African-Americans 'oppose what they see and hear from an ideological position as harmful, unpleasant, or distasteful media representations' (Davis and Gandy, 1999: 368).

Jorge Schement (1998) has examined the distinctions between racial and ethnic identification in relation to media segmentation. He suggests that the use of race as a category is to the advantage of Whites because, as the dominant group, they can use the language of race to stereotype, and thereby assign members of groups defined racially to a subordinate status. On the other hand, he sees ethnicity as a matter of choice, as reflecting greater autonomy and self-determination in the realm of identity. At the same time he recognizes that 'in the calculus of modern media, ethnicity has emerged as a potent determinant for organizing market segments' (Schement, 1998: 93).

Whether race, or ethnicity, or some unstable mix of the two forms the basis for the classification of groups, identification is also the product of a complex of influences that includes, but extends beyond those actors with a strategic, or instrumental interest in audiences. Castells (1997), for example, explores the ways in which ethnicity is being 'specified as a source of meaning and identity' which is different from the ways in which racial identification has been used as a 'source of oppression and discrimination' in the past (1997: 53). His charting of the evolution of African-American racial identity emphasizes the cleavages that have emerged within the population along class and ethnic lines. He finds a contemporary *ethnic* division among African-Americans based on religion that is being shaped by the growing importance of Islam in Black communities. Yet Castells still suggests that ethnicity does not have real potential as the basis for forming a common identity 'because it is based on primary bonds that lose significance, when cut from their historical context'. In the networked society that he sees developing, 'ethnic roots are twisted, divided, reprocessed, mixed, differentially stigmatized or rewarded' according to a logic 'that makes symbolic composites out of blurred identities' (Castells, 1997: 59).

Measurement

As Peterson suggests, 'the ways that media and market researchers measure audiences pervasively shape the ways that people in the media and advertising view those audiences. And at the same time, the ways that these communicators wish to view audiences shape the ways that researchers measure them' (Peterson, 1994: 171).

The social construction of audiences proceeds from mental images through the development of simple classifications that become 'facts' once captured by checkmarks on one official form or another. Estimates of the size of current population segments, and predictions regarding those to be encountered in the future are based on such facts.

For the most part, when Whites identify minority audience segments, either for commerce, or for public service, there is a tendency to be guided more by convenience than by consideration of the identities actually held by members of target populations. While the people who are identified as Asians in the United States, or Britain, or Australia may ultimately come to identify themselves in this way, it is clear that their personal identity departs from their official identification upon their arrival as an immigrant. The impact of official classification is widespread. For example, because the limited budgets of public service broadcasters such as the BBC have to be distributed among the major minority communities, the decision to 'serve' Pakistanis, Bangladeshis and Indians from East Africa by means of a single programme, like *Asian Magazine*, seems perfectly reasonable to White programme managers. The fact that this ethnic construction is rejected as unacceptable by the members of these ethnic communities is taken as further evidence of their unreasonable demands and insatiable appetite for special treatment (Husband and Chouhan, 1985).

The political economy of segmentation

The development of segmented audiences takes place in the context of an environment that is shaped by changes in technology, markets, and regulatory philosophy and practice that both reflect and are implicated in the transformation of global cultures (Mosco, 1996; Schiller, 1999). We are entering into an era in which regulation by so-called 'market forces' is replacing more direct forms of institutional control (Mosco, 1989: 85–94; Polic and Gandy, 1991). The reduction of regulatory barriers to the ownership of broadcasting entities has, somewhat ironically, reduced the number of stations owned by minorities at the same time that the number of stations targeted to those populations has increased (Siegelman and Waldfogel, 1998).

Differences between media

Understanding the construction of audience segments clearly requires consideration of the differences between media technologies that make the pursuit of distinctions within populations worthwhile. A primary constraint on the production of diversity within audiences is the availability of bandwidth, or channel capacity. An assumption of channel scarcity has historically been offered as a justification for regulatory control over access to the infrastructure of broadcasting. A given state of technical development, as well as politicized decisions about the allocation of spectrum to particular functions, has over time determined that less, rather than more, diversity would be the defining characteristic of national broadcasting systems.

It is unwise to think about communications technology independently of the regulatory systems and market structures that govern access to and control of production and distribution resources. For example, while it may be technologically feasible to dramatically increase the number of distinctly programmed channels it may not be economically or politically feasible to do so. The costs of owning and operating broadcasting entities have meant, historically, that members of minority groups have been excluded from positions of administrative authority. However, because operational control can be separated from ownership, members of minority communities have still been involved in the production of specialized content. Where the technology of networking makes it possible to consolidate small, isolated communities into an economically or politically viable segment, minority group members may be called upon, or invited, to produce and distribute targeted programme material. In the United States 'Black radio networks allowed blacks to write, produce, and broadcast news, sports, information, and entertainment exclusively for blacks' (Johnson, 1993/94: 183).

Of course, elitist assumptions about programme standards may serve to limit the involvement of racial and ethnic minority group members in the production of specific content within certain media. In Australia, ethnic radio broadcasters employed large numbers of individuals from targeted linguistic communities in the production of programmes, yet responsibility for the production of 'multicultural' programmes for the television service was reserved for professional organizations managed by Whites. Assumptions about differences in the skills required justified these distinctions (Patterson, 1990).

Because of the comparatively minor expenses required for the publication of a newspaper, magazine or newsletter, we observe numerous publications serving very small communities. This fact, in combination with the limited scope of distribution that geographic segmentation enables, has made it possible for such periodicals to be published for a specialized readership numbering only in the hundreds. With access to inexpensive computers and desktop publishing software, rather sophisticated examples of an ethnic community press have been produced.

While the economics that characterize the production and distribution of print media include incremental costs of paper, ink and fuel, which may still be a constraint on diversity, the economics of distribution for the Internet are quite different. This rapidly developing network makes it possible to imagine, develop and sustain a system of global distribution for any number of diasporic communities (Zhang and Xiaoming, 1999). Here the primary constraints are the economic limitations on access to minority audiences described as 'the digital divide' (Bikson and Panis, 1995; Ervin and Gilmore, 1999). The maxim size of the target audience is limited because most of its members have not invested in the equipment necessary to access the content. However, attempts to project the size, rate and extent of participation in the markets for new technology are both expensive and unreliable, even for the mainstream audience (Carey and Elton, 1996).

Demographics

Although the critical points at which an audience segment will be considered by observers to be too small to be worthy of attention will vary, the relative size, wealth and political power of the population within a defined segment is always important.

The problems involved in estimating the size of different racial and ethnic segments are substantial. Government statistics are a primary source of such estimates, but these figures are far from reliable. Depending on the way in which critical questions are asked, quite different estimates and projections can emerge. When framed in racial terms, projections of the US population in 2025 put the proportion of Whites at 78 per cent of the total. This estimate is inflated because of the fact that Hispanics have been classified racially as White. However, when people are asked to identify themselves in ethnic terms, Whites are projected to be less than 63 per cent of the population in 2025 (Schement, 1998: 94–95).

Part of the problem of estimation is to be found in a growing unwillingness on the part of many individuals to accept a biological basis for their classification by race (Gandy, 1998; Ratcliff, 1994). At the moment, the desire on the part of the children of interracial unions to reflect the racial heritage of both their parents by identifying themselves as 'multiracial' has been subordinated to the realities of identity politics. Articulate representatives of the communities with which they may or may not identify, have argued successfully that those communities would suffer the loss of 'strength in numbers' should these individuals choose to be counted as something other than Black or Asian, or Native American. Recently, the US Office of Management and Budget (OMB) introduced what can only be a temporary solution for the 2000 census. Officials have agreed to allow respondents to mark more than one racial category on their forms (1998).

Commercial estimates are no more reliable. In many communities, minority audiences remain invisible or poorly described because of the way they have been surveyed by the agencies responsible for estimating circulation and exposure to commercial messages. Severe under-counting persists in many of these markets because the leading agencies rely on estimation techniques that have been designed primarily for the mainstream audience.

While some of the under-counting and bias in the measurement of minority audience segments is based on the exclusion of eligible respondents from samples because of language, there are other distortions that reflect the influence of aversive racism. Failure to place diaries or meters because of real or imagined differences in security, reliability and maintenance of equipment continues to produce wildly varying estimates of audience size and composition.

Managers of minority media, and those who represented their interests, have used a variety of strategies to generate compelling evidence of population size and value. The more successful approaches generally involved contracting for special surveys by highly respected research firms. Even then, most of these surveys remained suspect because of the obvious self-interest reflected in the design of the surveys and the interpretation of the data.

Tastes and preferences

The identification of minority audience segments represents a classic 'chicken and egg' problem. Gathering evidence for the existence of unique audience segments depends in part on the availability of the types of content that would encourage their distribution to different sets of consumers (Barwise and Ehrenberg, 1988; Frank and Greenberg, 1980). Early attempts to determine whether revealed preferences indicated the existence of segments within the television audience were constrained by the relatively limited range of programme types available at any particular viewing hour. Barwise and Ehrenberg (1988: 36) concluded that 'in television there is nothing like the striking segmentation which is regularly reported for the readership of newspapers and magazines'. At the time of their report, the analyses reported by Frank and Greenberg (1980) represented the most comprehensive study of television audience tastes and preferences. Very little of the variance in revealed preference for different programme types was associated with either demographic or lifestyle characteristics of segments.

However, a subsequent analysis performed with the American public broadcasting system in mind (Frank and Greenberg, 1982) made use of the data to demonstrate the potential for programming for Black and Hispanic audience segments. Frank and Greenberg suggested that public broadcasting might serve minority audiences by producing programmes that were relatively more successful in attracting members of those population segments. They identified the interest segments that had relatively high proportions of Blacks and Hispanics; they also identified several programme types for which a Black or Hispanic viewing index was higher than that of the general population.

Historically, neither producers nor their primary clients have been willing to risk making substantial investments in programming in the absence of evidence that a sizeable audience segment exists. The balance between risk and opportunity shifts as a function of increased channel capacity, yet differential tastes and preferences can only be revealed in the context of a large number of options that are readily perceived as different.

As the number of distinct options increases, several possibilities for audience response present themselves. Consider the expansion of programme options that might accompany an increase in the number of channels available in a market with cable or satellite delivery. Members of the audience can be expected to spread their viewing choices across a greater number of channels and programmes. Others may increase their viewing of a subset of the programmes available. Increased polarization or greater intensity of viewing of a smaller number of programme types would be *de facto* evidence of the existence of segments definable by taste and preference (Webster and Phalen, 1997: 113). These might be definable as taste segments (Cantor, 1994).

Racial and ethnic segmentation is based on the assumption that the preference for specific content exhibited by members of one group differs substantially from the preferences exhibited by members of other groups defined by race or ethnicity. There is convincing evidence to suggest that there are real differences in the media preferences of particular racial and ethnic groups. It seems clear, for example, that Whites and African-Americans have quite different television preferences, even though members of both groups may be found in substantial numbers in the same audience for any programme or programme type. When their favourite programmes were compared in 1996, Black and White viewers had few programmes in common. Only *Monday Night Football* was in the top ten lists of both groups in the spring ratings sweep (Schement, 1998: 109).

Differences in racial group identification are also associated with revealed preferences for Black-targeted media. Younger and more racially oriented African-Americans have been observed to spend more time with, and to be less critical of, the programming on BET, the only national television network targeted to African-Americans (Jones, 1990). Bob Johnson, BET's chief executive and majority owner, is betting that the sharpening distinctions between the television preferences of Whites and African-Americans will increase his ability to exploit this audience segment (Black power, 1999).

As early as 1972, however, communication scholars questioned the usefulness of race as a basis for segmentation and targeting in all media. After noting that the audience for Black-oriented radio stations often contained a sizeable audience of White youth and college students, Surlin suggested that 'listener's behaviour is based more on psychological "blackness" than on physiological "blackness"' (Surlin, 1972: 297).

It is a matter of strategy, informed by resources, that determines what the relative proportion of an empirical audience needs to be of one race or ethnic group before the genre is associated reliably with a particular audience segment. It is a well-known fact that because of the relative size of the White population, and because of the popularity of rap and hip-hop music among White males, the audience for this music in urban centres often contains more White than Black listeners. One can predict with greater confidence that a young African-American male will be a fan of hip-hop music, than one can predict the musical preferences of a young White male. At the same time, the probability that the next purchaser of a hip-hop record will be Black, or even American, is necessarily quite low.

To date, there is only a woefully inadequate body of research that might be used to determine the extent to which audiences differ substantially in their preferences for media content. In the absence of a well-developed body of research on the tastes and preferences of minority audiences, producers and distributors have to rely on 'trial and error' (Neuman, 1991; Wildman and Karamanis, 1998).

Few studies have focused specifically on programme attributes expected to be at the base of racial and ethnic preferences. Not surprisingly, Frank and Greenberg (1980) did find that Blacks were more likely to view programmes that included African-American performers and situations. Given the segregated character of television programming, this may also explain the revealed preference of Blacks for music programmes in which African-American talent was most likely to be found.

It is also important to consider the extent to which members of the target community develop and maintain a sense of confidence or trust in the content provider. Despite their active use of mainstream media, African-Americans have historically expressed a higher level of trust in Black-targeted media in matters specifically related to the interests of African-Americans (Gibbons and Ulloth, 1982).

Market value

The construction and pursuit of minority audience segments is governed in large part by the logical calculus of expected value. Information about the expected value of any segment is often as unreliable as the information about its size and demographic composition.

Advertising agencies play a critical role in determining the perceived value of audience segments defined by race or ethnicity. The incentive for an agency to promote the value of the segment is to be found in its claim of special competence in reaching that segment. The value of the segment may be inferred in part from the number, visibility and reported billing of agencies that claim expertise in reaching those segments. Some entrepreneurs have chosen to specialize in ethnic audiences in particular, developing divisions that target Hispanics and Asians as well as African-Americans. In 1988, seventeen agencies, with billings in excess of $235 million, were listed as specializing in advertising to African-Americans (Wolseley, 1990: 335).

While it has long been argued that advertisers assign a lower value to Black and Latino audiences, it has been difficult to gather evidence in support of such a claim. In an unusual move, the Federal Communications Commission (FCC) financed an analysis of advertising rates and audience shares (Ofori, 1999). By comparing the share of advertising revenue to shares of audiences produced by different radio stations, different 'power ratios' could be computed. If stations within a given market received a share of revenue equal to their share of the audience in that market, the power ratio would be equal to one. If the ratios for segments of the market were less than one, a reasonable conclusion would be that their audiences were perceived to be less valuable to advertisers, or of interest to a smaller number of advertisers. The evidence is clear. Minority format stations had an average power ratio less than one, while non-minority format stations had an average power ratio that exceeded one. Other evidence of distortions in the market suggested that minority-owned stations had an even lower average power ratio than similarly targeted stations that were owned by Whites.

From time to time, advertisers have been accused of instructing their representatives not to 'make ethnic buys' or purchase time on stations that target minority audiences. Such decisions are of the sort defined as 'reasonable racism' (Armour, 1997). A variety of rationales might be offered as the basis for making 'reasonable' or legitimate business decisions to avoid media that attract members of particular racial and ethnic groups. In the absence of knowledge from experience or from research, stereotypes about the members of racial and ethnic groups leads advertisers to assume that the costs of producing a customer from within this group would exceed the additional revenue to be gained. Ignorance of the consumer leads to avoidance. A similarly uninformed rationale suggests that minority consumers can be reached just as easily and effectively through mainstream media channels.

There are also decisions that are based on fear of particular consumers. This fear has two related dimensions – both have a basis in racial prejudice. Aversive racism is assumed or projected upon the White consumer (Dovidio and Gartner, 1986). It is assumed that Whites will not want to eat or shop in the company of African-Americans. It is even assumed that White consumers will not want to be associated with commodities known to be preferred by Blacks or other ethnic group members who occupy lower rungs on the ladder of social status. Thus, a store owner or product manager is unwilling to risk trading the White customers he already has for the minority consumers he might attract through targeted ads. The reasonable racist avoids the minority consumer because he believes that Blacks and Hispanics will steal, tip less generously or otherwise prove to be less valuable customers (Armour, 1997; Ofori, 1999). Avoiding such customers is seen to make good business sense.

Ideology

The creation of minority audience segments is almost by definition a process of racial formation (Omi and Winant, 1994). As Omi and Winant suggest, racial categories are the products of a socio-historical process that reflects the differential power and influence of identifiable social groups. Members of these groups are engaged in a number of goal-oriented racial projects that are concerned with shaping the distribution of social and economic resources along racial lines. Roberta Astroff argues that efforts to define and then capture a Latino market required the subordination of racial distinctions among the Latinos living in the United States (Astroff, 1988/89). This strategy was particularly important because of the link between race and social class that finds Black Hispanics among the poorest members of this ethnic group. 'When race, language, and culture are collapsed into each other, their social nature and origins can be safely ignored', and this, she argues, is precisely what occurred in the formation of the Latino segment in the United States (Astroff 1988/89: 169).

Nationalism is another ideological influence that helps to shape the development of audience segments. For immigrant groups, there is some period of time during which they are expected to overcome their characterization as foreign. Yet, in many cases, the children of migrant labourers will continue to be treated as immigrants by members of the dominant community. In Britain, the children of Asian, African and Caribbean migrants have consistently been conceived as 'aliens within' by White Britons (Husband and Chouhan, 1985).

Racism, nationalism and xenophobia come together to shape the ways in which the social demography of these groups develops (Baumgartl and Favell, 1995). The concentration of newcomers into urban ghettos or enclaves is commonplace. The racial hierarchy that differentiates immigrant groups enables some to become more easily diffused into suburban communities, even though African-Americans remain highly segregated (Denton and Massey, 1993).

The political leaders in those nations whose recent history has been marked by substantial immigration have been repeatedly forced to choose between integrationist and pluralist national models. In many cases, an explicit policy in support of multiculturalism has been expressed and implemented. Such policies reflect an effort by the nation-state to overcome the crippling influence of xenophobic opposition to economic and political claims made by ethnic minorities (Baumgartl and Favell, 1995). As one observer puts it, 'Ethnic radio and multicultural television did not just happen because they seemed like a good idea at the time' (Jakubowicz, 1989: 109). The move towards multiculturalism in Australia was in part a reaction to anxieties generated by news of racial strife in Britain. The national broadcasting system was called upon to help maintain some semblance of social cohesion in a nation of immigrants.

In other cases, a multicultural policy evolves as a reflection of an underlying ethos of a broadcasting establishment that favours celebration over conflict. 'The ideological virtue of multiculturalism is that whilst it allows for the recognition of cultural difference it ignores relations of power and domination' (Husband and Chouhan, 1985: 285). As a result, programming falls far short of expressing the full range of anger and resentment that many minorities feel.

To a great extent, the minority press has traditionally been an oppositional press. Often, its critical function has been to provide an alternative construction of the challenges and opportunities faced by its primary audience. This oppositional stance has been part of a continuing 'war of images' between Blacks and Whites (Dates and Barlow, 1993). A continuous stream of persons of colour – who came to the United States as slaves, indentured labourers or immigrants – has been subjected to biased and distorted representation in the news media (Keever *et al.*, 1997), and the ethnic press has sought to set the record straight.

The decision to increase the supply of targeted programming to meet the interests and perceived needs of minority communities has often meant increasing the participation of members of these communities in critical production decisions. This has generally meant increasing their employment through the enforcement of 'equal employment opportunity' regulations. Less often, policies sought to increase their operational control through greater ownership of communications facilities. In 1978, the US Federal Communications Commission (FCC) initiated a policy encouraging minority ownership of broadcasting facilities. The general assessment of this policy is that it has failed to achieve its goals. Indeed, in the wake of the Reagan counter-revolution, minority ownership has actually slipped back towards the conditions that marked the origins of the policy (Ofori *et al.*, 1997).

A question that is rarely addressed is whether a policy in support of the development of capitalism along racial or ethnic grounds should have been expected to produce a result in the market which would be any different from that which the existing market provides. Should we expect that minority capitalists would be more or less successful than Whites in squeezing profits out of the market? If they did, would it be because they possessed specialist knowledge of minority segments that had been gained from their own experience of minority status? In the absence of irrationality (and the inefficiencies associated with racism), we would have to assume that this specialized knowledge would also be available to White programmers within the market (Wildman and Karamanis, 1998). However, the best evidence suggests that the real market devalues whatever expertise minority programmers might have. Thus, restrictions in the supply of content designed specifically for its minority segments will continue to exist (Ofori, 1999; Siegelman and Waldfogel, 1998).

Targeting Blacks

The evolutionary development of an African-American segment may serve as a model for other segments based on race or ethnicity. African-Americans who were ignored by the mainstream were served primarily by an alternative press motivated by a social mission. The construction of African-Americans as consumers following the Second World War marked the emergence of a growing commercial interest in the segment. The success of the civil rights movement brought about a degree of integration and assimilation of African-Americans into the dominant culture that was nearly matched by the assimilation of African-American culture into the mainstream. Yet, today, in what might be considered to be the twilight of a rather long day in the life of American media history, considerable uncertainty remains about the status of an African-American audience segment.

It is clear that American advertisers are faced with a quandary. Marketing to African-Americans has become problematic. The industry is unsure about 'whether to see them as a separate cultural entity, like Hispanic Americans, or to target them with the white population according to distinctions in income, gender, age, and other characteristics' (Turow, 1997: 80). To a considerable extent, it was Black media executives, and the managers of advertising agencies that specialized in reaching the African-American market, who have been complaining about the 'mainstreaming' of Black America. Critics suggest that newly emerging television networks had merely 'used' the African-American viewer as a way to establish themselves within the industry. These networks quickly abandoned the segment once they were able to move on to more lucrative markets (Carter, 1996; Trescott, 1996; Wynter, 1998). It wasn't always that way.

For my people

The Black press in the United States historically provided both leadership and support for African-Americans in their continuing struggle for civil rights (Wolseley, 1990). The flagship paper *Freedom's Journal* and some fifty other Black newspapers were established between 1827 and 1865 in support of the abolitionist movement (Brie, 1977/78). Even during the twentieth century, the

Black press consistently rose to the challenge of defending its readers against oppression (Owens, 1996).

The Black press in the United States has been motivated by service rather than profit for most of its history. Because neither circulation nor advertising could be relied upon to finance these publications, the publishers used income from donations and from personal employment to sustain the enterprises (Brie, 1977/78). Of course, there were exceptions, such as Robert Abbott's Chicago *Defender*, which reported a national circulation of 200,000 by 1917. It wasn't until the 1940s, however, that the Black press evolved into a cornerstone of Black capitalism.

Magazines, highly dependent upon advertising for their success, developed an editorial style that was designed to attract the Black middle class. John Johnson, publisher of *Ebony* magazine, developed a special, non-confrontational editorial standard for his magazine. From its earliest days, Johnson's publications revealed an editorial preference for stories that accentuated the positive and 'happier' aspects of Black life in the United States (Hirsch, 1968).

When surveyed in 1990, managers of African-American newspapers differed in their views regarding the factors that might determine their continued existence. Contrary to expectations, competition from either African-American or mainstream newspapers was not perceived as the primary threat to these weekly publications (Lacy *et al.*, 1991). In the view of its managers, the Black press will remain an alternative, rather than a direct competitor of mainstream newspapers. Few publishers believe that the need for a racially identified Black press will disappear in the foreseeable future.

Market value

Advertisers have never considered the African-American consumer to be an especially important market segment. The following reasons (Wolseley, 1990: 338–39) have been given for this assessment:

- African-Americans are poor, and are therefore not a viable market
- African-Americans are consumers of mainstream media and can be reached efficiently through those sources
- association with African-Americans is frowned upon by Whites, the primary market, and attracting Black consumers risks offence and loss of those more valuable consumers
- media targeted to African-Americans are likely to contain more confrontational, and non-traditional content that is generally of low quality; as a result, these media represent an unacceptable environment for mainstream products.

The fact that most of these reasons are based on ill-informed racial stereotypes does little to soften their impact on the behaviour of advertisers towards this audience segment.

There is some debate regarding the precise historical moment when the African-American consumer was seen to be worthy of any attention by mainstream advertisers (Brooks, 1995; Pride and Wilson, 1997). Yet, the process through which this market was assessed, and then constructed discursively, is not much different from the process that characterizes the exploitation of other ethnic markets. The first stage always involves efforts to estimate the size and cumulative value of the market. The African-American market, estimated at $4.8 million in 1942, was by that time being discussed in the trade press as a market that should not be ignored.

Eventually government statistics, such as those produced by the Department of Commerce and the Bureau of the Census, would be relied upon in estimating the size and quality of the African-American market. But specialized market research was needed to generate initial interest in this segment. The publisher of the Afro-American newspapers, in co-operation with the Urban League, contracted for the first comprehensive assessment of the Black consumer market in 1945. Also important were agents who were able to bridge the gap between Black and White communities. William Ziff, a White entrepreneur who later became the head of the Ziff-Davis publishing empire, served as a publisher's representative who specialized in obtaining advertising for the Black press (Pride and Wilson, 1997). The purchase of advertising with media targeted specifically to the Black audience by a major advertiser could be taken as an indicator that the segment had achieved an improved status. A decision by the Hoover Company to advertise its vacuum cleaners in *Ebony* magazine in 1951 was precisely that kind of historical landmark (Brooks, 1995).

Black radio

The history and contemporary status of radio programming targeted to African-Americans underscores the importance of the intersection between racism and the political economy of media in the United States (Newman, 1988). Because of the economics of radio, and historic limitations on the accumulation of wealth among African-Americans, radio programmes designed to appeal to Blacks were produced largely under the control of Whites.

The Black radio audience was built largely on the basis of Black on-air talent and recordings of Black performers. Its development was financed initially by a small, but growing, number of advertisers. The market expanded dramatically following the Second World War. White owners of Black-format stations had been led into this market by periodic reports and columns in the trade press that also provided guidance for those 'adventurers' who might take a chance in this market. One source, *Sponsor* magazine, was especially helpful in reporting surveys of the African-American audience and providing lists of special 'dos and don'ts' for success with this segment (Newman, 1988).

It seems ironic that during a period in which the United States was just beginning to dismantle its formal structure of racial segregation, black-oriented radio actually helped to heighten segregation within the radio audience. The heightening of Black racial identity and pride coincided with an appreciation of the economic value of audience segmentation. Black radio programming, including popular rhythm and blues music, helped to reinforce racial pride, as well as the salience of racial identity. Both would reach a historic peak in the 1960s and 70s.

The establishment of interconnected networks was the most effective way to transform a widely dispersed audience into a segment that might be of interest to advertisers. Although it was short-lived, the National Negro Network was established by a Black entrepreneur, Leonard Evans, in 1953. Tobacco marketer, Philip Morris, was among the network's primary sponsors (Johnson, 1993/94).

A news service, the Black Audio Network, was established in 1968. The network relied on Black journalists and emphasized African-American newsmakers. During its heyday, it convinced upwards of 90 stations to carry its reports.

Changes in FCC policy towards minorities produced a rapid expansion in the number of radio ventures organized by and for African-Americans. The Mutual Black Network, the National Black Network and Sheridan Broadcasting emerged during the 1970s. Not long afterwards, however, a decline in government support, in addition to changes in the organization of media industries in the United States, led to the consolidation of several previously independent Black networks.

During this period when the dramatic growth in Black networks supplying targeted programming took place, there were only 13 stations that were actually owned by African-Americans. By 1995, in response to a shift in FCC policy, African-Americans had come to own some 203 radio stations. The majority of these stations were targeted to Black listeners. At the same time, however, the stations owned by African-Americans represented only a fraction of the stations that reported Black-oriented programme schedules. Those Black-owned stations captured a comparatively smaller share of the revenue derived from marketing this segment to advertisers (Ofori *et al.*, 1997).

Following the passage of the Telecommunications Act of 1996 that allowed for an expansion in the number of stations that could be owned in any broadcast market, the numbers of stations owned by African-Americans declined sharply. The profitability of those remaining under Black control was also threatened severely by aggressive, direct competition from group-owned stations (Ofori, 1999). The movement of White entrepreneurs into an improved position may be indicative of an increased assessment of the value of the audiences produced by Black-format radio. However, the conclusion that the market value of the audiences produced by Black-oriented television has declined (Wynter, 1998) suggests that the political economy of audiences is far more complex than one might assume.

Linguistic segmentation: American Hispanics

There is a large and growing body of literature on the development of Spanish language media in the United States; however, attention within the scholarly community does not match the growing interest in this segment being shown by investors, advertisers and others who might benefit financially from its exploitation (Gutiérrez, 1977). Commercial interest in the Hispanic market reflects its present size, its rate of growth, its geographic concentration and its primary distinction from other segments on the basis of language. There has also been considerable historical interest in the development of Spanish-language television because of the unique role that Mexican investors have played in shaping American telecommunications policy.

Demography

Advertiser's interest in that aspect of the Hispanic market defined by Spanish language usage has increased dramatically since the 1960s. Despite the problems inherent in estimating the size of the Hispanic population, the US Census Bureau continues to report and to project dramatic growth in the Hispanic population. Since 1980, the Hispanic population has been seen to increase at five times the rate of the general population in the United States (Goodson and Shaver, 1994). While estimates of the date at which the boundary would actually be crossed differ, few doubt that the size of the Hispanic population will have exceeded that of African-Americans by not long after the turn of the century (Soruco, 1996).

The fact that this market was growing rapidly was cited most often (82 per cent of respondents) among the reasons given for targeting Hispanics by Spanish-language advertisers in 1986. An even larger majority of these advertisers were confident that the market would 'continue to grow and become more important in years to come' (Albonetti and Dominguez, 1989: 14). In addition to estimates of the size and amount of disposable income available to this segment as a whole, it was also important for those governed by market considerations to be able to estimate the costs of reaching this audience. Population density is a critical component of those costs.

The geographic distribution of Hispanics in the United States into ethnic enclaves is reflected in concentrations of groups from different regions of the Americas into particular urban centres. The circumstances that led to the migration of Hispanic groups over time helps to explain their concentration in different regions. Over 50 per cent of the Latino population is concentrated in California and Texas (Downing, 1992). Large concentrations of Puerto Ricans can be found in New York City and in the surrounding region. Miami became the centre of life for Cuban immigrants to South Florida, while Los Angeles houses the largest group of Mexican-Americans.

Linguistic sleight of hand

Although there are substantial scale economies or efficiencies that make reaching audiences that are as highly concentrated as Hispanics in the United States profitable, even greater efficiencies can be realized through network distribution across several population centres. In the case of Latinos in the United States, this has required programmers to erase, or ignore, many of the linguistic and historical distinctions that would ordinarily set these communities apart.

There is considerable diversity among those who speak Spanish. A relatively small number, primarily recent immigrants, speak only Spanish. A far larger number, perhaps 50 per cent, speak Spanish only part of the time. There are a relatively large number of people who are identified as Hispanic by heritage who have almost no knowledge or competence in Spanish (Aquirre and Bustamente, 1993). Differential linguistic ability and preference has been identified as an important predictor of whether an individual will be a regular user of Spanish-language media (Faber *et al.*, 1986).

Rodriguez (1997) suggests that the decision to produce an idealized Hispanic who would be attractive to mainstream advertisers required the invention of a pan-ethnic Spanish language. The resulting 'Walter Cronkite Spanish' that came to be used in the widely viewed newscast, *Noticiero Univisión*, was stripped of the distinguishing accents and intonations that might otherwise identify the national origin of the speaker.

To the degree that the development of an economically viable Hispanic segment depended upon the creation of a common Hispanic identity, this linguistic invention may have contributed to that goal. In the absence of cues to the contrary, members of the audience identified the programme's newscasters as having come from their own region, if not from their own social class. In addition, the journalistic scripts were crafted with a common identity in mind. The choice of collective personal pronouns like '*ustedes*' and '*Nosotros*' was strategic. For Rodriguez, '*Univisión*'s use of collective personal pronouns signals that journalists and pan-ethnic audience together are the insiders, the legitimated actors' in the newscast (Rodriguez, 1996: 66).

The creation of a pan-ethnic identity in order to achieve some criterion size for the Hispanic news audience has parallels in other media markets. Mahan (1995) discusses the 'Latinization' of New York Puerto Rican salsa as part of a marketing strategy developed by Fania Records. The Cuban heritage of the music, as well as its oppositional character, was lost as its commercialization progressed.

The loss of ethnic/cultural distinctions within the United States as a result of the implementation of a marketing strategy shares an ironic relationship with the historic expression of concerns about cultural imperialism that identified US-based media as the primary threat.

Internal colony

Around the time that many in the community of nations were organizing their resistance to the domination of American media products (Read, 1976), and many were demanding a New World Information and Communication Order (McPhail, 1987), a group of American policy scholars struggled to bring public attention to bear on an unusual counter-example. Félix Gutiérrez claimed that the Spanish International Network (SIN) had established a dominant position in the Spanish language television market in the United States in the 1960s. SIN moved beyond its primitive status as a 'bicycle' network that shuttled imported Mexican programmes from station to station, to an unparalleled position of power on the basis of direct satellite feeds from Mexico City (Gutiérrez, 1979). The Latino market had generally been ignored by domestic advertisers who tended to think of people who spoke Spanish in the United States as both foreign and poor in comparison with Hispanics in Latin America. Mexican entrepreneurs saw this same segment as a relatively wealthy population that could serve as a secondary market for Mexican film and video (Rodriguez, 1997).

While this example was presented to scholars and policy actors as a unique example of media imperialism (Gutiérrez and Schement, 1981 and 1994; Sinclair, 1990), the case of SIN also demonstrates the important role played by technology in developing the vital chain of supply that links immigrants to their homelands.

Market value

Astroff (1988/89) describes the process of transforming Chicanos and other Latino communities into valuable commodities as one marked by challenges and difficulties that went far beyond definition and measurement. She notes that the changes in the ideology of broadcast regulation in the 1980s made it difficult, if not impossible, to support the development of Spanish-language broadcasting on either cultural or political grounds. Instead, 'Latinos had to be presented as a lucrative and untapped market' (Astroff, 1988/89: 160). Article after article in the market-oriented press presented wildly optimistic and greatly varying estimates of the size and collective wealth of this market (Downing, 1992). At the same time, it was necessary for the advocates of this market to create a convincing image of Hispanics as consumers. Initially, some rather innovative stunts were used to convince advertisers of this fact. KCOR, a Spanish-language station in San Antonio Texas, asked its listeners to send in box tops, empty containers and other proofs of purchase in order to convince national advertisers that there were loyal customers who should not be ignored (Schement and Flores, 1977). In the process of enhancing the commercial value of this segment, reliance on traditional stereotypes of Latinos meant that 'all cultural values and experiences were translated into consumer preferences and behaviours' (Astroff, 1988/89: 163). What had been criticized as stubborn traditionalism became an enhancement when it was reconfigured strategically as an assurance of brand loyalty.

The Hispanic audience segment continues to be defined and differentiated by social class and linguistic preference across media, markets and categories of consumer goods. What remains to be seen is the extent to which the process of assimilation that generates the dissolution of ethnic segments in general will determine the future of the expanding Hispanic segment and the Asian segment that is just beginning to be defined.

Note

1. The author acknowledges the research assistance of Nancy Duda and the financial support of the Annenberg Public Policy Centre at the University of Pennsylvania.

References

'BLACK POWER. America's sharpening racial divide may be good for Robert Johnson, head of Black Entertainment Television', 1999: *The Economist* (10 April), 65.

ALBONETTI, J. and DOMINGUEZ, L., 1989: 'Major influences on consumer-goods marketers' decision to target US Hispanics', *Journal of Advertising* 21(1), 9–21.

ANDERSON, J., 1996: 'The pragmatics of audience in research and theory' in Hay, J., Grossberg, E. and Wartella, E. (eds), *The Audience and its Landscape*, Boulder, CO: Westview, 75–93.

ANG, I., 1991: *Desperately Seeking the Audience*, London: Routledge.

AQUIRRE, A. and BUSTAMENTE, D., 1993: 'Critical notes regarding the dislocation of Chicanos by the Spanish-language television industry in the United States', *Ethnic and Racial Studies* 16(1), 121–32.

ARMOUR, J., 1997: *Negrophobia and Reasonable Racism*, New York: New York University Press.

ASTROFF, R., 1988/89: 'Spanish gold: Stereotypes, ideology, and the construction of a US Latino market', *The Howard Journal of Communications* 1(4), 155–73.

BARWISE, P. and EHRENBERG, A., 1988: *Television and its Audience*, London: Sage.

BAUMGARTL, B. and FAVELL, A. (eds), 1995: *New Xenophobia in Europe*, London: Klewer Law International.

BENJAMIN, I., 1995: *The Black Press in Britain*, Staffordshire, UK: Trentham Books.

BIKSON, T. and PANIS, C., 1995: 'Computers and connectivity: Current trends' in Anderson, R., Bikson, T., Law, S. and Mitchell, B., *Universal Access to E-Mail. Feasibility and Societal Implications*, Santa Monica, CA: RAND, 13–40.

BRIE, H.L., 1977/78: 'Black newspapers: The roots are 150 years deep', *Journalism History* 4(4), 111–13.

BROOKS, D., 1995: 'In their own words: Advertisers' construction of an African-American consumer market, the World War II era', *The Howard Journal of Communications* 6(1–2), 32–52.

CALABRESE, A., 1997: 'Creative destruction? From the welfare state to the global information society', *Javnost* (The Public) 4(4), 7–24.

CANTOR, M., 1994: 'The role of the audience in the production of culture: A personal research retrospective', in Ettema, J. and Whitney, D.C., *Audiencemaking: How the Media Create the Audience*, Thousand Oaks, CA: Sage, 159–70.

CAREY, J. and ELTON, M., 1996: 'Forecasting demand for new consumer services: Challenges and alternatives', in Dholakia, R., Mundorf, N. and Dholakia,. *New Infotainment Technologies in the Home: Demand-side Perspectives*, Mahwah, NJ: Lawrence Erlbaum Associates, 35–57.

CARTER, B., 1996: 'Two upstart networks courting Black viewers', *The New York Times* (7 October): New York, C11.

CASTELLS, M., 1997: *The Power of Identity*, Malden, MA: Blackwell Publishers.

CORNELL, S. and HARTMANN, D., 1998: *Ethnicity and Race: Making Identities in a Changing World*, Thousand Oaks, CA: Pine Forge Press.

COTTLE, S., 1998: 'Making ethnic minority programmes inside the BBC: Professional pragmatics and cultural containment', *Media, Culture & Society* 20(2), 295–317.

DATES, J. and BARLOW, W. (eds), 1993: *Split Image: African-Americans in the Mass Media*, Washington DC: Howard University Press.

DAVIS, J. and GANDY, O., 1999: 'Racial identity and media orientation. Exploring the nature of constraint', *Journal of Black Studies* 29(3), 367–97.

DENTON, N. and MASSEY, D., 1993: *American Apartheid: Segregation and the Making of the Underclass*, Cambridge: Harvard University Press.

DERVIN, B., 1989: 'Users as research inventions: How research categories perpetuate inequities', *Journal of Communication* 39(3), 216–232.

DOVIDIO, J. and GARTNER, S. (eds), 1986: *Prejudice, Discrimination and Racism*, Orlando, FL: Academic Press.

DOWNING, J., 1992: 'Spanish-language media in the Greater New York region in the 1980s', in Riggins, S., *Ethnic Minority Media: An International Perspective*, Newbury Park, CA: Sage, 256–75.

ERVIN, K. and GILMORE, G., 1999: 'Traveling the superinformation highway. African-Americans' perceptions and use of cyberspace technology', *Journal of Black Studies* 29(3), 398–407.

EWAN, S., 1976: *Captains of Consciousness. Advertising and the Social Roots of the Consumer Culture*, New York: McGraw-Hill.

FABER, R., O'GUINN, T. *et al.*, 1986: 'Diversity in the ethnic media audience: A study of Spanish language broadcast preferences in the US', *International Journal of Intercultural Relations* 10, 347–59.

FRANK, R. and GREENBERG, M., 1980: *The Public's Use of Television*, Beverly Hills, CA: Sage.

——, 1982: *Audiences for Public Television*, Beverly Hills, CA: Sage.

FRASER, N., 1993: 'Rethinking the public sphere. A contribution to the critique of actually existing democracy' in Robbins, B., *The Phantom Public Sphere*, Minneapolis, MN: University of Minnesota Press, 1–32.

GANDY, O. and SIGNORIELLI, N., 1981: 'Audience production functions: A technical approach to programming', *Journalism Quarterly* 58, 232–40.

GANDY, O.H., 1998: *Communication and Race. A Structural Perspective*, London and New York: Edward Arnold and Oxford University Press.

GIBBONS, R.A. and ULLOTH, D., 1982: 'The role of the Amsterdam News in New York City's media environment', *Journalism Quarterly* 59(3), 451–55.

GOODSON, S. and SHAVER, M., 1994: 'Hispanic marketing: National advertiser spending patterns and media choices', *Journalism Quarterly* 71(1), 191–98.

GUTIÉRREZ, F. and SCHEMENT, J.R., 1981: 'Problems of ownership and control of Spanish-language media in the United States: National and international policy concerns' in McAnany, E., Schnitman, J. and Janus, N., *Communication and Social Structure: Critical Studies in Mass Media Research*, New York: Praeger, 181–203.

GUTIÉRREZ, F. and SCHEMENT, J.R., 1984: 'Spanish International Network. The flow of television from Mexico to the United States', *Communication Research* 11(2), 241–58.

GUTIÉRREZ, F., 1977: 'Spanish-language media in America: Background, resources, history', *Journalism History* 4(2), 34–41, 65–68.

——, 1979: 'Mexico's television network in the United States: The case of Spanish International Network' in Dordick, H., *Proceedings of the Sixth Annual Telecommunications Policy Research Conference*, Lexington, MA: Lexington Books, 135–59.

HALLER, H., 1988: 'Ethnic-language mass media and language loyalty in the United States today: The case of French, German, and Italian', *WORD* 39(3), 187–200.

HIRSCH, P., 1968: 'An analysis of *Ebony*: The magazine and its readers', *Journalism Quarterly* 45(2), 261–70, 292.

HUSBAND, C. and CHOUHAN, J., 1985: 'Local radio in the communication environment of ethnic minorities in Britain' in Dijk, T.V., *Discourse and Communication: New Approaches to the Analysis of Media Discourse and Communication*, Berlin: Walter de Gruyter, 270–94.

HUSBAND, C., 1994: 'General introduction: Ethnicity and media democratization within the nation-state' in Husband, C., *A Richer Vision: The Development of Ethnic Minority Media in Western Democracies*, Paris: UNESCO, 1–19.

JAKUBOWICZ, A., 1989: 'Speaking in tongues: Multicultural media and the constitution of the socially homogeneous Australian' in Wilson, H., *Australian Communication and the Public Sphere*, South Melbourne: MacMillan Co. of Australia, 105–27.

JHALLY, S. and LIVANT, B., 1986: 'Watching as working: The valorization of audience consciousness', *Journal of Communication* 36(3), 124–43.

JOHNSON, F., 1993/94: 'A history of the development of Black radio networks in the United States', *Journal of Radio Studies* 2, 173–87.

JONES, F., 1990: 'The Black audience and the BET channel', *Journal of Broadcasting and Electronic Media* 34(4), 477–86.

KARIM, K., 1997: 'Relocating the nexus of citizenship, heritage and technology', *Javnost* (The Public) 4(4), 75–86.

KEEVER, B., MARTINDALE, C. *et al.* (eds), 1997: *US News Coverage of Racial Minorities: A Sourcebook, 1934–1996*, Westport, CT: Greenwood Press.

LACY, S., STEPHENS, J. *et al.*, 1991: 'The future of the African-American press', *Newspaper Research Journal* 12(3), 8–19.

MCPHAIL, T., 1987: *Electronic Colonialism*, Newbury Park, CA: Sage.

MCQUAIL, D., 1992: *Media Performance: Mass Communication and the Public Interest*, London: Sage.

MAHAN, E., 1995: 'Culture industries and cultural identity: Will NAFTA make a difference?', *Studies in Latin American Popular Culture* 14, 17–35.

MEEHAN, E., 1993: 'Commodity audience, actual audience: The Blindspot Debate' in

Wasko, J., Mosco, V. and Pendakur, M., *Illuminating the Blindspots: Essays Honoring Dallas W. Smythe*, Norwood, NJ: Ablex: 378–97.

MOSCO, V., 1989: *The Pay-Per Society*, Norwood, NJ: Ablex.

——, 1996: *The Political Economy of Communication*, London: Sage.

MYRICK, H. and KEEGAN, C., 1981: *In search of Diversity*, Symposium on minority audiences and programming research: Approaches and applications, Washington DC: Corporation for Public Broadcasting.

NEUMAN, W.R., 1991: *The Future of the Mass Audience*, New York: Cambridge University Press.

NEWMAN, M., 1988: *Entrepreneurs of Profit and Pride. From Black Appeal to Radio Soul*, New York: Praeger.

OFORI, K., *et al.*, 1997: *Media Ownership Concentration and the Future of Black Radio*, Brooklyn, NY: Medgar Evers College Press.

OFORI, K.A., 1999: 'When being No. 1 is not enough: the impact of advertising practices on minority-owned and minority-formatted broadcast stations', Washington DC: Civil Rights Forum on Communications Policy.

OMI, M. and WINANT, H., 1994: *Racial Formation in the United States from the 1960s to the 1990s*, New York: Routledge.

OWEN, B. and WILDMAN, S., 1992: *Video Economics*, Cambridge, MA: Harvard University Press.

OWENS, R., 1996: 'Entering the Twenty-First Century: Oppression and the African-American Press' in Berry, V. and Manning-Miller, C., *Mediated Messages and African-American Culture: Contemporary Issues*, Thousand Oaks, CA: Sage, 96–116.

PATTERSON, R., 1990: 'Development of ethnic and multicultural media in Australia', *International Migration* 28(1), 89–103.

PETERSON, R., 1994: 'Measured markets and unknown audiences: Case studies from the production and consumption of music' in Ettema, J. and Whitney, DC, *Audiencemaking: How the Media Create the Audience*, Thousand Oaks, CA: Sage, 171–85.

POLIC, J.G. and GANDY, O.H., 1991: 'The emergence of the marketplace standard', *Media Law and Practice*, 55–64.

PRIDE, A. and WILSON, C., 1997: *History of the Black Press*, Washington DC: Howard University Press.

RATCLIFF, P., 1994: 'Conceptualizing "race", ethnicity and nation: towards a comparative perspective' in Ratcliff, P., *Race, Ethnicity and Nation*, London: UCL Press, 2–25.

READ, W., 1976: *America's Mass Media Merchants*, Baltimore, MD: Johns Hopkins University Press.

RIGGINS, S., 1992: 'The media imperative. Ethnic minority survival in the age of mass communication' in Riggins, S., *Ethnic Minority Media: An International Perspective*, Newbury Park, CA: Sage, 1–22.

RODRIGUEZ, A., 1996: 'Objectivity and ethnicity in the production of the *Noticiero Univisión*', *Critical Studies in Mass Communication* 13, 59–81.

——, 1997: 'Commercial ethnicity: Language, class and race in the marketing of the Hispanic audience', *The Communication Review* 2(3), 283–309.

SCHEMENT, J. and FLORES, R., 1977: 'The origins of Spanish-language radio: The case of San Antonio, Texas', *Journalism History* 4(2), 56–58, 61.

SCHEMENT, J., 1998: 'Thorough Americans: Minorities and the new media' in Garmer, A., *Investing in Diversity: Advancing Opportunities for Minorities and the Media*, Washington, DC: Aspen Institute, 87–124.

SCHILLER, D., 1999: *Digital Capitalism. Networking the Global Market System*, Cambridge, MA: MIT Press.

SIEGELMAN, P. and WALDFOGEL, J., 1998: 'Race and radio: Preference externalities, minority ownership, and the provision of programming to minorities', Philadelphia, PA: Wharton School, University of Pennsylvania.

SINCLAIR, J., 1990: 'Spanish-language television in the United States: Televisa surrenders its domain', *Studies in Latin American Popular Culture* 9, 39–63.

SMITH, N. C. and COOPER-MARTIN, E., 1997: 'Ethics and target marketing: The role of product harm and consumer vulnerability', *Journal of Marketing* 61(3), 1.

SORUCO, G., 1996: *Cubans and the Mass Media in South Florida*, Gainesville, FL: University Press of Florida.

SUBERVI-VELEZ, F., 1986: 'The mass media and ethnic assimilation and pluralism. A review and research proposal with special focus on Hispanics', *Communication Research* 13(1), 71–96.

SURLIN, S., 1972: 'Black-oriented radio: Programming to a perceived audience', *Journal of Broadcasting* 16(3), 289–98.

TRESCOTT, J., 1996: 'In the black. Small networks seek to win minority audiences', *Washington Post* (15 September): Washington DC, G1.

TUROW, J., 1997: *Breaking up America: Advertisers and the New Media World*, Chicago: University of Chicago Press.

US OFFICE OF MANAGEMENT AND BUDGET, 1998: 'Revisions to the standards for the classification of Federal data on race and ethnicity', Washington DC.

WEBSTER, J. and PHALEN, P., 1994: 'Victim, consumer, or commodity?' in Ettema, J. and Whitney, D.C., *Audiencemaking: How the Media Create the Audience*, Thousand Oaks, CA: Sage.

——, 1997: *The Mass Audience. Rediscovering the Dominant Model*, Mahwah, NJ: Lawrence Erlbaum Associates.

WILDMAN, S. and KARAMANIS, T., 1998: 'The economics of minority programming in Garmer, A., *Investing in Diversity: Advancing Opportunities for Minorities and Media*, Washington, DC: Aspen Institute, 47–65.

WOLSELEY, R., 1990: *The Black Press, USA*, Iowa City, IA: Iowa State University Press.

WYNTER, L., 1998: 'TV Programmers drop "Black-block" lineups', *Wall Street Journal* (2 September): Eastern US, B1.

ZHANG, K. and XIAOMING, H., 1999: 'The Internet and the ethnic press: A study of electronic Chinese publications', *The Information Society* 15(1), 21–30.

4

Culture, Communications and Political Economy

Peter Golding and Graham Murdock

Everyone, from politicians to academics, now agrees that public communications systems are part of the 'cultural industries'. The popularity of this tag points to a growing awareness that these organizations are both similar to and different from other industries. On the one hand, they clearly have a range of features in common with other areas of production and are increasingly integrated into the general industrial structure; on the other, it is equally clear that the goods they manufacture – newspapers, advertisements, television programmes and feature films – play a pivotal role in organizing the images and discourses through which people make sense of the world. A number of writers acknowledge this duality rhetorically, but go on to examine only one side, focusing either on the construction and consumption of media meanings (e.g. Fiske, 1989) or on the economic organization of media industries (e.g. Collins, Garnham and Locksley, 1988). What distinguishes the critical political economy perspective outlined here is precisely its focus on the interplay between the symbolic and economic dimensions of public communications. It sets out to show how different ways of financing and organizing cultural production have traceable consequences for the range of discourses and representations in the public domain and for audiences' access to them.

Critical political economy of communications – straw men and stereotypes

Some terms become notoriously loose in practice, acquiring the status of cliché or slogan rather than analytical precision. One such term in our field is 'critical' analysis, often (and wearily) contrasted with 'administrative' research. The dichotomy between empirical (often implying simply quantitative) work and more theoretical concerns became equated rather loosely with the distinction between administrative (meaning commissioned by the media companies by and large) and critical work (meaning broadly marxisant). The dichotomy was always false and has been much lamented and regretted.

The approach we are outlining here is clearly critical, but in a sense that necessarily engages with empirical research, and which has no qualms about
addressing issues of pragmatic and policy concern. It is critical in the crucial
sense that it draws for its analysis on a critique, a theoretically informed understanding, of the social order in which communications and cultural phenomena
are being studied.

This is a characteristic that it shares with another major tradition of research:
cultural studies. Both work within a broadly neo-marxist view of society, both are
centrally concerned with the constitution and exercise of power, and both take
their distance from the liberal pluralist tradition of analysis with its broad acceptance of the central workings of advanced capitalist societies (Curran, 1990: 139).
But this shared general stance conceals long-standing differences of approach,
generated by the divergent intellectual histories of these traditions, and sustained
by their very different locations on the contemporary academic map.

Whereas critical political economy has been institutionalized within faculties
of social science – and draws its major practitioners from the ranks of people
trained in economics, political science and sociology – departments and programmes of cultural studies are still mostly situated in humanities faculties and
pursued by scholars drawn from literary and historical studies. As a result, the
two groups tend to approach communications with rather different interests and
reference points, even when there is a strong desire to cut across disciplinary
boundaries, as there often is.

Work on communications from within a cultural studies perspective 'is centrally concerned with the construction of meaning – how it is produced in and
through particular expressive forms and how it is continually negotiated and
deconstructed through the practices of everyday life' (Murdock, 1989a: 436).
This project has generated work in two distinct, but related, areas. The first, and
by far the largest, concentrates on the analysis of cultural texts, including those
produced by the media industries. In contrast to transportation models, which
see media forms such as thrillers, soap operas or documentary films as vehicles
for transmitting 'messages' to consumers, cultural studies approaches them as
mechanisms for ordering meaning in particular ways. Where content analysis
sees the meaning of, say, a violent act in a television drama, as definable in
advance and detachable from its position in the text or the programme's relation
to other texts, cultural studies insists that its meaning is variable and depends
crucially on the contexts supplied by the overall narrative, the programme's
genre and the previous publicity surrounding the show and its stars.

This emphasis on the relational dimensions of meaning and its consequent
mutability is pursued in a second major strand in cultural studies research which
is concerned with the way that audience members interpret media artefacts and
incorporate them into their worldviews and lifestyles. This ethnographic thrust
celebrates the creativity of consumers (see, e.g., Willis, 1990) and views audience
members as active subjects, continually struggling to make sense of their situation, rather than as passive objects of a dominant production system. This
thrust is part of cultural studies' wider attempt to retrieve the complexity of
popular practices and beliefs. As a powerful counter to the simpler notions of
'effects' and the dismissive critiques of popular culture as trivial and manipulative, it is clearly a very considerable gain. However, as we shall see, it can easily
collude with conservative celebrations of untrammelled consumer choice.

In common with liberal defenders of the 'free' market, some influential currents within cultural analysis have emphasized the moment of exchange, when the meanings carried by texts meet the meanings that readers bring to them. In both styles of analysis, this encounter is removed from its wider contexts and presented as an instance of consumer sovereignty. For writers like John Fiske, it is also a signal of popular resistance, of 'ideology countered or evaded; top-down power opposed by bottom-up power, social discipline faced with disorder' (Fiske, 1989: 47). This romantic celebration of subversive consumption is clearly at odds with cultural studies' long-standing concern with the way the mass media operate ideologically, to sustain and support prevailing relations of domination. But even if this wider perspective is restored there is still the problem that cultural studies offers an analysis of the way the cultural industries work that has little or nothing to say about how they actually operate as industries, and how their economic organization impinges on the production and circulation of meaning. Nor does it examine the ways in which people's consumption choices are structured by their position in the wider economic formation. Exploring these dynamics is the primary task for a critical political economy of communications. In doing so we would be following Raymond Williams' injunction that 'we should look not for the components of a product but for the conditions of a practice' (Williams, 1980: 48).

Critical work, then, is not the opposite of administrative research, nor is it unambiguously opposed to the methods or concerns of cultural studies. Two central features of critical analysis take us a little nearer to a meaningful demarcation, first in terms of epistemology, second in terms of historicity.

The critical perspective assumes a realist conception of the phenomena it studies in the simple sense that the theoretical constructs it works with exist in the real world – they are not merely phenomenal. For this reason critical analysis is centrally concerned with questions of action and structure, in an attempt to discern the real constraints that shape the lives and opportunities of real actors in the real world. In this sense critical theory is also materialist, in its focus on the interaction of people with their material environment and its further preoccupation with the unequal command over material resources and the consequences of such inequality for the nature of the symbolic environment.

In addition, critical analysis is historically located. It is specifically interested in the investigation and description of late capitalism, which it defines as both dynamic and problematic, as undergoing change and as substantially imperfect. This historical anchoring of critical analysis is distinct from any approach, which is essentialist, detached from the specifics of historical time and place.

In this chapter, however, we have a less ambitious objective, which is to describe the basic tenets of a critical political economy of the media. While this approach assumes a critical analysis of contemporary society, it is far from a full account.

What is critical political economy?

Critical political economy differs from mainstream economics in four main respects: first, it is holistic; second, it is historical; third, it is centrally concerned with the balance between capitalist enterprise and public intervention; and, finally – and perhaps most importantly of all – it goes beyond technical issues of efficiency to engage with basic moral questions of justice, equity and the public good.

Whereas mainstream economics sees the 'economy' as a separate and specialized domain, critical political economy is interested in the interplay between economic organization and political, social and cultural life. In the case of the cultural industries we are particularly concerned to trace the impact of economic dynamics on the range and diversity of public cultural expression and its availability to different social groups. These concerns are not, of course, exclusive to critical commentators, they are equally central to political economists on the Right. The difference lies in the starting points of the analyses.

Liberal political economists focus on exchange in the market as consumers choose between competing commodities on the basis of the utility and satisfaction they offer. The greater the play of market forces, the greater the 'freedom' of consumer choice. Over the last two decades, this vision has gained renewed credence with governments of a variety of ideological hues. Born again in their faith in Adam Smith's hidden hand of 'free' competition, they have pushed through programmes of privatization of public services designed to increase consumer choice by extending the scale and scope of market mechanisms. Against this, critical political economists follow Marx in shifting attention from the realm of exchange to the organization of property and production, both within the cultural industries and more generally. They do not deny that cultural producers and consumers are continually making choices, but point out that they do so within wider structures.

Where mainstream economics focuses on the sovereign individuals of capitalism, critical political economy starts with sets of social relations and the play of power. It is interested in seeing how the making and taking of meaning is shaped at every level by the structured asymmetries in social relations. These range from the way news is structured by the prevailing relations between press proprietors and editors or journalists and their sources, to the way that television viewing is affected by the organization of domestic life and power relations within the family. These concerns are of course widely shared by researchers who are not political economists. What marks critical political economy is that it always goes beyond situated action to show how particular micro-contexts are shaped by general economic dynamics and the wider structures they sustain. It is especially interested in the ways that communicative activity is structured by the unequal distribution of material and symbolic resources.

Developing an analysis along these lines means avoiding the twin temptations of instrumentalism and structuralism. Instrumentalists focus on the ways that capitalists use their economic power with a commercial market system to ensure that the flow of public information is consonant with their interests. They see the privately owned media as instruments of class domination. This case is vigorously argued in Edward S. Herman and Noam Chomsky's book, *Manufacturing Consent: The Political Economy of the Mass Media* (1988). They develop what they call a 'propaganda model' of the American news media, arguing that 'the powerful are able to fix the premises of discourse, to decide what the general populace is allowed to see, hear and think about, and to "manage" public opinion by regular propaganda campaigns' (1988: xi). They are partly right. Government and business elites do have privileged access to the news; large advertisers do operate as a latter-day licensing authority, selectively supporting some newspapers and television programmes and not others; and media proprietors can determine the editorial line and cultural stance of the papers and broadcast stations they own. But by focusing on these kinds of strategic intervention they overlook the contradictions in the system. Owners, advertisers and key political personnel cannot always do as they would wish. They operate within structures that constrain as well as facilitate, imposing limits as well as offering opportunities. Analysing the nature and sources of these limits is a key task for a critical political economy of culture.

At the same time, it is essential to avoid the forms of structuralism that conceive of structures as building-like edifices – solid, permanent and immovable. Instead, we need to see them as dynamic formations that are constantly reproduced and altered through practical action. In his review of news studies, Michael Schudson argues that political economy relates the outcome of the news process directly to the economic structure of news organizations, and that 'everything in between is a black box that need not be examined' (Schudson, 1989: 266). This is a misreading. Although some studies confine themselves to the structural level of analysis, it is only part of the story we need to tell. Analysing the way that meaning is made and re-made through the concrete activities of producers and consumers is equally essential to the perspective we are proposing here. The aim is 'to explain how it comes about that structures are constituted through action, and reciprocally how action is constituted structurally' (Giddens, 1976: 161).

This, in turn, requires us to think of economic determination in a more flexible way. Instead of holding on to Marx's notion of determination in the *last* instance, with its implication that everything can eventually be related directly to economic forces, we can follow Stuart Hall in seeing determination as operating in the *first* instance (Hall, 1983: 84). That is to say, we can think of economic dynamics as playing a central role in defining the key features of the general environment within which communicative activity takes place, but not as a complete explanation of the nature of that activity.

Critical political economy is also necessarily historical, but historical in a particular sense. In the terms coined by the great French historian, Fernand Braudel, it is interested in how 'the fast-moving time of events, the subject of traditional narrative history' relates to the 'slow but perceptible rhythms' that characterize the gradually unfolding history of economic formations and systems of rule (Burke, 1980: 94). Four historical processes are particularly central to a critical political economy of culture: the growth of the media; the extension of corporate reach; commodification; and the changing role of state and government intervention.

What Thompson describes as 'the general process by which the transmission of symbolic forms becomes increasingly mediated by the technical and institutional apparatuses of the media industries' (1990: 3–4) makes the media industries the logical place to begin an analysis of contemporary culture.

Media production, in turn, has been increasing commandeered by large corporations and moulded to their interests and strategies. This has long been the case, but the reach of corporate rationales has been considerably extended in recent years by the push towards 'privatization' and the declining vitality of publicly funded cultural institutions. Corporations dominate the cultural landscape in two ways. First, an increasing proportion of cultural production is directly accounted for by major conglomerates with interests in a range of sectors, from newspapers and magazines, to television, film, music and theme parks. Second, corporations that are not directly involved in the cultural industries as producers, can exercise considerable control over the direction of cultural activity through their role as advertisers and sponsors. The financial viability of commercial broadcasting together with a large section of the press depends directly on advertising revenue, whilst more and more of the other 'sites where creative work is displayed', such as museums, galleries and theatres, 'have been captured by corporate sponsors' and enlisted in their public relations campaigns (Schiller, 1989: 4).

The extension of corporate reach reinforces a third major process: the commodification of cultural life. A commodity is a good that is produced in order to be exchanged at a price. Commercial communications corporations have always been in the business of commodity production. At first, their activities were confined to producing symbolic commodities that could be consumed directly, such as novels, newspapers, or theatrical performances. Later, with the rise of new domestic technologies such as the gramophone, telephone and radio set, cultural consumption required consumers to purchase the appropriate machine (or hardware) as a condition of access. This compounded the already considerable effect of inequalities in disposable income, and made communicative activity more dependent on ability to pay. Before they could make a telephone call or listen to the latest hit record at home, people needed to buy the appropriate equipment. As we shall see, the higher a household's income, the more likely it is to own key pieces of hardware – a telephone, a video recorder, a home computer – and hence the greater its communicative choices.

At first sight, advertising-supported broadcasting seems to be an exception to this trend, since anyone who has a receiving set has access to the full range of programming – they do not have to pay again. However, this analysis ignores two important points: first, audiences do contribute to the costs of programming in the form of additions to the retail price of heavily advertised goods; second, within this system, audiences themselves are the primary commodity. The economics of commercial broadcasting revolves around the exchange of audiences for advertising revenue. The price that corporations pay for advertising spots on particular programmes is determined by the size and social composition of the audience it attracts. And in prime-time, the premium prices are commanded by shows that can attract and hold the greatest number of viewers and provide a symbolic environment in tune with consumption. These needs inevitably tilt programming towards familiar and well-tested formulas and formats, away from risk and innovation, and anchor it in common sense rather than alternative viewpoints. Hence the audience's position as a commodity serves to reduce the overall diversity of programming and ensure that it confirms established mores and assumptions far more often than it challenges them.

The main institutional counter to the commodification of communicative activity has come from the development of institutions funded out of taxation and oriented towards providing cultural resources for the full exercise of citizenship. The most important and pervasive of these have been the public broadcasting organization, typified by the British Broadcasting Corporation (BBC) which has distanced itself from the dynamics of commodification by not taking spot advertising and by offering the full range of programming equally to every-one who has paid the basic annual licence fee. As the BBC's first Director-General, John Reith, put it: public broadcasting 'may be shared by all alike, for the same outlay, and to the same extent . . . there need be no first and third class' (Reith, 1924: 217–18).

As we shall see, however, this ideal has been substantially undermined in the last decade as the Corporation has responded to a fall in the real value of the licence fee by expanding its commercial activities in an effort to raise money. In a marked departure from the historic commitment to universal and equal pro-vision, these include plans to launch subscription channels for special interest groups.

At the same time, the Corporation has also come under intensified political pressure, particularly in the areas of news and current affairs. Its always fragile independence from government has been challenged by a series of moves, rang-ing from well-publicized attacks on the 'impartiality' of its news coverage to police seizures of film and, for several years until 1994, a government ban on live interviews with members of a range of named organizations in Northern Ireland, including the legal political party Sinn Fein.

These attempts to narrow the field of public discourse and representation are part of a wider historical process whereby the state in capitalist societies has assumed a greater and greater role in managing communicative activity. From its inception, political economy has been particularly interested in determining the appropriate scope of public intervention. It is therefore inevitably involved in evaluating competing policies. It is concerned with changing the world as well as with analysing it. Classical political economists and their present-day follow-ers start from the assumption that public intervention ought to be minimized and market forces given the widest possible freedom of operation. Critical polit-ical economists on the other hand point to the distortions and inequalities of market systems and argue that these deficiencies can only be rectified by public intervention, though they disagree on the forms that this should take.

Arguments within political economy on the proper balance between public and private enterprise are never simply technical, however. They are always underpinned by distinctive visions of what constitutes the 'public good'. Adam Smith ended his career as a professor of moral philosophy. He saw markets not simply as a more efficient, but as morally superior. Because they gave consumers a free choice between competing commodities, only those goods that provided satisfaction would survive. At the same time, he saw very clearly that the public good was not simply the sum of individual choices, and that private enterprise would not provide everything that a good society required. He saw particular problems in the sphere of culture, and recommended various public interven-tions to increase the level of public knowledge and provide wholesome enter-tainment. Critical political economy takes this line of reasoning a good deal further, linking the constitution of the good society to the extension of citizen-ship rights.

The history of modern communications media is not only an economic his-tory of their growing incorporation into a capitalist economic system, but also a political history of their increasingly centrality to the exercise of full citizen-ship. In its most general sense, citizenship is 'about the conditions that allow people to become full members of the society at every level' (Murdock and

Golding, 1989: 182). In an ideal situation, communications systems would contribute to these conditions in two important ways. First, they would provide people with access to the information, advice and analysis that would enable them to know their rights and to pursue them effectively. Second, they would provide the broadest possible range of information, interpretation and debate on areas that involve political choices, and enable them to register dissent and propose alternatives. This argument has been elaborated by the German theorist, Jurgen Habermas, in his highly influential notion of the 'public sphere'.

His historical narrative explains that in the early capitalist period a range of practices and institutions were evolved which facilitated rational and critical discussion of public affairs (Habermas, 1989; Golding, 1995). This open arena of debate, in which the emerging newspaper press paid a prominent role (especially in Britain), was, so Habermas argues, a feature found throughout industrializing western Europe. As critics have pointed out, however, his view of the past is highly idealized. In the first place, like early enthusiasts of a 'free' commercial press, he is 'far too sanguine about the capacity of market competition to ensure the universal access of citizens to the media of communication' and fails to examine 'the inevitable tension between the free choices of investors and property owners and the freedom of choice of citizens receiving and sending information' (Keane, 1989: 39). Second, this historic public sphere was an essentially bourgeois space, which largely excluded the working class, women and ethnic minorities.

Nevertheless, the idea of the public sphere is worth retaining, provided that we add that it needs to be open enough that all groups in the society can recognise themselves and their aspirations as being fairly represented. This general ideal of a communications system as a public cultural space that is open, diverse and accessible, provides the basic yardstick against which critical political economy measures the performance of existing systems and formulates alternatives.

Political economy in practice: three core tasks

In order to illustrate the concerns and distinctive priorities of a critical political economy of communications we will briefly outline three areas of analysis. The first is concerned with the production of cultural goods, to which political economy attaches particular importance in its presumption of the limiting (but not completely determining) impact of cultural production on the range of cultural consumption. Second, we examine the political economy of texts to illustrate ways in which the representations present in media products are related to the material realities of their production and consumption. Finally, we assess the political economy of cultural consumption, to illustrate the relation between material and cultural inequality which political economy is distinctively concerned to address.

The production of meaning as the exercise of power

Philip Elliott, in a bleak reading of developments in Britain in the early 1980s, suggested that the public sphere has been seriously eroded by recent developments. Technological and economic developments were promoting 'a continuation of the shift away from involving people in societies as political citizens of nation states towards involving them as consumption units in a corporate world'. Intellectuals, in particular, were being robbed of those public forums in which they could engage in their culture of critical discourse (Elliott, 1982: 243–44). A focal question for the political economy of communications is to investigate how changes in the array of forces that exercise control over cultural production and distribution limit or liberate the public sphere.

This directs attention to two key issues. The first is the pattern of ownership of such institutions and the consequences of this pattern for control over their activities. The second is the nature of the relationship between state regulation and communications institutions. We will briefly review each of these in turn.

The steadily increasing amount of cultural production accounted for by large corporations has long been a source of concern to theorists of democracy. They saw a fundamental contradiction between the ideal that public media should operate as a public sphere and the reality of concentrated private ownership. They feared that proprietors would use their property rights to restrict the flow of information and open debate on which the vitality of democracy depended. These concerns were fuelled by the rise of the great press barons at the turn of the century. Not only did proprietors like Pulitzer and Hearst in the United States and Northcliffe in England own chains of newspapers with large circulations, they clearly had no qualms about using them to promote their pet political causes or to denigrate positions and people they disagreed with.

These long-standing worries have been reinforced in recent years by the emergence of multimedia conglomerates with significant stakes across a range of central communications sectors. Time Warner, one of the world's top three media companies, is a textbook illustration of this trend in action. Originally formed in 1989 when the major American magazine publisher, Time, merged with the audio-visual interests grouped around the Warner film studios, it has since made a number of strategic acquisitions, including Ted Turner's television company in 1996. As a consequence it is now a major international player in book publishing, recorded music, feature film production and exhibition, satellite and cable television programming (through the CNN news channel, the Home Box Office and Cinemax movie channels, and the Cartoon Network), and animation, video games and children's toys (through the Hanna-Barbera studios, a 23 per cent stake in Atari and a 14 per cent share in Hasbro). Time Warner has also recently merged with the internet giant AOL.

This combination of key holdings is repeated, with variations, in the portfolios of Time Warner's major global competitors, Bertelsmann and News International. Bertelsmann, has used its extensive German publishing interests as a launch pad for diversification into commercial television, recorded music and American book publishing (through the 1998 acquisition of Random House) whilst Rupert Murdoch has assembled a diversified audio-visual empire on the back of his dominant Australian and British press holdings. This currently stretches from the Twentieth Century Fox film studios and the Fox television network in the United States, to three major satellite television systems: Star, which operates across Asia and the Middle East; BSkyB, which dominates the sector in the UK; and Latin Sky Broadcasting, a joint venture with the American telecoms and cable giant AT&T and the two major broadcasting conglomerates operating in Latin America – Televisa based in Mexico and Globo based in Brazil (see Herman and McChesney, 1997, Chapter 3).

The rise of communications conglomerates adds a new element to the old debate about potential abuses of owner power. It is no longer a simple case of proprietors intervening in editorial decisions or firing key personnel who fall foul of their political philosophies. Cultural production is also strongly influenced by commercial strategies built around 'synergies' that exploit the overlaps between the company's different media interests. The company's newspapers may give free publicity to their television stations or the record and book divisions may launch products related to a new movie released by the film division. The effect is to reduce the diversity of cultural goods in circulation. Although in simple quantitative terms there may be more commodities in circulation, they are more likely to be variants of the same basic themes and images.

In addition to the power they exercise directly over the companies they own, the major media moguls also have considerable indirect power over smaller concerns operating in their markets or seeking to break into them. They establish the rules by which the competitive game will be played. They can use their greater financial power to drive new entrants out of the market-place by launching expensive promotional campaigns, offering discounts to advertisers, or buying up key creative personnel, whilst firms that do survive compete for market share by offering similar products to the leading concerns and employing tried and tested editorial formulae.

The powers of the major communications corporations and their cultural and geographical reach are currently being extended by the move towards digital technologies coupled with the worldwide romance with 'free' markets (see Murdock, 1994b). For the first time, all forms of communication – written text, statistical data, still and moving images, music and the human voice – can be coded, stored and relayed using the same basic digital array of zeroes and ones, the language of computing. As a result, the boundaries that have separated different communications sectors up until now are being rubbed away. We are entering the era of convergence. The potentials are impressive. Cultural products flow between and across media in an increasingly fluid way. New combinations become possible. Consumers can use the upgraded telecommunications and cable networks to call up materials of their choice from vast electronic archives and libraries in the combinations and sequences they desire whenever they wish. Enthusiasts present these possibilities as ushering in the transfer of power from owners to audiences. One of the most vocal celebrants is Rupert Murdoch, one of the most powerful of the present-day media moguls. As he told a conference in September 1993, 'I must add (with maybe a tiny touch of regret) that this technology has liberated people from the once powerful media barons' (quoted in Greenslade, 1993: 17). Because, in the age of digital technology, he believes 'anybody will be able to start media, or get anything they want for the price of a phone call' there will be no place for him or his fellow media barons (quoted in Bell, 1993: 25).

The spectacle of Rupert Murdoch cheerfully writing his own business obituary is attractive but deeply flawed. The fact that consumers will have access to a wider range of cultural goods, provided they can pay (a point we shall come back to presently) does nothing to abolish the power of the media moguls. In the emerging environment, power will lie with those who own the key building blocks of new communications systems, the rights to the key pieces of technology and, even more importantly, the rights to the cultural materials – the films, books, images, sounds, writings – that will be used to put together the new services. And in the battle for command over intellectual properties, the media moguls have a sizeable advantage since they already own a formidable range of the expressive assets that are central to public culture, and this range is steadily increasing through acquisitions, mergers and new partnerships.

Over the last five years, the major companies' scramble to position themselves to maximum advantage in a rapidly moving communications environment, has produced the biggest wave of mergers and acquisitions in media history. This movement has been greatly aided by the removal or relaxation of the regulatory barriers that previously prevented consolidation across major sectors. In the United States, for example, we have seen the increasing integration of the Hollywood film studios with the major commercial television networks, producing an unprecedentedly powerful force in the global audio-visual market-place, which Jeremy Tunstall has dubbed 'Hollyweb' (Tunstall, 1998).

The process began in 1994, when Viacom, which controls thirteen US television stations, bought the Paramount studio, and was massively strengthened in 1995 when Disney purchased one of the top three television networks, ABC/Capital Cities for $19 billion (which, at the time, was one of the biggest acquisitions in American corporate history). Consolidation within the media and cultural industries is, however, only part of the story. Arguably, the recent entry of major players from the telecommunications and computing sectors may prove significant in the long run. This has been prompted by two developments: the technological convergence produced by digitalization and the permissive business environment created by more relaxed regulatory regimes. In 1999, for example, AT&T, the third largest US telecommunications company (as measured by market capitalization) acquired the country's second largest cable television group, Tele-Communications, Inc. (TCI), giving it the potential to deliver home entertainment as well as high-speed local phone services and internet access.

The very rapid growth of the internet, which has been the major communications phenomenon of the second half of the 1990s, has prompted a particularly concentrated flurry of activity as major corporations have belatedly grasped its enormous potential as a 'platform' for delivering broadcast services and organizing electronic transactions such as home banking, shopping and pay-per-view. Bill Gates, who has established a dominant position in the global computer software market, has been particularly active in exploring these possibilities. In an early move in 1997, his major operating company, Microsoft, bought up WebTV, a California-based company that had pioneered technology which allowed viewers to surf the net using their television sets rather than a personal computer. In 1998 WebTV joined up with BT, the leading British telecommunications company, to develop trials of the system in the UK, and in 1999 Microsoft and BT signed a general agreement to develop internet access for mobile telephone users.

Moreover, the geographical reach of these conglomerates and strategic alliances are being rapidly extended as governments around the world embrace privatization and 'free' market economies, allowing the major communications companies access to previously closed or restricted markets and increased scope for action. The opening up of markets in the former territories of the Soviet

Empire and in China are simply the most substantial instances in a general trend.

Historically, the main interruptions to this process have come from state intervention. These have taken two main forms. First, commercial enterprises have been regulated in the public interest with the aim of ensuring diversity of cultural production, including forms that would be unlikely to survive in pure market conditions. British commercial television companies, for example, are required to make a range of minority interest programmes, even though they are not profitable. Second, cultural diversity has been further underwritten by various forms of public subsidy.

Over the last two decades, however, this system has been substantially altered by privatization policies. Major public cultural enterprises, such as the French TF1 television network, have been sold to private investors. Liberalization policies have introduced private operators into markets that were previously closed to competition, such as the broadcasting systems of a number of European countries. And regulatory regimes have been altered in favour of freedom of operation for owners and advertisers. The net effect of these changes has been to greatly increase the potential reach and power of the major communications companies and to reinforce the danger that public culture will be commandeered by private interests. Charting these shifts in the balance between commercial and public enterprise and tracing their impact on cultural diversity is a key task for a critical political economy.

There are several dimensions to this process. First, state agencies such as the army and police have become major users of communications technologies, both for surveillance and for their own command and control systems. Second, governments and state departments have become increasingly important producers of public information in a variety of forms ranging from official statistics and daily press briefings to public advertising campaigns. Third, governments have extended their regulatory functions in relation to both the structure of the media industries (through restrictions on ownership and pricing, for example) and the range of permissible public expression (through regulations relating to areas such as obscenity, incitement to racial hatred and 'national security'). Lastly, and most important of all, liberal democratic governments have widened the range of cultural activities that they subsidize out of the public purse: either indirectly, by not charging value added tax on newspapers, for example; or directly, through various forms of grants. These range from the monies provided for museums, libraries and theatres to the compulsory annual licence fee for television set ownership which funds the BBC.

Broadcasting in Britain has evolved as a quasi-public institution, in which the ideals of public service have been translated into both law and custom and practice. The BBC, particularly under its first Director-General John Reith, construed itself as undertaking a mission to inform, educate and entertain, in a potent if indistinct ideology which has been readily adopted by commercial broadcasting. Both see themselves as performing a role more akin to education or health than to conventional purveyors of commodities in the market-place. The patrician overtones in such a self-assigned role, and the contradictions it generates for a medium dependent on advertising revenue, have undermined the credibility of this conception of broadcasting, and the enterprise culture of 1980s Conservatism enthusiastically challenged the idea that broadcasting should be protected from the disciplines of the market, arguing that consumer choice and cultural independence were best guaranteed by liberating the broadcast media from state regulation.

Defenders of public service broadcasting have found themselves wrong-footed, appearing to support a bureaucratic and statist conception of communications which was far from the ideals of the 'public sphere'. In addition, they seem to be ignoring the boundless potential of new technologies which might deliver the choice and communicative opportunities of an ideal 'public sphere' far more readily than the dead hand of state intervention.

The contribution of political economy to this debate is to analyse how and in what ways the relation between the media and the state has consequences for the range of expression and ideas in the public arena. The present dilemma of the BBC in Britain, provides an instructive case in point. After a long and often ill-tempered debate, the government finally published its plans for the Corporation's future in July 1994. The document was greeted with a sigh of collective relief from the BBC's supporters. The Royal Charter (under which the BBC operates) was to be renewed for a further ten years when the present one expired in 1996. The vocal lobby in favour of privatizing the Corporation had been routed. It appeared to be business as usual. But a closer look reveals a rather less clear-cut outcome (Murdock, 1994a). The licence fee (which provides the great bulk of the BBC's income) is only renewed for five years and will be reviewed 'before then in the light of technological and other developments'. In particular, there will be continuing consideration of the possibility of transferring 'all or some of the BBC's services to a subscription system'. By converting them from public goods, equally available to all, into commodities accessible only at a price this would transform the Corporation into a major commercial company in the international media market-place (HMSO, 1994: 31).

Indeed, this move is already under way. The government has nominated the BBC as a 'national champion' and encouraged it to capitalize on its reputation as vigorously as possible in the expanding global market-place for television programming created by the growth of home video, satellite and cable systems. To enable the Corporation to 'create and sustain a United Kingdom presence in an international multi-media world' . . . 'the Government has encouraged' it 'to develop its commercial activities, seeking private sector partners and finance' (HMSO, 1994: 24). The Corporation has pursued this challenge with increasing enthusiasm in recent years, through its Enterprises division, now renamed BBC Worldwide. In a major deal, signed in 1997, Flextech (a subsidiary of Tele-Communications, Inc.) was given preferential rights to past and future BBC programming for a period of thirty years, in return for a substantial investment in production. The first fruits of this partnership were four themed advertising-supported channels using BBC material and marketed as UK TV. In a separate deal, signed with the American Discovery Channel (in which TCI has a substantial investment), Discovery was given exclusive rights of 'first sight' over a range of BBC factual programming ideas in the areas of science, history, natural history and documentaries, in return for a guaranteed investment in production over five years.

These initiatives have bifurcated the BBC. On the one side stand the established national free-to-air channels paid for by the licence fee and available to all. On the other, a proliferating series of commercial services supported by subscription and/or advertising and aimed primarily at the international television market. The same pattern is repeated in the BBC's recent efforts to establish a significant presence on the internet, with a freely accessible website running alongside a subscription service. This dual structure poses serious problems for the Corporation's long-term survival as a publicly funded service. The more successful its commercial operations and the more revenues they generate, the weaker the case for retaining the licence fee. A House of Commons Committee had already identified this contradiction in a report on the BBC's economic future written before the recent flurry of deals. As it pointed out: 'should the BBC find a new, profitable commercial role . . . it might be very difficult, if not impossible, to justify the existence of the licence fee at all' (National Heritage Committee, 1993: para. 105).

But the state is not only a regulator of communications institutions. It is itself a communicator of enormous power. How this power is exercised is of major interest to a political economy of culture. Governments are inevitably anxious to promote their own views of the development of policy, and to ensure that legislative initiatives are properly understood and supported. In recent years this desire has fostered a rapid growth in communications activity, so that by 1990 the government was the second biggest advertiser in the country (see Golding, 1990: 95). Between 1986 and 1992 government advertising increased in real terms by 16 per cent, and more or less doubled in the previous decade (Deacon and Golding, 1994: 6). Communications researchers have commonly analysed this process as one of agenda-building, in which the state effectively gives subsidies to media organizations by reducing the effort required to discover and produce information for their audiences. As Gandy defines the term, an information subsidy 'is an attempt to produce influence over the actions of others by controlling their access to and use of information relevant to those actions' (Gandy, 1982: 61). In an increasingly public relations state the provisions of such subsidies can range from the entirely healthy distribution of essential information with which to explain and facilitate public policy to the nefarious management of news in which 'being economical with the truth' becomes an accessory of political life (see Golding, 1986 and 1994).

The production of communications is not, however, merely a simple reflection of the controlling interests of those who own or even control the broad range of capital plant and equipment which make up the means by which cultural goods are made and distributed. Within the media are men and women working within a range of codes and professional ideologies, and with an array of aspirations, both personal and social. These ambitions can be idealized; much cultural production is routine, mundane and highly predictable. But the autonomy of those who work within the media is a matter of substantial interest to political economists. Their aim is to discover how far this autonomy can be exercised given the consequences of the broad economic structure we have described above, and to what extent the economic structure of the media prevents some forms of expression from finding a popular outlet and audience.

An example can illustrate the point. Successive Royal Commissions have remarked on the significant absence within the British media of a popular newspaper with political sympathies to the radical left. The last Royal Commission on the Press, for example, concluded that, 'There is no doubt that over most of this century the labour movement has had less newspaper support than its right-wing opponents and that its beliefs and activities have been unfavourably reported by the majority of the press' (House of Commons, 1977: 98–99). 'There is no doubt', it went on, 'that there is a gap in political terms which could be filled with advantage' (110). Many journalists would sympathize with this view. As senior Fleet Street commentator Tom Baistow has lamented, 'For millions of Left, Centre and agnostic Don't Know readers there is no longer any real choice of newspapers' (Baistow, 1985: 57). To explain this, political economists will examine the impact of shifts in advertising support and ownership to discover why this gap exists and why, therefore, opportunities for the expression of radical views of the political left do not routinely find space in the organs of the British national press. In 1997 the general election in the UK returned a Labour Government under Tony Blair with a huge landslide majority, a quite extraordinary shift in the political landscape accompanied by dramatic changes in the apparent political affiliations and enthusiasms of some national newspapers (Deacon *et al.*, 1998: 146). Plainly this did not happen because large number of journalists had a common and sudden reverse in political vision. But some proprietors, in keen recognition of the collapse in popular support for the Conservative Government of John Major, were swift to recognize the need to back a winning horse, and indeed to anticipate their own future needs in relation to the next government's likely inclinations in the field of media regulation. The complex impact of proprietorial and other economic imperatives alongside the creative autonomy of journalists is but one dimension of cultural production needing the attention of critical political economists. For this they will wish to go beyond broad structural features, however, to asses the consequences for daily practice, routine news gathering and processing, journalistic recruitment and professional ideology, of these larger structures. This will require detailed study of the work of journalists, the way sources of varying power and authority engage in 'agenda-building', and the link between what industrial sociologists have traditionally characterized as market situation and work situation.

The political economy of cultural production, then, is concerned with the concrete consequences for the work of making media goods of the broad patterns of power and ownership which are their backdrop. To see where this takes us in the analysis of what gets produced we need to move on to the political economy of media output.

Political economy and textual analysis

As we noted earlier, research in cultural studies has been particularly concerned with analysing the structure of media texts and tracing their role in sustaining systems of domination. As it has developed, this work decisively rejected the notion that the mass media act as a transmission belt for a dominant ideology and developed a model of the communications system as a field or space, in which contending discourses, offering different ways of looking and speaking, struggle for visibility and legitimacy. But outside of televised political speeches, discourses are seldom available for public consumption in their 'raw' state. They are reorganized and recontextualized to fit the particular expressive form being used. Discourses about AIDS, for example, might well feature in a variety of television programmes, ranging from public health advertisement, to news items, investigative reports, studio discussion programmes, or episodes of soap operas or police series. Each of these forms has a major impact of what can be said and shown, by whom, and from what point of view. In short, cultural forms are mechanisms for regulating public discourse.

We can distinguish two dimensions to this process. The first has to do with the range of discourses that particular forms allow into play: whether they are organized exclusively around official discourses, or whether they provide space for the articulation of counter-discourses. The second concerns the way that the available discourses are handled within the text: whether they are arranged in a clearly marked hierarchy of credibility which urges the audience to prefer one over the others, or whether they are treated in a more even-handed and indeterminate way which leaves the audience with a more open choice.

If cultural studies is primarily interested in the way these mechanisms work within a particular media text or across a range of texts, critical political economy is concerned to explain how the economic dynamics of production structure public discourse by promoting certain cultural forms over others. Take, for example, the increasing reliance on international co-production agreements in television drama production. These arrangements impose a variety of constraints on form as the partners search for subject matter and narrative styles they can sell in their home markets. The resulting bargain may produce an Americanized product which is fast moving, based on simple characterizations, works with a tried and tested action format, and offers an unambiguous ending. Or it may result in a variant of 'televisual tourism' which trades on the familiar forms and sights of the national cultural heritage (Murdock, 1989b). Both strategies represent a narrowing of the field of discourse and inhibit a full engagement with the complexities and ambiguities of the national condition. The first effects a closure around dominant transatlantic forms of story-telling with their clearly marked boundaries and hierarchies of discourse. The second reproduces an ideology of 'Englishness' which excludes or marginalizes a whole range of subordinate discourses.

This general perspective, with its emphasis on the crucial mediating role of cultural forms, has two major advantages. First, it allows us to trace detailed connections between the financing and organization of cultural production and changes in the field of public discourse and representation in a non-reducible way, that respects the need for a full analysis of textual organization. Indeed, far from being secondary, such an analysis is central to the full development of the argument. Second, by stressing the fact that media texts vary considerably in their degree of discursive openness, it offers an approach to audience activity that focuses on structured variations in response. However, in contrast to recent work on audience activity produced within cultural studies, which concentrates on the negotiation of textual interpretations and media use in immediate social settings, critical political economy seeks to relate variations in people's responses to their overall location in the economic system (Murdock, 1989c). Of course, this cannot explain everything we need to know about the dynamics of response, but it is a necessary starting point.

Consumption: sovereignty or struggle?

For political proponents of a free market philosophy, communications goods are like any other. Since the best way of ensuring adequate distribution and production of the general commodities people want is through the market, so too, the argument follows, is this true for cultural goods. It is the truth or otherwise of this proposition that provides the analytical target for a political economy of cultural consumption.

Curiously, an influential version of this free market philosophy has had considerable currency in some work within recent cultural studies. In an attempt to contest the apparent simplistic determinism of a view that sees audiences as the passive dupes of all-powerful media, some writers have asserted the sovereignty of viewers and readers to impose their own meanings and interpretations on material which is 'polysemic' (that is, capable of generating a variety of meanings). This analysis has tempted writers of very varying political or social presuppositions. For liberal pluralists it has refurbished the view that the checks and balances of cultural supply and demand, though admittedly uneven, are far from bankrupt. The customer, though perhaps a little bruised, is still ultimately sovereign. For writers with more critical or radical instincts, it is a view that has unleashed a populist romance in which the downtrodden victims caricatured by crude economic determinists are revealed as heroic resistance fighters in the war against cultural deception.

Consumer sovereignty is in any total sense clearly impossible – nobody has access to a complete range of cultural goods as and when they might wish, without restriction. The task of political economy, then, is to examine the barriers that limit such freedom. It construes such barriers as being of two kinds: material and cultural. We will examine each of these in turn.

Where communications goods and facilities are available only at a price there will be a finite capacity to have access to them, limited by the disposable spending power of individuals and households. Spending on services generally has grown significantly in the last generation. In 1953/54 spending on services made up 9.5 per cent of household expenditure; by 1986 this proportion had risen to 12.7 per cent, and by 1993 to 19.6 per cent (Central Statistical Office, 1994). Between 1971 and 1997 all household spending increased by 91 per cent. But spending on recreational and other activities grew by 110 per cent, and on other services by 130 per cent (Office for National Statistics, 1999a: 106). Within this global figure, spending within the home has risen as a proportion, linked most significantly to the television set as an increasingly dominant hub of leisure time and expenditure. On average British adults in the 1990s spent 26 hours a week watching television broadcasts, and an as yet uncertainly calibrated amount of time using television for related activities, such as viewing videos or playing computer games. However, as the range of hardware required for such activities grows, so too does the demand on private expenditure necessary to participate in them.

These shifts in expenditure patterns reflect a gradual change in lifestyle across the population, but these are experienced very differentially among different groups. In 1997/98 the poorest tenth in the UK spent £5.50 on household services per week while the richest tenth spent three times as much. However, leisure services take up 15 per cent of the spending of the top group, but only 5 per cent of the spend of the poorest group, which spent less on food and alcoholic drink together than the richest tenth spent on drink (Office for National Statistics, 1999b). The disposable spending required for communication and information goods and services is tilted radically and increasingly towards more affluent groups. This has radical implications for the availability of such things if they remain commodities in the market-place rather than services in the public sphere.

As Table 4.1 shows, ownership of and access to communications is sharply differentiated by income within the UK population. This becomes more sharply true for recent innovations in information and communications technology. This gap has also become a matter of intense policy debate in the United States, where a series of reports by the National Telecommunications and Information Administration has charted what it tellingly terms the 'digital divide'. The most recent such report notes that – although, in general, ownership of computers and access to the internet has increased – by the start of 1999 households with incomes of $75,000 and higher were over twenty times more likely to have access to the internet than those at the lowest income levels, and more than nine times as likely to have a computer at home. More significantly this gap is widening – the gap between white and black households increased by 6 per cent between 1994 and 1998, and between the lowest and highest income groups by 29 per cent (US Dept of Commerce, 1999: chart I-14). Table 4.2 shows the digital divide in the UK at the end of the 1990s (see Golding, 1998: 2000).

This apparent worsening divide is not a blip in the statistics. Unlike domestic household goods that came gradually into general use among most households in previous decades, this gap is unlikely to diminish substantially, due to two factors. First, income and wealth differentials themselves have sharply widened

Table 4.1 Household ownership of selected communications facilities, UK 1997–98

Consumer goods	Proportion of households owning item (%) in each quintile group by income					
	Lowest 20%	Second Quintile	Third Quintile	Fourth Quintile	Highest 20%	All
Telephone	79	92	96	98	100	93
Mobile phone	3	6	12	21	38	16
Satellite dish	7	16	20	26	28	19
Home computer	8	12	22	34	57	27
VCR	65	76	91	94	97	84

Source: Golding (2000)

Table 4.2 Demographic correlates of internet access, UK 1998

Socio-economic group	% with a PC at home	% with internet access
AB	64	27
C1	50	17
C2	41	9
DE	26	6
All (15+)	44	14

Source: British Market Research Bureau (1999: 5, 7)

in the last decade. Between 1979 and 1998 in the UK the number of employees with earnings below the Council of Europe 'decency threshold' rose from 7.8 million (38 per cent) to 10.6 million (49 per cent) (Low Pay Unit, 1999: 11). Between 1971 and the late 1990s the gap between low and high incomes rose substantially; between 1980 and 1990 incomes grew by 47 per cent among the top tenth, but by only 6 per cent among the poorest tenth. Between 1979 and 1996 the total share of incomes fell for all groups in the lower half of the income distribution while large increases were registered among the best-off groups. The bottom half of the population accounted for 33 per cent of total income in 1979, 26 per cent in 1996 (Dept of Social Security, 1998: 97–98). Inland Revenue figures show that in the most recent year for which estimates were available in 1999 (namely 1995) the most wealthy 10 per cent in the UK owned half the total wealth, while the least wealthy half owned only 8 per cent of the total. The disposable spending power of different groups in the population is thus significantly polarized.

The second reason to anticipate the digital gap being widened is rooted in the nature of information and communications goods themselves. Such goods require regular updating and replacement, disadvantaging groups with limited spending power and cumulatively advantaging the better off. Owning video or computer hardware requires expenditure on software, owning a phone means spending money on using it. Owning a PC generates demand for add-ons – a modem, a printer, a scanner, additional software and, in time (probably no more than four years), the need to replace the basic machine. Thus limited spending power is a deterrent, not only to initial purchase but to regular use. Not surprisingly these figures disguise even sharper divisions among social groups. For example, telephone ownership among single parents with more than one child falls to well below 80 per cent. In other words nearly one in four such households is excluded from a communication resource for which they might be argued to have a particular need.

However, not all expenditure on communications goods involves the expensive acquisition of equipment. Television programmes can be viewed once you have a set to watch them on, as most people do, while many cultural materials are available as public goods; they are paid for from taxation as a common resource (public library books, for example). This is not a static situation, however. For political economists a shift in the provision and distribution of cultural goods from being public services to private commodities signals a substantial change in the opportunity for different groups in the population to have access to them. If television channels, or individual programmes, are accessible by price, as was envisaged for much of the new television structure heralded by the Broadcasting Act 1990, then consumption of television programmes will be significantly governed by the distribution of household incomes. The growth of multiple-channel television and pay-per-view services will impose increasing demands on limited disposable incomes and, increasingly, will differentiate the diet of material realistically accessible to various groups across the income gradient. Similar considerations would come into play if, for example, public libraries were to make greater use of powers to charge, as was proposed in a government Green Paper in 1988, even though, at the time, such proposals were shelved (Office of Arts and Libraries, 1988). By imposing the discipline of price on cultural goods they acquire an artificial scarcity that makes them akin to other goods of considerably greater scarcity. It is for this reason that the political economy of cultural consumption has to be especially concerned with material inequalities.

Critical political economy is not only concerned with monetary barriers to cultural consumption, however. It is also interested in the ways in which social location regulates access to other relevant resources. Central to this analysis is the attempt to trace the consequences of differing positions in the system of 'production', understood not simply as paid labour but as the complex intersection of waged work and domestic labour, including the work of caring. Three kinds of non-material resources are relevant to a fuller understanding of consumption and audience activity – time, space and the cultural competencies required to interpret and deploy media materials in particular ways.

Time, particularly true leisure time, is a highly unevenly distributed resource, and as much research in domestic settings has shown, access to unaccounted for time (time for oneself) is strongly stratified by gender. Women's prime responsibility for the 'shadow work' (Illich, 1981) of shopping, cleaning, cooking and nurturing has fundamental consequences for their relation to the mass media. Not only are their choices often constrained by the prior demands of husbands and children, but the fact that no one else in the family is regenerating their affective resources leads them to look for other ways of maintaining psychological support. For example, where men mostly use the telephone instrumentally, to 'get things done', women often use it expressively, to sustain social networks. What appears from the outside as trivial gossip, is experienced from the inside as an emotional life-saver. Time budget studies consistently confirm the strongly gendered distribution of non-work time. An official British survey conducted in the spring of 1995, for example, showed that on an average day working women spent a total of 2 hours 38 minutes cooking, caring for children and adults, and doing routine housework, as against the 51 minutes working men spent on these tasks. Women also spent considerably longer than men (1 hour 5 minutes as against 48 minutes) keeping in contact with friends and family by telephone or in person. Not surprisingly, this unequal attention to nurturing family members and sustaining social networks was reflected in significant differences in the time spent listening to the radio or watching TV. Whereas men devoted 2 hours and 4 minutes to these activities, women could only manage 1 hour and 49 minutes (Office for National Statistics, 1998: Table 13.2, 216).

Access to space is also a key resource which structures communicative choices, though it has so far been relatively little studied. The experience of watching television will differ depending on whether it is viewed in 'a room of one's own', in a living room, kitchen or other communal family space, or in a public site such as a bar. What is at issue here is the shifting spatial organization of privatized and sociable consumption and its implications for media experience. In order to map these varying mixes of spatial zones we need to trace their links to the dynamics of production and the patterns of geographic mobility and immobility, social separation and solidarity, and psychological identification and antipathy, that these generate.

An analysis of 'production' is also central to understanding the differential distribution of cultural competencies. One of the strongest empirical traditions within cultural studies – running from studies of youth subcultures to research on differential 'readings' of television texts – has concerned itself with how social locations provide access to cultural repertoires and symbolic resources that sustain differences of interpretation and expression (Morley, 1983). But critical political economy needs to go a stage further to explore how access to systems of meaning, particularly those offering frameworks of interpretation that cut across the grain of the cultural mainstream, is linked to involvement in the social sites that generate and sustain them, and how these sites in turn are being transformed by political economic changes more generally, as contemporary 'production' moves, shifts and recomposes. What happens to the micro-cultures of neighbourhoods in the face of urban redevelopment? How does de-industrialization and the shift from manufacturing to services alter occupational cultures and the critical cultures produced by the labour movement? How are the cultural relations between local and global formations reshaped by the migratory and diasporic movements of labour? These questions can only be tackled by reconnecting the political economy of communications with the political economy and cultural sociology of the contemporary world.

Conclusion

People depend in large measure on the cultural industries for the images, symbols and vocabulary with which they interpret and respond to their social environment. It is vital, therefore, that we understand these industries in a comprehensive and theoretically adequate way which enables the analysis of communications to take its place at the heart of social and cultural research. We have argued that a critical political economy provides an approach that sustains such an analysis, and in so doing have illustrated, in a preliminary way, the origins, character and application of such an approach. Much remains to be done, both theoretically and empirically, however, before we can claim to have fully established a critical political economy of communications.

References

BAISTOW, T. (1985) *Fourth Rate Estate: An Anatomy of Fleet Street.* London: Comedia.
BELL, E. (1993) 'Days of the Media Baron are Over', *The Observer Business News,* 5 September, 25.
BRITISH MARKET RESEARCH BUREAU (BMRB) (1999) *Is IT For All?* London: BMRB.
BURKE, P. (1980) *Sociology and History.* London: George Allen and Unwin.
CENTRAL STATISTICAL OFFICE (1994) *Family Spending 1993.* London: HMSO.
COLLINS, R., GARNHAM, N. and LOCKSLEY, G. (1988) *The Economics of Television: The UK Case.* London: Sage Publications.
CURRAN, J. (1990) 'The new revisionism in mass communication research: a reappraisal', *European Journal of Communication* 5(2–3), 135–64.
DEACON, D. and GOLDING, P. (1994) *Taxation and Representation: The Media, Political Communication, and the Poll Tax.* London: John Libbey.
DEACON, D., BILLIG, M. and GOLDING, P. (1998) 'Between Fear and Loathing: National Press Coverage of the 1997 British General Election' in Denver, D. *et al.*, *British General Elections and Parties Review. Vol. 8: The 1997 General Election.* London: Frank Cass, 135–49.
DEPARTMENT OF SOCIAL SECURITY (1998) *Households Below Average Income.* London: DSS.

ELLIOTT, P. (1982) 'Intellectuals, the "information society", and the disappearance of the public sphere', *Media, Culture and Society* Vol. 4, 243–53.

FISKE, J. (1989) *Understanding Popular Culture*. London: Unwin Hyman.

GANDY, O. (1982) *Beyond Agenda-Setting: Information Subsidies and Public Policy*.

GIDDENS, A. (1976) *New Rules of Sociological Method*. London: Hutchinson.

GOLDING, P. (1998) 'World Wide Wedge: Division and Contradiction in the Global Information Infrastructure' in Thussu, D.K. (ed.) *Electronic Empires: Global Media and Local Resistance*. London: Arnold, 135–49.

——, (1986) 'Power in the Information society' in Muskens, G. and Hamelink, C. (eds) *Dealing with Global Networks: Global Networks and European Communities.* Tilburg: IVA.

——, (1990) 'Political communication and citizenship: the media and democracy in an inegalitarian social order' in Ferguson, M. (ed.) *Public Communication: The New imperatives*. London: Sage Publications.

——, (1994) 'Telling Stories: Sociology, Journalism and the Informed Citizen', *European Journal of Communication* Vol. 9 No. 4, 461–84.

——, (1995) 'The mass media and the public sphere: the crisis of information in the "information society"' in Edgell, S., Walklate, S. and Williams, G. (eds) *Debating the Future of the Public Sphere*. Aldershot: Avebury.

——, (2000) 'Features: Information and Communications Technologies and the Sociology of the Future', *Sociology* 34(1).

GREENSLADE, R. (1993) 'Sky is not the limit', *New Statesman and Society,* 10 September, 16–17.

HABERMAS, J. (1989) *The Structural Transformation of the Public Sphere*. Cambridge: Polity Press.

HALL, S. (1983) 'The problem of ideology – Marxism without guarantees' in Matthews, B. (ed.) *Marx: A Hundred Years On*. London: Lawrence and Wishart, 57–85.

HERMAN, E.S. and CHOMSKY, N. (1988) *Manufacturing Consent: The Political Economy of The Mass Media.* New York: Pantheon Books.

HERMAN, E.S. and MCCHESNEY, R.W. (1997) *The Global Media: The New Missionaries of Global Capitalism.* London: Cassell.

HMSO (1994) *The Future of the BBC: Serving the Nation Competing World Wide*. London: HMSO, Cmnd 2621.

HOUSE OF COMMONS (1977) *Royal Commission on the Press: Final Report.* London: HMSO, Cmnd 6810.

ILLICH, I. (1981) *Shadow Work*. London: Marion Boyars.

KEANE, J. (1989) '"Liberty of the press" in the 1990s', *New Formations* 8, summer, 35–53.

Low Pay Unit (1999) 'How Britain Spends', *The New Review* 56, 9–10.

MORLEY, D. (1983) 'Cultural transformations: the politics of resistance' in Davis, H. and Walton, P. (eds) *Language, Image, Media.* Oxford: Basil Blackwell, 104–17.

MURDOCK, G. (1989a) 'Cultural Studies: Missing Links', *Critical Studies in Mass Communication*, Vol. 6, No. 4, December, 436–40.

——, (1989b) 'Televisual Tourism' in Thomsen, C.W. (ed.) *Cultural Transfer or Electronic Colonialism?*. Heidelberg: Carl Winter-Universitatsverlag, 171–83.

——, (1989c) 'Audience Activity and Critical Inquiry' in Dervin, B. *et al.* (eds) *Rethinking Communication Volume 2: Paradigm Exemplars*. London: Sage Publications, 226–49.

——, (1994a) 'Money Talks: Broadcasting Finance and Public Culture' in Hood, S. (ed.) *Behind the Screens: The Structure of British Television in the Nineties*. London: Lawrence and Wishart, 155–83.

——, (1994b) 'The New Mogul Empires: Media Concentration and Control in the Age of Convergence', *Media Development,* Vol. XLI No. 4, 3–6.

MURDOCK, G. and GOLDING, P. (1974) 'For a Political Economy of Mass Communications' in Miliband, S. and Saville, J. (eds) *The Socialist Register 1973*. London: Merlin.

MURDOCK, G. and GOLDING, P. (1989) 'Information poverty and political inequality: citizenship in the age of privatised communications', *Journal of Communication*, Vol. 39, No. 3, summer, 180–95.

NATIONAL HERITAGE COMMITTEE (1993) *The Future of the BBC. Volume 1: Report and Minutes of Proceedings House of Commons Session 1993-4*. London: HMSO.

NORWOOD, NJ: Ablex.

OFFICE FOR NATIONAL STATISTICS (1998) *Social Trends,* No. 28. London: HMSO.

——, (1999a) *Social Trends,* Vol. 29. London: HMSO.

——, (1999b) *Family Spending 1997–1998.* London: HMSO.

OFFICE OF ARTS AND LIBRARIES (1988*) Financing our Public Library Service: Four Subjects for Debate.* London: HMSO, Cmnd 324.

REITH, J. (1924*) Broadcast Over Britain.* London: Hodder and Stoughton.

SCHILLER, H.I. (1989) *Culture Inc: The Corporate Takeover of Public Expression.* New York: Oxford University Press.

SCHUDSON, M. (1989) 'The sociology of news production', *Media, Culture and Society*, Vol. 11, No. 3, July, 263–82.

THOMPSON, J.B. (1990) *Ideology and Modern Culture: Critical Social Theory in the Era of Mass Communication.* Cambridge: Polity Press.

TUNSTALL, J. (1998) 'Hollywood Network Cartel in the World', paper presented to the International Conference on Questioning, International Communication School of Journalism, Carleton University, Ottawa, 29 May to 1 June.

US DEPARTMENT OF COMMERCE (1999*) Falling through the Net: Defining the Digital Divide.* Washington: National Telecommunications and Information Administration.

WILLIAMS, R. (1980) *Problems in Materialism and Culture.* London: Verso.

WILLIS, P. (1990) *Common Culture.* Buckingham: Open University Press.

5

The Global and the Local in International Communications

Annabelle Sreberny

Introduction

> After three thousand years of explosion, by means of fragmentary and mechanical technologies, the Western world is imploding. During the mechanical ages we had extended our bodies in space. Today, after more than a century of electric technology, we have extended our central nervous system itself in a global embrace, abolishing both space and time as far as our planet is concerned . . . As electrically contracted, the globe is no more than a village.
>
> (Marshall McLuhan, 1964, 11–12)

> A Third World in every First World
> A Third World in every Third World
> And vice-versa
>
> (Trinh Minh-ha, 1987)

Contemporary rhetoric suggests that we live in a unitary world in which space and time have collapsed and the experience of distance imploded for ever. The antagonistic blocs of East and West are giving way to international markets, moneys and media. Germany is unified. A new and expanding 'Europe' looms. The centrifugal force of 'globalization' is the catchphrase of the 1990s. Yet at the very same time, in the same but different world, the centripetal forces of old and new tribalisms and nationalisms are at work and ethnic struggles are breaking out all over. Armenians confront Azarbaijanis, Serbs fight Croats, Hutu and Tutsi kill each other; Hindu-Moslem relations in India and Black-Jewish relations in the USA are strained; Jews and Moslems, Turks and Somalis worry about racism across Europe; and Sarajevo, Grozny, Kigali become part of the international lexicon of tragedy and terror. Far from the 'loss of the subject', identity seems to lie at the heart of politics in the late twentieth century.

Giddens (1990: 64) defines globalization as 'the intensification of worldwide social relations which link distant localities in such a way that local happenings are shaped by events occurring many miles away and vice versa'. For Giddens, what he calls 'time-space distanciation' (p. 64), a theme developed at length in

Harvey (1989), helps to create 'complex relations between *local involvements* (circumstances of co-presence) and *interaction across distance* (connections of presence and absence). In this stretching process of relations, there are numerous modes of connection between different regions and contexts. Appadurai (1990) has described five such 'scapes' of interaction as the ethnoscape, the technoscape, the infoscape, the financescape and the mediascape – which are interconnected, even overlapping.

Much theoretical debate centres on how the current situation should be conceived and labelled. Some argue that there is a discernibly 'new' kind of economic-cultural structure to be called 'post-modernity' (Harvey, 1989) while others argue that the evident changes of the last fifteen years simply reflect the supreme development and natural extension of global capitalism and prefer to call this structure 'late capitalism' (Jameson, 1990) or 'high modernity' (Giddens, 1990). What is significant throughout these debates is that the role of communication and information have been finally and generally recognized as crucial elements in the new world order. Yet the role and shape of communications in the 1990s is by no means very fixed or very clear, and neither are our theoretical models for explaining/exploring communications on an international scale. The rapidity and complexity of change in the media environment during this decade seems to require a newer set of terms and vantage points than are offered by older perspectives, which often seem frozen in a bygone era. This chapter explores the dynamic tension between the global and local levels of analysis, as suggested by Giddens, as a provocative and useful construct which can help us uncover the deeply contradictory dynamics of the current moment. In the twin yet opposing processes of globalization versus localization, media play a central role and reveal the tensions between the macro and micro levels of socio-economic structures, cultures, and development dynamics.

A brief reprise of older models in international communication:

Since the 1960s, the field of International Communication has been dominated by three intellectual paradigms: that of 'communications and development', that of 'cultural imperialism' and currently by a revisionist 'cultural pluralism' which is still searching for a coherent theoretical shape. It will be argued here that this third construct is itself full of contradictions, and that the 'global/local' model at least has the merits of putting 'contradiction' at the core of its construct. A brief reprise of these models is useful, both as intellectual history and to understand the different theoretical bases and implications of the models for current understanding.

'Communications and Development' emerged out of developmentalist thinking in the early 1960s. After the Second World War, the emergence of independent national political systems such as India, Algeria, Ghana, out of the grip of varied European colonialisms, spawned debates among Western academics about the nature of 'development' and the obstacles within such newly-independent nations to development. Some arguments focused on the lack of capital for investment, prompting such practical solutions as the World Bank and interest-bearing loans, under which results many developing nations are still groaning. Other arguments examined the lack of entrepreneurial vision and trained manpower, spawning education exchanges and training programs. The arguments developed by Daniel Lerner (1958) and Wilbur Schramm (1964) focused instead on the Weberian/Parsonian 'mentalities' or conjeries of attitudes that were supportive or obstructive to change. They suggested that the traditional values of the developing world were the central obstacles to political participation and economic activity, the two key elements of the development process. The 'solution' for their analysis was the promotion of the use of communications media to alter attitudes and values, embodied in 'media indicators' (minimum numbers of cinema seats, radio and television receivers, and copies of daily newspapers as a ratio of population necessary for development), which were adopted by UNESCO and widely touted in the developing world. This perspective has been roundly criticized for its ethnocentrism, its ahistoricity, its linearity, for conceiving of development in an evolutionary, endogenist fashion and for solutions which actually reinforced dependency rather than helping to overcome it.

The 'dependency' paradigm, developing initially in Latin America and building on older critiques of imperialism (Gunder-Frank, 1964) instead recognized the global structures and interrelationships conditioning the 'development' of the Third World, particularly the multiple and diverse legacies of colonialism. It was particularly critical of the post-independence economic dynamics which kept Third World states in economic hock to the ex-imperial powers, and argued that 'development' could not be mere mimicry of Western structures but had to be conceived as an autonomous, self-chosen path that built on the rich/ancient cultures of the Third World. From within this broad, critical framework, the specific model of 'cultural imperialism' argued that, far from aiding Third World nations to develop, the international flows of technology transfer and media hardware coupled with the 'software' flows of cultural products actually strengthened dependency and prevented true development. The great merit of the models of 'cultural imperialism' (Schiller, 1976; Mattelart, 1979) and 'media imperialism' (Boyd-Barrett, 1977) was their recognition of *global* dynamics and relationships, taking their cue from much older models of imperialism, and the suggested linkages between foreign policy interests, capitalist expansion and media infrastructures and contents. This theoretical model spawned a wide variety of empirical studies which documented the imbalanced flow of media products – from news (Galtung and Ruge, 1965) to films (Guback and Varis, 1982) to television programming (Varis, 1974/1984) – as well as the export of organizational structures (Katz and Wedell, 1977) and professional values (Golding, 1977) from the developed to the Third World. Behind its structuralist analysis and the descriptive mapping of international communications dynamics, a central assumption was that western cultural values (often conflated to 'American' values) such as consumerism and individualism, expressed implicitly in a variety of media genre as well as directly through advertising, were being exported to and decisively altering Third World cultural milieux. Fears of 'cultural homogenization' and 'cultural synchronization' (Hamelink, 1983) were voiced, and arguments made for Third World 'cultural disassociation' along the lines of Samir Amin's 'delinking' from the global capitalist system as the only way toward autonomous development and protection of indigenous cultures. Criticism of this position have been made from quite divergent historical perspectives. One argument, looking back in time, suggests that the very term 'cultural imperialism' tends to obscure the many deep and diverse *cultural* effects of imperialism itself, including the export of religion, educational systems and values, European languages, and administrative practices, all of which have long ago and irretrievably altered the cultural milieux of the colonized (Sreberny-Mohammadi, 1996). Such an argument questions the utility of terms such as 'authenticity' and 'indigeneity' within a lengthy history of cultural contact, absorption and recreation, and suggests that a cultural debate which focuses mainly on modern media neglects other much older and deeper structures which may embody 'foreign' values but may also be the pillars of modernity.

Another strand of critique, looking forward to the new realities of the 1990s, suggests that, like the earlier arguments for 'communications and development', the 'cultural imperialism' model was based on a situation of comparative global media scarcity, limited global media players and embryonic media systems in much of the Third World. The speed-up of history, evidenced in the rapidity of changes in many areas of social life, is especially evident in the global spread of communication and information technologies and the advent of many new and diverse media actors over the past decade or so. In the 1990s, it is clear that the international media environment is far more complex than that suggested by the 'cultural imperialism' model whose depiction of a hegemonic media pied piper leading the global media mice appears frozen in the realities of the 1970s, now a bygone era.

Empirically there is a more complex syncopation of voices and a more complicated media environment in which western media domination has given way to multiple actors and flows of media products. More nations of the south are producing and exporting media materials, including film from India and Egypt, television programming from Mexico and Brazil. For example, *TV Globo*, the major Brazilian network, exports telenovelas to 128 countries, including Cuba, China, the former Soviet Union, East Germany, earning export dollars for Brazil, and its productions outnumber those of any other station in the world (Tracey, 1988). Indeed the flow of televisual materials from Brazil to Portugal is one example of how contemporary cultural flows reverse the historic roles of imperialism, while Latin American telenovelas on Spanish television channels in the USA has been called 'reverse cultural imperialism' (Antola and Rogers, 1984). In another region and medium, the Indian film industry has an international reputation as the most productive – more than nine hundred films in 1985 – with an extensive export market (Dissanayeke, 1988). India has also managed to keep a somewhat dualistic yet productive tension between high art film and a popular cinema, creating movies that reflect and reinforce different elements of India's rich cultural past as well as indigenizing invasive foreign elements into a distinctive Indian style (Binford, 1988). Television, too, has been successful at translating ancient Indian culture into popular contemporary televisual fare, the Hindu epic, the Ramayana, clearing urban streets and creating a huge demand for additional episodes over the fifty originally planned (Chatterji, 1989). These Third World producers have become not only national producers but international exporters of cultural products, a process which revisionists claim has altered any one-way flow of western material and the 'hegemonic' model of cultural imperialism (McNeely and Soysal, 1989). These 'global pluralists' adopt an optimistic voice regarding the diversity of media producers and locales and the many loops of cultural flows that have merged (Tracey, 1988; Boyd, 1984).

But the very rapidity of change on the international media scene makes it hard to discern long-term trends. The 'global cultural pluralists' are correct to note the coming of age of many Third World media producers and the localization of some media production. Yet at the same time even stronger tendencies toward greater globalization and conglomeratization can be discerned, which I will document shortly.

There is also a conceptual challenge to the 'cultural imperialism' model, stemming from new modes of analyzing media effects which question the 'international hypodermic needle' assumption proferred by the 'hegemonic' model. Arguments about 'the active audience' and 'polysemy' (e.g. Fiske, 1987) inserted into international communications debate suggest that diverse audiences bring their own interpretive frameworks and sets of meaning to media texts, thus resisting, reinterpreting and reinventing any foreign 'hegemonic' cultural products, the details of which we will again explore later. The 'global cultural pluralism' model seems to suggest many independent and happy producers, somewhat evacuating issues of dominance, cultural appropriation and media effects. I think we need a fourth perspective, one that essentially recognizes and does justice to the dynamic tension between the global and the local, as suggested by Giddens, and the shifting terrains that they encompass. After Trinh Minh Ha (1987), I will call this outlook 'the global in the local, the local in the global' and use the rest of the chapter to explore some of the evident contradictions and tensions between these two poles in different contexts.

We could divide globalization in the media sphere into four separable elements: the globalization of media forms, of media firms, of media flows and of media effects. I will examine them in turn.

1 Globalization of media forms

It is claimed that more and more of the world is wired as a global audience with access to electronic media. The 'success' of the spread of media distribution and reception systems is in evidence – by the end of the 1980s radio signals were globally available and transistors had overcome lack of infrastructure, while nationally based television services had been established in all but the smallest and poorest of African and Asian countries. Globally, the number of television receivers rose from 192 million in 1965 to 873 million in 1992. There are antennae in the Amazon jungle. China is the third largest producer of television receivers. Beyond RTV reception, video players/recorders (vcrs) have *potential* global reach (Alvarado, 1988; see also Boyd et al., 1989). Thus, at least in terms of national involvement in electronic media production and distribution of public access to communications infrastructure, there has been significant development over the past three decades.

However, distribution is still extremely unequal. The global 'average' of 160 television receivers per 1000 population actually ranges from a high of 800 per thousand in North America to a low of 23 per thousand in the non-Arab states of Africa. The global trend is in place, yet by no means 'achieved'. Global still does not mean universal.

Table 5.1 Television receivers, 1970–92.

| Continents, major areas and groups of countries | Number of television receivers | | | | | | | | | |
| | Total (millions) | | | | | per 1000 inhabitants | | | | |
	1970	1975	1980	1985	1992	1970	1975	1980	1985	1992
World Total	298	407	558	689	873	81	100	125	142	160
Africa	1.6	2.7	8.2	15	26	4.5	6.6	17	26	38
America	108	153	202	260	302	211	273	331	392	408
Asia	41	54	98	137	235	20	23	38	48	73
Europe (including former USSR)	144	192	243	268	300	205	264	324	349	381
Oceania	3.8	5.6	6.8	8.6	10	187	264	296	348	375
Developed	273	365	478	550	616	259	331	416	463	498
Developing	25	42	80	139	257	10	14	24	38	61
Africa (excl. Arab states)	0.4	0.7	3.6	6.0	12	1.4	2.2	10	14	23
Asia (excl. Arab states)	40	52	94	130	224	19	23	37	47	72
Arab states	2.6	4.2	9.3	16	25	21	30	56	82	105
Northern America	92	130	166	204	226	405	548	661	774	800
Latin America and the Caribbean	16	23	36	56	76	57	70	99	139	166

2 Globalization of media firms

Central to any discussion of globalization has been the rise of global markets and the role of transnational corporations (TNCs) in adapting to, producing for and profiting from that. The media sphere has long had its global firms, which tend to become bigger and more powerful as the century winds to an end (Bagdikian, 1990). Media moguls such as Rupert Murdoch, Silvio Berlusconi and Henry Luce with the Warner Brothers have created corporate structures that span continents, combine holdings in broadcast, print and film production and also control distribution facilities such as satellites and cable networks. As an example, the merger in March, 1989, between Henry Luce and Harry and Jack Warner made Times Warner the largest media corporation in the world. It had an assessed value of $18 billion, a workforce approaching 340,000, a corporate base in the USA, with subsidiaries in Australia, Asia, Europe and Latin America (Time Warner Inc., 1990). Revenues were over $10 billion during 1989 from activities in magazine and book publishing, music recording and publishing, film and video and cable television. Time Warner is thus a prime example of a growing global corporate structure which is highly vertically integrated – controlling the production process from the conception of a film idea to the building in which it will be shown, for example – and diversifying horizontally to have stakes in other related leisure and information holdings. By Time Warner's own analysis, vertical integration has numerous benefits, including 'creative synergies' and economies of scope and scale; 'optimal levels of promotion' which prevents separate companies having a '"free ride" on the promotional activities of others'; enables companies to 'be responsive to the desires of consumers'; and allows companies to accept greater financial risk than firms which operate in individual industry segments, thus being able to support projects of questionable commercial value. Access to global markets essentially reinforces and multiplies the economies of scale.

Time Warner's own materials readily describes the company as 'a vertically integrated global entity' (Time Warner, 1990: 47). Indeed, large corporations have not been slow to recognize the positive public value attached to the notion of 'globalization' as a unifying process of recognition of a common humanity, and coolly to adopt it for their own purposes. Thus, as part of its own self-marketing, on Earth Day – April 22, 1990 – a day devoted to global awareness and ecological concern, Time Warner launched a new logo and a new motto: 'The World is Our Audience'. In similar fashion, Sony justifies its development of American-based holdings by appropriating a famous radical grassroots slogan 'Think Globally, Act Locally' for its own purposes. Thus Sony USA writes 'It is Sony's philosophy that global corporations have a responsibility to participate actively in the countries in which they operate, a philosophy of "global localization". This means thinking globally while acting locally – being sensitive to local requirements, cultures, traditions and attitudes' (Sony USA, 1990: 1). (Note that Sony employs 100,000 worldwide, enjoys an annual consolidated sales of about $16.3 billion, and has its stock sold on exchanges in ten countries.) These global giants clearly see themselves as part of a current phenomenon and are quick to point out the increasingly international activities of competitors.

Some try to debate the extent of this process of consolidating a few vertically

integrated global media giants and their power to control the creation, production and distribution of worldwide information and communication. Thus,
Murdoch's News Corporation argues against the notion that the emergent pattern is of 'international media holdings by relatively few media forms', by arguing that 'multinational media companies have emerged but they are too
numerous to be characterized as "few"' (NTIA, 1990: 5). But this appears nothing more than a quibble; of the thousands of corporations active in the media
business worldwide, this group of global media moguls is clearly no more than
a handful. While accurate and extensive comparative data is still hard to find, a
UNESCO-compiled table for seventy-eight firms listed for their total 1987
media turnover (including press and publishing, television, radio and cinema)
shows that only seven had turnover of more than three billion dollars, with 15
having turnover of more than 2 billion dollars (UNESCO, 1989: 104).

Of the seventy-eight firms listed in the complete table, not one was based in
the Third World. Forty-eight were US or Japanese, while the rest were western
European, Canadian or Australian. Already in 1988, the combined revenue of
five such giants (Bertelsmann AG; News Corp; Hachette; and pre-merger Time
inc. and Warner) was estimated at $45 billion, or 18 per cent of the $250 billion
worldwide information industry (see Table 5.2).

Many of these corporations are American, and for many sectors of the
American culture industries international sales are now a crucial source of
income. In 1989 foreign revenues accounted for 38 per cent of total revenues for

Table 5.2 Selected major information and communication groupings. Total
media turnover – Top 15 Corporations out of 78 listed by UNESCO, 1989.

Group	Country	Ranking-media	Media sales	Press, publishing, recording (%)	Radio, TV, motion pictures (%)	Period
Capital Cities/ABC	USA	1	4440	23	77	
Time	USA	2	4193	61	39	
Bertelsmann	Germany	3	3689	54	18	June 87
News Corp	Australia	4	3453	58	32	June 88
Warner Communications	USA	5	3404	49	51	
General Electric	USA	6	3165		25	
Gannett	USA	7	3079	88	12	
Times Mirror	USA	8	2994	85	11	
Gulf + Western	USA	9	2904	37	63	
Yomiuri Group	Japan	10	2848	63	23	86
CBS	USA	11	2762		100	
ARD	Germany	12	2614		100	
NHK	Japan	13	2541		100	March 88
Advance Publications	USA	14	2397	92	8	
MCA	USA	15	2052	8	92	

NB   Of the 78 firms listed by UNESCO i*n the complete table* not one was based in the
Third World.

the American motion picture industry and helped to keep the value gap between imported film and film exports at $3 billion dollars. Ted Turner's Cable News Network is received by the Kremlin and the Islamic Republic, and *Baywatch* enjoys an international audience.

Yet clearly in the 1990s not all this global expansion is conducted by American or European-based firms, the usual assumption of the 'cultural imperial' thesis. There is considerable inter-capitalist rivalry, and foreign interests have discovered both the lucrative domestic US market, still the single largest in the world, and the global resonance of American popular culture. A few recent examples would be the globalization of Hollywood, involving the purchase of Columbia Pictures and Tri-Star Pictures by Sony, the Japanese giant which had already bought Columbia Records in 1988 (the context for the Sony America slogan discussed above); the purchase of MGM/United Artists by Pathe SA, an Italian company; the purchase of 20th Century Fox by Rupert Murdoch's Australian-based News Corporation, and in November 1990, the purchase of MCA Inc, which includes Universal Studios, Universal Pictures and MCA Records by the Japanese firm Matsushita.

The dynamic of foreign firms buying US media outlets extends well beyond film-making into many other media: Murdoch's News Corporation owns newspapers in Boston and San Antonio, Harper Row books, and Triangle Publications which publishes *TV Guide*, the largest circulation magazine in the USA; International Thomson Group, based in Canada, owns 116 daily newspapers in the USA; the British-based Maxwell Communications owns Macmillan Books; Bertelsmann AG, the German giant, owns RCA and Arista Records, while the Dutch firm N. V. Philips owns Polygram, Island and A&M Records.

The increasing complexity and transnationalization of global media markets were the focus of a study by the National Telecommunications and Information Administration (NTIA), a section of the US Department of Commerce in Washington, DC. Entitled *Comprehensive Study on the Globalization of Mass Media Firms*, in February 1990 it invited input in order to 'better formulate US communications policy in a rapidly changing information environment' (NTIA, 1990). Culling through the responses, it rapidly becomes clear that the US-based media/culture corporations are concerned essentially with two phenomena that affect their access to international media markets. The first is the newly defined and instituted European cultural policy which they interpret as a set of trade barriers to the free flow of American cultural products. The second is the problem of media piracy, significantly but not solely in the Third World. Yet it is abundantly clear that Europe is viewed as the most promising media market, with very little interest paid to or in media development in the Third World, other than chagrin at the media free ride that many Third World societies have enjoyed. Thus these frequently cited examples of media 'globalization' actually reveal its very limited coverage. These processes involve corporate actors of the north, interested in northern media products and audiences, with marginal amounts of the production or circulation occurring among the peoples of the south. It seems quite evident that the production and promotion strategies of these global media firms would do little to alleviate the global imbalance in media availability, and rather exacerbate the global imbalances between the media rich and the media poor.

3 Global media flows

Globalization has often been applied to the spread of western mediated products across the globe, from which few places seem immune. There is much anecdotal evidence of the use of western cultural products, sometimes in somewhat improbable and erstwhile 'remote' places. Ouderkirk (1989) describes trekking up the highest Guatemalan mountains in search of some remote and authentic Qeche Indians and hearing some stirring music which as she approached turned out to be old Beatles tapes! Pico Iyer's (1989) travelogue talks about 'video nights in Kathmandu' and elsewhere in Asia, encountering 'Ike and Tuna Turner' sandwiches in the heart of the People's Republic of China, Burmese musicians playing songs by the Doors, as well as countless Asian remakes of Rambo movies. The film *Bye Bye Brasil* amusingly reflects on the public abandonment of traditional performing arts for television as it spread into the hinterland of Brazil. Visits to the Islamic Republic of Iran revealed considerable use of American videos such as *Robocop* and *Maximum Overdrive* and audiotapes of Madonna and Michael Jackson, all brought in via the black market from Dubai (Sreberny-Mohammadi and Mohammadi, 1994).

As already mentioned, much early work supportive of the 'cultural imperialism' hypothesis provided descriptive mappings of unequal global flows, and much international debate in the 1970s–80s focused on this notion, as an indicator of global domination and threat to indigenous cultural survival. This culminated in the UNESCO Mass Media Declaration, the report of the Macbride Commission and the formulation of a tenet of the New International Information Order as moving from a merely 'free' flow to a 'free and balanced' flow of communication (although no adequate empirical measures of such balance have ever been devised).

Trade Barriers and Piracy: Local Strategies vis à vis the Global

Two different strategies have been devised to deal with the imbalanced flow: trade barriers to cultural imports and piracy. Limits on the amount of imported programming and vetting of imported materials exist in Brazil, India, Iran and elsewhere in the Third World. But it was Europe's move toward an albeit voluntary continental policy for 1992 that worried transnational corporations. Time Warner argued that it faced formidable trade barriers, 'some of which are clothed in the garb of "cultural" measures ostensibly designed to protect the cultural sovereignty and artistic heritage of the country in question'. (Time Warner, 1990: 48). The corporation proclaimed a certain sensitivity: 'Although we must be sensitive to the cultural environment and needs of every locale in which we operate, trade barriers can only be justified to the limited extent that they are truly necessary to protect indigenous cultures that would otherwise be overwhelmed by the cultural products of other countries' but in the very next paragraph the tone changed: 'The cultural issue is appearing with alarming frequency in the international marketplace, and must be roundly rejected' (Time Warner, 1990: 48). Its main concern, shared by other media multinationals, was the European initiative in the *Television without Frontiers* directive which suggested a 50 per cent quota on imported programming by October 1992 where possible (although this is non-binding) and defines a 'European' television company, one where the production and control of production is in an EU state or as a majority of the total cost of production is borne by a producer or co-producer from the EU states or those states privy to the Council of Europe convention. Thus even the possibility of transnationals developing coproductions with Europeans is limited to a minority financial and creative capacity, a trade limitation in Time Warner's eyes. There are also European Union initiatives to promote the EU audiovisual industry and cultural uniqueness of member states as well as the development and standardization of hardware such as HDTV. France's impressive ability to get film included in the remit of the GATT talks is well known; though cultural importation remains a point of controversy within the EU. While Koreans were chastized for putting live snakes in cinemas showing US-made films, and Brazil and Egypt were noted for developing policies promoting homemade cultural production, from the statements of Time Warner and other corporations it was evident that essentially they saw Europe as the problem, not the Third World. The former presented an already well-developed media market with a substantial population possessing considerable disposable income, a market to which US-based firms want ready access. Thus a closer examination of corporate 'globalization' strategies reveals highly preferred locales and areas of acute disinterest, depending on the already existing level of insertion of the populations within global capitalism.

The Third World was problematic to transnationals mainly because of its video piracy, an ingeniously literal understanding of the 'free flow' concept. It is apparent that the still limited and unregulated media markets of the Third World are not especially attractive to transnational culture brokers, which perhaps ironically gives Third World media systems a chance to produce for themselves and escape the western cultural net, a *force majeure* for delinking.

Media Localization

At the same time as these dynamics of globalization have been established, an opposing tendency is concurrently at work, as a consequence of, and often in reaction to, the former; that is the dynamic of localized production and the indigenization of cultural products already referred to above. The evidence about such trends is patchy and somewhat contradictory. Varis (1984) in his two studies of television flows in 1973 and 1984 concluded that few national systems had made major transitions to self-reliance in television programming. Yet more recent research comparing Europe with Asia by Sepstrup and Goonasekera (UNESCO, 1994) reveals some interesting trends. Of the nine countries studied, two Asian countries – India and Korea – revealed the highest amounts of domestically produced television, about 92 per cent of their respective televised programming (Sweden 81 per cent, Netherlands 78 per cent, Hungary 70 per cent, the Philippines produces 67 per cent, Bulgaria 61 per cent), while Italy (58 per cent), and Australia (46 per cent) had the lowest proportions of domestically produced programming. But Latin American researchers argue that, despite the proliferation of media, television programming has become more North American; that 99 per cent of the films shown on Brazilian television are American, and that cheap packages of old movies and TV shows are 'dumped' and thus flood the Latin American media scene (Osava, 1990). Oliveira argues that Brazilian homemade television is even more commercial than American programming with 'merchandizing' of products a central part of telenovela content, encouraging a consumerist way of life of which the USA is the most advanced example (Oliveira, 1990). The same can be said of Peruvian media. India's film industry is being severely challenged by the spread of vcrs and video piracy, the importation of western movies and the closure of cinemas as running costs rise and audiences dwindle (Mohan, 1990). Cross-fertilization between western cinema and television – predominantly American and British – with the popular Indian cinema is creating more 'hybrid' cultural forms, like a new film genre wryly described as the 'curry eastern' (Jain, 1990).

Some evidence suggests that when a choice is available domestic production is preferred over imported. Telenovelas garner larger audiences than imported American soaps not only in Brazil but elsewhere in Latin America (Antola and Rogers, 1984). But evidence from Sepstrup and Goonasekera's research (UNESCO, 1994) shows a more complicated picture: Indian audiences are the most loyal to domestic programming (99 per cent of daily viewing) while audiences in the two eastern European countries chose the largest daily proportion of foreign programming (Hungary 47 per cent and Bulgaria 42 per cent). Presumably a mix of demographic variables such as gender, education, urban dwelling, linguistic background, coupled with different patterns of work, leisure and actual programming schedules, may all play a role in accounting for the diet of programmes viewers actually chose when offered a mixed menu of foreign and domestic materials. This makes generalizations about audience behaviour difficult, and suggests much work remains to be done regarding audience preference structures. Fears of hybridization and creolization exist, that the 'authenticity' of a culture is damaged and undermined in its contact with western culture industries and its adoption of genres foreign to domestic cultural tradition. Some counter that the Latin telenovela is a truly indigenous and independent genre (Straubhaar, 1981), building on internal cultural forms and breaking with the mimicry of western genre. Tunstall in *The Media are American* (1977) pointed out that the importation of media systems to the Third World included not only media hardware but also western forms and genres, which he suggested would lead to precisely such 'hybrid' concoctions. But Oliveira (1990) argues that this 'indigenization' of media often seems to enhance not diversity but domination by domestic corporate concerns. But, we must ask, what is this pristine image of culture that lurks behind this argument? Human history is a history of cultural contact, influence and recombination, as is in evidence in language, music, visual arts, philosophical systems; perhaps media flows merely reinforce our mongrel statuses.

More to the point, evidence suggests that the 'newer' model of cultural indigenization may have been severely overstated and certainly presented in far too naive a manner. Much of this so-called indigenous production is created by large corporations, and deeply infused with consumption values, one of the basic critiques of the 'cultural imperialism' perspective. Another point of direct relevance to the 'localism' claim is that the level of this media production is at the level of the nation, either through state-supported or national corporate networks. Thus in such arguments the 'local' is really the 'national', while the truly local (subcultural, grassroots, etc) is ignored. This 'national' culture may privilege urban lifestyles over rural, may barely represent minority languages and tastes, even disallowing such diversity in the name of 'national unity'; it may produce mediated culture within a narrowly defined ideological framework that fits the politics of the regime of the day. The case of Iran suggests that tradition required defending at the moment that it was already challenged, so Islam as 'cultural identity' was constructed to oppose the Shah and the influx of foreign cultural values and products, only to be used after the revolution as an ideological weapon against all political opponents (Sreberny-Mohammadi, 1991). National agendas are not coincidental with truly 'local' agendas, and real concerns arise as to whether 'national' media cultures adequately represent ethnic, religious, political and other kinds of diversity. In international relations, the 'national' level may be local *vis à vis* the global level, but in domestic relations the 'national' is itself a site of struggle, with a variety of 'local' identities and voices in contention.

Cultural products in the global economy

The new revisionism also seems to have exaggerated the size/amount of this 'localized' production, which is perhaps of financial significance for national economies in the Third World, but is barely yet reflected in international statistics. There are immense difficulties involved in cross-national calculations and comparisons of media, information and cultural production and flow statistics. UNESCO has made a major effort to compile international data in *World Communication Report* published in 1989. Taking this information for the moment at face value, it provides important indicators of the extent of the changes the 'global pluralists' suggest. For example, information on 'total turnover for information and communication' for selected major information and communications groupings which includes equipment, services, and cultural products, clearly shows the continuing dominance of US and Japanese firms (see Table 5.3).

These comprise 67 per cent of the top 25 companies, 66 per cent of top 50 companies and 67 per cent of the top 100 companies; European firms, by contrast, comprise 28 per cent of top 25, and 26 per cent of the top 50 (with Canada the only other nation included), and 26 per cent of the top 100 companies. Other Commonwealth countries begin to appear in the second 50, while Korea and Brazilian companies appear at positions 83, 91 and 94. Of 304 organizations listed by UNESCO in a ranked table of major information and communication groupings, Globo placed 301. Thus the example of *Rede Globo* and Brazilian cultural production as a counter to 'cultural imperialism' as a net exporter of cultural products is cut to size. Simply summarized, corporations based in the USA, Japan and western Europe dominate.

If hardware and software areas are parcelled out, does the picture look any different? Not significantly. The table for 'total media turnover' for major information and communication groupings provides a remarkably similar picture to the above.

Half of the first 25 companies, of the first 50, and of the total of 78 companies for which statistics are presented, are US companies (see Table 5.2). No Third World media corporation penetrates this 'top 78'. Now, of course, such figures represent the total dollar value of communications output, and say nothing specific about *export* dollar values, but they do dampen the optimistic hailing of major Third World cultural producers. While the map of global cultural

Table 5.3 Selected major information and communication groupings. Total turnover for information and communication.

Group	Country	Ranking-information and communication	Information and communication sales	Total sales	Information and communications (%)	Period
IBM	USA	1	54217	54217	100	March 88
NTT	Japan	2	40926	40926	100	March 88
ATT	USA	3	37458	33598	111	
Matsushita	Japan	4	24683	34832	71	March 88
Deutsche Bundespost	Germany	5	20185	28960	70	March 88
NEC	Japan	6	19622	19622	100	March 88
Philips	Netherlands	7	19253	26023	74	March 88
British Telecom	UK	8	17344	17344	100	March 88
France Telecom	France	9	16650	16650	100	
Toshiba	Japan	10	16106	17824	90	March 88
Lucky Gold Star	Korea, Rep. of	83	2791	11474	24	86
CBS	USA	84	2762	2762	100	
TRW	USA	85	2721	6821	40	
Apple	USA	86	2661	2661	100	September 87
ARD	Germany	87	2614	2614	100	
US Sprint	USA	88	2592	2592	100	
TDK	Japan	89	2586	2586	100	November 87
Toppan Printing	Japan	90	2584	3800	68	May 87
Samsung	Korea, Rep. of	91	2581	14193	18	85
NHK	Japan	92	2541	2541	100	March 88
Ford Motor	USA	93	2500	71643	3	
IBL	UK	300	501	501	100	86
Globo	Brazil	301	500	500	100	86
Nippon Telcommunication Construction	Japan	302	500	500	100	March 87
Talt	USA	303	500	500	100	
JTAS (Jydske Telefon)	Denmark	304	500	500	100	

Groups 11–82 and 94–299 have not been included in this table.

flows is more complex in the 1990s, it is not as yet fundamentally realigned. But what about the question of 'effects'?

4 Global media effects?

Media effects is one of the most disputed areas of domestic media research so there is no reason to expect any greater unanimity about effects at the international level. The 'cultural imperialism' thesis did tend to suggest a 'hypodermic needle' model of international effects, 'American' values being injected into Third World hearts and minds. Recent work, building on reception theory and models of the active audience, is giving a more nuanced view of international effects as mediated by pre-existing cultural frameworks and interpretative schema. Thus, despite their book's title (*The Export of Meaning*), Leibes and Katz (1990) argue that meaning is not exported *in* western television programming but created *by* different cultural sectors of the audience in relation to their already formed cultural attitudes and political perceptions. Others (Beltran, Oliveira) argue that it is not so much national American values that are exported but rather more generalized capitalist consumption values (which, of course, America best epitomizes) reinforced by advertising and prevailing development orientations. For them, globalization portends homogenization which, while useful for milk, produces a culture that tastes bland and is not even good for you!

What is often omitted from discussions on effects, are the deeper shifts in cultural orientations and patterns of sociability, in modes of perception and information-processing, that the advent of media create everywhere, albeit in different forms relative to the pre-existing local culture; that is to say it is the very 'fact of television', as Cavell (1982) calls it, in our social lives, not so much its content, that is most often overlooked.

The arrival of media in Third World settings is finally being examined by anthropologists (although there is never an index listing for 'media' or 'television' in a cultural anthropology textbook, despite the fact that most Third World societies are now mediated in some way) and communications researchers. Ethnographic studies are beginning to show the rich play between the pre-existing culture and the new quasi-international culture and the shifts in social relations that the latter may foster. In an ethnographic study conducted in various sites across Brazil, Kottak (1990) explored how television alters patterns of sociability, usage of time, creates conflicts within the family and alters the gender balance, themes also explored in the comparative work on family use of television compiled by Lull (1988). Kottak suggests the need to investigate media impact over time, finding in Brazil an early mesmerization with the television set with a later development of selectivity and critical distance, negative attitudes toward television increasing with higher income and years of exposure. Political context and dramatic events also impinge on media usage: global news viewing was high during the Gulf War, while domestic attention to international channels grew during the Iranian revolution (Sreberny-Mohammadi and Mohammadi, 1994) and in China under martial law (Lull, 1991). News carried by international media channels can open up the range of information and interpretation available to audiences, be a major irritant to governments, challenge state censorship and perhaps help democratic movements.

Other ethnographic work suggests the slippery boundaries of the 'global' and 'local'. Abu-Lughod (1989) has studied the impact of what she calls 'technologies of public culture' on the Awlad 'Ali, the Western Desert Bedouin in Egypt. Although these Bedouin have been quite marginal to mainstream Egyptian culture, they were by no means culturally or politically untouched before these technologies arrived; indeed, they often made their money from selling post-war scrap metal and from smuggling goods between pre-Qaddafi Libya and Egypt. Abu-Lughod examines the impact of tape-players, radios and television on Awlad 'Ali life, saying that their use does not eliminate sociability but in fact brings people together for long periods of time. Such use does realign social relationships, mixing the sexes and tempering age differences at home, while video shows in local cafes kept young men away from the home and gave them greater exposure to media. In line with reception theory, she argues too that these technologies do not destroy distinctive cultures because 'it is not just that people themselves seem to embrace the technologies and actively use them for their own purposes, but that they select, incorporate and redeploy what comes their way' (p. 8) although she notes that so far at least the amount of truly *foreign* programming available is extremely limited. If anything, new technologies such as cassettes have helped to revitalize Bedouin identity as distinct from Egyptian culture through recordings of poetry and song. The urban middle-class Egyptian lifestyles revealed on soap operas present a different set of options to Bedouin women, especially the possibility of marrying for love and living independently of the extended family, so that the dominant Egyptian mediated culture is used as a language of resistance against the authority of tribal elders. Also embedded in such programming are consumer values, for electronic durables as well as products for a newly sexualized femininity, drawing the Bedouin further into the Egyptian political economy. Yet at the same time, in a contradictory manner, Egyptian radio and television carries more transnational messages about Islam, which is gaining in popularity, and which provides an antidote both to capitalist urban Egyptian values as well as the local Bedouin identity (Abu-Lughod 1989: 11; 1993).

Hannah Davis (1989) describes life in a small Moroccan agricultural town of 50,000 people and notes how 'symbols from different worlds overlap: a picture of the king of Morocco hangs next to a poster of the Beatles. The sounds of a religious festival outside . . . mingle with the televised cheering of soccer fans . . . in the morning we watch a holy man curing a boy, then stop off at the fair where we see a woman doing motorcycle stunts; in the evening we watch an Indian fairy tale or a Brazilian soap opera or an Egyptian romance' (p. 13). She remarks 'it is not the contrast between the elements that is striking; it is the lack of contrast, the clever and taken-for-granted integration' (p. 12). As in much of the Middle East, public space is male space, and thus it is the women who gather round the television and vcr at night, watching Egyptian, Indian and 'French' – here the generic term used for western – films. Egyptian films were romances that reduced the women to tears, while the western films elicited 'gasps of surprise, horrified hiding of the eyes, fascination or prurience', with American sexual shamelessness being both admired and feared, imitated and denigrated. The transcultural mix of symbols is apparent when one young girl organizes a traditional religious feast yet defiantly appears wearing a denim skirt and earrings; thus, such symbols may be used in personal struggles to 'define, test or transform the boundaries' of local lives (p. 17).

Such examples reveal the complex (re)negotiation of identity(ies) vis à vis the 'dominant' and the 'foreign' cultures, both of which shift in focus depending on the specific locale of the actor. The above examples pose a number of different pairs of relations in which the site of the 'local' and the image of the 'global' are differently defined: rural/urban; Bedouin/Egyptian; Moroccan/Egyptian; Bedouin/French; Moroccan/American and so forth. This work reveals again the postmodern 'bricolage' of assorted cultural icons from different locations and time periods which circulate inside the non-industrialized world, yet invites no simple reading of the effects of these encounters. Iran is again a useful example of the way in which cultural icons can become deeply invested with one set of ideological connotations in one moment of political struggle, and invested with completely the opposite connotations at a subsequent but differently defined political moment. Thus religious language, traditional symbolism and mythology were popularly (re-)adopted as part of the revolutionary struggle against the Shah, but with the new repression of the Islamic Republic a popular cultural underground began to produce hard liquor and circulate western videos as part of a new resistance (Sreberny-Mohammadi and Mohammadi, 1994). Thus a 'sign' of resistance – the veil, for example – at one point in time can become a 'sign' of oppression at another. The details of such anthropological/ethnographic work extend the 'localist' focus, and show the complexity and range of reactions to and uses of contemporary global cultural encounters. They warn us against generalized assumptions about media/cultural effects, that the 'foreign' may emanate from the urban capital, a western country other than the USA and perhaps even from a Third World media producer of very different cultural background but whose depictions of social life in the process of development can reverberate across the south.

One other basic shift that the global flow of mediated products and the establishment of culture industries in the Third World creates is that documented by Horkheimer and Adorno toward consumption of mass-produced culture. That is culture, from being local lived experience, becomes media product, with the implicit danger that what is not reflected on television no longer has cultural worth. One last neglected 'effect' is important to consider. It has been argued that media development in the west has moved through a set of 'stages' during which one form of communication and its preferred modality of discourse has been dominant. These have been described by Ong (1982) as orality, chirography/typography and the period of the dominance of electronic media which he labels 'secondary orality'. Yet in the Third World there is evidence that the middle stage, at least as measured by mass literacy and circulation of printed materials, may be 'jumped', with societies moving directly from a predominantly oral culture directly into the 'secondary orality' of electronic media. We have paid little attention to this new and different kind of cultural formation. The 'communications and development' model tended to collapse history, suggesting the development of newspapers, cinemas, radio and television all at once, while the 'cultural imperialism' model has given most attention to electronic media. Yet if print is connected to the development of rational logical thinking (Ong), to the development of modern ideologies not linked to church or aristocracy (Gouldner), and the growth of a public sphere, open debate and active citizenry (Habermas), then the limited if non-existent development of this mode of communication in developing countries has profound political and social consequences which have barely been acknowledged.

Change in the 1990s

Over the past few years, new tendencies have developed and older ones have become exaggerated.

Greater but not Equal Access

The greatest changes in the media environment have occurred in Asia, as a result of both national (Freedom Forum, 1993) and transnational activities (Chan, 1994a). Recent figures (*Screen Digest*, April 1994) suggest that nine Asian countries from Pakistan to China have between them 62 terrestrial television channels, 18 of which were launched since 1990. In Hong Kong, Malaysia, Singapore and Taiwan over 90 per cent of homes have television; China and the Philippines have over 50 per cent penetration, although India and Pakistan still have only around 20 per cent of homes with television.

Asia has become part of the 'global village'. Since most economic forecasts anticipate a massive growth in the Asian middle class, an estimated 250 million people in India alone (*Guardian*, March 25, 1995), the further media penetration of households, increased satellite programming and increased advertising seem likely. In 1994–95 there were over 15 international conferences held in Asia about various aspects of broadcasting and telecommunications in the continent, just one indication of the increasing importance of the continent for these industries.

But the media impact is unequal. There are huge disparities between countries, and there are equally great disparities between rural and urban communities within countries. For example, in Indonesia, the fifth most populous country in the world, urban dwellers are 30 per cent of population but own 65 per cent of the televisions; only 23 per cent of rural areas have TV, and the bulk of those are black and white sets. Yet the calculations are that the middle class is 3 per cent of population, which still gives advertisers over 5 million people to target (*Multichannel News International*, March 1995), so a fifth commercial TV channel began in January 1995 with Soeharto family members playing a key role in the commercial media game.

There remains significant global inequality of access to print, to radio and to television – though these are no longer simply regional disparities. Table 5.4 shows the global inequalities in numbers of newspapers, books and amount of newsprint consumed. Illiteracy is increasingly recognized as the biggest barrier to development, with a strongly skewed gender pattern (Sreberny-Mohammadi, 1994). Research on the relationship (if any) between access to electronic media and patterns of literacy is needed; perhaps instead of arguing against television we should concentrate more on the value of literacy. The inequality in access to telephony is shocking, while provision of such services are of far more direct social utility than developments in broadcasting. Nor does the presence of television imply the availability of other indicators of development; for example, it is estimated that over 50 per cent of households in China have television, while only 1 per cent has running hot water.

The other geographic area where there has been a dramatic change in the media environment is the Middle East. The Gulf War brought 24-hour American news coverage to the region, found eager audiences and created pressure for change in the regional media industries. This, coupled with a postwar economic boom,

Table 5.4 Selected global media consumption, 1987–92.

	Radios (per 100 people) 1990	Televisions (per 100 people) 1990	Annual cinema attendances (per person) 1988–91	Annual museum attendances (per person) 1987–91	Registered library users (%) 1987–91	Daily newspapers (copies per 100 people) 1990	Book titles published (per 100,000 people) 1988–91	Printing and writing paper consumed (metric tons per 1000 people) 1990	Letters posted (per capital) 1991	Telephones (per 100 people) 1990–92	International telephone calls (minutes per capital) 1990–92	Motor vehicles (per 100 people) 1989–90
Aggregates												
Industrial	113	54	2.3	0.8	–	30	74	95	401	48	31	50
Developing	18	6	3.0	–	–	4	5	4	13	3	–	3
World	35	15	2.8	–	–	9	15	20	105	13	–	15
OECD	126	60	2.4	0.9	–	31	94	106	406	64	36	54
Eastern Europe and former Soviet Union	–	–	–	–	–	–	–	–	–	15	–	–
Eastern Europe only	41	29	1.6	0.6	22.0	25	34	10	–	18	6	19
European Community	81	44	1.7	0.6	18.2	25	92	82	249	54	39	42
Nordic	92	48	1.8	1.5	11.8	51	161	128	–	74	73	45
Southern Europe	55	37	1.6	0.1	–	10	66	45	116	48	21	43
Non-Europe	164	72	3.0	1.1	–	35	–	122	486	71	27	63
North America	201	80	3.8	1.4	–	25	–	135	648	79	34	73
All developing18 countries	5.5	3.0	–	–	4.4	5.2	4.0	13.4	3.1	–	3.1	–
Least developed countries	10	0.9	–	–	–	0.6	1.8	0.3	3.2	0.3	–	0.2
Sub-Saharan Africa	15	2.5	–	–	–	1.2	2.7	1.5	3.3	1.5	–	2.6
Industrial countries	113	54.4	2.3	0.8	–	30.3	74.4	95.2	401.0	47.8	–	50.1
World	35	14.7	2.8	–	–	9.2	15.1	20.3	104.9	13.0	–	15.4

Compiled from *Human Development Report 1994*, pp. 160, 161, 193.

has fostered a more open media environment (Warwick, 1995). 1994 saw the launch of no less than 20 satellite-delivered television channels in the region (*Media International*, 1995) including Egyptian Satellite Channel (ETC), ORBIT, MBC, and five channels of ART from Saudi Arabia. Video penetration is also estimated at over 90 per cent in many countries.

Continued growth of media conglomerates: the conquest of heaven

A renewed frenzy of US-centered media mergers was seen in 1995. For a while in August, the Walt Disney take-over of Capital Cities/ABC gave that conglomerate the status of the world's largest media entertainment corporation. But that was rapidly eclipsed in the autumn when Time-Warner regained its position as the world's giant by merging with Turner Broadcasting, the owners of CNN. Other mergers and joint ventures include: Microsoft with NBC; Westinghouse with CBS; Seagram with MCA. The search for 'synergy' is creating ever fewer giant media corporations, the new mega-moguls or multicoloured behemoths.

God's biggest current problem is not being in geostationary orbit. The celestial spheres have been purchased and occupied by satellites, the technological form that has done most to revolutionize global broadcasting and telecommunications and create a borderless world, at least for images and information if not for the movement of peoples. STAR beams over Asia; ORBIT over the Middle East; SKY and ASTRA over Europe. The transnational media moguls have shifted from ignoring the south to recognition of the potential spending power of Third World middle classes, hence the expansion of satellite provision, fast-changing takeovers and buyouts of media companies, and the testing of new formats (*Index on Censorship*, 1994; Rusbridger, 1994; Shawcross, 1995). STAR TV (launched by Hutchison Whampoa but purchased by Murdoch in 1992) had already by 1995 reached 54 million homes with a footprint that stretches from Israel and the UAE to China, Hong Kong and Korea. CNN, BBC WORLD, and MTV have all found satellite distributors and southern audiences.

However the new mogul invaders are beginning to be met with more resistance than their old eponymous counterparts.

'Domesticating' output

As has already been mentioned, local or regional programming is often far more popular than western programming. ZEE TV, developed by the Indian trading group Essel and broadcasting in Hindi, rapidly became more popular than Murdoch's STAR and the state-sponsored and dull Doordashan. In 1993 Murdoch bought a 49 per cent share in the company, MTV left, and, acknowledging the need to 'indigenize' programming, STAR has developed a Hindi music channel, Channel V.

Thus even the major media players have come to realize the need for 'cultural sensitivity' and to recognize the different taste cultures within regions. So far this often tends toward a 'Cinema Paradiso' approach to programme content, cutting out the anticipated 'naughty bits' while conveniently forgetting that entire programmes are deeply imbued with non-local values and attitudes regarding family life, relations across the generations, gender roles, lifestyle, even political participation.

Reverse flows

In early 1995 ZEE TV took over the satellite television company TV Asia in the UK for an estimated ú10m, giving it access to the approximately 2 million Asians in the UK, and 8 million in Europe. ORBIT, out of Rome, and MEBC, out of London, broadcast not only to the Middle East, but also to Arab speakers across Europe and North America. Emirates Dubai TV (EDTV) in the UAE has been broadcasting to the estimated 8 million Arabs in Europe and the 8 million in the US since December 1993, offering a 24-hour channel of news and entertainment including children's programming and sport that is 70 per cent in Arabic, sourced from the Arab world and supported by two Dubai-based production houses. Slowly the south is broadcasting to the north.

Going global

Other southern channels are also going global: India's Doordashan will lease capacity on PanAmSat PAS 4 over the Middle East and Europe; China Central Television (CCTV) is set to launch the world's first 24-hour Chinese television service and Chinese News and Entertainment (CNE) already serves an estimated one-million-strong Chinese community in Europe. WETV also aims to globally distribute programmes from the south, by women, by non-commerical groupings with a dedicated satellite, Mondiale, in the planning stage (Fountain, 1995).

Such developments mean that global flows do not only flow out from the West, but increasingly flow in. The issues of international communication described here are not just concerns of the south but increasingly of the north as well, and connect to debates about multiculturalism and diversity in North American and European contexts. Indeed, it is ironic to note how Third World concerns about cultural identity, so scorned by western countries in the 1970s, are now articulated by those very countries in the 1990s.

Forms of resistance

Governments have reacted to the heavenly invasions in different ways. None have tested the 'prior consent' principle accepted by WARC to limit the incursions of satellite signals (Chan, 1994b). Some have banned satellite dishes (Singapore, Malaysia, Saudi Arabia, Iran); dishes are produced by People's Liberation Army in China while technically banned, the ban being ignored in rural China. The encryption of signals limits access; ORBIT, broadcasting from Rome to the Middle East, uses an encrypted signal which requires a decoder. Other controls on distribution have also been devised; for example, Bahrain utilizes an MMDS delivery system, taking in outside satellite channels but feeding them to the domestic population via cable, allowing for a governmental point of control over what is distributed. The satellite distributor may also clash with the programme maker: STAR bumped BBC World from its China footprint when the Chinese authorities objected to BBC coverage of human rights issues but Murdoch wanted to maintain his positive relationship with the Chinese authorities. Despite curbs and regulations in many states, economic, political and cultural resistance are variously expressed through piracy, illegal dishes, illegal cable, etc.

Conclusion: global, regional, national, local

If nothing else, the chapter has shown the complexity of the global contemporary media/culture spectrum at the start of the twenty-first century, and the range of theoretical constructs that have been used to explain, and base policy on the international role of media, particularly in the 'Third World'. The 'mood' of contemporary analysis can be quite varied. One position is that of the happy postmodernist who sees that many kinds of cultural texts circulate internationally and that people adopt them playfully and readily integrate them in creative ways into their own lives, and that cultural bricolage is the prevailing experience as we enter the twenty-first century. Another is the melancholy political economist who sees the all-pervasive reach of the multinationals and wonders how long distinctive cultures can outlast the onslaught of the western culture industries. Somewhere in between lies the cautiously optimistic fourth-worlder who sees in the spread of media the possibilities for revitalization of local identities (ethnic, religious, class, etc) and their use as tools of political mobilization *vis à vis* both national and global forces. But we have also seen the slippery nature of the linguistic terms used in international communications analysis: that 'global' rarely means 'universal' and often implies only the actors of the north; that 'local' is often really 'national' which can be oppressive of the 'local'; that 'indigenous' culture is often already 'contaminated' through older cultural contacts and exists as a political claim rather than a clean analytic construct. The bi-polar model suggests either imbalance/domination, the political-economy perspective, or balance, the 'global pluralist' perspective, whereas the real world reveals far greater complexity.

Cultural boundaries are not etched in stone but have slippery divisions dependent on the self-adopted labels of groups. What seems clear is that, far from an end to history, or the loss of the subject, identity politics and cultural preservation are going to be amongst the hottest issues of the next century that will be fought out internationally and intra-nationally, with profound political and economic consequences. The apparent triumph of late capitalism in 1989–90 and the demise of the so-called second world of state socialism suggest that ideological politics in the classic sense is going to be less important than the revival of identity politics in the future. Yet at the same time as the demise of a single master narrative of global progress is trumpeted in some quarters, in others the old indicators of a single path to 'development' are still utilized, and even adopted with greater eagerness by Third World societies yearning for 'progress'. It is likely that in the next decade we shall see a revival of intense debate about development, and the unresolved role of culture within that process, neo-Lernerian arguments for the positive role of media systems as part of national development encountering arguments for more thoroughgoing Third World economic disassociation and delinking from the global capitalist economy (Amin, 1990), as well as fourth world/indigenist culture arguments for the maintenance of local identities (Verhelst, 1990). These levels may themselves be in conflict, for a strong 'national' position taken in relation to international economic and cultural forces may lead to repression of 'local' forces and voices in relation to that 'national' level. Interstate relations are not coterminous with intercultural relations, and the political and conceptual agenda of the twenty-first century is going to be how to cope with these various levels of actors and processes. It is here that conceptual leakage in the global/local framework of analysis is most evident, highlighted by the particularly complex set of issues raised by mediated cultural flows which poignantly reveal in their electronic presence the absence or porousness of boundaries. In the bipolar model it is the 'national' level of analysis that becomes invisible. Yet it is national policy-making that helps define a cultural identity, provides the regulatory framework for media organizations – the state providing direct funding and control in many Third World nations – and cultural trade policy, as well as defining the domestic public sphere and the extent to which diverse voices will or will not be heard. As Giddens himself underscores in much of his work, nation-states are the key political systems of the modern world, controlling the structures – legal, administrative, financial, military, surveillance, and informational – in which we all live and which are now involved in transnational dynamics – a capitalist world economy, the world military order, systems of inter-governmental organizations, transnational political movements, etc – which both press in on and explode the meaning of national boundaries (Giddens, 1985). Indeed, as Giddens argues, the worldwide system of nations states exists in constant tension with the global capitalist economy.

In the mid-1990s the global media picture is more complex than ever. Transnational media co-exist with domestic, and compete for audiences; domestic production can become even more commercial, garish and explicit than the western 'originals'; but perhaps new programming formats, indigenized media products, alternative news frames, might also develop. Pressures for democratization, variety, entertainment, are strong, and it seems a form of Eurocentric hubris to deny others what we enjoy in the name of some questionable 'high culture' purity. It is an exciting time in media development, when the paternalistic preoccupation of the past twenty years might give way to a realization that the creativity, energy and indeed entrepreneurship of the south is at least equal to that of the north. Southern media environments need to be taken as seriously as northern sites, and studied with as varied and contextualized approaches, and that must now include flows and actors on many levels: the global, the regional, the national, and the local, since all of these might constitute the loci of the 'imagined communities' (Anderson, 1983) of the future.

Epilogue

The original version of the preceding essay was written in 1990, and was probably one of the first to address directly the relationship between the global and the local in international communication, or in any social sphere for that matter. Since then there has been an avalanche of books on globalization in general and on the globalization of the media in particular. As my grandmother used to say about Christmas turkeys, if I had a penny for every book published in the last ten years with globalization in its title, I'd be a rich woman by now.

The essay was revised and updated in 1995 and has enjoyed a good life, widely used and cited in academic research as well as providing the basis for pedagogic review in Jones and Jones' book on the media (1999), and Fulcher and Scott's introductory text *Sociology* (1999).

The essay stands, as does a lot of academic work, as a sign of the times. When

I read it now, even its title seems to be premised on too binary a division – the global versus the local; whereas now I might suggest that the global is usually a rather abstract level of analysis, which is best explored through particular instances, that is through the mutual interpenetration of the global and the local, or 'glocalization' as Robertson calls it.

The approach of the essay is historical, trying to present emergent models of international communication, but tending to suggest that one paradigm is simply surpassed by another. It would be better to say that elements from all the models are to be found across the huge swathe of contemporary literature, and that the debates between paradigms continue, rather than being resolved.

Indeed, perhaps the most significant thing about the current (1999) international media environment is that conflicting tendencies are evident, so the legalistic jargon of 'on the one hand' and 'on the other' does seem appropriate. On the one hand, there are tendencies towards increasing size, the CBS–Viacom merger producing the latest conglomerate to claim 'biggest in the world' status for a moment. The United-Carlton merger in November 1999 produced the largest commercial television company in Britain with pretensions to address the global market. On the other hand, there are tendencies towards cultural, linguistic and religious particularity, with the emergence of significant cultural markets in Spanish, Chinese and Arabic product. Such linguistically based markets are not only supported by nationally based forms of media production but also through the work of different kinds of diasporic communities which maintain affiliation and a sense of identity through the production and circulation of many kinds of mediated products, including newspapers, music video, poetry journals and film. On yet another hand, more territories are joining the televisual revolution, like St Helena; more countries seem to be moving towards democratization, like Tunisia, in which a free press and media access are recognised as staples of the process; there's more production from within the south. Yet there's on-going concern about inequality of access to media caused by urban-rural divides, by class divisions and by gender disparities, as much within countries as across them.

An end-of-the-century accounting of gains and losses in communication would have been fascinating and I begin to wonder what kind of data and analysis that would produce: for example, how many millions of people are literate (still not everyone) and how many people have now made their first phone call (still not everyone)? Technological Luddism has given way to a perhaps overly positive attitude towards new technologies with insufficient appreciation of the profound cultural change that they bring. Old models of economic development are being supplanted by more complex models in which political indicators are central, in which democratization and gender equality are increasingly key concerns.

Most of the theorizing and debate in international communications is a post-Second World War phenomenon, the final half of a tumultuous century. If we take a millennial view, then the speed up of change is so marked as to be breathtaking, and reminds us of the overly-fast rush to judgements in our field since it also changes so visibly in front of our own eyes. Slower, more tempered, judgements and a longer historical purview all seem necessary; and I'm well aware of talking to myself here too.

Globalization implies a paradigm shift, a world in which notions of national sociologies, national cultures and national media models do not work as simply any longer. We are just beginning to work and live through its implications.

References

ABU-LUGHOD, L., 1989: 'Bedouins, Cassettes and Technologies of Public Culture', *Middle East Report*. 159, 4, 7–12.
——, 1993: 'Finding a Place for Islam: Egyptian Television Serials and the National Interest', *Public Culture* 5, 3, 493–514.
ALVARADO, M., (ed.), 1988: *Video World-Wide: An International Study, London/Paris*: Unesco/John Libbey.
AMIN, S., 1990: *Delinking*, Monthly Review Press.
ANDERSON, B., 1983: *Imagined Communities*. London: Verso.
ANTOLA, L. and ROGERS, E. M., 1984: 'Television Flows in Latin America', *Communication Research*, 11, 2, 183–202.
APPADURAI, A., 1990: 'Disjuncture and Difference in the Global Cultural Economy', *Public Culture*. 2, 2, 1–24.
BAGDIKIAN, B., 1990: 'Lords of the Global Village', *The Nation*, 248, 23, 805–20.
BINFORD, M. R., 1988: 'Innovation and Imitation in the Indian Cinema' in W. Dissanayeke (ed.) *Cinema and Cultural Identity*. Maryland, University Press of America.
BOYD, D., 1984: 'The Janus Effect? Imported Television Entertainment Programming in Developing Countries', *Critical Studies in Mass Communication*, 1, 379–91.
BOYD, D., Straubhaar, J. D. and LENT, J. A., (eds), 1989: *Videocassette Recorders in The Third World*, New York: Longman.
BOYD-BARRETT, O., 1977: 'Media Imperialism: toward an international framework for the analysis of media systems', in J. Curran, M. Gurevitch and J. Woollacott (eds), *Mass Communication and Society*. London: Edward Arnold.
CAVELL, S., 1982: 'The Fact of Television', *Daedalus*, III, 4, 75–96.
CHAN, J. M., 1994a: 'Media Internationalization in China: Processes and Tensions', *Journal of Communication* 44, 3, 70–88.
——, 1994b: 'National Responses and accessibility to STAR TV in Asia', *Journal of Communication* 44, 3, 112–33.
CHATTERJI, P. C., 1989: 'The Ramayana TV serial and Indian secularism', *InterMedia*, 17, 5, 32–34.
DAVIS, H., 1989: 'American Magic in a Moroccan Town', *Middle East Report*, 159: 19, 4, 12–18.
DISSANAYEKE, W., 1988: 'Cultural Identity and Asian Cinema', in W. Dissanayeke (ed.), *Cinema and Cultural Identity*. Maryland: University Press of America.
FABRIKANT, G., 'Studios look to Foreign Markets', *New York Times*, March 7, 1990, Section D1.
FISKE, J., 1987: *Television Culture*. New York: Methuen.
FOUNTAIN, A., 1995: 'Global Visions: two versions', *Free Press (CPBF)* 85, March–April.
FULCHER, J. and SCOTT, J., 1999: *Sociology*, Oxford: Oxford University Press.
FREEDOM FORUM, 1993: *The Unfolding Lotus: East Asia's Changing Media*. New York: Freedom Forum Media Studies Center, Columbia University.
GALTUNG, J. and RUGE, M., 1965: 'The Structure of Foreign News', *Journal of Peace Research*, 1, 64–90.
GIDDENS, A., 1985: *The Nation-State and Violence*. Cambridge: Polity Press.
——, 1990: *The Consequences of Modernity*. Stanford University Press.
GOLDING, P., 1977: 'Media Professionalism in the Third World: the transfer of an ideology' in J. Curran, M. Gurevitch and J. Woollacott (eds), *Mass Communication and Society*. London: Edward Arnold/Open University.

GUBACK, T., and VARIS, T., 1982: *Transnational Communication and Cultural Industries.* (Reports and Papers on Mass Communication No. 92) Paris: UNESCO.

GUNDER-FRANK, A., 1964: 'The Development of Underdevelopment' in *Capitalism and Underdevelopment in Latin America*, New York: Monthly Review Press.

HAMELINK, C., 1983a: *Finance and Information*, New Jersey: Ablex.

——, 1983b: *Cultural Autonomy in Global Communications*, New York: Longman.

HARVEY, D., 1989: *The Condition of Postmodernity*, Oxford: Basil Blackwell.

HOBSBAUM, E., 1990: *Nations and Nationalism since 1780*, Cambridge: Cambridge University Press.

Human Development Report 1994, 1994: Oxford: Oxford University Press.

Index on Censorship, 1994: 'Media Moguls', September/October.

IYER, P., 1989: *Video Nights in Kathmandu*, New York: Vintage Press.

JAIN, M., 1990: 'The Curry Eastern Takeaway', *Public Culture* 2, 2.

JAMESON, F., 1984: 'Postmodernism, or the cultural logic of late capitalism', *New Left Review*, 146, 53–92.

——, 1992: *Postmodernism, or The Cultural Logic of Late Capitalism.* Durham: Duke University Press.

JONES, M, and JONES, E., 1999: *Mass Media*, Basingstoke: Macmillan.

KATZ, E. and WEDELL, G., 1977: *Broadcasting in the Third World*, Massachusetts: Harvard University Press.

KOTTAK, C. P., 1990: *Prime-Time Society: An Anthropological Analysis of Television and Culture*, California: Wadsworth.

LERNER, D., 1958: *The Passing of Traditional Society*, New York: Free Press.

LIEBES, T. and KATZ, E., 1990: *The Export of Meaning*, Oxford University Press.

LULL, J. (ed.), 1988: *World Families Watch Television*, California: Sage Publications.

——, 1991: *China Turned On*, London: Routledge.

MATTELART, A., 1979: *Multinational Corporations and the Control of Culture*, England: Harvester Press and New Jersey: Humanities Press.

MCLUHAN, M., 1964: *Understanding Media*, London: Routledge Kegan Paul.

MCNEELY, C. and SOYSAL, Y. M., 1989: 'International Flows of Television Programming: A Revisionist Research Orientation', *Public Culture*, 2, 1: 136–45.

Media International, 1995: '1995 Special: The Year Ahead' January, 17.

MINH HA, T., 1987: 'Of Other Peoples: Beyond the "Salvage" Paradigm', in H. Foster (ed.), *Discussions in Contemporary Culture Number One*, Seattle: Bay Press.

MOHAN, A., 1990: 'Cinema fall prey to video pirates', *Development Forum.*

NTIA (National Telecommunications and Information Administration), 1990: *Comprehensive Study of the Globalization of Mass Media Firms*, US Dept. of Commerce.

OLIVEIRA, O.S., 1990: 'The Three-Step Flow of Cultural Imperialism: A Study of Brazilian Elites', paper presented at ICA Conference, Dublin, Ireland.

——, 1990: 'Brazilian Soaps Outshine Hollywood: Is Cultural Imperialism Fading Away?' Paper presented at ICA Conference, Dublin, Ireland.

ONG, W., 1982: *Orality and Literacy*, London: Metheun.

OSAVA, M., 1990: 'Foreign domination of TV perplexes Latin Americans', *Development Forum.*

OUDERKIRK, C., 1989: 'Modern-day Mayans', *World Monitor*, 2, 7.

RUSBRIDGER, A., 1994: 'Television's new world order: The moghul invasion', *Guardian Weekend*, April 9.

SCHILLER, H., 1976: *Communication and Cultural Domination*, White Plains: International Arts and Sciences Press.

SCHRAMM, W., 1964: *Mass Media and National Development*, California: Stanford University Press.

SHAWCROSS, W., 1995: 'Reaching for the Sky', Special Supplement on 'Whose News: Democracy and the Media', *New Statesman and Society*, 24 March.

SONY, USA, 1990: *Comments in Response to Notice of Inquiry on Globalization of Mass Media Firms*, NTIA/OPAD.

SREBERNY-MOHAMMADI, A., 1991: 'Media Integration in the Third World: An Ongian Look at Iran', in B. Gronbeck, T. Farell and P. Soukup (eds), *Media, Consciousness and Culture*, California: Sage Publications, in press.

——, 1994: *Women, Media and Development in a Global Context*, UNESCO, June.

SREBERNY-MOHAMMADI, A. and MOHAMMADI, A., 1991: 'Hegemony and Resistance: Cultural Policies in the Islamic Republic of Iran', *Quarterly Review of Film and Video* (special issue on World Television) 12, 33–61.

——, 1994: *Small Media, Big Revolution: Communications, Culture and the Iranian Revolution*, Minnesota: University of Minnesota Press.

——, 1995: 'The Many Faces of Cultural Imperialism', in P. Golding, P. Lewis, and N. Jayaweera (eds), *Beyond Cultural Imperialism: The New World Information Order Debate in Context*, London: Sage Publications.

STRAUBHAAR, J. D., 1981: 'Estimating the Impact of Imported versus National Television Programming in Brazil', in S. Thomas (ed.), *Studies in Communication and Technology*, vol. 1, New Jersey: Ablex.

TIME WARNER INC., 1990: *Comprehensive Study of the Globalization of Mass Media Firms*, Response to National Telecommunications and Information Administration Request for Comments, NTIA/OPAD.

TRACEY, M., 1988: 'Popular Culture and the Economics of Global Television', *Intermedia*, 16, 2.

TUNSTALL, J., 1977: *The Media are American*, London: Constable.

UNESCO, 1989: *World Communication Report*, Paris: UNESCO.

——, 1994: *Television Transnationalization: Europe and Asia* (P. Sepstrup and A. Goonesekera) Reports and Papers, No. 109, Paris: UNESCO.

VARIS, T., 1974: 'Global Traffic in Television', *Journal of Communication*, 24, 102–109.

——, 1984: 'The International Flow of Television Programs' *Journal of Communication*, Winter, 143–52.

VERHELST, T., 1990: *No Life Without Roots: Culture and Development*, London: Zed Press.

WARWICK, M., 1995: 'Arabsat', *Middle East Broadcasting and Satellite*, January, 9.

6

Rethinking Media and Democracy

James Curran

Introduction

New times call for new thinking. Dictatorships of left and right have given way to multi-party democracies around the world. New communications technology has ostensibly offered greater choice. These political and technical changes are an open invitation to rethink 'media and democracy', a subject where discussion has become repetitive and wrapped in the cobwebs of time.[1]

This chapter attempts, therefore, to do more than; merely provide a textbook-style exposition of traditional liberal thought.[2] It also assesses its relevance for today. Much liberal analysis derives from a period when the 'media' consisted principally of small-circulation, political publications and the state was still dominated by a landed elite. The result is a legacy of old saws which bear little relation to contemporary reality.

Critical evaluation of liberal thought will be linked to discussion of policy. Anachronistic ideas from a frock-coated world of the past were deployed to redefine media policy in the 1980s and 1990s, and were endorsed by key public bodies from the American Supreme Court to the European Commission. Sceptical appraisal of this liberal legacy is thus not simply an academic activity: it involves questioning the central thrust of current policy-making in the communications arena.

This reappraisal concludes with new proposals for reformulating liberal argument and for organizing a democratic media system. These may well be rejected in favour of better considered alternatives. But whatever view is taken, this much seems clear: the literature on media and democracy needs a removal van to carry away the unwanted lumber accumulated over the centuries. What should be removed, what should take its place, and how the intellectual furniture should be rearranged, needs to be thought about in a new and critical way.

Free market watchdog

The principal democratic role of the media, according to liberal theory, is to act as a check on the state. The media should monitor the full range of state activity, and fearlessly expose abuses of official authority.

This watchdog role is said to override in importance all other functions of the media. It dictates the form in which the media system should be organized. Only by anchoring the media to the free market, in this view, is it possible to ensure the media's complete independence from government. Once the media becomes subject to public regulation, it may lose its bite as a watchdog. Worse still, it may be transformed into a snarling Rottweiler in the service of the state.

This orthodox liberal view is especially well entrenched in the United States. For instance Kelley and Donway, two American political scientists of conservative sympathies, argue that any reform of the media, however desirable, is unacceptable if it is 'at the cost of the watchdog function. And this is the inevitable cost. A press that is licensed, franchized or regulated is subject to political pressures when it deals with issues affecting the interests of those in power' (Kelley and Donway, 1990: 97). This reservation is restated by the centrist political theorist, Stephen Holmes, as a rhetorical question: 'Doesn't every regulation converting the media into a "neutral forum" lessen its capacity to act as a partisan gadfly, investigating and criticising government in an aggressive way?' (Holmes, 1990: 51). Even American analysts with strongly reformist views share the same fear: 'I cannot envision any kind of content regulation, however indirect,' writes media critic, Carl Stepp, 'that wouldn't project government into the position of favouring or disfavouring some views and information over others. Even so-called structural steps aimed at opening channels for freer expression would post government in the intolerable role of super-gatekeeper' (Stepp, 1990: 194).

This free market argument was deployed with great effect in the United States during the 1980s to justify broadcasting deregulation. Television channels were 'freed' from the fairness doctrine that required them to cover important issues and present alternative views on controversial matters of importance (Baker, 1998). Rules restricting media concentration were also relaxed (Croteau and Hoynes, 1997; Tunstall and Machin, 1999).

A parallel campaign was mounted in Britain. As the media magnate, Rupert Murdoch (1989: 9) succinctly put it, 'public service broadcasters in this country [Britain] have paid a price for their state-sponsored privileges. That price has been their freedom' (Murdoch, 1989: 9; see also Adam Smith Institute, 1984; Veljanovski, 1989). Although this rhetoric encountered more opposition in Britain than in the United States, it influenced the government of the day. Regulation of commercial broadcasting content was reduced, and anti-monopoly restraints were eased during the 1990s (Goodwin, 1998).

The liberal watchdog argument was effective partly because it invoked a premise which was widely accepted in relation to the press.[3] Newspaper regulation, other than through the 'ordinary' law of the land, was vehemently opposed in both the United States and Britain on the grounds that it would muzzle criticism of government. Thus, the American Supreme Court struck down in 1974 a press right of reply law in Florida on the grounds that it would inhibit free speech, and 'chill' critical scrutiny and debate (Barron, 1975). Similarly, the last Royal Commission on the Press in Britain opposed in 1977 any form of selective newspaper subsidy because 'it would involve in an obvious way the dangers of government interference in the press' (Royal Commission on the Press, 1977: 126).

Market liberals had only accepted more extensive regulation of broadcasting on the grounds that the limited number of airwave frequencies made it a 'natural monopoly' (Royal Commission on the Press, 1977: 9; see also Horwitz, 1991). When the number of television channels multiplied with the introduction of advanced cable and satellite, this 'special case' argument was undermined. What was right in principle for the press was now applicable, it was argued, to broadcasting. Television should be set free.

Attention has focused for convenience on Britain and the United States. However, a very similar sequence of argument and pressure occurred in many other countries especially in mainland Europe, Asia and Australasia. The same freedom rhetoric was invoked; the same opportunities beckoned with the development of new television channels; and a shift towards broadcasting deregulation followed (Avery, 1993; Aldridge and Hewitt, 1994; Raboy, 1996; Weymouth and Lamizet, 1996; Humphreys, 1996; Herman and McChesney, 1997; Ostergaard, 1997; Robins, 1997; Tracey, 1998; Catalbas, 2000; Curran and Park, 2000).

Time-worn arguments

The traditional public watchdog definition of the media thus legitimates the case for broadcasting reform, and strengthens the defence of a free market press. At first glance, this approach appears to have much to commend it. After all, critical surveillance of government is clearly an important aspect of the democratic functioning of the media. Exposure of the Watergate scandal during the Nixon presidency or lesser-known exploits (outside their country) such as disclosure of state involvement in the illegal sale of Bofors guns in Sweden or Nikiforov's exposure of local state corruption in the former USSR, leading to his murder in 1989, are all heroic examples of the way in which the media performed a public service by investigating and stopping malpractice by public officials.

However this argument is not as clear-cut as it seems. While the watchdog role of the media is important, it is perhaps quixotic to argue that it should be paramount. This conventional view derives from the eighteenth century when the principal 'media' were public affairs-oriented newspapers. By contrast, media systems in the early twenty-first century are given over largely to entertainment. Even many, so-called 'news media' allocate only a small part of their content to public affairs – and a tiny amount to disclosure of official wrong-doing.[4] In effect, the liberal orthodoxy defines the main democratic purpose and organizational principle of the media in terms of what they do *not* do most of the time.

The watchdog argument also appears time-worn in another way. Traditionally, liberal theory holds that government is the sole object of press vigilance. This derives from a period when government was commonly thought to be the 'seat' of power and main source of oppression. However, this traditional view takes no account of the exercise of economic authority by shareholders. A revised conception is needed in which the media are conceived as being a check on *both* public and private power.

This modification diminishes the case for 'market freedom' since it can no longer be equated with independence from all forms of power. A growing section of the world's media has been taken over by major industrial and commercial concerns such as General Electric, Westinghouse, Toshiba, Fiat, Bouyges, and the Santo Domingo groups, in a development that extends from the United States and Japan to Hungary and Colombia (Bagdikian, 1997; Herman and McChesney, 1997; Ostergaard, 1997; Tunstall and Machin, 1999; Curran and Park, 2000). A number of media organizations have also grown into huge leisure conglomerates that are among the largest corporations in the world. The issue is no longer simply that the media are compromised by their links to big business: the media *are* big business.

The conglomeration of news media mostly took place during the last three decades. It gave rise sometimes to no-go areas where journalists were reluctant to tread for fear of stepping on the corporate toes of a parent or sister company (Hollingsworth, 1986; Bagdikian, 1997; Curran and Seaton, 1997). It is also claimed plausibly that the media are in general less vigilant in relation to corporate than public bureaucracy abuse because they are part of the corporate business sector (McChesney, 1997).

Market corruption

The classic liberal response to these criticisms is that the state should be the main target of media scrutiny because the state has a monopoly of legitimated violence, and is therefore the institution to be feared most. For this reason, it is especially important to establish a critical distance between the media and the governmental system through private media ownership.

What this seemingly persuasive argument fails to take into account is the way in which the market is now a source of corruption that can subdue critical oversight of government. This is because the nature of the relationship between private media and government has been transformed since the early eighteenth century when 'Cato' (1983 [1720]) set out with such powerful eloquence the press watchdog thesis. The sphere of government has been enormously extended since his day, with the result that politicians and public officials are now routinely involved in decision-making that can affect the profitability of private media enterprises. Media organizations are also in general more profit-oriented, have more extensive economic interests and have more to gain from business-friendly government. In turn, governments are now more in need of government-friendly media because they have to woo and retain mass electoral support.

These cumulative changes have given rise to a relationship that is increasingly prone to corruption. This is highlighted by Chadwick's (1989) pioneering research which shows that a number of media entrepreneurs formed a tactical alliance with the Labour Government in Australia in the late 1980s as a way of securing official permission to consolidate their control over Australia's commercial TV and press. This resulted in an unprecedented number of editorial endorsements for the Labour Party in the 1987 election, as well as opportunistic fence-sitting by some traditionally anti-Labour papers. Similarly, Rupert Murdoch removed in 1994 the critically independent BBC World News service from his Asian Star satellite system, and later vetoed HarperCollins' publication of ex-Hong Kong Governor Chris Patten's memoirs, in order to avoid offending the Chinese Government when he was seeking to expand into the Chinese broadcasting market. In much the same way the Argentine media tycoon,

Eduardo Eurnekian, axed a critical TV report on the building of an expensive airstrip on President Menem's private property. At the time, Eurnekian was bidding for (and duly obtained) a major stake in Argentina's privatized airports (Waisbord, 2000).

Indeed, the potential for media corruption was enormously increased by the deregulatory policies that were pursued in the 1980s and 1990s. Lucrative broadcasting and telecommunications franchises were disposed of; new arrangements were made for their operation, which affected their costs and profitability; and the rules governing media acquisitions and cross-media ownership were changed. Whether leading media corporations became much bigger, more dominant and more profitable depended, in part, on political and bureaucratic consent. This encouraged a number of non-aggression pacts typified by the tacit understanding that was reached between Tony Blair, as leader of the Labour opposition in Britain, and Rupert Murdoch in the mid-1990s. Tabloid hounds pursuing Labour were called to heel in return for very strong signals that a New Labour Government would not attack Murdoch's monopolist empire (Curran and Leys, 2000).

In other words, the market can give rise not to independent watchdogs serving the public interest but to corporate mercenaries that adjust their critical scrutiny to suit their private purpose.

Market suppression

Still more serious is the way in which the market can silence media watchdogs altogether. Many privately owned media organizations supported right-wing military coups in Latin American countries (Fox, 1988; Waisbord, 2000). This collusion was typified by *El Mercurio*, which backed the military coup in Chile, loyally supported the Pinochet dictatorship and largely overlooked its violation of human rights. Similarly, the Globo TV network gave unconditional support to the military regime in Brazil, while most of Argentina's privately owned media failed to investigate state-sponsored 'disappearances' during the period of military rule. Less dramatically, private media in Taiwan 'not only accepted authoritarian rule', according to Lee (2000: 125), 'but also helped to rationalize it' during the period before 1987. In each case, these media collaborations with authoritarian states arose because media owners were part of the national system of power.

Even in societies where market-based media have a more independent and adversarial relationship to government, appearances can still be deceptive. Media attacks on official wrong-doing can be manipulative or pull their punches. 'Fearless' investigative journalism, in these circumstances, can be viewed as little more than an elite transaction.

For example, a seven-person team from Northwestern University examined six investigative stories exposing official fraud, failure or injustice that appeared in the American media in the period 1981–88 (Protess *et al.*, 1991). All these stories, it turned out, were initiated and sourced by well-positioned power holders. In most cases, tip-offs to the media were part of a conscious agenda-building strategy by 'policy elites' who were preparing the ground for reform or were engaged in image-building. In most cases media disclosure can be best understood, according to this debunking account, as an integral part of media management.[5]

Even the Watergate investigation (exposing high-level Republican involvement in the 1972 break-in at the Democrat headquarters and President Nixon's
subsequent cover-up, leading to his forced resignation), cited earlier as an example of heroic media vigilance, is not immune from this demythologizing
approach. It has gone down in legend as an example of intrepid journalists
doggedly tracking down the truth and changing the course of history. In fact,
most of the press's independent investigation took the form of receiving pre-
culled information from state officials. Furthermore 'the moving force', conclude Gladys and Kurt Lang (1983: 301), 'behind the effort to get to the bottom
of Watergate came neither from the media nor public opinion but from political
insiders' who maintained pressure for the story to be pursued and to be recognized as important. This insider guidance resulted in the media defining
Watergate primarily as a legal-juridical issue. This restrictive definition encouraged the adoption of very inadequate reforms in the wake of Watergate.

What all these examples point to is the inadequacy of the liberal model which
explains the media solely in terms of market theory. The media are assumed to
be independent, and to owe allegiance only to the public, if they are funded by
the public and organized through a competitive market. This theory ignores the
many other influences that can shape the media, including the political commitments and private interests of media shareholders, the influence exerted through
news management and the ideological power of leading groups in society. In
short, this extremely simplistic theory fails to take into account the wider relations of power in which the media are situated. This is a key point to which we
shall return when we consider other aspects of the media's functioning in the
democratic system.

State control

If private media are subject to compromising constraint, so too of course are
public media. There is no lack of examples where public broadcasters have acted
as little more than mouthpieces of government (Downing, 1996; Sparks, 1998;
Curran and Park, 2000a). These cautionary experiences reveal the variety of different pressures that have been applied. Public broadcasters have been censored
by restrictive laws and regulations; undermined by being packed with government supporters; squeezed by refusals to increase public funding; intimidated by
public and private criticism; and crushed through sackings of staff and the
threat of privatization.

However, a qualifying note needs to be introduced at this point. The radical
media literature is bedevilled by system logic which assumes that state-
controlled media serve the state and corporate-controlled media serve business
corporations. This ignores, or downplays, countervailing influences. Privately
owned media need to maintain audience interest in order to be profitable; they
have to sustain public legitimacy in order to avoid societal retribution; and they
can be influenced by the professional concerns of their staff. All these factors
potentially work against the subordination of private media to the political
commitments and economic interests of their shareholders. Likewise, the long-
term interest of public broadcasters is best served by developing a reputation for
independence that wins public trust and sustains political support beyond the
duration of the current administration. In many liberal democracies, the ideal of

broadcasting independence is not only pursued by broadcasting staff for professional reasons, but is supported also by the political elite partly out of self-interest. Senior politicians of all major parties know they will need access to broadcasting when they are voted out of office.

The autonomy of publicly regulated broadcasting is also supported by a system of checks and balances. While this varies from country to country, it usually includes, in western Europe, most of the following safeguards: a constitutional guarantee of freedom of expression; formal rules requiring broadcasting impartiality, enshrined in law; civic society or all-party representation on broadcasting authorities; hypothecated, index-linked public funding; competition between broadcasters, organized in different ways; and the devolution of editorial authority within broadcasting organizations through formal or informal structures (Humphreys, 1996; Raboy, 1996). These safeguards are further underwritten by public support for broadcasting independence.

Since these qualifying arguments run counter to the tenor of conventional radical accounts (such as those provided by Herman and Chomsky, 1988, and Herman, 1998), perhaps they should be exemplified by two, 'mini' case studies. The first concerns journalistic resistance to corporate control. In April 1984, the chief executive of Lonrho, Tiny Rowland, intervened to protect the corporation's profitable investments in Zimbabwe. One of Lonrho's many newspapers, the London-based *Observer*, was about to report that the Zimbabwe army had massacred civilians in the country's dissident Matabele province. Lonrho's relations with the Zimbabwe Government were already strained since Lonrho had backed the losing party in the recent election. The corporation had also been widely attacked in Zimbabwe as a relic of colonial power. Anxious to avoid further trouble, Rowland told his editor, Donald Trelford, not to run the story. Trelford refused and was backed by the paper's staff and independent directors. The dispute at the paper was leaked and Rowland was widely criticised. He hastily backed down to avoid further public censure (Curran and Seaton, 1997).

The second example illustrates journalistic resistance to state control. In 1988, Thames Television, part of Britain's publicly regulated ITV network, made a programme, *Death on the Rock*, which alleged that a British army SAS unit had unlawfully killed unarmed members of an IRA active service unit in Gibraltar. The programme also claimed that the official version of this event was misleading. The Foreign Secretary, Sir Geoffrey Howe, asked the commercial television regulatory authority, the IBA, to veto the programme on the technical grounds that it would prejudice the official inquest that was due to take place. The IBA refused and the programme was transmitted on 28 April 1988.

This was not the end of the story. Prime Minister Margaret Thatcher was furious, and her displeasure was echoed by much of the press: 'TV Slur on the SAS' was the *Daily Star*'s headline (29 April 1988); 'Fury Over SAS "Trial by TV"', reported the *Daily Mail* (29 April), which also published a TV review calling the programme 'a woefully one-sided look at the killings'; *The Sunday Times* ran several articles which impugned the reliability of the programme's main witness and cast doubt on the programme's claims.

This public flak failed to intimidate. Thames Television ordered an internal inquiry which hailed the programme as 'trenchant' and its makers as 'painstaking and persistent' (Windlesham and Rampton, 1989: 143). The programme was subsequently given the top annual (BAFTA) award of the television industry in a symbolic act that deliberately snubbed both the government and the Conservative press. Thames Television then rubbed salt in political wounds by repeating the programme in May 1991, as an example of outstanding journalism.

But if these two examples illustrate professional aspirations for independence in both the public and private sectors, it should be remembered that these aspirations are not equally supported. The political culture of liberal democracies is very alert to the threat posed by governments to the freedom of public media, but is much less concerned about the threat posed by shareholders to the freedom of private media. Government ministers are attacked if they seek to dictate the content of public television, yet proprietors are not exposed to equivalent criticism if they seek to determine the editorial line of their media properties. Elaborate checks and balances have been established in old liberal democracies to shield public media from the state. Yet, equivalent checks have not yet been developed to shield private media from their corporate owners.[6]

In sum, an unthinking, catechistic subscription to the free market is not the best way to secure fearless media watchdogs that serve democracy. Instead, practical steps should be taken to shield the media from the corruptions generated by *both* the political and economic system.

Settling of accounts

Since the discussion so far has followed a number of twists and turns, it may be helpful to reiterate here its central argument. The conception of the media as a democratic watchdog is important but it does not legitimate, as neo-liberals claim, a free market system. Market pressures can lead to the downgrading of investigative journalism in favour of entertainment. Corporate ties can also subdue critical surveillance of corporate power. More importantly, the owners of private media can be aligned to those in power, or have a mercenary relationship to government, in a way that silences critical exposure of official wrong-doing.

Pressures can also be brought to bear to silence state-linked watchdogs. But elaborate defences have been developed to prevent this, in contrast to the much weaker protections that have been constructed against shareholder abuse. Therefore a strategy is needed that defends the media from both public and private power, and enables the media to serve the wider public through critical surveillance of all those in authority.

Information and debate

The watchdog perspective of the media is defensive. It is about protecting the public by preventing those with power from overstepping the mark. However, the media can also be viewed in a more expansive way, in liberal theory, as an agency of information and debate that facilitates the functioning of democracy. The media brief the electorate and assist voters to make an informed choice at election time. The media also provide a channel of communication between government and governed, which helps society to clarify its objectives, formulate policy, co-ordinate activity and manage itself.

All this can best be achieved, in the liberal view, through the free market. This secures the media's independence as an intermediary, and generates a wide-ranging and inclusive debate. The freedom of the market allows anyone to publish an opinion; this ensures that all significant points of view are aired, and that information is made available from varied sources.

In this way participation in public debate is extended. Good government is also fostered because decision-making processes are exposed to the interplay of opposed opinion. As the American jurist, Oliver Holmes, declared in a much-quoted statement, 'the best test of truth is the power of the thought to get itself accepted in the competition of the market . . .' (quoted in Barron, 1975: 320).

As with the watchdog perspective, there is much to commend this approach. It assumes that democracies need informed and participant citizens to manage their common affairs. It also believes that public debate is more likely to produce rational and just outcomes if it takes account of different views and interests. At the heart of this liberal – or what is called, in the United States, republican – tradition is thus an admirable stress on active self-determination, reasoned debate and social inclusion.

There is, however, one central flaw at its centre: its wide-eyed belief in the free market. Its espousal of neo-liberalism undermines what it sets out to achieve in four different ways.

First, the free market now restricts the effective freedom to publish. When liberal press theory was first framed, it really was the case that ordinary people could set up their trestle table, so to speak, in the main market-place of ideas because it was cheap to publish. Great national newspapers were launched in 1830s Britain, for example, with minimal outlay (Curran, 1977). Now at least £20 million is needed to establish a new national broadsheet, and over £15 million to establish a new popular cable TV channel in Britain.[7] While there are still some media sectors where costs are low, these tend to be marginalized or have low audiences. A lone website on the internet is virtually free but it does not have the same communicative power as owning a mass television channel or newspaper. The central square of the public sphere has been rendered inaccessible, in short, by the high cost of market entry.

Second, the free market reduces the circulation of public information and renders people less well informed. The dynamics of this process are explored by Curran, Douglas and Whannel (1980) in relation to the British press. Pioneer market research undertaken for publishers over a 40-year period showed that human interest stories consistently obtained the highest readership scores because they appealed to all categories of reader, whereas public affairs had only a minority following concentrated among certain social groups. Competitive market pressure to maximize sales resulted therefore in human interest content displacing public affairs coverage. Indeed, by the late 1970s, public affairs accounted for less than 20 per cent of the editorial content of the national popular press. A comparable process has occurred in popular television. News has tended to be banished to the margins of prime-time, to make way mainly for fiction, whenever mass television has been deregulated. Thus, in Britain, news was shunted in 1999 to 6.30pm and 11pm slots on the main commercial channel, ITV, to give a clear run for top-rated programmes.

Third, the free market restricts participation in public debate. It generates information-rich media for elites, and information-poor media for the general public. The result, in many countries, is a polarization between prestige and mass newspapers. Something rather similar is now developing in the public space being constructed around the emergent Euro-polity, where only the Euro-elite is being specifically catered for by informative newspapers, magazines and television channels (Schlesinger, 1999). While this recurring pattern reflects inequalities in society, the market confirms rather than challenges these.

Fourth, the market undermines intelligent and rational debate. Market-oriented media tend to generate information that is simplified, personalized, decontextualized, with a stress on action rather than process, visualization rather than abstraction, stereotypicality rather than human complexity (Epstein, 1973; Inglis, 1990; Iyengar, 1991; Gitlin, 1990 and 1994; Hallin, 1994; Liebes, 1998). This is a by-product of processing information as a commodity. The first inkling of this came as a terrible shock to liberals like Mathew Arnold (1970) who reacted with horrified amazement to the market-oriented 'new journalism' of the 1880s. More than a century later, we have rather less reason to be surprised.

Ironically, successful public service broadcasting systems come closest to embodying the liberal ideal of informed, rational and inclusive public debate. They give prominence to public affairs programmes, reasoned discussion and (in some systems) pluralistic representation. This is because they put the needs of democracy before those of profit, and are supported in this by government legislation. This approach means deserting eighteenth-century notions of the leviathan state, and recognizing that governments, elected by the people and subject to constitutional constraints, can potentially act in the public interest.

Voice of the people

Representing people to authority is, in liberal theory, the third key democratic function of the media. In one version, this is the culmination of the media's mission. After having briefed the people and staged a debate, the media relay the public consensus that results from this debate to government. In this way, the government is supervised by the people between elections. As Thomas Carlyle (1907) put it, the press is 'a power, a branch of government with an inalienable weight in law-making', derived from the will of the people.

The introduction of opinion polls took some of the wind out of this 'fourth estate' argument. More often now, the claim is made simply that the media speak for the people, and represent their views and interests in the public domain. The assumption is that 'the broad shape and nature of the press is ultimately determined by no one but its readers' (Whale, 1977: 85) because the press must respond in a competitive market-place to what people want, and express their views and interests. As a consequence the privately owned press – and, by extension, the privately owned broadcasting system – speak up for the people.

This argument is so frequently advanced that it is necessary to explain in some detail why it is fundamentally flawed. In the first place, it invokes an idealized view of market competition. In reality, most media markets have developed in ways that weaken consumer influence.

Market failures

The influence of the consumer is reactive rather than proactive. It is exerted through choosing between what is available in the market rather than, as in the case of the producer, through direct expression. The extent of real market choice is consequently central to how much power the consumer really has. If that choice is curtailed, consumer influence is correspondingly diminished.

Up until the early 1980s, consumer choice was strongly constrained by media oligopoly. The press systems in most countries developed in a highly monopolistic form (Hoyer, Hadenius and Weibull, 1975; Commission of the European Communities, 1992; Sanchez-Tabernero *et al.*, 1993; Bagdikian, 1997). Radio and television offered only a few competing channels. The media sectors that first became globalized – news agencies, film and music – were dominated by a relatively small number of companies (Herman and McChesney, 1997).

This stable, controlled media landscape was transformed in the 1980s and 1990s by the diffusion of new communications technologies. Fibre-optic cable, high-powered satellite, digitalization, personal computers and the internet offered new communications 'pipelines' into the home. Some also crossed national frontiers. This expanded the range of media products, established new niche markets and introduced new sources of competition. For a time it seemed as if oligopolistic market control would be ended, and the consumer would be greatly empowered.

The response of leading media producers to this threat was a well-judged combination of political lobbying and market adaptation. They pressed for a relaxation of anti-monopoly controls by arguing initially that market expansion diminished the need for regulation, and subsequently that concentration was necessary in order to compete effectively in the global market. The success that greeted their efforts in many countries (including, crucially, the United States) enabled them to embark on an extended merger and acquisition spree supported by generous bank credit. Out of market fragmentation there developed a new pattern of multimedia concentration.

In the United States, film and television companies merged to establish a new axis for large vertical media corporations, around which other media interests were grouped. The key landmarks in this change were the pioneer coupling of the film major Twentieth Century Fox and Metromedia (television) under Rupert Murdoch in the mid-1980s, followed by Viacom's acquisition of Paramount and Blockbuster in 1994, Disney's purchase of the ABC television network in 1995, and the merger of Time Warner (itself the result of a 1989 merger) with Turner Broadcasting in 1996, among other marriages of convenience (Herman and McChesney, 1997; Tunstall and Machin, 1999). Almost certainly a new portent of things to come was the merger of the telecommunications giant, AT&T, with the cable TV giant, TCI, in 1998, and that of Time Warner with America OnLine (AOL) in 2000. This presaged the arrival of telecommunications and net companies as two further players in the game of happy families that is reshaping the American media system.

The number of corporations dominating the United States media shrank from an estimated fifty in 1983 to ten in 1997, with another twelve having major positions in particular media markets (Bagdikian, 1983 and 1997). These mega-corporations typically control film and television production companies, a 'bouquet' of television channels delivered through different systems, and a portfolio of media and leisure interests (such as books, newspapers, magazines, cinemas, music labels, sports teams and theme parks). In addition, these corporations tend to be bankers and distributors for so-called 'independent' media companies, and are involved in multiple joint ventures in e-commerce, digital services and other new communications applications. Their activities now conform to a classic oligopolistic pattern. They compete against each; sell to each other; swap assets with each other; and have co-ownership, revenue-sharing, co-production and co-purchasing deals with each other. This enables them to increase profitability through economies of scale and scope, share the cost of risk-taking and, above all, limit competition. While this is good for large media companies, it limits the effective power of consumers through an informal system of market regulation (Tunstall and Machin, 1999).

What happened in the United States was duplicated, with national variations, in numerous other countries. In Britain, where there is almost no film industry left, the main new axis for media concentration is a partnership between press and television, around which other media interests are grouped. Once again, Murdoch led the way by ducking and weaving through anti-monopoly controls. His press group acquired rival titles to become the biggest in Britain, and to this he added a pioneer satellite television system which became a British monopoly through the BSkyB merger in 1990. During the 1990s, fifteen ITV companies also merged to become three, and expanded by gaining part of the new Channel 5, cable television channels, OnDigital terrestrial television, and national and local press titles. In late 1999 two of these giants, Carlton and United News and Media, announced a proposed merger, with the third declaring its intention to construct an alternative merger package. A similar pattern of press and television businesses combining to form the core of new mega-corporations is still more advanced in Germany (Herman and McChesney, 1997).

If one defensive response to market fragmentation was corporate concentration, another was attempted global conquest. The introduction of new ways of delivering television programmes provided an opportunity to break into formerly protected national markets, while privatization policies led to the sale of state media assets. However, this global expansionist strategy ran into mounting resistance. New centres of media production, from Taiwan to Brazil, developed to challenge the might of the transational 'majors', mostly headquartered in the United States (Sinclair *et al.*, 1996). In many countries, television audiences showed a strong preference for their national product. The adaptive response of transnational media corporations to these setbacks was, increasingly, to 'think global but act local'. They formed alliances with leading national media corporations, in this way strengthening the forces of national oligopoly. They brought to these alliances formidable weapons: additional financial resources, cross-media promotion, popular production formulae, accumulations of stock and often a global distribution network.

The first key factor limiting consumer influences is, thus, an enormous increase in the concentration of media ownership, and of the resources that giant media corporations are able to bring to bear in limiting competition and managing demand. The second factor, already referred to, is high market entry costs. This is interpreted in traditional liberal analysis in a restricted way as tending to exclude insights that might enhance public enlightenment. This overlooks its key significance as an invisible form of censorship that excludes social groups with limited financial resources from competing in the main media sectors. The result is a market system that is not genuinely open to all, and which tends to be controlled by right-wing leadership.

A long list of right-wing media tycoons – for example, the Australian-American Rupert Murdoch, the Canadian Conrad Black, the German Leo Kirch, or the Italian Silvio Berlusconi – is not matched by a corresponding list on the left (save for pro-market social democrats). These right-wing media controllers are even more free to give expression to their views than before because the increase of entertainment content has weakened the link that used to exist between media and public opinion. Increasingly, audiences seek to be diverted rather than represented. The relative autonomy this can confer on media controllers is illustrated by the career of Rupert Murdoch. He has always been willing to rein in his ideological commitments in order to gain regulatory favours from politicians, to conform to state-imposed impartiality rules, or to woo audiences, if the situation required it. But informing his last 30 years, and indeed giving to it a principled continuity, has been a steadfast determination to promote, wherever possible, right-wing values (Munster, 1985; Leapman, 1983; Shawcross, 1993). As one of his closest lieutenants, Andrew Neil, records: 'Rupert expects his papers to stand broadly for what he believes: a combination of right-wing republicanism from America mixed with undiluted Thatcherism from Britain' (Neil, 1996: 164), a view echoed by other senior Murdoch employees (Evans, 1983; Giles, 1986).

The third limitation on the influence of individual consumers applies only to some of them – minorities and the ones with least money. Mass media markets are oriented towards majorities as a way of maximizing sales and effecting scale economies (that is, spreading high expenditure on the 'first copy' over subsequent copies to reduce unit costs). While niche provision has increased, this is geared more towards affluent than low-income minorities. This distortion is further accentuated by advertising funding of terrestrial television, magazines and newspapers, which exerts a gravitational pull towards upscale, profitable audiences (Curran, 1986; Baker, 1994; D'Acci, 1994). In short, market democracy is a universe where individuals do not have equal votes.

The claim that market expansion has led to more consumer choice thus needs to be viewed critically. More media outlets does not necessarily mean 'more of the same', as some left-wing critics maintain. But what it does mean is that choice is always *pre-structured* by the conditions of competition. In a contemporary context, this means provision for unequal consumers, in oligopolistic markets where entry is restricted. The constraints this imposes are well illustrated by the development of American television and the British press.

American television is the most mature, multi-channel market system in the world. Instead of being dominated, as in the 1970s, by three organizations, it is now dominated by six. Whereas before it offered mainly formulaic network programmes for mass audiences, now it offers an enormous range of specialist programmes, including stand-up alternative comedy, tub-thumping religious sermons, interactive shopping, Hollywood classics, sitcom classics, 24-hour news, differentiated sports coverage, new American films, children's cartoons, history programmes, natural science programmes, classical opera, soap opera for Korean viewers and much else besides. But while there has been a spectacular increase in the genre variety of American television, there has not been a corresponding increase in its ideological range (Entman, 1989; Kellner, 1990; Croteau and Hoynes, 1997; McChesney, 1999).

The British press gives the appearance of being one of the most competitive

in the world. In contrast to the monopolistic local structure of most press systems, it has a dominant national press boasting no less than twenty (general)
daily and Sunday titles[8] – a number significantly boosted by the adoption of
'new' printing techniques in the mid-1980s. However, appearances can be deceptive. Just five groups control over 90 per cent of national newspaper circulation.
No new national newspaper launched in the last 80 years has been able to stay
independent. Moreover, the ideological range of this press has contracted over
the last 30 years, while remaining much more right-wing than its public. During
the 1980s and early 1990s, the Conservative press's share of national daily circulation was some 50 per cent more than that of the Conservative Party in general elections (Seymour-Ure, 1996: 217–18). On numerous issues, the leaders of
the national press have reproduced a remarkably narrow arc of opinion, indeed
sometimes only one opinion (Curran and Seaton, 1997).

Comparative perspective

If privately owned media are not automatically the voice of the people, who
then do they represent? The answer to this question depends crucially upon the
configuration of power to which the media are linked. We will consider below
four ideal-typifications that shape media output.

In the first model, the economic elite is the leading group in society, and exerts
influence over the political system through its power base in the economy, control of private media, funding of political candidates and informal channels of
access to the state. Perhaps the country that most resembles this ideal-type is
contemporary Russia (McNair, 2000) where the economic elite has a leading
position in the economy, dominates privately owned media and has a strong
influence within the state. A key moment when this power group flexed its mus-
cle was in 1996 when the main commercial television channels joined public
broadcasting in providing partisan support for the oligarchy's chosen candidate,
Boris Yeltsin, and helped to secure his election despite his obvious frailty. In this
model, then, private media are primarily conduits of economic elite influence on
both government and public opinion.

In the second ideal-type, the leading group is the political elite. The main circuit of influence passes from this elite through the media system to other groups
and power centres in society. The political elite generally uses state power to
develop a clientelist system of patronage and influence. Its usual method of control over privately owned media is a combination of carrot and stick: the award
of television franchises to allies; generous state loans, subsidies and government
advertising to lubricate media goodwill; the waiving of monopoly controls to
boost the growth of friendly media groups; state posts for top media people; and
highly restrictive laws enabling the imprisonment of dissident journalists who
stray outside this system of control. This broadly corresponds to the situation
in contemporary Malaysia (Nain, 2000), and to that – until quite recently – in
Korea (Park *et al.*, 2000) and Taiwan (Lee, 2000).

The third ideal-type is a relationship of relative parity between political and
economic elites leading to a sometimes uneasy alliance between the two. The
media, in this model, represent the elite consensus, and seek to win popular
acceptance of it. This seems to describe the situation in a number of Latin

American countries where there is a strong national state (Waisbord, 2000). The key interaction that influences the media is not that between media and consumers but that between elites. For example, Hallin argues that it was primarily pressure from a reformist faction within Mexico's political elite rather than consumer pressure that led the commercial broadcaster 'kicking and screaming' into reluctant pluralism in the late 1980s (Hallin, 2000: 103).

The fourth model is liberal corporatism, based usually on a three-way relationship between organized capital, labour and the state. This produces a system of power-sharing and consensus that powerfully influences the discursive terms of reference of the media. This is typified by contemporary Sweden (Dahlgren, 2000) and until the 1980s by Britain (Curran and Leys, 2000). Liberal corporatism is the norm in northern Europe, although it is perhaps now in decline because globalization has produced a shift from political to economic power, and weakened organized labour.

One key variable in all these models is the degree to which the leading power network coheres. If disagreements develop within it, these are generally reproduced in the media. This can give the appearance of liberal theory 'working': the media can indeed be galvanized into watchdog activity, public debate and representing the resulting 'public opinion'. However, the initial impetus in this process of representation comes not from the 'people' but from within the power structure.

The second key variable is the extent to which the central power network is able to frame public debate within its terms of reference and shape public attitudes. An energized civil society, well-developed alternative networks of ideas and communication, professional oriented media staffs, and consumer pressure can combine to detach part of the media from the prevailing power system (Curran, 1996). In this situation (in important respects resembling that in early nineteenth-century Britain when liberal press theory was refined), part of the media can indeed represent critical public opinion and become an emancipatory force.

This is a necessarily condensed alternative view to that of private media as tribunes of the public. What it stresses is the need to take account of the full range of influences shaping the media, in social contexts that are different and cannot be reduced to a single, liberal economistic explanation of the media as the voice of the consumer.

Habermas and the public sphere

So far this essay has provided a critical exposition of liberal theories of media and democracy, and argued both that they are conceptually flawed and that their objectives cannot be realized through a free market programme. Two other aspects of the liberal tradition need to be reviewed: its tacit understanding of the democratic system, and its idealist legacy.

Traditional liberal theory perceives the political system to be constituted primarily by government and individuals. In this theory the media protect, inform, gather together and represent private citizens, and enable them to supervise government through the agency of public opinion.

This approach clings to an archaic understanding of polity largely developed in the late eighteenth century. It fails to recognize that people are represented primarily through political parties, interest groups and the myriad structures of civil society. These are the principal building blocks of contemporary liberal democracy. A theory of media and democracy needs to be related, in other words, to the collective and institutional forms of the modern political system.

It is worth turning in some detail to the writing of Jürgen Habermas because it represents a clever attempt to do precisely this. However, the attention of media studies has centred on Habermas's early work which is not very helpful in terms of updating liberal theory because the relevant part of it is steeped in traditional liberalism. Habermas's first study argued that a 'bourgeois public sphere' came into being in the eighteenth century (Habermas, 1989 [1962]). This consisted of privileged private citizens who debated public affairs in a free, rational and (in principle) disinterested way through personal interaction and debate in the press, and reached a consensus that influenced government. However, this public sphere was limited, according to Habermas, by being socially restricted. It was corrupted subsequently by the corporate organization of public life and the commodification of culture, in a process of 'refeudalization'.

This account has been both enormously influential and widely attacked.[9] The debate it triggered has given rise to a normative conception of the contemporary public sphere as a neutral space within society, free of both state or corporate control, in which the media should make available information affecting the public good, and facilitate a free, open and reasoned public dialogue that guides the public direction of society (Scannell, 1989; Hallin, 1994; Corner, 1995). In effect, this conception seeks to recreate Habermas's idealized notion of eighteenth-century public life in an enlarged and egalitarian form. However this approach (with a few exceptions like Dahlgren, 1995) does not take adequate account of the intermediary structures of modern democracy. It also seems to invite us, on the basis of a very unreal view of the past, to see public debate as a mass version of a university seminar conducted through socially responsible media.

Habermas has since shifted his position. His more recent work represents an ambitious attempt to reconceptualize the media and public sphere in a contemporary context. Abandoning his early, impressionistic, account of twentieth-century 'refeudalization' (Habermas, 1992), he now invokes a more conventional understanding of the workings of democracy (Habermas, 1996 [1992]). At its centre, Habermas argues, is government, the civil service, judiciary, parliament, political parties, elections and party competition. Outside this core system is an inner periphery of institutions (such as regulatory agencies) with powers delegated by the state. The outer periphery is made up of two sorts of organization that can be broadly categorized as 'customers' (business associations, labour unions and private organizations) and 'suppliers' (voluntary associations, churches, new social movements and public interest groups). According to Habermas, social concerns should be transmitted – ideally – from the periphery of society to the centre.

A second key shift in Haberman's analysis is his revised understanding of the public sphere. This is no longer conceived of as private individuals coming together as a single public but 'as a network for communicating information and points of view' that connects the private world of everyday experience to the political system (Habermas, 1996: 360). The public sphere is also viewed as being much more differentiated, pluralistic and organized than before. Its key activists are said to be public interest groups and also radical professionals who identify, draw attention to and interpret social problems, and propose solutions. They are the 'sensors' of society who detect neglected issues, rise potentially above self-interest, and generate countervailing influence on behalf of the disadvantaged. Their interventions can also lead, with the aid of press and broadcasting mediation, to critical debate coalescing into 'topically specified *public* opinions' (Habermas, 1996: 360, original emphasis), and sustained pressure for a considered response from the political system.

This analysis is much more optimistic than Habermas's earlier, more frequently cited work. It implies greater confidence in the capacity of civil society to offset concentrations of power, greater hope that the media will facilitate meaningful debate, and greater faith in the critical independence of media audiences. However, this optimism is conditional upon the public sphere being mobilized so that 'the balance of power between society and the political system then shifts' (Habermas, 1996: 379). When the public sphere is 'at rest', influence tends to flow, in Habermas's view, from administrative and social power at the core of the political system to the periphery.

Three things are worth noting about this account. It plays down class conflict, which causes Habermas to downgrade the role of organized labour as an agency of popular representation. It does not consider how the media should be organized to best serve the needs of democracy. It also offers an account of the contemporary public sphere which seems, for very understandable reasons, unfinished.

Whereas, before, the public sphere was viewed by Habermas as being co-extensive with the nation state (Habermas, 1989), it is now presented as 'a highly complex network that branches out into a multitude of overlapping international, national, regional, local, and subcultural arenas' (Habermas, 1992: 373). While this reformulation is clearly an advance on his original conception, its detail is still left vague. Especially underdeveloped is Habermas's reference to the 'emerging global public sphere' as a key development that may conceivably be a harbinger of a 'new universalist world order' (Habermas, 1992: 444).

This allusion draws attention to something that is important. A system of 'global governance', through organizations like the United Nations, World Trade Organisation and International Monetary Fund, has begun to emerge. Flows of communication have become more globalized. And public interest groups operating on an transnational basis have had a growing impact through appeals to the international community in a number of areas: most notably human rights, environmental protection, relief of world poverty, world peace and global market regulation. Yet, the inter-relationships between these different phenomena are still unclear and require further investigation.

However, what does seem clear is that the global public sphere is best understood not as a single global space of democratic exchange – what Marshall McLuhan (1964) memorably called a 'global village' – but as a series of interlocking public spaces. This is the implication, for example, of Sonia Serra's illuminating study of the campaign against the killing of street children in Brazil (Serra, 1996 and 2000). What made the campaign effective, she argues, was the way in which local Brazilian reformers teamed up with transnational agencies. This generated coverage in national press and television outlets around the world, and gave rise to political pressure funnelled largely through national governments (in addition to the United Nations and the Catholic Church). This had a profound impact on the media, public opinion and government of Brazil, and led to a change in the law. This case study thus acknowledges the national partitioning of global space, a point reinforced by a companion essay in this volume (Lee *et al.*, see Chapter 14) which shows that the media of different countries represented the return of Hong Kong to China in markedly divergent ways, seemingly reflecting differences in their political culture, national interest and collective memory. However 'national partitioning', though useful as an image, fails to capture the complexity of the interlocking spaces of the global public sphere. As another essay in this volume points out, globalization also involves the forging of new conjunctions between the global and the local in ways that weaken the national (Sreberny, see Chapter 5).

International civil society has long been a political force, as the remarkable nineteenth-century campaign against slavery demonstrates. Yet, the number and influence of transnational public interest groups like Greenpeace seem to have grown during the last two decades. However, powerful national states still continue to enjoy privileged media access and formidable resources in the battle for international opinion. This is well illustrated by a study of television coverage of the Reagan-Gorbachev summits in 1985–88. This offered only 'a semblance of an international public sphere', according to Daniel Hallin (Hallin, 1994: 161), because participation in the televised dialogue was dominated by the then superpowers, and largely excluded grass-roots organizations.

Without getting caught up in recent globalization debates, which have been summarized elsewhere,[10] it is perhaps sufficient to register one key point. A new global communications order is developing in a lopsided, uneven way which is clearly connected to wider inequalities of power and resources in the world. It is within this distorting context that an international (rather than global) public sphere is taking shape.

This is contested by those who argue that the internet is creating a global public space that exists independently of nation, distance and power. Cyberspace is incubating, it is argued, a new world order based on international communication, reciprocal understanding and popular empowerment (Negroponte, 1996). What this fails to take into account is the ways in which relations of inequality in society enter into and structure cyberspace. In 1997, 92 per cent of internet hosts were derived from OECD countries, reflecting the superior wealth and communications infrastructure of the developed world (Patelis, 2000: 92). The fastest-growing communications on the internet are now e-commerce and business-generated messages, due to the enormous resources available to the corporate business sector. What the internet seems to reveal is the way in which external relations of power shape communications, rather than the other way round.

Idealist legacy

A critical revision needs to think further not only about the functioning of the public sphere, but also about the idealist premises of liberal theory. The traditional justification for media pluralism – that truth will automatically confound error in open debate – now seems implausible. As Chafee (1983: 294) wryly puts it, 'I can no longer think of open discussion as operating like an electric mixer. ... Run it a little while and truth will rise to the top with the dregs of error going down to the bottom.' His reservations were based on distortions in the distribution of information and the subjective element in making judgements. This last point has been highlighted by research emphasizing the highly selective ways in which people assimilate information and form opinions (Graber, 1988; Corner *et al.*, 1990; Neuman *et al.*, 1992). To these misgivings should be added a further reservation: the 'best' argument, in the sense of one best supported by evidence and logic, does not necessarily prevail against arguments that have more publicity and are more congenial to those in power. Yet, the liberal idea that media should offer a plurality of opposed opinion still seems essential, and defensible, for other reasons. It is a way of promoting not truth but public rationality based on dialogue; not rule devoid of error but a system of self-determination informed by freedom, choice and a tradition of independence that comes from civic debate.

This raises the question of how media plurality should be conceptualized. The traditional liberal approach, still dominant in American jurisprudence, is to equate it with the free trade of ideas. This has given rise to the rule-of-thumb yardstick which measures media pluralism in terms of the number of competing media outlets or the division of market shares. The assumption is that if there is a significant level of competition, there is no lack of pluralism. This is a view regularly endorsed in American legal judgements (Horwitz, 1991; Baker, 1997a), and increasingly by the European Commission (Commission of the European Communities 1992 and 1994).

This ignores *where* opinion comes from, and brackets out the question of social access. Indeed, usually absent from this market competition approach is a recognition that ideas and systems of representation are part of the discursive arsenal competing groups use to advance their interests. This argument can be pitched in a simple and rudimentary way in terms of party agendas. Political parties on the right tend to emphasize tax, law and order and defence, while those on the left tend to stress welfare provision and employment because these are areas where they are traditionally perceived to be strong by voters. Rival political parties consequently vie with each other at election time to get television to make their 'issues' the dominant ones of election coverage.

A comparable but more complex process of contestation takes place between rival social groups at the level of ideology. Different ways of making sense of society, different codes and explanatory contexts, different premises and chains of association privilege some social interests as against others. The media's role is never solely confined to imparting information, but necessarily involves arbitrating between the discursive frameworks of rival groups. Which frameworks are included or excluded matters because over time it can affect collective opinion and, indirectly, the allocation of social resources in society.

For this reason, pluralism cannot just be equated with competition. It needs to mean more than this: namely, media diversity supported by an *open* process of contest in which different social groups have the opportunity to express divergent views and values. This broader definition implies a commitment to extending freedom of expression, broadening the basis of self-determination, and promoting equitable outcomes informed by awareness of opposed opinions and interests.

It also means accepting a greater degree of conflict played out in the media. In idealist liberal argument, conflicts are resolved through good communication and goodwill. Its belief is that society is homogeneous and harmonious, and people are able to identify through the application of reason the common good. From this is derived the assumption that media debate culminates in agreement. However, this approach ignores the existence of conflicts of interest between social groups that cannot be dissolved magically through discussion. It also pays too little attention to the ways in which material interests can be cloaked in altruism. Indeed, the 'reasonableness' that this liberalism extols can be used to exclude the 'irrational' (for example, 'emotional' women or the 'loony left'), and justify bracketing out their terms of reference, producing a civilized debate that conveniently reaches conclusions favourable to established privilege. This idealist tradition is in fact nothing like as benign and civilized as it appears to be, although some notion of universality and civic virtue derived from it needs to be retained.

Another issue raised by the liberal inheritance is the democratic status of media entertainment. The conventional liberal approach is to exclude from consideration entertainment on the grounds that it is not part of rational exchange and does not belong to the political arena; or to see it as an enemy of republican democracy that is poisoning the body politic. Both responses now seem increasingly inadequate for different reasons.

Collective self-management does not only take place in the bounded world of politics, it also takes the form of social regulation expressed through shared understandings of what is acceptable and unacceptable in social behaviour, supported in the first instance through social interactions registering approval or disapproval. These understandings are debated, affirmed and revised through collective dialogue conducted partly through media entertainment. For example, much human interest news is about deviancy, about where shifting boundaries are or should be drawn, and about what happens to those who flout society's moral rules (Ericson *et al.*, 1987). It has the same normative and regulatory dimension within a complex, differentiated society as gossip in traditional village communities.

The exclusion of entertainment as being outside the political domain also looks increasingly unsatisfactory on several counts. First, media fiction offers cognitive maps of reality, and furnishes social understandings that have political implications. For example, whether crime is regularly portrayed, in television and film drama, as arising primarily from social conditions or individual evil has a bearing potentially on attitudes towards law and order. Second, media entertainment is bound up with debates about social values and identities (McGuigan, 1996), which are two key determinants of voting behaviour. Third, media entertainment is a vehicle of debate about certain 'political' issues. Thus, television soap opera is an important forum of discussion about race and gender relations, single parenthood and sexual minorities, all areas which are subject to public legislation or regulation (Geraghty, 1995; Goldsmiths Media Group, 2000). Fourth, entertainment (and in particular popular music) is an important way in which disempowered groups are able to register their opposition to dominant structures and ideologies (Hebdige, 1979; Gelder and Thornton, 1996). Rap music, in the words of Chuck D (formerly of the group Public Enemy), is 'the CNN black people never had' (cited in Cross, 1993: 108).

But if entertainment should be recognized as a positive part of the media's contribution to the democratic process, traditional liberal objections centring on rationality and participation are not all misplaced. Soap opera can extend democratic insight and understanding, but it is not an ideal way of debating the relative merits of alternative policy options. An entertainment-only diet displacing public information and political debate is a recipe for passivity and social control, something that is welcomed by a particular style of paternalistic leadership. As Emilio Azcarraga, head of Mexico's main commercial television network, memorably observed in 1991: 'Mexico is a country of a modest, very fucked class, which will never stop being fucked. Television has an obligation to bring diversion to these people' (cited in McChesney, 1998: 17). People who are informed and active participants in civil society are a much more formidable and less biddable force than those who are only 'active' at the level of consumption. The disadvantaged who 'fight back' through cultural subversion of popular entertainment are, in the absence of concerted action in the political domain, engaged in seeking an essentially 'magical' solution to their social situation. At some level, public information and political involvement are the prerequisites of exerting collective influence for change. In the succinct words of the American political theorist, Alexander Meikeljohn (1983: 276): 'self-government is a nonsense unless the "self" which governs is able and determined to make its will effective'.

An alternative approach

If the conventional liberal approach has a number of flaws, how might it be replaced with something better? Perhaps the first step in rethinking liberal theory is to break free from the assumption that the media are a single institution with a common democratic purpose. Instead, different media should be viewed as having different functions within the democratic system, calling for different kinds of structure and styles of journalism.

Edwin Baker (1998) makes the important point that the democratic purpose of one part of the media system is to assist social groups to constitute themselves and clarify their objectives.[11] How their interest as a social group is best served is not something that springs pre-formed into peoples' consciousness as a consequence of their social circumstances. It needs to be explored through internal group processes of debate.

A democratic media system needs, therefore, to have a well-developed, specialist media tier, serving differentiated audiences, which enables different social groups to debate issues of social identity, group interest, political strategy and normative understanding on their own terms. For some subordinate groups in particular this will be liberating because they will have the space and media arsenal to question social arrangements that restrict the social resources available to them and curtail their life chances. They will also be empowered by being able to question dominant discourses that legitimate their subordination, and will be in a position to develop alternative arguments that advance their interests.

This specialist tier also has a secondary democratic purpose of enhancing the political effectiveness of different social groups. It should include media that assist collective organizations to recruit support; provide an internal channel of communication and debate for their members; and transmit their concerns and policy proposals to a wider public. In other words, the representative role of the media includes helping civil society to exert influence on the governmental system.

Above this specialist sector is a general media sector, reaching heterogeneous publics. This should be organized in a way that enables different groups in society to come together and engage in a reciprocal debate. This should be staged in a way that promotes mutual understanding,[12] and furthers a common search for solutions. However, by offering an open public dialogue, this sector should also help people to identify adequately their self-interest, and weigh this in the balance in relation to competing definitions of the common good. In addition, this general media sector should facilitate democratic procedures for defining agreed aims and regulating conflict. In a national context, this includes adequately informing the electorate about the political choices involved in elections, in a way that helps to constitute these as defining moments for collective decision. General media need also to keep open agenda-setting channels between civil society and the governmental system, not least by being responsive to public interest group initiatives, and maintaining pressure for adequate responses to them.

The design of this media system will make the attainment of collective agreement more difficult. In most societies, the media are linked to the hierarchy of power and tend to promote social integration on its terms. An approach that seeks, by contrast, to destabilize this link, and allocate effective communications resources to subordinate and minority groups, is liable to promote fissiparous tendencies at a time when general societal ties appear to be weakening. However, general media remain a source of general social cohesion in this model. They will tend to draw people together through the sharing of the same cultural experiences, and reproduce ritualized events that affirm common identities, values and memories (Peters, 1989; Dayan and Katz, 1992; Liebes and Curran, 1998).

Built into this conception of a democratic media system is a desire to maintain some kind of equilibrium between conflict and conciliation, fragmentation and unity. The intention is to create spaces in which differently constituted groups can communicate effectively with themselves in order to facilitate the self-organization needed to advance their sectional interests. At the same time, these divergent groups need also to be brought into an arena of common discourse where reciprocal debate can take place in order to facilitate an agreed compromise. Informing this approach is the hope that tacit acceptance of an inegalitarian social order will be replaced by the building of a new, more equitable social settlement, regulated by an informed, unbiddable public, in which powerful economic forces are confronted by well-organized political ones.

What might this media system look like in terms of structure and organization? What kinds of journalism would it foster? These questions beg further questions in that the design of any media system needs to take into account the generation of pleasure and rewarding cultural experience, which are issues that lie outside the terms of reference of this essay. Any prescription based on what serves the democratic needs of society can only be a partial imput to a larger debate. But with this qualification in mind, let us consider what a re-evaluation of the democratic functioning of the media implies in terms of public policy.

Towards a working model

The outline that follows may seem to American eyes detached from political reality. But although it does not exist in any country as a single functioning model, it draws upon and composites features derived from the practice of different European countries. Indeed, it is proposed in this form precisely because it works with the grain of what is attainable.

The model can be viewed at a glance in Figure 6.1. It has a core sector, constituted by general interest TV channels that reach a mass audience. This is where different individuals and groups come together to engage in a reciprocal debate about the management of society. Contrary to fashionable argument which asserts that contemporary media systems have become irrevocably fragmented, the main four television channels in a large number of developed countries account for between half and three-quarters of total viewing (Ostergaard, 1997; Curran, 1998 and 2001). These popular television channels are still the central meeting places of contemporary society. If they lose this status, this model of a democratic media system will have to be modified.

This core sector is fed by peripheral media sectors, three of which are intended to facilitate the expression of dissenting and minority views. The *civic* media sector consists of channels of communication linked to organized groups and social networks. The *professional* media sector occupies a space wholly independent of both the state and the market in which professional communicators relate to the public on their own terms, with the minimum of constraint. The *social market* sector subsidizes minority media as a way of promoting market diversity and consumer choice. To this is added a conventional *market* sector which relates to the public as consumers, and whose central rationale within the media system is to act as a restraint on the over-entrenchment of minority concerns to the exclusion of majority pleasures.

This media system is designed to promote the expression of diversity. Its constituent parts are organized in different ways, and connect to different parts of

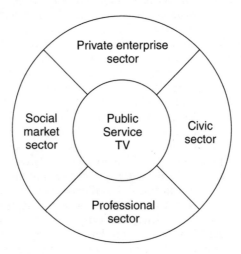

Fig 6.1

society. Publicly accountable in multiple ways, the media system is also intended to be broadly representative of the society it serves. Above all, its architecture is designed to create spaces for the communication of opposed viewpoints, and a common space for their mediation. Both the detail and thinking behind this outline are further explored below.

Core media: public service solutions

The core media sector should be entrusted to public service organizations (whether publicly owned or publicly regulated). Potentially, this offers the best way of establishing an open public forum because public service television is governed by fairness and access rules. It is also a way of ensuring that core media promote public information since this is a central objective of the public service approach. The universalist method of funding public service television also prevents the creation of second-class citizens excluded by price. By contrast, a fully deregulated television system will tend to give low priority to public affairs, sacrifice depth for ratings, charge extra for premium services and be more prone to partisanship.

While the actual practice of public service broadcasting does not always correspond to theory, there are – as mentioned earlier – well-tested strategies for preventing government control. Of these, four are especially important: independent funding through a licence fee; a block on unmediated government appointments to broadcasting authorities; the dispersal of power within broadcasting organizations; and a climate of freedom, supported by a written constitution.

Public service broadcasting can also be unresponsive to public demand. However, experience has shown this to be particularly true of public service monopolies. Where there is regulated competition between publicly owned and publicly regulated commercial broadcasters, public service broadcasting has been much more attuned to public preferences (Tracey, 1998).

The public service approach takes a number of different forms. The *social franchising* approach, typified by Dutch television, allocates airtime and technical facilities to organizations judged to be representative of leading groups in society (such as liberals, socialists and conservative Protestants) on the basis of their membership and/or subscription to their programme magazines. Each of these groups assemble packages of programmes, funded by public finance, advertising and membership dues, within public service guidelines (Brants and McQuail, 1997; Nieuwenhuis, 1993; McQuail, 1992).

The second model is *liberal corporatism* (typified by German television, with Scandinavian variants). This has the same objective as the social franchising model – the creation of a television system that reflects the plurality of society – but adopts a different strategy for achieving this. Whereas the Dutch model leases parts of the television system to different 'pillars' of society, the liberal corporatist model seeks to secure pluralism through social partnership. The first approach delivers representation through group rivalry, the second through group power sharing.

In Germany, representatives of different social and political groups work together as members of broadcasting authorities. These are especially influential within the public sector. Depending upon the locality, appointees to broadcasting authorities are nominated by leading groups and institutions in society (such as business, labour, political parties, environmentalists, science, pensioners, consumers etc.), or by the local state assembly (with balanced political representation), or by a mixture of the two methods (Sandford, 1997; Humphreys, 1994; Hickethier, 1996).

The third approach, exemplified by British television, is based on a *civil service* model. This seeks to establish television as a neutral, autonomous zone that stands above partisan politics and social interest. Those appointed to broadcasting authorities are, in British parliamentary jargon, 'national trustees' representing the British people. To some extent, these authorities are a fig leaf – a façade of public accountability – which allows producers considerable creative autonomy within the framework of public service objectives (Curran and Seaton, 1997; Tunstall, 1993).

What can be learned from these different experiments? Both the civil service and social franchising approaches have distinctive strengths that seem best suited to the needs of other media sectors (see below). They are less well adapted to staging a collective debate, the prime democratic purpose of the core sector. The Dutch experience suggests that the pivotal organizations around which the public service system is constructed are inadequately representative of society as a whole at a time of rapid social change (Ang, 1991). The civil service approach, at least in Britain, is inadequately pluralistic for the different reason that representative pluralism is not one of its central objectives (Curran, 1998). By contrast, the liberal corporatist approach is ideally suited to reproducing the perspective of different groups in society in a coherent dialogue.

Lessons can be derived from different examples of the liberal corporatist approach. The German version of it is not free of problems: in particular, it needs to have fewer party nominees, and more representatives from new social movements and social minorities like 'guestworkers'. But it has the distinctive strength, as a consequence of a Constitutional Court ruling, of seeking to reflect pluralism of value and perspective in its entertainment as well as public affairs content. This reflects a sophisticated understanding of the role of fiction in informing democratic discourse.

Civic media sector

The civic media sector supports organizations that are the life force of democracy. These are political parties, new social movements, interest groups, and subcultural networks that relay the concerns of society and propose policy initiatives for consideration by the political system. Especially important in parliamentary democracies, and now greatly in need of democratic rejuvenation, are political parties that have a pivotal position as organizations that aggregate interests, distribute costs, define electoral choices and offer channels of general (rather than single-issue) influence.

The civic media sector has three main segments. The first consists of media (such as party-controlled newspapers) which provide a link between civic organizations and the wider public. They are generally adversarial, and seek to build support for a partisan understanding of society and set of objectives. The second segment consists of subcultural media (such as gay or lesbian magazines) which relate to a social constituency rather than an organized group. These can have an important 'constitutive' function that ultimately facilitates organized effectiveness: in particular, they can promote a sense of social cohesion and common identity, and clarify values and goals through internal processes of discussion (Gross, 1998). The third segment consists of intra-organizational media (such as trades union journals) whose purpose is to reinforce the loyalty of its members, hold leaderships to account, assist in the sharing of relevant information and experience, and provide a forum for developing new ideas and initiatives.

The civic media sector is in trouble. Party-controlled newspapers have been in decline throughout the western world for a very long time. Many politically aligned journals of opinion have an uncertain future due to their limited utility to advertisers and the expansion of the prestige press. The development of intra-organizational media has also been skewed by the large investment made in top-down, company magazines and corporate videos. Only subcultural media, in some areas, are flourishing.

There are two ways in which the civic media sector can be reinvigorated. One strategy is to adapt the social franchising approach, mentioned earlier, to supporting organized minority voices. Some local radio stations, cable and digital television channels could be allocated, either through lease or time-share arrangements, to organizations that represent significant groups in society.

The second (but not necessarily mutually exclusive) strategy is to subsidize the existing media of major organized groups. The case for doing this is the same as for funding political parties. It is a way of facilitating the working of democracy, and supporting collective organizations as a public interest counterweight to private corporate interests. Thus, the weekly journals of political parties, immigrant groups and other organizations receive financial support in Norway (£2.6 million in 1995 (Murschetz, 1998: 297)), which enhances both their quality and influence. Support could be extended also to civic sector communications on the internet, where professional journalistic and design skills are needed to increase their impact.

Professional media sector

The professional media sector should be composed of media that are under the control of professional communicators, or organized in a form that gives staff maximum creative freedom. It should be publicly funded, but free of public service requirements.

This is the only part of the proposed media plan that does not already exist in prototype, and for this reason may seem especially fanciful. Precedents could be cited in the form of individual media organizations that operate as public trusts, co-operatives or supported public interest ventures (Dowmunt, 1993; Downing, 1984). However, the 'professional sector' conception really derives from a romantic view that British public service television fosters producer freedom (Tunstall, 1993), to a greater degree than either the representative-driven model of northern European television or the market-driven system of the United States. In fact, the British 'civil service' model is subject to increasing corporate and market constraints. But what this proposal seeks to do is distil the *logic* of the British approach to broadcasting, and develop it as a concept for a new media sector.

It could be pioneered as a public trust which commissions programmes (the

British Channel 4 model) or as a broadcasting organization under democratic staff control. It needs to be adequately publicly funded in order to be insulated from market pressure (through, for example, a tax on media advertising, or a spectrum charge on licensed broadcasters or through a new digital licence fee). Without secure public funding, and control over a major national television and radio channel, it will never be able to fulfil its remit.

The creation of this professional sector would strengthen the media system's oversight of power centres in society. While public service and market media are linked respectively to the state and big business, and the civic sector is tied to organized interests, the professional sector would be entirely autonomous. Its unqualified independence would make it an especially effective public watchdog.

The professional sector would also enhance the diversity of the media system since it would connect to the public in a different way from other sectors. It would relate to society not on the basis of state-defined objectives, the maximization of profit, or the advancement of an organized group, but solely on terms defined by professional communicators.

This should promote a distinctive style of public affairs coverage. Journalists working for market media are increasingly entertainers; those working for civic media are advocates; while those in public service broadcasting are constrained by an obligation to mediate a 'balanced' debate. By contrast, journalists in the professional sector would be guided solely by truth-seeking, and would be free to judge everything on its merits.

Above all, the professional sector should preside over a revival of television drama. Already, public service television has generated memorable fiction; notably, social realist soap opera of the quality of *EastEnders* and multiple-episode dramas, like *Heimat* and *Our Friends in the North*, which interpret a whole era and exploit the distinctive potential of television as a medium. In a more creatively free environment, television dramatists and production teams should be able to rise to still greater heights. Just as novelists in the second half of the nineteenth century expanded the boundaries of conscience and understanding, and offered arresting interpretations of social change that galvanized public debate, so television dramatists should occupy a similar place in the imaginative landscape of contemporary society, and generate comparable public reflection about the direction in which society is moving.

Private enterprise sector

A private enterprise media sector should also be part of this blueprint. It will make the media system as a whole more responsive to popular pleasures. It will also enhance its diversity since it will tend to privilege right-wing perspectives, thereby helping to balance centrist and left voices emanating from other parts of the media.

A third reason is that it will contribute potentially to critical oversight of political power. This may not be the case in countries where there is a close alliance between big business, private media and the state. However, in some countries, private media are more independent of the state than public media. Including a private sector thus potentially enhances the critical surveillance role of the media.

An unregulated private enterprise sector should be present in all parts of the media industry, with one qualified exception. A deregulated commercial, over-the air TV sector should not be established because it would undermine the pluralism of the rest of the television system. It would scoop advertising revenue needed to sustain alternatives, and generate pressure on its rivals to converge towards the middle ground.

There is also a strong case for fostering greater devolution of power within commercial media corporations in order to shield media staff from compromising corporate interest, and from the pressures for uniformity generated by concentration of ownership. This could be achieved by legally underwriting the freedom of editors and their equivalents, and introducing new procedures for staff participation in their appointment (Curran, 1995). Another approach, adopted in the Austrian press, is for the editorial independence of journalists to be protected in legally binding contracts.

Social market sector

The social market sector takes the form of minority media, operating within the market, which are supported by the state. It has come into being in a number of countries as a way of promoting competition and consumer choice.

In Europe, social market support takes two main forms. One is a drip-feed of selective subsidy targeted towards minority media. This is typified by selective press subsidies in Sweden, Norway and (on a smaller scale) France which compensate small papers for their limited scale economies and advertising support (Murschetz, 1998; Skogerbo, 1997). In Sweden, for example, this takes the form of graduated production grants paid to 'secondary' papers in each market, and subsidies to encourage cost-cutting co-operation in printing and distribution. These are distributed neutrally by a public body, with all-party representation, and benefit both left- and right-wing papers. Their effect has been to sustain competition between policiticized local newspapers that would not have survived in free market conditions (Gustafsson and Hulten, 1997).

The second form of aid facilitates market entry. This includes quota legislation, as in Britain where all terrestrial television organizations are required by law to buy 25 per cent of their programmes from independent production companies. It also takes the form of preferential loans for new media ventures, from the acquisition of plant and premises in the case of the Austrian press to 'front money' for film production provided by the Media 2 Programme of the European Union. Experience suggests that financial aid for production can be ineffective unless it is accompanied by measures facilitating distribution. Thus, the creation of Channel 4 in Britain has been successful in promoting innovation because it offers programme-makers two things: money and access to the public. Similarly, municipal ownership of cinemas in Norway ensures that state-supported Norwegian films get screened in their domestic market (along with film products from around the world, not just from Hollywood).

In fostering market competition, social market policies have also contributed to media diversity. However, there is a case for making this approach more explicitly directed towards the objective of sustaining media variety in a form that benefits the democratic process. Greater priority in the allocation of start-up loans could be given to resource-poor groups, and innovatory forms of media organization – such as self-managing enterprises, co-operatives and organizations with consumer or community representation – as a way of promoting a greater plurality of voices in the media. The traditional areas where aid is provided – newspapers and films – could be extended to include low-cost sectors like specialist book publishing, local radio and even music production, all of which contribute, potentially, to the democratic process.

The social market approach is associated with legislative curbs on media concentration. These need to be strengthened in the interests of democracy rather than relaxed in the interests of market competitiveness. They also need to be made more effective by being enforced through supra-national agencies – in the case of Europe through the European Union and Council of Europe – in order to prevent evasion of monopoly curbs through relocation to 'safe havens'.

Conclusion

Implicit in this outline is a complex set of requirements for a democratic media system. It should empower people by enabling them to explore where their interest lies; it should foster sectional solidarities and assist the functioning of organizations necessary for the effective representation of collective interests; it should sustain vigilant scrutiny of government and centres of power; it should provide a source of protection and redress for weak and unorganized interests; and it should create the conditions for real societal agreement or compromise based on an open working through of differences rather than a contrived consensus based on elite dominance. This can best be realized through the establishment of a core public service broadcasting system, encircled by private enterprise, social market, professional and civic media sectors. These latter will strengthen the functioning of public service broadcasting as an open system of dialogue, and give added impetus to the collective, self-organized tradition of civil society.

Notes

1.   This chapter is the third version I have written for successive editions of this book. Revising it is like getting a 10-year-old car past its roadworthy (MOT) test. This time round, I have done more than merely paint over rust-marks on the body work: I have tried to supply a new engine. My thanks go to the staff and students at the Department of Communications, University of California, San Diego, for helpful suggestions incorporated into the original essay.

2.   'Liberal' is a confusing word, meaning different things in Britain and the United States. It is used here in its British historical sense of thought associated with the Liberal Party, emphasizing individualism, freedom, tolerance and free trade.

3.   In Britain, there is press-specific regulation in only one area – monopoly law.

4.   Estimates for the proportion of public affairs content in mass media are provided by Curran and Seaton (1997); Strid and Weibull (1988); and Neuman (1986) quoted in Abramson (1990).

5.   In its key last chapter this admirable, thought-provoking book fails to distinguish between progressive and conservative elites, and their different relationships to other social groups in society – something that seems called for especially in its chapter 5. This distinction is one way of rescuing investigative journalism from the authors' debunking.

6.   In this context it is worth noting that the *Observer*, when it was owned by Lonrho, was different from most privately owned media in having 'independent directors' largely selected by staff who played a key role in resisting corporate corruption.

7.   These estimates are based on the start-up and run-in costs, respectively, of the *Independent* and *Live TV*, as disclosed by senior executives working for these ventures.

8.   These figures exclude the *Sport, Sunday Sport* and *Sunday Business* on the grounds that they are specialist publications, and the *Morning Star* because it is rarely stocked by newsagents and is therefore not nationally available.

9.   Especially useful commentaries on this book, or the debates that arise from it, are Scannell (1989), Keane (1991), Calhoun (1992), Negt and Kluge (1993), Thompson (1995), Dahlgren (1995) and Corner (1995).

10.   Recent contributions to, and reviews of, globalization debates include Morley and Robins (1995), Waters (1995), Braman and Sreberny-Mohammadi (1996), Herman and McChesney (1997), Thussu (1998), Stevenson (1999), Curran and Park (2000b), and representing an important and neglected perspective, Panitch and Leys (1999).

11.   Useful starting points for rethinking media and democracy, in addition to Habermas, are Garnham (1986), Keane (1991), Dahlgren (1995), McChesney (1999), and the publications of an American radical lawyer, Edwin Baker (Baker, 1989, 1997a, b, 1997 and 1998) which deserve a much wider audience than American lawyers and law students. Baker shows how productive it is to synthesize media research with alternative theories of democracy. Those wanting to follow the same route might start with Held (1996), who offers a good overview of models of democracy. Like the literature he reviews, Held barely mentions the mass media.

12.   A minor but telling illustration of the way in which different groups can be ignorant of what the other thinks, even though they live cheek by jowl in ostensibly integrated communities, occurred when I conducted jointly two group discussions in an East Anglian village for the Eastern Counties Newspapers Group. The first group of working-class couples said that they were worried about the lack of good job prospects for their children, the lack of leisure facilities for the young and the problem of social discipline among teenagers. The second group of middle-class couples were mainly concerned about the environment and the threat of increased urbanization in the area (which would generate a wider range of jobs and more leisure facilities) and were convinced that the first group fully shared their concerns. When informed that this was not the case, they were visibly taken aback, with some arguing rightly that the local paper should have alerted them to what other people in the community were feeling. This may seem to illustrate an aspect of rural, socially stratified England. But other monopoly papers also fail to provide an adequate channel of communication between social classes in their local community. For example the *Los Angeles Times* was remarkably uninformative about Los Angeles' black ghettos in 1990, giving little indication of the smouldering resentments that were to erupt in 1992 in one of the most serious riots in twentieth-century America.

References

ABRAMSON, J., 1990: 'Four Criticisms of Press Ethics' in J. Lichtenberg (ed.) *Mass Media and Democracy*, New York: Cambridge University Press.

ADAM SMITH INSTITUTE, 1984: *Omega Report: Communications Policy*, London: ASU.

ALDRIDGE, A. and HEWITT, R. (eds), 1994: *Controlling Broadcasting*, Manchester: Manchester University Press.

ANG, I., 1991: *Desperately Seeking the Audience*, London: Routledge.

ARNOLD, M., 1970: *Selected Prose*, Harmondsworth: Penguin.

AVERY, R. (ed.), 1993: *Public Service Broadcasting in a Multichannel Environment*, White Plains, NY: Longman.

BAGDIKIAN, B., 1983: *The Media Monopoly*, Boston: Beacon Press.

——, 1997: *The Media Monopoly*, 5th edn, Boston: Beacon Press.

BAISTOW, T., 1985: *Fourth-Rate Estate*, London: Commedia.

BAKER, C., 1989: *Human Liberty and Freedom of Speech*, New York: Oxford University Press.

——, 1994: *Advertising and a Democratic Press*, Princeton, NJ: Princeton University Press.

——, 1997a: 'Giving the Audience What it Wants', *Ohio State Law Journal* 58(2).

——, 1997b: 'Harm, Liberty, and Free Speech', *Southern Law Review* 70(4).

——, 1998: 'The Media that Citizens Need', *University of Pennsylvania Law Review* 147(2).

BARRON, J., 1975: *Freedom of the Press for Whom?*, Ontario: Midland Book.

BRAMAN, S. and SREBERNY-MOHAMMADI, A. (eds), 1996: *Globalization, Communication and Transnational Civil Society*, Cresskill, NJ: Hampton Press.

BRANTS, K. and MCQUAIL, D., 1997: 'The Netherlands' in B. Ostergaard (ed.) *The Media in Western Europe*, 2nd edn, London: Sage.

CALHOUN, C. (ed.), 1992: *Habermas and the Public Sphere*, Cambridge, MA: MIT Press.

CARLYLE, T., 1907: *On Heroes, Hero-Worship and the Heroic in History*, London: Chapman and Hall.

CATALBAS, D., 2000: 'Broadcasting Deregulation in Turkey: Uniformity Within Diversity' in J. Curran (ed.) *Media Organisations in Society*, London: Arnold.

CATO, 1720: 'Of Freedom of Speech: That the Same is Inseparable from Publick Liberty', *Cato's Letters*, No. 15, 4 February. Reprinted in H. Bosmajian (ed) 1983: *The Principles and Practice of Freedom of Speech*, 2nd edn., Lanham: University Press of America.

CHADWICK, P., 1989: *Media Mates*, Melbourne: Macmillan.

CHAFEE, Z. JNR, 1983: 'Does Freedom of Speech Really Tend to Produce Truth?' in H. Bosmajian (ed.) *The Principles and Practice of Freedom of Speech*, 2nd edn., Lanham: University Press of America.

COMMISSION OF THE EUROPEAN COMMUNITIES, 1992: *Pluralism and Media Concentration in the Internal Market*, Brussels: CEC.

——, 1994: *Follow-up to the Consultative Process Relating to the Green Paper on 'Pluralism and Media Concentration in the Internal Market'*, Brussels: CEC.

CORNER, J, 1995: *Television and Public Address*, London: Arnold.

——, RICHARDSON, K. and FENTON, N., 1990: *Nuclear Reactions*, London: Libbey.

CROSS, B., 1993: *It's Not About a Salary*, London: Verso.

CROTEAU, D. and HOYNES, W., 1997: *Media/Society*, Thousand Oaks, CA: Pine Forge.

CURRAN, J., 1977: 'Capitalism and Control of the Press, 1800–1975' in J. Curran, M. Gurevitch and J. Woolacott (eds) *Mass Communication and Society*, London: Edward Arnold.

——, 1986: 'The Impact of Advertising on the British Mass Media' in R. Collins *et al.* (eds) *Media, Culture and Society: A Critical Reader*, London: Sage.

——, 1995: *Policy for the Press*, London: Institute for Public Policy Research.

——, 1996: 'Rethinking Mass Communications' in J. Curran, D. Morley and V. Walkerdine (eds) *Cultural Studies and Communications*, London: Arnold.

——, 1988: 'The Crisis of Public Communication: A Reappraisal' in T. Liebes and J. Curran (eds) *Media, Ritual and Identity*, London: Routledge.

——, 2001: *Media and Power*, London: Routledge.

CURRAN, J. and LEYS, C., 2000: 'Media and the Decline of Liberal Corporatism in Britain' in J. Curran and M-Y Park (eds) *De-Westernizing Media Studies*, London: Routledge.

CURRAN, J. and PARK, M-Y. (eds), 2000a: *De-Westernizing Media Studies*, London: Routledge.

CURRAN, J. and PARK, M-Y., 2000b: 'Beyond Globalization Theory' in J. Curran and M-Y. Park (eds) *De-Westernizing Media Studies*, London: Routledge.

CURRAN, J. and SEATON, J., 1997: *Power Without Responsibility: The Press and Broadcasting in Britain*, 5th edn. London: Routledge.

CURRAN, J., DOUGLAS, A. and WHANNEL, G., 1980: 'The Political Economy of the Human-Interest Story' in A. Smith (ed.) *Newspapers and Democracy*, Cambridge, MA: MIT Press.

D'ACCI, J., 1994: *Defining Women*, Chapel Hill, NC: University of Carolina Press.

DAHLGREN, P., 1995: *Television and the Public Sphere*, London: Sage.

——, 2000: 'Media and Power Transitions in a Small Country: Sweden' in J. Curran and M-Y. Park (eds) *De-Westernizing Media Studies*, London: Routledge.

DAYAN, D. and E. KATZ, 1992: *Media Events*, Cambridge, MA: Harvard University Press.

DOWMUNT, T., 1993: *Channels of Resistance*, London: British Film Institute.

DOWNING, J., 1984: *Radical Media*, Boston: South End Press.

——, 1996: *Internationalizing Media Theory*, London: Sage.

ENTMAN, R., 1989: *Democracy Without Citizens*, New York: Oxford University Press.

EPSTEIN, E., 1973: *News from Nowhere*, New York: Random House.

ERICSON, R., BARANEK, P. and CHAN, J. 1987: *Visualizing Deviance*, Milton Keynes: Open University.

EVANS, H., 1983: *Good Times, Bad Times*, London: Weidenfeld and Nicholson.

FOX, E. (ed.), 1998: *Media and Politics in Latin America*, London: Sage.

GARNHAM, N., 1986: 'The Media and the Public Sphere' in P. Golding, G. Murdock and P. Schlesinger (eds) *Communicating Politics*, Leicester: Leicester University Press.

GELDER, K. and THORNTON, S., 1996: *The Subcultures Reader*, London: Routledge.

GERAGHTY, C., 1995: 'Social Issues and Realist Soaps: A Study of British Soaps in the 1989s and 1990s' in R. Allen (ed.) *To Be Continued*, London: Routledge.

GILES, F., 1986: *Sundry Times*, London: John Murray.

GITLIN, T., 1990: 'Blips, Bites and Savvy Talk: Television and the Bifurcation of American Politics' in P. Dahlgren and C. Sparks (eds) *Communication and Citizenship*, London: Routledge.

——, 1994: *Inside Prime Time*, revised edn, London: Routledge.

GOLDSMITHS MEDIA GROUP, 2000: 'Media Organisations in Society: Central Issues' in J. Curran (ed.) *Media Organisations in Society*, London: Arnold.

GOODWIN, P., 1998: *Television Under the Tories*, London: British Film Institute.

GRABER, D., 1988: *Processing the News*, 2nd edn, White Plains, NY: Longman.

GROSS, L., 1998: 'Minorities, Majorities and the Media' in T. Liebes and J. Curran (eds) *Media, Ritual and Identity*, London: Routledge.

GUSTAFSSON, K. and HULTEN, O., 1997: 'Sweden' in B. Ostergaard (ed.) *The Media in Western Europe*, 2nd edn, London: Sage.

HABERMAS, J., 1989 [1962]: *The Structural Transformation of the Public Sphere*, Cambridge: Polity.

——, 1992: 'Further Reflections on the Public Sphere' in C. Calhoun (ed.) *Habermas and the Public Sphere*, Cambridge, MA: MIT Press.

——, 1996 [1992]: *Between Facts and Norms*, Cambridge: Polity.

HALLIN, D., 1994: *We Keep America on Top of the World*, London: Routledge.

——, 2000: 'Media, Political Power, and Democratization in Mexico' in J. Curran and M-Y. Park (eds) *De-Westernizing Media Studies*, London: Routledge.

HEBDIGE, D., 1979: *Subculture*, London: Sage.

HELD, D., 1996: *Models of Democracy*, 2nd edn, Cambridge: Polity.

HERMAN, E., 1998: 'The Propaganda Model Revisited' in R. McChesney, E. Wood and J. Foster (eds) *Capitalism and the Information Age*, New York: Monthly Review Press.

HERMAN, E. and CHOMSKY, N., 1988: *Manufacturing Consent*, New York: Pantheon.

HERMAN, E. and MCCHESNEY, R., 1997: *The Global Media*, London: Cassell.

HICKETHIER, K., 1996: 'The Media in Germany' in T. Weymouth and B. Lamizet (eds) *Markets and Myths*, London: Longman.

HOLLINGSWORTH, M., 1986: *The Press and Political Dissent*, London: Pluto Press.

HOLMES, S., 1990: 'Liberal Constraints on Private Power?: Reflections on the Origins and Rationale of Access Regulation' in J. Lichtenberg (ed.) *Mass Media and Democracy*, New York: Cambridge University Press.

HORWITZ, R., 1991: 'The First Amendment Meets Some New Technologies: Broadcasting, Common Carriers, and Free Speech in the 1990s', *Theory and Society*.

HOYER, S., HADENIUS, S. and WEIBULL, L., 1975: *The Politics and Economics of the Press*, London: Sage.

HUMPHREYS, P., 1994: *Media and Media Policy in Germany*, Oxford: Berg.

——, 1996: *Mass Media and Media Policy in Western Europe*, Manchester: Manchester University Press.

INGLIS, F., 1990: *Media Theory*, Oxford: Blackwell.

IYENGAR, S., 1991: *Is Anyone Responsible? How Television Frames Political Issues*, Chicago: University of Chicago Press.

KEANE, J., 1991: *Media and Democracy*, Cambridge: Polity.

KELLEY, D. and DONWAY, R., 1990: 'Liberalism and Free Speech' in J. Lichtenberg (ed.) *Mass Media and Democracy*, New York: Cambridge University Press.

KELLNER, D., 1990: *Television and the Crisis of Democracy*, Boulder: Westview Press.

LANG, G. and LANG, K., 1983: *The Battle for Public Opinion*, New York: Columbia University Press.

LEAPMAN, M., 1983: *Barefaced Cheek*, London: Hodder and Stoughton.

LEE, C., 2000: 'State, Capital and Media: The Case of Taiwan' in J. Curran and M-Y. Park (eds) *De-Westernizing Media Studies*, London: Arnold.

LIEBES, T., 1998: 'Television's Disaster Marathons: A Danger for Democratic Processes?' in T. Liebes and J. Curran (eds) *Media, Ritual and Identity*, London: Routledge.

LIEBES, T. and CURRAN, J., 1998: *Media, Ritual and Identity*, London: Routledge.

MCCHESNEY, R., 1997: *Corporate Media and the Threat to Democracy*, New York: Seven Stories Press.

——, 1998: 'The Political Economy of Global Communication' in McChesney, R., Wood, E. and Foster, J. (eds) *Capitalism and the Information Age*, New York: Monthly Review Press.

——, 1999: *Rich Media, Poor Democracy*, Urbana: University of Illinois Press.

MCGUIGAN, J., 1996: *Culture and the Public Sphere*, London: Routledge.

MCLUHAN, M., 1964: *Understanding Media*, London: Routledge and Kegan Paul.

MCNAIR, B., 2000: 'Power, Profit, Corruption, and Lies: The Russian Media in the 1990s' in J. Curran and M-Y. Park (eds) *De-Westernizing Media Studies, London: Routledge.*

MCQUAIL, D., 1992: 'The Netherlands: Safeguarding Freedom and Diversity Under Multichannel Conditions' in J. Blumler (ed.) *Television and the Public Interest*, London: Sage.

MEIKELJOHN, A., 1983: 'The Rulers and the Ruled' in H. Bosmajian (ed.) *The Principles and Practice of Freedom of Speech*, Lanham: University Press of America.

MORLEY, D. and ROBINS, K., 1995: *Spaces of Identity*, London: Routledge.

MUNSTER, G., 1985: *Rupert Murdoch*, Ringwood, Australia: Viking.

MURDOCH, R., 1989: *Freedom in Broadcasting* (MacTaggart Lecture), London: News International.

MURSCHETZ, P., 1998: 'State Support for the Daily Press in Europe: A Critical Appraisal', *European Journal of Communication* 13(3).

NAIN, Z., 2000: 'Globalized Theories and National Controls: The State, the Market, and the Malaysian Media' in J. Curran and M-Y Park (eds) *De-Westernizing Media Studies*, London: Routledge.

NEIL, A., 1996: *Full Disclosure*, London: Macmillan.

NEGHT, O. and KLUGE, A., 1993: *Public Sphere and Experience*, Minneapolis: University of Minnesota.

NEGROPONTE, N., 1996: *Being Digital*, London: Coronet.

NEUMAN, W., 1986: *The Paradox of Politics*, Cambridge, MA: Harvard University Press.

NEUMAN, W., JUST, M. and CRIGLER, A., 1992: *Common Knowledge*, Chicago: University of Chicago Press.

NIEUWENHUIS, A.J., 1993: 'Media Policy in the Netherlands: Beyond the Market?', *European Journal of Communications* 7(2).

OSTERGAARD, B., (ed.) 1997: *The Media in Western Europe*, 2nd edition, London: Sage.

PANITCH, L. and LEYS, C., (eds.) 1999: *Global Capitalism Versus Democracy*, Rendlesham: Merlin.

PARK, M-Y., KIM, C-N. and SOHN, B-W., 2000: 'Modernization, Globalization, and the Powerful State: The Korean Media' in J. Curran and M-Y. Park (eds.) *De-Westernizing Media Studies*, London: Routledge.

PATELIS, K., 2000: 'The Political Economy of the Internet', in J. Curran (ed.) *Media Organisations in Society*, London: Arnold.

PETERS, J., 1989: 'Democracy and American Mass Communication Theory: Dewey, Lippmann, Lazardsfeld', *Communication*, 11.

PROTESS, D. *et al.*, 1991: *The Journalism of Outrage*, New York: Guilford Press.

RABOY, M. (ed.), 1996: *Public Broadcasting for the 21st Century*, Luton: University of Luton Press.

ROBINS, K. (ed.), 1997: *Programming for People*, Newcastle: Centre for Urban and Regional Studies, University of Newcastle.

ROYAL COMMISSION ON THE PRESS 1974–77 FINAL REPORT, 1977: London: HMSO.

SANCHEZ-TABERNERO, A. *et al.*, 1993: *Media Concentration in Europe*, Manchester: European Institute for the Media.

SANDFORD, J., 1997: 'Television in Germany' in J. Coleman and B. Rollet (eds) *Television in Europe*, Exeter: Intellect.

SCANNELL, P., 1989: 'Public Service Broadcasting and Modern Public Life', *Media, Culture and Society* 11(2).

SCHLESINGER, P., 1999: 'Changing Spaces of Political Communication: The Case of the European Union', *Political Communication* 16.

SERRA, S., 1996: 'Multinationals of Solidarity: International Civil Society and the Killing of Street Children in Brazil' in S. Braman and A. Sreberny-Mohammadi (eds) *Globalization, Communication and Transational Civil Society*, Creskill, NJ: Hampton Press.

——, 2000: 'The Killing of Brazilian Street Children and the Rise of the International Public Sphere' in J. Curran (ed.) *Media Organisations in Society*, London: Arnold.

SEYMOUR-URE, C., 1996: *The British Press and Broadcasting Since 1945*, 2nd edn, Oxford: Blackwell.

SHAWCROSS, W., 1993: *Murdoch*, London: Pan.

SINCLAIR, J., JACKA, E. and CUNNINGHAM S., 1996: *New Patterns in Global Vision*, Oxford: Oxford University Press.

SKOGERBO, E., 1997: 'The Press Subsidy System in Norway', *European Journal of Communication* 12(1).

SPARKS, C., 1998: *Communism, Capitalism and the Mass Media*, London: Sage.

STEPP, C., 1990: 'Access in a Post-Responsibility Age' in J. Lichtenberg (ed.) *Mass Media and Democracy*, New York: Cambridge University Press.

STEVENSON, N., 1999: *The Transformation of the Media*, Harlow: Longman.

STRID, I. and WEIBULL, L., 1988: *Mediesveridge*, Goteborgs: Goteborgs University Press.

THOMPSON, J., 1995: *The Media and Modernity*, Cambridge: Polity.

THUSSU, D., 1998: *Electronic Empires*, London: Arnold.

TRACEY, M., 1998: *The Decline and Fall of Public Service Broadcasting*, Oxford: Oxford University Press.

TUNSTALL, J., 1993: *Television Producers*, London: Routledge.

TUNSTALL, J. and MACHIN, D., 1990: *The Anglo-American Connection*, Oxford: Oxford University Press.

VELJANOVSKI, C., 1989: 'Competition in Broadcasting' in C. Veljanovski (ed.) *Freedom in Broadcasting*, London: Institute of Economic Affairs.

WAISBORD, S., 2000: 'Media in South America: Between the Rock of the State and the Hard Place of the Market' in J. Curran and M-Y. Park (eds) *De-Westernizing Media Studies*, London: Routledge.

WATERS, M., 1995: *Globalization*, London: Routledge.

WEYMOUTH, T. and LAMIZET, B. (eds), 1996: *Markets and Myths*, Harlow: Longman.

WHALE, J., 1977: *The Politics of the Media*, London: Fontana.

WINDLESHAM, L. and RAMPTON, R., 1989: *The Windlesham/Rampton Report on Death on the Rock*, London: Faber and Faber.

7

Rethinking the Study of Political Communication

Jay G. Blumler and Michael Gurevitch

Introduction

Different fields of study call for different degrees of re-thinking and revision. Consequently, scholars working in diverse disciplines may be differentially obliged to take retrospective looks at the conceptual underpinnings of their fields. In part, this has to do with the 'hardness' or 'softness' of the fields concerned; in part it hinges on the pace of change in the societal, technological and intellectual environments in which their enquiries are situated. Whether a field of study is 'hard' or 'soft' is, of course, a matter of judgement, but it could be argued that the less the basic paradigm of a field of enquiry needs to adapt to the impact of external change, the more it could claim 'hardness'; the more vulnerable the conceptual structure of a given field to the vagaries of external change, the 'softer' it is and the greater the need to reconsider and re-frame it in the light of changing conditions.

Gauged by this criterion, the physical sciences are clearly less exposed to sources of paradigm shift than the social sciences. The seeming immutability of the laws of nature offers greater protection to the paradigms on which those sciences are based and to their theoretical underpinnings. Of course, as Thomas Kuhn has taught us, the physical sciences are also subject to paradigmatic change, but these arise more from accumulating weaknesses in the explanatory power of a given paradigm than from changes in their objects of study. The social sciences, by comparison, clearly require greater theoretical and conceptual alertness. Processes of social, political and cultural change are bound to impact on the conceptual frameworks developed and deployed by sociologists, economists and political scientists, since the phenomena they examine and the issues they study are continually being transformed. It is more difficult to discern enduring structures, rules and generalizations when the societal kaleidoscope keeps revolving, confronting us with ever-changing, new and different patterns.

A good case in point is the field of political communication, the scholars and practitioners of which must continually adapt to changes both in the communication technologies by which political messages are produced and disseminated, and in the structure and culture of the surrounding social and political system.[1] Thus, Blumler and Kavanagh (1999) maintain that over the relatively short period since the end of the Second World War, the organization of political communication has passed through three successive, if overlapping, phases in many western democracies. First was a time (in the late 1940s and 1950s) when much political communication, reflecting partisan positions and beliefs associated with relatively strong and stable political institutions, enjoyed fairly ready access to the mass media. Next came the age of limited-channel nationwide television, expanding the mass political audience and elevating the news media to ever more powerful institutional standing *vis-à-vis* parties and governments. The third, current and still emerging, period is marked by a proliferation of the main means of communication both within and beyond the mainstream mass media and is therefore an age of communication abundance.

This latest transition is a confusing time for the study of political communication. Swanson (1999: 205) finds it particularly 'complex, volatile and ... chaotic'. Four impulses appear most responsible for such unsettlement.

First, the communication problems of political parties, the prime seekers of electoral support in representative democracies, have been acutely aggravated by profound social changes. The huge reservoirs of social support on which they relied in the past – relatively coherent and party-minded social class, workplace and neighbourhood groupings – have dried up or dwindled. Instead politicians have had to court backing from a more consumerist, individualistic, volatile and sceptical electorate on the basis of issues and appeals of the moment. Trying to implement and sustain an effective strategy for communicating to such a public must often seem like an unceasing scramble.

Second, advances in audio-visual technology have instituted a more elaborate, fragmented, competitive and commercially geared media system. This not only hosts many more channels but also an exploding variety of journalistic formats and services, ranging from news flashes to conventional bulletins to 24-hour news, as well as an equally diverse set of 'infotainment' formats, talk shows and the like. This has increased uncertainty for all wishing to get their political messages into circulation – over where best to place them and how they might fare in the maelstrom of follow-up questioning, comment and criticism. Moreover, the responses to all this of individual citizens, who are better placed than ever before to relate to both politics and to communication as they personally choose, are more difficult to predict and master.

Third, new – though still embryonic – modes of political communication are being injected into the system via the surging dissemination of the internet and other interactive sources of information and opinion. Many questions with no clear answers as yet arise from this. How will the hitherto dominant political and media institutions adapt their offerings to it? Will they be seriously rivalled by other forces keen to exploit it? Will the internet mainly supplement the mainstream news media or increasingly supplant them? Will the availability of large stores of information, easy access to a wide range of sources, and mechanisms for the exchange of views and information transform people's expectations of how they should be addressed and served as citizens? Will present inequalities between the information-rich and information-poor be increased or levelled? Will representative democracy itself be challenged by more participatory, plebiscitary or populist models? Although the answers to these questions are still hidden in the future, the forecasters are divided at present into two camps – the optimists and the sceptics. Optimists maintain that the internet will usher in an era of liberated and empowered citizens, turning consumers of political messages into originators and producers of political communication. The sceptics (such as Davis, 1999) claim that, thus far, the internet has not proven to be a revolutionary innovation and that as yet there is little evidence of the expected rosy future. Obviously, only time will tell.

Fourth, the geography of communication is also in flux. National boundaries no longer define communication systems so distinctly, as the organization and flow of mass communications are being internationalized. Satellite technology has extended and speeded coverage of events throughout the world. Media economics – escalating production costs allied to limits on domestic revenues – has increased the importance of foreign markets. New genres packaged for global sale (e.g. MTV, CNN) have emerged (Ferguson, 1990). A few giant media conglomerates are vying for transnational supremacy. Many people have increasing access to non-national sources of entertainment, information, play, sociability – and politics. Politicians and pressure groups increasingly strive to reach and influence international audiences. Every now and then the contours of a global public sphere seem to be emerging.

If we are to make sense of such a turbulent scene, we need to select some key points of anchorage from which to view and analyse it. What might these be? Much of our own past work (see Gurevitch and Blumler, 1977; Blumler and Gurevitch, 1981; Blumler and Gurevitch, 1995) was predicated on the view that an understanding of the processes of political communication required a systemic perspective, i.e. one in which the different components of the system – media institutions and professionals; political institutions, parties and political advocates; audience members placed at the receiving end of the output produced by these institutions; and the surrounding socio-political environment – interact and impact upon each other, such that change in one triggers adaptive changes in the rest of the system. We believe that the application of such a framework to present conditions – considering how each of the elements in this model is being affected by the various changes outlined above – could still be clarifying.

The shifting political communication terrain

Political advocates

Our point of departure here is the 'competitive struggle to influence and control popular perceptions of key political events and issues' which takes place in all democracies nowadays among politicians and spokespersons of other interests and causes wishing to shape public policy (Blumler, 1990: 103). Much of this involves a 'competition for access' to the major communications media of the time, in which the 'material and symbolic advantages' of the various advocates 'are unequally distributed' (Schlesinger, 1990: 77).

Several developments in such publicity competition have stemmed from the waning of party loyalties and deference to authority among members of the public. First, effective communication to the electorate through the mass media has become even more important for government leaders and vote-seeking politicians, needing to gain each day (as it were) the approval they formerly could count on over longer stretches of time. This has impelled a thorough-going professionalization of the parties' communication activities, in which specialist consultants assume responsibility for proactive news management, campaign and message design, and research-based political marketing (Mayhew, 1997; Mancini, 1999a). Second, pressure groups and other sources of advocacy have put relatively less emphasis than in the past on lobbying inside governments, legislatures and parties and more on communication of their concerns and stands through the mass media. This helps them to build and sustain membership support and to create agendas to which governments must respond. And third, the terms of politicians' involvement in competition for media access have shifted to their disadvantage.

Until the 1980s the prevailing system tended to give 'a rather privileged position in political communication output to the views of already established power holders' (Blumler and Gurevitch, 1981: 489). Although political leaders had to heed the demands of other groups as well, they often managed this by incorporating their representatives into networks of formal and informal consultation, in which broadly shared assumptions about policy goals, and how conflict over them should be negotiated, prevailed. More radical groups, moved by different normative stances and policy priorities, tended to be excluded, not only from policy discourse but also from media access – unless they engaged in newsworthy protests and demonstrations, in which case they risked provoking pejorative coverage depicting them as disruptive and violent extremists (see McLeod, 1995).

But latterly the pecking order of political voices in the news has altered. For one thing, the political newshole is shrinking. In the United States, Britain and other advanced democracies, the main news media are devoting relatively less space and time to the activities of governments and statements of politicians (Lee, forthcoming; Negrine, 1999; OECD, 1996). For another, politicians face increased competition for media publicity from a much wider range of advocates who operate outside the political parties, including advertisers, pollsters, interest groups and diverse social causes and movements. It is true that certain material and symbolic advantages still accrue to leaders of political institutions due to their authority as elected representatives of the people and their power to make laws and execute policies affecting society as a whole. Nevertheless, 'official' politicians must fight harder to get their messages noticed and passed on in their preferred terms, while media tolerance has apparently increased for stances that would previously have seemed beyond the pale. At times the central publicity tussle pits a government or political party against a well-organized, well-resourced and media-savvy pressure group or social movement rather than the opposing party. In 1999 Britain, for example, some of the Blair government's most difficult communication struggles arose from conflict with consumer groups and the environmental lobby (over genetically engineered foods), the Countryside Alliance (over fox-hunting, farmers' reduced incomes and rural decline generally), and the campaign for freedom of information (over the initially modest terms of its proposals for abolishing the Official Secrets Act). Another example is the big publicity battle that raged, during the Seattle conference later in the same year of the World Trade Organisation, between governments of the richer countries and a disparate alliance of ecologists, human rights groups and trades unionists.

Many factors underlie this shift in the structure of media access for political advocates. One is increased journalistic scepticism about politicians' claims and assertions, which is reinforced by their belief that many members of the public are also unwilling to take politicians' utterances at face value. Related to this is the affronted sensitivity of journalists to leading politicians' attempts to manage the news in their favour, an effort they can sometimes neutralize by bringing in other critical voices. In the prevailing atmosphere of political disenchantment, coverage of party conflict, organized as government vs opposition, may have also lost some of its appeal – as if too often stale and predictable.

Flows of communication to and through the media have also been affected by trends in the overall relationship of modern society to the political arena. On the one hand, a heightened awareness has developed in recent years of every citizen's entitlement to a decent life in a wide range of spheres – at work, in health, education, social security, public transport, the environment, etc. But on the other hand, a host of problems have arisen in most of these areas, which are not amenable to immediate solution and which, at best, politicians can only hope to ameliorate gradually over the longer term. As Bennett *et al.* (1999: 18) summarize:

> First, rising standards of living and security may encourage people to be less likely to defer to authorities, be they government or media. Second, the bar of public expectations for institutions and their leaders may have been raised over time.

This tension between personal expectations and social conditions affords alert non-party pressure groups many opportunities to publicize their values and demands in the media – for example, through coverage of research they may have sponsored on worsening social trends in their fields or of opinion surveys they have conducted on people's experiences and problems in such fields.

Finally, today's much-expanded media system has helped to prise open the previously rather narrow funnel of access to electoral audiences. There are now many more outlets in which groups can try to place their messages in the hope of eventually achieving their wider circulation throughout the rest of the system as well.

Professional mediators

Like politicians, professional political journalists have also been slipping down a salient pecking order – that of access to news time and space for their reports inside their media organs. Of course demand for their contributions fluctuates in response to the flow of events – increasing during election campaigns, at times of high political crisis, or when controversy rages over weighty decisions of state. But the intensified competitive pressures on media organizations arising from communication abundance and increased commercialism have tended to diminish political journalists in two ways.

First, they have lost status. This is partly because they no longer address the entire attentive nation through a small number of authoritative channels; there are now many more outlets through which people can follow politics, none of which can rule the roost as before. It is also partly because politics must compete with the increased availability in most of those outlets of entertainment, sport and other more beguiling fare. This has been accompanied by an upsurge of other forms of specialist journalism, which compete with political journalism for resources, space and appeal – financial journalism, sports journalism, celebrity journalism and fashion journalism for instance.[2] The loss of status also stems, in part, from the increased exposure of many journalists' media employers to a market logic, which subjects politics like everything else to the levelling impact of a profit and loss calculus. This calls into question the previously sheltered position political journalism used to enjoy inside many media organizations.

Several consequences flow from this loss of standing. 'Sacerdotal' approaches to political coverage, wherein certain political events are regarded as inherently deserving of ample and serious coverage, have become less common. Politics must fight for its place in reporting and scheduling more often on the basis of its news value or likely audience appeal. Examples include drastic reductions of party convention coverage by the US networks, similar reductions in verbatim reporting of parliamentary debates by Britain's broadsheet press, and the near-demise of long-form analytical documentaries in many national broadcasting systems. Another consequence is the blurring of past distinctions between the 'quality' and 'tabloid' press and an upsurge of 'infotainment' approaches to politics. To get noticed, political journalists must learn to accommodate civic with hedonistic values. In addition, as market competition intensifies and politics is knocked off its pedestal, the ethics of political journalism becomes less careful and less closely policed. Davis and Owen (1998) ascribe the decline in traditional standards in part to the fact that many of the new media outlets are not bound by any notion of public service or by the norms of objective journalism. More generally, political coverage in the new conditions comes more often under review and pressure to demonstrate its compatibility with media organizations' goals, entailing a retailoring of such output if necessary.

Second, as with political advocacy, so too has the range of significant actors involved in the professional mediation of politics been broadened. The more or less bounded and coherent circle of political journalists who in the past boarded the same 'bus' to follow the same political personalities (Crouse, 1972) has been diluted and bypassed. The big players of political journalism no longer command the field they once dominated so prominently. They are now jostled by many new and less inhibited makers and breakers of news, sources of commentary, and investigative pursuers and purveyors of scandal in talk shows, tabloids and websites. One of the more significant developments here is the role played by entertainers and popular culture professionals in the political arena (e.g. stand-up comics and talk show hosts) as well as the tabloidization of news and current affairs magazines. The professional political journalist now shares the stage with media professionals who come from the entertainment side of the industry, whose celebrityhood provides them with considerable clout, and with whose perspectives and offerings they must somehow engage.

The audience for political communication

This component of the political communication process is changing in three important respects: in structure; modes of reception; and in role.

First, new media conditions tend to fragment the political audience, though

to what extent and along what lines is not entirely clear and needs to be empirically monitored over time. With the multiplication of channels and outlets, the
size of the mass audience for political news is undoubtedly reduced, and a diversification of political communication forms, catering for more distinct audience
sectors, is facilitated. 'Balkanization' is probably an overly extreme metaphor for
present-day audience structure. The saturation of our media environment with
round-the-clock coverage of the top stories of the day ensures that almost everyone, even some who 'don't want to know', will be reached by news about major
political events and conflicts. What may differ most across outlets and their
audiences is how those stories are framed, analysed and followed up in diverse
arenas and styles of commentary and discussion.

Nevertheless, two fault lines of audience differentiation may deepen with the
advance of communication abundance. Political communication may increasingly address the particular identities and concerns of culturally distinct sub-
groups – though such a process may vary cross-nationally according to how far
the societies concerned are already culturally segmented and polarized. And the
audience may be structured even more than at present by variables of political
stratification (interest, knowledge, and a propensity actively to seek out more
information), as some in the population absorb little more than the daily political headlines and occasional tabloid stories, while others use the internet to
explore the panorama of political issues and ideas more widely and deeply.

Second, media abundance is likely to change how political messages are
received by audience members, though again research is needed to clarify along
what lines. Much audience reception in the new conditions may turn on a tension between a greater freedom to choose, and an increased inability to avoid,
political materials. Thus, with so many communication channels and forms
available, it is obviously easier for people to look for and stay with that which
interests them and to turn off whatever does not. Yet because political communication often blends with a flow of other materials nowadays, people can be
exposed to it inadvertently as it crops up in genres and formats not usually designated as 'political'. All that said, however, media abundance does appear to
introduce a greater element of flexibility into people's approaches to political
communication. By multiplying and diversifying the possibilities of audience
patronage across a wide range of media and information sources, it allows some
individuals to be 'specialists', spending extensive amounts of time consuming
favourite materials, and other individuals to be 'eclectics', sampling a broader
miscellany of media fare. Again a potential for restructuring the audience arises
here, differentiating political cognoscenti from 'hit-and-run' followers of public
affairs and from 'anti-politicals', who may try, as far as possible, to close their
eyes and ears to politics in the media.

But a third audience-related shift may be even more important than the others.
Until recently, much political communication was a straightforwardly top-down
affair. The issues of the day were mainly defined and discussed by politicians,
journalists, experts and interest group leaders for reception and consideration by
voters. The former were predominantly actors, the latter recipients of political
communication. But today it sometimes seems as if the 'audience' has broken out
of that pigeonhole into a different role – like that of a 'producer' or an 'actor'
(though lacking the focused intentionality of other actors in the system).[3]

In part this change stems from the increased choice inherent in an expansion of media abundance that can cater more closely for individual preferences. Thus, a combination of the decline of network news, the coming of 24-hour news, and the emergence of the web as a news medium have arguably shifted 'some of the editorial process to the viewers' (Pope, 1999: 57). But it is an outcome as well of those strong currents of populism that have lately been suffusing the worlds of both politics and the media. These also emanate from the expansion of media outlets, which 'has created new opportunities and pitfalls for the public to enter the political world' (Delli Carpini and Williams, 2000). But they derive additionally from the decline of ideology, leaving a sort of legitimacy gap that populism helps to fill; from the growth of political marketing as an adjunct to campaign strategy; and from the diminished standing of political, media and other elites in popular eyes.

Consequently, communicators who wish to inform, persuade or simply hold the attention of their auditors must adapt more closely than in the past to what ordinary people find interesting, relevant and accessible. More efforts are made to engage voters in news stories by featuring the comments of ordinary citizens. The voiced opinions of men and women in the street are being tapped more often in a veritable explosion of populist formats and approaches: talk shows; phone-ins; solicitation of calls, faxes and e-mails for response by interviewed politicians; studio panels confronting party representatives; larger studio audiences putting questions to politicians through a moderator; and town meetings of the air, deliberative polling and televised 'people's parliaments'. Moreover, leading political and media organizations regularly conduct research into ordinary people's preferences, tastes and images of their own efforts and personalities – to help them keep in touch with the public mood and to stand a better chance of winning electoral support or audience share respectively.

All this may be transforming the agenda-setting process, giving the audience-public (or its 'public opinion' as presented in polls, market research and media reports) a more active role in it than was previously the case. Although the news media are frequently depicted as front-line 'agenda setters', one can always ask: Who sets the agenda for them? When a partial answer refers to the initiatives and statements of politicians, the same question can be raised: Who puts the words in the politicians' mouths? And when the answer to that question is cast in terms of politicians' advisers, communication experts and pollsters, again the question can be put: From where do these people get their ideas? Presumably a main source is poll results, focus groups and so on – i.e. members of the public. We thus have a sort of circle of agenda setting, to which the audience element now appears at least as contributory as that of the others.

The surrounding environment

As much of the above has intimated, the socio-political field in which political communicators operate has become far more complex and fluid than before. Curtin (1999) even terms the present situation an 'era of indeterminacy' for all involved in cultural and political expression. This heightens their difficulties of comprehension, adaptation and control.

In part this arises from the increased intractability of the central problems of politics, such as those of economic management, safeguarding the environment, escalating demands and costs of social provision, and rising rates of crime, drug abuse and other indicators of social breakdown. In part, it stems from the intensified competition by which all communicators are affected. But it is also the product of a host of increased uncertainties. When voters' loyalties are more volatile, what policies and messages stand the best chance of bringing them into your camp – and for how long? When people have more identities to assume, through which ones are they most likely to respond to particular events, initiatives and appeals? When the issues on the publicity agenda are more numerous and diverse, to which should communicators give highest priority? When the voices accorded access to the media are more numerous and diverse, which are most likely to ring sympathetic bells with the general public? When more outlets for political communication are available in our elaborated media system of television, press, radio, news magazines and the internet, how can messages be most effectively designed to suit their diverse 'demand characteristics' and to appeal to their diverse audiences? And when the very boundaries that previously structured the political communication field seem to be dissolving – e.g. between 'political' and 'non-political' popular culture genres, between 'quality' and 'tabloid' approaches to politics, between journalists serving audiences as 'informers' and as 'entertainers', and between 'mass' and 'specialist' audiences – how can one know what to say most persuasively to whom through what channel?

A new form of political communication system?

Out of the convergence of many recent trends – especially the continuing advance of media innovation and abundance, the acceleration of social change with its numerous unpredictable consequences, the fragmentation of social orders, the dethroning of political institutions, people's increased expectations of personal autonomy, and the resulting proliferation and diversification of communicators, issue agendas and media outlets – a new form of political communication system does seem to be emerging. How might it be most appropriately characterized? Although it is too early to discern its ultimate shape, three broad, and possibly enduring, features stand out at this stage in contrast to past arrangements.

Porous politics

First, what counts as 'political' has become less clear-cut than previously. Highly significant in this respect has been the entry of popular culture into politics. At the time of writing, for example, the question of George W. Bush's intellectual suitability for presidential office was being pursued in the US by jokes from talk show hosts Jay Leno and David Letterman.[4] Earlier in the year President Clinton was the butt of their (and others') jokes about his involvement with Monica Lewinsky. Was he being treated thereby as a politician, or an ordinary man with the usual sex drives, or both? At any rate, entertainment has become a more significant source of people's perceptions of politics. This development can be expressed in various ways – as a matter of politics being 'cut down to size', or of the 'de-ghettoization of politics'. But politics has undoubtedly broken out of the shells of respect, deference and distance from people's daily lives in which it had formerly been enclosed. There is now a less identifiable core of what counts in some delimited sense as 'the political'.

It follows that people's experiences of 'the political' may become more divergent as well. When there was a more identifiable core, most people would have tuned in to more or less the same personalities, ideas and problems that constituted politics in the media. But now they are more likely to follow those facets of a more sprawling and amorphous political field which they individually notice or that happen to have reached them when using the media for other purposes.

As part and parcel of the same tendency, there has been an increased politicization of other domains of life – as with sex, gender and family relations. Politics is increasingly a prime definer of many other areas of social life and is consequently being viewed through a multiplicity of other lenses. Thus, virtually everything becomes in principle raw material for treatment as a public issue. Politics is more all-embracing.

Might such an expanded notion of 'the political', less tightly focused and more entertainment-laced, affect people's ability to make choices as citizens and their ability to find material in the media designed to clarify those choices? Such a question may be less pressing at election time. For when politicians campaign for support, when the media cover their campaigns, and when voters respond to them, all tend to revert to the more 'official' sense of what politics and citizenship are about, a core set of top-of-the-agenda choices and issues for determination through the established political institutions. But whether such a compartmentalization can be sustained – and how completely if at all – is an open question in the new scheme of things.

Thus, 'third-age' political communication could be said to pivot on a master tension between 'infinite' politics (politics is everything and is open to all modes of communication – entertaining as well as informing) and a more conventionally 'bounded' politics (that which is characteristically processed through the official institutions and departments of state).

System integration

Second, for many reasons, democratic political communication systems are less closely integrated than formerly. In part, this is due to the sheer abundance of the present media system, in which there are many 'more channels, chances and incentives to tailor political communication to particular identities, conditions and tastes' (Blumler and Kavanagh, 1999: 221). Partly it is because the aggregating power of the major parties – their ability to draw into themselves and to co-ordinate a broad range of political demands under a few alternative umbrellas – has weakened. They are more often buffeted by a multiplicity of conflicting demands, posed from the outside – in the media and on the streets, as it were. And in great part, it is because the mutual understandings, ground rules and informal networks that once prevailed between political and journalistic elites, shaping much of their behaviour and output, are no longer so influential. In increasingly fragmented and competitive political and media markets, such understandings tend to lose their binding force (Sanders, Bale and Canel, 1999). There is also the fact that each side of the old 'political-media complex' (Swanson, 1992) has become less dependent on the other: journalists can turn to many other sources than politicians to keep their stories moving; and politicians have a wider choice of media outlets in which to place their messages.

In addition, a marked divergence seems to be surfacing in the new political communication system between the processes and assumptions that underlie the institutions of territorial representative democracy and the goals and assumptions that animate the increasingly assertive and media-aware organizations of so-called 'civil society'. Britain, for example, is said by Alderman (1999: 128) to 'have become two nations politically: on the one hand, that of [the] two parties which continue to monopolize power at the parliamentary and governmental level and, on the other, that of the single issue groups and protest movements, whose membership has long since outstripped the active grassroots support the parties can call upon'. Beck (1992 and 1997) terms the latter 'arrangements from below' or 'subpolitics', when referring to the politicizing activities of social movements, advocacy and pressure groups which coalesce and vie with each other in attempts to influence the exercise of political power by mobilizing communication pressures on its holders through media-reported events, protests, statements, surveys and agitation (Eide and Knight, 1999). Their increased visibility and clout are potentially disintegrative, because the *raison d'être* of such bodies is to promote particular values, interests and demands with little regard for their relations to other values and claims or to the availability of resources in the public purse.

This divergence has attracted polarized evaluations among commentators. Some tend to celebrate the upsurge of subpolitics, regarding its welter of clubs, professional associations, causes and pressure groups as a more vigorous and authentic alternative to the machinations of politicians and the alleged failure of the state as a moral and participatory project (McLellan, 1999). But others tend to deplore the new state of affairs, because, in contrast to party-controlled politics, which can make 'the whole greater than the parts', interest group politics is intrinsically single-minded and divisive, involving the 'accumulation of mere enthusiasms with no certainty of overall coherence' (Seymour-Ure, 1999: 49).

Perhaps the divergence between these two arenas should not be exaggerated. After all, governments and parties are still in the business of trying to build supportive coalitions of multiple interests. But this has undoubtedly become more difficult. Governments have more often to take decisions on contested issues in the face, simultaneously, of party-political opposition, interest group pressures and media-framed coverage. This is a complex and multi-faceted terrain, which communication research has tended to neglect. Although the literature is full of studies of government-media relations on the one side, and includes many studies of how the media have portrayed various social movements and interest groups on the other, there is a dearth of work that focuses on the interplay of all these elements. Case studies of the interrelations among government, media and active interest groups in high-profile issue areas are much needed.

But the question of system integration may also be considered from two other angles. One concerns the staying power of the so-called 'political-media complex'. As Swanson (1999: 205) points out:

> From the 1960s forward . . . political communication has been . . . explained by scholars essentially as the product of a well-understood dynamic between political actors and parties on the one hand, and mainstream news media on the other hand, with both soliciting the attention and consideration of the public.

Despite the recent destabilization of both these communicators, it would be premature to close the scholarly books on them. Leading politicians still enjoy unique authority as elected law-makers, just as top professional journalists still enjoy unique prestige arising from their regular access to such figures. And neither group will submit passively to all the new-found challenges to their positions. Indeed, recent research has documented how assiduously the best-funded candidates and largest media organizations in the United States have been adapting their strategies and offerings to the new medium of the internet, in order to maintain their dominance as primary players in the flow of political communication and information. The author of this research (Davis, 1999: 5–6) consequently predicts that the news organizations and government entities with the 'most influence on the mass news dissemination business' will hitch the web so successfully to their wagons that their materials 'will become the primary information sources for Internet users of the future'.

Otherwise, we should not lose sight of certain interconnecting influences by which key institutions and actors are affected and constrained in even our more loosely organized political communication systems. Three important sources of such system-wide 'integration' may be identified.

One arises from the imperative for most attempts to influence political opinion to be funnelled nowadays through a 'media-constructed public sphere' (Schulz, 1997). As Castells (1997) puts it:

> It is not that the media 'controls' politics as such, rather that they have come to create and constitute the space in which politics now chiefly happens for most people in so called 'advanced' societies. . . . Whether we like it or not, in order to engage in the political debate we must now do so through the media.

As noted in the section on political advocacy, however, it has become an increasingly demanding task to operate effectively in this space, one for which expert assistance is now regarded as indispensable. Neither publicity amateurs nor subject specialists can manage this on their own. Consequently, almost *all* would-be political advocates – not only political parties and candidates but also the leading cause and interest groups that compose 'civil society' – must *professionalize* their approaches to media publicity and hire the services of personnel skilled in such activities as planning campaigns, conducting and interpreting opinion research, adapting to the schedules and formats of diverse media outlets, and addressing the news values and working practices of journalism. Despite its increased social and political fragmentation, then, the new political communication system is as if integrated by the impact of an increasingly commanding and self-confident elite of professional communicators, whose members work for all political publicity seekers and share perspectives, strategies and insights across those diverse sponsors, not only domestically but also internationally (Plasser, 1999).

Second, it follows that in a media-constructed public sphere, certain formative characteristics of *media organization* will exert cross-system influences on a society's flow of political communications. How far the media are commercially organized or oriented to public service and their social responsibilities, for example, will tend to shape that flow, as will the intensity of the competition that prevails among the main media for audiences and revenues.

Finally, how political advocates and professional mediators fashion their communications for optimal reception by their audiences will be affected by certain system-spanning tenets of *political culture*, which may vary across different societies. For example, political cultures may differ: 'in the degree to which they value the political sphere itself as a dignified and important realm of activity, informed involvement in which deserves to be promoted' (Gurevitch and Blumler, 1977: 283); 'in the degree to which they embrace or resist populism – or the principle of *vox populi, vox dei'* (Blumler and Gurevitch, 2000); and in the basic stock of historically derived 'ideas in good currency' (Shon, 1971), on which rivals in the battle for public opinion may periodically draw when striving to frame contested issues in terms they hope will appeal to journalists and their target publics.

Democracy and the media

Third, the new political communication system is hosting many explorations of new meanings, expectations and potentials of 'democracy' and 'citizenship'. In Hannerz' (1999: 403) words:

> These days the notion of 'citizenship' is coming into prominence again; not only in a legal sense, but as a key word in debates over desirable combinations of rights, responsibilities and competences in the late 20th century, soon 21st century, world.

Three root sources have combined to fuel this process: a widespread belief that democracy as conventionally interpreted is in trouble and that shortcomings of mainstream media coverage of politics are largely to blame for its 'crisis' (Blumler and Gurevitch, 1995); the rising tide of populism in cultural, political and media quarters, which upgrades the value of heeding the views and preferences of ordinary people; and an impression that certain qualities of the new media could be enlisted behind more active forms of political participation. Often mentioned as potentially redemptive features of the new media are: the availability of large stores of information for citizens to tap without the prior intervention of media gatekeepers or other mediators; more emphasis on the substance of political conflict in contrast to conventional journalists' heavy treatment of it as a 'game'; interactivity, enabling citizens to find things out for themselves rather than passively receiving or ignoring what is given; and the creation of virtual forums, enabling exchanges between citizens and officials and discussions of current issues among citizens themselves.

The new democratic strivings have been expressed in many ways, both normatively and practically. Most influential among the normative manifestations has been Habermas's (1989) concept of the 'public sphere', depicted as a space in which people can discuss civic issues on their merits without distortion by pressures of state or market institutions. This is put forward as an ideal, in light of which existing political communication arrangements can be criticized, their reform conceived and certain practices approximating the desired standards welcomed. Thus, Livingstone and Lunt (1994) have discussed the conformity of talk shows and audience discussion programmes to Habermas's standards, while Larson (1999: 143) contends that the increased coverage of 'people in the street' by US network news during the 1996 presidential campaign 'was consistent with the notion of a public sphere'. Another normative expression is the civic journalism movement in the United States, which urges news organizations to assume some responsibility for revitalizing public communication, notably by identifying voters' most pressing concerns, creating forums in which those concerns can be aired, and obliging politicians to address them.

In practical terms, not only have the schedules of broadcasting organizations been peppered with discursive formats centring on ordinary people's political views and experiences (as itemized in the section on the audience above). In many countries the governmental process itself has been opened to new participatory efforts through public consultations over national and local issues. Pratchett (1999), for example, notes the recent development in Britain of a wide-ranging 'public participation agenda', including the creation by public bodies of citizens' panels, citizens' juries, focus groups and community planning forums. Similarly, Tambini (1999) has surveyed the emergence in Europe and the United States of 'civic networks' – i.e. attempts to use new media technology, particularly the internet, to improve participation in local democratic processes. Describing this as 'a global trend', he states that, 'New information systems and civic networks' are being 'opened by local authorities every week' (1999: 308).

Much of this is in its infancy, and the jury is still out on the exercises concerned, some of which have in any case been conceived as trials and experiments. This is not the place to consider their detailed implementation, achievements and problems. In conclusion we would only make two points that have been somewhat neglected in recent discussions of democracy and the media.

One is to warn against unthinking adherence to tacitly anarchic notions of civic communication. Democratic deliberation and participation can be significantly advanced only through institutions and procedures that are specifically designed to realize such goals. For example, the mere creation of more space in the news for coverage of the forces of 'civil society' should not be taken as a sign that the mass media are becoming exemplars of Habermas's public sphere, especially if what is mainly reported are demonstrations, confrontations with the police, emotional outpourings and slogans, lacking placement in some broader framework of considered debate. This point is underscored by a recent study of discussion forums on the internet (Davis, 1999: 162–63) in which there is apparently little real exchange of views. Instead, discrete assertions by scattered individuals tend to predominate in an atmosphere that favours 'the loudest and most aggressive' contributors. For their part, the possibility that some promoters of populist and participatory schemes in broadcasting or national and local government are going through such motions chiefly for their own instrumental ends (to attract large audiences, to appease critics, or just to seem accessible) rather than to enrich democracy, cannot be excluded. Much empirical research and sifting of evidence about motives, structures, practices and outcomes, are therefore needed before the prospects for deploying new communication technologies to enhance the constructive involvement of citizens in public affairs can properly be assessed.

Second, amidst all the revisionist ferment, time should also be spared to consider a new sort of normative issue posed by key features of the new political communication system. With social change proliferating advocates and issues for consideration, and with media change creating more channels for them to appear and be aired in, in such a system there may be more chances for more numerous voices to be heard, more problems to be brought to people's attention, and more chances for people to find what they want to hear, see or know about.

But it may also be more difficult to put all this together 'at the centre'. The contrast could be between a public sphere of cacophony and one of coherent communication: How can the system as a whole and the individuals holding diverse roles within it sort out the cacophony when making their respective choices? And how many will be deterred by the apparent 'embarrassment of riches' and give up the effort altogether?

Buddy, can you paradigm?

The introductory theme of this chapter was the relative vulnerability of paradigms prevalent in the social sciences to the vagaries of change. There, however, the full implications of such 'softness' for our particular field were left open. How should they be faced? Does turbulence in the technological and social environment in which processes of political communication are conducted today require its scholars to go back to the conceptual drawing board? Clearly there have been many changes in the phenomena of political communication and in the issues raised for research and evaluation. But has its generative ground altered so fundamentally as to demand a new paradigm of political communication analysis?

Our answer to this question is both a 'yes' and a 'no'!

On the one hand, new concepts and research approaches are needed to take account of the increased diversification that is affecting political communication at all levels.[5] Such diversification applies, for example, to: the instruments by which political communications are carried and therefore shaped (ranging from television to the internet); the main sources of political advocacy; the numerous issues such advocates place on the societal agenda and the differing perspectives on political reality they project; expansion of the range of media practitioners beyond the ranks of traditional political correspondents to include not only notionally 'non-political' genres in mainstream media but also originators of messages from outside the familiar media organizations; models of democracy (including representative and direct, 'top-down' and 'bottom-up' variants); and ways in which citizens may tap into, process and use the multiplicity of available streams of information and ideas. Consequently, all theories of political communication impact that have presumed mass exposure to relatively uniform bodies of political content – such as those of agenda-setting, the spiral of silence and the cultivation hypothesis – must be re-thought.

On the other hand, it appears from our detailed review that a 'systems' perspective on political communication processes is still valid and useful. In taking stock of what has been happening, it was clarifying to focus on a triad of actor types (advocates, mediators and audiences) situated in an environmental field, to specify possible influences on their mutual relations, and to identify overall patterns that may be resulting from their interactions. It is true that political communication systems have become more fluid and hence more difficult to comprehend at any given moment, before the kaleidoscope turns and they change again. Yet so long as we acknowledge that fluidity, and are prepared to incorporate it into our analytical efforts, the approach presented here should continue to serve us well into the foreseeable future.

Notes

1. For a fuller discussion of the main sources of change in political communication systems, see Blumler and Gurevitch (1995: 204–6).

2. Citing a content survey of regional dailies over several recent decades, Simons (1999) notes that in the United States in recent years 'business news has been, far and away, the fastest-growing editorial segment in the nation's newspapers, if not in all media'.

3. See Rhodes (1996) for a rigorous discussion of the problems involved in representing collectivities (such as 'the public' or 'the audience') as actors.

4. According to Bruni (1999), Bush 'is the one whose failure on a televised pop quiz about lesser-known world leaders launched a thousand quips, helping to turn him into Leno's favourite target. "George Bush released his new slogan today: He'll get tough with What's-His-Name," Leno joked last month. This month, Letterman cracked, "The guy may have bonehead stamped all over him".'

5. For a fuller discussion of diversification, see Blumler and Kavanagh (1999: 221–23) and Mancini (1999b).

References

ALDERMAN, K., 1999: 'Parties and Movements', *Parliamentary Affairs*, 52 (1), 128–30.

BECK, U., 1992: *Risk Society: Towards a New Modernity*, London, Newbury Park and New Delhi: Sage.

BECK, U., 1997: *The Reinvention of Politics: Rethinking Modernity in the Global Social Order*, Cambridge: Polity Press.

BENNETT, S.E., RHINE, S.L., FLICKINGER, R.S. and BENNETT, L.M., 1999: '"Video Malaise" Revisited: Public Trust in the Media and Government', *Press/Politics*, 4 (4), 8–23.

BLUMLER, J.G., 1990: 'Elections, the Media and the Modern Publicity Process' in Ferguson, M. (ed.), *Public Communication: The New Imperatives*, London, Newbury Park and New Delhi: Sage.

BLUMLER, J.G. AND GUREVITCH, M., 1981: 'Politicians and the Press: An Essay on Role Relationships' in Nimmo, D.D. and Sanders, K.R. (eds), *Handbook of Political Communication*, Beverly Hills and London: Sage.

——, 1995: *The Crisis of Public Communication*, London and New York: Routledge.

——, 2000: 'Americanization Reconsidered: UK-US Communication Comparisons across Time' in Bennett, W.L. and Entman, R.M. (eds), *Mediated Politics in the Future of Democracy*, Cambridge and New York: Cambridge University Press.

BLUMLER, J.G. and KAVANAGH, D., 1999: 'The Third Age of Political Communication: Influences and Features', *Political Communication*, 16 (3), 209–30.

BRUNI, F., 1999: 'Jabs at Bush Put Focus on Question of Intellect', *New York Times on the Web*, 8 December, 1999.

CASTELLS, M., 1997: *The Power of Identity*, Oxford: Blackwell.

CROUSE, T., 1972: *The Boys on the Bus*, New York: Ballantine Books.

CURTIN, M., 1999: 'Feminine Desire in the Age of Satellite Television', *Journal of Communication*, 49 (2), 55–70.

DAVIS, R., 1999: *The Web of Politics: The Internet's Impact on the American Political System*, Oxford and New York: Oxford University Press.

DAVIS, R. and OWEN, D., 1998: *New Media and American Politics*, Oxford and New York: Oxford University Press.

DELLI CARPINI, M.X. and WILLIAMS, B.A., 2000: *Mediated Politics in the Future of Democracy*, Cambridge and New York: Cambridge University Press.

EIDE, M. and KNIGHT, G., 1999: 'Public/Private Service: Service Journalism and the Problems of Everyday Life', *European Journal of Communication*, 14 (4), 525–47.

FERGUSON, M., 1990: 'Electronic Media and the Redefining of Time and Space' in Ferguson, M. (ed.), *Public Communication: The New Imperatives*, London, Newbury Park and New Delhi: Sage.

GUREVITCH, M. and BLUMLER, J.G., 1977: 'Linkages between the Mass Media and Politics: A Model for the Analysis of Political Communication Systems' in Curran, J., Gurevitch, M. and Woollacott, J. (eds), *Mass Communication and Society*, London: Edward Arnold.

HABERMAS, J., 1989: *The Structural Transformation of the Public Sphere: An Enquiry into a Category of Bourgeois Society*, Cambridge, MA: MIT Press.

HANNERZ, U., 1999: 'Reflections on Varieties of Culturespeak', *European Journal of Cultural Studies*, 2 (3), 393–407.

LARSON, S.G., 1999: 'Public Opinion in Television Election News Beyond Polls', *Political Communication*, 16 (2), 133–45.

LEE, M., forthcoming: 'Reporters and Bureaucrats: Public Relations Counter-Strategies by Public Administrators in an Era of Media Disinterest in Government', *Public Relations Review*, 35 (4).

LIVINGSTONE, S. and LUNT, P., 1994: *Talk on Television: Audience Participation and Public Debate*, London and New York: Routledge.

MCLELLAN, D., 1999: 'Then and Now: Marx and Marxism', *Political Studies*, 47 (5), 955–66.

MCLEOD, D.M., 1995: 'Communicating Deviance: The Effects of Television News Coverage of Social Protest', *Journal of Broadcasting and Electronic Media*, 39 (1), 4–19.

MANCINI, P., 1999a: 'New Frontiers in Political Professionalism', *Political Communication*, 16 (3), 231–45.

——, 1999b: 'A "Technology Theory" of Political Communication', paper presented to a Conference on Technological Innovation and Political Communication, Perugia, December 1999.

MAYHEW, L. H., 1997: *The New Public: Professional Communication and the Means of Social Influence*, Cambridge and New York: Cambridge University Press.

NEGRINE, R., 1999: 'Parliaments and the Media: A Changing Relationship?', *European Journal of Communication*, 14 (3), 325–52.

ORGANISATION FOR ECONOMIC COOPERATION AND DEVELOPMENT, 1996: *Ministerial Symposium on the Future of Public Services*, Paris: OECD.

PLASSER, F., 1999: *Tracing the Worldwide Proliferation of American Campaign Techniques*, Vienna: Center for Applied Political Research.

POPE, K, 1999: 'Network and Cable TV', *Media Studies Journal*, 13 (2), 52–7.

PRATCHETT, L., 1999: 'New Fashions in Public Participation: Towards Greater Democracy?', *Parliamentary Affairs*, 52 (4), 616–33.

RHODES, R.A.W., 1996: 'The New Governance: Governing without Government', *Political Studies*, 44 (4), 652–67.

SANDERS, K., BALE, T. and CANEL, M.J., 1999: 'Managing Sleaze: Prime Ministers and News Management in Conservative Great Britain and Socialist Spain', *European Journal of Communication*, 14 (4), 461–86.

SCHLESINGER, P., 1990: 'Rethinking the Sociology of Journalism: Source Strategies and the Limits of Media-Centrism', in Ferguson, M. (ed.), *Public Communication: The New Imperatives*, London, Newbury Park and New Delhi: Sage.

SCHULZ, W., 1997: 'Changes of the Mass Media and the Public Sphere', *Javnost – The Public*, 4 (2), 57–71.

SEYMOUR-URE, C., 1999: 'Are the Broadsheets Becoming Unhinged?' in Seaton, J. (ed.), *Politics and the Media: Harlots and Prerogatives at the Turn of the Millennium*, Oxford: Blackwell.

SHON, D., 1971: *Beyond the Stable State*, London: Temple Smith.

SIMONS, L.M., 1999: 'Follow the Money', *American Journalism Review*, 21 (10), 55–68.

SWANSON, D.L., 1992: 'The Political-Media Complex', *Communication Monographs*, 59, 397–400.

SWANSON, D.L., 1999: 'About This Issue' (introduction to a Symposium on a Third Age of Political Communication), *Political Communication*, 16 (3), 203–7.

TAMBINI, D., 1999: 'New Media and Democracy: The Civic Networking Movement', *New Media and Society*, 1 (3), 305–29.

SECTION II

Media Production

8

The Sociology of News Production Revisited (Again)

Michael Schudson

A prefatory note is in order for this fourth version of an essay originally published in 1989 and then twice revised and updated for earlier editions of this anthology. Ten years ago, the essay sought primarily to organize and clarify different approaches to studying the social manufacture of news. As I revised it, I emphasized the ways that cultural explanations of news are not entirely reducible to social, political, or economic causes and that the cultural dimension of news deserved greater attention. Today, if any of the perspectives discussed here needs special advocacy, it may well be the social or social-organizational one. The conventionalized opposition in media studies programmes between 'political-economic' and 'cultural' approaches has too often neglected the specific social realities that can be observed at the point of news production. This is where news sources, news reporters, news organization editors and the competing demands of professionalism, the market-place and cultural traditions collect around specific choices of what news to report and how to report it.

At the same time, studies of news production that focus narrowly on news institutions themselves, and are not broadly aware of how they evolve in relationship to other social institutions, especially political institutions, will have to escape their self-imposed confinement. Journalism is of course important as a constitutive element of public life. Media institutions, like any other institutions, are obviously governed by traditions and dynamics of their own. But in the broader ecology of public life, news institutions do not define politics any more than political structures fully determine the news; there is ongoing interaction. It is, to be sure, an interaction in which the media seem to be increasingly an autonomous force, independent of political parties. Gianpietro Mazzoleni has called this development in Italy a 'Copernican revolution' in political communication – 'yesterday everything circled around the parties, today everything circles around, and in the space of, the media' (1995: 308). At its best, this 'mediatization' of politics is one in which journalism is 'capable of standing as spokesperson for civil society, of challenging political arrogance and political roguery', but media institutions, unlike parties whose weakening hold on popular loyalties has afforded new space for media aggrandizement, are not accountable to the public

(Mazzoleni, 1995: 309, 315). The growing interest of political scientists and com-munication scholars alike in a field of 'politics and media' or 'media and politics' is welcome. Both the neglect of the news media in political studies and the media-centricity of communication studies should be speedily abandoned.

Social scientists who study the news speak a language that journalists mistrust and misunderstand. They speak of 'constructing the news', of 'making news', of the 'social construction of reality'. 'News is what newspapermen make it', according to one study (Gieber, 1964: 173). 'News is the result of the methods newsworkers employ', according to another (Fishman, 1980: 14). News is 'man-ufactured by journalists' (Cohen and Young, 1973: 97) in the words of a third. Even journalists who are critical of the daily practices of their colleagues and their own organizations find this talk offensive. Such language propels journal-ists into a fierce defence of their work, on the familiar ground that they just report the world as they see it – the facts, facts and nothing but the facts – and, yes, there's occasional bias, sensationalism, or inaccuracy, but a responsible journalist never fakes the news.

   That's not what we said, the scholars respond. We didn't say journalists fake the news, we said journalists make the news:

> To say that a news report is a story, no more, but no less, is not to demean news, nor to accuse it of being fictitious. Rather, it alerts us that news, like all public documents, is a constructed reality possessing its own internal validity.
>
> (Tuchman, 1976: 97)

In the most elementary way, this is obvious. Journalists write the words that turn up in the papers or on the screen as stories. Not government officials, not cul-tural forces, not 'reality' magically transforming itself into alphabetic signs, but flesh-and-blood journalists literally compose the stories we call news. Journalists make the news. (Would you say, the journalist might respond, that scientists 'make' science rather than 'discover' it or report it? Yes, the conscientious scholar must answer, we would say precisely that, and sociologists of science do say precisely that.)

   This is not a point of view likely to make much headway with professional journalists. 'News and news programmes could almost be called random reac-tions to random events' a British reporter told sociologist Graham Murdock. 'Again and again, the main reason why they turn out as they do is accident – accident of a kind which recurs so haphazardly as to defeat statistical examina-tion' (1973: 163). The study of the generation of news aims to find an order behind this sense of accident (and to understand as ideology journalists' failure to acknowledge such an order).

   The sociology of the production of news goes back at least to Max Weber (1921/1946), who wrote of the social standing of the journalist as a political per-son; Robert Park (1922, 1923), an ex-journalist himself, who wrote about the US immigrant press and news itself as a form of knowledge; and Helen MacGill Hughes (1940), who wrote an early study of human interest stories. But the formal study of how news organizations produce news products dates to 'gate-keeper' studies in the 1950s.

   Social psychologist Kurt Lewin coined the term 'gatekeeper' and several social scientists (White, 1950; Gieber, 1964) applied it to journalism. David

Manning White studied a middle-aged wire editor at a small American newspaper. For one week, 'Mr Gates' (as White called him) made available to the researcher every piece of wire copy, both those he rejected and those he selected to print in the paper. He then wrote down a reason for rejection on every story he turned down. Some of these reasons were not very illuminating: 'not enough space'. Others were technical or professional: 'dull writing' or 'drags too much'. Still others were explicitly political: 'propaganda' or 'He's too Red'. These last greatly influenced White's interpretation of gatekeeping although political reasons for rejection accounted for just 18 out of 423 cases. Mr Gates admitted that he did not like President Harry Truman's economic policies, that he was anti-Catholic and that these views affected his news judgement. White concludes that 'we see how highly subjective, how based on the "gatekeeper's" own set of experiences, attitudes and expectations the communication of 'news' really is'.

If Mr Gates' judgements can be attributed to personal subjectivity, we should expect some variation among wire editors if a larger sample were studied. Walter Gieber found otherwise in a study of sixteen wire editors in Wisconsin. All the editors selected news items in essentially the same way. They were not doing politics in selecting the news, they were doing a rote task. The typical editor was 'concerned with goals of production, bureaucratic routine and interpersonal relations within the newsroom' (1964: 175). Gieber's analysis is a refutation, not an extension, of White's.

The term 'gatekeeper' is still in use. It provides a handy metaphor for the relation of news organizations to news products. But, surprisingly, it leaves 'information' or 'news' sociologically untouched. Who gets to be a gatekeeper, and why? Who writes the news items that reach the gatekeepers, and how? Under what constraints and with what expectations? The gatekeeper metaphor minimizes the complexity of news-making. It tries to fix news-making at one point along a circuit of interactions and does not examine the circuit as a whole.

What approaches might work better, then? Three perspectives on news-making are commonly employed. The first is the view of political economy that relates the outcome of the news process to the structure of the state and the economy, and to the economic foundation of the news organization. This view appears in its most theoretically sophisticated and self-critical form in British media studies (Murdock, 1982).

The second approach comes primarily out of sociology, especially the study of social organization, occupations and professions, and the social construction of ideology. This perspective tries to understand how journalists' efforts on the job are constrained by organizational and occupational demands.

Third, a 'cultural' approach emphasizes the constraining force of broad cultural traditions and symbolic systems, regardless of the structure of economic organization or the character of occupational routines.

All three of these approaches have strengths and weaknesses I will discuss here. All of them, even taken together, have so far fallen short of providing adequate comparative and historical perspectives on news production. All of them recognize (or, at any rate, should) that news is a form of culture. It is a structured genre, or set of genres, of public meaning-making. But this is not to suggest that it floats in a symbolic ether. It is a material product and there are political economic, social and cultural dimensions to understanding its production, distribution and appropriation by audiences (Garnham, 1990: 10).

The value of each of the three perspectives varies depending on what aspect of 'news' one wants to explain. Is it the conservative, system-maintaining character of news? Or is it the very opposite – the extent to which the press in liberal societies is adversarial or even nihilistic, system attacking or system denigrating, cynical about government or derisive of a society's core values? Analysts may want to understand finer features of the news: why does it focus on individuals rather than systems and structures? Why is news so heavily dependent on official sources? Why has there been a 'tabloidization' of news around the world in the past decades? An especially complex question concerns whether one should find distressing, and try to explain, the deviation of the media from 'fair' and 'objective' reporting or, instead, should find disturbing and try to understand how it is that 'fair', 'objective' reporting presents a portrait of the world in tune with the view of dominant groups in society. Thus critics have objected to the Glasgow Media Group's studies for castigating television news bias when the more important point may be that broadcast news programmes 'achieve their ideological effectivity *precisely through* their observation of the *statutory* requirements of balance and impartiality' (Bennett, 1982: 306). Each of the perspectives I will now review may be more useful with some of these questions than with others.

The political economy of news

The link between the larger political economy of society and day-to-day practices in journalism is, as Graham Murdock has observed, 'oblique' (Murdock, 1973: 158). The link between ownership of news organizations and news coverage is not easy to determine – and it grows more difficult by the day as public and commercial systems of ownership mix, blend and intersect in a growing variety of ways (Noam, 1991). Can patterns of ownership be tied to specific habits of reporting? In some cases, this makes sense. Curran *et al.* (1980) ask why elite and mass-oriented newspapers in Britain provide such different fare even though reader surveys find that different classes prefer to read similar materials. They explain that advertisers find value in papers that attract small, concentrated elite audiences; the expense of reaching an 'upscale' audience is lower if a large share of this audience can be addressed through a single publication without having to pay the expense of reaching thousands of extraneous readers.

In other cases, a link between ownership and market structure on the one hand and news content on the other is not apparent. In Europe, it is not clear that public and private broadcasters differ systematically in the ways they present political news and current affairs (Brants, 1998: 328). Research on the impact of chain ownership compared to independent ownership of American newspapers on news content has been either inconclusive, as David Demers found in a useful literature review (1996) or, as C. Edward Baker puts it, 'tepid, hardly motivating any strong critique of chain ownership or prompting any significant policy interventions' (Baker, 1994: 19).

Some scholars write as if corporate ownership and commercial organizations necessarily compromise the democratic promise of public communication (McChesney, 1997), but the evidence is more nearly that the absence of commercial organizations, or their total domination by the state, is the worst-case scenario. In Latin America, government officials benefited more from state-controlled media than did the public; for Latin American policy-makers in the recent wave of democratization, 'strong control, censorship, and manipulation of the mass media during authoritarian and democratic regimes have deeply discredited statist models' (Waisbord, 1995: 219). South Korean journalism is more free since political democratization began in 1987 than it was under the military regime of the early 1980s when 700 anti-regime journalists were dismissed, the Minister of Culture could cancel any publication's registration at will, security agencies kept the media under constant surveillance and the Ministry of Culture routinely issued specific guidelines on how reporters should cover events (Lee, 1997). Still, in the new Korean media system, market considerations create new forms of internal censorship and old expectations of politicians – that they should receive favourable media treatment – persist.

Not that market-dominated systems and state-dominated systems are easy to distinguish these days. Yuzhei Zhao offers a detailed and persuasive account of the blending of commercial and state-controlled media in post-Tiananmen Square China (Zhao, 1998). After Tiananmen Square, the government tightened controls on the media, closed down three leading publications whose coverage it judged too sympathetic to the protesters, replaced editors at other newspapers, and required all news organizations to engage in self-criticism. The state continues to monitor political news, but pays less attention to coverage of economic, social and environmental issues. In all cases, self-censorship rather than heavy-handed party control is the operating system (Polumbaum, 1997).

Despite the tightening of party control, there has also been a rapid commercialization of the popular press and a proliferation of sensational, entertainment-oriented tabloids that are serious competitors to the established press for advertising revenues. Media outlets in the 'commercial' sector remain political organs, catering to the party's propaganda needs but trying to 'establish a common ground between the Party and the people' through the choice of what topics to cover (Zhao, 1998: 161). The commercial media have grown rapidly while the circulation of the traditional party organs has dropped. Party control remains substantial in leading news organizations throughout China, but even at Central China Television, the most influential station in the country, novel and aggressive news formats have tested the limits and sought to please the public as well as the party leadership. 'Focus', an innovative programme begun in 1994, has raised critical issues, has spoken on behalf of the poor and has investigated corruption in both business and government. Still, the department that produces it aims to make all the journalists share the same perspective and refrain from airing any segment that could induce political instability. The journalists are 'dancing with chains on' (Zhao, 1998: 121).

The new blends of state, independent and commercial news media, the mixed patterns of ownership and control, do not even have names, let alone theories to explain them. Zhao, for lack of any better term, describes the Chinese system as a 'propagandist/commercial model' of the media (1998: 151). Nor is there any accounting in media theory for what Zhao suggests may be 'China's unique contribution to world journalism' – the degree and extent of its corruption. News sources routinely pay for journalists' travel, hotels and meals when they report out-of-town events ('three-warranty reporting'), some journalists moonlight as public relations agents for businesses, and journalists and news organizations receive cash, negotiable securities, personal favours and gifts not only from business clients but even from government clients seeking favourable coverage (1998: 72–93). Journalists' salaries are low and 'few ... can resist the temptation offered by one paid news report that can bring in a red envelope with as much as a whole month's salary, not to mention an advertising deal worth years of salary' (1998: 87). There are not only a variety of political-economic structures of news production, but each gives rise to its own characteristic evasions, collusions and corruptions.

Fewer and fewer corporations control more and more of the American news media (Bagdikian, 1997). Major media conglomerates control more and more of the world's media. Where media are not controlled by corporations, they are generally voices of the state. Under these circumstances, it would be a shock to find the press a hotbed of radical thought. But, then, critical or radical thought in any society at any time is exceptional. In all political and economic systems, news 'coincides with' and 'reinforces' the 'definition of the political situation evolved by the political elite' (Murdock, 1973: 172). This basic intuition seems incontestable. The greatest research interest lies in determining its limits and specifying what structural and cultural features of the media can work to keep news porous, open to dissident voices and encouraging of genuine debate.

If scholars take too rigid a view of how powerful elites control news, then much of the media's output, not to mention much of recent world history, cannot be understood. Is it wise to accept the flat-footed functionalism of Edward S. Herman's and Noam Chomsky's *Manufacturing Consent* (1988), that the media 'serve to mobilize support for the special interests that dominate the state and private activity' (1988: xi) and that the propagandistic role of the American press is not in any essential way different from the role *Pravda* played in the Soviet Union? This would make many of the most dramatic moments in US media history in the past half-century inexplicable, from the role of the press in publicizing the civil rights movement to its coverage of opposition to the Vietnam War. A view that sees large corporations and the media working hand in glove to stifle dissent or promote a lethargic public acceptance of the existing distribution of power cannot explain why corporations in the early 1970s should have been so incensed at how the US media covered politics, the environment and business (Dreier, 1982).

One might prefer a more flexible theoretical stance – that the media reinforce the 'cultural hegemony' of dominant groups, that is, that they make the existing distribution of power and rewards seem to follow from nature or common sense and so succeed in making oppositional views appear unreasonable, quixotic, or utopian – perhaps even to the dissenters! This would explain how the culture industry keeps progressive social change from happening and so would explain why eastern Europe is ruled today by the Communist Party, why women in western democracies do not hold office, why African-Americans in the United States failed to win civil rights, why no coverage of gays and lesbians can be found in the news media today, and why Thatcher rules in Britain, Franco in Spain, Berlusconi in Italy and Nixon in the United States.

In short, 'hegemony' explains far too much. Handy a concept as it has sometimes been, it requires more critical consideration and more subtle deployment. The ability of a capitalist class to manipulate opinion and create a closed system of discourse is limited; ideology in contemporary capitalism is contested terrain. The ability of a socialist bureaucracy to create a closed system has limits, too, although its direct efforts to create one have often been stronger, have certainly been more explicitly advanced and have faced fewer legal or political impediments. The question to ask is what role the media play in the midst of or in relationship to social change. The behaviour of the American press in questioning the Vietnam War may have emerged precisely because the political elite did not know its own mind. It was deeply divided. Even then, the press seems largely to have gone about its normal business of citing official leaders – but at a time when officials were at odds with one another (Hallin, 1986). The result was that the media did not reinforce existing power but amplified elite disagreements in unsettling and unpredictable ways.

Both state and market limit free expression, but this does not make the comprehensiveness and severity of their means, the coherence of their motives, or the consequences of their controls the same. Public criticism of state policy is invariably easier in liberal societies with privately owned news outlets than in authoritarian societies with state or private ownership. In China, published criticism of the state has been tightly constrained; newspapers, it is said in China, 'swat flies but don't beat tigers' (Polumbaum, 1994: 258). Reporters have some freedom to write articles critical of high officials, but they must then circulate these as internal documents (*neibu*) not available in the public press (Grant, 1988).

The political economy perspective in Anglo-American media studies has generally taken liberal democracy for granted and so has been insensitive to political and legal determinants of news production. In a sense, it has been far more 'economic' than 'political'. Increasingly, this is recognized as a serious deficiency. In the 1980s in Europe, in the face of a threat to public broadcasting from conservative governments sympathetic to commercialization, scholars came increasingly to see in public broadcasting a pillar of a free public life (Garnham, 1990: 104–14). Increasingly, there have been efforts to articulate a view of 'civil society' where the media hold a vital place and attain a degree of autonomy from both state and market – as in the best public service broadcasting (Keane, 1991).

This correctly suggests that, within market societies, there are various institutional forms and constitutional regimes for the press. Rosario de Mateo's (1989) sketch of the newspaper industry in Spain during the Franco regime, the transition to democracy and the full restoration of democracy makes it clear that private, profit-making newspapers put ideological purity as their first priority under Franco. After Franco, however, the same private, profit-making press has emphasized profits first while providing more opportunity for freedom of expression. Where state-operated media in authoritarian political systems serve directly as agents of state social control, both public and privately owned media in liberal societies carry out a wider variety of roles, cheerleading the established order, alarming the citizenry about flaws in that order, providing a civic forum for political debate, acting as a battleground among contesting elites. Pnina Lahav and her colleagues have usefully surveyed press law in seven democratic societies. Lahav concludes that Sweden and the United States protect free expression better than the United Kingdom, France and the Federal Republic of Germany with 'a more elitist attitude toward the press' (Lahav, 1985: 4).

The distinction between 'market' and 'state' organization of media, or between commercial and public forms of broadcasting, is vital but masks important differences within each category. Public broadcasting may be a quasi-independent corporation or directly run by the government, its income may come from fees only (Japan, Britain and Sweden), or also from advertising (Germany, France, Italy), or from the government treasury (Canada). In Britain, cabinet ministries determine fee levels while in Japan, France and Germany, parliament makes the decision (Krauss, 2000). Each of these variations creates (and results from) a distinct politics of the media. In Norway, since 1969, and in Sweden, France and Austria since the 1970s, the state has subsidized newspapers directly, especially to strengthen those newspapers offering substantial political information but receiving low advertising revenues. These policies have sought to stop the decline in the number of newspapers and so to increase public access to a diversity of political viewpoints. The size of the subsidies has fallen off in recent years as governments have come to place more faith in market principles and the virtues of economic efficiency (Skogerbo, 1997; Murschetz, 1998). The 'state versus market' distinction gives no purchase whatever for assessing or understanding any of these variations.

When there is serious ideological contestation in liberal democracies, how does it take place? What institutional mechanisms or cultural traditions or contradictions of power provide room for debate and revision? Daniel Hallin, borrowing from the work of Jurgen Habermas, has argued that the opportunity for the media to offer dissenting views and to publicize scandalous news arises in part because they must attend as much to their own legitimation as to furthering the legitimation of the capitalist system as a whole (Hallin, 1984). If they fail to attend to their own integrity and their own credibility with audiences, they may in fact 'simply become ineffective ideological institutions'. This, it appears, is exactly what happened to official media in eastern Europe; readers there were famous for recognizing that the only reading worth doing is reading 'between the lines'.

The relation of news organizations to new information technologies is a feature of political economy that has occasioned more discussion in the news business than research among scholars. There are, of course, grand generalizations about how audio cassettes made possible Khomeini's revolution in Iran or how photocopiers, short-wave radio, CNN, satellite microwave relays and fax machines fuelled the end of the Soviet regime and helped keep Boris Yeltsin in control during the 1991 attempted coup (Shane, 1994: 261–67). But there has been little academic attention to the concrete consequences of the technological transformation of news production, both in print and in television. Indeed, as newspapers embrace both computer and telecommunications capabilities, the gap between broadcast and print newsrooms narrows. Where broadcasting always relied on print media for information and ideas, increasingly print relies on broadcast as well, and CNN is part of the taken-for-granted background noise in American newsrooms.

Beginning in the 1970s, newspapers have seen the introduction of VDTs, pagination (the electronic assembly of pages), online and database research, remote transmission and delivery, digital photo transmission and storage. The technologies are generally introduced to lower labour costs and to provide the technical capability to make the newspaper more 'user-friendly', with more interesting and attractive page design. The question for the sociology of news is what influence, overall, any of this has on the news product. Anthony Smith was probably the first to draw comprehensive attention to the issue (1980) but his work has not been followed up with the same analytic skill. We know that the new technology has moved elements of newspaper production from the 'back-shop' to the newsroom, has increased the amount of time editors spend on page make-up and has improved spelling. But has it changed the news product in any more fundamental ways? Some observers suggest that the ability of foreign correspondents to send home copy by satellite has led to more and shorter stories on timely events rather than fewer, longer, more analytic and less time-bound work. This may decrease the quality of news (Weaver and Wilhoit, 1991: 158–59). But hard evidence on how new technology affects the news, or even hypotheses about it, are limited.

Both scholars and critics, including critics in or close to the news business itself, view recent technological and market changes with alarm. When a 'new news' responds to corporate concerns and technological imperatives, the ethics of professional journalism seems under ever-growing assault (Kalb, 1998). The anecdotal evidence here is sobering, but the baseline of comparison is feebly depicted. The worst incidences of contemporary journalism get compared to the remembered best of another era; there is a need for more careful comparison and more broadly conceived research frameworks. It is very likely that some of the worst instances of contemporary journalism are made possible by some of the same forces – particularly the force of semi-independent professionalism and a declining deference to authority in public culture – that creates the best (Schudson, 1999).

The social organization of newswork

In an influential essay, Harvey Molotch and Marilyn Lester (1974) created a typology of news stories according to whether the news 'occurrence' is planned or unplanned and, if planned, whether its planners are or are not also promoting it as news. If an event is planned and then promoted as news by its planners, this is a 'routine' news item. If the event is planned by one person or organization but promoted as news by someone else, it is a 'scandal'. If the event is unplanned, it becomes news as an 'accident'.

This defines news by the way it comes to the awareness of a news organization. For Molotch and Lester, it is a mistake to try to compare news accounts to 'reality' in the way journalism critics ordinarily do, labelling the discrepancy 'bias'. Instead, they seek out the purposes that create one reality instead of another. The news provides a 'reality' that is 'the political work by which events are constituted by those who happen to currently hold power' (1974: 111). Molotch and Lester reject what they call the 'objectivity assumption' in journalism – not that the media are objective but that there is a real world to be objective about. For them, the news media reflect not a world 'out there' but 'the practices of those who have the power to determine the experience of others' (1974: 54).

In 1974 this strong statement of the subordination of knowledge to power announced a liberating insight. A quarter-century later, Molotch and Lester's basic claim too often has been lifted off its social foundation in writings on the media that ignore how journalists operate within a set of real constraints – among them, the constraint of having to write 'accurately' about actual (objectively real) occurrences in the world, whoever planned them and however they came to the media's notice. The reality-constructing practices of the powerful will fail (in the long run) if they run roughshod over the world 'out there'.

Still, the basic orientation that takes news-making as a reality-constructing activity governed by elites has proved enormously useful. Mark Fishman conducted a participant-observation study at a middle-sized California newspaper to find that journalists are highly attuned to bureaucratic organizations of government and that *'the world is bureaucratically organized for journalists'* (1980: 51). That is, the organization of 'beats' is such that reporters get the largest share of their news from official government agencies. 'The journalist's view of the society as bureaucratically structured is the very basis upon which the journalist is able to detect events' (1980: 51). One of the great advantages of dealing with bureaucracies for the journalist is that the bureaucracies 'provide for the continuous detection of events' (1980: 52). The bureaucrat provides a reliable and steady supply of the raw materials for news production.

One study after another comes up with essentially the same observation. It matters not whether the study is at national or local level – journalism, on a day-to-day basis, is the story of the interaction of reporters and government officials, both politicians and bureaucrats. Some analysts claim that officials have the upper hand (Gans, 1979: 116; Cohen, 1963: 267; Bennett, 1994: 23–29; Dorman, 1994: 76; Schlesinger and Tumber, 1994). Some media critics, including many government officials, say that reporters have (Hess, 1984: 109). But there is little doubt that the centre of news generation is the link between reporter and official, the interaction of the representatives of the news bureaucracies and the government bureaucracies (Sigal, 1973).

This is apparent in the daily practices of journalists. 'The only important tool of the reporter is his news sources and how he uses them', a reporter covering state government in the United States told Delmer Dunne (1969: 41). Stephen Hess confirms this in his study of Washington correspondents. He found reporters 'use no documents in the preparation of nearly three-quarters of their stories' (Hess, 1981: 17–18). Hess does not count press releases as documents – these are, of course, another means of communication directly from official to reporter. It is clear that the reporter–official connection makes news an important tool of government and other established authorities. Some studies accordingly examine news production from the viewpoint of the news source rather than the news organization (Cook, 1989) or focus on the links between reporters and their sources in 'source–media analysis' (Schlesinger and Tumber, 1994: 28).

A corollary to the power of the government source or other well-legitimated sources is that 'resource-poor organizations' have great difficulty in getting the media's attention (Goldenberg, 1975). If they are to be covered, as Todd Gitlin's study of American anti-war activities in the 1960s indicated, they must adjust to modes of organizational interaction more like those of established organizations (Gitlin, 1980).

The significance of reporter/source studies lies not only in detailing the dynamics of news production but in evaluating the power of media institutions as such. Media power looms especially large if we assume that the portrait of the world the media present to audiences stems from the preferences and perceptions of publishers, editors and reporters unconstrained by democratic controls. However, if the media typically mirror the views and voices of established (and democratically selected) government officials, then the media are more nearly the neutral servants of a democratic order. To note a recent instance, policy experts widely attacked American television news for forcing the United States to intervene with military force in Somalia in 1992 by showing graphic scenes of starving people. But Jonathan Mermin's research shows that the networks picked up the Somalia story only after seven senators, a house committee, the full house, the full senate, a presidential candidate and the White House all publicly raised the issue. When the networks finally got to it, they framed it very much as Washington's political elites had framed it for them (Mermin, 1997: 397). This does not mean the TV stories made no difference – clearly they rallied public interest and public support for intervention. But where did the TV story come from? Not from thin air, and not from reporters, but from established, official sources.

The consistent finding that official sources dominate the news is invariably presented as a criticism of the media. If the media were to fulfil their democratic role, they would offer a wide variety of opinions and perspectives to encourage citizens to choose among them in evaluating public policies. But there is an alternate view also consistent with democratic theory. What if the best to hope for in a mass democracy is that people evaluate leaders, not policies? What if asking the press to offer enough information, history and context for attentive citizens to make wise decisions on policies before politicians act is asking the impossible? It may be a more plausible task for the media, consistent with representative democracy, that citizens assess leaders after they have acted (Zaller, 1994: 201–02).

There has been more attention to reporter–official relations than to reporter–editor relations, a second critical aspect of the social organization of newswork. Despite some suggestive early work on the ways in which reporters engage in self-censorship when they have an eye fixed on pleasing an editor (Breed, 1952/1980 and 1955), systematic sociological research has not been especially successful in this domain. Certainly case studies of newswork regularly note the effects – usually baleful – of editorial intervention (Crouse, 1973: 186; Gitlin, 1980: 64–65; Hallin, 1986: 22) Frands Mortensen and Erik Svendsen (1980) pay explicit attention to various forms of self-censorship in Danish newspapers. Generally, however, studies do not look at the social relations of newswork from the editor's desk.

Most research, then, has focused on the gathering of news rather than on its writing, rewriting and 'play' in the press. This is unfortunate when research suggests that it is in the *play* of a story that real influence comes. Hallin (1986), Herman and Chomsky (1988) and Lipstadt (1986) all argue that in the press of a liberal society like the United States lots of news, including dissenting or adversarial information and opinion, gets into the newspaper. The question is *where* that information appears and how it is inflected. Hallin suggests there was a 'reverse inverted pyramid' of news in much reporting of the Vietnam War. The nearer the information was to the truth, the further down in the story it appeared (1986: 78).

If more work develops on the relations of reporters and editors inside the newsroom, it can learn much from the comparative studies initiated by Wolfgang Donsbach and Thomas Patterson, reported by Donsbach (1995), and further developed in a careful British-German comparison by Esser (1998). Where there are many job designations in a British newsroom, all personnel in a German newsroom are '*Redakteurs*' – editors or desk workers – who combine the tasks of reporting, copy-editing, editorial or leader writing and commentary. Where editors read and edit the work of reporters in a British or American newspaper, what a *Redakteur* writes goes into print without anyone's exercising supervision. Different historical traditions have led to different divisions of labour and different understandings of the possibility and desirability of separating facts from commentary.

If one theoretical source for the sociology of news has been symbolic interactionism or social constructionist views of society (as in the work of Molotch and Lester, Tuchman and others), a complementary source has been organizational or bureaucratic theory. If, on the one hand, the creation of news is seen as the social production of 'reality', on the other hand it is taken to be the social manufacture of an organizational product, one that can be studied like other manufactured goods. This latter point of view is evident, for instance, in Edward Jay Epstein's early study (1973) that grew out of a political science seminar at Harvard on organizational theory. That seminar took its working assumption to be that members of an organization 'modified their own personal values in accordance with the requisites of the organization' (1973: xiv). One should therefore study organizations, not individuals, to analyse the 'output' they produce – in this case, news. Epstein's study, based on fieldwork at national network news programmes in 1968 and 1969, emphasized the organizational, economic and technical requirements of television news production in explaining the news product. Epstein found the technical constraints of television news particularly notable. These, of course, have changed radically and rapidly in the past two decades – a serious historical account of this technological revolution remains to be written. A broadly comparative sociology of news would observe how the absence of some technical and logistical features of news production taken for granted in advanced economies limits news coverage in developing nations. In Ghana, for instance, poor communication between cities and rural areas, including the frequent breakdown of lorries carrying newspapers to the countryside, has helped confine reporting to urban areas and issues (Twumasi, 1985).

Who are the journalists in news organizations who cover beats, interview sources, rewrite press releases from government bureaus and occasionally take the initiative in ferreting out hidden or complex stories? If organizational theorists are correct, it does not matter. Whoever they are, they will be socialized quickly into the values and routines of daily journalism. A cross-national survey by Colin Sparks and Slavko Splichal (1989) apparently supports this view: despite different national cultures, despite different patterns of professional education, and despite different labour patterns of journalists (some in strong professional associations or unions, some not), the stated professional values of the journalists do not differ greatly. Surveys in Germany by Lutz Hagen likewise find relatively modest differences in journalists' occupational norms between those trained in the West and those whose education and professional socialization was entirely in the state and party-run schools and media organizations of the former German Democratic Republic (East Germany). West and East

German journalists equally (89 per cent and 84 per cent respectively) aspire to be 'neutral reporters' (Hagen, 1997: 14).

It is best to be cautious about this survey data. Twice as many East Germans as West Germans (25 per cent to 11 per cent) say that a journalist should be a 'politician using alternative means' (Hagen, 1997: 14). Even when journalists uphold the same nominal values, they may do so for different reasons. In communist Poland, journalists were strongly attached to professionalism, not out of occupational autonomy but as a refuge from 'the unpleasant push and pull of political forces' (Curry, 1990: 207). Professionalism was a set of values and practices that protected the Polish journalist from manipulation by the Communist Party, government bureaucrats and the sponsoring organization of each newspaper or journal. Even so, Karol Jakubowicz observes that it has proved difficult for journalists in eastern Europe to shed a sense of journalism as a form of political advocacy (1995: 136–37). We may simply not comprehend the discrepancy between 'professional values' revealed in surveys and actual journalistic practice (de Smaele, 1999: 180).

Whether there is a convergence of journalistic practices and precepts is an important question. There are signs of a shared professional culture, promoted by what has been called 'the global newsroom' (Gurevitch, Levy and Roeh, 1991). There is evidence that political journalists from different countries (Italy, the Soviet Union, the United States) covering the same international event all adopt common themes and a common orientation to addressing 'humanity' rather than particular national audiences (Hallin and Mancini, 1991). Convergence may increase as western public agencies, private corporations and non-profit organizations promote a liberal model of market-based journalism in eastern Europe and the former Soviet Union (Mickiewicz, 1998).

Journalists at mainstream publications everywhere accommodate to the political culture of the regime in which they operate. Still, ideals of journalistic professionalism may incline journalists toward acting to support freedom of expression. In China, some journalists have developed a professional devotion to freedom of expression and have been a pressure group for the liberalization of press laws (Polumbaum, 1993; Zhao, 1998). In Brazil under military rule in the 1960s and 1970s, reporters grew adept at sabotaging the government's efforts at censorship (Dassin, 1982: 173–76).

Some American scholars have insisted that professional values are no bulwark against a bias in news that emerges from the social backgrounds and personal values of media personnel. S. Robert Lichter, Stanley Rothman and Linda S. Lichter (1986) made the case that news in the United States has a liberal 'bias' because journalists at elite news organizations are themselves liberal. Their survey of these journalists finds that many describe themselves as liberals and tend to vote Democratic. This is a moderate liberalism, at most, and only within the peculiar American political spectrum: the group is more socially liberal (53 per cent say adultery is not wrong) than economically liberal (only 13 per cent think government should own big corporations). American elite journalists fully accept the framework of capitalism although they wish for it a human face.

The Lichter, Rothman and Lichter approach has been criticized for failing to show that the news product reflects the personal views of journalists rather than the views of the officials whose positions they are reporting (Gans, 1985). American journalists, more than their counterparts in Germany, are committed to their ideology of dispassion, their sense of professionalism, their allegiance to fairness or objectivity (Donsbach, 1995). They have a professional commitment to shielding their work from their personal political leanings. Moreover, their political leanings tend to be weak. Several close observers find leading American journalists not so much liberal or conservative as apolitical (Gans, 1979: 184; Hess, 1981: 115).

Critics and activists who advocate the hiring of more women and minorities in the newsroom share the intuition of Rothman and the Lichters that the personal values journalists bring to their jobs from their social backgrounds will colour the news they produce. New hiring practices to develop a newsroom more representative of the population by gender and ethnicity should thus transform the news product itself. News should become more oriented to groups often subordinated or victimized in society. Some anecdotal evidence (Mills, 1990) suggests that a changing gender composition of the newsroom does influence news content, but other reports suggest that definitions of news have not dramatically changed (Beasley, 1993: 129–30). In the United States there has been more fear that the growing affluence of national journalists who report by fax and phone and access databases from their computers will remove them from direct contact with the poor, than there has been hope that more minorities and women in the newsroom will make the press more responsive to a broader constituency.

What is fundamental in organizational approaches, as opposed to the social recruitment/personal values approach of Rothman and the Lichters, is the emphasis on (a) constraints imposed by organizations despite the private intentions of the individual actors and (b) the inevitability of 'social construction' of reality in any social system. Both points are crucial. As for the first, it should be noted that constraints come not only from the news organizations reporters work for directly but from patterns of news-gathering that bring reporters from different publications under the influence of one another. In the United States, there is criticism of 'pack journalism', where reporters covering the same beat or story tend to emphasize the same angle and adopt the same viewpoint. In Japan, a kind of bureaucratized 'pack journalism' has become entrenched. 'Reporters' clubs' are organizations of reporters assigned to a particular ministry, and most basic news comes from reporters in these clubs. Since most clubs are connected to government agencies, news takes on an official cast. The daily association of reporters at the clubs contributes to a uniformity in the news pages; reporters are driven by what is described as a 'phobia' about not writing what all the other reporters write (Feldman, 1993: 98, 120–23; Krauss, 2000; Freeman, 2000).

As for the second point, analysts from a social organizational perspective hold that news is not a report on a factual world but 'a depletable consumer product that must be made fresh daily' (Tuchman, 1978: 179). It is not a gathering of facts that already exist; indeed, as Tuchman has argued, facts are defined organizationally – facts are 'pertinent information gathered by professionally validated methods specifying the relationship between what is known and how it is known. . . . In news, verification of facts is both a political and a professional accomplishment' (1978: 82–83). I am now inclined to add 'yes, but': events in the world do not magically transform themselves into news, yes; but the process of news production interacts with a set of actual occurrences that news producers and news sources do not entirely control or anticipate. Hurricanes happen, wars break out, elections take place. The news media can, of course, frame these events in different ways, but they can also embarrass themselves or disgrace themselves by ignoring the facts or representing them in ways that belie common observation.

Little has been said here about the differences between print and television news. There is much to say, of course, but in terms of basic news-gathering tasks, less than meets the eye. Most television news stories come from print sources, especially the wire services (Krauss, 2000). American evidence suggests that, at least for national news, print and television journalists share a great deal in their professional values. Separate studies of how print and TV journalists use experts, for instance, reveal that in foreign policy coverage, both prefer former government officials to other kinds of experts (Steele, 1995; Hallin, Manoff and Weddle, 1993). What Janet Steele calls the 'operational bias' in TV news – selecting for experts who personally know the key players, who have strong views on a limited range of policy alternatives and who will make short-term predictions are also characteristics print journalists seek. Even the television preference for experts who can turn a good phrase is one that print journalists also share.

For all the acclaim CNN won for its coverage of the 1991 Gulf War, in 1996 it had just twenty bureaux and thirty-five correspondents outside the United States, compared to about a hundred bureaux for each of the leading global wire services: Agence France-Presse, Associated Press and Reuters, each employing between 300 and 600 correspondents and photographers (Moisy, 1996). News outlets, both print and television, rely overwhelmingly on these services.

Cultural approaches

In social organizational approaches, the fact that news is 'constructed' suggests that it is *socially* constructed, elaborated in the interaction of the news-making players with one another. But the emphasis on the human construction of news can be taken in another direction. Anthropologist Marshall Sahlins has written in a different context that 'an event is not just a happening in the world; it is a *relation* between a certain happening and a given symbolic system' (1985: 153). Social-organizational approaches do not focus on the cultural givens within which everyday interaction happens in the first place. These cultural givens, while they may be uncovered by detailed historical analysis, cannot be extrapolated from features of social organization at the moment of study. They are a part of culture – a given symbolic system within which and in relation to which reporters and officials go about their duties.

Most understandings of the generation of news merge a 'cultural' view with the social organizational view. It is, however, analytically distinct. Where the organizational view finds interactional determinants of news in the relations between people, the cultural view finds symbolic determinants of news in the relations between 'facts' and symbols. A cultural account of news helps explain generalized images and stereotypes in the news media – of predatory stockbrokers just as much as hard-drinking factory workers – that transcend structures of ownership or patterns of work relations. In Paul Hartmann's and Charles Husband's analysis of British mass media coverage of racial conflict, for instance, they note that, 'The British cultural tradition contains elements derogatory to foreigners, particularly blacks. The media operate within the culture and are obliged to use cultural symbols' (1973: 274). Frank Pearce, in examining media coverage of homosexuals in Britain (1973), takes as a theoretical starting point anthropologist Mary Douglas's view that all societies like to keep their cultural concepts clean and neat and are troubled by 'anomalies' that do not fit the pre-conceived categories of the culture. Homosexuality is an anomaly in societies that take as fundamental the opposition and relationship of male and female; thus homosexuals provide a culturally charged topic for storytelling that seeks to preserve or reinforce the conventional moral order of society – and its conceptual or symbolic foundation. News stories about homosexuals, says Pearce, may be moral tales, 'a negative reference point . . . an occasion to reinforce conventional moral values by telling a moral tale. Through these means tensions in the social system can be dealt with and "conventionalized"' (1973: 293).

A cultural account of this sort can explain too much; after all, news coverage of homosexuality has changed enormously since Pearce wrote his article, a universal cultural anxiety about anomalous categories notwithstanding. A 1996 study of US news coverage concludes that gays and lesbians appear much more in the news than fifty years ago, are covered much more 'routinely' as ordinary news subjects rather than moral tales, and that while coverage is not free of anti-gay prejudice, it is generally fair (Alwood, 1996: 315).

Similarly, broad cultural explanations of the prevalence and character of crime news (Katz, 1987) must also be evaluated with some caution. While it makes sense that broad and long-lasting phenomena – like heavy news coverage of crime over two centuries across many societies – will have deep cultural roots, it is also important to recognize fashions, trends and changes in crime coverage. Joel Best (1999) provides a useful account of why some newly defined crimes receive only occasional or episodic press coverage and others, with better institutionalized support in a 'victim industry', receive more systematic and ongoing treatment. What is at stake here is the interaction of general cultural and specific social-organizational dimensions of news.

Journalists may resonate to the same cultural moods their audiences share even if they typically know little about their audiences. American journalists underestimated the size of their working-class audience (Gans, 1979: 238–39). Soviet journalists overestimated the education level of their readers and underestimated the proportion of women in their audience (Remington, 1988: 167). Herbert Gans found that the reporters and editors he studied at US news weeklies and network television programmes 'had little knowledge about the actual audience and rejected feedback from it'. They typically assumed that 'what interested them would interest the audience' (1979: 230). It would be instructive to know more about the image of the reader in the journalists' minds.

A cultural account of news is also relevant to understanding journalists' vague renderings of how they know 'news' when they see it. The central categories of newsworkers themselves are 'cultural' more than structural. Stuart Hall has tried to define the indefinable 'news values' or 'news sense' that journalists regularly talk about. He writes:

'News values' are one of the most opaque structures of meaning in modern society. All 'true journalists' are supposed to possess it: few can or are willing to identify and define it. Journalists speak of 'the news' as if events select themselves. Further, they speak as if which is the 'most significant' news story, and which 'news angles' are most salient are divinely inspired. Yet of the millions of events which occur every day in the world, only a tiny proportion ever become visible as 'potential news stories': and of this proportion, only a small fraction are actually produced as the day's news in the news media. We appear to be dealing, then, with a 'deep structure' whose function as a selective device is un-transparent even to those who professionally most know how to operate it.

(Hall, 1973: 181)

This is exactly right, at least for journalism in liberal societies. In the Soviet Union, the matter was much simpler – 'the party's conception of newsworthiness becomes the journalists' (Remington, 1988: 169; Davis, Hammond and Nizamova, 1998: 84), although there is evidence even in pre-Gorbachev days that Soviet journalists held professional values distinct from party directives (Mills, 1981). Gaye Tuchman's observation on American journalists parallels Hall's on the British when she writes that 'news judgement is the sacred knowledge, the secret ability of the newsman which differentiates him from other people' (1972: 672).

The cultural knowledge that constitutes 'news judgement' is too complex and too implicit to label simply 'ideology' or the 'common sense' of a hegemonic system. News judgement is not so unified, intentional and functional a system as these terms suggest. Its presuppositions are in some respects rooted much more deeply in human consciousness and can be found much more widely distributed in human societies than capitalism or socialism or industrialism or any other particular system of social organization and domination can comprehend. Patriarchal and sexist outlooks, for instance, may well be turned to the service of capitalism, but this does not make them capitalist in origin nor does it mean that they fit capitalist structures especially well.

A specific example may illustrate the many dimensions of this problem. Why, Johan Galtung and Mari Ruge (1970) ask, are news stories so often 'personified'? Why do reporters write of persons and not structures, of individuals and not social forces? They cite a number of possible explanations, some of which are 'cultural'. There is cultural idealism – the western view that individuals are masters of their own destiny, responsible for their acts through the free will they exercise. There is the nature of story-telling itself, with the need in narrative to establish 'identification' There is also what they call the 'frequency factor' – that people act during a time span that fits the frequency of the news media (daily) better than do the actions of 'structures' that are much harder to connect with specific events in a 24-hour cycle.

Is this last point a 'social structural' or a 'cultural' phenomenon? In some respects, it is structural – if the media operated monthly or annually rather than daily, perhaps they would speak more often of social forces than of individuals. Indeed, examining journalism's 'year-end reviews' would very likely turn up more attention to social trends and structural changes than can be found in the daily news. But, then, is the fact that the press normally operates on a daily basis structural or cultural? Is there some basic primacy to the daily cycle of the press, of business, of government, of sleeping and waking, that makes the institutions of journalism inescapably human and person-centred in scale?

Or might there be some more or less universal processes of human perception that lead to an emphasis on the individual? Does this have less to do with some-thing peculiarly American or western or capitalistic than it does with what psy-chologists refer to as the 'fundamental attribution error' in human causal thinking – attributing to individuals in the foreground responsibility or agency for causation that might better be attributed to background situations or large-scale trends or structures? That news definitions and news values differ across cultures can be demonstrated by comparative research. For instance, the Soviet media, like western media, operated on a daily cycle, but very little of the news treated happenings in the prior 24 hours (Mickiewicz, 1988: 30). Soviet news organizations operated according to long-range political plans and stockpiled stories and editorial to meet political needs (Remington, 1988: 116). The sense of immediacy taken by western media to be a requirement of news (and often taken by critics to be an ideologically loaded weakness of journalism) is not, the Soviet case would suggest, an invariant feature of bureaucratic organization, occupational routines or a universal diurnal human rhythm. It is rooted instead in a nation-specific political culture.

So one need not adopt assumptions about universal properties of human nature and human interest (although it would be foolish to dismiss them out of hand) to acknowledge that there are aspects of news generation that go beyond what sociological analysis of news organizations is normally prepared to handle. Richard Hoggart has written that the most important filter through which news is constructed is 'the cultural air we breathe, the whole ideological atmosphere of our society, which tells us that some things can be said and that others had best not be said' (Bennett, 1982: 303). That 'cultural air' is one that, in part, rul-ing groups and institutions create but it is also, in part, one in whose social con-text their own establishment takes place.

The cultural air has both a form and content. The content, the substance of taken-for-granted values, has often been discussed. Many studies, in a number of countries, have noted that violent crimes are greatly over-reported in relation to their actual incidence (Katz, 1987: 57–58). Over-reporting takes place not only in the popular press but (to a lesser degree) in the mid-market and quality press, too (Schlesinger and Tumber, 1994: 185). Gans (1979) describes the core values of American journalism as ethnocentrism (surely a core value in journal-ism around the world), altruistic democracy, responsible capitalism, small-town pastoralism, individualism and moderatism. These are the unquestioned and generally unnoticed background assumptions through which news in the United States is gathered and within which it is framed.

If elements of content fit conventional notions of ideology or the common sense of a hegemonic system (Gans calls them 'para-ideology'), aspects of form operate at a more subtle level. By 'form', I refer to assumptions about narrative, story-telling, human interest, and the conventions of photographic and linguis-tic presentation in news production. Weaver (1975) has shown some systematic differences between the inverted-pyramid structure of print news and the 'the-matic' structure of television news; Schudson (1982) has argued that the inverted-pyramid form is a peculiar development of late nineteenth-century American journalism, and one that implicitly authorized the journalist as polit-ical expert and helped redefine politics itself as a subject appropriately discussed by experts rather than partisans; Hallin and Mancini (1984) demonstrate in a comparison of television news in Italy and the United States that formal conventions of news reporting, often attributed to the technology of television by analysts or to 'the nature of things' by journalists, in fact stem from features of a country's political culture. Schudson (1994, 1995) shows that even the familiar social practice of interviewing, and the conventions of news-writing connected to it, has specific roots in late nineteenth-century American culture. Chalaby (1996) goes so far as to claim that journalism itself is 'an Anglo-American invention', an extravagant claim that none the less rightly calls attention to the role of English and American culture in promoting a fact-centred, report-centred journalism. All of this work recognizes that news is a form of literature and that among the resources journalists work with are the traditions of story-telling, picture-making and sentence construction they inherit from their own cultures, with a number of vital assumptions about the world built in.

Reporters breathe a specifically journalistic, occupational cultural air as well as the air they share with fellow citizens. The 'routines' of journalists are not only social, emerging out of interactions among officials, reporters and editors, but literary, emerging out of interactions of writers with literary traditions. More than that, journalists at work operate not only to maintain and repair their social relations with sources and colleagues but their cultural image as journalists in the eyes of a wider world. Robert Manoff shows how television news reporters deploy experts in stories not so much to provide viewers with information but to certify the journalist's 'effort, access, and superior knowledge' (1989: 69). Barbie Zelizer (1990) has demonstrated the ways that reporters in American broadcast news visually and verbally establish their own authority by suggesting their personal proximity to the events they cover. Regardless of how the news was in fact 'gathered', it is presented in a style that promotes an illusion of the journalists' adherence to the journalistic norm of proximity. The reality journalists manufacture provides not only a version and vision of 'the world' but of 'journalism' itself.

Cultural form may also refer to language itself. Prognostications of a 'global village' unified by new globe-spanning satellite communications founder on the persistent strength of local and regional language loyalties and national identities. While CNN (Cable News Network) was by 1993 available in 140 countries, relatively small proportions of viewers regularly tune in. Euronews, similarly if on a smaller scale, is a five-language satellite-transmitted news channel launched in 1994 and available to millions, that is already experiencing the difficulties of one-world broadcasting in a multinational, multicultural human scene (Parker, 1994).

Most research on the culture of news production takes it for granted that, at least within a given national tradition, there is one common news standard among journalists. This is one of the convenient simplifications of the sociology of journalism that merits critical attention, and might indeed be a point at which a lot of current assumptions about how journalism works begin to unravel. Reporters who may adhere to norms of 'objectivity' in reporting on a political campaign (what Daniel Hallin calls the 'sphere of legitimate controversy') will not blink to report gushingly about a topic on which there is broad national consensus (the 'sphere of consensus') or to write derisively on a subject that lies beyond the bounds of popular consensus (the 'sphere of deviance') (Hallin, 1986: 117). It is as if journalists were unconsciously multilingual, code-switching from neutral interpreters to guardians of social consensus and back again without missing a beat. Elihu Katz and Daniel Dayan have noted how television journalists in Britain, the United States, Israel and elsewhere who narrate live 'media events' rather than ordinary daily news stories abandon a matter-of-fact style for 'cosmic lyricism' (1992: 108). Yoram Peri shows that the same code-switching took place in Israeli print journalism in covering the martyred Prime Minister Yitzhak Rabin. In life, Rabin walked in the sphere of legitimate controversy, but in death he was absorbed into the sphere of consensus (Peri, 1997).

Conclusions

The approaches to the study of news I have reviewed all have great strengths. All three approaches have greatly advanced our understanding of the media by focusing on the specific institutions and the specific processes in those institutions responsible for creating news. They have sought to abandon functionalist guidelines that understand the media by positing some general social function the media serve (although the political economy perspective is not yet free of a functionalist orientation). Still, an implicit normative functionalism has been smuggled into many studies: the idea that the news media *should* serve society by informing the general population in ways that arm them for vigilant citizenship. I am sympathetic to this as one goal the news media in a democracy should try to serve but it is not a very good approximation of what role the news media have historically played – anywhere. The news media have always been a more important forum for communication among elites (and some elites more than others) than with the general population.

In the best of circumstances, the fact of a general audience for the news media provides a regular opportunity for elites to be effectively embarrassed, even disgraced, as Brent Fisse and John Braithwaite show in their cross-national study of the impact of publicity on corporate offenders (1983). The combination of electoral democracy with a free press, economist Amartya Sen has argued, has prevented famines even when crops have failed (Sen and Dreze, 1989). But even here the 'audience' or the 'public' has a kind of phantom existence that the sociological study of news production has yet to consider in its theoretical formulations.

The three perspectives have their weaknesses, too. They are typically ahistorical, and ignore possibilities for change in the nature of news. They tend to be indifferent to comparative as well as to historical viewpoints. Comparative research is cumbersome, of course, even in the age of word processors and computer networking. And it is conceptually bedevilling. How can news be compared across countries when, in one country, the press is primarily national and in the next regional and local? How can comparison be made between the news media in a country where intellectual life is concentrated in a few media outlets and another where is it highly dispersed? Media studies are genuinely linked to national political issues – they are an academic meta-discourse on the daily defining of political reality. The motive for research, then, is normally conceived in isolation from comparative concerns. If this strengthens the immediate political relevance of media studies, it weakens their longer-term value as social science.

None of the three perspectives, by itself, can account for all that we might want to know. Take just one important example. There is a shift, reported in a number of studies from around the world, towards reporting styles that are more informal, more intimate, more critical and more cynically detached or distanced than earlier reporting. British television interviewing changed from a style formal and deferential toward politicians to a more aggressive and critical style that makes politicians 'answerable to the public through the television news interview' (Scannell, 1989: 146). Japanese broadcasting changed in a similar direction under the influence of news anchor Kume Hiroshi, whose 'alienated cynicism and critical stance toward society and government' appears to have charmed a younger, more urban and more alienated generation (Krauss, 1998: 686). Kume's style moved toward a type of politics 'more cynical and populist' than the old bureaucratic conservatism, but one that 'offers little in the way of the framing of real political alternatives' (Krauss, 1998: 686). In fact, Ellis Krauss argues, the Japanese political establishment now 'relies as much on a form of cynical inertia as on strong belief and allegiance to any positive values' (1998: 690).

Meanwhile, a new investigative aggressiveness in Latin American journalism may be a related development. In Brazil, Argentina and Peru, revelation of government scandals emerges not from old-fashioned partisan journalism but from a new, more entertainment-oriented journalism that adopts stock narratives and a telenovela-style personality-focused moralizing style. In Silvio Waisbord's view, the results do not contribute to a public accounting of the moral order but come from and reinforce cultural pessimism. Scandal becomes a form of entertainment at best, and contributes to political cynicism (Waisbord, 1997: 201).

Evidence of a more aggressive, less deferential style in American television news (Hallin, 1984) seems related. So, too, Norway's most popular newspaper, *Verdens Gang*, has adopted the melodramatic framework of tabloid journalism in covering politics. 'Politicians in a way become human beings, while the voters become customers' (Eide, 1997: 179). There is something at work here consistent with the developments in The Netherlands that Liesbet van Zoonen refers to as 'intimization' in the news (van Zoonen, 1991). This increased critical informality in journalism may be a feature of what social theorist Norbert Elias might see as part of the 'informalization' trend of the twentieth century (Elias, 1996).

Are these changes explained by shifts in political economy? Or social organization? Or culture? Clearly, all are involved. A future sociology of news production has to integrate them.

References

ALWOOD, E. (1996) *Straight News: Gays, Lesbians, and the News Media.* New York: Columbia University Press.

BAGDIKIAN, B. (1997), 5th edn, *The Media Monopoly.* Boston: Beacon Press.

BAKER, C.E. (1994) *Ownership of Newspapers: The View from Positivist Social Science.* Cambridge, MA: Joan Shorenstein Center on Press, Politics, and Public Policy, Research Paper R-12, Harvard University.

BEASLEY, M. (1993) 'Newspapers: Is There a New Majority Defining the News?' in P.J. Creedon, (ed.) *Women in Mass Communication.* Newbury Park, Ca: Sage.

BENNETT, T. (1982) 'Media, "Reality," Signification' in M. Gurevitch, T. Bennett, J. Curran and J. Woollacott, *Culture, Society and the Media*. London: Methuen, 287–308.

BENNETT, W.L. (1994) 'The News About Foreign Policy' in W.L. Bennett and D.L. Paletz (eds), *Taken by Storm: The Media, Public Opinion, and US Foreign Policy in the Gulf War*. Chicago: University of Chicago Press, 12–40.

BEST, J. (1999) *Random Violence: How We Talk About New Crimes and New Victims*. Berkeley: University of California Press.

BRANTS, K. (1998) 'Who's Afraid of Infotainment?', *European Journal of Communication* 13, 305–35.

BREED, W. (1952/1980) *The Newspaperman, News and Society*. New York: Arno Press.

——, (1955) 'Social Control in the Newsroom: A Functional Analysis', *Social Forces* 33: 326–55.

CHALABY, J.K. (1996) 'Journalism as Anglo-American Invention' in *European Journal of Communication* 13, 303–26.

COHEN, B.C. (1963) *The Press and Foreign Policy*. Princeton: Princeton University Press.

COHEN, S. and YOUNG, J. (eds) (1973) *The Manufacture of News: A Reader*. Beverly Hills: Sage.

COOK, T.E. (1989) *Making Laws and Making News: Media Strategies in the US House of Representatives*. Washington, DC: Brookings Institution.

CROUSE, T. (1973) *The Boys on the Bus*. New York: Ballantine.

CURRAN, J., DOUGLAS, A. and G. WHANNEL (1980) 'The Political Economy of the Human-Interest Story' in A. Smith (ed.), *Newspapers and Democracy*. Cambridge, MA: MIT Press, 288–342.

CURRY, J.L. (1990) *Poland's Journalists: Professionalism and Politics*. Cambridge: Cambridge University Press.

DASSIN, J. (1982) 'Press Censorship and the Military State in Brazil' in J.L. Curry and J.R. Dassin, *Press Control Around the World*. New York: Praeger, 149–86.

DAVIS, H., HAMMOND, P. and NIZAMOVA, L. (1998) 'Changing Identities and Practices in Post-Soviet Journalism: The Case of Tarstan', *European Journal of Communication* 13, 77–97.

DE MATEO, R. (1989) 'The Evolution of the Newspaper Industry in Spain, 1939–87', *European Journal of Communication* 4, 211–26.

DE SMAELE, H. (1999) 'The Applicability of Western Media Models on the Russian Media System', *European Journal of Communication* 14, 173–89.

DEMERS, D. (1996) 'Corporate Newspaper Structure, Editorial Page Vigor, and Social Change', *Journalism and Mass Communication Quarterly* 73, 857–77.

DONSBACH, W. (1995) 'Lapdogs, Watchdogs and Junkyard Dogs', *Media Studies Journal*, Fall: 17–30.

DORMAN, W.A. and LIVINGSTON, S. (1994) 'News and Historical Content: The Establishing Phase of the Persian Gulf Policy Debate' in W.L. Bennett and D.L. Paletz (eds), *Taken by Storm: The Media, Public Opinion, and US Foreign Policy in the Gulf War*. Chicago: University of Chicago Press, 63–81.

DREIER, P. (1982) 'Capitalists vs the Media: An Analysis of an Ideological Mobilization Among Business Leaders', *Media, Culture and Society* 4, 111–32.

DUNNE, D.D. (1969) *Public Officials and the Press*. Reading, MA: Addison-Wesley.

EIDE, M. (1997) 'A New Kind of Newspaper? Understanding a Popularization Process', *Media, Culture and Society* 19, 173–82.

ELIAS, N. (1996) 'Changes in European Standards of Behaviour in the Twentieth Century' in N. Elias, *The Germans*. New York: Columbia University Press, 23–43.

EPSTEIN, E.J. (1973) *News From Nowhere*. New York: Random House.

ESSER, F. (1998) 'Editorial Structures and Work Principles in British and German Newsrooms', *European Journal of Communication* 13, 375–405.

FELDMAN, O. (1993) *Politics and the News Media in Japan*. Ann Arbor: University of Michigan Press.

FISHMAN, M. (1980) *Manufacturing the News*. Austin: University of Texas Press.

FISSE, B. and BRAITHWAITE, J. (1983) *The Impact of Publicity on Corporate Offenders*. Albany: State University of New York Press.

FREEMAN, L.A. (2000) *Closing the Shop: Information Cartels and Japan's Mass Media*. Princeton: Princeton University Press.

GALTUNG, J. and RUGE, M. (1970) 'The Structure of Foreign News: The Presentation of the Congo, Cuba and Cyprus Crises in Four Foreign Newspapers' in J. Tunstall, (ed.) *Media Sociology: A Reader*. Urbana: University of Illinois Press, 259–98.

GANS, H.J. (1979) *Deciding What's News: A Study of CBS Evening News, NBC Nightly News, Newsweek and Time*. New York: Pantheon.

——, (1985) 'Are US Journalists Dangerously Liberal?' *Columbia Journalism Review* (November/December), 29–33.

GARNHAM, N. (1990) *Capitalism and Communication*. London: Sage.

GIEBER, W. (1964) 'News Is What Newspapermen Make It' in L.A. Dexter and D. Manning, *White, People, Society and Mass Communications*. New York: Free Press.

GITLIN, T. (1980) *The Whole World is Watching*. Berkeley: University of California Press.

GOLDENBERG, E. (1975) *Making the Papers*. Lexington, MA: DC Heath.

GRANT, J. (1988) 'Internal Reporting by Investigative Journalists in China and Its Influence on Government Policy', *Gazette* 41, 53–65.

GUREVITCH, M., LEVY, M.R. and ROEH, I. (1994) 'The Global Newsroom: Convergences and Diversities in the Globalization of Television News' in P. Dahlgren and C. Sparks (eds) *Communication and Citizenship*. London: Routledge.

GUREVITCH, M., BENNETT, T., CURRAN, J. and WOOLLACOTT, J. (eds) (1982) *Culture, Society and the Media*. London: Methuen.

HAGEN, L. (1997) 'The Transformation of the Media System of the Former German Democratic Republic After the Reunification and Its Effects on the Political Content of Newspapers', *European Journal of Communication* 12, 5–26.

HALL, S. (1973) 'The Determination of News Photographs' in S. Cohen and J. Young (eds) *The Manufacture of News: A Reader*. Beverly Hills: Sage, 176–90.

HALLIN, D.C. (1986) *'The Uncensored War': The Media and Vietnam*. New York: Oxford.

——, (1984). *We Keep America on Top of the World*. London: Routledge.

HALLIN, D.C. and MANCINI, P. (1984) 'Speaking of the President: Political Structure and Representational Form in US and Italian Television News', *Theory and Society* 13, 829–50.

——, (1991) 'Summits and the Constitution of an International Public Sphere: The Reagan-Gorbachev Meetings as Televised Media Events', *Communication* 12, 249–65.

HALLIN, D.C., MANOFF, R.K. and WEDDLE, J.K. (1993) 'Sourcing Patterns of National Security Reporters', *Journalism Quarterly* 70, 753–66.

HARTMANN, P. and HUSBAND, C. (1973) 'The Mass Media and Racial Conflict' in S. Cohen and J. Young (eds) *The Manufacture of News: A Reader*. Beverly Hills: Sage, 270–83.

HERMAN, E.S. and CHOMSKY, N. (1988) *Manufacturing Consent*. New York: Pantheon.

HESS, S. (1984) *The Government/Press Connection*. Washington, DC: The Brookings Institution.

——, (1981) *The Washington Reporters*. Washington: Brookings Institution.

HUGHES, H.M. (1940) *News and the Human Interest Story*. Chicago: University of Chicago Press.

JAKUBOWICZ, K. (1995) 'Media Within and Without the State: Press Freedom in Eastern Europe', *Journal of Communication* 45 (4), 125–39.

KALB, M. (1998) 'The Rise of the "New News": A Case Study of Two Root Causes of the Modern Scandal Coverage', Cambridge, MA: Joan Shorenstein Center on Press, Politics, and Public Policy, Discussion Paper D-34.

KATZ, E. and DAYAN, D. (1992) *Media Events: The Live Broadcasting of History*. Cambridge, MA: Harvard University Press.

KATZ, J. (1987) 'What Makes Crime "News"?' *Media, Culture and Society* 9, 47–76.

KEANE, J. (1991) *Liberty of the Press*. Cambridge: Polity Press.

KRAUSS, E. (1998) 'Changing Television News in Japan', *Journal of Asian Studies* 57, 663–92.

——, (2000) *Broadcasting Politics in Japan: NHK TV News*. Ithaca, NY: Cornell University Press.

LAHAV, P. (ed.) (1985) *Press Law in Modern Democracies: A Comparative Study*. New York: Longman.

LEE, J. (1997) 'Press Freedom and Democratization: South Korea's Experience and Some Lessons', *Gazette* 59 (2), 135–49.

LICHTER, S.R., ROTHMAN, S. and LICHTER, L.S. (1986) *The Media Elite: America's New Powerbrokers*. Bethesda, MD: Adler and Adler.

LIPSTADT, D. (1986) *Beyond Belief: The American Press and the Coming of the Holocaust 1933–1945*. New York: Free Press.

MCCHESNEY, R.W. (1997) *Corporate Media and the Threat to Democracy*. New York: Seven Stories Press.

MANOFF, R.K. (1989) 'Modes of War and Modes of Social Address: The Text of SDI', *Journal of Communication* 39, 59–84.

MAZZOLENI, G. (1995) 'Towards a "Videocracy"? Italian Political Communication at a Turning Point', *European Journal of Communication* 10, 291–319.

MCCHESNEY, R.W. (1997) *Corporate Media and the Threat to Democracy*. New York: Seven Stories Press.

MERMIN, J. (1997) 'Television News and American Intervention in Somalia: The Myth of a Media-Driven Foreign Policy', *Political Science Quarterly* 112, 385–403.

MICKIEWICZ, E. (1988) *Split Signals: Television and Politics in the Soviet Union*. New York: Oxford.

——, (1998) 'Media, Transition, and Democracy: Television and the Transformation of Russia' in R.G. Noll and M.E. Price (eds) *A Communications Cornucopia*. Washington, DC: Brookings Institution Press, 113–37.

MILLS, K. (1990) *A Place in the News*. New York: Dodd, Mead.

MILLS, R.D. (1981) 'The Soviet Journalist: A Cultural Analysis', PhD dissertation, University of Illinois. Ann Arbor: University Microfilms International.

MOISY, C. (1996) 'The Foreign News Flow in the Information Age', Cambridge, MA: Joan Shorenstein Center on Press, Politics, and Public Policy, Discussion Paper D-23.

MOLOTCH, H. and LESTER, M. (1974) 'News as Purposive Behavior: On the Strategic Use of Routine Events, Accidents, and Scandals', *American Sociological Review* 39, 101–12.

MORTENSEN, F. and SVENDSEN, E.N. (1980) 'Creativity and Control: The Journalist Betwixt His Readers and Editors', *Media, Culture and Society*, 2, 169–77.

MURDOCK, G. (1973) 'Political Deviance: The Press Presentation of a Militant Mass Demonstration' in S. Cohen and J. Young (eds) *The Manufacture of News: A Reader*. Beverly Hills: Sage, 156–75.

——, (1982) 'Large Corporations and the Control of the Communications Industries' in M. Gurevitch, T. Bennett, J. Curran and J. Woollacott, *Culture, Society and the Media*. London: Methuen, 118–50.

MURSCHETZ, P. (1998) 'State Support for the Daily Press in Europe: A Critical Appraisal', *European Journal of Communication* 13, 291–313.

NOAM, E. (1991) *Television in Europe*. New York: Oxford University Press.

PARK, R.E. (1922) *The Immigrant Press and its Control*. New York: Harper.

——, (1923) 'The Natural History of the Newspaper', *American Journal of Sociology* 29, 273–89.

PARKER, R. (1994) 'The Myth of Global News', *New Perspectives Quarterly* 11, 39–45.

PEARCE, F. (1973) 'How To Be Immoral and Ill, Pathetic and Dangerous, All At the Same Time: Mass Media and the Homosexual' in S. Cohen and J. Young (eds) *The Manufacture of News: A Reader*. Beverly Hills: Sage, 284–301.

PERI, Y. (1997) 'The Rabin Myth and the Press: Reconstruction of the Israeli Collective Identity', *European Journal of Communication* 12, 435–58.

POLUMBAUM, J. (1993) 'Professionalism in China's Press Corps' in R.V. Des Forges, L. Ning, and W. Yen-bo (eds) *China's Crisis of 1989*. Albany: SUNY Press, 295–311.

——, (1994). 'To Protect or Restrict: Points of Contention in China's Draft Press Law' in P.B. Potter (ed.) *Domestic Law Reforms in Post-Mao China*. Armonk, NY: ME Sharpe, 247–69.

——, (1997) 'Political Fetters, Commercial Freedoms: Restraint and Excess in Chinese Mass Communications' in C. Hudson (ed.) *Regional Handbook of Economic and Political Development*, Vol. 1, Chicago: Fitzroy Dearborn.

REMINGTON, T.F. (1988) *The Truth of Authority: Ideology and Communication in the Soviet Union*. Pittsburgh: University of Pittsburgh Press.

SAHLINS, M. (1985) *Islands of History*. Chicago: University of Chicago Press.

SCANNELL, P. (1989) 'Public Service Broadcasting and Modern Public Life', *Media, Culture and Society* 11, 135–66.

SCHLESINGER, P. and TUMBER, H. (1994) *Reporting Crime: The Media Politics of Criminal Justice*. Oxford: Clarendon Press.

SCHUDSON, M. (1982) 'The Politics of Narrative Form: The Emergence of News Conventions in Print and Television', *Daedalus* 111, 97–113.

——, (1994) 'Question Authority: A History of the News Interview in American Journalism, 1860s–1930s', *Media, Culture & Society* 16, 565–87.

——, (1995) *The Power of News*. Cambridge: Harvard University Press.

——, (1999) 'Social Origins of Press Cynicism in Portraying Politics', *American Behavioral Scientist* 42, 998–1008.

SEN, A. and DREZE, J. (1989) *Hunger and Public Action*. Oxford: Clarendon Press.

SHANE, S. (1994) *Dismantling Utopia: How Information Ended the Soviet Union*. Chicago: Ivan R. Dee.

SIGAL, L.V. (1973) *Reporters and Officials*. Lexington, MA: Lexington Books.

SKOGERBO, E. (1997) 'The Press Subsidy System in Norway', *European Journal of Communication* 12, 99–118.

SMITH, A. (1980) *Goodbye Gutenberg*. New York: Oxford University Press.

SPARKS, C. and SPLICHAL, S. (1989) 'Journalistic Education and Professional Socialisation', *Gazette* 43, 31–52.

STEELE, J.E. (1995) 'Experts and the Operational Bias of Television News: The Case of the Persian Gulf War', *Journalism and Mass Communication Quarterly* 72, 799–812.

TUCHMAN, G. (1972) 'Objectivity as Strategic Ritual: An Examination of Newsmen's Notions of Objectivity', *American Journal of Sociology* 77, 660–79.

——, (1976) 'Telling Stories', *Journal of Communication* 26 (Fall), 93–97.

——, (1978) *Making News: A Study in the Construction of Reality*. New York: Free Press.

TWUMASI, Y. (1985) 'Social Class and Newspaper Coverage in Ghana' in F.O. Ugboaja (ed.) *Mass Communication, Culture and Society in West Africa*. München: K.G. Saur, Hans Zell Publishers, 219–20.

VAN ZOONEN, L. (1991) 'A Tyranny of Intimacy? Women, Femininity and Television News' in P. Dahlgren and C. Sparks (eds) *Communication and Citizenship*. London: Routledge, 217–35.

WAISBORD, S. (1995) 'Leviathan Dreams: State and Broadcasting in South America', *Communication Review* 1, 201–26.

——, (1997) 'The Narrative of Exposes in South American Journalism', *Gazette* 59, 189–203.

WEAVER, D. and WILHOIT, G.C. (1991), 2nd edn, *The American Journalist*. Bloomington: Indiana University Press.

WEAVER, P. (1975) 'Newspaper News and Television News' in D. Cater and R. Adler (eds) *Television as a Social Force*. New York: Praeger.

WEBER, M. (1921/1946) 'Politics as a Vocation' in H. Gerth and C.W. Mills (eds) *Max Weber: Essays in Sociology*, 77–128.

WHITE, D.M. (1950) 'The Gatekeeper: A Case Study in the Selection of News', *Journalism Quarterly* 27, 383–90. Also reprinted in L.A. Dexter and D.M. White (eds) (1964) *People, Society, and Mass Communications*. New York: Free Press.

ZALLER, J. (1994), 'Elite Leadership of Mass Opinion: New Evidence from the Gulf War' in W.L. Bennett and D.L. Paletz (eds) *Taken by Storm: The Media, Public Opinion, and US Foreign Policy in the Gulf War*. Chicago: University of Chicago Press, 186–209.

ZELIZER, B. (1990) 'Where is the Author in American TV News? On the Construction and Presentation of Proximity, Authorship, and Journalistic Authority', *Semiotica* 80, 37–48.

ZHAO, Y. (1998) *Media, Market, and Democracy in China: Between the Party Line and the Bottom Line*. Urbana: University of Illinois Press.

9

Entertainment

Simon Frith

Introduction

'Entertainment' is a term that always seems to be used with a hint of disdain: entertainment is always just entertainment. There are two implicit contrasts involved here. One rests on an aesthetic judgement: entertainment (fun, of the moment, trivial) is being contrasted to art (serious, transcendent, profound). The other rests on a political judgement: entertainment (insignificant, escapist) is being contrasted with news, with reality, with truth.

The media themselves – the press and broadcasting, at least – have historically built such contrasts into their own organizational framework. News rather than entertainment is the way to editorial or corporate power (if not to wealth and stardom); news rather than entertainment is the source of public influence. One effect of this is the suggestion, widespread in Europe at least, that the 'devaluation' of broadcasting caused by deregulation can be measured by the rise of entertainment shows at the expense of news and documentaries. Press commentators, too, tend to describe the decay of the tabloid press in terms of a shift from news to entertainment pages. 'Dumbing down' thus describes both a confusion of news and entertainment values (in docu-soaps, talk shows like Jerry Springer's, the press coverage of media personalities) and the increasing influence on newspaper and broadcasting policy of entertainment and 'lifestyle' editors.

Any academic account of the media and entertainment must, then, take account of the way in which 'entertainment' occupies an ideological place within media structures, but there is a further difficulty here: the implicit disdain for entertainment in conventional media argument has been reinforced by an even greater disdain for entertainment in conventional media sociology. Academic researchers may be well aware, in the abstract, of the importance of entertainment as a socio-cultural force, whether this is measured in the economic terms of wealth creation, employment, investment and so forth, or in the anthropological terms of its importance for our everyday lives, identities and patterns of sociability. Media sociologists are equally well aware, in research practice, that the boundaries between entertainment and art or between entertainment and news are anyway difficult to draw. It remains the case, however, that sociological research focuses on the 'heavy' rather than the light output of, say, television; there is still far more systematic scholarly analysis of news values than of popular taste.

In my *Sociology of Rock* (Frith, 1978), I remarked that if sociologists could not exactly ignore the record players, tape recorders and transistor radios found (alongside the TV set) in most households in Britain and North America by the end of the 1960s, they could still write thousands of articles about mass communication as if music played no part in it. Records did begin to be included in textbook lists of the mass media, but that was the only mention they got. I don't believe the situation has changed much since then. Media sociology, at least in the Anglo-American tradition, is still focused on the press and broadcasting (rather than on film, music or computer games); and it still tends to treat newspapers and broadcasters primarily with reference to 'real' issues – to political power, the democratic process, the public sphere.

It is not surprising, then, that the best analytic and research work on entertainment in the last 15 to 20 years has come from different academic fields with different theoretical perspectives altogether. Feminist scholars, for example, working within the theoretical frame of women's studies, pursued their interest in the everyday construction of gender values and differences into pioneering studies of television entertainment (Modleski, 1982; Hobson, 1982; Ang, 1985), cinema entertainment (Johnston, 1973; Gledhill, 1987), and print entertainment (Ferguson, 1983; Radway, 1984). Cultural studies, meanwhile, defined its interest in media consumption – in subcultural style, the politics of the everyday, the meaning of 'the popular' – against the 'positivist' approach of media and communication studies (Hebdige, 1979; Bennett, 1981); while it was from film studies' semiotic approach to the mass media text that the first applied studies of television entertainment (Fiske and Hartley, 1978), advertisements (Williamson, 1978), and even music videos (Kaplan, 1987) emerged.

By the end of the 1980s academic media analysis thus reflected a clear political and methodological bifurcation, a bifurcation that was hardly challenged in the 1990s. Sociologists and communications theorists, using conventional empirical methods, focused on issues of economics, production, message, effects; scholars in the overlapping fields of cultural studies, women's studies and film studies, using a variety of semiotic readings and 'ethnographies', addressed issues of consumption, meaning, pleasure, identity. What these different approaches share is a model of communication in which the media process is divided into three: production (the site of debates about ownership, influence and power); consumption (the site of debates about effects, taste and 'resistance'); and meaning (the site of debates about ideology, 'Americanization' and national identity).

This model draws on both the classic American mass communication question of 'who says what to whom' (Schramm, 1954) and the Frankfurt School's account of mass culture as culture industry (Adorno, 1991), but as an approach to entertainment it has two problems. First, it produces an over-bureaucratized account of production in which it is assumed that the culture industries are as economically 'rational' as any other form of capitalist enterprise. In fact, the most remarkable aspect of the media production of entertainment is the level of failure involved – the vast majority of books published, music recorded and films scripted do not recover their costs (or even reach an audience), and any account of the economics of entertainment has to take account of the effects of fashion, novelty and boredom, matters that are not easily rationalized. It is perhaps worth noting in this context that 'youth', an audience category that describes not simply a stage of life but also a restless, fickle, obsessive attitude to media consumption, is a key market target for all entertainment media, whether pop music, the Hollywood film, the TV scheduler or the *Sun* newspaper.

The conventional media model produces, second, an over-politicized account of consumption, in which the central debate treats the consumer almost entirely in terms of discursive power, dominant and oppositional values, the 'cultural dope' versus the resistant reader, rather than by reference to, say, aesthetic judgements or sensual pleasures. The meaning of entertainment is thus always ideological. If cultural studies rescued popular media pursuits from the condescension of sociology, it did so by suggesting that they are really, politically, serious.

In this media model, in short, entertainment is studied (or dismissed) as a form of political communication, involving power, influence and manipulation. What concerns me about this approach is that it makes no sense of entertainment as a kind of sociability with a long human history. Entertainment, something that (in the *Chambers Dictionary* definition) 'holds the attention pleasurably', is not the product or result of the mass media, and even today mediated entertainment must take its place in the flux of the everyday – we hear as many good stories from friends as from professionals; we are as likely to play games and music for ourselves as to pay to have other people play them for us (Finnegan, 1989).

In this chapter, then, I want to suggest an approach to the entertainment industry that starts out from the problem of entertainment not as communication but as commodity. The question that interests me is how money is made out of social activities and domestic pleasures that long predate the mass media. Entertainment is obviously an industry now; the points originally made by the Frankfurt School about the serial production of art, the standardization of music, and the ownership and exchange of culture are still pertinent. I want to examine them with a model (taken from the history of music, the oldest form of entertainment) in which the key factors are not production, consumption and meaning, but storage, retrieval and occasion.

Entertainment describes events and activities that pass the time, that are by their nature fleeting, but to be commodified such events and activities have, nevertheless, to be objectified. How is entertainment given material form as property and for exchange? At the same time there has to be some social agreement as to when such exchange is appropriate, when it will have the desired social effects. How is entertainment as commodity exchange placed in the everyday? With these questions in mind I will approach entertainment from the perspective of technology (and storage and retrieval) on the one hand, and leisure (and occasion) on the other.

Technology

The starting point here has to be history. It is undeniable that the development
of mass-mediated entertainment has been dependent on technological innovations that have made the serial production of entertainment goods economically
feasible. Printing thus made possible the book, newspaper and magazine trade,
just as twentieth-century entertainment is tied up with the use of photography,
the phonograph, the film camera and the wireless, the TV, the video and the personal computer. In common-sense terms, indeed, the technology *is* the entertainment: we talk of watching television, listening to records, going to the
cinema, playing computer games and surfing the web. It is, nevertheless, misleading to assume that technology determines the form or content (or use or
ideology) of entertainment, for at least two reasons. On the one hand, inventors
and manufacturers have rarely anticipated the eventual use of their devices
(Edison, to give the most notorious example, first marketed the phonograph as
a kind of dictating machine and explicitly rejected the idea that it might have
entertainment value); on the other hand, the essential conservatism of both producers and consumers means that technological advance is almost always in the
name of doing more efficiently or profitably or conveniently what is done
already. This is one reason why artists, particularly self-defined avant-garde
artists, have been so unexpectedly important in the technical shaping of mass
entertainments: they are the only people fully committed to using new means of
symbolic production experimentally.

From this perspective the 'revolutionary' impact of electronic technology has
been overstated. A visitor from the mid-nineteenth century might be amazed by
how we are now entertained but would not be very surprised by what entertains
us: our sense of plot and drama, comedy and tragedy, sensation and excitement,
heroism and villainy, what we mean by a good tune, a good story, has not
changed much – there are as many aesthetic continuities as there are technical
differences between the nineteenth-century penny paper and twentieth-century
tabloid, the nineteenth-century stage melodrama and the twentieth-century
Hollywood film, the nineteenth-century novel and the twentieth-century best-
seller, the nineteenth-century street ballad and the twentieth-century pop song.
Even the computer games industry is as dependent on good storylines as on the
electronic engineers who realize such stories graphically.

Writing the history of entertainment in terms of storage and retrieval clarifies
the effects of technology, a point I can best illustrate with the example of music.
Music (an obviously time-based medium, existing only as it is experienced) has
been through three broad storage stages. Initially it was 'stored' in the mind and
body of a person (and in his or her musical instrument). The first professional
musical entertainers were people paid to 'retrieve' music in their own performances (though they no doubt soon had their own supporting entourage of
agents and promoters).

Following the invention of printing, music could, in a second stage, be stored
easily too in the form of notes, in the score. To be realized as music, such notes
still had to be played, but there were now new players in the musical economy –
composers and publishers as well as performers could make money out of this
new storage device, the printed score or sheet music. Musicians were still at the
core of the music business, but the economic opportunities had clearly

expanded: the composers and publishers profited now too from amateur performers, from the domestic use of musical instruments (the market for which in turn expanded, giving piano manufacturers, for example, a new impetus to apply industrial technology to mass production).

In the third stage, following the invention of the phonograph, music came to be recorded, stored as sound on a 'carrier' which became in its evolving forms (phonogram, record, cassette tape, compact disc) the basic musical commodity. Again, though, this did not displace professional performers from the centre of musical entertainment nor, in the end (a point to which I will return), lessen the economic importance of music publishing. In terms of musical form, indeed, one could say that it was precisely the development of recording (and broadcasting) technology that enabled eighteenth- and nineteenth-century concert hall art to be sold in the twentieth century as the mass entertainment now known, somewhat misleadingly, as 'classical music'.

This framework is, I think, applicable to other media (for example, in the movement from story-teller to book author to film producer) and it certainly helps us to understand the three central issues in the economics of entertainment: talent, copyright and the relationship of hardware and software.

Talent

All entertainment industries see themselves as talent industries: they define their activities as discovering, nurturing and exploiting talent (and remain, in this respect, imbued with the ideology of early nineteenth-century Romanticism). A number of consequences flow from this.

First, all entertainment businesses are organized around the idea of stardom. The star is central to the entertainment market, most obviously in the figures of the film and pop star (film projects have to be sold on the back of their potential stars; record company profits depend on their star signings) but equally importantly in publishing (through the build-up of a best-selling author's name, for example) and broadcasting (the first question asked of even the most straightforward documentary proposal is thus 'who will present it?'). One way in which news is seen (dismissively) to be becoming entertainment is through this star effect – as newsreaders are paid more than news editors, and as even the most serious broadsheets sell themselves on their 'name' columnists.

Second, it follows that competitive entertainment corporations are committed above all to finding stars, nurturing them, making them happy. Hence the importance in the music industry, for example, of contract lawyers and artist managers, and the increasingly dominant role of the agent in publishing and sport. One aspect of this is that we have to understand the economic logic of entertainment companies (their investment patterns, for example) by reference to the exigencies of long-term star-making as well as to those of recovering the immediate costs of a particular star vehicle. In the record industry, as Keith Negus has pointed out, this can mean in-house tensions between an A&R department's career strategies and the marketing department's attempts to maximize the sales of the product to hand (Negus, 1992). In publishing it has meant the rise of 'packaging' and books 'authored' (but not necessarily written) by star sportsmen, politicians, models, comedians or even serial killers. In all media it has led to the increasing importance of merchandising – product endorsement can produce as much income as direct sales, an image on a T-shirt as much as a performance on stage or record. Merchandising is nothing new – it was, for example, a way in which P.T. Barnum made money from (and helped to promote) the Swedish soprano, Jenny Lind, in the USA in the mid-nineteenth century (Barnum, 1967) – but it is notable that these days the most successful 'tie-in' sales campaigns (aimed primarily at children) use cartoon characters like Wallace and Gromit or The Simpsons or techno-toys from blockbuster films like *Star Wars* rather than stars as such (see Engelhardt, 1986). Disney is obviously the master of the co-ordinated marketing of cartoon characters in film, video, book, television programme, magazine, theme park and any amount of merchandise, but its strategy is the norm now of the entertainment business. Indeed, in merchandising terms, the biggest star attraction at the end of the 1990s seemed to be the 'subversive' characters from *South Park*.

The point I want to stress here is different, however. The economics of entertainment may be organized around star quality and talent, but what makes someone a star in the first place is mysterious. Few stars have been created by the entertainment industry from scratch. Star quality is, it seems, discovered – or revealed – by the public, and only then exploited by the business. There is, in short, something essentially irrational at the core of commercial entertainment, and it is misleading to regard the 'culture industry' as a super-efficient regulator of public taste. It has to be seen, rather, as an industry organized around the fickleness of the public. Entertainment companies necessarily carry a high level of failed projects (nine out of ten records, for example), and necessarily tolerate the eccentricity of their successful acts. What matters is to make as much money as possible out of what does work and, in the end, stars are crucial for the entertainment industry because they are the only tangible evidence of what the public does want. This gives them significant bargaining power. In the British television industry, for example, a clear difference emerged in the 1990s between flourishing star-based production companies, offering a variety of entertainment formats, and precarious ideas-based companies, simply surviving from project to project. The economic dependence of entertainment companies on stars is equally a feature of music and book publishing.

Copyright

Copyright is the basis of property rights in the entertainment business and therefore the basis of entertainment as a capitalist industry. In the music industry, for example, songs are 'properties' (like books in the publishing industry, films in the movie industry, and game-show formats in the TV industry), properties in which companies own 'baskets of rights' (Frith, 1993). The owners of a music copyright (the writer and publisher) charge a fee for its use – whether as a recording or in live performance, on a film soundtrack or as an advertising jingle, on the radio or in a shopping mall.

Two important points follow from this. First, the entertainment industries are particularly dependent for their profitability on laws that restrict the uses to which a work may be put and define those which must be licensed by the copyright holders. A recurring problem for the entertainment industry, then, is how to rewrite copyright law to take account of changing circumstances. This problem is most obvious in technological terms: each new way of using an image, song or story needs to be specifically restricted. In the case of music, for example, the development of recording at the beginning of the twentieth century raised the question of the rights of composers and publishers in the broadcast or other public use of their songs on record; the rapid spread of cassette players in the 1980s raised the question of the rights of record companies in the domestic copying of their music; while the use of digital technology in the 1990s raised the question of who owns sounds.

Copyright laws have duly been amended to reflect changing technological conditions, but it is by no means the case that different national legislatures are agreed on what should be done. In Britain, for example, it was eventually ruled that the 1911 Copyright Act gave record companies the right to restrict the public use of recordings (just as song publishers could restrict the public performance of songs). In the USA this has never been accepted: to own a record there is to have the right to do what one likes with it. Similarly, while in the 1980s many European countries accepted the record industry argument that home taping should be formally 'licensed' (via a fee paid on the purchase of a blank tape or a tape recorder), this was rejected by the 1988 British Copyright Act, and has certainly not been accepted in the USA, where a similar battle was fought – and lost – by Hollywood studios against home taping on VCRs (Lardner, 1987).

The difference between countries' copyright rules has been a problem for the entertainment business since its goods first crossed national boundaries, and there is a long history of publishers, record companies and film studios seeking to have copyright law standardized (and enforced) to their best advantage internationally. Such lobbying began with European publishers' nineteenth-century campaigns for legislation to protect their authors from US piracy and continue with global corporations' determination to protect their music, film and computer software from Third World piracy, whether through national legislation or 'terms of trade' agreements. (One point worth noting in this context is that a not insignificant sector of the entertainment business is illegal.)

If changes in copyright laws, nationally and internationally, reflect the effects of technology and exchange on cultural storage and retrieval, they also determine the economic effects of cultural mediation. This is my second point: the most significant source of income in the entertainment industry is not the manufacture and exchange of goods to individual customers for cash (though this is obviously important) but the fee income from licensing the rights to various uses of the property (including the right to put it on a carrier – a record, a tape – to be sold to the public on an individual basis). The implications of this are more obvious in some industries than others: until the development of the domestic VCR, for example, individual consumers could not buy films (or TV programmes) as such; their 'authors' thus made their money licensing their use by exhibitors or television stations. Now, by contrast, money can be made out of films in a variety of ways, not just from rental to theatres or from deals with broadcasters, but also from transmission on cable and satellite and from 'selling through' to the public (film-makers now make more money from video than cinema formats). Even those entertainment industries (like book publishing) that seem to depend exclusively on individual consumption are, in fact, making money out of a variety of licences. The financial return on a best-selling novel, for example, is likely to be as great in terms of film and television rights, serialization and condensation rights as from sales as such; and the music industry almost certainly now makes as much money from licensing its properties for mediated use (on radio, television and film soundtrack; as the background noise of public places) as it does from domestic CD sales. Hence the continuing economic importance of music publishers and the 'back catalogue': songs, like books, may be exploited throughout their copyright period, as they are revived, repackaged and articulated in new technological forms; 'classic' rock records get a new life as boxed-set CDs just as 'classic' Hollywood films get a new life as domestic videos. The digital television channels that now give us the chance to choose between hundreds of programmes confine most of these choices to old programmes, old films, old footage from the archives.

Hardware/software

One peculiarity of the twentieth-century entertainment industry is that it rests on two different sorts of sales process: first, people have to be persuaded to buy hardware, a permanent piece of domestic furniture (a gramophone or cassette or CD player; a radio or television set; a satellite dish or digital decoder; a personal computer); second, they have to be persuaded to buy software, to continue to purchase music, watch programmes, rent videos, buy computer games and subscribe to services to use on their machinery. There is obviously a complementary process here: there is no point in buying hardware unless there is software available to use on it; there is no point in buying software without having the hardware in place.

This is obvious enough. What is less obvious, perhaps, is that the historical relationship between hardware and software manufacturers keeps shifting and is not necessarily harmonious. Hardware manufacturers, for example, can expect to move from an initial high-risk, highly competitive market in which even the largest technological investment may turn out to have been futile (as with quadraphonic sound or the Betamax video system), to a buoyant period in which mass acceptance of a new device means an essentially monopolistic position and huge profits, to a tailing off in demand as the market is exhausted. Software manufacturers, by contrast, respond to market conditions and, when a new technology does take off, have an ever-growing market as the new goods spread from the most affluent consumers to the general public.

If hardware and software manufacturers thus occupy different business cycles there are also fluctuations in the negotiation of what we might call cultural power. Hardware manufacturers (who have historically come from outside the established entertainment industry) need access to software rights if their goods are to have consumer appeal. They are, in this respect, utterly dependent on existing rights owners (and so Sony took over CBS to ensure it had films and sounds available). This accounts for the essential conservatism of the entertainment business (new hardware simply makes more easily accessible familiar software), and for the recurring tensions between hardware manufacturers and software rights holders, who are initially apt to see any new way of exploiting rights as a threat to customary money-making ways (the MP3 device for downloading music from the internet is the latest example as I write).

This is the context in which we can observe two different corporate strategies among entertainment companies. On the one hand, they may seek to combine hardware and software interests, using the economic dependence of each on the other – this is the strategy of Sony-CBS and Microsoft; on the other hand, they may decide (like Time Warner, Rupert Murdoch's News International and the German Bertelsmann group) to be publishers, exploiting their software interests through the ownership or control of all possible means of transmission, such that the same property can be simultaneously sold as a comic book, a paperback, a film and a video, a record and a visual image, each different sort of 'carrier' working to promote all the others. Neither strategy is necessarily stable – at the end of the 1990s the electronic companies Matsushita and Philips both sold their software interests, MCA and Polygram, to the Canadian company Seagram, which, as Universal, thus became a major global entertainment corporation having started out in whisky.

Leisure

I come now to the question of when entertainment is appropriate. In broad terms we associate entertainment with leisure, with non-work times, with relaxation and play, though in practice this boundary has become blurred as music is used, for example, as part of the soundtrack of the workplace, and given the increasing economic importance of consumer service industries in which one person's leisure is another person's work. Entertainment, that is to say, must be judged socially appropriate as a matter of both time and space (Scannell, 1996).

From this perspective two aspects of mass media entertainment stand out. There is, first, what we might call the routinization of the special event. If entertainment was once marked as a special moment – a festival or rite, a wedding or birthday – such 'specialness' is now a part of the everyday: the evening, the weekend, the break; all 'spare' time is now an opportunity for entertainment, whether skimming a paper or watching TV in the morning, listening to a Walkman or car radio on the way to work, or reading a magazine or paperback in the lunch hour. Entertainment was once defined by the social situation that produced it; now it defines a quality of experience, a kind of pleasure or relaxation that may be available in any place at any time. This is one of the issues that confuses the high/low culture debate. High culture is claimed to describe in itself a 'special' experience – something transcending the everyday; such specialness is harder and harder to maintain not so much because high culture is itself a commodity but because its enjoyment too has been routinized – in the use of classical records and radio programmes, prints of great paintings, paperback classics and so forth.

It follows, second, that there is now no clear distinction between public and domestic entertainment, between personal and social rituals. For most people public entertainment is in fact mostly experienced in the home (as we listen to the radio or CD player, watch TV, read the newspaper; as theatrical and sports and musical events from around the world are on offer day and night in the corner of the living room). The history of musical entertainment thus seems marked, at least technologically, by a drive towards privatization. The early Victorian pub piano became the late Victorian domestic piano which became (via the player piano) the family phonogram then radiogram, which became in turn the portable record player and the transistor radio and thus, eventually, the Walkman. There is something of the same development in film entertainment:

films are more likely to be watched in the home than in the cinema now, and not even there by the family as a whole. And one of the often predicted uses of the internet is that it will enable us to tailor even newspapers to our individual needs, each issue digitally edited to our specific information requirements as *The Daily Me*.

What is going on here is a shift in the meaning of entertainment from a description of a particular sort of social experience to the articulation of a certain kind of individual market choice: the magazine market (a title for every taste; a niche for every member of the family) has become the model for radio and television, for film as video, for music as CD. The point is not that entertainment has ceased to be a sociable affair, but that the 'society' involved is a 'taste public', an aspect of the entertainment fantasy itself – most obvious, perhaps, in the men's 'lifestyle' magazines that rose to prominence in the 1990s.

The implications of this can best be discussed under two headings: mediation and taste.

Mediation

Just as record companies refer to primary and secondary musical rights (distinguishing between the primary right to put a song on record and sell it to the public and the secondary right to exploit that record as a source of entertainment in itself) so I want to distinguish between primary and secondary entertainment. Many entertainment goods, that is, are not provided directly for the public itself but for people who seek to entertain the public – cinema exhibitors, television companies, radio programmers. Such secondary 'entertainment' is thus framed by pre-readings of the market and by instrumental interests, as radio and TV stations, for instance, use musical artefacts to attract certain sorts of viewer/listener for certain sorts of advertiser. (Newspaper and magazine publishing has long depended economically on titles attracting advertisers rather than readers as such; or, rather, on titles attracting the readers the advertisers want.)

Analysts of television thus talk of the 'audience commodity' (Ang, 1991): 'entertainment' in this context does not describe the sort of work sold to an audience, but the sort of audience sold to an advertiser, an audience at leisure, having a good time. Karl Marx once noted that the successful capitalist manufacturer did not just make goods for a market but, just as importantly, created a market for his goods. This is particularly necessary for entertainment goods, the demand for which is both irrational (a matter of taste, fad and fancy) and competitive (not just in terms of other leisure goods but also by reference to other uses of leisure time). The promotion of entertainment goods is thus just as important – and costly – as their production in the first place. The promotional budget for Hollywood films matches their production costs; the promotional budget for a new album release matches recording costs.

This has three effects that are worth noting. First, marketing departments have become increasingly important in terms of corporate power and influence. Their task these days is less to devise the best means of selling whatever books or sounds or films the editorial or 'creative' departments come up with than to ensure that whatever is created is, indeed, marketable. No signing is made, no package approved, no studio go-ahead given without consideration of its potential market. It follows, second, that the entertainment business is obsessed with audience research, with sales figures and sales charts, with viewing patterns and reactions. Entertainments come to us imbricated with theories of what we want. (And one irony here is that since Paul Lazersfeld's pioneering work for NBC in the 1940s academic media studies have therefore been a significant strand of media market research.) But, third, the entertainment business still needs 'live' audiences as well as those hypothesized by audience researchers. This is perhaps most obvious in sport. As sports rights have become centrally important to the marketing of new TV services, so sports themselves have had to adapt to the needs of their new paymasters (Whannel, 1992). At the same time, though, the appeal of sport to the television audience (and to its sponsors) still rests on it being a real spectacle with a real crowd: the paying customers for a Manchester United game are necessary for the team's credibility. Mediated entertainment, in short, must still make reference to unmediated sociability, whether in the laugh track for sitcoms, the studio audience in talk shows, or the DJ's crew in 'zoo radio'.

Taste

For the industry, public taste means 'taste publics', patterns of leisure interest and activity that can be mapped on to other social characteristics – age and gender, class and ethnicity, sexuality and occupation, spending power. 'Taste', an ideological gesture at the liberal myth of free individual market choice, is redescribed in terms of demographics, sociographics, niche marketing. In this model what the public wants is effectively determined by who the public are, and this assumption remains essential to the day-to-day practices of the entertainment business even though, on the one hand, the public does not want most of what is offered to it and, on the other, the biggest profits tend to come from books, films and records that create their own, unexpected audiences, which 'cross over' (thus creating a new taste map, a new blueprint for formulaic production).

From a sociological perspective the interesting issue here is not so much taste as taste formation (Bourdieu, 1984). Rather than treating the social structure as the site on which cultural goods must be sold, sociologists treat entertainment as the site in which the dynamics of social relations are enacted: it is through the expression of taste that we articulate sameness and difference, subjective and social identity. It is not so much that because people have certain (socially determined) tastes they choose certain leisure goods and activities, but that in choosing these goods and activities they reveal and define their tastes, and hence their sense of their social position. Cultural capital can only be accumulated (and realized) in cultural exchange, and from this perspective taste is the key to the formation of social groups and alliances (Thornton, 1995).

Entertainment, to put this another way, is valuable primarily as a source of symbolic goods and a setting for symbolic activity and if, from an academic point of view, such activity can be understood as in some sense 'subversive' of dominant ideology, from an industry point of view what people make of leisure goods matters less than that they routinely consume them – entertainment corporations are happy to take their cut of gangsta rap, kung fu movies, comic cults and ecstasy-driven dance records. One further point should be made here:

analysts of all sorts are apt to use the raw data of leisure consumption (sales figures and box office returns) as measures of popular taste and value: to watch a film or TV show is to like and somehow 'agree' with it. This makes a nonsense of the everyday experience of entertainment in which much of what we consume is, indeed, 'disappointing'. Consumption is not the same thing as discrimination, and one of the more foolish consequences of the distinction between art and entertainment is the suggestion that to be entertained is to suspend all moral or aesthetic judgement (Shrum, 1996).

This is to raise questions about the value of entertainments and entertainers which take us away from problems of media analysis to problems of aesthetic analysis which I have dealt with elsewhere (Frith, 1996). Here I want to conclude by focusing instead on the political issues raised by the organization of entertainment as an industry. One striking aspect of the entertainment business, for example, is the resonance of the idea of 'independence' – whether this is defined against state organizations, as in the case of 'independent' radio or TV, or against major corporations, as in the case of 'independent' film or record production. There is clearly some confusion here between institutional and ideological terms: a technical description (how a company works in terms of production and distribution; its size) is taken to describe what it produces (adventurous, radical films, programmes and music; the unstandardized). This argument does not stand up to much scrutiny, not least because independent entertainment companies depend ultimately on fitting market niches unoccupied by the major companies and are thus, if anything, more likely to produce to formula, more likely to think in terms of 'taste publics'. The paradox here, in fact, is that in as far as independent production companies are radical and adventurous it is in their *de facto* role as the R&D departments of the major corporations, which use them (often with their own substantial investment) to test new acts and forms and markets, moving in on success through their domination of the means of distribution (and this is not confined to music industry practice   acting talent is snatched by TV and film producers from experimental theatre companies and alternative comedy clubs; writing talent is taken over by major publishers from small imprints; eccentric magazine ideas (like *Wallpaper*) are exploited by the corporations once their sales potential has been established).

Globalization

From the very earliest days of the international entertainment industry – with the rise of Tin Pan Alley at the end of the nineteenth century, for example – there has been a recurrent fear of 'Americanization', whether articulated in defence of existing European culture or as an attack from the third world against 'cultural imperialism', and it is easy enough to envisage a media future in which MTV is on every TV screen, a Hollywood film in every movie theatre, Disneyland on every continent, Mariah Carey on every radio station, and *Penthouse* and *Cosmopolitan* in every newsagent. How seriously should we take this picture?

Applying the model of storage and retrieval described above, one can certainly describe the trade in twentieth-century entertainments in terms of technological logic. As sounds, for example, came to be stored in wax grooves, so the inventors and manufacturers of recording devices spread first hardware then software (at a price) around the world. No music-making or listening community was unaffected, and a pioneer recording man like Fred Gaisberg, pushing his way stolidly across Europe and Asia, establishing local recording industry after local recording industry at the behest of his master's voice back in the USA, can be seen as a cross between a missionary and a merchant capitalist, exchanging recording technology for exotic sounds to record, establishing a new kind of musical map, a flow of sound for local pressing and distribution.

It is equally easy to misread this story, however, and music thus becomes a useful case study for the globalization thesis. The point is not that a new technology produced a new world culture, but rather that music's own essential mobility enabled the new technology to flourish – and shaped the way it worked. There are a number of reasons why music, by its nature, crosses boundaries. On the one hand, its value and use is less dependent on language than print media (or, for that matter, film and television); on the other hand, people and peoples can take their music with them when they themselves move. Music, that is, defines migration: in nearly all societies, north and south, east and west, the most popular sounds come from the social margins (the Americanization of global pop is thus better labelled African-Americanization); for nearly all transported ethnic and cultural communities music is the central expression of their continued national identity, is the enacted form of the sociability that binds communities in their understandings of sameness and difference (Slobin, 1996).

From this perspective it is clear that the development of a technologically driven recording industry did not transform some previously pure 'national' music. Rather, it was the peculiar qualities of music – a cultural form unconstrained by national boundaries, mobile in time and place, the source of our most intense emotional experience of both social and individual identities – that allowed the record industry to take off, as an industry that was from the beginning not really organized or regulated nationally. (The music industry thus stands in clear contrast to broadcasting which was, partly for technological reasons, instrumental in defining twentieth-century nations.) This point has been reinforced by the digital revolution.

For a start, multinational corporate control of music now clearly describes the control of distribution rather than content – hence the declining relevance of the old model of cultural imperialism in which Anglo-American music (as well as capital) was taken to dominate the world. Globally successful sounds may now come from anywhere, and what matters for the world's major music corporations (of which only Time Warner is headquartered in the USA) is that they own the rights to all possible uses of such sounds, and that they can co-ordinate their exploitation across all music media, all music 'carriers', all media systems. The development of 'global music' is, in this respect, an aspect of the development of global television via cable and satellite and of deregulated radio broadcasting; more simply, it reflects the global spread of consumption, of shopping and 'leisure' and advertising, all musical activities.

It follows that the concept of a 'local' pop market is increasingly problematic not just in the sense that all localities are now awash with global sounds but also because local musicians now perceive their potential audience in international terms. The pop sales trend by the end of the 1990s was for local charts to be dominated by local acts, but these acts have their own global perspectives. What, from the mid-1960s to the mid-1980s, was primarily a fantasy for Anglophone groups – making it in America or Japan – is now built in to what it means to be 'a musician', whether in Holland or Honduras, Australia or Angola. If all musical communities are now crossed by global forces, all local musicians now dream (however vainly) of worldwide success (Robinson, 1991).

Digital technology has certainly made all sounds, whatever their source, more easily available to record producers, wherever they are. 'Music on record', like many other current cultural goods (films and television programmes, books and magazines), is thus a multinational product, literally. No longer the record of an event, a music made in one space at one time, it has become a way of internationally co-ordinating information. What we finally hear is a work constructed from a variety of parts (a bass drum here – London; a steel guitar there – Nashville; back-up voices there – Soweto). From this perspective, 'global music' describes a sound – an aesthetic – as well as a sales process.

For the industry the central impetus of globalization has been less that everyone in the world should be listening to the same music than that every country in the world should have the same copyright laws, and in terms of corporate structure globalization thus describes a process more complex than it may at first seem. It has certainly meant the take-over of the more successful local recording and music publishing companies (there are few significant independent record companies left in Europe, for example), but it has not necessarily meant the systematic imposition of American stars on European audiences. Rather, it has led to new sorts of A&R competition within music corporations, competition between nationally and regionally defined divisions, each responsible for uncovering their own talent and turning it from local to global success, competition between different genre divisions (such as country, rap and salsa) for national and international promotional resources (Negus, 1999). The new focus on distribution and promotion as the core activity of the multinational music industry, together with a technology that allows globally marketable sounds to be produced just about anywhere, means that production, as such, can still be remarkably small-scale. The creative basis of the music business (writers, musicians, engineers, production companies) is, on the whole, not of direct interest to the majors (this anyway tends to be the most unstable, high-turnover end of the industry), and small, local companies are, as I have already suggested, useful structurally just in terms of research & development.

Where 'global' factors come into play is in music marketing, in the mediation of music's meanings on radio and television, by advertisers and journalists, and it is here that the term 'globalization' has a greater resonance, describing the integration of entertainment activities across both media and national boundaries. What is at issue here, I think, is not whether all peoples are watching the same films or listening to the same records (or whether these films and records are American) but whether all are involved in the same sort of activity. The 'globalization' of leisure, in other words, describes not the success of international marketing but the effect of broad social changes in the organization of work and family life. It is because of these changes that entertainment goods become internationally marketable not vice versa.

The politics of entertainment

This is the context in which a number of governments have sought to develop national cultural policies (Smith, 1998). These have taken a variety of forms, but I will classify them loosely under three headings.

Protecting/promoting national entertainment industries

The emphasis here is on state subsidy for local producers, state support for international marketing and state protection against cultural imports. The problem with all such policies is the assumption that the international leisure market is made up of competing national industries (under the dominance of the biggest, the USA). In fact, the culture industries are not organized nationally, and, while there is evidence that state support does have a positive effect on the international career of local artists and performers, there is little indication that this has helped maintain national culture industries as such – internationally successful Danish or Australian or Irish or Canadian stars or goods or formats are simply signed to multinational labels and studios (this is a necessary aspect of their success).

Just by entering the game of international leisure marketing, one has to abandon the nation as the playing field. One aspect of this is that policies designed to promote 'national' films or music or TV production tend to lead to local versions of Anglo-American pop, the Hollywood film and TV show. Hence a second sort of policy, as follows.

Protecting/promoting a national culture

Policies here revolve around the subsidy of particular sorts of performer and performance – performance and performers who might otherwise be redundant commercially, though one could also point to the use of language regulations (by the French, for example). The problem is how a national culture is to be defined. Most so-called 'folk' forms, for instance, are simply frozen moments in the history of hybrid sounds and drama, and folk policy more often involves the invention of tradition (for political or tourist or 'heritage' reasons) than any commitment to the culture's continuing vitality and change (one needs only look to the break-up of Yugoslavia and the sudden emergence of previously unheard national folk traditions to make this point).

Leisure-as-national-culture policies tend to define entertainment formally, whether in terms of aesthetic value or distinctive styles, neither of which are, in fact, necessarily national qualities. An alternative approach is to ensure that people have the resources and opportunities to express themselves (their national situation) in whatever manner seems appropriate and to be seen and heard (which means having some guaranteed access to the media). Policy here means the following.

Protecting/promoting national cultural resources and spaces

Governments have thus got involved in supporting theatres and studios, broadcasters and publishers, in providing training and entrepreneurial advice, and if such policy remains hands-off it is probably effective. The difficulty (especially

when choices have to be made) is to disentangle aesthetic and market judgements as to who should be supported, a problem exacerbated by the fact that
nationally supported cinema, music or literature is often highly critical of (or
uninterested in) 'the nation'.

I would draw two conclusions from such political activity. First, entertainment is clearly essential to identity if that is defined in terms of ethnicity or
sociability or personality. It does not, though, seem to have much to do with
national identity, precisely because its value is as a way of crossing borders,
whether literally or ideally.

Second, fears of globalization (or Americanization) should be treated for
what they are: anxieties about the effects of market forces, and in terms of entertainment these are not easy to read. It is difficult, for example, to explain the rise
of rap as entertainment in the USA in the 1980s in terms of corporate policy
and media control, or its spread around the world in terms of American foreign
policy, and the global influence of reggae seems to have been despite, rather than
because of, the policies of either international record companies or the
Jamaican Government. I still have a sense that the music industry is organized
to exploit, belatedly, ideas that come from elsewhere, rather than to develop such
ideas for itself, and music is thus still a mass medium in which unofficial voices
may regularly be heard. There are obvious reasons for this – music is for educational reasons more accessible than print, for technological reasons more accessible than film or television. There is something else involved here, too, a more
general point: precisely because music-as-entertainment is not taken seriously by
the media or academic establishment, it can be by everyone else.

References

ADORNO, T.W., 1991: *The Culture Industry. Selected Essays on Mass Culture.* London:
   Routledge.
ANG, I., 1985: *Watching Dallas: Soap Opera and the Melodramatic Imagination.* London:
   Methuen.
——, 1991: *Desperately Seeking the Audience.* London: Routledge.
BARNUM, P.T., 1967: *The Struggles and Triumphs of P.T. Barnum Told By Himself* [1882].
   London: MacGibbon and Kee.
BENNETT, T. (ed.), 1981: *Popular Television and Film, A Reader.* London: British Film
   Institute.
BOURDIEU, P., 1984: *Distinction. A Social Critique of the Judgement of Taste.* London and
   New York: Routledge and Kegan Paul.
ENGELHARDT, T., 1986: 'Children's Television. The Shortcake Strategy' in Todd Gitlin
   (ed.), *Watching Television.* New York: Pantheon.
FERGUSON, M., 1983: *Forever Feminine.* London: Heinemann.
FINNEGAN, R., 1989: *The Hidden Musicians. Music-Making in an English Town.* Cambridge:
   Cambridge University Press.
FISKE, J. AND HARTLEY, J., 1978: *Reading Television.* London: Methuen.
FRITH, S. (ed.), 1993: *Music and Copyright.* Edinburgh: Edinburgh University Press.
——, 1978: *The Sociology of Rock.* London: Constable.
——, 1996: *Performing Rites. The Value of Popular Music.* Cambridge, MA: Harvard
   University Press.
GLEDHILL, C. (ed.), 1987: *Home is Where the Heart Is. Studies in Melodrama and the
   Woman's Film.* London: British Film Institute.

HEBDIGE, D., 1979: *Subculture. The Meaning of Style*. London: Methuen.

HOBSON, D., 1982: *Crossroads. The Drama of a Soap Opera*. London: Methuen.

JOHNSTON, C., 1973: *Notes on Women's Cinema*. London: SEFT.

KAPLAN, E.A., 1987: *Rocking Around the Clock. Music Television, Postmodernism and Consumer Culture*. New York and London: Methuen.

LARDNER, J., 1987: *Fast Forward. Hollywood, the Japanese, and the VCR Wars*. New York: Norton.

MODLESKI, T., 1982: *Loving with a Vengeance. Mass-Produced Fantasies for Women*. Hamden, CN: Archon Books.

NEGUS, K., 1992: *Producing Pop. Culture and Conflict in the Popular Music Industry*. London: Edward Arnold.

——, 1999: *Music, Genres and Corporate Culture*. London: Routledge.

RADWAY, J., 1984: *Reading the Romance. Women, Patriarchy and Popular Literature*. Chapel Hill, NC: University of North Carolina Press.

ROBINSON, D.C. *et al.*, 1991: *Music at the Margins. Popular Music and Global Cultural Diversity*. Newbury Park CA and London: Sage.

SCANNELL, P., 1996: *Radio, Television and Modern Life*. Oxford: Blackwell.

SCHRAMM, W. (ed.), 1954: *The Process and Effects of Mass Communication*. Urbana, IL: University of Illinois Press.

SHRUM, W.M., (1996): *Fringe and Fortune*. Princeton, NJ: Princeton University Press.

SLOBIN, M. (ed.), (1996): *Retuning Culture*. Durham, NC: Duke University Press.

SMITH, C., (1998): *Creative Britain*. London: Faber & Faber.

THORNTON, S., (1995): *Club Cultures: Music, Media and Subcultural Capital*. Cambridge: Polity Press.

WHANNEL, G., (1992): *Fields in Vision. Television, Sport and Cultural Transformation*. London: Routledge.

WILLIAMSON, J., 1978: *Decoding Advertisements. Ideology and Meaning in Advertising*. London: Boyars.

10

Commercialism and Professionalism in the American News Media

Daniel C. Hallin

In October 1993 Dan Rather created a brief sensation with a speech at the Radio and Television News Directors Association, where he railed against the current state of the institution he has personified for the past decade or so. 'They've got us putting more and more fuzz and wuzz on the air, cop-shop stuff, so as to compete not with other news programs but with entertainment programs, including those posing as news programs, for dead bodies, mayhem and lurid tales' (Viles, 1993).

The following Sunday (17 October) Walter Goodman, television critic for *The New York Times*, ridiculed 'Parson Rather' for his 'sermon' on journalistic responsibility:

> The ratings may not be all that scientific, but the bottom-liners have learned that they are more reliable guides to the nation's taste than high-minded journalists. Corporate executives are not by and large suicidal. If they were persuaded by the figures that news from other countries, economic news and serious, substantive news of any kind would bring in more money than game shows or crime shows, America would have an hour's worth of such nourishment every night. The problem faced by Mr Rather and his allies is that mass merchandising does not permit much in the way of boutique programming. That's the reason for public television. . . . [T]he fat cats he is fighting have nothing more devious in mind than catering to the enormous audience he wants to serve. . . . He has to hope that the watering down and dolling up of the 'CBS Evening News' do not increase its ratings, for otherwise he may be driven to flee the studio and charge about the land, trying to stir up new hurricanes against old windmills.

What is remarkable here is not so much Rather's speech as its reception by the *Times*. For perhaps twenty years, from the early 1960s to the early 1980s, it was taken for granted that television news was *not* simply show business. Any television executive, any broadcast journalist, and certainly a critic for *The New York Times*, could be counted upon to repeat that the journalist indeed had an obligation higher than the ratings, that television news served the public, not simply the market. What was a commonplace of journalistic ethics a few years ago is now increasingly regarded as the modern equivalent of knight errantry.

The American media have been essentially commercial since the penny press of the 1830s, save the small institution of public broadcasting, created in 1967 and always very marginal. But commercial logic has never been completely dominant. In the case of broadcasting it was modified by government regula-tion, which imposed an obligation, modest and somewhat vague to be sure, to serve the 'public convenience and necessity'. In the case of journalism generally, it was modified in the nineteenth century by the political commitments of own-ers and editors, and then in the twentieth by the growing culture of profession-alism. At the end of the twentieth century, government regulation of broadcasting had been, for the most part, swept away and the culture of profes-sionalism was clearly in decline. Is it possible that in the twenty-first century commercial logic will finally rule the American media without challenge? If it is, what would this mean for American culture?

The nature of professionalism

In the late 1940s, the Commission on Freedom of the Press articulated the argu-ment for what came to be called the 'social responsibility' theory of the press (Siebert, Peterson and Schramm, 1956). The commission was concerned with increasing concentration of media ownership, which, it felt, meant that the pub-lic interest could no longer be protected simply by preventing government inter-ference with the 'market-place of ideas'. It was concerned both with the danger that media owners would exclude political views contrary to their own, and the danger that commercialization would undermine responsible reporting. It advo-cated certain forms of government action to encourage competition, as well as action by non-profit institutions, which it hoped would supplement the com-mercial media as communicators. Nevertheless, deeply rooted in the American liberal tradition, it looked above all to the press itself for the solution: 'We sug-gest', a Commission representative wrote, 'that the press look upon itself as per-forming a public service of a professional kind.' Adding that, 'there are some things which a truly professional man will not do for money' (Commission on Freedom of the Press, 1947: 92).

In calling for professionalization, the Commission was endorsing a trend that was already well under way. It happened gradually and is hard to date. It had its roots in the 'information' model of journalism that developed near the turn of the twentieth century, led in part by *The New York Times* after its purchase in 1896 by Adolph Ochs (Schudson, 1978). Into the 1960s, the change was still in progress. Among the last major papers to make the transition were the *Los Angeles Times*, which was still clearly a Republican paper through the 1950s, but in 1960, to the great consternation of Richard Nixon, gave essentially even-handed coverage to Kennedy's campaign and to his, and the *Chicago Tribune*, which remained faithful to Colonel Robert McCormick's politics into the 1970s (Squires, 1993: 29–32). It is probably fair to say, though, that professionalization was mostly consolidated by the mid-1940s when the Commission on Freedom of the Press was preparing its report. In the intervening years most journalists and most commentators on the American media came to see this model of jour-nalism as stable and permanent, the end product of the 'natural history' of journalism. Now it seems we have to ask whether the era of professionaliza-tion might prove to be a brief, anomalous phase, a period of a little more than a generation when the contradictions between the different roles of the news media – economic, political and cultural – seemed resolved, but were so only in a temporary or illusory way. It is not likely that the professional model of journalism will disappear from the scene altogether. It is too deeply rooted in the culture for that; even 'tabloid news', which we will explore later, is parasitic on it in many ways, borrowing its forms and authority. But professionalism is also not likely to continue with the sense of confidence in its own identity and its dominance of the American media scene that it has enjoyed for the past generation or two.

It has often been pointed out that the notion of the journalist as a 'professional' is vague and in many ways dubious. Many journalists would characterize their job as a craft rather than a profession; in a number of cases journalists have gone to court to argue that they should not be considered professionals under labour laws, but ordinary wage-workers engaged in routine activities under close supervision – and therefore eligible for overtime pay. Many toilers in the media industry indeed fit this description, and many, at the top levels of journalism, do not. Journalism is also very different from the 'classical' professions – law, medicine, architecture, engineering – in that its practice is not based on any systematic body of knowledge. A degree in journalism is optional – and probably more necessary for employment at the bottom than the top of the profession; no licences or exams are required, and no peer review boards judge one's competence.

What I mean by professionalization here is, first of all, that journalism, like other professions, developed an ethic of 'public service'. The professionalization of journalism was part of a general trend, beginning in the Progressive Era, away from partisan politics as a basis for public life, and towards conceptions of administrative rationality and neutral expertise. The journalist was supposed to serve the public as a whole, and not particular interests, whether the partisan causes journalists had championed in the nineteenth century, or the narrow commercial interests of advertisers and owners. The notion of the 'public interest' is very much under assault today, from a number of sides, and this shift in political culture is one of the factors cutting the ground from beneath the professional model. The ideology of public service was connected with the notion of objectivity, the faith that it was possible to report 'events' from a non-political and non-sectarian standpoint, relying on neutral criteria of 'newsworthiness' to make the inevitable choices media 'gatekeepers' must make. This notion is also under assault. It was also connected with an important change in the structure of the news organization: owners stepped back to some degree from day-to-day control of news operations and journalists were given relative autonomy to make most news decisions.

Professionalization certainly never eliminated the underlying contradictions of journalistic practice. There was always, for example, an ambiguity over how the need to interpret news to make it comprehensible to the audience could be reconciled with the demand for objectivity. There was also recurring tension over the line between the owner's prerogative and journalistic autonomy. Yet it did provide a provisional resolution that seemed to most of those involved – journalists, owners, readers, politicians – to work well enough. Morale was high in news organizations; the media were growing in prestige and there was relatively little controversy over their ethics or their political role.

I have called this period the 'high modernism' of American journalism (Hallin, 1992a). I use the term with some hesitation, because I do not mean to drag in all the baggage of postmodernist theory. I do think that this period in the history of the news media has much in common with what is often called the 'high modernist period' in art and architecture (Harvey, 1990): a belief in progress, rationality and universal truths or standards, as well as a conviction that it is possible to be part of the 'establishment', with wealth, access and prestige, and simultaneously independent – an avant-garde in art, a watchdog in the media. The current fragmentation of the news media, with Geraldo Rivera and *The New York Times* both claiming the mantle of journalism, the increasingly blurred line between news and entertainment, and the journalists' growing uncertainty about their voice and standpoint – should they, for example, just give the facts, or say to people, 'I feel your pain'? – all these things clearly fit the description of postmodern culture.

Why is this change taking place? It seems to me that the causes are of two kinds. The first, and most obvious, is a change in the economics of the news media, which has shifted the balance between business and journalism, bringing into question the equilibrium on which the professional model was based. The second, and more complex, set of factors has to do with changes in politics and culture that have undermined the rather special conditions under which professionalism flourished.

Market-driven journalism

The pressures towards commercialization are strongest in the case of television, but they affect print media as well. I will begin with the latter.

The 'total newspaper'

The separation between journalism and business so dear to the heart of the 'traditional' journalist is increasingly giving way to the concept of 'total newspapering': the idea that circulation, sales and editorial efforts must be integrated, all directed towards the project of marketing news-information (Towles, 1984; Underwood, 1993; Squires, 1993; Kurtz, 1993a; Rappleye, 1998). A *Business Month* profile of Knight-Ridder's chairman bore the headline: 'Customers First: After a Year as CEO, Jim Batten is Campaigning to Get Every Knight-Ridder Employee Thinking Like a Marketer' (quoted in Underwood, 1993: 17). Editors are increasingly expected to have business training, and market research increasingly influences editorial decisions. Often there is considerable tension between the cultures of journalism and marketing. 'Nobody with a reporter's mentality was allowed in these meetings,' said Wayne Ezell, editor of the *Boca Raton News*, referring to strategy sessions in which the Florida publication was forged into a particularly pure example of the market-driven paper (Kurtz, 1993b: 86). The results of this shift are plain to see in any American paper, though their extent varies considerably. They include shorter stories, colour and graphics, and a shift in the news agenda away from traditional 'public affairs' and towards lifestyle features and 'news you can use'. Surveys of American journalists have also found a substantial decline in job satisfaction, which seems to be in part a response to diminished autonomy on the job (Weaver and Wilhoit, 1991; Underwood, 1993).

Why has this shift come about? There are two major schools of thought on this issue, which might be called the 'readership theory' and the 'stockholder theory'. The readership theory holds that newspapers are doing what they must to respond to a dangerous decline in readership, becoming more responsive in an effort to hold on to 'customers' who can choose between a number of sources of information. Newspaper readership is indeed declining. Between 1967 and 1991, the percentage of American adults reporting they read a newspaper every day declined from 73 to 51 (Kurtz, 1993b: 62), with the sharpest decline among younger age groups. In the late 1950s newspaper circulation reached a peak at 1.3 papers sold per household. By the late 1980s it was down to 0.7 per household (Bogart, 1989: 16). Given these facts, according to the readership theory, newspapers had no choice but to find out what modern readers wanted and give it to them.

For the readership theory, the story begins with the introduction of television in the 1950s. For the stockholder theory, it begins in the late 1960s, with the trend towards 'public' ownership of newspaper companies. In 1967 the Gannett chain, which now owns over 90 newspapers, began selling stock on the New York Stock Exchange. At that point, only Dow Jones, publisher of *The Wall Street Journal,* and Times Mirror, publisher of the *Los Angeles Times*, were publicly traded, though they, like other newspaper companies, remained essentially family-controlled.

Gannett, under the leadership of Al Neuharth, demonstrated to Wall Street that newspapers could be, as he put it, 'a dependable profit machine in good times and bad' (quoted in Squires, 1993: 21). His were mostly monopoly papers, not the competitive urban papers of the past. They were aggressive at introducing the technology that has cut newspaper production staffs by roughly half from the 1970s to the 1990s, and were leaders in the introduction of market research and the shift toward softer news. Gannett's *USA Today,* launched in 1982, is the classic case of the consumer-oriented paper, and the main competitor to the *New York Times* model of what a newspaper should be. Even as newspaper readership declined, Gannett's papers made spectacular profits, often in the 30 per cent range, far above the average in other industries. Since 1970, as formerly family-owned papers have sold out to chains or have themselves gone public, American newspapers have increasingly been oriented towards Wall Street's expectations, and as this has happened, according to the stockholder theory, public service notions of journalism have been pushed aside. Traditional newspaper owners wanted to make money, of course. But they were often satisfied with profit margins of 5–7 per cent, and were strongly oriented towards the prestige and public standing of their papers. It was in that economic context, according to this view, that journalistic professionalism thrived; with Wall Street calling the shots it is not clear it can survive.

The two theories diverge over, among other things, the question of how to account for the decline of readership. According to the readership theory, it results from forces outside the control of the newspaper industry. The most important is the rise of television as an alternative source of information. Increasing time pressure has also been cited as an important factor: people are working more, the argument goes, in part because of the trend towards households with two wage earners, and perhaps also playing more; they therefore have less time for reading the paper (Denton, 1993). The time explanation draws some support from the fact that Sunday newspaper circulation has not declined as weekday circulation has. Finally, demographic changes are often cited, particularly the increase in minority populations often with weak literacy skills in English and without the cultural habit of newspaper reading – though here it should be pointed out that immigration is hardly a new phenomenon in the United States, including extensive immigration from regions of the world (eastern and southern Europe, particularly) where newspaper readership was limited.

According to the stockholder theory, on the other hand, newspapers themselves bear much of the responsibility for the decline in readership: in pursuit of short-term profits they have cut quality and raised price, alienating the reader in the process. They have also in many cases made a choice to serve a smaller, more affluent readership for which they can demand premium advertising rates, rather than attempting to maximize circulation in the population as a whole. James Squires, who edited the *Chicago Tribune* and the *Orlando Sentinel* and later served as media adviser for Ross Perot's presidential campaign, has argued this position most forcefully, underlining the fact that readership and profits have moved in opposite directions, with profit margins increasing from around 8–12 per cent in the 1960s to 15–20 per cent in the 1980s, even as readership had declined (Squires, 1993: 72–102). One other explanation for this pattern might be that the trend towards monopoly accounts for both high profits and low circulation: perhaps a single newspaper simply cannot serve the diverse urban community in the way that competing newspapers could (the newspapers that disappeared in this period were mostly afternoon papers serving a working-class readership).

From broadcast journalism to reality-based programming

In television, the heyday of professionalism was briefer and its decline has been more dramatic. Many popular accounts push the 'golden age' of broadcast journalism back to the 1950s, when Edward R. Murrow and his associates held forth at CBS. There were indeed distinguished journalists in television in this era, carrying into that new medium journalistic traditions established in print and in radio. Far more characteristic of this period, however, was NBC's *Camel News Caravan*, a slight, 15-minute bulletin largely drawn from wire reports, anchored by John Cameron Swayze, hired by a Reynolds Tobacco account executive who thought he had a pretty face (Matusow, 1983). It was in the early 1960s that the journalistic professionalism became firmly institutionalized at the networks. In 1963 CBS and NBC expanded their evening news broadcasts from 15 minutes to half an hour, and began to devote increasing resources to public affairs programming. The news divisions that produced this programming were to a large extent insulated from commercial pressures. They were run largely by journalists, who identified far more with their colleagues in the print press than with network headquarters or the people in Hollywood who produced commercial television. They were not expected to make money, and indeed lost millions. Why did these businesses engage in an activity that lost such sums? News did provide some indirect economic benefits. News personnel became visible, prestigious symbols of network identity, useful for marketing the network to viewers, advertisers and affiliates. It seems unlikely, though, that the news divisions would have enjoyed the size and autonomy they did if broadcasting had not been a regulated industry, and the networks therefore concerned to show that they were more than routine businesses, that they were responsible institutions, fulfilling the public service mandate of the Federal Communications Act and deserving of protection under the First Amendment. To all of this it should be added that they could easily afford it, as a highly profitable oligopoly.

By the mid-1980s, the networks were moving to eliminate the special status of the news divisions, supervising them more closely and forcing them, like any other division of the corporation, to contribute to the bottom line. It was this move, of course, that produced Dan Rather's outburst. As outlined below, the change resulted from a number of factors.

Increased competition

This began in the 1970s, as ABC News moved to compete with the other networks. Then in the 1980s the entire structure of the television market began to change with the growth of cable, direct broadcast satellite TV, the Fox network – which had 11 per cent of the prime-time audience in 1998–99 – and the smaller WB and UPN networks. The three-network share of the television audience declined from about 90 per cent in the 1970s to 43 per cent (during prime-time) for the 1998–99 season.

Deregulation

In the 1980s the FCC eliminated a working requirement that stations devote 5 per cent of broadcast time to news and public affairs, and generally moved towards treating broadcast licences as private property. Broadcasters now feel little pressure to show they are serving the 'public convenience and necessity'.

The rise of local TV news

In the 1970s, local TV stations discovered that news could make money. They began expanding their news operations and developed a much more market-driven model of television journalism than that produced by the networks. The public service culture of network and newspaper journalism, with its corresponding hostility to letting commercial considerations intrude into the newsroom, is not entirely absent in local television news, but it is much weaker: sometimes with embarrassment and sometimes – especially among news directors and other top personnel – with defiance or with bland matter-of-factness, local TV people are usually quick to explain that they are in the television business and that ratings are the ultimate arbiter of news judgement. Local TV news is extremely important for a number of reasons. It is more watched than the network news. One 1988 estimate put the nightly audience of network news at 47 million, as compared with 80 million for local news (McManus, 1994: 10). It is also now the primary training ground for network news personnel, who in earlier years typically spent some time working in print journalism. It is also an attractive model to network executives who would like to remake news in a more profitable form.

The rise of 'reality-based programming'

The term originated in the 1980s, but the trend can be dated to 1968, when *60 Minutes* went on air. Within a few years this hybrid of news and entertainment was among the most successful shows on television, competing for ratings with the top entertainment programmes, and becoming the most profitable television series ever produced (Campbell, 1993). Because news magazines are cheaper to produce than entertainment programmes and because they are fully owned by the networks rather than licensed from Hollywood production companies, they have become extremely important to network profitability. By the 1998–99 season the networks were producing 14 hours of prime-time news magazine programming a week. These shows have deeply affected the network news divisions, 'breaking down the corroded barriers' between news and entertainment, as a CBS executive said about *48 Hours* (Haithman, 1988). They exert a strong pull on the evening news programmes, once the *raison d'être* of the news divisions, both because the evening news is increasingly used to promote news magazines appearing later the same night and, most important, because production of the magazines is gradually coming to be the news divisions' primary activity, shaping the recruitment and socialization of TV journalists (Zurwick and Stoehr, 1993 and 1994).

Meanwhile, other forms of 'reality-based programming' were developed entirely outside the networks. These included, most notably for our purposes, the 'tabloids' – *Hard Copy*, *A Current Affair* and *Inside Edition* – which borrow the forms of journalism, but are produced strictly as commercial products with minimal connection to the traditional professional culture. These programmes had their heyday in the late 1980s and early 1990s and have declined in recent years. But they too have played a central role in transforming TV news – indeed, their decline is due in part to the fact that both local news and network news magazines have appropriated much of their agenda and technique.

Corporate culture

Finally, in the 1980s, each of the networks was either involved in a major merger, or taken over by a larger corporation. Many accounts of these mergers and acquisitions argue that the new owners thought of broadcasting more strictly as a business than previous owners, and approached news in those terms (Auletta, 1991; Boyer, 1989; Mazzocco, 1994).

The effects of these changes include substantial budget cuts at the network news divisions, with Washington bureaus, for example, being reduced from near 30 correspondents to less than half that number (Kimball, 1994: 23), and an increased focus on stories that provide 'moments' of emotional involvement (Boyer, 1989).

Political and cultural change

It is probably no accident that the period of 'high modernism', in the news media as in other branches of culture, coincided with the aftermath of the Second World War. The nation had been through two profound crises, the great depression and the war. In each case, people had looked to political leadership, particularly in Washington, for solutions. The prestige of public affairs was high, and there was a strong sense of a national interest that transcended partisan, commercial and sectarian interests. To some degree, these attitudes towards public life carried over into the early years of the Cold War, though by the 1960s it was clear that they had begun to erode. The collapse of the professional model of journalism coincides with the passing of what Putnam (1996) calls the 'long civic generation', born between 1910 and 1940, which was characterized by unusually high levels of civic engagement, including a high rate of newspaper readership.

Besides a strong sense that public affairs was important and worth attending to, two related characteristics of the political culture of the post-war period made professionalism more plausible as a model of journalism. This was a period of relatively strong political consensus, and also of high public confidence in political authority. Foreign policy dominated political thinking; in journalism the 'national security' beats were the most prestigious, and in many ways provided the model for the rest of reporting. In this arena bipartisanship was the political watchword, and a strong conviction prevailed that power and justice were united: the president and his chief advisers made decisions on behalf of the nation as a whole and indeed on behalf of the Free World. Those decisions were conceived as essentially above politics, and the men who made them were regarded with real awe. In domestic policy, consensus prevailed on the basic outlines of New Deal politics – a consensus strengthened by robust economic growth and a conviction that the modern economy was close to eliminating class divisions. Surveys showed strong public confidence in political leaders and institutions and there was a widespread belief that neutral expertise could solve social problems.

In this context it was easy for journalists to settle in as part of the political 'establishment' without feeling that they were compromising their independence or their relationship with the ordinary citizens who formed their audience. It was easy, too, to believe in 'objectivity': official statements could be reported 'straight' – that is, at face value – and basic political assumptions were widely enough shared that they could be taken for granted. The consensus of Cold War liberalism and the faith in political authority that went with it were broken by Vietnam, Watergate, the struggles over race and gender, and the deteriorating position of the blue collar 'middle class', to name just a few of the forces of change.[1] This had two major consequences for the news media. First, it undermined the credibility of 'objective journalism' and pushed the news media towards more interpretative forms of reporting. Second, it left journalists with a problem of how to position themselves: were they insiders or outsiders? Did they identify with the elite, or with the increasingly alienated mass public?

The trend towards interpretative reporting deserves further comment. The idea is hardly new: Walter Lippmann and Curtis MacDougall argued for interpretative reporting in the 1920s and 1930s. But 'straight' reporting clearly dominated during the height of the professional era. 'Today, subtly, without any clear consensus', in the words of *Los Angeles Times* media writer Tom Rosenstiel (1993), 'the idea of straight reporting is giving way to something else. Many of the nation's newspapers are shifting uneasily toward a new era of subjectivity.'

There are many reasons for the shift. Partly it represents a reaction to the decline of political authority. In practice, straight journalism meant taking official statements at face value; but if those become 'inoperative', as Nixon's did during Watergate, journalists feel pressure to fill the void. Partly it arises from competition and commercialization. Part of the appeal of the tabloid news shows is that the journalists take sides and emote along with the audience. Network television had already moved during the 1970s from a particularly narrow form of 'straight' reporting towards thematic, packaged stories with strong 'storylines' (Hallin, 1992b). The rise of the magazine shows is likely to push TV news further in the direction of subjectivity. An ABC producer said of the magazine-style 'American Agenda' segment that appears on *World News Tonight*: 'American Agenda pieces are by definition supposed to offer a solution to the problem being covered. If not a solution, a point of view. It's easier to connect with the audience that way' (quoted in Kimball, 1994: 20).

Newspapers, meanwhile, in their effort to appeal to younger readers, have moved in the direction of commentaries and features (Diamond, 1994: 274–83). There is also some tendency for the voice of interpretative reporting to change: from the 'voice of God' adopted by *Time* magazine or the top Washington columnists of the Cold War era, to the 'voice of the people' of tabloid news, or to a more obviously subjective voice.

In much of Europe it has long been assumed that journalism is an exercise in interpretation, and necessarily involves adopting a political point of view. But American journalism has been based on a denial of this kind of subjectivity, and the traditional style of American news writing is in large part designed to conceal the voice of the journalist. So the move to subjectivity creates considerable confusion among American journalists about what the rules of the game are now to be.

A number of other social changes have also served to undercut the professional model. I will focus on three.

Multiculturalism

It is common today to assume that newsrooms are more diverse than they once were. This is true in at least one respect: there are significantly more women among the ranks of journalists – an increase, according to Weaver and Wilhoit (1991: 22), from 20 per cent in 1971 to 34 per cent in 1982–83. Gays are also now openly present in many major news organizations. It is not clear, on the other hand, that newsrooms are more diverse in ethnic terms. Only something like 9 per cent of newsroom employees are from ethnic minority groups, with most studies showing little progress over time (Gilliam, 1991; Weaver and Wilhoit, 1991). Diversity is mainly thought of today in terms of gender and ethnicity, not class, and there is little information about trends in the class background of journalists; some have suggested it is more uniformly middle class today than a generation ago. It is certainly true, though, that in the wake of the cultural revolution of the 1960s and 1970s, there is greater consciousness of the cultural roots of news judgement, a consciousness that is often manifested in sharp debates over particular news decisions (Kurtz, 1993a). This makes it harder to sustain the notion of professional neutrality.

Blurred boundaries between the public and private domains

This is most obvious in the recurring problem of how far to go in covering politicians' private lives. In the 1940s journalists used to call Republican politician Wendell Willkie at the home of his lover, *New York Herald-Tribune* literary editor Irita Van Doren, but none would have thought of reporting that relationship; by the 1980s the *Miami Herald* was staking out the apartment of

Democratic presidential hopeful Gary Hart to catch him with his lover, and *The New York Times* was sending a questionnaire to every presidential candidate, asking if he or she had committed any private 'indiscretion' (Sabato, 1993). The media are far from passive observers of this change, but they did not create it by themselves: it results in part from the challenge posed by the women's movement to the separation of public and private – the notion that 'the personal is political' – and in part from the breakdown of traditional rules of the political game as the elite community of Washington has become less 'clubby' and more individualized (Kernell, 1993). At any rate this change too undermines the professional model: it tarnishes the journalist's aura of high-mindedness, thrusts the subjectivity of news judgement to the forefront, and undermines the division of labour between the 'serious press' concerned with public affairs, and the tabloids and internet gossip sheets, which major news organizations increasingly find themselves following or imitating. The Watergate scandal hurt the prestige of the presidency but enhanced that of the media; the Lewinsky scandal tarnished both (Wolff, 1998).

The rise of new media

New media make it possible for news-makers to communicate with the mass public without the mediation of journalists. This trend began much earlier, with radio, which made it possible for the president to address the public 'directly'. But the number of channels has multiplied considerably with the recent explosion of 'infotainment' media. H. Ross Perot launched his presidential campaign through talk shows and magazine programmes, reaching 20 per cent support in the polls before the mainstream news media took note of him (Rosenstiel, 1993: 164–65; Zaller with Hunt, 1994). Clinton holds 'electronic town meetings' rather than press conferences. The police reporter of old is replaced by *Cops*, and *Real Stories of the Highway Patrol*, syndicated shows on which the main narrators are policemen, not journalists (Katz, 1993). The trend towards live reporting, led by local news and by CNN, and increasingly important with the growth of internet news sites, also tends to remove the journalist from the role of gatekeeper and interpreter, and thrust either the images themselves or other communicators to the forefront. In the case of the Gulf War and the war in the Balkans, live coverage meant that military briefers partly supplanted journalists as providers of information and commentary.

These new forms of media are often described as providing 'unmediated' communication. This is clearly not accurate: they are often carefully structured as commercial products, each with its own logic of selection and emphasis. Conventional news media, moreover, are still very powerful, as Zaller and Hunt (1994) demonstrate in the case of the Perot campaign. But these new media do decentre the process of communication in important ways, and encourage people to ask, 'What do we need journalists for, anyway?'

Decline or Utopia?

Are we witnessing the decline of public life, or the dawn of a more democratic age of multiple voices and responsiveness to popular taste? The answer, I think, is complex.

I am not convinced by the view, most often articulated by elite journalists of the 'high modernist' period, that the transformation of the American media represents a downhill slide from a 'golden age'. Journalistic professionalism, for one thing, is far from dead, and in certain ways is stronger than ever. The journalism of the golden age was most of the time extremely passive, particularly in its handling of official information. Today's more analytic journalism is often much more sophisticated. The journalism of the golden age was event-oriented in the extreme: 'hard news' was what happened yesterday, and long-term trends or underlying conditions were ignored. Today there is at least a modest tendency towards more thematic, less event-centred reporting (Barnhurst and Mutz, 1997).

The rise of the new media, moreover, does seem to represent real democratization in certain ways. Many journalists denounced the move towards 'talk show democracy' in the 1992 presidential election. With presidential candidates avoiding the press and appearing instead on *Larry King Live* and MTV, they would never have to face tough questions from people who had enough background knowledge to put them on the spot, and the image-makers would have a field day – so went the argument. There are, to be sure, plenty of problems with talk shows as a political forum. Clinton's 'electronic town meetings' were more like royal audiences than town meetings: individuals came to ask the President for help, not to exchange ideas among themselves. And the commercial character of the new media certainly affects their agenda. When Clinton, during his 1992 campaign, appeared on the Phil Donahue show, Donahue tried aggressively to push the discussion on to Clinton's alleged affair with Gennifer Flowers. Donahue's *audience*, however, objected vociferously, applauding a woman who insisted the discussion should focus on public policy. In the second of the three presidential debates that same year, which broke with political tradition by employing a talk-show format rather than a panel of journalists, audience members again insisted that the candidates address the economy rather than Gennifer Flowers and Clinton's draft record; in the third debate, with the journalists back in charge, attention turned again to the personal charges, as well as to the kind of 'inside baseball' analysis of polls and political tactics favoured by the professional journalist. There is also, it seems to me, considerable symbolic importance simply in the fact that the candidates are seen interacting with ordinary voters, and that members of the mass public see people like themselves speaking out in the political arena. Perhaps the increased public interest in the 1992 election was in part a result of the fact that the campaign was carried out in forums where ordinary voters felt more at home. The mainstream media do not have a very good record in recent years of including the ordinary citizen in the representation of political life (Hallin, 1992b).

Even the shift towards a more market-driven form of journalism, and the blurring of the lines between news and entertainment that goes with it, are positive developments in many ways. News and entertainment have never been absolutely separate, and there is no reason why they should be. The best journalists have always been good story-tellers. Story-telling is essential to journalism because it generates popular interest. It is central, as well, because news has never been only about providing information in the narrow sense, but also a contribution to dialogue about values and collective identity, and that kind of dialogue is carried on largely through narrative (Campbell, 1991).

The traditional agenda of 'hard news', moreover, was always narrow, and in important ways elitist. It was extremely Washington-centred, preoccupied with inside-the-beltway discussion of limited relevance to most audience members. It was heavily focused on the activities of elites (Gans, 1979). It reflected the gender, class and race biases of the elite journalists who produced it. It also tended to define issues 'from the top down', privileging the point of view of the policy-maker over the more experiential point of view of the citizen who would live with the policy (Hallin, 1986).

In a recent *Columbia Journalism Review* cover story on 'How Pressure for Profit is Perverting Journalism', one journalist gave the following illustration of declining standards of news judgement:

> If someone from the entertainment side or the promotion department came to us and suggested we do a piece about a lesbian coming out in a prime-time sitcom, we would have yelled, 'Forget about it!' It's unbelievable how much of that junk gets on the air.
>
> (Hickey, 1998b: 34)

He was referring, of course, to the extensive media attention that surrounded the episode in which the protagonist of the popular sitcom *Ellen* came out as a lesbian. But was this, in fact, poor news judgement? Couldn't one argue that the coming-out episode of *Ellen* represented a cultural change of considerable significance, more important to public life than many of the Washington-based events that defined the world of news for the professional journalist of old? If there are more stories today about education, health, the media, or the politics of personal life – domestic violence, for instance – so much the better: this represents a much-needed broadening of our sense of what constitutes a public issue.

Once we reject the notion of the golden age, however, once we accept that there is plenty of room for change in the professional culture of American journalism, there is still much in the trend towards commercialization of news that is deeply disturbing. If the news agenda has been broadened in certain ways, it has been trivialized in others. An extreme example can be found at local TV stations during the 'sweeps' – the four months of the year when ratings are determined for all local markets. The kinds of story routinely featured during this period would have been considered the wildest parody of commercialization 15 years ago; a few recent ones in the San Diego market include week-long series on local nudist colonies, private eyes who use hidden cameras to spy on spouses suspected of infidelity, and a giggly, voyeuristic series on S&M sex (the latter generated considerable community protest). At newspapers, there is often pressure to focus on news that will 'help the new-value consumer seek the full, rich life' in the words of an executive of Harte-Hankes Communication (Underwood, 1993: 8). The editor of the *Boca Raton News* once boasted, '"[Champagne] prices soon to explode" – we're the only paper in America to do an eight-inch story on that. For baby boomers who go to a lot of [champagne] parties, that's more interesting than what [Republican politician] Jack Kemp had to say today' (quoted in Kurtz, 1993b: 86).

In other ways, meanwhile, the news agenda has been narrowed. There is, for example, considerably less international news, both in newspapers, where it has declined from 10.2 per cent of the newshole in 1971 to 2.6 per cent in 1988 (Emery, 1989), and on television. The focus on international reporting that char-

acterized the Cold War era is certainly open to criticism. Much of that reporting reflected the journalists' status as insiders, and their often uncritical acceptance of an ideology that saw threats to 'national security' in every political
development around the world. But international reporting is declining at a time
when increased economic interdependence is making world politics in many
ways more, not less, relevant to the lives of ordinary people.

The trend from 'hard news' to 'sensationalism' is often referred to as
'tabloidization', and it makes sense to consider specifically the influence of the
new television tabloids. Appropriately enough, these shows tend to generate
debates among media critics which resemble the shouting matches of the Geraldo
Rivera and Jerry Springer shows. For journalism traditionalists they are the
purest manifestation of evil; for some popular cultural theorists of postmodern
bent they represent, 'a place where ideological forces of the powerful may be
challenged by oppositional or popular forces' (Glynn, 1990: 32; see also Fiske,
1992). Obviously a bit more subtlety is needed in understanding these shows.
Like every form of popular culture, there is clearly a story to be told about
why and how they appeal to their audience. It is also clearly true that – like
other 'infotainment' forms – they sometimes provide a vehicle for voices normally marginalized by the 'serious' news media (Hallin, 1994: 92–97). Louise
Mengelkoch, a journalist who served as an informal media adviser for a victim
of a gang rape whose father was tried for killing one of her attackers, puts it this
way: 'As gatekeepers [the tabloids are] lousy, and that's often fortunate for those
who need them most. They will listen to your story when nobody else will, if it
has the elements and angles they're looking for' (Mengelkoch, 1994).

But to present these products of the media industry as a form of popular
resistance to oppression – the modern equivalent of Bakhtinian carnival – is
rather far-fetched. They have their own principles of exclusion: '*A Current
Affair,*' reports a former tabloid producer, 'didn't like doing stories about gays,
people of color, or unattractive women' (Bradford, 1993: 41). They also, of
course, don't like doing stories about politics: an individual rape victim might
find a hearing on the tabloids; an *organization* dedicated to defending the interests of rape victims is far more likely to succeed with traditional journalism.
Like their print forerunners, the supermarket tabloids (Bird, 1992), they tend to
be quite traditional in their worldview: they focus, to be sure, on transgressors
of social norms, but typically with strong moral condemnation. It would make
far more sense to defend them on conservative grounds, as reinforcing social values, than as 'exposing the cracks in the hegemony of the normal' (Glynn, 1990:
29). There are plenty of reasons to worry about the effect of tabloidization on
the wider culture. The tabloids, to give just one example, depend heavily on the
exploitation and amplification of fear. The local television promotion reproduced in Figure 10.1, advertising a tabloidized sweeps-month feature, illustrates
an important consequence: the dichotomy drawn in this genre between the
forces of order and the outgroups – represented here by the hairy wild man –
who threaten it and must be controlled.

Those who celebrate the tabloids as a form of social resistance typically identify journalistic professionalism as a form of oppression, a tool of the 'power-
bloc' in Fiske's words (1992: 49), which 'hides its disciplinarity under notions of
objectivity, responsibility and political education.'[2] In fact, it is just as simple-
minded to identify traditional journalism as purely top-down communication as

Fig. 10.1

to identify the tabloids as purely bottom-up. Journalistic professionalism is as contradictory in its relations to the powerful and powerless as any other branch of popular culture. In the name of professionalism, to be sure, a correspondent in Central America may be admonished that what s/he has learned from a peasant must be confirmed by an 'authoritative' source; a Black reporter pushing for greater coverage of the African-American community may be asked, 'are you Black first, or a reporter?' But it is also in the name of professionalism that reporters will resist the dictates of marketers to report on suburban champagne parties, and insist instead on covering the inner city. Professionalism, moreover, is by no means the sole possession of elite journalists in Washington bureaus: thousands of rank-and-file journalists around the country hold it dear as a protection of the 'privilege' of a rather modest autonomy. I have often been struck in talking to local television people at the anger expressed, often most strongly in lower ranks, among camera crews, for example, at the pressure for tabloidization; within local TV stations there is no question that tabloidization is imposed from the top, while professionalism provides the language of resistance from below.

It is in the name of professionalism, too, that journalists will often resist pressures to shape the news to fit the political interests of the owners, and that the latter will often be inhibited from attempting such influence. And the decline of professionalism therefore raises the question about whether the connection between ownership and political power might become more direct in the future. Professionalization did not, of course, eliminate the ability of media owners to influence the political content of the news. After all, Warren Breed's famous essay, 'Social Control in the News Room' (1955) was written at a time when professionalization was largely consolidated. Subtle influence has always flowed from the top down in media organizations. Diamond (1994: 124) quotes Arthur Sulzberger, Jr, publisher of *The New York Times*, as saying, 'I don't believe in telling editors and reporters what to do. But I do believe in long, philosophic conversations with my editors about where the paper, the city and the country are going.' The 'Darts and Laurels' column of the *Columbia Journalism Review* typically features one or two current examples of more heavy-handed intervention in the news process. Still, professional norms have, over the last generation, significantly limited the manipulation of news by owners seeking to push their particular political convictions or interests.

The news culture changes slowly, and we are not yet back to the days when politically ambitious owners reserved the right to use the news columns to shape public opinion whenever they pleased. But there are signs of change. In the magazine industry there is clearly considerable pressure from advertisers for greater control over content (Baker, 1997). The new Fox news division, meanwhile, reflects the politics of owner Rupert Murdoch in a way we have not seen at a major news organization since the death of *Time* founder Henry Luce (Hickey, 1998a). If journalists become increasingly accustomed to deferring to management in matters of marketing (Underwood (1993) reports a trend towards a sort of fill-in-the-blanks journalism, in which reporters, rather than being sent to find out 'what the story is' are assigned to supply part of a package devised by marketers) it certainly seems conceivable that the inhibitions against political interference might gradually die out.

Conclusion

Mark Fowler, chairman of the FCC under Ronald Reagan, once said, 'the public interest is that which interests the public'. This is the dominant view in discussions of the media today: that the media are industries producing a consumer product like any other, and that the market can be the only basis for deciding what kind of product that should be. The *Times'* Walter Goodman echoes that view, and so, in an interesting way, do those who express the particular brand of postmodernism cited above, who also argue that whatever succeeds on the market is by definition 'the popular,' and any criticism can only be elitist.

This view, however, runs into tremendous difficulties, both logical and empirical, once one tries to think out what it really means. Mr Fowler's comment seems like a clever line, and not a nonsensical tautology, only because users of the English language are perfectly capable of distinguishing between different senses of the word 'interest': what captures one's attention at a particular moment and what one has a stake in, in a more lasting way. Donahue's audience recognized this when they insisted that they did not want to hear about Gennifer Flowers during the election campaign, or, to put it in terms of the related distinction between public and private life, that they wanted to be treated for the moment as citizens rather than consumers. These distinctions are properly the subject of considerable debate today, but they are not for all that meaningless. A number of scholars have offered critiques of the notion of consumer sovereignty applied to the media, including Curran (in this volume), McManus (1994) and Gitlin (1985) in his analysis of the role of audience 'feedback' in production decisions in the television industry. The issues involved are too complex to be summarized fully here; suffice it to say that if ever there were an industry that involved what economists call 'externalities' it is the cultural industry, with the news media as a particularly obvious case. The nation's political agenda, its stock of social knowledge, its style of political discussion, all are shaped by the news media, and there is no reason to suppose that they will be 'optimized' by profit-seeking programmers and advertisers.

Professionalized news media will not, of course, disappear. They will always have a market, at least among wealthier people who feel they have a stake in public affairs. It is possible, however, that we will see a division of the news audience into one wealthier segment that watches news produced on traditional journalistic lines, and another part that watches only news produced in a tabloid style. In principle, differentiation of the news market could be a force for greater democracy; different parts of the community have different concerns, and the news has never served them all equally or in a satisfactory way. Unfortunately, however, what seems most likely – if 'serious news' indeed becomes what Goodman calls 'boutique programming' – is a kind of differentiation that reinforces social barriers, in effect excluding working-class audiences from the information about public affairs, and 'interpellating' them as private, 'emotional' and properly outside the world where public power is exercised.

If we are to avoid the collapse of news media with some sense of public service, two things will probably have to happen. First, journalism will have to change. The 'high modernist' conception of professionalism is clearly no longer viable and needs to be rethought in important ways. For one thing, as Carey (1993) has argued, journalists will probably have to shift from conceiving of themselves as, in effect, a representative or stand-in for a unitary but inactive public, to a role of facilitating and publicizing public dialogue. Second, we will need a new public debate over the question asked more than 50 years ago by the Commission on Freedom of the Press: what can be done, through public policy or the structuring of media institutions, to 'free the press from the influences which now prevent it from supplying the communication of news and ideas needed by the kind of society we have and the kind of society we desire' (1947: 79).

Notes

1.   It is interesting that similar changes have taken place in most western countries, suggesting that deeper processes are at work behind these specific events.
2.   See also Pauly (1988), who, though he does not characterize tabloid news as popular resistance, interprets mainstream journalists' criticism of it as nothing more than a defence of their privileges, and dismisses professionalization as a 'simulation of social responsibility'.

References

AULETTA, K. (1991) *Three Blind Mice*. New York: Random House.
BAKER, R. (1997) The Squeeze. *Columbia Journalism Review*, September/October: 30–36.
BARNHURST, K. and MUTZ, D. (1997) 'American Journalism and the Decline in Event-Centered Reporting', *Journal of Communication*, Vol. 47, No. 4: 27–53.
BIRD, S.E. (1992) *For Inquiring Minds: A Cultural Study of Supermarket Tabloids*. Knoxville, TN: University of Tennessee Press.
BOGART, L. (1989) *Press and Public: Who Reads What, When, Where and Why in American Newspapers*. Hillsdale, NJ: Erlbaum.
BOYER, P. (1989) *Who Killed CBS? The Undoing of America's Number One News Network*. New York: St Martin's.
BRADFORD, K. (1993) 'The Big Sleaze', *Rolling Stone*, 18 February: 39–44, 69.
BREED, W. (1955) 'Social Control in the Newsroom', *Social Forces*, Vol. 33: 326–35.
CAMPBELL, R. (1991) *60 Minutes and the News: A Mythology for Middle America*. Urbana, IL: University of Illinois Press.
——, 1993) 'Don Hewitt's Durable Hour', *Columbia Journalism Review*, September/October: 25–28.
CAREY, J.W. (1993) 'The Mass Media and Democracy: Between the Modern and the Postmodern', *Journal of International Affairs*, Vol. 47, No. 1: 1–21.
COMMISSION ON FREEDOM OF THE PRESS (1947) *A Free and Responsible Press*. Chicago: University of Chicago Press.
DENTON, H. (1993) 'Old Newspapers and New Realities: The Promise of the Marketing of Journalism', in *Reinventing the Newspaper*. New York: Twentieth Century Fund.
DIAMOND, E. (1994) *Behind the Times: Inside The New York Times*. New York: Villard Books.
EMERY, M. (1989) 'An Endangered Species: The International Newshole', *Gannett Center Journal*, Vol. 3, No. 4 (Fall).
FISKE, J. (1992) 'Popularity and the Politics of Information', in P. Dahlgren and C. Sparks (eds), *Journalism and Popular Culture*. Thousand Oaks: Sage.
GANS, H. (1979) *Deciding What's News*. New York: Pantheon.

GILLIAM, D.B. (1991) 'Harnessing the Assets of a Multicultural Future', *Media Studies Journal*, Vol. 5, No. 4: 127–35.

GITLIN, T. (1985) *Inside Prime-time*. New York: Pantheon.

GLYNN, K. (1990) 'Tabloid Television's Transgressive Aesthetic: *A Current Affair* and the 'Shows that Taste Forgot'', *Wide Angle*, Vol. 12, No. 2: 22–44.

HAITHMAN, D. (1988) 'CBS' '48 Hours' Hopes to Break Down Barriers', *Los Angeles Times*, 19 January.

HALLIN, D.C. (1986) 'Cartography, Community and the Cold War' in R.K. Manoff and M.S. Schudson (eds), *Reading the News*. New York: Pantheon.

——, (1992a) 'The Passing of the 'High Modernism' of American Journalism', *Journal of Communication*, Vol. 42, No. 3: 14–25.

——, (1992b) 'Sound Bite News: Television Coverage of Elections, 1968–1988', *Journal of Communication*, Vol. 42, No. 2: 5–24.

——, (1994) *We Keep America on Top of the World: Television Journalism and the Public Sphere*. London and New York: Routledge.

HARVEY, D. (1990) *The Condition of Postmodernity*. Cambridge, MA: Blackwell.

HICKEY, N. (1998a) 'Is Fox News Fair?' *Columbia Journalism Review*, March/April: 30–35.

——, (1998b) 'Money Lust: How Pressure for Profit is Perverting Journalism', *Columbia Journalism Review*, July/August: 28–36.

KATZ, J. (1993) 'Covering the Cops: A TV Show Moves In Where Journalists Fear to Tread', *Columbia Journalism Review*, January/February: 25–30.

KERNELL, S. (1993) *Going Public: New Strategies of Presidential Leadership*. Washington, DC: Congressional Quarterly Press.

KIMBALL, P. (1994) *Downsizing the News: Network Cutbacks in the Nation's Capital*. Washington, DC: The Woodrow Wilson Center Press.

KURTZ, H. (1993a) *Media Circus: The Trouble with America's Newspapers*. New York: Times Books.

——, (1993b) 'Yesterday's News: Why Newspapers Are Losing Their Franchise', in *Reinventing the Newspaper*. New York: Twentieth Century Fund.

MCMANUS, J. (1994) *Market-Driven Journalism: Let the Citizen Beware?* Thousand Oaks, CA: Sage.

MATUSOW, B. (1983) *The Evening Stars: The Making of the Network News Anchor*. New York: Ballantine.

MAZZOCCO, D. (1994) *Networks of Power: Corporate TV's Threat to Democracy*. Boston: South End Press.

MENGELKOCH, L. (1994) 'When Checkbook Journalism Does God's Work', *Columbia Journalism Review*, November/December: 35–38.

PAULY, J.J. (1988) 'Rupert Murdoch and the Demonology of Professional Journalism' in J.W. Carey (ed.), *Media, Myths and Narratives: Television and the Press*. Beverly Hills: Sage.

PUTNAM, R.D. (1996) 'The Strange Disappearance of Civic America', *The American Prospect*, Winter: 34–48.

RAPPLEYE, C. (1998) 'Cracking the Church-State Wall: Early Results of the Revolution at the Los Angeles Times', *Columbia Journalism Review*, January/February: 20–23.

ROSENSTIEL, T. (1993) 'Reporters Putting Their Own Spin on Events', *Los Angeles Times*, 25 November: A1.

SABATO, L. (1993) *Feeding Frenzy: How Attack Journalism Has Transformed American Politics*. New York: Free Press.

SCHUDSON, M. (1978) *Discovering the News: A Social History of American Newspapers*. New York: Basic Books.

SIEBERT, F.S., PETERSON, T. and SCHRAMM, W. (1956) *Four Theories of the Press*. Urbana, IL: University of Illinois Press.

SQUIRES, J. (1993) *Read All About It! The Corporate Takeover of America's Newspapers.* New York: Random House.

TOWLES, D.B. (ed.) (1984) *Promoting the Total Newspaper.* Reston, VA: International Newspaper Marketing Association.

UNDERWOOD, D. (1993) *When MBAs Rule the Newsroom: How the Marketers and Managers are Reshaping Today's Media.* New York: Columbia University Press.

VILES, P. (1993) 'Dan Rather Blasts TV News', *Broadcasting & Cable*, 4 October: 12.

WEAVER, D.H. and WILHOIT, G.C. (1991) *The American Journalist: A Portrait of US News People and Their Work.* Bloomington, IN: Indiana University Press.

WOLFF, M. (1998) 'Bad News for the Media Elite', *New York*, 23 November: 30–34, 120.

ZALLER, J. with HUNT, M. (1994) 'The Rise and Fall of Candidate Perot: Unmediated Versus Mediated Politics, Part I', *Political Communication*, Vol. 11, No. 4: 357–90.

ZURWICK, D. and STOEHR, C. (1993) 'Money Changes Everything', *American Journalism Review*, April: 26–30.

——, (1994) 'Eclipsing the Nightly News', *American Journalism Review*, November: 32–38.

11

In Defence of Objectivity Revisited

Judith Lichtenberg

Introduction

In these postmodern times, the ideal of objectivity may seem a bit tattered around the edges, but American journalists still embrace it as one of the fundamental norms of their profession. The distinction between news, where objectivity is thought possible and desirable, and opinion, where objectivity is thought impossible, is deeply entrenched in the journalistic culture. Inextricably intertwined with truth, fairness, balance, neutrality, the absence of value judgements – in short, with the most fundamental journalistic values – objectivity is a cornerstone of the professional ideology of journalists in liberal democracies.

Yet the objectivity of journalism has come increasingly under fire in recent years. The criticisms come from a variety of quarters and take several forms. Some say that journalism *is not* objective; others that it *cannot be* objective; and still others that it *should not be* objective. Odd as it may seem, sometimes the same critic seems to be making all of these charges at the same time.

One challenge comes from critics – from across the political spectrum – who claim that the media have misrepresented their views or have not reported their activities impartially. Some say that the media have a 'liberal bias', that they overemphasize unrest and dissent, or look too hard for muck to rake. Other critics contend that, on the contrary, the press serves the conservative interests of government and big business. Aggrieved individuals and groups of all kinds charge that news coverage of this or that issue is unfair, biased, or sensational.

Those who attack journalism on these grounds seem to share one crucial assumption with those they criticize. Charges of bias or unfairness suggest that objectivity is at least possible. How can one complain of bias, after all, unless *un*bias can be imagined? But many contemporary critics, not only of journalism but of every other form of inquiry, reject this assumption. Journalism is not objective, they say, nor could it be. As one recent textbook puts it, objectivity 'is a false and impossible ideal', and although all media writers claim it in some way, 'they are all wrong' (Kessler and McDonald, 1989: 24, 28).

This view has its roots in the sociology of knowledge and today finds its fullest expression in postmodernism; it is shared by many sociologists, humanists, legal scholars and other social critics. They believe that the idea of objectivity rests on an outmoded and untenable theory of knowledge, according to which objective knowledge consists in correspondence between some idea or statement and a reality 'out there' in the world. 'Objectivity', in the words of a former journalism school dean, 'is an essential correspondence between knowledge of a thing and the thing itself' (McDonald, 1975: 69). According to the critics, however, reality is not 'out there'; it is 'a vast production, a staged creation – something humanly produced and humanly maintained' (Carey, 1989: 26). Reality, on this view, is 'socially constructed', and so there are as many realities as there are social perspectives on the world. There is no 'true reality' to which objective knowledge can be faithful.

One might have expected at least that those reaching such conclusions would do so with a certain regret or disappointment. 'Wouldn't it be good if true knowledge were possible, and isn't it sad that it isn't?' Yet the same people who believe objectivity is impossible often hold also that it is an undesirable and even a dangerous ideal. Objectivity is a strategy of hegemony used by some members of society to dominate others (MacKinnon, 1982: 537); a 'strategic ritual' enabling professionals to 'defend themselves from critical onslaught' (Tuchman, 1972); even 'the most insidious bias of all' (Schudson, 1978: 160).[1] At best, objectivity 'is a cultural form with its own set of conventions' (Schiller, 1981: 5).

The compound assault on objectivity

On the face of it, there is a certain oddness in this compound assault on objectivity – that journalism is not objective, that it could not be, that it should not be – for the charges are essentially incompatible. Thus, although often a single critic makes more than one of these accusations, no two of them taken together makes sense. Why not?

1   The sincere complaint that a piece of journalism is not objective makes sense only against the background assumption that objectivity is possible (why bother complaining about the inevitable?).
2   The insistence that journalism cannot be objective makes superfluous the view that objectivity is undesirable (why bother denouncing the impossible?).
3   The assertion that objectivity is not desirable makes senseless the complaint that journalism is not objective (what is the complaint?).

These apparent confusions do not result from simple muddleheadedness. Ultimately we will find that the different charges levelled against objectivity are really charges levelled against different understandings of objectivity.

Let us begin by trying to reconstruct roughly the chain of reasoning to the all-encompassing conclusion that objectivity in journalism does not, could not, and should not exist:

- Experience continually confronts us with examples of clashes of belief (between individuals, between cultures) that we cannot resolve – we do not know how to decide which belief is true.
- No one can totally escape his or her biases; no one can be completely objective.

- Therefore, the idea that there could be an objective, true account of things is a fiction.
- Anyone who sincerely thinks there could be such an account is deluded by a faulty understanding of the relation between mind and the world.
- This faulty understanding has significant practical consequences; belief in objectivity and adherence to practices thought to be implied by it reinforces existing power relations and cultural and political chauvinism.
- Therefore, the aspiration to objectivity, whether innocent or not, serves as a prop in an ideological agenda.
- So, in other words, real objectivity is impossible and its attempted manifestations are either naive or insidious or both.

Who is this enemy that makes such strange bedfellows, uniting critics from left and right and bringing together the most abstruse of academics with worldly politicians, advocates, and journalists? The alleged enemy is no single entity. In elevating objectivity to an ideal one may be endorsing any of several different ends, or the supposed means of attaining them. It is for this reason that the attack on objectivity can represent a variety of different complaints. Since the values captured by the term 'objectivity' vary greatly – in the extent to which they are possible, probable, actual, or desirable – the legitimacy of the complaints varies as well.

In what follows I have two aims. One is to show that in its core meaning we cannot coherently abandon the ideal of objectivity, and that, whatever they may think, objectivity's critics do not abandon it either. The other is to acknowledge, and to explore, the critics' genuine insights. I shall argue, then, that those detractors of objectivity who enlighten us about the defects and pitfalls of journalism (or other forms of inquiry) themselves covertly rely on the idea of objectivity. Their real target is something else. It may be a value such as neutrality – something commonly associated with objectivity but distinct from it; or it may be a practice or method commonly thought to attain objectivity. There may be good reasons for repudiating these values or practices or methods, but they do not, I shall argue, mean that we should repudiate objectivity in its core sense.

Metaphysical questions

Our most fundamental interest in objectivity is an interest in truth. We want to know how things stand in the world, or what happens, and why. In this sense, to claim that a particular piece of journalism *is not* objective is to claim that it fails to provide the truth or the whole truth. In addition, to deny that objectivity is *possible* is at least to deny that there is any way of getting at the truth, on the grounds that all accounts of things are accounts from a particular social, psychological, cultural or historical perspective and that we have no neutral standpoint from which to adjudicate between conflicting accounts. To deny that objectivity is possible is often also to insist, not only that we can never get at the truth, but also that for precisely this reason it makes no sense to think there is any such thing. Even to speak of 'truth' or 'the facts', these critics strongly suggest, demonstrates a certain naiveté.

To doubt that objectivity is possible, then, is to doubt that we can know how things *really* are or what *really* happens, where 'really' means something like 'independently of our own perspective'. But there is a crucial ambiguity in the phrase 'our own perspective'. One way to doubt the objectivity of a story or an account of things is to challenge the particular perspective from which it is told. So, for example, one might doubt that American news accounts of the Gulf War told an objective story. When our worries take this form, we may be doubting that a particular account or set of accounts is objective – i.e. true or complete – but we need not be denying that it is possible to tell an objective, or at least a more objective, story. Indeed, we typically have specific ideas about how to go about getting one. We seek out foreign press reports of these events, compare them to each other and to American news reports, and evaluate inconsistencies within and between stories in light of a variety of standards. We inquire into a news organization's sources of information, likely obstacles to the reliability of its judgements, whether it has interested motives that might give it reason to distort the story. So, for example, in attempting to understand what happened in the Gulf War, the cautious inquirer will question the American media's reliance on US military reports and press conferences as a source of credible information, and will attempt to find other sources of information with which to compare and assess US reports. These sources will be subjected to the same kind of scrutiny.

We have, in short, a multitude of standards and practices for evaluating the reliability of information. This is not to say that we can often determine the whole truth and nothing but the truth, particularly in the quick-and-messy world that journalists cover. It is rare, however, that we have no guidance at all. We know how to distinguish between better and worse, more or less accurate accounts.

Often, however, the challenge to objectivity connects to deeper philosophical worries, to the centuries-old debate between realists and idealists. The metaphysical realist says that there is a world or a way things are 'out there', i.e. existing independently of our perspective. Traditionally, 'our' perspective meant not yours or mine or our culture's, but the human perspective, or even the perspective of any possible consciousness. The ideal of knowledge presupposed by this view holds that objects or states of affairs in the world are 'intrinsically' or 'independently' a certain way, and that knowledge consists in somehow 'mirroring' the way they are.

The metaphysical idealist denies that we can know what the world is like intrinsically, apart from a perspective. The world is our construction in the sense that we inevitably encounter it through our concepts and our categories; we cannot see the world concept- or category-free. Kant, the father of the contemporary idealist critique, described universal categories shaping our perception of the world that are necessary for human beings to experience the world at all. The sense for Kant in which we cannot get outside our perspective is unthreatening, because by 'our' perspective Kant meant not that of our clan or culture but that of all human consciousness. So understood, idealism poses no threat to objectivity. The idealist can make all the distinctions the realist can make: between the real and the illusory, what is 'out there' and what is 'in here', the objective and the subjective. Lions are real and unicorns mythical; trees and sky are 'out there' and stomach-aches and beliefs are 'in here'. Idealism leaves everything as it is (Luban, 1986: 708–11).

But Kant opened the door to a more threatening relativism. For having admitted that our knowledge of the world is relative to a framework, it was a natural step to the view that the categories moulding our experience depend partly on concrete and particular conditions that vary from culture to culture, community to community, even person to person. When twentieth-century thinkers took this step, arguing not simply that reality is constructed but that it is socially constructed – constructed differently, therefore, by different groups and cultures – they repudiated Kant's consolation that we could accept idealism while preserving objective, because universal, knowledge.

Global doubts and local doubts

When critics tell us that reality is socially constructed by way of explaining that our news accounts of events are not objective, what are they saying? That our culture, our political and other interests do much to structure and determine the way we (whoever 'we' may be) look at the world, and that our news reports reflect, reinforce, and even create these biases? Of course this is true. Yet some of the sharpest critics of the press make this latter argument without calling into question the possibility of objectivity; indeed they rely on it, as I would argue they must (Chomsky, 1969). But the assertion that reality is socially constructed means something more than this. There is a finality and inevitability about it: we believe what we believe because of our gender or class or cultural attachments; others with other attachments believe differently, and there is no adjudicating between our beliefs and theirs, for there is no neutral standpoint.

Yet surely the critics do not mean that we can never get outside our perspective in this sense, outside the particular world-view in which we have been raised, that we can never look at it, criticize it, judge it. They have, after all. How do they know that American news accounts of the Gulf War are partial, except by comparison with some other actual or possible accounts? The judgement of partiality rests partly on other sources of information, which taken separately or taken together have, they believe, proved more consistent or coherent.

The point is that it makes no sense to criticize a statement or description as biased or unobjective except against the background of some actual or possible contrast, some more accurate statement or better description. We have a variety of means to settle differences between conflicting beliefs or to establish one view as superior to another. We get more evidence, seek out other sides of the story, check our instruments, duplicate our experiments, re-examine our chain of reasoning. These methods do not settle all questions, but they settle many. In showing us how, say, British news stories construct reality, critics of necessity depend on the possibility of seeing and understanding alternative versions of the same events. And if no means existed to compare these alternative 'realities', the charges would have no bite. For the critics' point is not that these alternative 'realities' are like so many flavours of ice cream about which *de gustibus non disputandum est* but that those who see things in one way are missing something important, or getting only a partial view, or even getting things wrong.

Typically, the social constructionist critique vacillates between two incompatible claims: the *general*, 'global' assertion that objectivity is impossible because different people and cultures employ different categories and there is no way of deciding which framework better fits the world; and the charge that *particular* news stories or mass media organizations serve ideological interests or represent the world in a partial or distorted or otherwise inadequate way. It is crucial to see that these charges are incompatible. In so far as objectivity is impossible there can be no sense in the claim – certainly none in the rebuke – that the media are ideological or partial, for these concepts imply the possibility of a contrast. Conversely, in so far as we agree that the media serve an ideological function or bias our vision, we implicitly accept the view that other, better, more objective ways are possible.

Transcultural communication

Lurking in the assault on objectivity is the assumption that different cultures possess radically different worldviews, worldviews so different they are impermeable to outside influence. On this view, different cultures cannot engage in genuine conversation with each other, because they speak different conceptual and evaluative languages and employ different standards of judging. And there are no available yardsticks external to the culture by which to judge these internal standards of judgement.

This claim is overstated, however. Two points are important. First, despite all the talk about differences in worldview, we share a great deal even with those from very different cultures. Second, even where we see things differently from those of other cultures we can see *that* we see things differently and we can see *how* we see things differently. So our worldviews are not hermetic: others can get in and we can get out. As we shall see, the two points are not wholly separable: the distinction between sharing a perspective and being able to understand another's perspective is not sharp.

It is easy to fall under the sway of the doctrine of cultural relativism. At a certain point in our intellectual development – often in late adolescence – we are struck with the realization that language plays a crucial role in shaping the experience and worldview of individuals and even whole cultures. But the truth in this insight has been misunderstood and exaggerated. For one thing, what impresses us depends partly on the premise that different 'worldviews' take the same underlying stuff, the same data of experience, and shape it differently. The 'aha experience' of relativism depends, then, on the commonsense recognition of one world out there – something that, paradoxically, the relativist is often at pains to deny.

Furthermore, the differences between worldviews can be exaggerated. Even those from very different cultures can agree, despite their deeply different conceptions of time, to meet at ten and to come together at what all recognize as the negotiating table. Intractable disputes between cultures arise sometimes because their values diverge; equally often, however, such disputes arise precisely because their values coincide. Both the Israelis and the Palestinians invest Jerusalem with sacred and irreplaceable value. In what sense do their worldviews clash? As Francis I is supposed to have said about Henry VIII: 'Henry and I agree about everything: we both want Calais.'

Even where our points of view clearly differ, what should we make of this fact? As Donald Davidson puts it (1984: 184).

Whorf, wanting to demonstrate that Hopi incorporates a metaphysics so alien to ours that Hopi and English cannot, as he puts it, 'be calibrated', uses English to convey the contents of sample Hopi sentences. Kuhn is brilliant at saying what things were like before the revolution using – what else? – our postrevolutionary idiom.[2]

Our worldviews, then, are not unalterable and hermetic. We can and do come to see things as others see them – not just others from our culture but from radically different ones. Thucydides brings the agony of the Athenians' war to life; Ruth Benedict gets us to see 'the uses of cannibalism'; Faulkner shows us how things look to an adult with the mind of a child. The possibility of communication between cultures is perhaps inseparable from the first point: from the outset different cultures possess points of commonality and contact, and these enable us to travel back and forth. Could there be a point to history, anthropology, literature, journalism, biography, if this were not so?

Of course, some people and some cultures are easier to understand than others. Sometimes, at the limit, we remain after all in the dark. Generally, however, we can succeed more or less in overcoming the barriers. We can see the world as others see it.

Deconstructing 'the social construction of reality'

If other 'realities' are not hermetic and impermeable, that takes much of the wind out of the assertion that reality is socially constructed. For the usual connotations of the word 'reality' are exhaustive and exclusive: reality is all, and all there is. If instead there are many possible realities, and ways to get from one to the other, then we can see into each other's worlds, and our realities can thereby be altered.

Perhaps the claim is that even when we seem to escape the determination of our vision by a particular social construction, even when we seem to see things in a new light, that new vision is also socially constructed. Suppose, for example, that, partly as a result of changes in American news accounts, over the last twenty years or so Americans have come to understand the Palestinian point of view in the Middle East conflict better than they had before.[3] It might be argued that these changes result from differences in the American political establishment's view of its own geopolitical interests. On this view, the changes are themselves socially constructed out of the web of American ideology.

No doubt changing American interests partly explain the changes in perception; but to insist that apparently divergent views *always and only* derive from the push of the dominant culture's interests, from the powers that be, amounts to an unfalsifiable conspiracy theory. The claim that reality is socially constructed is then in danger of becoming empty. If, on the other hand, it is acknowledged that other sources, apart from the powers that be, can be responsible for changes in our views, then the question is what work the concept of social construction is doing. Is the point simply that ways of looking at the world do not come into being *ex nihilo*, but are rather the product of . . . of *something* – the total social-political-economic-cultural-psychological-biological environment? And is this anything more than the claim that everything has a cause? Beyond these extremely general assertions the view that reality is socially constructed seems to add nothing. For if every view is socially constructed but no view could *not* be socially constructed we learn nothing of substance when we know that reality is socially constructed.

This is not to deny that the media sometimes or even often present events in a distorted, biased or ideological way. It is rather to insist that we can only explain this fact on the assumption that there are better and worse, more and less faithful renderings of events, and that, despite our own biases, preconceptions, 'conceptual schemes', we can escape our own point of view sufficiently to recognize the extent to which it imposes a structure or slant on events that could be seen differently.

The word 'reality' is to blame for some of the confusion. By her own account, one crucial theme of Gaye Tuchman's book *Making News* is that 'the act of making news is the act of constructing reality itself rather than a picture of reality' (Tuchman, 1972: 12). Tuchman's point trades on ambiguities in the term 'reality'.

News can illuminatingly be said to construct reality rather than a picture of it in two senses. First, some events are genuine media creations. When *Newsweek* in the 1980s proclaimed on its cover that 'Nixon Is Back', then in a crucial sense Nixon *was* back. To have arrived on *Newsweek's* cover is to be back from whatever realm of nonbeing one formerly inhabited. We have here a variation on the Pirandellesque insight that 'It's the truth if you think it is': 'It's the truth if they (the major media) say it is'. But this rule applies to only a very limited fraction of our beliefs, a tiny portion of the total news product.

Second, the act of reporting news is an act of constructing reality in the sense captured by the sociological commonplace that 'if a situation is defined as real it's real in its consequences'. If people believe that news stories of an event are accurate, they will behave accordingly, and for certain purposes those stories function as 'reality'. This is sometimes simply a matter of the bandwagon effect: when a news story describes college-bound students' scramble for admission to elite institutions, more students may panic and start scrambling.

Nevertheless, journalists purport to represent an independent reality, and, although they often fall short, if we abandon the concept of a reality independent of news stories we undermine the very basis on which to criticize their work.

The existence and meaning of facts

Most people have a crude picture of what objectivity means, and this partly explains its bad name. Belief in objectivity does not mean that every question that can be posed, or about which people might disagree, has a single determinate right answer. If it did we would be wise to reject it.

What, then, does belief in objectivity commit us to? At the very least it means that some questions have determinate, right answers – and that all questions have wrong answers. So, for example, it is a fact that Bill Clinton is currently the President of the USA, and that in 1995 the New York State legislature reinstated the death penalty.

Do objectivity's critics deny that Bill Clinton is President or that the death penalty was reinstated in New York? Let us hope not. How, then, do they reconcile these unassailable facts with their repudiation of objectivity? We find several strategies.

1   One is to insist that nevertheless such facts are socially constructed. What does this mean? No reasonable person would deny that for there to be such a thing as a President of such a thing as the USA, a wide variety of complex social institutions must be in place. If that is all it means to say this fact is socially constructed, nothing significant turns on admitting it. Typically, however, the point of emphasizing the constructedness of a fact is to undermine its truth or credibility. Yet however constructed 'Bill Clinton is President' may be, it is no less true or credible for that.

A variation on the theme that all facts are socially constructed is the claim that they are all 'theory-laden'. Certainly every factual statement can be understood to imply decisions about the usefulness or appropriateness of categorizing things in one way rather than another. If we want to dignify even the most commonsensical of such categorizations with the label 'theory', who is to stop us? But then we must keep in mind that there are theories and theories. 'The human fetus is a person' and 'The PLO is a terrorist organization' are laden with controversial theories. 'The earth revolves around the sun' and 'The lion is a mammal' are laden with theories not seriously contestable in modern times. Facts, then, may be theory-laden; but whether they therefore lack objectivity depends on the particular theories they carry as freight. 'Bill Clinton is President' may in some sense rest on a theory or conceptual framework, but it is one so widely shared and innocuous that the label 'theory-laden', usually brought as an accusation, loses its bite. Without an account of the faulty theory embedded therein, we can rest content: when our theories are good, theory-ladenness is nothing to fear.

It may be said that the facts just mentioned are not interesting facts, and that this weakens the point they are used to illustrate. In what sense are they not interesting? Surely New York's reinstatement of the death penalty is in many respects interesting. In claiming these facts are not interesting the critic must mean that it is uncontroversial that these *are* facts. With that we would agree; but to have gained the critic's agreement on this point is itself a victory. For the social constructionists sometimes seem to include all facts, however humdrum, in the realm of the constructed (and to be deconstructed). To acknowledge that these 'uninteresting' facts *are* facts is to concede what seemed to be a point of disagreement.

2   An alternative strategy for the relativist is to exempt such facts from the realm of the socially constructed, but to insist that they are trivial and that all non-trivial 'facts' of the kind prominent in news stories are socially constructed in an interesting sense. Yet to admit this is more significant than it looks. First, there will be *lots* of these trivial facts, perhaps an infinite number of them. Second, such facts will serve as a crucial check constraining all the non-trivial, socially constructed 'facts' that are supposed to comprise the bulk of the news. In this sense it is hard to see how the apparently innocuous facts can be trivial, even if taken one by one they seem to lack a certain cosmic weightiness. Finally, having admitted the existence of some non-socially constructed facts, it will prove difficult to draw the line between these and the socially constructed ones, especially given the constraints the former place on the latter. So the camel of objectivity gets its nose in the tent.

3   A third strategy is to admit the independence of some facts from socially produced theories, but to insist that nevertheless these facts will be inter-

preted differently by members of different groups or cultures, and that these interpretations, themselves social constructions, will invest the same facts with different meanings. This claim can be understood in at least two ways.

(a) In one sense there is no disputing that these facts will be interpreted differently by different people. We all agree that the New York State legislature reinstated the death penalty, but we disagree about the reasons for it and about the agents ultimately responsible, its consequences, its symbolic significance.

Yet our disagreements about these matters of 'interpretation' will in turn depend partly on other facts, such as people's beliefs about crime and about the efficacy of capital punishment. The constraint of facts will rule out some interpretations as wrong, even if it typically leaves room for reasonable disagreement about which interpretation is right. The web of expectations on which everyday life depends rests on the possibility of knowing all sorts of things 'beyond a reasonable doubt'. So the insistence that an interpretation of the facts is beyond the reach of objective evaluation is simply overstated. There may generally be room for disagreement, but not all the room in the world. Some interpretations are better than others, and some are simply wrong.

(b) A second sense in which it may be said that different people and groups will invest the same facts with different meanings can be illustrated by a study of British, American and Belgian coverage of elections in Ireland. The study found that the BBC story focused on the potential consequences of the vote for British-Irish relations; the CBS story used the election as a peg to talk about Irish unemployment and its potential consequences for immigration to the USA; and the Belgian account focused on the role of the Catholic Church in Irish politics, the relation between church and state being an important issue in Belgium (Gurevitch et al., 1991). It makes sense to say that each story took the same set of facts but interpreted them differently; each invested the facts with different meanings.

The point is important, and we should not underestimate the significance of this 'meaning construction' function of the mass media; it bears extensive examination. Those who stress this point, however, often seem to misunderstand its relevance (or lack of it) to the question of objectivity. The British, American and Belgian news reports invest the Irish election with different meanings – they see it as signifying different things – but they all refer to the same events and agree about certain crucial facts, such as who won the elections. Indeed, the three stories may be perfectly compatible with each other. It is no surprise to find that the same events have different significance for people of varying histories, cultures or interests. We might put this point by saying that the issues raised here go *beyond* the question of objectivity, but they do not subvert objectivity. I conclude that these challenges pose no threat to the existence of objective facts.

Beyond objectivity?

Belief in objectivity does not mean that about every question we might ask (or everything that reporters report) there is a single right answer. The interesting question is how extensive the realm of objective facts is. Imagine a continuum of objectivity along which to locate the variety of subjects and statements news reporters investigate. At one end we find the relatively straightforward and uncontroversial facts of the kind we have just been discussing. In the middle we find statements about which clearly there is a truth, a 'right answer', but where to a greater or lesser extent the answer is difficult to discover. How did the dinosaurs become extinct? Who were the high-ranking Communists in MI5? Did O. J. Simpson murder Nicole Simpson and Ronald Goldman? The answers to some of these questions may depend partly on what we mean by certain terms (like 'murder'), but even assuming consistent usage we may reasonably disagree about the answers. Still, no one doubts that there are definite answers.

The line is sometimes thin between cases where clearly there is a truth about the matter although we have difficulty finding out what it is, and those where it cannot be said that there is a truth about the matter. For many of the complex goings-on between people, both at the 'macro' political level and at the 'micro' interpersonal level, the language of truth and objectivity may be thin and inadequate. When, for example, we have heard in detail 'both sides of the story' from quarrelling lovers or friends, we may sort out some clear truths about what happened, but in the end we may still be left with a residue of indestructible ambiguity, where it is plausible to say not simply that we do not know for sure what happened but that at the appropriate level of description there is no single determinate thing that happened.

Now it seems clear that examples of this kind of ambiguity and indeterminacy abound for the most interesting and important subjects covered in the news. Did Clarence Thomas sexually harass Anita Hill? Uncertainty may depend partly on insufficient evidence and doubts about the credibility of witnesses. Disagreement may, however, depend on other things as well: on different understandings of how sexual harassment should be defined, and on related questions about the meaning of certain gestures, expressions and interactions. Depending on the framework in which we embed the bits of evidence, the gestures and utterances, we will get different answers. And the question 'Which framework is the appropriate one?' may not always have a determinate answer.

On the other hand, sometimes it does. Once we know the context of a given utterance or action, the ambiguous often becomes unambiguous. 'Did he or didn't he?' The answer is yes or the answer is no.

So the defender of objectivity can perfectly well agree with Stanley Fish – perhaps to his dismay – that 'no degree of explicitness will ever be sufficient to disambiguate the sentence [for example, what he said to her] if by disambiguate we understand *render it impossible to conceive of a set of circumstances in which its plain meaning would be other than it now appears to be*' (Fish, 1980: 282–83). As long as we can know what context, framework, or set of conventions actually governed the circumstances – which often we can – we will be entitled to conclude that in *these* circumstances he meant x or did y.

Questions about the application of concepts such as sexual harassment or racism reside in the murky area where fact meets value, description meets evaluation. Some who would describe themselves as objectivists would reject the view that values are objective. To the extent, then, that sexual harassment and racism are evaluative rather than descriptive concepts, these objectivists would deny that there can be a truth about such matters as whether a remark is racist or a person has sexually harassed another. Facts can be objective, they would say, but value judgements cannot.

Yet our commonsense understanding of concepts like racism and sexual harassment supports the view that they can be applied or misapplied: that it can be true or false that a remark is racist or that someone sexually harassed another. Facts and values are not so neatly separable. Their inseparability of facts and values is commonly taken to support the anti-objectivist position: facts are not that 'hard', because they are infused with values. But the shoe can be placed on the other foot: values are not that 'soft', because they are infused with facts.

I cannot take up the larger question lurking here of the objectivity of value judgements. But two points are worth making. First, the realm in which this question is relevant forms a limited part of the object of journalistic investigation. Journalists are typically concerned with issues at the more factual end of the continuum. Second, the more important point is that the journalist (and indeed anyone who hopes to understand the world) must arrive at the conclusion of indestructible ambiguity or indeterminacy very reluctantly, only after the arduous search for the truth has been found not fully realizable.

We must, in other words, proceed on the assumption that there is objective truth, even if sometimes in the end we conclude that within a particular realm the concept of truth does not apply, or that in any case we will never discover it. It is not irrelevant to note that the vehemence with which defenders of both Thomas and Hill (a category that came to include a large number of Americans and other observers) made their respective cases reveal that *they* had no doubt that there was a right answer to the harassment question. Perhaps they were deluded. But it is significant that people behave and think as if there were a truth about these matters.

They cannot, I would argue, do otherwise. The concepts of objectivity and truth function for us as 'regulative principles': ideals that we must suppose to apply, even if at the limit they do not, if we are to possess the will and the ways to understand the world.[4] And we do possess, even if to an imperfect degree, the will and the ways.

The politics of objectivity

I hope to have shown in the foregoing discussion not only why we must make the assumption that objectivity is possible, but also why critics have thought otherwise. Nevertheless, we still do not have a complete answer to the question (although hints are strewn along the way) why many of these critics not only deny that objectivity is possible but express hostility toward the idea. Why are they angry rather than sorry?

The main reason is that they see the claim of objectivity as the expression of an authoritarian, power-conserving point of view. Michael Schudson (1978: 160) describes this attitude, as it arose in the 1960s:

> . . . 'objective' reporting reproduced a vision of social reality which refused to examine the basic structures of power and privilege. It was not just incomplete, as critics of the thirties had contended, it was distorted. It represented collusion with institutions whose legitimacy was in dispute.[5]

Is this view right? I think in many ways it is. But there are a variety of accusations implicit here that need to be sorted out.

First the assertion of objectivity seems to heighten the status of claims to which it attaches. To insist not only that the enemy is winning the war, but that this statement is objective seems to elevate it to a higher plane of truth or credibility. The assertion of objectivity then appears to involve a certain arrogance, a setting-up of oneself as an authority. Now in one sense this is silly. Ordinarily when we say 'The sky is blue' we imply 'It's an objective fact (for all to see) that the sky is blue'. My belief that what I say is true or objective adds nothing to the belief itself. At the same time, to the extent that we are convinced of our own objectivity or that of others, we are less likely to be open to other points of view. Belief in one's own objectivity is a form of smugness, and may lead to a dangerous self-deception. Belief in the objectivity of others (such as the news media) enhances their credibility, often unjustifiably.

So acceptance of the ideology of objectivity – the view that institutions like the news media are generally objective and are sincerely committed to objectivity – has significant political consequences, as the critics suggest. Your belief that a newspaper always and only publishes true and objective information will serve as an impediment to your political and intellectual enlightenment, whether you are a consumer or a producer of news. However, for the ideology of objectivity to have the political consequences the critics suggest, we must add a further premise: not only that people believe the press is objective, but also that the news provided favours the powers-that-be. (We can imagine an alternative: an opposition press with a great deal of authority and credibility.)

Is the press biased in favour of the powers-that-be? One reason to think so is that mass media organizations are vast corporate entities; they are *among* the powers-that-be, and so have interests in common with them. I am interested here in a different question, however. Does the commitment to objectivity *itself* create biases in favour of the conservation of political power? This is the implicit claim of some of objectivity's critics: that the methods associated with the ideal of objectivity contain an inherent bias toward established power.

One reason for thinking that objectivity is inherently conservative in this way has to do with the reporter's reliance on sources. Among the canons of objective journalism is the idea that the reporter does not make claims based on her own personal observation, but instead attributes them to sources.[6] Yet sources must seem credible to perform the required role, and official, government sources – as well as other important decision-makers in the society – come with ready-made credentials for the job. In addition, they often have the skills and the resources to use the news media to their advantage. Yet such sources are not typically disinterested observers motivated only by a love of truth.

Journalists therefore confront a dilemma. If they provide to such sources an unfiltered mouthpiece, they serve the sources' interests. In order not to provide an unfiltered mouthpiece, journalists must make choices about which of the sources' statements are sufficiently controversial to call for 'balancing' with another point of view, and they must choose the balancing points of view. If, in cases where the official view is doubtful, they merely balance the official source's view without even hinting at the probable truth, they mislead the audience. Each of these policies raises troubling questions about objectivity.

The first alternative, simply to provide an unfiltered mouthpiece, characterizes the press's response to Joseph McCarthy in the 1950s. This example, widely cited by objectivity's critics, has helped tarnish its reputation. Although we can see why journalists might have worried about challenging McCarthy's accusations, however, it is just as clear that leaving them unanswered does not satisfy any intelligent conception of objectivity. We care about objectivity because we care about truth; giving credibility to baseless charges – whether by commission or omission – cannot count as objective.[7]

It follows that journalists must make judgements about the credibility of sources and what they say. Objectivity does not mean passivity. But when does a source's statement invite challenge? The obvious answer is: when it seems controversial. What seems controversial, however, depends on the consensus existing in the culture at a given time. That consensus derives partly from powerful ideological assumptions that, while unchallenged in the culture, are by no means unchallengeable. So it is that I. F. Stone argues that 'most of the time objectivity is just the rationale for regurgitating the conventional wisdom of the day' (quoted in Hertsgaard, 1989: 65–66). What goes without saying may be dogma rather than truth.

Supposing, however, that, the journalist does recognize that an official view is sufficiently controversial to invite challenge, she must choose which opposing sources to cite and how to frame the debate between the opposing points of view. Is the dispute taken to span a fairly narrow range of the political spectrum? If so, the press may be criticized for perpetuating the status quo by reproducing the conventional wisdom. Is the opposing point of view chosen an 'extreme' one?[8] In that case the press may sensationalize the matter at hand or marginalize the opposition by making them seem like crazies. Either way, the journalist cannot avoid exercising judgement.

These dilemmas explain another of the standard criticisms of journalism's commitment to objectivity: not that it necessarily favours established power, but that it leads to a destructive agnosticism and scepticism.[9] Objectivity must be 'operationalized', and this is done through the idea of balance. In exploring controversial issues, the journalist does not himself commit to a view, but instead gives voice to different sides of the story. The reader is left to judge the truth. If the journalist truly balances the views, however, there may be no rational way for the reader to decide between them. So she comes to the conclusion that 'there's truth on both sides' – or neither. Every view is as good as every other. Rather than connecting with truth, objectivity, according to this way of thinking, leads to cynicism and scepticism.

Yet both these criticisms – that objectivity favours established power, and that it leads to scepticism and indecision – suffer from too mechanical a conception of objectivity. It is easy to see how the problems they address arise in the transition from objectivity-as-an-ideal to objectivity-as-a-method. In part, they stem from a confusion between objectivity and the appearance of objectivity. Questioning the remarks of an important public figure may look partisan, while leaving them unchallenged does not; but the appearance is misleading and only skin-deep. Similarly, leaving two opposing points of view to look equally plausible where one has the preponderance of reason and evidence on its side is a charade of objectivity. It reflects the common mistake of confusing objectivity and neutrality. The objective investigator may *start out* neutral (more likely, she is simply good at keeping her prior beliefs from distorting her inquiry), but she does not necessarily *end up* neutral. She aims, after all, to find out what happened, why, who did it. Between truth and falsehood the objective investigator is not neutral.

The confusion between objectivity and neutrality arises, I think, because of the belief alluded to earlier that 'values' are not objective, true, part of the 'fabric of the universe'. According to the positivist outlook of which this is part, the objective investigator will therefore remain 'value-neutral' and his inquiry will be 'value-free'. Yet the identification of neutrality and objectivity within a given realm depends on the assumption that there is no truth within that realm. Leaving aside the question of whether values are objective, if facts are objective the objective investigator will not be neutral with respect to them.

As a journalistic virtue, then, objectivity requires that reporters not let their preconceptions cloud their vision. It does not mean they see nothing, or that their findings may not be significant and controversial. Nevertheless, it is easy to see why many people confuse objectivity and neutrality. Often the outsider cannot easily tell the difference between a reporter who has come to a conclusion based on a reasoned evaluation of the evidence, and one who was biased toward that conclusion from the start. The safest way to seem objective, then, may be to look neutral.

The inevitability of objectivity

We have good reasons, then, to suspect claims to objectivity. People who insist on their own objectivity protest too much; they are likely to be arrogant, overconfident, or self-deceived. In fact, those who acknowledge their own biases and limitations probably have a better chance of overcoming them than those who insist they are objective. Those who have faith in the objectivity of others may be complacent or dangerously naive. They fail to see the many obstacles – inborn and acquired, innocent and insidious, inevitable and avoidable – on the way to truth.

My defence of objectivity, moreover, in no way amounts to the claim that the press (in general or in any particular manifestation) is in fact objective or free of ideological or other bias. Sometimes the biases of the press result from overt economic or political purposes, as when news organizations suppress damaging information about corporations to which they belong; sometimes from structural or technological features of media institutions, such as television's reliance on good pictures. It is also true that, paradoxically, the aspiration to objectivity can contain biases of its own, by advantaging established sources or by encouraging an artifical arithmetic balance between views and tempting reporters to maintain the appearance of neutrality even in the face of overwhelming 'non-neutral' evidence. These tendencies are genuine, although not, I have been arguing, insuperable.

To believe in objectivity is not, then, to believe that anyone *is* objective. My main purpose has been to show that, nevertheless, in so far as we aim to understand the world we cannot get along without assuming both the possibility and value of objectivity. That the questions reporters ask have answers to which people of good will and good sense would, after adequate investigation, agree is the presupposition that we make, and must make, in taking journalism seriously.

Notes

1. I should add that although Schudson is sympathetic to this view, in this passage he is characterizing it rather than espousing it.
2. Whorf's views can be found in Whorf (1956). For a clear critique of Whorfian relativism, see Devitt and Sterelny (1987: 172–84).
3. For evidence of this change, see Schmidt (1990: A1), reporting a New York Times/ CBS News Poll on changes in American attitudes toward Israel and the Palestinians.
4. The idea of a regulative principle or ideal comes from Kant: 'the ideal in such a case serves as the *archetype* for the complete determination of the copy . . . Although we cannot concede to these ideals objective reality (existence), they are not therefore to be regarded as figments of the brain; they supply reason with a standard which is indispensable to it, providing it, as they do, with a concept of that which is entirely complete in its kind, and thereby enabling it to estimate and to measure the degree and the defects of the incomplete' (Kant, 1965: 486 [A569 B597]).
5. See also Hallin (1986: 63–75). For a good discussion see West (1990).
6. This is not strictly speaking true: as an eyewitness to events, the reporter often enunciates facts directly; even when not an eyewitness, he does not attribute every statement made to a source. Reporters could not get their stories off the ground if they had to attribute every statement to a source. The question of when a statement is thought sufficiently important and controversial to require attribution goes to the heart of disputes about objectivity and the appearance of objectivity, as I. F. Stones's remark, quoted on p. 239, illustrates.
7. Note in this connection Schudson's discussion of Bob Woodward and Carl Bernstein's approach in the Watergate investigation. Schudson believes that the ideal of objectivity implies the conventional, passive model of journalism associated with the press's response to McCarthy. Yet he remarks that Woodward and Bernstein 'insisted that they did nothing exceptional. They denied that their manner of reporting was distinctive; to them, "investigative reporting" is just plain reporting . . . They make a case for a journalism true to an ideal of objectivity and false to the counterfeit conventions justified in its name' (Schudson, 1978: 188–89). Even Schudson, one of objectivity's influential detractors, here acknowledges (what Woodward and Bernstein have no trouble seeing) that much of what goes under the name of objectivity reflects a shallow understanding of it. The distinction often manifests itself in the use of quotation marks: is it objectivity or 'objectivity' that's the culprit?
8. Obviously what we characterize as extreme depends again on the prevailing consensus at the time, and may therefore involve controversial political judgements. The dilemmas – and journalists' common capitulation to the prevailing political consensus – are hilariously illustrated in Cockburn (1987).
9. The criticisms are not unconnected. If Nature abhors a vacuum, then even a precise balancing between two opposing views will give the advantage to the more prestigious view that is associated with established power.

References

CAREY, J. W., 1989: *Communication as Culture: Essays on Media and Society*. Boston: Unwin Hyman.
CHOMSKY, N., 1969: 'Objectivity and Liberal Scholarship'. In *American Power and the New Mandarins*. Harmondsworth: Penguin.
COCKBURN, A., 1987: 'The Tedium Twins'. In *Corruptions of Empire*. London: Verso.
DAVIDSON, D., 1984: 'The Very Idea of a Conceptual Scheme'. In *Inquiries into Truth and Interpretation*, New York: Oxford University Press.

DEVITT, M. and STERELNY, K., 1987: *Language and Reality*. Cambridge, MA: MIT Press.

FISH, S., 1980: *Is There a Text in This Class?* Cambridge, MA: Harvard University Press.

GUREVITCH, M., LEVY, M. and ROEH, I., 1991: 'The Global Newsroom', in P. Dahlgren and C. Sparks (eds), *Communication and Citizenship: Journalism and the Public Sphere in the New Media Age*. London: Routledge.

HALLIN, D., 1986: *The 'Uncensored War': The Media and Vietnam*. New York: Oxford University Press.

HERTSGAARD, M., 1989: *On Bended Knee: The Press and the Reagan Presidency*. New York: Schocken Books.

KANT, I., 1965: *Critique of Pure Reason*. New York: St. Martin's Press.

KESSLER, L. and MCDONALD, D., 1989: *Mastering the Message: Media Writing with Substance and Style*. Belmont, California: Wadsworth.

LUBAN, D., 1986: 'Fish v. Fish or, Some Realism About Idealism', *Cardozo Law Review* 7.

MACKINNON, C., 1982: 'Feminism, Marxism, Method, and the State: An Agenda for Theory', *Signs* 7.

MCDONALD, D., 1975: 'Is Objectivity Possible?'. In Merrill, J. C. and Barney, R. D. (eds), *Ethics and the Press: Readings in Mass Media Morality*. New York: Hastings House.

SCHILLER, D., 1981: *Objectivity and the News*. Philadelphia: University of Pennsylvania Press.

SCHMIDT, W. E., 1990: 'Americans' Support for Israel: Solid, But Not the Rock It Was', *New York Times*, July 9.

SCHUDSON, M., 1978: *Discovering the News: A Social History of American Newspapers*. New York: Basic Books.

TUCHMAN, G., 1972: 'Objectivity as Strategic Ritual', *American Journal of Sociology* 77.

WEST, R., 1990: 'Relativism, Objectivity, and the Law', *Yale Law Journal* 99.

WHORF, B. L., 1956: *Language, Thought and Reality*. Cambridge, MA: MIT Press.

12

The Return to Cultural Production Case Study: Fashion Journalism

Angela McRobbie

The 'Hollywoodization' of work

By drawing on the case of contemporary UK fashion journalism (newspapers and magazines) this article seeks to outline the constituent features of what might be described as a return to cultural production as a key question for media and communications study. Why return? And to what extent does a return necessitate a different kind of language developed explicitly to account for the changing conditions that now prevail in this sector of journalism? The answer to the first question is that for too long in feminist media studies there has been a concern with media texts and their various meanings at the expense of any detailed sociological consideration of those who actually make these texts. Valuable though this work is, this has, none the less, created a one-sided understanding of contemporary media and has provided no basis for considering the means by which media representations of women, for example, have changed (or indeed remain unchanged) in anything other than speculative terms. The eclipse of issues around production also marks the decline of sociological perspectives, creating an unbalanced gendered division of labour in media and communications studies, with women predominating in the arts and humanities-based topics and approaches, and men maintaining a grasp on issues of political economy, locally and globally.

Of course there are exceptions in both camps, but it is also around this axis of gender that the main antagonisms in media, cultural and communications studies have been fought. It is possible nowadays to almost lose count of the number of angry denunciations of the 'textual turn' in media studies by the almost exclusively male political economists of media (for the most recent outburst see Ferguson and Golding, 1997). Cultural studies, ambivalently placed midway between the social sciences, with their aspiration to define the terrain of political engagement for the whole field (in particular policy issues), and the humanities and arts areas with their focus on psycho-analytical approaches and close textual readings, also attracts a good deal of hostility. This is partly because of the obstinate straddling of 'big' global political issues with an equally energetic commitment to the politics of meaning as manifest at the micro-social level on the part of key thinkers including Stuart Hall, Gayatri Chakravorty Spivak and Judith Butler.

This article modestly locates itself within the cultural studies tradition. It attempts to re-assert the necessary connectedness in the field between, on the one hand, the political issues of new gender labour markets in culture and the media, and on the other hand with the consequences these have for the kinds of media we consume and the configuration of media power. So, in answer to the second question, regarding the need for a new vocabulary, the issue will be how, at the relatively local level of London-based media labour markets, the intensification of casualization and freelance work impacts on the media world of fashion journalism through the existence of the 'network'.

However there are few working models for how such an analysis might proceed, for the very reason that cultural studies, despite in principle occupying this middle space, has not in recent years produced the kind of studies that concretely map out movements of people in and out of new labour markets. There has also been a neglect of the terrain of experience, that is to do with how, in this case, cultural workers make sense of what they do and with how they explain their own pathways through the insecure and volatile fields of creative labour. For example, in my own recent study of young women fashion designers, this absence of interest in labour markets and in the experience of new worlds of work, in cultural studies and indeed in the mainstream of media and communication studies, forced me to look towards the recent sociological writings of Giddens (1997), Beck (1999), and Lash and Urry (1994) to help make sense of the material the interviews were producing (McRobbie, 1998). Giddens was useful for his analysis of the 'opaque futures' that characterize this changing field of employment. Beck talked about 'capital without jobs' which I then inverted to describe the 'jobs without capital' which these young women were creating for themselves as self-employment out of the shadow of unemployment. Lash and Urry provided the insight of 'disorganized capitalism' which was also a convenient way of characterizing the spectrum of tiny 'micro-economies' of fashion design set up by the fashion graduates and concentrated in a few sites across London.

Alongside this new sociological work was an emerging current which, under the influence of Foucault sought to understand how different regimes of meanings were organized to produce new subjectivities in the workplace – that is a new kind of disciplined but also creative worker, and also new kinds of cultural economy. For example Paul Du Gay demonstrated how the discourses of 'enterprise culture' during and after the Thatcher years, shifted the whole ethos of work away from its social relations to the individual subject (Du Gay, 1996). The 'enterprising subject' could be 'shaped up' through a range of guiding discourses. A different kind of worker but also one more willing to be flexible and to bend to the requirement of the new working environment could be engendered by these disciplinary practices, many of which were couched in the language of self-realization. What underlies this is the requirement of the person to take responsibility for him or herself as an individual worker. The new self-image of the creative worker who loves his or her work with a passion – let us say the writer, film director, fashion designer, or model with her 'portfolio' – becomes the template for us all. For example, the training programmes for Body

Shop sales assistants encourage the workforce to think of the floor as a stage or theatre, and in its earlier, more successful, days Body Shop invited job applicants to come for 'an audition'. This would be an apposite example of a trend Charles Leadbeater has called the 'Hollywoodization' of work (Leadbeater, 1999). The impact is to disaggregate the workforce into an army of individualized 'wannabes' seduced into extraordinary degrees of self-exploitation by their self-definitions as 'creatives' and by the hope that they will be lucky in the 'winner takes all' labour market. Work becomes a playground for enjoyment and a pathway to celebrity.

This provides a useful way of thinking about fashion journalists, and the intensely individualizing ways in which they work, and also their self definitions as all-round creative persons rather than simply professional journalists. However as I have argued elsewhere the problems with this approach are threefold. First, to interpret the willing commitment to working patterns which no employer could reasonably expect as evidence of the wholesale success of the Thatcherite attempt to transform working practices so that they are virtually unrecognizable from what they were less than 20 years ago, fails to recognize the agency of the young women for whom this appears to be a desirable option. Second, it is quite inattentive to the experience of working in these fields and how these experiences are understood and acted upon in the longer term. That is, we are provided with no sense of how, in being 'shaped up' in these ways, the new young cultural worker might reorganize working practices in an attempt to solve problems posed by the demands and expectations of the new work. There is no sense of the processes of work requiring the attention and reflexivity of agents themselves. Finally these accounts are inattentive to the specific gender dynamics of work and employment at a time when young women are entering the workforce as a lifelong endeavour. It is unwise to overlook, or indeed discount, the utopian thread that accompanies the simple desire on the part of young women to work and to achieve financial independence in ways that are also personally rewarding, even if that means longer hours than might be expected in a mainstream salaried job. In short it is also imperative that we have fuller accounts of the meanings brought to the workplace by young women for whom work now seems to represent an opportunity to achieve equality with men and an identity independent of men. These new horizons need to be documented even as they are also frustrated.

Questions of method . . . or 'How to study networks?'

Production studies require intense periods of immersion in the field of study. Even when this means simply interviewing media professionals rather than establishing a full-blown ethnographic study of workplace routines, it is a slow and unpredictable process. There is also the difficult business of getting access to powerful people and then getting their time for more than just an 'in and out' interview. But this alone does not fully explain the eclipse of studies of media workers in recent years. There are other reasons why what people say about what they do, and how they do it, has dropped down the agenda. Garnham has argued that a good deal of research needs to be done on media production processes and organizations. But he quickly adds that existing work often 'succumbs to the superficial glamour', taking at face value what media personnel say about the creative aspects of the work they do (Garnham, 1990: 11). He implies that research would need to dig more deeply, gaining familiarity as well as insight, so that the respondents would drop their professional images and speak more directly about the reality of their working conditions.

What is clearly at stake here is the interpretative mode as well as the methodological procedures employed in this kind of research. Garnham is concerned that media producers use the interview situation to describe and promote their own creative talents. This, he implies, misses the point of production studies, which presumably is to explore relations of power, decision-making, control, organization and administration. However I would propose that it is precisely the creative dimension, the dynamics of self-promotion and also the sociological nature of 'the glamour' that now ought to be the focus of attention in studies of cultural workers. In my own recent study of fashion designers (McRobbie, 1998) I argued that the rhetoric of creativity and glamour together played a key role in the professional and promotional strategies needed to bring the work to the attention of the market (and mediated through the fashion magazines and press). So in this case it was important to examine the instrumental interplay between creativity, craft and glamour as components in the volatile careers of independent designers as well as being part of a process of 'aesthetic self-actualization'. It was also important to recognize the role of the network of contacts, colleagues, acquaintances and friends which functioned as support group and employment agency at the same time and which came together around the glamour/creativity constellation.

Garnham is also aware of the limitations of traditional ethnographic studies, particularly those that adopt a micro-social approach where the fine details of social interaction in, say, the putting together of a news bulletin fail to recognize the more structural constraints that dictate in advance the nature and shape of such a process. As he puts it, such work emphasizes human agency but often at the expense of social structure. Likewise this kind of work can often convey the field of study as being more autonomous and more cut off from the network of powerful institutions that are its conditions of existence. But his fears here are misplaced. The need for work that shows the complexity of decision-making in contemporary media and communication practice far outweighs the fear of disappearing into the minutiae of ethnomethodological detail. The fact is that more data would be invaluable because, as Garnham also says, 'the bibliography of the producers of culture is scandalously empty' (Garnham, 1990: 12). I am arguing therefore for a renewed commitment to production studies, but from a position that acknowledges the scale of the changes that have swept through the culture and media industries to the point that working practices within this vast sector are almost unrecognizable compared to those that prevailed when sociologists talked convincingly about the routines and daily practices of media professionals as they worked alongside each other in a relatively stable TV newsroom environment (Schlesinger, 1982).

There has been a substantial dissolving of boundaries of professional expertise in many media fields, and particularly in fashion journalism. Autonomy and professionalism has given way to being multi-skilled and flexible. Likewise corporate interests and sponsorship have recently entered into a more direct relationship with the working practices of journalists. As we shall see in the case of fashion journalism, the way in which the large fashion conglomerates erode the boundaries of conventional journalistic practice is instructive. Thus while Peter Golding and Graham Murdock have argued that there is an 'oblique relation between theories of political economy and practices of journalism', fashion journalism allows us the opportunity to explore the way in which the limits that have divided professional practice from corporate interests are being continually stretched (Golding and Murdock, 1996). Other writers have already shown how certain specialist fields of journalism, particularly those associated with consumer affairs – such as motoring – often share closer interests with companies and manufacturers than with news reporting or political journalism (Elliott, 1977; Tunstall 1971). But in the media in the 1990s especially, with the growth of public relations and corporate sponsorship, the spider's web of commercial interests has spread to almost every corner of journalism. By looking at fashion we can see one example of how this works and to what effect.

The construction of meaning in fashion journalism is shaped by these larger interests, while by convention it is also open and ambivalent. The editorial content of fashion magazines, for example, comprises mainly of the fashion spread: a series of visual images composed around a range of clothes, models, settings and accessories. None of these items is presented as advertising copy, designers are instead credited in small print usually at the bottom of the page. The glossy fashion magazines are expected, by advertisers representing the vast beauty and fashion conglomerates, to provide the right kind of enhanced, or luxury, environment within their fashion pages, and to complement the advertising pages through deploying the aesthetic codes of fashion in such a way as to sustain and continually renew the interest of the relevant band of consumers. It is about delivering and directing consumers to the advertisers through the visual pleasure of the fashion pages. Advertisers know that, for leading magazines, the 'art work' of the fashion pages, produced in-house by the fashion team, is what makes the magazine distinctive, gives it a brand identity and is its main selling point. *Vogue* fashion means something rather different from *Marie-Claire* fashion or *Elle* fashion, but each magazine is known primarily for its fashion none the less.

While it might be difficult, sociologically, to pin down the relation between the requirements of the advertising media planners who purchase the pages for their clients and the distinctive landscape of meanings of the fashion shots laid out across the centrefolds of the magazines, it is not impossible. But it would require a different kind of 'step by step' research than has been carried out in recent years. This would mean not only participant observation or interviews with decision-makers and planners inside the media companies who work for the advertising agency (who, in turn, work for the clients), but also inside the magazines and alongside the fashion editorial team whose job it is to create the visual style of the publication as a whole. In short it would mean trailing, tracking and mapping out the networks that connect the enormous chain of activities involved in creating one issue of one magazine. This process is so multimediated and extended across such a wide range of personnel, organizations, institutions and other agencies, that research of this type – seeking to explore the relation between the sources of capital and the image on the page – would entail a more complex 'multi-site' methodology than has so far emerged in media studies.[1] This gives rise to two outstanding questions: first, how to develop a methodology to encompass the way in which cultural production is now organized on a day-to-day basis, largely by networks of individuals; and second, how to consider the impact that networks of creative individuals have on media power and media forms. The remainder of this chapter attempts to begin to answer both of these questions, albeit within the limited field of the fashion press.

'The page is art'

By a process of trial and error it became apparent to me in the mid-1990s that the only way to access the experience of work in the new cultural and creative sector was through the modest tool of the interview. Consequently I carried out a series of interviews with a range of people working in the fashion media. This was part of a broader study of career pathways in fashion design. I wanted to explore the relationship between fashion design and the fashion media. Several commentators had suggested that the success of British fashion design from the mid-1980s had partly depended on the support and publicity it received from the expanding fashion press, including the newly launched glossies *Elle* and *Marie-Claire*, the style magazines *The Face* and *i-D* and the more generous space given over to fashion in the daily newspapers, tabloid and broadsheet, as part of their attempt to win more women readers. During this time I interviewed almost all the well-known fashion editors currently working in the UK. I also talked with a number of young fashion journalists and interviewed women working in fashion PR, who in turn introduced me to a new band of workers in the fashion media known as stylists. Even at this preliminary stage, the existence of a network indicated an expansive but informal field of 'contacts'.

Although I was aware that the methodology of the interview was very different from doing participant observation inside the offices of the magazines and newspapers, I encountered first hand the difficulties participant observation posed, for the reason that the personnel doing this kind of work were highly mobile, most likely to be employed on a freelance or temporary contract, and consequently individualized in their outlook and rather isolated in their working practices. In the course of the day, and from week to week, they moved with speed through a large number of working environments. These included the magazine offices, various foreign destinations, the photographer's studio, their agents offices, their own homes where they also worked, and various other locations including cafés and bars where they had business meetings. They were quite literally always 'on the move', and their peripatetic working identities discounted regular day-to-day contact with the same people over a lengthy period of time. In the absence of this, and as a counter to isolation, they relied on the network of colleagues and agents with whom they spoke on the phone throughout the day.

The various working practices I outline below constitute the distinctive career pathways that prevail in fashion journalism. This raises three questions: How new are these and to what extent are they different from the those that governed this as a field of work in the past? How representative are these as recognizable practices of cultural production in other sectors of the media? What role does gender play in determining the conditions of this field of work?

Inevitably, history and tradition play some role in shaping the occupational parameters in fashion. This is apparent in the training of fashion journalists. Those who trained in art colleges alongside the designers adhered to the ideas of fashion as fine art and the fashion media as part of the *Vogue* tradition. Those who had university degrees and had completed a postgraduate training in journalism with a specialism in fashion media were more interested in fashion as lifestyle and as part of the consumer culture.

The *Vogue* tradition is unashamedly elitist. With most of the early editors and journalists coming from 'society' backgrounds, their embracing of fashion and fashion photography as modern art was, and continues to be, part of an attempt to secure for fashion a recognized place within the realms of high culture. The *Vogue* tradition elevates the artist to the status of creative genius, and one of its missions is to achieve the same status for the great fashion designers. This image of the artist has no expectations or requirements that art be in any way connected with politics or society. Indeed any connection with wider social issues would spoil fashion's love of theatricality and drama. The combination of spectacle and fantasy so beloved by designers like Galliano and McQueen ensures that the journalists confirm the special status of fashion as 'extraordinary'. The contemporary influence of this tradition has filtered down and represents the dominant strand in fashion journalism. It is epitomized in the writing style of celebrated *Vogue* editor Anna Wintour and also in the work of Sally Brampton who was the founding editor of British *Elle*. In both these cases the work as editor has been similar to that of patron of the arts. Wintour introduced the work of Galliano to an international audience and helped him secure financial backing. Brampton wrote regular extended features on him and brought his name to the attention of a wide middle-class readership through the pages of the broadsheet UK press: 'One only needs to look at the collection of John Galliano . . . to appreciate the mastery of fantasy, sometimes wantonly perverse and sometimes lyrically beautiful – that this culture can produce' (Brampton, 1996).

But despite these efforts, the specialist nature of fashion journalism and its marginal status elsewhere in the media makes it relatively inward-looking, resistant to change, frequently defensive and fiercely loyal to its own traditions. Its low status in the eyes of Oxbridge-educated journalists and news journalists in general, is reflected in a brief comment by Jonathan Glancey of the *Guardian* following the death of Versace. He said, 'Why all the bother . . . over a preening victim of fashion, who belongs to the fashion press, not to Fleet Street?' (Glancey, 1995). For this reason it is extremely rare for a young woman fashion journalist to move, for example, to BBC2's high-status programme *Newsnight*. But although cut off from the mainstream of journalism, the working practices of the young women I interviewed display all the marks of the insecure patterns of employment now evident right across the media and culture industries (including *Newsnight*). Like other sectors of the culture industries, it has undergone substantial expansion in recent years and this is also reflected in the growth of the undergraduate courses specializing in 'fashion communication'.[2]

Given the strenuous attempts on the part of the newspaper industries to gain more women readers, a pattern also being duplicated across terrestrial, cable and satellite television, it follows that the space devoted to fashion features has increased noticeably in quite a short space of time. The overall impact has been to make careers in fashion, including journalism, more recognized pathways which are then presented to girls at school and in college as realizable ambitions. One consequence of this is that the tradition of this being a 'nice job' for well-bred girls from the upper classes has been replaced by more open access. This has swollen the ranks of those attempting to gain a foothold in this world and often willing, as a result, to work for nothing. In short the fashion media represent one recognized site among the landmarks of 'glamorous jobs for young women today'. Study of the fashion media therefore provides an excellent opportunity to examine an occupational field which can be understood as part of the feminization of the media.

Fashion journalism comprises of a number of activities. The fashion team led by the editor is responsible for putting together the fashion pages. This is largely a visual job. The written text accompanying the images is usually a headline, caption or a few evocative sentences. Fashion writing includes a number of conventionalized practices: the designer profile, fashion reporting of the collections, the consumer overview (as in *Marie-Claire*'s well-known feature '100 Best Buys') and the single-item feature ('This year's new shirt' etc.). Together these require the services of a wide range of personnel, including editors and writers, art directors and fashion assistants, stylists, make-up artists, models, photographers and set designers. Many of these jobs are, however, interchangeable. For this reason the labour process of fashion journalism is best understood first in terms of *fluidity and mobility* and second through the ethos of *creativity*.

In the 18 months that elapsed before the completion of the interviews with fashion media workers and the writing up of the research, every single woman who participated had moved from the job they were doing at the time. Although it is now widely recognized that media jobs have an immensely high turnover, (in advertising most people do not stay in one job longer than two years), this inevitably produces a different kind of relationship to workplace and employer, and indeed to colleagues. These young women are representatives of the process of 'individualization'. As the labour force has become more fragmented and as large institutions have become deregulated, more and more people are detached from the older structures of workplace, family and community and are encouraged instead to become 'entrepreneurs of the self' (Du Gay 1996). The long-term consequences of 1980s' neo-liberalism in the workplace and post-industrialization in the West are producing a more self-reliant, opportunistic workforce, an increasing number of whom work for themselves. All of these features were visible in the army of freelancers I met in the course of this study. Their working identities were defined within a 'time space compression' like that described by David Harvey (Harvey, 1989). They worked at a faster pace on more than one job at the same time and also moved rapidly through a range of different working environments located in different parts of the world.

Capital has thus unburdened itself of the responsibility for the health and safety, insurance and other social costs of a workforce by encouraging self-employment and cultural entrepreneurialism. Nowhere is this more apparent than in the media and communications industry and it is certainly the case in the fashion media. Even editors of large-circulation magazines owned by multinational conglomerates were frequently employed on 3- to 4-days-a-week contracts. The entire staff of these magazines (most on similar contracts) rarely rises above ten in total. Otherwise there is a vast network of part-timers, freelancers and 'contributing editors'. The ethos is consequently one of networking – 'keeping in with the right people' – and committed self-interest. Only one of the people I interviewed belonged to a trade union, although several indicated the need for more protection; most, however, claimed not to have the time to get involved.

There is no doubt that their working schedules represented an intensification of labour. They worked long hours for unreliable rewards and most of them were willing to take on extra unpaid work if it helped their creative profile. This style of working is summed up in the comments by two young fashion journalists, one at the time employed as fashion editor for the *Guardian* newspaper, the other a freelance fashion stylist.

> I have worked for five years as a journalist, after completing the one-year postgraduate course at City University. I started in design journalism first on *World of Interiors* magazine for six months, then I went into *Fashion Weekly* as menswear editor. I was there for two years. In 1992 I was freelance and won the Jackie Moore award in the *Vogue* writing competition. I went back to *Fashion Weekly* which was superb training for the whole fashion industry, and while I was there I was also freelancing for *Elle* and *Vogue*, and also doing some designer interviews for *i-D*. I started doing some bits for Louise Chunn who was then fashion editor at the *Guardian* and then I took over from her when she left.
>
> (Harriet Quick, interviewed in July 1995)

This constitutes eight jobs in five years (albeit some of them part of the 'freelance portfolio'). It is also relevant that all the work she mentions – carried out on a freelance basis for style magazines including *i-D*, *The Face*, *Dazed and Confused* – is unpaid. The reward is publicity and the possibility that the work will lead to more lucrative contracts from magazines and international fashion companies. The second respondent, Anna Cockburn, had already established a reputation as a talented stylist when I interviewed her in a café in London. Her commentary is worth quoting at length.

> I did two years at Central St Martins, but I knew I wasn't going to paint. I was much more interested in making images, so I left and worked as a fashion photographer's assistant, knowing nothing much about fashion. . . . Then I got a job at Joseph (the fashion retailer) . . . at that stage I didn't know what a stylist was. But I wanted a change and I heard there was possibly some work at *Harpers & Queen*, assistant to the fashion editor, and I got the job. During this time I was also working in a pub at night to pay the bills. At *Harpers* I found myself with six pages, and whether it was a collection I saw, a film or a dream, or a painting, it was the idea that was important . . . the stylist and the photographer can both be mavericks and it works. I got promoted to junior fashion editor and then the recession hit [1989/90] . . . you were forced to be less creative . . . I went to *Elle* . . . but I didn't really settle down. I then spent a year in America on various projects, came back as contributing editor to *Vogue* . . . it was a bit disappointing because everything had to be agreed and approved . . . it was all done at the level of 'house style'. Since then I've been freelance. The agent calls me up and says there is a job here or there. . . . At the same time right through this period I've worked for *The Face* and *i-D* who don't pay but it's exposure and it's advertising for people like myself. . . . It always costs me but it's worth it for the freedom, the exposure and the space. They are also generous with the credits which are more visible and bold.

In this case, eleven jobs in seven years, with pub work at night and unpaid work requiring outlay without any financial reward – in effect, she is paying to work for nothing! What each of these cases reveals – apart from the rapid turnover of jobs and the 'investment' in unpaid work – is the privatization of occupational identity. These are young workers whose 'unique talent' is what makes them attractive to employers. In such circumstances they can only afford to think on their own behalf. This, I would argue, also has repercussions for the kind of work they do; because they are so reliant on future jobs from unknown sources, and because they have already experienced periods of job insecurity they are forced to play safe. The fashion editor of the *Guardian* (who replaced Harriet Quick) said, a few months later in response to a telephone question of mine, that 'it would be more than my job's worth' to run a feature which suggested that major fashion houses in the United States were relying on a chain of sweated labour even though the story had surfaced across the American media and prompted immediate political responses.

The issue was not, she agreed, one of newsworthiness or reliable sources, but more that she needed to know that in the future she could talk with and gain access to the fashion houses in question as a source of fashion information and features. This was a 'professional judgement' since it is very common for fashion companies to refuse entrance to journalists to their shows and collections if they have written critically about them. At the same time, given the flow of ex-editors and journalists into in-house fashion PR for the major companies, often for huge salaries, it could also be surmised that self-interest in this volatile, high-turnover labour market also motivated her decision. Nor was this incident exceptional: on various occasions I was told of stories not running for similar reasons. The result in the fashion pages is inevitably timidity in the face of controversy and social conservatism on the politics of fashion.

The ethos of creativity

The editors and writers exonerated themselves from politics and social responsibility on the basis of their self-image as 'creatives'. On the one hand they were promoting the work of the designers by featuring their work in the magazines and newspapers, on the other hand they often actually defined themselves in the same artistic terms. They had adopted an equally creative identity that fuelled their ambition and also justified the long hours, low pay and even the lack of success ('misunderstood by critics and public alike'). In one case a fashion editor argued that it was the magazine and indeed the fashion pages that inspired the designers: 'the page is art'. The editor of *The Face*, Sheryl Garrett, makes a similar point:

> Fashion-wise we are pushing back the barriers; it's not a question of simply presenting clothes. Often we commission clothes to be designed to go with the overall art idea. It's more of an art direction approach to fashion. And because of this the best fashion photographers and stylists will work for us for free. *The Face* is a career ladder, a huge opportunity for creative people to get attention and show their work.

What was a consistent feature of the ethos of creativity was its individualizing focus and the way in which it was utilized as a mark of the self which was, in turn, a bargaining tool in the labour market. The editors, journalists, stylists and assistants all understood that what gave them an advantage, what sold them to an employer was their distinctive 'style', the way they envisaged and then produced the fashion pages, the images that came to be associated with their name. They were in effect 'auteurs' of fashion journalism. Garrett, for example, describes the pages she commissioned around the time of the release of the film *Reservoir Dogs*: 'Most of the magazines followed up Tarantino images with the men in suits, they played around with that. What we did was the blood issue, the fashion with blood story.' This, then, would become part of Garrett's portfolio; as editor with overall responsibility for the story, it would help her get her next job, for the reason that it attracted a lot of publicity, was seen by a lot of advertising agencies and possibly also helped the models, photographers, stylists and writers who did the whole 'test' to get more work.

There are limits which no editor or journalist I interviewed considered breaching and these had to do with the fashion industry itself and the conditions that prevail on the inside, including fashion manufacturing: 'It's not a *Marie-Claire* story'. Thus even in the style press which prided itself on its radical image, this went no further than documenting the look on the street and recording 'real fashion'. In these cases there was a pseudo-populist conviction that fashion was a subcultural and collective impetus rather than the inspiration of a Paris-based designer. All the more surprising, then, that these magazines proved no more able to dig deeper below the surface than their multinationally owned counterparts like *Marie-Claire*, *Elle* or *Vogue*. This confirms Dick Hebdige's argument that *The Face* displayed all the marks of postmodern knowingness in its ironic style and playful rhetoric, while remaining adamantly shallow and superficial (Hebdige, 1988). Politics remains a signifier that can be converted into an accessory, an idea for a fashion story, while the real – as Hebdige puts it, what happens on Planet One – is summarily dismissed.

I have argued here that the working conditions of the new strata of fashion journalists, in particular their freelance and independent status along with their perceived self-images as 'creative', provide a further explanatory frame for the avoidance of politics and the narrow visual conservatism of the fashion media. This converges around a staple diet of highly conventionalized images and text, and otherwise uncritical copy which could be described as broadly promotional. 'This is new, this is what looks good, and this is how much it costs'! On the one hand they perceive their low status and shallow 'airhead' image from the ranks of the serious journalists, and this produces a defensiveness and a determination to stick with their genre and aspire to achieving higher status by self-promotion and uncritical, unreflexive celebration of the form. On the other hand they are more locked within this narrow field and depend more for future work contracts from fellow editors, public relations companies in the field and also the big fashion companies themselves. This is the circuit and it is bound by rigid conventions about what can be said and what must remain unsaid. As Barthes, one of the few academics to subject fashion journalism to detailed scrutiny, said many years ago: 'Fashion's *bon ton*, which forbids it to offer anything aesthetically or morally displeasing, no doubt unites here with maternal language: it is the language of a mother who "preserves" her daughter from all contact with evil' (Barthes, 1967 (reprinted 1983): 261).

I conclude with a word in defence of the young women journalists. It is as much the emergent conditions of work that produce these patterns as it is the whims of editors-in-chief eager to keep circulation figures high, advertising revenue pouring in and, at the same time, keep the fashion world happy. Garnham pours scorn on this trend in the media field and culture industries to work for nothing: 'Often labour is not waged at all, but labour power is rented out for a royalty' (Garnham, 1990: 163). It is for him the ultimate self-sacrifice at the altar of creativity, it lets Capital off the hook, allows it to get away with offloading all the risks to this 'exploited sector'. . . 'without running the risk of labour unrest or bearing the cost of redundancy or pension payments. Their cup brimmeth over when, as is often the case, the workers themselves willingly don this yoke in the name of freedom' (1990: 163).

Of course he is quite right. And such a fragile precarious existence in turn creates a timid band of freelancers and self-employed people whose adventurousness goes no further than advocating the politics of shock within the 'art of the page'.[3] But we also have to be reminded that this is a historical phenomenon, these young women workers are testing the ground of the post-industrial creative economy in the UK. As I argue elsewhere (McRobbie, 1998), in most cases they have little to lose because this is also work carried out under the long shadow of unemployment. Journalists and designers alike had relied on support from the 'dole to work' programme – the Enterprise Allowance Scheme – introduced by Mrs Thatcher in 1983 and phased out ten years later. In these circumstances glamour is a compensatory mechanism that gives them the impetus to keep going, and networking replaces the sociability of the traditional workplace in this individualized and often isolated environment.

I am well aware that I have done no more than sketch out a provisional plan for the kind of research in media and communication studies which I have suggested urgently needs to be done. While the UK media economy appears to be buoyant, it is sustained at its outermost points, away from the offices of the chief executives, by a band of young workers whose patterns of employment are wildly different from the traditional expectations of what it is to have a job and earn a salary. Apart from pressing issues that are intrinsic to the conditions of their labour (low pay, limited social insurance, anxieties about time off through illness or maternity) I have also suggested that the nature of the network and the reliance on friends and on the grapevine for getting the next job discourages a more critical voice in this kind of journalism. Thus the risk-taking activity needed to keep afloat in the creative economy appears to minimize risk-taking in the broader field. There are few, if any, public voices of discontent, and across the millions of glossy pages and column inches I have not as yet come across a single recent piece of writing by a fashion journalist which subjects the fashion system to scrutiny. Indeed it is a noticeable feature of the few articles and news reports that describe the existence of child labour or other exploitative practices in the fashion industry, or that demonstrate the existence of racism within the world of modelling and the magazine business, that they are inevitably written by journalists from outside the field of fashion.[4]

Notes

1.   I envisage here a kind of interrogatory research which would ask the cultural producers involved at every step along the way, questions like: 'Why this image?' 'Why this way?' 'Why these clothes, these props, this setting, this style of make-up and hair etc.?'

Such research would also attempt to pinpoint the key decision-makers, the chain of authority and also the spaces of autonomy.

2. A quick glance down the list of staff and contributors in the fashion magazines and newspaper fashion pages reveals this to be a predominantly female field. Access to it has widened to include young women from less privileged backgrounds particularly through the BTEC route through college-based courses in fashion, art and design, and media and communications.

3. A good example of shock aesthetics is the 1993 *Vogue* fashion spread styled by Corinne Day which first introduced Kate Moss to the fashion world, and at the same time presented fashion and models alike in run-down, shabby settings. This gave rise to the notion of grunge fashion and so-called 'heroin chic' and had the desired effect of triggering a moral panic about hard drugs and anorexic models.

4. The *Guardian* (24 November 1999) reported overt racism among model agency executives following an undercover television documentary broadcast the previous evening on BBC television. Both the programme itself and the *Guardian* article were written and investigated by non-fashion journalists (Gillan and Younge, 1999).

References

BARTHES, R. (1967/83) *The Fashion System, Hill and Wang*: New York.

BECK, U. (1999) *Schone Neue Arbeits-Welt*, Campus Verlag Frankfurt.

BRAMPTON, S. (1996) 'Flight of Fantasy', *Guardian Weekend*, 3 February.

DU GAY, P. (1996) *Consumption and Identity At Work*, Sage: London.

ELLIOTT, P. (1977) 'Media Occupations: An Overview' in J. Curran, M. Gurevitch and J. Woollacott (eds) *Mass Communication and Society*, Edward Arnold: London, 142–74.

FERGUSON, M. AND GOLDING, P. eds (1997) *Cultural Studies in Question*, Sage: London.

GARNHAM, N. (1990) *Capitalism and Communication: Global Culture and the Economics of Information*, Sage: London.

GIDDENS, A. (1997) *Runaway Worlds*, ICA: London.

GILLAN, A. and YOUNGE, G. (1999) 'Race Bias Attack on Top Model Agency', *Guardian*, 24 November: 3.

GLANCEY, J. (1995) 'All Dressed Up By The Queen of Frock 'n' Roll', *Guardian*, 18 July, 19.

GOLDING, P. and MURDOCK G. (1996) 'Culture, Communications and Political Economy' in J. Curran and M. Gurevitch (eds) *Mass Media and Society*, 2nd edn, Edward Arnold: London 11–31.

HARVEY, D. (1989) *The Condition of Postmodernity*, Blackwell: Oxford.

HEBDIGE, D. (1988) *Hiding in the Light*, Routledge: London

LASH, S. and URRY, J. (1994) *The Economy of Signs and Spaces*, Sage: London.

LEADBEATER, C. (1999) *Living On Thin Air*, Viking: London.

MCROBBIE, A. (1998) *British Fashion Design: Rag Trade or Image Industry?*, Routledge: London.

SCHLESINGER, P. (1982) *Putting Reality Together*, Constable: London.

TUNSTALL, J. (1971) *Journalists at Work*, Routledge: London.

13

From Dead Trees to Live Wires: The Internet's Challenge to the Traditional Newspaper

Colin Sparks

This chapter looks at the impact of the internet on the newspaper press. In the last few years the oldest of the mass media has been forced to confront the newest form of communication, and attempt to adapt to these changed conditions. The challenge involves everything from styles of writing and presentation, through the ethics of journalism offline and online, to the business model of the newspaper. It is this last area with which I am concerned here. The contemporary press is almost everywhere primarily a commercial press, and a commercial press depends upon a stable and profitable business model. How to make sure that the news is profitable is, as Michael Schudson remarks, a recurrent problem (1996: 6). Unless the people who own commercial news media can make money out of them, then there will be no Fourth Estate, no investigative journalism, no public forum in which contemporary issues can be discussed. The outcome of an examination of the economic consequences of the internet for newspapers is thus fundamental to every aspect of their future.

The contemporary commercial newspaper press has lots of serious limitations from the point of view of democracy, but it nevertheless constitutes one of the main mechanisms by which citizens learn about their world. It is, to use a phrase much discussed elsewhere in this volume, one of the chief sites of the public sphere. Anything that alters the business model of the newspaper, for good or ill, thus has important consequences for political life. To the limited extent that citizens are able to influence the direction of society in a capitalist democracy, the newspaper is an essential aid to them. The issues at stake in this chapter are therefore ones that go far beyond the technical questions of what makes good online journalism, and extend to the degree to which the internet acts to affect the political structure of society.

The aim of this investigation might be summarized in an attempt to answer the question 'What is the significance of the internet for the democratic functions of the newspaper press?' Accordingly, I first look at the evidence for newspapers' engagement with the internet. Second, I consider the strengths and weaknesses of this development of online newspapers. Third, the online behaviour of news-seekers is considered. Next, I suggest some of the consequences of these shifts for the industry as a whole and try to identify possible responses from newspapers. Finally, an attempt is made to assess the overall impact of these changes. Because the development of the internet is such a recent phenomenon, it is too early to be reaching firm conclusions about its effect on any aspect of society, and what I say here should be regarded as tentative and subject to revision as the historical experience grows richer.

Going online

The existing mass media have certainly not been slow to develop a presence on the internet. According to one regular survey, there were, on 2 June 1999, 11,389 media sites, the vast majority of them on the World Wide Web (E&P, 02/06/99). This overall figure includes a wide range of different media, as Figure 13.1 shows. It is obvious that the printed media, and in particular newspapers and magazines, have found an internet presence extremely attractive. Together, these two categories account for well over half of the total.

Another important point to note is that what are quite different media in the offline world, for example newspapers and televisions stations, are nowhere near as distinct online. Instead of one being on paper and delivered by hand, and the other on a more or less dumb CRT and delivered by electromagnetic radiation, they are both delivered by the same technology of cabled transmission and received on the same, usually rather clever, CRT. Instead of one dropping in to your mailbox very early in the morning and the other droning on in the corner of the living room against the background of domestic life, they are both available at any time you want through the (usually) simple means of an electronic connection.

In the offline world, the printed and broadcast media function according to different economic logic. Even when, as in the USA, both are predominantly privately owned, they are regulated by different laws and codes. Although they are both 'media', they are distinct social phenomena, certainly from the point of

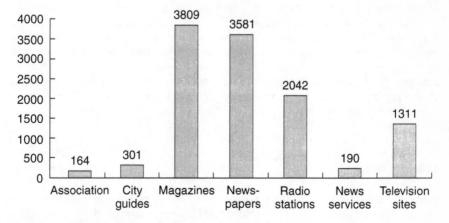

Fig. 13.1 Online media at June 1999
(Source: E & P, 1999)

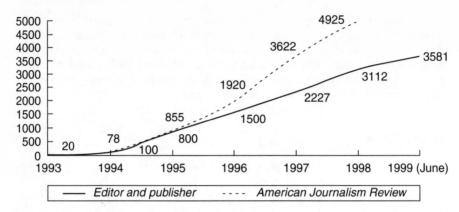

Fig. 13.2   The growth of online newspapers
(Sources: E & P 1993–99; Meyer, 1998)

view of the consumer. In the online world, on the other hand, they both have exactly the same status. An online presence elides the differences of form, of timing and of social consumption, which are the bases of the market positions of various different kinds of media.

This online presence is a very recent one, as Figure 13.2 demonstrates. The two sets of figures arise from the different definitions used by the organizations that generated them, and I have no grounds for suggesting that one is more accurate than the other. What matters for us, however, is not the exact number of online newspapers but the sequence of events and the apparent changes in magnitude. In these respects, the two sources tell very similar stories. Some newspapers and specialist news suppliers had long been available on dial-up services, but these latter were, and are, essentially subscription-based business tools that offered an electronic version of the offline texts of groups of newspapers and magazines. In 1993 there were hardly any freestanding electronic newspapers available. As reports from that period, which now seems to be in the distant past of the internet, clearly illustrate, it was by no means obvious, either to scholarly observers or to the industry itself, exactly what form the electronic newspaper would take. Different newspaper companies were exploring a range of possible delivery technologies, most of them proprietary, but these were all in the experimental stage. Late 1994 to early 1995 appears to have been the period when the real growth began, with hundreds of papers flooding online. It quickly became clear to everybody that the graphical capabilities of the World Wide Web made it overwhelmingly the medium of choice for the online newspaper.

Why go online?

It is quite legitimate to ask the question 'Why has there been this flood of titles online?' There are numerous possible secondary explanations – including enthusiasm for new technology and the general sense that one wishes to be part of the wave of the moment – but the fundamental reasons must surely be economic.

The people who own newspapers have, by and large, decided that the internet provides opportunities and challenges to which they need to respond.

Some of the opportunities are obvious. The offline newspaper is in part a process of manipulating symbols, and in part a straightforward industrial production process. Once the journalists and the advertising people have delivered the made-up, final copy, the newspaper undergoes a series of transformations that constitute the physical production and distribution of a commodity. Printers and printing presses produce thousands or millions of more or less identical physical copies of the newspaper. Dispatchers load the newspaper on to trucks, and drivers distribute it to wholesalers and then to retailers. They in turn either deliver it to the user, or put it on display next to the sweets and the cigarettes. All of this costs money for wages and equipment. It has been estimated that something like 50 per cent of the costs of a US newspaper are consumed by this physical process of production and distribution.

The online newspaper does not incur any of these costs. True, it requires some space on a server, but this is not a comparable expense to the printing presses and trucks needed for the physical product. The consumers themselves pay costs of distribution, buying the PCs and paying the telecommunications charges. The online newspaper offers the proprietors the prospect of substantial cost reductions (Sparks, 1996).

It also provides the possibility of new readers. One key constraint on the circulation of newspapers has always been physical distance. Particularly with a daily newspaper, there is a limit to how widely it can de distributed, and this limit is set by the time it takes a truck or a train to make the journey to the point of delivery. The major reason why no national daily newspaper could evolve in the USA before the advent of satellite transmission and remote printing is that the size of the country makes it impossible to publish a physical newspaper in, say, New York and distribute it the same day to homes in Dallas, or Seattle or Miami. Even with the technologies of the 1980s, distances were still so great that papers like the *Wall Street Journal*, *New York Times* and *USA Today* could not be in every home in every hamlet the morning after they were put together in New York. Telecommunications is, famously, one of the main engines of 'space-time compression', and it abolishes this tyranny of distance. It is now perfectly possible for readers in Seattle – or for that matter Tokyo, Delhi, Moscow and London – to access a New York-based newspaper more or less simultaneously with people in Brooklyn (Sparks, 1999a).

Newspapers are now freed of the physical limitations on their potential audience and can attempt to find readers around the world. One obvious example of this is that newspapers in regions of high emigration can reach people who have left the land of their birth but who still hanker after news of the 'old town' and the people who stayed behind. The electronic newspaper provides ties for diasporas that the older émigré media once provided much less efficiently. Other readers, particularly for the leading titles published in the main global centres, will be attracted by the depth and detail of the coverage of important events that are shaping the contemporary world, and that are not available in such detail in their own local newspapers. The *New York Times*, for example, found that half of its 3 million registered online users had never bought an offline copy of the paper (Brown, 1999a).

A further opportunity for expansion is provided by the opportunity for a newspaper to reach new social groups who previously did not buy the offline title. In countries with competitive newspaper markets, like the UK, national daily newspapers have strong brands that both attract and repel readers. One of the possibilities of an online edition is that it makes it feasible to modify a newspaper's image to that which becomes more attractive to those who found its offline embodiment repellent. An example of this process is the *Electronic Telegraph*, which consciously distanced itself from the elderly and reactionary image of its physical parent, the *Daily Telegraph*. More generally, the online audience is believed to be younger than the population as a whole, and it is precisely amongst younger age groups that newspaper reading is a less well-entrenched habit. The online edition provides a way to reach people who perhaps seldom or never purchased the offline edition.

The online newspaper also confers what journalists perceive as an important competitive feature in news-gathering as compared with working offline. Physical newspapers may produce several editions, but in general they only have one, or at most two, main publication points in any 24-hour period. The need to print and transport a physical product imposes strict time deadlines on the news day. This means that there is a risk that an important news development will occur too late to be put in to the newspaper on the day of its occurrence. Journalists think that covering these 'breaking stories' is a very important part of their work. Printed newspapers have long been thought to be at a disadvantage to radio and television, both of which offer the opportunity continuously to update news throughout the day, although observation suggests that this facility is used, at best, for a minority of items. The online newspaper, on the other hand, is free from these constraints. It can be updated as quickly and as continuously as a radio or television broadcast, and thus newspaper journalists are once again on an equal footing with their competitors (Kurz, 1999).

The advantages accruing from producing an online edition are summarized in Figure 13.3. The online news-gathering and production process is free from the arbitrary deadlines imposed by the physical constraints of printing and distributing a newspaper. There is no longer a lengthy period while the purely mechanical tasks of printing thousands of identical copies and distributing them throughout the circulation area are achieved. The news can pass straight from

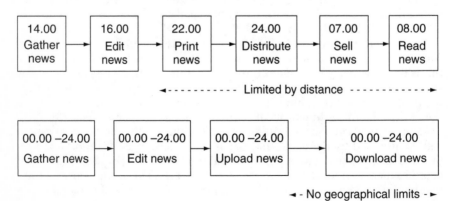

Fig. 13.3   From offline to online

the reporter to the desk editor and then directly into circulation, to be read at any hour of the day and night, and it can be updated and modified as events unfold and interpretations become clearer. For their part, the readers now have access to a much wider range of products, unconstrained by what is physically available in their particular location. They are free to pick and choose between different online products and to select those that seem important or attractive for a particular purpose. On the face of it, at least, it looks as though the internet promises newspaper proprietors new profits, print journalists new opportunities, and readers new freedoms. Everyone, except perhaps printers, transport workers and news vendors, will benefit from the new world.

In reality, the online world has its own problems, some of which are so severe as to pose very serious problems for the parent companies of offline titles as well. The basic difficulties are, first, that producing an online edition hardly ever means that it is possible to abandon the offline version and, second, that the development of online media causes problems for the revenue streams of offline media. In order to understand why that is the case, we need first to understand what makes an offline newspaper commercially viable, and why it takes the form that it does.

Smearing ink on dead trees

There are several available models of how an offline newspaper can be run, but the dominant one in the developed world is that of the commercial operation. It is true that various kinds of subsidy play a supporting role in some countries, but almost everywhere the newspaper is centrally and primarily a business. Like every other business, a newspaper company sells products to raise revenue, and in order to do so incurs costs when it buys the raw materials, labour and services needed to produce its products. For a successful newspaper company, of course, revenues exceed costs, and this we will crudely term 'profitability'.

The business model of the commercial newspaper is relatively well known (Sparks, 1999b), and I only need to summarize it here. Newspapers have two revenue streams: from subscription, the money paid when a customer purchases the newspaper; and from the sale of advertising space in the newspaper. Of these, the latter is usually by far the most important. In US newspapers, for example, it accounts for around 80 per cent of income. Of the advertising that is found in newspapers, one of the most important elements is the 'classified' section, which accounts for between 25 and 50 per cent of the advertising income of a US newspaper and around 30 per cent of total income (Brown, 1999a; Duncan, 1999). Classified advertising is dominated by three categories: jobs, cars and houses. The other major advertising staple for US newspapers is display advertising placed by local retailers, which has many of the same localized features as classified advertising proper. National display advertising is relatively unimportant in the US press, and elsewhere it is of secondary importance to the local press.

The offline newspaper is able to raise these two revenue streams because it is in a unique position. There is no way in which people who are interested in the daily news can find the range and depth of reporting other than in newspapers. On the other hand, there is no way that small-scale local advertisers can

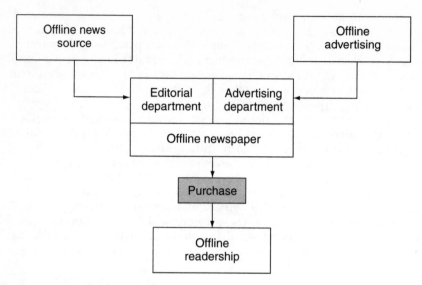

Fig. 13.4   The 'virtuous offline circle'

efficiently reach their target audience except by purchasing space in a newspaper. As Figure 13.4 shows, there is a peculiar 'virtuous circle' that applies to the offline newspaper. In order to attract readers who will purchase the newspaper, the proprietors have to invest in editorial material that will be of interest to them. In order to attract advertisers who will pay for space in their pages, the proprietors have to show that they can attract readers. The business model of the commercial press is one that seals advertising and editorial material indissolubly together. The newspaper is thus a bundle of two quite different kinds of symbolic material: journalism, which makes strong claims to separate fact and opinion; and advertising, which of course attempts to elide the two. A glance at the kinds of prose produced by a journalist and a real estate agent demonstrates the differences.

There is, however, another important twist to the business of the offline newspaper. For a variety of technical economic reasons, the market for newspapers is subject to powerful trends towards monopoly (Sparks, 1995; Picard, 1997; Furhoff, 1973). Some concentrated and wealthy markets – like Britain, for example – are able to support competing newspapers, but the norm is for single newspapers to be dominant in a particular region. The USA is the best example of this. The facts of geography discussed above have meant that newspapers mostly have only local circulation, and the vast majority of the 1,500 or so daily newspapers in the USA enjoy effective local monopoly.

Monopoly has two interesting effects on the behaviour of newspaper proprietors. In the first place, it means that they can set the price of advertising without reference to the behaviour of their competitors, so they usually set it high. Second, not all readers are equally valuable. While everyone pays their 25 cents, or whatever, to buy the paper, advertisers are much more interested in readers who have high disposable incomes, and will pay much more to reach them. Newspaper owners are thus interested in reaching rich readers, and will adopt policies that maximize such an audience. It has long been known that maximizing profits does not necessarily entail maximizing the total audience (Corden, 1953). A newspaper can decide that it is more profitable to concentrate only on a section of its readers rather than trying to serve the whole of the population. Economic analysis can show that it is unprofitable to print and distribute papers in poorer areas. It can also show that certain kinds of editorial material are particularly attractive to desirable (that is, rich) readers, and should therefore be developed at the expense of other copy. There is, then, a sound business reason for newspapers to try to 'superserve' their wealthier clients.

The overall effect of all of this is threefold. In the first place, the local monopoly has meant that newspapers have been able to sustain very high levels of profitability even when their circulation has been falling sharply, as is particularly the case in the USA but is more generally true of many developed countries (Picard, 1999). Second, newspapers have developed styles of journalism, most notably 'objective' reporting, that do not involve obvious bias for or against any influential group in society, since to do so would risk alienating important potential readers. Third, newspapers are disproportionately read by the upper social class and carry material that reflects the interests of that group.[1]

The commercial newspaper press has thus come to constitute the kind of 'bundle' of material that is illustrated in Figure 13.5. The newspaper is a clearly defined product, obviously different in its mode of delivery and periodicity from the magazine on the one hand and broadcasting on the other. Within the newspaper, there is a clear difference between editorial content and advertising content, both of which are produced by quite different people operating with distinct, and sometimes opposed, professional ideologies. Editorial content itself is divided between what is thought of as 'news' and other material. This partly consists of 'features' related to the news agenda, and partly of a miscellany of other material that appeals to different aspects of the lives of the readers. Advertising, for its part, consists partly of displays, but mostly of a wide range of classified ads.

This unique bundle has very far-reaching consequences. Because the known news tastes of elite readers include, although they are not exhausted by, detailed

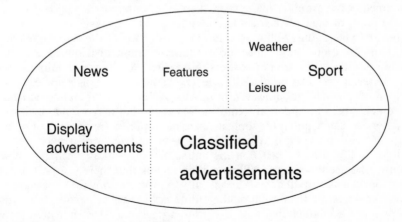

Fig. 13.5 The offline newspaper bundle

reporting and commentary on politics, economics, society, international affairs and so on, these kinds of material occupy a prominent place in monopoly newspapers.[2] In other words, it makes very good business sense for the newspaper to play the role of Fourth Estate, since it attracts rich readers and thus enables the sale of expensive advertising space. Commercial newspapers, therefore, have a powerful incentive – the profit motive – to act as part of the public sphere. Because an informed citizenry exercising genuine choices about the future of society is essential to most theories of democracy, it is not going too far to say that it is this extraordinary set of circumstances that provides the basis for democratic public life in contemporary societies.

Critics will immediately, and correctly, point out the limitations of this model. It is true that the definition of politics, the boundaries of the acceptable, the language and concerns present in the newspapers and so on, all reflect the interests and concerns of the elite. There is a host of ways, ranging from the kinds of sports that are covered, through the length of the sentences used in reports and features, to the crude physical realities of distribution patterns, which mean that these papers are distanced from the lives of the mass of the population, and are, often quite literally, unavailable to large sections of society. The commercial press is necessarily a bourgeois press that covers the world from the point of view of bourgeois democracy. Obviously, it is inadequate for any theory of democracy that seeks genuine equality for the whole of society. Equally obviously, it adopts a harsh stance to those within or without that it perceives as hostile to its interests. Certainly, it is not an agent of human liberation in any serious sense. Within the narrow limits of bourgeois democracy, however, the commercial press does do at least part of what ideologists of the Fourth Estate claim it ought to.

The road to surfdom

Going online threatens this fortuitous set of circumstances. The online world modifies both the cost bases and the revenue streams of newspaper operations in ways that threaten the link between editorial and advertising material. The development of the online newspaper, therefore, represents a major problem from the point of view of the democratic function of the press.

In the first place, going online adds to the overall costs of the newspaper company. Although online newspapers do not have the same distribution expenses as do offline titles, they are not costless to produce. At the very minimum, the offline material needs to be placed on a server and this entails some expense. This kind of 'shovelware', however, is very unattractive to the online audience and it quickly became apparent to most newspapers that they would be obliged to develop dedicated, and quite sophisticated, operations to produce their online editions (McAdams, 1995). While existing news and features can be 'repurposed' for online use, the fact that the online newspaper has a different news rhythm to the deadline-bound offline edition means that there is a pressure to employ journalists and other staff specifically to produce copy for the electronic version. Again, while the design of the offline newspaper has evolved over the years to suit the characteristics of the printed page, this does not necessarily work well in the world of the CRT, so it is necessary to hire designers to produce material that better fits the properties and characteristics of the web. These costs can be considerable for a serious online effort: the *Washington Post*, for example, spends around 10 per cent of group revenues on its electronic initiatives, which amounted to around US$37.8 million in 1998. The company has 180 'producers, coders, technicians and editors' in its *Washingtonpost.Newsweek Interactive* newsroom (Brown, 1999b).

It also needs to be stressed that these are additional costs. The fact that the online newspaper has almost zero distribution costs would only be a benefit to a newspaper company if it could abandon its offline editions, sell off its presses and lorries, and sack its printers and transport workers. So far, that has not proved practical for the vast majority of newspapers.[3] To the extent that the newspaper retains an offline audience and offline advertising, it continues to sustain offline costs. If the online edition erodes the audience for the offline newspaper, then those costs have to be borne by a slimmer revenue base. They thus become ever more onerous.

On the other hand, the online newspaper is not a very promising revenue stream. It has proved extremely difficult for newspapers to charge for access to their basic services. A number of newspapers have tried to introduce payment, but all except the *Wall Street Journal*, which provides specialized business services, have been forced to retreat. The *Wall Street Journal* made US$16.8 million in 1998 from its US$60-a-year subscription charge, and while this is a substantial sum, it is far from representing enough money to put the business on a viable footing. It might be possible for some other newspapers in the same niche market, for example the *Financial Times*, to introduce and sustain charges for content, but even very prominent titles like the internationally renowned *New York Times,* and the extremely web-oriented local newspaper for Silicon Valley, the *San Jose Mercury*, have been unable to make this strategy work. The best that can be achieved, so far, is to charge for specialized aspects of the newspaper, like access to its archive.

The other traditional source of revenue is advertising. At first sight, at least, this looks promising. Although still at a very low absolute level, advertising on the internet is increasing quickly. According to the estimates of the Internet Advertising Bureau, it was up from US$906.5 million in 1997 to US$1.92 billion in 1998, a rate of growth of 112 per cent (Afzali, 1999). The reason for this is that, novelty aside, the internet represents a valuable new medium for advertisers. First of all, while it is true that the technology is not particularly suited to display advertising, the fact that it is searchable means that classified advertisements are much more appropriately placed in this medium than in the physical world. You can find the ad for the used Ford you want to buy without having to wade enviously through pages of Lexuses, BMWs and Mercedes. As one industry enthusiast wrote: 'Classifieds translate well online, leveraging the inherent strengths of the medium, including searchability and database functionality, faster updated listings and more flexible word-and-line spacing relative to print' (Hyland, 1997: 2). The second positive feature is that it is much easier on the internet than it is in the offline world to be sure of the number of people who have seen your advertisement. Advertisers can therefore expect to be able to choose very precisely which media they use for particular campaigns, and control their costs much more directly in proportion to the reach of an advertisement. As one media buyer put it: 'the great thing about the internet is that it is a very trackable and accountable medium. Any advertiser or business setting up a website can tell how many different people have been into the site, how often they came, and which pages they have looked at' (Newing, 1999: 1). Third, the core online audience remains younger and richer than the population as a whole, and therefore constitutes a particularly attractive prospect for advertisers (NTIA, 1999).

Online editions of newspapers might seem to be well positioned to take advantage of these opportunities. In reality, the development of online advertising represents a considerable threat to the newspaper. As we noted above, newspapers are not the only media outlets to have moved enthusiastically on to the web. Not only have literally thousands of other offline media established online presences, but there have been quite a few new starts that exist only on the internet. In the online world, the hard and clear divisions between different media no longer exist. The online newspaper has the same form as the online radio station, the online television station and the online magazine. The online newspaper is no longer distinguished by the fact that it appears every morning or every evening, as opposed to the continuous flow of the broadcasters or the weekly and monthly periodicity of the magazines (Featherly, 1998). What is more, all of these different media now exist in exactly the same space. The geographic distances that previously segmented the market so powerfully have now been more or less abolished. The online reader can have access to any title, from anywhere in the world, at any time she wants. Conversely, the advertiser can gain access to the most dispersed readership through new media and in new ways. The upshot of all of this is that, for the first time in years, newspapers face serious competition in their core business. They no longer have the privileged relationship with readers, and thus with advertisers, that was the foundation of their success in the offline world.

The new competition affects both their editorial content and advertising. In the editorial field, the newspaper now faces direct competition from four types of rival. The first of these is competition from other newspapers. The effective abolition of distance means that no newspaper can now rely on being insulated by geographical location. Titles that had previously enjoyed undisputed domination of their tiny local market now face competition from other newspapers. Obviously, some of these are also small provincial operations that pose little threat, but others are the strongest brands in the newspaper business, like the *New York Times* and *Washington Post*. While newspapers like this might not be much of a threat to local news, they are certainly a strong challenge when it comes to the coverage of major national and international stories, since they can afford to dedicate many more resources, both online and offline, to such issues. The 10 per cent of group revenue that the *Washington Post* dedicates to its online activities translates into a much larger sum than the equivalent percentage of the revenue of a smaller news organization, and online they are in direct competition.

The second challenge comes from media that were previously delivered by different technologies, at different times and in different places, but which now occupy the same place as online newspapers. Some of these, like CNN, pose a threat similar to that of the big metropolitan newspapers, since they have very strong brands that are attractive to news consumers. Others, however, like radio and television stations, threaten to undermine the pre-eminence of the newspaper as source of local news and information in the online world. They can reasonably claim to have as much of a focus on the community as does the newspaper, and can offer the same kind of online news and feature material, as well as possible supplementary material, like sounds and images, derived from their different offline operations.

The third type of competition is from the proliferation of news sources on the internet. In order to have news and related material, it is not necessary to have an offline news presence. There are examples, particularly from specialist areas like technology, of enduring online news operations that are wholly web-based. Purely online news operations, because they do not have to invest in printing and distribution, are also cheaper and easier to set up than offline enterprises, so the entry barriers, particularly for the suppliers of special kinds of 'niche' news, are much lower. Specialist news, which previously was not economically viable, except either as part of a high-cost publication or as part of the general news provision of a newspaper, can thus have a better chance of existing independently and profitably online. The general news diet of newspapers is also under threat from large websites, for example the main portals, that also carry news which they obtain from traditional news wholesalers like Reuters. Given that these sites are amongst the most trafficked on the Web, they constitute an apparent threat to the attempt to offer online newspapers as spin-offs from offline operations.

The final type of competition comes from news sources themselves. The main generators of much of the standard news diet – like government bodies, large businesses, pressure groups and so on – no longer need the newspaper as an intermediary to reach the public. They can now publish their own material, selected, edited and presented in ways that they see fit, and offer it directly to the public in competition with the newspaper journalists' reports of their doings. They are freed from what they perceive as the restrictions imposed by conventional news values, which they often believe stress conflict, edit for brevity and, with marginal and oppositional groups, impose dominant meaning frames on activities. The best-known example is the online publication of the Starr Report, but there are many other, less sensational, examples. NASA, for example, has two goals with its network of sites: 'to cut the costs of communicating with news media and the public, and to disseminate the unfiltered "NASA version" of events' (Kirsner, 1997: 4). The interested citizen can now go straight to NASA, or the Congressional Record, or the SEC filing, or the Union strike bulletin, without any need for the reporter to select and filter it for her. If she is sufficiently interested, she can use a variety of software tools to allow her to receive regular supplies of material from and about her favourite topics, bypassing both online and offline newspapers altogether. In this respect, at least, the promise of the internet is realized: low entry barriers mean that smaller, and dissident, organizations can find a voice online that is often denied them offline.

The advertising content of newspapers also faces a severe challenge from the same types of competitor. In the web-based version of the display advertisement, the banner ad, the challenge comes from those large sites, whether portals or strongly branded news outlets, that are able to demonstrate that they can, in the industry jargon, 'aggregate the eyeballs' on a large scale. Much more importantly for the finances of the newspaper, classified advertisements can readily be migrated to the web, which even offers a better environment for them than does print. Quite apart from the new ability of online radio and television outlets to offer a home for classified advertising, there are a number of websites devoted exclusively to the publication of classified advertisements. They are particularly strong in the core areas of jobs (e.g. Monsterboard.com), cars (e.g. CarPoint.com), and real estate (e.g. Realtor.com). Since these sites are not burdened with the costs of a news operation, they can have lower running costs. They can thus translate capital and revenue into competitive advantage in terms of promotion and functionality. The chances are that they are in a position to offer both advertiser and customer 'more and better' than the newspaper.

And just as online news sources can dispense entirely with the services of a newspaper to reach their target audiences, so online advertisers can use the potential of the internet to avoid intermediaries. Newspapers in Iowa, for example, found that they had a new competitor for job advertising when the state Department of Economic Development launched a website (smartcareermove.com) offering much-reduced fees for in-state companies wishing to advertise vacancies (Noack, 1998). UK universities have similarly bypassed the traditional outlets for academic jobs by setting up their own recruitment site (www.jobs.ac.uk). Not only does the web allow brands to construct their own, independent presence in which they can display their products to the best advantage, and include material that would be intolerably expensive to distribute in the offline world, but it also provides them with a facility that amounts to a greatly enhanced direct mail operation targeted at people who have an interest in their sorts of goods.

Overall, then, the newspaper faces a serious challenge in the online world. As Figure 13.6 illustrates, it faces a 'vicious online circle' that contrasts in all respects with its virtuous offline cousin. Online, the newspaper faces serious competitors for the first time, which can offer some or all of its main products

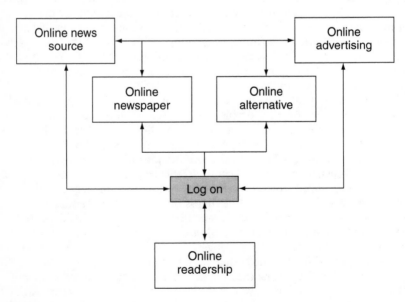

Fig. 13.6 The 'vicious online circle'

and services more cheaply or more efficiently. Some of these are other newspapers, which for the first time can compete directly online. Some are other media, which now find themselves in the same social and technical space as newspapers. Still others are new entrants to the market for news. The same new competitors are also hungry for the advertising revenue that the newspaper has traditionally enjoyed.

The newspaper faces the classic threat of 'disintermediation': the main suppliers of the components of its business model find that they can reach their intended clients directly, without the benefit of an intermediary. It also faces the problem of 'unbundling': the two main constituents of its offline business, public affairs and advertising, are no longer necessarily joined together in the online world. In a purely online world, the fortuitous combination of circumstances that produced the serious public affairs-oriented newspaper does not exist. The current basis of the press as Fourth Estate is under threat, and with it the claims of democratic political life.

The online news audience

Of course, such an apocalyptic claim needs immediately to be qualified and made more accurate. The extent to which the newspaper press experiences a crisis depends, in part at least, on what the news-consuming habits of the population will be in the future. This is true both for production costs and for revenue streams. If the appetite for online news is for expensive kinds of material, presented in novel ways, that are not easily subsidized by the news-gathering efforts of the offline editions, then the cost of running an online edition will escalate. If the number of visitors to newspaper websites is small, and their behaviour on the websites is such as to mean that they make short visits, then the chances of them being directed to advertising material of any substance is reduced.

Online news is an important element of people's internet usage, both at home and elsewhere. Although e-mailing (undertaken by 77.9 per cent of US persons who have internet access from home) is the most important home online activity, and the unspecific 'info search' (59.8 per cent) is the second most important, 'checking news', at 45.9 per cent, is a strong third preference (NTIA, 1999: 60). A separate survey, using equally respectable data also from December 1999, found that 41 per cent of respondents went online either at home or at work (or both). Of these, 25 per cent (or around 10 per cent of the total US population) went online to get news every day, and 64 per cent (or around 25 per cent of the total US population) did the same at least once a week. This online news usage had increased considerably since 1995, and had grown very sharply even between April and December 1998. Everyday users, as a proportion of all of those going online, for example, stood at 6 per cent in June 1995 and 18 per cent in April 1998. Of the 1998 respondents, however, only 16 per cent said they got more of their news from online rather than offline sources, while 75 per cent said that offline sources were more important (Pew Center, 1999: 17). It seems, therefore, that for the wired section of the population, access to online news is an important aspect of their internet usage, but it is seldom at the expense of offline media. Indeed, of those who got news online, 16 per cent claimed that they now used other news sources 'more often', as opposed to only 11 per cent who used

News type	%
Political news	43
Business news	58
Sports news	47
International news	47
Science news	43
Technology news	59
Weather news	64
Entertainment news	58
Local news	42
Health news	46

Fig. 13.7   News interests of online news consumers
(Source: Pew Center, 1999: 21–22)

them 'less often' and 63 per cent who thought that their usage was 'about the same' (1999: 17).

The same study also investigated the kinds of news that people say they seek online. The main results are summarized in Figure 13.7. These show that there is a substantial demand for a wide range of different kinds of news genres online. There is a relatively high degree of interest in business and technology, which may reflect the fact that the profile of the online audience is still dispro-portionately 'techie', and politics has quite a low score compared with its prominence in the offline US press. The picture, however, is one that, with a bit of rebalancing, is recognizably that of a newspaper. There are, nevertheless, one or two interesting aspects deserving of further attention. The high figure for international news may come as a surprise to some foreign observers, since it is part of established wisdom that US citizens are little interested in what happens outside of that country. The second is the very high figure for weather news, which emerges as the most popular form.

Figure 13.8 shows the percentage of those respondents who used the internet to 'get news and information about current events, public issues, or politics at least once every few weeks' that went to different kinds of sites. While it is clear that, in this particular case, there was considerable local interest, the fact is that the national sites were more attractive overall. We can supplement this with the finding of a commercial survey from June 1999 that recorded the total number of visitors to the top news sites. The results are presented in Figure 13.9.[4] These are, of course, a snapshot of web usage, and the ordering changes to a certain extent from month to month, but they do tend to confirm the overall picture. We cannot be definite about what this might mean without breakdowns of access on a regional basis (for example, the proportion of those in City X that access the *X Daily News* rather than msnbc.com). Overall figures for this do not yet exist in the public domain, but one of the most successful online newspaper operations, the *Access Atlanta* site, claims that it has an audience reach of 22.3 per cent of the users in its region (Runett, 1999: 1). If this is generally the case, then it is possible to draw two conclusions. First, the figures suggest that the key

News source	%
Websites of broadcast TV networks	22
Websites of national newspapers	16
Wall Street Journal home page	9
C-Span's website	8
MSNBC	18
CNN/Time All Politics	13
A website devoted to local community	16
Websites of national news magazines	13
Online-only magazines	3
PBS Online	9
House and Senate web pages	8

Fig. 13.8 Percentages of online news users visiting different sites
(Source: Pew Center, 1999: 23)

Ranking	Website	Unique users (000)
1	Msnbc.com	4,631
2	Weather.com	2,635
3	Cnn.com	2,244
4	Pathfinder.com	2,243
5	Espn.com	2,185
6	Abcnews.com	1,623
7	Sportsline.com	1,465
8	Pcworld.com	1,196
9	Usatoday.com	1,099
10	News.com	857

Fig. 13.9 Top ten news sites in June 1999
(Source: Business Wire, 1999)

entry point for news consumption on the web is national rather than local.[5] This is particularly striking in the case of weather: despite the fact that this is necessarily experienced on a local basis, a news site devoted primarily to this content nevertheless scores a high national rating. One of the explanations for this is surely that the offline 'brand strength' of national news organizations is higher than that of purely local products, and this is translated into the online world in which the physical obstacles to the wider exploitation of the brand do not exist. Another industry survey of visitors to newspaper sites found that more than 50 per cent go to national sites like MSNBC and CNN.com for national and international news. It is only with regard to the more local and immediate issues that a smaller newspaper can expect to retain any competitive advantage (CyberAtlas, 1999).

The second conclusion that we can draw is that the preferred types of news source tend to be those, like television sites, that are strongest on brief reports.[6] The view is often advanced that the internet is a technology that 'enables' the citizen, because it allows the interested individual to research stories in depth, to follow links and to compare contrasting accounts. This is true of the technology, but does not seem to correspond to the current social usage. Lots of people make visits to online news sites, but they go for brief accounts of events. This is misleadingly known in the industry as 'breaking news', since the model is the long-running story involving events that unfold over the course of a day or more. In practice, the economics and sociology of news-gathering mean that the news diet will remain relatively stable over a day in normal circumstances. The brief visits that online news-seekers make are, most likely, 'headline checking' rather than the systematic perusal of a news agenda.

Taken together, these early indications of people's online news behaviour do not spell disaster for the majority of newspapers. There is little evidence that online news-seeking leads to a decline in offline news consumption. On the other hand, the online news-seeker is more likely to go first to a national site than to a local one for the bigger stories. For the newspaper that is purely local, this could be a serious problem unless it is able to make sure that it is the essential starting point for those seeking local information. Most local newspapers are today part of national chains, so there are possibilities for attracting visitors first to a national site, provided that the group contains a suitable title that can act as a national magnet brand, and then providing the opportunity to 'drill down' to the more local titles. However true this may be, it also seems to be the case that people make relatively brief visits to news sites. There is little apparent basis for the kinds of detailed reporting that are the historical strength of the newspaper. Neither do these kinds of visit provide a very attractive environment for the sale of advertising space. News content now has to compete with a wide range of other material as an accompaniment to advertisements.

Reinventing the newspaper?

None of this means that the newspaper is finished as a form of social communication, but it most certainly means that there are severe pressures on the existing model of the newspaper. These are likely to lead to changes both to the overall shape of the industry and to the character of the newspapers of which it is made up. Because we are still at a very early stage in the process, it is difficult to say with any certainty what the exact outcomes will be, but it is possible to identify the points at which pressures are likely to arise, and to outline possible responses to them.

The first pressure point is that costs are likely to rise. Very few papers will be in a position to abandon their offline editions in the foreseeable future. The patterns of internet access and usage are likely to remain those that leave a substantial social and economic space for the offline newspaper. On the other hand, if newspapers abandon their online editions in order to cut costs, then they also abandon any attempt to win a share of the advertising that is certainly migrating online. No matter how unsuccessful they may turn out to be, online editions at least have some chance of attracting online advertising, while purely offline editions do not. The second pressure point is that the very fact that some advertising, and particularly classified advertising, is migrating online means that one of the main revenue streams for newspapers will be threatened. As Figure 13.10 shows, there are asymmetries of both costs and revenues between the online and offline versions of newspapers that mean there is no easy synergy between the two activities.

Rising costs and falling revenues mean that profit margins will be squeezed, and this can be expected to have several consequences. For those commercial newspapers that operate at the margins of viability, the effect could be closure. More likely, however, is that the pressures will lead to a strengthening of the well-established tendencies towards chain ownership, with smaller newspapers, and smaller chains, finding relief from a profit squeeze in the economies of scope and of scale that a larger organization brings. A big newspaper chain, particularly one with a prominent national news brand, can devote serious resources to meeting the challenge of the strongest brands, and perhaps provide a focal point for entry in to the world of both news and advertising. The consequence of this, however, is that the online national and international news agenda will be set by a small number of strong brands. Some of these will, no doubt, be related to newspapers and others to broadcast news organizations, but it is very likely that they will derive the bulk of their coverage, particularly their international coverage, from one or two of the main news wholesalers (Paterson, 1999). If the audience is accessing its national and international news from a few large sites, then obviously there is little point in other organizations, who are in any case experiencing cost pressures, continuing to hire journalists of their own to produce this kind of copy. One of the obvious ways for newspaper proprietors to reduce their running costs is to get rid of journalists whose material is

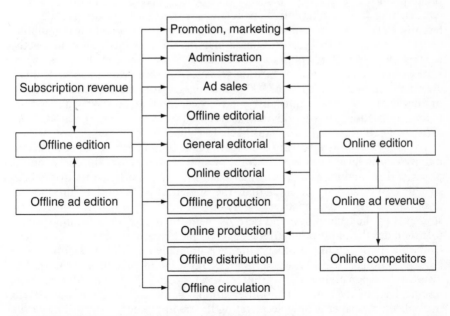

Fig. 13.10 Asymmetry of costs and revenues

no longer useful in the competitive struggle. As a consequence, the range of reporting of public events is likely to be reduced.

The other side of the coin of pressures on costs is that newspapers will be understandably tempted to play to their strengths. Offline newspapers do have very real strengths, some of which can be transported into the online environment. Both in terms of editorial and advertising copy, newspapers have a detailed knowledge of their locality that is not immediately available to other organizations. In terms of editorial copy, newspapers have long adopted a strategy of 'zoning', which in essence is an attempt to get closer to the immediate interests of defined communities by means of producing editions that are narrowly focused on particular places. In terms of advertising material, newspapers have a large and experienced sales force that has an intimate knowledge of local businesses and has established commercial relationships with them.

Both of these assets have been very useful when newspapers have faced the threat of a new entrant into their market. There are several examples of newspapers being able to construct their own highly focused web presences very quickly and to establish at least a strong presence in the online world. The best-known example is the *Orlando Sentinel*, which was faced with competition from the launch of a Microsoft *Sidewalk* city guide in its own circulation area and responded by developing its online presence into an entertainment and shopping guide called *Calendar Online*. This used the resources of the newspaper to provide what it claims is a richer diet of local information than its rival, and has apparently been very successful in raising advertising revenue (Bales, 1999).

On the other hand, just as experience suggests that it is not good enough simply to provide online access to sheets of copy designed for the offline world, so constructing such an alternative involves newspapers in doing things rather differently. In terms of journalism, the stress on the small area and the community leads to a move towards features-based material and towards community activities rather than towards politics. One example of this involves the news organization *New Jersey Online* in hosting websites for local youth soccer teams – eventually ending up with some 900 home pages. But to do this successfully the organization hired not a journalist but a 'soccer mom', who clearly understood much more about that world than a hot-shot graduate from J-School, with dreams of reporting the NFL, was likely to (Ulin, 1999).

The move towards involving the local offline community in the online community of the local newspaper involves a shift in the relationship between the paper and its audience, who become much more like participants in the construction of a shifting artefact than the audience for a finished product. In important ways, this constitutes a realization of the inherently interactive strengths of the technology, and permits the ordinary person a far more active role than did the old printed artefact, where 'participation' was at best confined to the letters page. On the other hand, it is an audience defined as 'folks', with kids, pets, houses, jobs, cars and holidays, rather than as 'citizens' with public duties and responsibilities. Those latter aspects are hived off to a different, more remote, level of the national and international news sources. In this, of course, the online newspaper is only accelerating the trend present in the offline world, which goes far wider than the content of the media and involves an alleged crisis of representative democracy. It is ironic that a technology that holds the promise of overcoming that very crisis is transformed by the pressures of the market into yet another of its causes.

The adaptation of advertising to the online world involves a shift of focus away from simply providing a conduit in which some people can announce that they have something for sale and other people can note that fact, into providing a market-place in which the different parties can carry out a transaction. In other words, the newspaper can attempt to enter that, actually rather small, part of the exploding world of e-commerce that is consumer-oriented. The problem newspapers face, however, is how to persuade companies that they should share some of the revenue arising from their transactions. The costs of developing one's own website are not so great, and there are plenty of competing hosts that offer at least as many potential customers, so the newspaper has no direct advantage. The obvious way around this problem is for the newspaper to develop forms of editorial writing that attract the right kinds of audiences and encourage them to engage in transactions. One example of this strategy is the development of a 'Beanie' site by Alice Sky at the Knight-Ridder-owned *Wichita (Kansas) Eagle*. This quickly proved as popular on its own as the newspaper as a whole, and became a central part of the overall group online strategy. The site combines material produced by its own journalists, material submitted by fans, and large amounts of promotional material, advertisements and so on. According to its founder: 'this is not journalism, it is a community, and that's the heart of journalism' (Blankenhorn, 1999: 3).

However, as this example clearly demonstrates, this strategy involves a re-orientation of the newspaper towards a discourse that is much more directly related to bringing together editorial writing and commercial transactions than has been the proclaimed norm for at least the last 50 years. Although offline newspapers have, in practice, long devoted large amounts of space to editorial material they know will attract advertising revenue, there has always been some genuine basis to the claim that these were quite separate functions, and that the latter did not influence the content of the former. Certainly, there is very little evidence that the main news and current affairs coverage was systematically adapted to the needs of particular advertisers, although it has been convincingly argued that newspapers have in general created a pro-advertiser climate (Baker, 1994). The new model takes as its starting point the need to produce editorial copy that will fit in with the interests of the advertisers and merchants who are to be attracted to pay for exposure in the online paper. The job of the 'journalist' becomes to collect material, some of it recognizably news and some of it recognizably promotional copy, and package it together with advertising and transactional material in order to attract readers and persuade them to buy some good or service – the transactional model only generates revenue if an actual sale is made.

Taken together, these developments suggest a new model of the online newspaper, which is outlined in Figure 13.11. In contrast with the model of the offline newspaper represented in Figure 13.5 and discussed above, the boundaries between a newspaper and other forms of publication are much less clear. The balance of both elements of the newspaper, the editorial and the commercial, has also shifted, with the introduction of transaction-based material as the major development in paid-for copy. The most significant development, however, is the

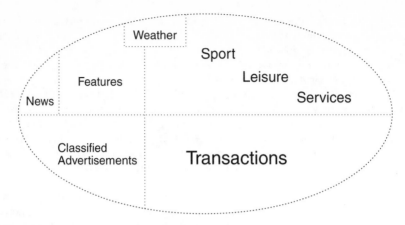

Fig. 13.11   The online newspaper bundle?

fact that the line between editorial and commercial material, once so clearly drawn (at least in theory), is now blurred.

Whether this emerging new model newspaper yet represents a viable business model is currently an open question. There are claims that some online news sites are making money: 25 per cent of newspaper and magazine sites 'reported operating in the black in 1998' according to one report (Stone, 1999: 1). How one interprets this is a matter of dispute. There appears to be some evidence at least that sites claiming to be profitable are still in fact receiving hidden subsidies from the offline editions, for example through the free or discounted use of news services and perhaps other overheads (Zollman, 1998: 5). Ominously, the most convincing claims for profitability come from those companies, like Knight-Ridder, that have been most innovative in incorporating transactions into their sites, and those, like Thomson, that have been most ruthless in pruning editorial inputs down to a minimum. It is likely that, over time, at least some sites will come to represent viable commercial propositions, but it is equally likely that they will, in content and presentation, be radically different from their remote offline ancestors.

Conclusions

The development of the internet thus provides a major challenge to the existing model of the newspaper, and to those elements of the public sphere that are dependent upon the Fourth Estate role of the press. The offline newspaper press developed its characteristic form as a bundle in which editorial and advertising material played mutually supportive roles. It was to the advantage of the owners that editorial material addressed the interests of elite social groups because these were the readers most interesting to advertisers. On that fortuitous basis the provision of public affairs news and commentary proved to be economically viable. The development of the online world provides four challenges to this model.

1. It introduces intense competition. By abolishing distance, it ensures that small local titles now have to win their readers in a battle with the leading national and international news brands. By homogenizing delivery mechanisms, it ensures that newspapers compete directly for attention with other news sources like radio and television organizations.
2. It dissolves the link between editorial and advertising material. It is now possible for would-be advertisers to reach audiences just as efficiently either through other media channels or directly through their own efforts. It is also now possible for news sources and interested individuals to reach each other without the intermediation of the newspaper. The interests of the elite readers can be serviced directly by news sources other than newspapers. Newspapers are now freer to devote their attention to less serious matters.
3. The combination of these pressures is likely to lead to an increasing concentration of sources of national and international news and the parallel development of new kinds of local newspaper. A possible model is a division of labour between large sites carrying the traditional kinds of public information and very localized newspapers moving more into a community service than a news-gathering role.
4. One response to the pressure on advertising revenue is for newspapers to develop relationships with other companies on the basis of facilitating electronic commerce. This has the consequence that it begins to erode the distinctions between editorial and commercial material.

Overall, these developments pose a threat to the stability of the offline newspaper model, and in particular to its historically strong commitment to extensive coverage of news and current affairs, and its function as a forum for public debate. Since these constitute two central aspects of contemporary democratic political life, it seems to follow that the development of the internet poses a threat to the highly imperfect contemporary public sphere. How severe that threat will be, and whether any substantive alternatives will emerge, it is too soon to say, but the early evidence is not good. A technology that evidently has the potential to overcome many of the limits of the mass media looks like evolving into one that exacerbates existing tendencies to separate politics and ordinary life, and to concentrate public debate and information in just a few hands. It will act thus to entrench the domination of unaccountable power.

Notes

1. In markets that are large enough to permit more than one newspaper, there is a tendency for the titles to stratify their editorial content and their readership. On the one hand, there is an upmarket press, with very heavy dependence on advertising revenue and restricted circulation. On the other hand, there is a downmarket press with very heavy dependence on subscription revenue and restricted income from advertising. The UK national daily press is the prime example of this kind of market. It is also noteworthy that this kind of press market is much less dominated by the practices of impartial journalism than are monopoly newspapers. In a competitive environment, partisanship is a minor aspect of product differentiation.
2. In competitive markets, this reporting occupies a prominent place in newspapers directed at elite groups: for example, the 'quality' press in the UK.

3.   So far as I can tell, only one newspaper – the *Orem Daily Journal* – has abandoned physical distribution. This was a free newspaper launched in October 1998 in offline and online form in the Orem-Provo area of Utah. The aim was to attack the advertising revenue of the local monopoly offline newspaper, the *Daily Herald*, published in Provo. It failed to make much headway in its physical form, and closed that operation at the end of July 1999. At the time of writing, the online edition continues. The main US industry analyst commented that: 'In effect, the publisher of an established weekly newspaper attempted to run a daily newspaper to compete with an entrenched daily, and found the challenge to be too great. But rather than pack up and go home, the internet offers perhaps another way for Journal Publication, which owns both papers, to compete' (Outing, 1999).

4.   According to the report: 'The following list is compiled using a proprietary software tool tracking "unique visitors" who go to a Website. Every visitor is counted only once, regardless of how many time the individual visits a site. This sample includes 55,000 home users who are not using the proprietary AOL browser. The total universe of non-AOL home internet users is approximately 50,000,000' (Business Wire, 07/14/99).

5.   Indeed, one could conclude that the high score for CNN explains the interest in 'international' news. Even though analysis shows that CNN's website is predominantly US-oriented, it is certainly perceived, even by the scholarly community, as an 'international' news source.

6.   It should be said that the *Washington Post* (12) and the *New York Times* (14) both scored relatively highly.

References

AFZALI, C. (1999) 'IAB: Internet Ad Revenues Reach $1.92 Billion for '98'. *Internet-News.com Advertising Report*, 3 May. At http://www.internetnews.com/IAR/print/0,1089,12_109931,00.html.

BAKER, C. (1994) *Advertising and a Democratic Press*. Princeton, NJ: Princeton University Press.

BALES, M. (1999) '*Orlando Sentinel* Shifts to 'Internet Time' for Microsoft City Guide Battle'. At: http://www.digitaledge.org/monthly/1999_07/Orlando.html.

BLANKENHORN, D. (1999) 'Online newspapers create niche content sites'. At http://www.adage.com/interactive/articles/19980727/article4.html.

BROWN, C. (1999a) 'Romancing the abyss'. From Part 12 of the *American Journalism Review*'s 'Special Report: The State of the American Newspaper'. At http://ajr.newslink.org/special/12-1.html.

——, (1999b) 'A computer game converted to a serious purpose'. From Part 12 of the *American Journalism Review*'s 'Special Report: The State of the American Newspaper'. At http://ajr.newslink.org/special/12-6.html.

BUSINESS WIRE (07/14/99) 'Top 20 News Sites'. *Business Wire*, 16 July.

CORDEN, W. (1953) 'The maximization of profit by a newspaper'. *Economic Studies 20*: 181–90.

CYBERATLAS (1999) 'Newspaper Sites Cut Into Other Media'. At http://cyberatlas.internet.com/big_picture/traffic_patterns/print/0,1323,5391_156111,00.html.

DUNCAN, E. (1999) 'The Internet v. the Press: Caught in the Web: The Internet is Bound to do Serious Damage to the Newspaper Business'. *The Economist*, 17 July: 21–23.

E&P (1999) *Editor & Publisher Media Links: Online Media Directory Current Database Statistics*, 2 June. At http://www.mediainfo.com/ephome/npaper/nphtm/statistics.htm.

FEATHERLY, K. (1998) 'TV's Threat Get Bigger on the Web'. In *MediaInfo.com*, 11 November 11. From *Editor & Publisher Online Archives*.

FURHOFF, L. (1973) 'Some Reflections on Newspaper Concentration'. *Scandinavian Economic History Review*, 21(1): 1–27.

HYLAND, T. (1997) 'Web Advertising A Year of Growth'. *IAB: Advertising ABC's*. At http://www.iab.net/advertise/content/webgrowth.html.

KIRSNER, S. (1997) 'The Space Race on the Internet'. *MediaInfo.com*, 5 May. From *Editor & Publisher Online Archives*.

KURZ, H. (1999) 'On Web, Newspapers Never Sleep'. *Washington Post*, 9 July: E1. At http://www.washingtonpost.com/wp-srv/business/daily/sept99/online7.htm.

MCADAMS, M. (1995) 'Inventing an Online Newspaper'. *Interpersonal Computing and Technology: An Electronic Journal for the 21st Century*, Vol. 3, No. 3, July: 64–90. Cited from: http://www.sentex.net/~mmcadams/invent.html.

MEYER, E. (1998) *AJR Newslink: An Unexpectedly Wider Web for the World's Newspapers*. At http://ajr.newslink.com.

NEWING, R. (1999) 'Viewpoint: Jane Ostler on Advertising on the Web'. In *The Financial Times Survey; Information Technology*, 3 March: 1.

NOACK, D. (1998) 'Iowa Papers Object to State's Classified Publication'. *Editor & Publisher Interactive*, 9 November. From *Editor & Publisher Online Archives*.

NTIA (1999) *Falling Through the Net: Defining the Digital Divide. A Report on the Telecommunications and Information Technology Gap in America*. Washington, DC: National Telecommunications and Information Administration of the US Department of Commerce, July.

OUTING, S. (1999) 'A Newspaper Dies, a Website is Born'. In *Stop the Presses! Online News Industry News and Analysis*, Monday, 2 August. At http://www.mediainfo.com/ephome/news/newshtm/stop/st080299.htm.

PATERSON, C. (1999) 'Internet News: Source Concentration and Cybermediation'. Paper presented at the Euricom Colloquium on the Political Economy of Convergence, University of Westminster, London, 5–8 September.

PEW CENTER (1999) *Online Newcomers More Middle-Brow, Less Work-Oriented: The Internet News Audience Goes Ordinary*. The Pew Research Centre for the People and the Press. At http://www.people-press.org/tech98mor.htm.

PICARD, R. (1997) 'Modeling the problem: De novo entry into daily newspaper markets'. *Newspaper Research Journal*, Vol. 18, Nos 3–4, summer/fall: 94–108.

——, (1999) 'Implications of the Changing Business Model of the Newspaper Industry'. *Quarterly Journal of International Newspaper Financial Executives*, Second Quarter: 2–5.

RUNETT, R. (1999) 'Online Newspapers Gaining Traction'. Report on the Newspaper Association of America's conference *Connections 1999* proceedings for Friday 6 July. At http://www.digitaledge.org/connections99/fri.html.

SCHUDSON, M. (1996) 'News in the Next Century: New Technology, Old Values . . . and a New Definition of News'. Report commissioned by the Radio and Television News Directors Foundation's *News in the Next Century Project*. At http://www.rtndf.org/rtndf/newtech.htm.

SPARKS, C. (1995) 'Concentration and Market Entry in the UK National Daily Press'. *European Journal of Communication*, Vol. 10, No. 2: 179–206.

——, (1996) 'Newspapers, the Internet and Democracy'. *Javnost* (The Public), Vol. III No. 3: 43–58.

——, (1999a) 'Newspapers, the Internet and the Public Sphere'. *Review of Media, Information and Society*, Vol. 4: 51–68.

——, (1999b) 'The Press' in Stokes, J. and Reading, A. (eds) *The Media in Britain: Current debates and developments*. Basingstoke: Macmillan.

STONE, M. (1999) 'News Websites Turning Towards Profitability'. *Editor & Publisher Interactive*, 20 February 20. From *Editor & Publisher Online Archives*.

ULIN, T. (1999) 'There's More to Community Publishing than Ad Revenues'. Report on the Newspaper Association of America's conference *Connections 1999* proceedings for Friday 6 July. At http://www.digitaledge.org/connections99/fri.html.

ZOLLMAN, P. (1998) 'The Numbers Racket'. *Mediainfo.com*, 25 July. From *Editor & Publisher Online Archives*.

SECTION III

Mediation of Meaning

14

National Prisms of a Global 'Media Event'

Chin-Chuan Lee, Joseph Man Chan,
Zhongdang Pan and Clement Y. K. So[1]

It is often claimed that media discourse represents 'a site of symbolic struggle', but what are the processes, significance and limits of that struggle? As a global 'media event' (Dayan and Katz, 1992), the transfer of Hong Kong from British to Chinese sovereignty on 1 July 1997 provides such a site and moment for opposing *national* media communities to express, and thus reinforce, their enduring values and dominant ideologies. More than 8000 journalists and 776 media organizations from around the world congregated in this bustling city to witness an event of presumed global significance. Journalists are interested not in Hong Kong *per se*, but in China. They participate in the embedded ideological struggle among various modern *-isms*: East versus West, capitalism versus socialism, democracy versus authoritarianism. What marks for China national triumph over colonialism is, in the eyes of most western journalists, 'a menacing, authoritarian Chinese government, its hands still stained by the blood of Tiananmen Square, riding roughshod over freewheeling, Westernized Hong Kong' (Chinoy, 1999: 394).

Foregrounding a barrage of news events as a rupture requires interpreting its meaning against a background of continuities. Van Ginneken (1998: 126) puts it well: 'What the fireworks of international news illuminate or leave in the dark is the historic panorama beyond them.' This essay examines from the perspective of comparative sociology of news-making how international journalists take part in a post-Cold War ideological discourse through making sense of a 'media spectacle' (Edelman, 1988). This event undergoes a transformation – thus robbed of conflict, suspense and theatrical appeal. This does not prevent the world media-cum-various national cultural arms from plunging into discursive struggles to promote the legitimacy of their national regimes.

Despite much talk about the growing globalization processes, we argue that international news-making is inherently domestic, paradoxically local and, above all, *national*: the same event may be given distinct media representations by various nations through the prisms of their dominant ideologies as defined by power structures, cultural repertoires and politico-economic interests. This is the process of 'domestication' (Cohen, *et al.*, 1996; Gans, 1979). Even though the set of people to be interviewed, mostly the elite and some token 'ordinary folks', is likely to be small and highly overlapping, different national narratives enable journalists to insert the present into a highly ideological perspective on the past and the future. Moreover, in most foreign policy issues, media differences across the ideological divide *within* a nation tend to be dwarfed by media differences *between* nations.

International news-making and discursive struggles

The handover of Hong Kong stands for a concentric circle of relevance and vested interest to various national discursive communities and is thus open to divergent media construction. International news-making follows the same logic of domestic news-making, but under different political conditions. It is widely accepted that the media produce and reproduce the hegemonic definitions of social order. There are four general claims to this overall thesis. First, 'news net' of the media (Tuchman, 1978) corresponds to the hierarchical order of political power and the prevailing belief system that defines this order. Occurrences outside the centralized organizations or standard genres would not be recognized as news. Second, even in a democratic society, news production must inevitably epitomize the capitalist mode of production and serve the financial-ideological structure and interests of the dominant class, race and gender (Mosco, 1996; Thompson, 1990). Third, the ideology of journalistic professionalism, as enshrined by the creed of objectivity, is predicated on an unarticulated commitment to the established order (Gitlin, 1980; Said, 1978; Schlesinger, 1979; Tuchman, 1978). News media 'index' the spectrum of the elite viewpoints as an essential tool for domestic political operation (Bennett, 1990; Cook, 1998). In a similar vein, Donohue, Tichenor and Olien (1995) maintain that the media perform as a sentry not for the community as a whole, but for groups having sufficient power and influence to create and control their own security systems. Fourth, when elite consensus collapses or is highly divided, or when there is strong mobilizing pressure from social movements, the media may have to reflect such opinion plurality (Page, 1996; Hallin, 1986; Chan and Lee, 1991). Such plurality does not, however, question the fundamental assumptions of power in society.

The international order being more anarchic, the *state* – rather than specific individuals, classes or sectors within a country – acts as the repository of 'national interest' (Garnett, 1994), as the principal maker of foreign policy, and as a contestant in international news discourse (Snyder and Ballentine, 1997: 65). Operating as 'little accomplices' of the state (Zaller and Chiu, 1996), the media rely on political authorities to report foreign policy-cum-national interest. Moreover, the media, the domestic authorities and the public tend to perceive the international news reality through shared lenses of ideologies, myths and cultural repertoire. The media revolve around the head of state, foreign ministry and embassies to make news because these institutions are assumed to have superior if not monopolistic access to knowledge about what national interest is abroad. Foreign news agendas are even more closely attuned to elite conceptions of the world than are domestic news agendas. The US media therefore tend to 'rally around the flag' in close alliance with official Washington

(Brody, 1991; Cook, 1998), especially when the country is in conflict with foreign powers. By this process of 'domesticating' foreign news as a variation on a national theme (Cohen *et al.*, 1996), the media serve to sharpen and legitimize national perspectives embedded in the existing order of power and privilege. Gans (1979) maintains that in the US media, foreign news stories are mostly relevant to Americans or American interests, with the same themes and topics as domestic news; when the topics are distinctive they are given interpretations that apply to American values. Media domestication is an integral part of the international political economy.

News media participate in a broader discursive process in constructing the domestic elite's images of 'the other' and legitimizing the state's effort in safeguarding geopolitical interests abroad (Said, 1981 and 1993). They produce a local narrative of the same global event through employment of unique discursive means of rhetoric, frames, metaphors and logic. In 'tangling' with distant contestants in the game of international news-making, they impute different causes and effects to reality to advance national interests and promote national legitimacy. During the Persian Gulf War, CNN became a stage for the US and Iraqi Governments to verbally attack each other, paving the way for and extending the eventual armed conflict (Kellner, 1992). Unlike the institutional struggle in which central authority allocates tangible material resources (Jabri, 1996: 72), the discursive struggle wins or loses symbolically in terms of expression of preferred values and orders. The latter may be mobilized into an institutional struggle while the former may derive its legitimacy from a discursive struggle (Edelman, 1971; Gamson, 1988; McAdam, McCarthy and Zald, 1996). During the Cold War, the superpowers contested over intangible public opinion, images and rhetorical discourse in order, ironically, to prevent the 'hot wars' of guns and missiles (Medhurst, 1990).

The making of a media event

The script for the handover had already been written in the Sino-British Joint Declaration in 1984. The predictability of its prescheduled nature facilitates 'calendar journalism' (Tuchman, 1978). Such events may neither require much enterprising journalistic effort (Sigal, 1973) nor satisfy the 'entertainment logic' of the television age (Altheide and Snow, 1979). Worse yet, since bad news is good news, the world media had concocted various hypothetical worst-case scenarios of communist takeover but the handover turned out to be smooth and peaceful. The large presence of international journalists in a crowded island became a story – a media spectacle – more important than the event itself. A Canadian journalist compares this 'thin massive event' to 'a small pellet of fish food being attacked by 8,000 piranhas'. *Newsweek*'s bureau chief, when asked, agrees that thousands of competitive egos probably end up talking to the same set of twenty to fifty people in town, but the *Daily Telegraph* reporter defends this practice as an inherent logic of journalism and no different from covering South Africa or Bosnia.

According to Dayan and Katz (1992), a media event may fall into one of three categories: a contest, a conquest or a coronation. In spite of the consuming efforts made by dismayed international journalists, the handover story did not seem to rise to various qualifications of a *spectacular* media event. As it began, the event seemed to contain all the exciting elements of a conquest or those of a contest. As the event went through a process of transformation during its life cycle, elements of a contest and conquest receded and the media began to focus on it more as a coronation.

First, a contest 'pits evenly matched individuals or teams against each other and bids them to compete according to strict rules' (Dayan and Katz, 1992: 33). Media events of this type should generate much excitement over the process of competition and reduce the uncertainty about its outcome. The Sino-British rows over sovereignty negotiations and Governor Patten's democratic reforms (Dimbleby, 1998) began to fade in significance as Hong Kong inched towards the handover.

Second, a conquest refers to great men and women with charisma who 'submit themselves to an ordeal, whose success multiplies their charisma and creates a new following' (Dayan and Katz, 1992: 37). Indeed, all of China's official and media proclamations hail Deng Xiaoping, the paramount leader, as the ingenious author of the 'one country, two systems' idea, through which the previously impossible task of reclaiming Hong Kong becomes a reality. Thus, Chinese heroes roundly beat British imperialist villains. As a favourite icon that 'provides an occasion for journalists and their sources to refigure cultural scripts' (Bennett and Lawrence, 1995), China's official television constantly shows a picture of Margaret Thatcher falling on the steps in front of the Great Hall of the People. The Prime Minister had just emerged from her first excruciating encounter with Deng, during which he lectured her that China would not take humiliation from foreign powers any more. That showdown forced both sides to embark on painful negotiations leading finally to the handover. This icon was coined in 1982, and by 1997 Thatcher had retired from public life and Deng was already dead, but the image lives on as a soothing symbol of conquest for China's injured national psyche. The PRC media are also fond of flexing military icons to relish the story of national strength in front of the doubting world.

A coronation, a third kind of media event, deals in 'the mysteries of rites of passage' which 'proceed according to strict rules, dictated by tradition rather than by negotiated agreement' (Dayan and Katz, 1992: 36). Media coverage of a coronation serves to pledge allegiance to the political centre and to renew contract with it. Persons of authority are signified and dignified by costumes, symbols, titles and rituals. Media presentation, which tends to be reverent and priestly, enacts the tradition and authority that are usually hidden from everyday life. A prime icon of Hong Kong's handover coronation is a picture of the brief moment at the midnight of 30 June, seemingly frozen in history. The Union Jack is being lowered and the Chinese flag raised. All principal actors – including Prince Charles, President Jiang, Governor Patten and Chief Executive Tung – are solemnly arrayed on the stage to commemorate a change in the authority structure and to usher in the formal absorption of Hong Kong into the motherland. In spite of its historical significance this still moment produces no lively journalism.

The media event thus transformed, journalists must do something to save the integrity of their paradigmatic structure: repairing part of the assumptions, culling more supporting data, dismissing contrary evidence, or trying to fit their stories into generic narrative structures of media events (Bennett, Gressett and

Haltom, 1985; Chan and Lee, 1991). Above all, they must 'hype up' the event in the hope that their domestic audiences may find reasons to participate in the media rites and rituals. Aronson (1983: 23) defines 'hype' as 'the merchandizing of a product – be it an object, a person, or an idea – in an artificially engendered atmosphere of hysteria, in order to create a demand for it, or inflate such demand as already exists'. Through the display of repetitive, familiar and exaggerated images, often out of context, hyping creates a mythical ritual that is confirming of the dominant ideological framework (Nimmo and Combs, 1990).

National media prisms

To understand these national narratives, we will take a 'constructionist' approach to 'framing analysis' (Gamson, 1988; Gamson and Modigliani, 1987 and 1989; Pan and Kosicki, 1993) and examine the newspaper and telecast accounts from two weeks before to one week after the handover. These frames serve as an organizing scheme with which journalists provide coherence to their stories and through which some critical issues can be discussed and understood. Gitlin (1980: 7) writes, 'media frames, largely unspoken and unacknowledged, organize the world both for journalists who report it and, in some important degree, for us who rely on their reports'. We will first deconstruct each national media account into what Gamson and Lasch (1983) call 'signature matrix', a device that lists the key frames and links them to salient signifying devices. We will then reconstruct their major theses into genotypical categories – or what Gamson calls 'ideological packages' – replete with metaphors, exemplars, catchphrases, depictions, visual images, roots, consequences and appeals to principle.

In a nutshell, national jingoism of China's mouthpiece contrasts sharply with the fear and doubt of all other national media systems. Western media accounts reveal a common commitment to democratic values and widespread ideological aversion to the PRC. But they also differ in matters of national interest. The US media bang the drum of democracy while the British media exhibit considerable imperial nostalgia. The Australian and Canadian media emphasize the unique significance of Hong Kong to their countries. The Japanese media are intensely concerned with economic interests but not democratic issues. The ideological gaps that stratify the media's taste cultures on domestic issues become blurred on a remote foreign reality like Hong Kong. All in all, several lines of ideological contestation are engaged.

China: nationalism and its discontent[2]

The Chinese authorities harness the media to a 'national ceremony' full of patriotic emotions but, mindful of historical precedents, are determined to contain mass euphoria. Media extravaganzas are tightly orchestrated. Of the sixteen media units chosen to cover the handover, the 'big three' – China Central Television (CCTV), the *People's Daily* and the Xinhua News Agency – account for the lion's share of the 610-member entourage. All of them must strictly follow official policy and news guidelines. The party-state accords special advantage on the big three and facilitates their access to pro-China sources in Hong Kong.

The media interpret reclaiming Hong Kong as the culmination of national triumph over western colonialism – a Chinese dream that could not have been realized without strong communist leadership. The event marks an end to 150 years of national humiliation and a beginning of the reunifying process with Macao and Taiwan into the big 'Chinese family-nation' (*guojia*). This framework places a micro local report about the handover in the macro context of Chinese history. The media adopt a linear historical script that starts with the British takeover of Hong Kong in 1840, flows continuously to unjust domination of a weak and corrupt China by western imperialists and ends up with the 'China is strong again' theme. Little mention is made of British achievements in Hong Kong. Nor is the handover put in the context of the general decolonization trend in the world. In fact, after 1949 Mao Zedong himself decided not to change British jurisdiction over Hong Kong because China needed the port to circumvent western blockade, and this later became a topic of Moscow's ridicule in the 1970s. The Chinese media do not acknowledge these historical interruptions.

The media recreate a highly politicized myth of the Chinese as a family-nation. National festivities being a family affair, patriotic expressions are mingled with the rituals of ancestral worship. CCTV features a family memorial of Lin Zexu, an official whose burning of confiscated British opium triggered the Opium War, with 300 descendants gathered in his hometown to read a eulogy and recite a pledge of patriotism to their distinguished ancestor. CCTV and the *People's Daily* emphasize that the handover is a day of national jubilation for all 'children of the Yellow Emperor' around the world who should be united as closely as 'flesh and bones' in the 'big motherland family'. For days, the *People's Daily* carries special sections featuring various overseas Chinese communities, one by one honouring the return of Hong Kong, taking special care to reflect geographic balance within a global appearance. CCTV sends twenty-two crews to cover strategically selected cities within China and from global Chinese communities, whose activities are synchronized to construct a mythical concept of 'Chinese' that transcends spatial divide, ethnic differences and political rifts.

The 'children of the Yellow Emperor' are to be embraced by Mother China from Beijing. Visually revealing is the 'countdown clock' at the centre of Tiananmen Square, where CCTV depicts the frantic scenes of national flags, fireworks, folk and ethnic dances, accompanied by the sound of the national anthem and thunderous acclamations from the crowd. CCTV's anchors declare that the countdown clock has 'erected a monument in people's heart forever' and this is a spectacular 'festival of the century' for the Chinese nation. The official media keep emphasizing that Hong Kong will be even more prosperous under the care of the motherland's 'one country, two systems' policy, and that Macao and Taiwan will follow suit.

In contrast, since the people in Hong Kong had no say over the fate that the PRC and Britain negotiated on their behalf, the media show enormous ambivalence about this forced union. While praising British achievements in the colony, they also pay lip-service to national dignity but evince little enthusiasm for becoming a member of the Chinese family-nation. The main concern now is whether China will indeed honour its promise to prevent 'one country' from interfering with 'two systems'. Hong Kong people identify with Chinese culture but reject the communist system, as an *Apple Daily* editorial (1 July) asserts. A columnist asks rhetorically (24 June), 'Why do so many people feel unsettled and alienated as Hong Kong bids farewell to colonial rule?' Public opinion polls are often reported to show widespread fear about losing liberty, democracy and human rights under Chinese rule, a fear that *Ming Pao* (1 July) attributes to the Tiananmen crackdown as its worst source. The *South China Morning Post* (1 July) editorially urges China to leave the 'Hong Kong virus' alone.

The defensive and subdued Taiwan media largely echo their government's rejection of the PRC's 'one country, two systems' policy as a solution to national division. Instead, Vice-President Lian Zhan, in a CNN interview, proposes to adopt what he calls 'one country, one system – a better system', meaning Taiwan's flourishing democracy. He tells NBC's Tom Brokow that Taiwan is 'part of China, but not part of the PRC' (*China Times*, 22 June). Appealing to international media for sympathy and rebuffing Beijing's nationalist lure, the leaders insist that Taiwan will not be absorbed as a province of the PRC, and that Taipei and Beijing be treated as two equal sovereign states under one nation. While expressing satisfaction at Hong Kong's return to 'the Chinese nation' (*minzu*), the head of Taiwan's Mainland Affairs Committee reiterates that Taiwan, unlike Hong Kong, is a sovereign state, not a local government of the PRC. If the PRC tries to link the 'nation' and the 'state' as one big happy family headed by Beijing, Taiwan's media seek to de-link them. Other pro-independence papers, such as the *Liberty Times*, even treat China and Taiwan as two separate political entities; to them, the distinction between a nation and a state is irrelevant. It prominently reports a 'Say No to China' rally (24 June) with a headline that reads, 'Opposing Chinese Annexation'.

The United States: new guardian of democracy

The United States views itself as 'a righter of wrongs around the world, in pursuit of tyranny, in defense of freedom no matter the place or cost' (Said, 1993: 5). The collapse of the Soviet Union has left the United States the only super-power and made the People's Republic of China (PRC) a major hurdle to reconstructing the US-dominated international order (Burchill, 1996). In a controversial thesis, Fukuyama (1992) asserts that the end of the Cold War marks the total exclusion of viable systemic alternatives to western liberalism that is the 'only coherent political aspiration'. As the *Chicago Tribune* laments in a typical editorial (1 July, 1997), 'There is sadness in seeing this jewel of Asia transfer to the hands of a dictatorial regime, only 10 years after the fall of the Berlin Wall.' This postulated East–West contest is given credence by vivid memories of the Tiananmen crackdown, which stand out as the most potent point of media reference. Because of, or notwithstanding, its human rights abuse, China has now stepped in to fill the psychological void of the United States for a new enemy.

The media proclaim that the United States has taken over Britain's 'guardian responsibility'. President Bill Clinton pledges to link the preservation of Hong Kong's freedoms to Washington's policy towards China; but his 'positive engagement' policy, aiming to 'draw China in' rather than to 'shut China out', is widely criticized (in, for example, the *Washington Post*, June 24) for sniffing up a version of the old 'quiet diplomacy' excuse for doing nothing about China's human rights or Hong Kong's freedoms. With the British gone, the conservative Republican chairman of the Senate Foreign Relations Committee, Jessie Helms, writes in the *Wall Street Journal* (25 June) urging the United States to 'employ tactics well beyond legal challenges' until China lives up to its commitments.

This 'new guardian' role is obviously based not on sovereignty or territorial claims, but is justified on ideological grounds. CBS News casts Hong Kong's handover as part of a big story about China striving to be a world superpower. Not only does its serious-looking anchor, Dan Rather, travel to Hong Kong by way of revisiting, reminiscing about and reporting from Tiananmen Square, thus linking the handover to the crystallized symbol of communist repression, a key member of the network's coverage team is Bob Simon, a 'war correspondent' renowned for his coverage in the Middle Eastern and Bosnian theatres but with little knowledge of China. Wearing a safari suit, he tells Rather that 'a communist regime gets control of a piece of real estate without firing a shot'. The *South China Morning Post* gives the four globe-trotting US celebrity anchors a simple test on name recognition and finds them 'decidedly hazy on some general knowledge of Hong Kong' (Beck, 1997). Ignorance makes them even more reliant on stereotypes.

The *Washington Post* doubts editorially (1 July) that 'authoritarian China' can succeed in using Hong Kong as a model to bring 'democratic Taiwan' back to the fold, and urges that the people of Taiwan be allowed to decide their own future. Citing China's violation of agreements with Tibet, a writer implores that 'policy-makers in the free world' keep a 'vigilant watch on Hong Kong' (2 July). The *Washington Post* compares the Hong Kong handover to communist North Vietnam's takeover of the capitalist south, even though the British do it with style or – in the words of CBS correspondent Simon– 'without tail between legs'. Next to the Tiananmen crackdown, Singapore and its authoritarian patriarch, Lee Kuan Yew, emerge as a favourite media metaphor. Singapore's *Straits Times* chides 'the British nation's surrogate mourner [in Hong Kong] – the western media, human rights lobbyists and crusading politicians in Washington and parts of the European Union'. The *New York Times* notes editorially new Chief Executive Tung's fondness for Singapore's system (29 June) which is, in the view of a correspondent (Chinoy, 1999: 396), 'wholly out of touch'. Governor Patten gets a lot of media mileage from lashing out at Lee Kuan Yew as an 'eloquent advocate of authoritarian government', not particularly Asian or Confucian (The *Washington Post*, 25 June). Thus, international politicians and media fight an ideological battle at the site of Hong Kong on the occasion of its sovereignty transfer.

The new Cold War is translated into a local fight over the erosion of Hong Kong's fragile democracy (especially the dismantling of the elected legislature) and existing freedoms. A *New York Times* editorial (1 July) declares, 'By *habit* and *ideology*, Beijing is quite capable of quashing freedom in Hong Kong' (emphasis added). It predicts (25 June) that China's critics will have 'a major confrontation in the next few years with communist hardliners who never met a publication that they did not like to censor'. The media repeat Patten's railing against Hong Kong's business elite, most of them having obtained foreign passports, for a switch of allegiance to Beijing. Major democratic leaders like Martin Lee are media icons. *Wall Street Journal* editorials (26 June and 1 July) criticize harshly Beijing's behaviour in seeking to gain 'absolute control' in Hong Kong, and condemn German, French and British leaders for kowtowing to Beijing (2 July).

While it is common to see Hong Kong as the recipient of abuse and negative influence from China, the US media also invoke a complementary frame – deriving from the well-known Greek 'Trojan Horse' mythology – to suggest that Hong Kong will be a harbinger of economic, even political, change for China. The *New York Times* (1 July) states that the Red Star over Hong Kong may mark the end of Maoism. On the same day, Foreign Affairs columnist Thomas Friedman argues that Hong Kong is the future of China 'when it grows up'. He also warns (3 July) that if China does not live up to its obligation, it 'will be punished by that most brutal, efficient and immediate of diplomatic tools: the ATM machine'. He refers to the more than $100 billion in foreign investment in Hong Kong – most of it in highly liquid funds. In a similar vein, former Prime Minister Thatcher writes in the *Wall Street Journal* (27 June) that Hong Kong will mark 'a new impulse toward freedom and democracy in China and the rest of Asia'. She also refers to Hong Kong in a CNN interview as a 'small crystal ball for a big solution' and 'an example and a flagship of what the Chinese can accomplish'.

Britain: imperial nostalgia

The Tiananmen crackdown provided an impetus for Britain to harden its policy towards China. When Chris Patten arrived in 1992 as the last Governor he vowed to abandon a decade of British appeasement and acquiescence policy and, instead, to implement last-minute democratic reforms as a British legacy in the colony. China was so infuriated that it denounced him as 'sinner of the millennium' (Dimbleby, 1998; Patten, 1998). Verbal warfare was daily media fare. Patten's rhetorical eloquence did much to inspire local and international media conjecture about the horrible scenarios of life under Chinese rule.

The British media seldom broach, much less apologize for, the history of the Opium War. Displaying considerable imperial nostalgia, they claim that their small island nation generally 'brought civilization to the world' and, specifically, left good legacies – liberty, prosperity, the rule of law, and a clean and efficient civil service – in Hong Kong. Former Prime Minister Thatcher, calling herself 'an unashamed defender of the record of the British Empire', argues in the *Wall Street Journal* (27 June) that Hong Kong's lifestyle would be 'an impulse toward freedom and democracy in China'. Extolling Hong Kong as 'a Chinese success story with British characteristics', Governor Patten (1997) emphasizes in his monthly radio programmes and public speeches that Hong Kong is the only decolonized place with less democracy. 'Because men who set off from our islands conquered the world,' the *Daily Telegraph* asserts editorially (30 June), English is now the world language of commerce, law, science and a universal model for good government. 'Hong Kong is Britain's creation,' it continues. To the *Financial Times* (30 June), Hong Kong people under British rule enjoy better government and greater opportunities than Beijing has yet provided for its own people. 'If this is a [national] disgrace,' it asks, 'whose is it?' These media depictions, while substantially true, present a truncated and skewed history that loses sight of Britain's own anti-democratic record in the colony and typifies what Said (1978, 1981 and 1993) portrays as the imperial construction of Orientalism.

The BBC calls Hong Kong 'the best run' and the 'most successful' of the countries of the British Empire. All major media accentuate Britain's presumed role in safeguarding Hong Kong's freedom – by echoing official rhetoric or by personifying Patten. On the day of the handover, the *Daily Telegraph* prominently quotes Prince Charles, in headline and text, as saying, 'We shall not forget you.' Patten is the symbol of ability, character and political courage to 'stand by the principle of liberty against the angry power of China' (*The Times*, 1 July). Both the BBC and ITV underscore Patten's characteristically strong rhetoric: 'Hong Kong people are to rule Hong Kong. That's the promise. That's the unshakeable destiny.' (Patten also exchanges fire in the British media with his detractors, those 'China Hands' in the Foreign Office who accuse him of being belligerent to Beijing and detrimental to British interests.) *The Times* claims that Britain has secured a firm commitment from world leaders to watch over China (23 June). It depicts Prime Minister Tony Blair as someone who 'talks tough with Beijing leaders' and Foreign Secretary Robin Cook as 'freedom's watchdog in [the] former colony' (1 July). The *Guardian* observes more soberly in an editorial (30 June), 'After all the superlatives have been spoken, we must not let our attention [to this matter] drift away.'

Patten had wanted to convince British and international public opinion of Britain's ability to withdraw from Hong Kong 'with at least a modicum of dignity and honour' (Dimbleby, 1998). He appears to have achieved this mission in view of the overwhelmingly celebratory, if also sad and sentimental, media characterization. The media use pictures and tidbits related to British cultural icons or colonial symbols. A Black Watch soldier is shown rehearsing a Highland dance for a Hong Kong farewell concert. The pageantry is filled with coloured uniforms, military bands, regiments in formation and the Union Flag. Above all, the BBC praises the departing royal yacht with the tone of a romantic lover: 'Thousands of various kinds of ships move through [the glass canyon of Hong Kong] every day, but none is as pretty as *Britannia*! After 80 state visits in her 47 years of service, she has not seen a quite as emotional departure as this one'. Of the British departure, a *Times* (1 July) subheader reads: 'tears mingle with the rain as retreat is beaten'. The *Daily Telegraph* spreads a headline across pages two and three: '*Britannia* sails into the night as the flag of freedom is lowered forever.' The *Financial Times* is less emotional and more Britain-centred in its coverage.

Canada and Australia: the diaspora

The media in Australia and Canada – Hong Kong's new diaspora – share western pessimism but also develop their own news agendas. Neither country is a global power. Canada has absorbed more than one million immigrants, mostly affluent middle-class professionals who were willingly uprooted from Hong Kong to escape the prospect of communist rule. Australia too has absorbed Hong Kong immigrants to a lesser extent, and many Australians remember Hong Kong fondly as their first take of the East. The Australian media call for a foreign policy more independent from the United States and Britain, while the Canadian media stress their special ties with Hong Kong.

The Australian media focus on what China can do to harm Hong Kong as well as what Hong Kong can do to change China. The best-case scenario would be for China to become more like Hong Kong, and the worst-case scenario would be for Hong Kong to sink into a mainland mire of corruption, disrespect for the rule of law, and restraint on press and other freedoms. An Australian Television (ABC) programme contrasts 'modern' Hong Kong people's 'despising' view of China with 'backward' mainland Chinese people's patronizing view of Hong Kong. Two of its feature stories (17 and 30 June), one with footage of the Tiananmen Square massacre, mock Hong Kong business for working with 'their new communist bosses rather than run[ning] for cover with their second passports'. The third special feature story (1 July) is introduced by asking if the Red Flag over Hong Kong 'signals a new game plan for organized crime and its export to Australia'. One in four of ABC's stories makes reference to Taiwan's position.

Australia has been striving for a more independent foreign policy. Earlier in 1997 it refused to support the United States and Britain in condemning China's human rights at a United Nations forum in Geneva. In attending the swearing-in ceremony of Hong Kong's Provisional Legislature, Foreign Minister Alexander Downer puts it bluntly: 'Gone are the days when Australia does just what Washington and London want us to do' (*Weekend Australian*, 14–15 June). Former Prime Minister Malcolm Fraser writes in the *Australian* (17 June) charging that 'British and US attempts to establish a western-style enclave in Hong Kong and to impose western conditions on China will contribute nothing to stability in East Asia and the western Pacific.' He calls for an open appraisal of western policy in this region. In response, a historian comments that Australia's position is not on higher moral ground, but simply based on 'a different set of national interests to pursue in the international arena' (20 June).

As neighbours and allies, Canada has much in common with the United States but has always struggled to come out from Big Brother's shadow and establish its own identity. The Canadian media are characteristically suspicious of China's respect for liberty and democracy. In a CBC Pacific Rim Report (20 June), after China's Minister for Hong Kong Affairs Lu Ping gives a speech, a local businessman reacts that he trusts Lu in terms of business but not human rights. The programmes' host remarks that 'the right to make money will be protected, but [I'm] not sure about human rights'. The media favour Hong Kong's democratic camp; but, privately, many Canadian journalists have found fault with their American colleagues for 'carrying the Holy Grail' as 'the only interpreters' of democracy.

The media stress the special ties between Canada and Hong Kong. Not only do Toronto and Vancouver have a distinct Chinese flavour, Cantonese is now the third most widely spoken language in Canada. So, what happens in Hong Kong has a direct bearing on what happens in Canada. Jonathan Manthorpe of the Southam News says: 'Hong Kong is a domestic story for us. I sometimes feel I am in the Richmond West bureau of the *Vancouver Sun*.' There are so many Canadians living in Hong Kong (estimates say 200,000) that it is impossible for journalists not to bump into their fellow citizens. CBC is keen to mention the Canadian identity of its interviewees in Hong Kong, ranging from a radio broadcaster, a newspaper columnist and a lawyer, to a billionaire. The *Globe and Mail* (3 July) quotes Chief Executive Tung as telling the visiting Foreign Affairs Minister Lloyd Axworthy about his wish to strengthen the special bilateral relationship, as they attend Canada Day celebrations together – a day that also happens to be the first of Tung's administration. One editorial theme of Fairchild

Television Canada is the 'Canada–Hong Kong sentiment' while another illustrates how Canadian commodities, interests and technology have taken root in Hong Kong.

Japan: money, not democracy

As befits their international image, the Japanese media are intent on preserving much of Japan's economic benefit in the region, while demonstrating little concern for local democratic aspirations. It has been observed that elite integration between the Japanese Government, commercial–industrial conglomerates and the media is so powerful – much more so than in the United States – that the media tend to echo the government-corporate views (Pharr and Krauss, 1996). Historically, Japan's 'least offensive' policy in foreign diplomacy has placed economic benefits above ideological interests (Ozaki and Arnold, 1985). Inasmuch as human rights are not a guiding spirit of Japan's foreign policy, its leaders have questioned the idea of applying western standards of democracy to countries like China (Kesavan, 1990). During the Tiananmen crackdown, US media zealously sided with the protesters as if to score an ideological victory, but the Japanese media were reluctant to challenge the Chinese authorities in order to protect Japan's economic gains (Lee and Yang, 1995).

Most western media that had been based in Hong Kong to report about China moved their offices up to Beijing after the PRC normalized its relations with the United States in 1979. But the Japanese have continued to maintain a large contingent of reporters in Hong Kong – efficiently, if quietly, gathering economic intelligence about South China. They do not get excited about China's democracy or human rights unless politics means money and trade. During the Hong Kong handover, a *Yomiuri Shinbum* reporter confides that his editor would have scolded him for wasting the space if he dwelled on the themes of democracy. For this reason, when he requests an interview with Democracy Party leaders he is given the cold shoulder. Several of his Japanese colleagues have provided corroborated accounts. However, the democratic concerns in Hong Kong are too intense for the Japanese journalists to ignore, so they say that western media have focused their attention on Hong Kong's democracy.

Conclusion

International news-making is a form of ideological contestation. Media domesticate foreign news in the light of their own national interests and cultural assumptions. Three outstanding theses – and discursive battles – can be revisited. First, what is the nation-state? The international media are uneasy about the PRC's strengthened role in the geopolitical order. But within Chinese societies, it provokes heated debate about the political and cultural meanings of China and being Chinese. In laying claim to official legitimacy, the PRC media construct China as a unified nation-state that is centred in Beijing yet supposedly inclusive of global Chinese communities as common descendants of mythical ancestry. The helpless Hong Kong media display ambivalence about being part of the Beijing-defined nation-state. The Taiwan media seek to de-link 'the nation' from 'the state', claiming that there are two equal sovereign states within one Chinese nation (Pan, Lee, Chan and So, 1999).

The second theme regards the interpretation of colonialism and nationalism. Media tie their narratives selectively to larger historical frameworks to achieve interpretative coherence. Holding the Opium War as *the* point of historical reference, the echo chamber of the PRC media tries to *essentialize* British colonialism as evil while upholding nationalism as supreme; the handover of Hong Kong is touted as a national triumph over western imperialism. History is thus made invariant, decontextualized, temporally frozen and incapable of change and rupture. On the contrary, the British media seek to *de-essentialize* colonialism by emphasizing that the British have created in Hong Kong a stable and prosperous enclave against relentless national turmoil in the PRC (Patten, 1997 and 1998). This media framing directs attention towards reassessing the virtues of nationalism and colonialism in the context of concrete and changing historical experiences rather than fixed ideological assumptions. On the receiving end, the Hong Kong media are reminiscent about positive British legacies; while accepting Chinese nationalism as a cultural goal, they distrust its political practice. As the next target of China's pressure, the media in Taiwan endorse putting British colonialism to an end but reject the PRC brand of nationalism as expansionist and hegemonic. Interestingly, US, Canadian and Australian media all refer tangentially to their own British colonial past but defend British accomplishments in Hong Kong as part of western civilizations.

Finally, the handover energizes media struggles between systems and ideologies. The PRC finds itself being renewed as a villain in the post-Tiananmen era and in the post-Cold War order, while both US and British media underscore their new and old guardian roles towards Hong Kong. The PRC media contend that the 'one country, two systems' approach will protect Hong Kong's capitalism within China's socialism as if 'two systems' were totally compatible with 'one country'. On the contrary, prevailing scepticism drives the international media to make three sorts of prognosis. First, democracy and human rights will be seriously eroded under authoritarian Chinese rule. Second, Hong Kong will become another Singapore in being economically prosperous but politically controlled. Third, Hong Kong's capitalist prosperity won't be viable without democracy.

So, what will happen? Time will be the best judge. But even in the unlikely event of unequivocal evidence, media struggle will continue to refract differing ideological lights.

Notes

1. Chin-Chuan Lee drafted this chapter, based on the results of joint research with Joseph Man Chan, Zhongdang Pan and Clement Y.K. So. They are grateful to the Universities Research Grants Committee in Hong Kong for support with funding and to Winnie Kwok for research assistance.

2. This section is based on Pan, Lee, Chan and So (1999).

308   *Chin-Chuan Lee* et al.

References

ALTHEIDE, DAVID L. and ROBERT P. SNOW (1979), *Media Logic*. Beverly Hills, CA: Sage.

ARONSON, STEVEN M.L. (1983), *Hype*. New York: William Morrow.

BECK, SIMON (1997), 'Anchors aweigh in the great ratings war', *South China Morning Post*, 30 June, 23.

BENNETT, W. LANCE (1990), 'Toward a theory of press-state relations in the United States', *Journal of Communication*, 40, 103–25.

BENNETT, W. LANCE and REGINA G. LAWRENCE (1995), 'News icons and the mainstreaming of social change', *Journal of Communication*, 45, 20–39.

BENNETT, W. LANCE, LYNN GRESSETT and WILLIAM HALTOM (1985), 'Repairing the news: A case study of the news paradigm', *Journal of Communication*, 35, 50–68.

BRODY, RICHARD A. (1991), *Assessing the President: The Media, Elite Opinion, and Public Support*. Stanford: CA: Stanford University Press.

BURCHILL, SCOTT (1996), 'Liberal internationalism', in Scott Burchill and Andrew Linklater (eds), *Theories of International Relations*. New York: St. Martin's Press, 28–66.

CHAN, JOSEPH MAN and CHIN-CHUAN LEE (1991), *Mass Media and Political Transition: The Hong Kong Press in China's Orbit*. New York: Guilford Press.

CHINOY, MIKE (1999), *China Live*. Lanham, Maryland: Rowman and Littlefield.

COHEN, AKIBA A., MARK R. LEVY, ITZHAK ROEH and MICHAEL GUREVITCH (eds) (1996), *Global Newsrooms, Local Audiences: A Study of the Eurovision News Exchange*. London: J. Libbey.

COOK, TIMOTHY E. (1998), *Governing with the News: The News Media as a Political Institution*. Chicago, IL: University of Chicago Press.

DAYAN, DANIEL and ELIHU KATZ (1992), *Media Events: The Live Broadcasting of History*. Cambridge, MA: Harvard University Press.

DIMBLEBY, JONATHAN (1998), *The Last Governor*. London: Warner Books.

DONOHUE, GEORGE, PHILLIP J. TICHENOR and CLARICE OLIEN (1995), 'A guide dog perspective on the role of media', *Journal of Communication*, 45, 2, 115–32.

EDELMAN, MURRAY (1971), *The Politics of Symbolic Action*. New York: Academic Press.

——, (1988), *Constructing the Political Spectacle*. Chicago, IL: University of Chicago Press.

FUKUYAMA, FRANCIS (1992), *The End of History and the Last Man*. New York: Free Press.

GAMSON, WILLIAM A. (1988), 'A constructionist approach to mass media and public opinion', *Symbolic Interactionism*, 11, 161–74.

GAMSON, WILLIAM A. and ANDRE MODIGLIANI (1987), 'The changing culture of affirmative action', in Richard G. Braungart and Margaret M. Braungart (eds), *Research in Political Sociology*, Vol. 3, Greenwich, CN: JAI Press, Inc., 137–77.

——, (1989), 'Media discourse and public opinion on nuclear power: A constructionist approach', *American Journal of Sociology*, 95, 1–37.

GAMSON, WILLIAM A. and KATHRYN E. LASCH (1983), 'The political culture of social welfare policy', in Shimon E. Spiro and Ephraim Yuchtman-Yaar (eds), *Evaluating the Welfare State: Social and Political Perspectives*. New York: Academic Press, 397–415.

GANS, HERBERT J. (1979), *Deciding What's News: A Study of CBS Evening News, NBC Nightly News, Newsweek and Time*. New York: Pantheon Books.

GARNETT, J.C. (1994), 'The national interest revisited', in Kenneth W. Thompson (ed.), *Community, Diversity, and a New World Order*. Lanham, MD: University Press of America, 87–110.

GITLIN, TODD (1980), *The Whole World is Watching*. Berkeley, CA: University of California Press.

HALLIN, DANIEL (1986), *The 'Uncensored' War*. New York: Oxford University Press.

JABRI, VIVIENNE (1996), 'A structurationist theory of conflict', *Discourses on Violence: Conflict Analysis Reconsidered*. Manchester, UK: Manchester University Press, 54–89.

KELLNER, DOUGLAS (1992), *The Persian Gulf TV War*. Boulder, CO: Westview Press.

KESAVAN, K.V. (1990), 'Japan and the Tiananmen Square incident', *Asian Survey*, 30, 7, 681–699.

LEE, CHIN-CHUAN and JUNGHYE YANG (1995), 'National interest and foreign news: Comparing US and Japanese coverage of a Chinese student movement', *Gazette*, 56, 1–18.

MCADAM, DOUG, JOHN D. MCCARTHY, and MAYER N. ZALD (eds) (1996), *Comparative Perspectives on Social Movements: Political Opportunities, Mobilizing Structures, and Cultural Framing*. New York: Cambridge University Press.

MEDHURST, MARTIN J. (1990), 'Rhetoric and cold war: A strategic approach', in Martin J. Medhurst, Robert L. Ivie, Philip Wander and Robert L. Scott (eds), *Cold War Rhetoric: Strategy, Metaphor, and Ideology*. New York: Greenwood Press, 19–27.

MOSCO, VINCENT (1996), *The Political Economy of Communication*. London: Sage.

NIMMO, DAN and JAMES E. COMBS (1990), *Mediated Political Realities*. New York: Longman.

OZAKI, S. and W. ARNOLD (1985), *Japan's Foreign Relations: A Global Search for Economic Security*. Boulder, CO: Westview Press.

PAGE, BENJAMIN (1996), *Who Deliberates? Mass Media in Modern Democracy*. Chicago, IL: University of Chicago Press.

PAN, ZHONGDANG and GERALD M. KOSICKI (1993), 'Framing analysis: An approach to news discourse', *Political Communication*, 10, 55–75.

PAN, ZHONGDANG, CHIN-CHUAN LEE, JOSEPH MAN CHAN and CLEMENT Y.K. So (1999), 'One event, three stories: media narratives of the handover of Hong Kong in Cultural China', *Gazette*, 61, 99–112.

PATTEN, CHRIS (1997), *Letters to Hong Kong*. Hong Kong: Government Printer.

——, (1998), *East and West*. London: Macmillan.

PHARR, SUAN and ELLIS S. KRAUSS (eds) (1996), *Media and Politics in Japan*. Honolulu: University Press of Hawaii.

SAID, EDWARD W. (1978), *Orientalism*. New York: Pantheon.

——, (1981), *Covering Islam: How the Media and the Experts Determine how we see the Rest of the World*. New York: Pantheon.

——, (1993), *Culture and Imperialism*. New York: Knopf.

SCHLESINGER, PHILIP (1979), *Putting 'Reality' Together: BBC News*. London: Constable.

SIGAL, LEON V. (1973), *Reporters and Officials: The Organization and Politics of Newsmaking*. Lexington, MA: DC Heath.

SNYDER, JACK and KAREN BALLENTINE (1997), 'Nationalism and the marketplace of ideas' in Michael Brown, Owen Cote, Jr, Sean M. Lynn-Jones and Steven E. Miller (eds), *Nationalism and Ethnic Conflict*. Cambridge, MA: MIT Press, 61–91.

THOMPSON, JOHN B. (1990), *Ideology and Modern Culture*. Stanford, CA: Stanford University Press.

TUCHMAN, GAYE (1978), *Making News: A Study in the Construction of Reality*. New York: Free Press.

VAN GINNEKEN, JAAP (1998), *Understanding Global News*. Thousand Oaks, CA: Sage.

ZALLER, JOHN and DENNIS CHIU (1996), 'Government's little helper: US press coverage of foreign policy crisis, 1945–1991', *Political Communication*, 13, 385–405.

15

Media, Citizenship and Civic Culture

Peter Dahlgren

Democracy is a visionary concept that is often both invoked and contested. Allegiance to its ideals is espoused continually, but there can be much disagreement about how these ideals are to be interpreted and applied. In the empirical real world, we find that democracy is difficult to implement, always in need of active support if it is to flourish, and presently undergoing significant changes. The social conditions for its existence in late modern life are evolving, and many observers express frustration over how it is functioning. In most appraisals of democracy's condition today the media figure prominently. All this can also be said about a key corollary concept, namely citizenship, though it is only in recent years that this notion has become an object of attention from the standpoint of social and cultural theory, and has moved beyond its status as a largely formal category. As the concept of citizenship increasingly comes into the limelight as a specific angle of vision on democracy, the media's significance here, too, must be elucidated. The same holds true, I would suggest, for the idea of a civic culture, understood as an analytic extension of the idea of citizenship. Exploring theoretically and empirically the interplay between the media on the one hand, and citizenship and civic culture on the other, in the historical context of late modernity, will help shed important light on specific features of contemporary democracy.

In what follows I will try to pull together and extend some current strands of thinking in this domain. I first offer some reflections on the often-noted declining participation and trust in formal political systems, and on the rise of what is called lifestyle politics. There is both good news and bad news for democracy in these developments. My premise is that it is important to grasp the ambivalence within the current political malaise in coming to grips with questions about citizenship, civic culture and the media. This brief discussion on the current condition of democracy thus attempts to contextualize the analytic presentation of citizenship and civic culture that follows. The theme of citizens and democracy has traditionally been framed to a large extent by perspectives from political science. In my treatment I try to integrate these with newer contributions from cultural theory and cultural studies, in particular the notion of identity. What emerges is a framework that can help us probe, analytically and empirically, some of the key connections between the media and the functioning of democratic institutions.

Disengaged – or redirected – citizens?

The signs are everywhere. Around the world, the established democracies are witnessing a decline in vitality. The formal political systems are not able to mobilize the support and engagement of citizens as in the past. Even in the domain of civil society, we observe a decrease in participation in organized associational life, which in turn is seen as eroding the social capital necessary for democratic participation (Putnam, 1993, is a key text about this matter; see also Putnam, 1996). Political knowledge among citizens is seemingly on the decline and voter turnouts are diminishing. In the United States, recent presidential elections have elicited the votes of about half the citizens, with the winner entering the White House with about a quarter of the voters behind him. (This is a fact the media tend not dwell on, since it could evoke issues of political legitimacy or otherwise serve to impede governance.) Studies by the UCLA/American Council on Education among first-year college students in the United States reveal an all-time low in the mid-1990s, when less than 32 per cent said that keeping up with political affairs was an important goal for them (cited in Rimmerman, 1997). Even in a country like Sweden, which has in the past had consistently high voter turnouts and high levels of political knowledge, as well as very impressive levels of involvement in the associations of civil society, one sees a decline (Petersson, 1998). Similarly, opinion polls show a marked downturn in political trust in Sweden (Holmberg, 1999).

On the surface, citizens in western democracies thus appear to be losing interest in politics. This is unquestionably troubling, and there is a growing concern about how to renew their involvement (see Sandel, 1996; Dahl, 1998; Fullinwider, 1998; Institute for the Study of Civic Values). Certainly it can be argued that a degree of scepticism towards the formal political system and towards major institutions is ultimately healthy. Too much trust is not good for democracy; it can turn into an incentive for corruption. However, many observers today sense that scepticism is turning into cynicism and the climate of political life is becoming corrosive (Blumler and Gurevitch, 1995).

Yet there is important counter-evidence to the political disengagement thesis, warning against a simplified, one-sided view. One important element here is the increase in extra-parliamentarian politics in recent decades. This is witnessed by various forms of collective action, ranging from opinion-mobilization by international NGOs, to social movements concerned with such issues as gender, ecology and peace, as well as those with more culturally expressive orientations (see e.g. Melucci, 1996). Politically, this is a mixed bag: we cannot, for example, ignore the presence of racist and Fascist groups in this context. However, more generally we observe that, especially via the internet, the conventional political spectrum is being broadened by the entry of many new voices into the public realm (Hill and Hughes, 1998). One can conclude that these participants, albeit a small minority of the population, manifest not a declining interest in politics *per se*, but rather a decision to work in political arenas outside the conventional representational system. Moreover, it can be argued that such movements constitute an important step towards the renewal of democracy, precisely because they contribute to redefining the political terrain in the face of stagnant institutions.

More generally, some social theorists, while observing the decline in traditional civic and political engagement, also point to counter-evidence in altered forms of involvement, including changing notions about what politics actually is. This has varyingly been termed a shift toward 'anti-politics' (Mulgan, 1994), 'life politics' (Giddens, 1991), or, more elaborately, the 'internalisation of freedom' coupled with a 'disavowal of politicians' (Beck, 1998). The newer social movements are often seen as one, but far from the only, expression of this pattern. What such views emphasize is that if support for traditional political parties, interest group politics and (in western Europe) corporatist structures and processes is declining, engagement is being redirected to issues and themes that are seen as having closer personal meaning. People are mobilizing around questions that apparently have more direct bearing on their lives, their life plans, morality and/or identity. There is in other words a tendency that politics is becoming more expressive of people's self-conception and worldviews. Lifestyle politics has a vast array of manifestations, including such diverse issues as abortion, the contents of schooling, vegetarianism, the environment and many topics related to consumption: quality, prices, availability and so on. Group-based identity politics, based on factors such as ethnicity, gender and sexual preference, have been a mushrooming dimension of lifestyle politics. People increasingly tend to build temporary alliances rather than offer long-term allegiance to traditional political organizations. The world of traditional politics is contracting, with engagement becoming less institutionalized and political agendas becoming less stable and less predictable; at the same time, more individualistic forms of political expression are beginning to manifest themselves (these developments are neatly summarized in Gibbins and Reimer, 1999).

These changes need to be understood against the larger backdrop of late modern culture, which according to many theorists (see e.g. Fornäs, 1995) heralds significant alterations in, among other things, perceptions of politics and the social world, as well as the psychic composition of the self. Gibbins and Reimer (1999) argue that what is taking place is not just a shift in values, but also a loosening of the patterns and structure of values. They and others see a drift towards the ad-hocing, mixing and individualization of values, where people today are more prone to personally combine value elements to construct their own frameworks rather than inherit culturally received 'packages'. This, logically, coincides with the trend towards lifestyle politics. All this is not simply a massive retreat to the private sphere and selfish concerns, as some critics claim, even if that dimension is clearly present. Bennett (1998) finds in extensive survey data indications that even if civic and political involvement via group membership and participation has declined in the United States, individual civic involvement such as volunteer work remains high. Also, he notes that while support for politicians and government has eroded, public interest in politics remains high, though other data suggest this is less so among the young.

Media angles

It is important to retain some perspective on both the decline in traditional politics and the rise of lifestyle politics. What we see thus far represent shifts, tendencies; they do not by any means describe the full realities of late modern democracy. Yet, as trends, they need to be taken seriously. From the standpoint of conventional party politics – not to mention Marxian class politics – it may be tempting to take a dismissive stance towards lifestyle politics. One may see it as frivolous, opportunist, lacking in larger societal visions and so forth. Such depictions are no doubt true in many instances, but that is not the point. Conventional party politics is not doing so well, and class politics is doing even worse. Whatever one's own political views, one is still stuck with the task of trying to analyse the historical present, and here lifestyle politics has become an important feature.

Analysts with a traditional view of politics may lean more towards pessimism, while those of a more postmodern temperament may feel more optimistic. We should, however, remember that 'lifestyle politics' and similar labels, while convenient, are somewhat glib. They pull together very diversified tendencies and activities. Further analysis of political life may render the label inconvenient and/or prove it to be the product of a transient phase in the history of democracies. For example, there is not always a clear distinction between lifestyle politics and traditional politics. Many issues having to do with lifestyle politics touch upon the themes of traditional politics, such as the distribution of material benefits. In any case, what disengagement and lifestyle politics point to at present do have an important bearing on the evolving notions of citizenship and civic culture, as we shall see. First I want to discuss how these trends can be understood in relation to the media (see also Dahlgren, 2000).

Researchers in political communication and journalism look, of course, to the modes of representation in the media in order to comprehend current political trends. One familiar stream of analysis posits a strong correlation between media output and the growing lack of interest in political life (Fallows, 1997; Franklin, 1997). Given the centrality of the media as a dominant space of politics today (Castells, 1997), their role in the shaping of contemporary democracy can hardly be dismissed. Critics find that the increasing commercial pressures of the media's political economy (Herman and McChesney, 1997) foster a drift towards sensationalism, trivialization, personal drama and sports metaphors. Scandal moves to the fore (Lull and Hinerman, 1997), while journalism and entertainment become blurred, undercutting the coverage of serious issues and fanning the flames of cynicism. Another theme put forth is that the ongoing differentiation of social worlds and the erosion of community, as well as the growing 'niches' of consumerist culture, all serve to undercut political life on the larger scale, and the media are implicated in this. The traditional mass media can be said to have reinforced patterns of horizontal fragmentation and vertical segmentation of audiences – though in fact the media both promote and follow social patterns of differentiation. This has whittled away at national public space, thereby reducing engagement with the traditional political arena. Such tendencies are greatly amplified by the newer media, including desktop publishing and the internet, that offer inexpensive possibilities for reaching specialized audiences. In keeping with these trends, the emerging practices within political communication of 'targeting' messages to ever more specialized and smaller groups also serves to undercut a common public culture (see Gandy, 2000).

Such perspectives give very plausible interpretations of the media's role in the deficit side of democracy's developments and remind us of the central importance of attending to media policy from the horizons of democracy (see Calabrese and Burgelman, 1999). However, to account for the media's contribution to the newer manifestations of lifestyle politics, to the growth of the 'personalized polity', we need to look at the media with different lenses, albeit not without some ambivalence. Indeed, certain aspects of the mass media's output that may have been deemed negative in regard to civic disengagement can in this context have a positive valence. Thus, features of what is often loosely called 'popularization' trends can possibly serve to mobilize engagement, even if in non-traditional ways. For instance, the increasing porosity of the boundaries between the genres of news, entertainment, drama and advertising may result in discursive frames that are more accessible to broader audiences. Issues may be grasped in less analytic ways, but the conceptual links to one's own everyday life may be made more apparent.

These media developments appear to readily invite particular involvement in topics having to do with values, morality, lifestyle and daily living more so than does 'serious' or 'hard news', with its traditional treatment of conventional politics. The focus on the concrete, rather than the abstract, on persons rather than institutions, on events and incidents rather than on social processes, is also an obvious 'popular' device that makes the world accessible for more personalized engagement. Moreover, the media's contribution to opening up the boundaries between public and private fits well with the political trend noted above. This is particularly manifested in the growing interactive media domains in, for example, some television talk shows and radio phone-in programmes. Here topics from the sphere of private life often become public and discursively framed as political, and the experiences of non-elite people are accorded legitimacy, often in the face of contrasting testimony by 'experts' (Livingstone and Lunt, 1994, clearly make this point). Partly what is at stake here is not just professional values about what is good journalism, but more systemic concerns over the boundaries of the political field. Seen in a positive light, elements of popular journalism and even infotainment can contribute constructively to a revitalization of democracy's public sphere.

Yet, the ambivalence of how to view such developments in the media hangs thick in the air. I have argued elsewhere (Dahlgren, 1995) against a knee-jerk rejection of popular forms of journalism and quasi-journalism. They can help to extend the public sphere by engaging people who may feel remote from more traditional forms of news and current affairs and by serving as discursive gateways where other kinds of topics can become formulated and enter into political life. However, one has to make distinctions, and not give a generalized carte blanche here. Much of this kind of media output is clearly counter-productive to democracy, not least on account of values that are implicitly fostered (exploitation, voyeurism and cynicism, for example). One must also ask in just which topics or issues citizens are invited to engage themselves in these popular ways and about the political significance of these issues. How we are to judge is not always clear in all cases; hindsight may even prove our initial reactions to have been off the mark. I will return to this theme below.

The internet, with its innumerable newsgroups and chatrooms, as well as networking possibilities, must also be seen as an important factor in the alteration of political life today, even if there is some tendency towards exaggerated claims. While the spread of the internet since the mid-1990s has truly been an astounding media development, we must not forget that the patterns vary significantly among the western democracies. All serious prognoses anticipate that access will ultimately be far from universal, generating in turn a situation that is very problematic from the standpoint of democracy (see Loader, 1998). The situation in the developing world is another matter entirely, with such nations accounting for only a small percentage of the computers on the planet. Also, we must keep in mind that the use of the internet for anything having to do with politics and the public sphere comes very low on the list of the purposes to which it is put (Hill and Hughes, 1998).

That said, it is none the less clear that the net is having an important impact on political life. Hill and Hughes (1998) argue that conventional politics has not undergone a dramatic permutation as a result of the net. However, it is clear that the net has become a central tool for many social movements and non-governmental organizations involved in networking, opinion-building and activism. That it has become so pervasive throughout western society (Castells, 1997; Kitchin, 1998), impacting on our understanding of community (see also Smith and Kollock, 1999; Holmes, 1997; Jones, 1998) indicates that it cannot but help to alter relations of power among individuals, groups and institutions (Hague and Loader, 1999; Jordan, 1999). The mass media themselves are undergoing transformation, as they move towards digital convergence in various aspects of their operations, including, not least, their increasing presence on the net. If we should be cautious about how much faith we should place in the internet's capacity to rejuvenate the public sphere (Dahlgren, 2000), we can at least be alert to the fact that it is at present involved in redefining the boundaries of the political. It is thereby contributing both to a problematizing of traditional politics and to openings towards new politics.

Other social realities

Important as they are, the media can never be the whole story here. Analysts also point to shifts in social structure and demographics as explanations of declining disengagement in conventional politics and the emergence of lifestyle politics; the young in particular are at the forefront of many of the trends. Others note the paucity of new political ideas, while some speak of the growing structural gaps between organized political life and people's everyday realities, and cite evidence of a sense of powerlessness among citizens as well as corruption among officials. Postmodern theorists emphasize how traditional structures of government and politics are out of step with contemporary cultural patterns and identity processes. All of these interventions have something to contribute to our understanding about political life today, even if the relative weight that should be attributed to the varying factors may be disputed (and largely linked to paradigmatic preferences). Further, several of these factors in turn relate to the impact of the increasing power wielded by private enterprise to shape the social terrain in the era of global capitalism.

In this regard, one particular line of analysis on political disengagement that I would emphasize calls attention to how economic factors can impact on political behaviour. Bennett (1998) has examined major studies of the American workforce and concludes that a good deal of the political lack of interest we observe today can be attributed to the profoundly stressful circumstances under which large segments of the population live. The major transformations to globalized, post-Fordist economies often wreak havoc on personal, family, social and civic life. While aggregate statistics suggest that 'the economy' has been doing better in recent years, other research points to a different social reality. This has to do with the harsh demands that working life, often coupled with extensive economic insecurities (the threat of unemployment, low wages and the rising costs of social services), place on families. Child-rearing, personal relationships, long-term planning, leisure time – these and other dimensions of private life come under severe strain. For the unemployed, of course, the situation is still more grim. Data on psychological and emotional disorders and the massive use of prescription (not to mention illegal) drugs paints a picture of deep distress within large segments of the population of the industrialized nations, a situation that borders on the psycho-socially pathological. This line of thought, about the pervasive psychic devastation of late modernity, tends all too often to be absent in contemporary social and cultural theory. (A useful introduction to such a critical psychology of modernity, linking mental suffering to contemporary social, economic and cultural patterns, can be found in Sloan, 1996.)

This argument does not claim to be a total explanation for anti-politics or for why political communication via the mass media is less likely to resonate with today's 'personalized polity'. It does, however, posit that material circumstances and consequent stresses must be understood as significant factors for the conditions of civic and political engagement. It also evokes a type of argument about the social welfare prerequisites for citizenship. Today, the economic and sociopsychological realities of large segments of the *employed* population, not just the unemployed, impede their participation as citizens. The economists Bluestone and Rose (quoted in Bennett, 1998) summarize the situation succinctly. They say that people 'will not find a better balance between work and leisure, between earning a living and spending time with loved ones, between being a wage earner and "civic engagement" until the economy provides long-term employment and rising wages'.

Despite the difficult circumstances in which many people find themselves, and despite growing distrust towards government and electoral politics in many countries of the world, the contemporary political malaise does not appear to have shaken people's commitment to democratic values. Large-scale transnational studies suggest that what is happening in the industrialized nations is that the value orientations prevalent among citizens increasingly tend to reject hierarchical authority, but not democracy. This tends to correlate strongly with socio-economic development, and is interpreted as an important cultural resource for the future of democracy (Inglehart, 1997 and 1999). Researchers see the emergence of 'critical citizens' (Norris, 1999), who are dissatisfied and disillusioned with their leaders and with conventional politics, but not with the basic premises of how a democratic society should function. Though there is considerable national variation from these aggregate results, this must be taken as encouraging. The tendency to reject hierarchical authority (assuming it has legitimacy) may, however, prove to be a problematic tendency for the functioning of democracies in complex societies.

Contemporary democracy finds itself at a period of transition, with a variety of forces – having to do with political economy, social structure, culture and, not least, the media – shaping the forms and degrees of citizen engagement. We can surmise that 'citizenship' is changing, and indeed remarks of this kind are often heard in discussions about democracy today. Let us probe further what the concept itself can point to.

Citizenship: formal status and social agency

What is citizenship? There are a number of ways to answer that question. At one level it is relatively simple. The concept traditionally builds upon a set of rights and obligations, historically evolved in society, and underscores universalism and equality. In the modern world it has usually been linked to the nation-state. In this sense, citizenship can be treated as a formal, legal framework that undergirds democracy. The post-war writing of T.H. Marshall (1950) in Britain provided a re-orientation in contemporary thinking about citizenship (Bulmer and Rees, 1996). In the context of welfare societies struggling with class inequalities, he underscored three by now familiar dimensions of citizenship, that have defined much of contemporary discussion: the *civil*, which aims to guarantee the basic legal integrity of society's members; *political*, which serves to ensure the rights associated with democratic participation; and *social*, which addresses the general life circumstances of individuals. In the case of social citizenship, Marshall's thought was that if people fall below certain levels of well-being they are unable to function in their role as citizens, a theme that takes on new relevance in the light of the decline of the welfare state. A number of commentators today, in the context of multicultural and multi-ethnic societies in a global context, argue that *cultural* citizenship must also be added to the list. This category would include, for example, the rights to have one's own traditions and language, as well as a series of rights that particularly link up with both the common good and minority needs in relation to the modern media (see also Murdock, 1999; Stevenson, 1999, Chapter 4).

These definitions function as important bedrock for democratic society. They specify citizenship as a formal status, providing a starting point for the debates over exactly which rights and obligations are to be included, and for the struggles to implement genuine universality and equality. One can say that the formal status of citizenship conceptually frames much of political life in modern democracies. How we define citizenship is inseparable from how we define democracy and the good society; it thus remains highly contested.

At another level, when we transpose these definitions to concrete social reality, the picture becomes more complex. The normative and the empirical do not always mesh very well, and citizenship can thus become an analytic tool for critical analysis. Indeed, citizenship has increasingly become an object of social theory and social analysis (see also Turner, 1993; van Steenbergen, 1994; Beiner,

1995; Janoski, 1998), not least from the standpoint of feminist horizons and the obstacles to women achieving equality and universalism (see also Voet, 1998; Dean, 1997). Much of this literature casts citizenship in terms of social agency, as particular sets of practices and the circumstances around them. Traditional social science research has already done this in some ways, emphasizing the importance of certain values and norms being internalized as a prerequisite for citizenship. More recent work has taken a somewhat different, though largely complementary, route. Based in cultural theory (e.g. Preston, 1997; Isin and Wood, 1999) as well as political philosophy (e.g. Clarke, 1996; Mouffe, 1993; Trend, 1996; Smith, 1998), these contributions have highlighted the dimension of identity as a key to understanding citizenship as a mode of social agency. In short, in order to be able to act as a citizen, it is necessary that one can see one-self as a citizen, as subjectively encompassing the attributes this social category may involve.

Just which attributes are relevant is a question that has become more and more complicated. In the emerging modern world, for example, citizenship was defined by its relevance for the public realm. However, the neat boundaries between public and private have become increasingly problematic (see e.g. Weintraub and Kumar, 1997). Today, citizenship still generally evokes the notion of a subjectivity positioned publicly – even if a 'public' context can be very small-scale. Yet, with the public and private having become intertwined, citizenship as an identity becomes interlaced with other dimensions of the self. However, if citizenship is a dimension of the self, this does not mean that people necessarily give the word 'citizen' a meaning that resonates with them; they may have other vocabularies. From the standpoint of research one has to be sensitive to people's own discursive strategies for making sense of and participating in democracy.

One of the hallmarks of late modern society is the emergence of the self as a reflexive project, an ongoing process of the shaping and reshaping of identity, in response to the pluralized sets of social forces, cultural currents and personal contexts encountered by individuals. Moreover, the identity is understood as plural: in our daily lives we operate in a multitude of different 'worlds' or realities; we carry within us different sets of knowledge, assumptions, rules and roles for different circumstances. Some of these elements reside more towards the core of our identity, others more in the periphery. Yet, all of us are, to varying degrees, composite people. The idea of composite identities also pertains to citizenship. Democracy's health is seen as linked to citizenship, understood as a significant element of the construction of our multiple selves; Gellner (1994) uses the metaphor 'modular man' (*sic*) to capture this idea. People's identities as citizens (however defined), with their sense of belonging to – and perceived possibilities for participating in – societal development becomes a crucial element in the life of democracy. To see citizenship as one dimension of identity may also help us to avoid letting our democratic ideals generate a predefined, one-size-fits-all portrait of citizenship that is sociologically and psychologically unrealistic. If democracy were to presuppose that the majority of the population be turned into a corps of adult scouts, the prospects would be bleak, indeed.

In practical terms, I see citizenship as central to the fundamental issues of social belonging and social participation. Identities of membership are not just subjectively produced by individuals, but evolve in relation to institutional mechanisms in society. Citizenship thus serves as an analytic entry into the study of the dynamics of social inclusion and exclusion. It invites us to consider democracies' ideals of universalism and equality and to confront the discrepancies between these ideals and prevailing social realities. In so doing, we have to look concretely at specific societal domains and identify the collectivities for which membership and participation are relevant in terms of democratic theory.

To which collectivities do we, or might we, want to belong? Citizenship has traditionally been associated with the nation-state (cf. Calhoun, 1997) but, increasingly, debates about citizenship refer to a variety of entities. The neighbourhood, the city, the associations and organizations of civil society, the region, even global society, are invoked. Within diasporic communities many people experience multiple loyalties, multiple identities and, increasingly, even insist on multiple citizenship. In Sweden, for example, children of second- and third-generation immigrants can see themselves as bicultural, as Greek-Swedes, Turk-Swedes, etc. Within some regions of the EU, new embryonic compound identities may be appearing. The growing integration of the greater Copenhagen area and southern Sweden is one example of this phenomenon. Yet distinctions are always made: what mechanisms of inclusion and exclusion operate in different domains? Here we see the need to relate the identity aspect of citizenship to structural ones: democratic membership and participation cannot function in the absence of institutional structures – legal, social, economic, cultural – that can solidify citizenship in the respective domains. For example, members of immigrant populations may be accorded some, or even full, formal citizenship rights, but cultural and economic mechanisms may operate to hinder the genuine development of an identity as a member of the new society. Alternatively, even if many people feel that they are 'citizens of the world', this does not in itself secure them democratic rights and procedures on a global scale. Merely positive identity processes cannot compensate for the weakness of institutional guarantees at this level.

To highlight citizenship in terms of identity can be seen as a type of 'cultural turn', which invites further extension and development. The next step is to situate citizenship identity in a scheme that relates it to other significant factors that shape the daily life of democracy. This leads us to the concept of civic culture.

Dimensions of civic culture

Civic culture is not a completely unproblematic concept. It contains both empirical and normative elements. It also has a past: since the ancient Greeks, reflection on the cultural preconditions of politics has been an integral part of political thought. After the Second World War, American political scientists began to try to draw lessons about democracy's cultural variables. Based in the political climate of the Cold War, and using large-scale survey techniques coupled with Parsonian views on social integration, they launched the notion of the civic culture as the foundation of a major cross-national research effort (Almond and Verba, 1963 and 1980). My points of departure are somewhat different; in using the concept, I wish to update it and would thus avoid what I take to be elements of psychological reductionism and ethnocentrism. Also, my view of culture is constructionist and materialist, rather than systemic.

We can schematically make a distinction between a formal democratic system, with its institutional structures, laws, parties, elections, etc., and a complex, multi-dimensional civic culture, anchored in everyday life and its horizons. Civic culture both reflects and makes possible this democratic system, while at the same time it is dependent upon the system for its institutional guarantees and parameters. My notion of civic culture can thus be seen as an important region of the habermasian life-world, with its negotiation of norms and values. As such, it is vulnerable to colonization from the system of politics and economics, yet can potentially also impact on the norms and values that guide those spheres. The political system (but to a lesser degree the economic system) and a civic culture are, in principle, mutually dependent: both evolve in relation to each other. A civic culture is thus both strong and vulnerable: it generates the normative and cultural resources required for a functioning democracy, yet it sits precariously in the face of political and economic power. It can be shaped by citizens, but can also shape them, since various 'technologies of citizenship', as Cruikshank (1999) calls them, such as government and education – and I would add the media (see also Dahlgren, 1997) – can serve to empower or disempower citizens via the civic culture. As Cruikshank underscores, citizens are 'subjects' in both senses of the word: potentially sovereign individuals as well as individuals under the authority or control of others.

We would be more correct to think in terms of civic cultures in the plural, given the patterns of diversity among citizens, though this would be linguistically awkward in the long run. A civic culture does not presuppose homogeneity among its citizens, but in the spirit of civic republicanism does suggest minimal shared commitments to the vision and procedures of democracy, and that entails a capacity to see beyond the immediate interests of one's own group. Needless to say, this may be a tricky balance to maintain at times. However, different social and cultural groups can express civic commonality in different ways, theoretically enhancing democracy's possibilities. Groups and their political positions are always to some extent in flux, and individuals can embody multiple group loyalties; the boundaries of 'we-ness' in heterogeneous modern democracies can shift. The tasks of making democracy work in societies characterized by pervasive social differentiation, not least along ethnic and cultural lines, is perplexing (Kymlicka, 1995; Spinner, 1994), but struggles for a pluralistic civic culture are an important way to frame the problems and strive for solutions.

The notion of civic culture thus points to those features of the socio-cultural world that constitute everyday preconditions for all democratic participation: in the institutions of civil society; engagement in the public sphere; and involvement in political activity, broadly understood. These preconditions involve cultural attributes prevalent among citizens that can in various ways facilitate democratic life (including the processes whereby the definitions of democratic life are defined and translated into politics). As a concept, then, the civic culture is not new, and even my reformulation carries over traditional elements from political science/political communication. It is the connection with cultural theory that in my view enhances its utility, connecting perspectives from constructionism and sense-making with the framework from traditional social science. We can distinguish between four dimensions – empirical elements – of civic culture. Each of these can in turn serve as starting points for interrogating the media.

Relevant knowledge and competencies

This is obvious, this is basic. People must have access to reliable reports, portrayals, analyses, discussions, debates and so forth about current affairs. Here the media's role is central, yet also problematic. Accessibility has to do not just with technical and economic aspects, but also with linguistic and cultural proximity. The sources of knowledge and the materials for the development of competencies must be comprehensible, cast in modes that communicate well with different collectivities. This of course reiterates the need for multiple public spheres – or a highly heterogeneous overarching one – characterized by sufficient autonomy and diversity to address and incorporate different groups. Some degree of literacy is essential; people must be able to make sense of that which circulates in the public sphere, and to understand the world in which they live. They also have to have the ability to express their own ideas if they are to partake in the public sphere's processes of opinion-formation and/or engage in other political activities; communicative competencies are indispensable for a democratic citizenry. Education, in its many forms, will thus always retain its relevance for democracy, even if its contents and goals often need to be critically examined. Sociological realism tells us that it is unlikely that the necessary levels of knowledge and competence for all members of society can be attained; also, citizens certainly must have the right to not be engaged. However, the principle of universalism underscores that any systematic mechanisms of exclusion in this regard are antithetical to democracy and must thus be challenged. Precisely what kinds of knowledge and competencies are required for the vitality of a civic culture can never be established once and for all, but must always be open for discussion.

Loyalty to democratic values and procedures

Democracy will not function if such virtues as tolerance and willingness to follow democratic principles and procedures do not have a grounding in everyday life. Even support for the legal system (assuming it is legitimate) is an expression of such virtue: democracy will not survive a situation of profound lawlessness. Just what are the best or real democratic values, and how they are to be applied, can of course be the grounds for serious dispute – and it is precisely in such situations that the procedural mechanisms take on extra importance. The resolution of conflict, striving for compromise in situations where consensus is impossible, is a key task for a democratic society and requires a commitment to the rules of the game. The media largely tend to reinforce the commitment to democratic values (even by invoking them in sensationalist scandals), and in particular it can be argued that support for the democratic rights of individuals is something that is spreading globally via media representations. Schudson (1998) in his historical survey of citizenship in the United States argues that, in particular, the cementation of the values of individual offers grounds for a qualified optimism regarding democracy's future.

Practices, routines, traditions

Democracy must be embodied in concrete, recurring practices – individual, group and collective – relevant for diverse situations. Such practices help generate personal and social meaning to the ideals of democracy, and they must have an element of the routine, of the taken-for-granted about them, if they are to be a part of a civic culture. Elections can be seen as a form of practice in this regard, but a civic culture requires many other practices, pertinent to many other circumstances in everyday life, to civil and political society. For example, how to hold a meeting, manage discussion, even how to argue, can be seen as important features of the life-world that have a bearing on civic culture. The interaction among citizens is a cornerstone of the public sphere, and the kinds of established rules and etiquette that shape such interaction either promote the practices of public discussion or contribute to their evaporation. (See Eliasoph, 1998, for a detailed ethnographic study of inhibiting discursive practices in American civic culture.) Across time, practices become traditions, and experience becomes collective memory; today's democracy needs to be able to refer to a past, without being locked in it. New practices and traditions can and must evolve to ensure that democracy does not stagnate. Again, we can see how the lack of practices and traditions is an obstacle in many societies attempting to develop their democratic character. The media obviously contribute here by their representations of ongoing political life, including its rituals and symbols, yet increasingly also take on relevance as more people make use of the newer interactive possibilities and incorporate these as part of their civic culture practices.

Identities as citizens

Here we return to the theme of people's subjective view of themselves as members and participants of democracy. These four dimensions should be seen as a circuit of mutually reinforcing factors, not a list of separate items. For people to see themselves as citizens, and for a civic culture to flourish, involves thus the mutual interdependence of knowledge and competencies, loyalty to democratic values and procedures, as well as established practices and traditions. While a civic culture rests upon citizens' ways of doing and thinking in everyday life, the media can foster or hinder this circuit.

Media linkages

The political trends in modern democracy articulate in complex ways with the evolution of the media. The dimensions of civic culture offer ways to organize analyses of how the media, via their modes of representation as well as the newer forms of interactivity that they offer, are contributing to the decline of traditional political life and the emergence of newer forms of involvement. We have a theoretically and empirically larger analytic toolkit to work with. This does not promise that we will get any easier answers, but it can help us to formulate questions and stake out research directions. I cannot in detail pursue the many possibilities here, but I can suggest some lines of enquiry. If we begin with the first dimension, of knowledge and competencies, we quickly encounter a number of questions at the centre of concerns about the media today.

That democracy needs an informed citizenry and the media are the chief vehicles for achieving is an established platitude, though none the less relevant because of its conventionality. The low degree of political knowledge has been a source of lament since the very start of such research in the early decades of this century. Today, however, the problem is seemingly compounded by the patterns of media use, especially among young people, further calling into question the level of knowledge among citizens (see Buckingham, 1997, for an excellent review of the issues and debates around this theme; see also Graber, 2000). Younger citizens are drifting away from the daily newspaper and more towards television, away from journalism and more towards entertainment. Also, there seems to be an increase in 'surfing' patterns: younger people are less prone to manifest a loyalty to specific journalistic outlets and instead use a variety of outlets, with sporadic patterns.

Discussions of these trends have tried to avoid gloom by mobilizing the arguments about lifestyle politics and, not least, new paths towards political knowledge. This argument underscores the idea that people are attending more to popular issues to do with individuals' micro-worlds. In keeping with lifestyle politics, they are simply orienting themselves with different kinds of knowledge. Yet, as Buckingham (1997) notes, there is no reason why a focus on micro-concerns should necessarily exclude awareness of macro ones. Political power is still operating on that level as well, and ignoring this won't serve democracy. The ambivalence of lifestyle politics remains.

Another line of argument puts weight on the newer modes of representation. They are faster, more visually oriented, less dependent on print culture. However, Buckingham (1997) also points to data that show a strong correlation between newspaper reading and political knowledge; those who use only television as a source of news clearly fare less well in this regard. There is just no way that we can dismiss the need for accurate information about the world. Information is necessary, though not sufficient. It must be made meaningful and must be related to previous understandings in order to become knowledge. (Information in the media is not always accurate or relevant, or may carry ideological dimensions, but that is another matter.) Cultural studies' emphasis on how people subjectively relate to media portrayals is thus very important, but so is the question of what they actually learn, in cognitive terms, about the world. Knowledge is still closely associated with power, not least in civic contexts, and for knowledge we need both information and meaning. The complementary character of these perspectives is an important item on the research agenda.

Yet, the issue of precisely what kinds of knowledge and competencies are relevant for civic culture remains, and this needs to be investigated further. The assumption that it is fundamentally the informational, journalistic output about current affairs in the media that is of relevance for civic culture is probably still largely true, but increasingly less so. Given the growing hybridization of media genres, the question of what media output is of relevance for civic culture takes on considerable significance. Within the ubiquitous media culture, the distinction between 'popular culture' and consumption on the one hand and 'public knowledge' and politics on the other is not always obvious (see, for instance, Dahlgren and Sparks, 1992). Also, it is becoming more difficult to discount the political significance of much fiction and other entertainment in the media (Street, 1997).

Turning to the dimension of loyalty to democratic values and procedures, conventional wisdom suggests that these qualities are largely determined by the home and other institutions of 'primary socialization' in the 'private sphere', and by the educational system; people then approach the mediated public sphere as 'fully formed' citizens. This relates strongly to liberalism's view of the free-floating, choice-making individual, socially and culturally disembedded and unencumbered. (It also implies a very rationalist mode of attention towards the media.) Such views are sociologically quite shaky, as we observe precisely how the media increasingly contribute to the formation of identity and subjectivity, from early childhood onwards (see also Grodin and Lindlof, 1996). The media milieu is deeply implicated in the formation of citizens' values. This is by no means a one-way, causal relationship, as the past two decades of research on reception and sense-making in relation to the media remind us. The point is, however, that people attend to the media and to civic culture with frames of reference and discursive competencies to a great extent pre-structured by the media. (That the hours young people in some western countries spend in front of television have begun to bypass the number of hours they spend in the classroom takes on added significance in this context.) The increasingly referential symbolic media universe has become a significant agency of socialization in the modern world, and social experience becomes increasingly interwoven with media experience, or at least interpreted in terms made available by media discourses.

The dimension of practices and routines opens up another field of enquiry. If the boundaries of the political are less clear today, so too are the definitions of the practices and traditions of political relevance. Especially in relation to the media, many questions arise. The research tradition on media uses perhaps, at times, tended to predefine the answer to this question. Today it would seem to be an important task to develop fresh perspectives on how various kinds of media uses – including the mass media and the newer interactive media – relate to the development of civic culture. Are new traditions emerging? Is it the case that the realm of civic-relevant practices is shrinking, or are we faced with the challenge of fundamentally redefining the boundaries of political relevance?

From the horizons of daily life, evidence suggests that journalism is not experienced as neatly demarcated from the rest of the media's output. Barnhurst (1998), for example, finds that among young citizens, the processes of identity formation involve an extensive bricolage approach to the media, blending the serious and the popular, to form citizens' identities that are rooted in the personal and the local. For these young people, civic engagement with the media involves both an instrumental orientation and pleasure, and an ongoing shifting of subject positions. In other words, the practices of civic culture may well be fundamentally evolving, in keeping with the changes in the media landscape.

Finally, returning to the dimension of identities as citizens, two themes have become prominent here, both of which I have already alluded to: nationalism/globalization and consumerism. Historically, modern democracy evolved with the formation of the nation-state, and the concept of 'citizen' was anchored firmly in this entity. Thus, even today, for the vast majority of people in western society, the primary locus of their membership and participation as citizens is the nation-state. Despite the march of globalization, the power of nationalism in the modern world scarcely needs reiteration. Visions of using the media to foster, for example, 'pan-European' identities have had to face the sobering realities of national loyalties (cf. Richardson and Meinhof, 1999). However, there are signs that a European identity is gaining ground in some of the EU countries, and even if a civic culture on this scale is still far in the future, this is an important element to watch.

The notions of global citizenship and transnational civic culture are undeniably attractive, yet have be met with realism. Discussions about globalization often invoke the idea of the diminishing role of the nation-state. This is, of course, valid, but it becomes all too easy to exaggerate this point. The nation-state is being reconfigured, but is not about to leave the historical scene and nor are politics centred on the nation-state by any means obsolete. Globalization, not least of the political economy, obviously warrants attention and critical intervention, but political engagement in transnational matters must operate within less solidified institutional structures, an important factor in identity formation. Even the EU, while a highly developed construction, is still in the process of evolving its democratic mechanisms, which – in comparison with national structures – still have a long way to go. Yet, the globalization of civic culture has begun. People in NGOs, social movements, political groups, diasporic and postcolonial networks, activist alliances and so on are increasingly operating across national borders, to a large extent with the aid of newer media. New identities of citizenship are taking shape. Research needs to follow these developments.

Consumerism raises a different set of questions. In the media, political, social and consumerist discourses become more and more intertextual (Slater, 1997; Miles, 1998). With the boundaries between journalism and mediated popular culture becoming increasingly porous, and people often disregarding the traditional borders between the socially serious and the playful in their identity work as citizens, we inevitably confront the relationship between civic and consumer culture. Many of the reflexive identity processes of late modernity go via consumption. The circulation of goods, the material and symbolic meanings of commodities, and the dominant position of advertising in all of its many variants in the media seemingly make civic culture very diminutive by comparison. This becomes obvious if we simply reflect on the extent to which the media address us as consumers compared with how much they address us as citizens. It is undeniable that consumerist discourses have a strong position in the current global political order, where market forces have such a large degree of freedom in shaping the social landscape as well as the contours of conventional politics. Civic culture is something that will increasingly have to be defined and constructed both in relation to and against consumer society.

While the consumer is structurally integrated into the market and the citizen belongs to a collectivity characterized by the principles of universalism and equality, they cannot be seen as radically distinct in all cases. Consumption can quickly take on political attributes; lifestyle politics often hover around issues of consumption. Citizens need to consume, and consumer identities can readily shift into citizenship; they become intertwined in certain contexts. Postmodern notions of the 'consumer citizen' may suggest that lifestyle politics centres around issues of consumption rather than production. This is true to an extent, but its total realization is dependent on the absence of deprivation, which is hardly a probable condition for any society today. We should note that the citizen–consumer interface is far from stable, and can change with the vicissitudes of material circumstances. The material constraints on consumption mean that it is not safely beyond the reach of the old-style politics of distribution; not everyone in western society is, or will be, an affluent, postmodern subject, a 'consumer citizen'. Indeed, this label may begin to signify something quite different, something critical, if citizens develop a democratic concern with the social realities of inequality associated with consumption.

I noted above that democracy's evolution cannot be understood in exclusively media-centric terms, that we have also to situate it against the backdrop of larger material, social and cultural conditions. From this vantage point, we see a variety of forces challenging the boundaries between the political and the non-political. Civic culture can be viewed as encompassing a force-field, where conventional political thinking tries to contain and demarcate the boundaries of the political, while newer trends serve to disperse the older partitions. It is not a question of a full collapse of difference, but rather a blurring at the edges, but it has by now become sufficiently problematic from the standpoint of conventional politics (van Zoonen, 1998). We have not arrived at a situation where everything is political; rather, it is the case that more and more features of social and cultural reality have become *potentially* political.

The media are inexorably entwined with the declining engagement in conventional politics, as well as with the emergence of newer, lifestyle politics. While empirical and normative ambivalence about these developments remains, we can choose to underscore the encouraging fact that individuals and groups are finding new ways of doing – and imagining – democracy.

References

ALMOND, GABRIEL and SIDNEY VERBA (1963) *The Civic Culture*. Princeton: Princeton University Press.

ALMOND, GABRIEL and SIDNEY VERBA, eds (1980) *The Civic Culture Revisited*. Princeton: Princeton University Press.

BECK, ULRICH (1998) *Democracy Without Enemies*. London: Sage.

BEINER, RONALD, ed. (1995) *Theorizing Citizenship*. Albany: State University of New York Press.

BENNETT, LANCE (1998) 'The uncivic culture: communication, identity, and the rise of lifestyle politics', *Political Science and Politics*, Vol. 31, No. 4, December, 741–61 (also available at: www.apsanet.org/PS/dec98/).

BENNETT, LANCE and ROBERT ENTMAN, eds (2000) *Mediated Politics: Communication in the Future of Democracy*. Cambridge: Cambridge University Press.

BLUMLER, JAY and GUREVITCH, MICHAEL (1995) *The Crisis of Public Communication*. London: Routledge.

BUCKINGHAM, DAVID (1997) 'News media, political socialization and popular citizenship: toward a new agenda', *Critical Studies in Mass Communication* 14(4) 344–66.

BULMER, MARTIN and ANTHONY M. REES, eds (1996) *Citizenship Today: The Contemporary Relevance of T.H. Marshall*. London: University College London Press.

CALABRESE, ANDREW and JEAN-CLAUDE BURGELMAN, eds (1999) *Communication, Citizenship and Social Policy: Rethinking the Limits of the Welfare State*. Lanham, MD: Rowman and Littlefield.

CALHOUN, CRAIG (1997) 'Nationalism and the public sphere' in Weintraub, Jeff and Krishan Kumar, eds, *Public and Private in Thought and Practice: Perspectives on a Grand Dichotomy*. Chicago: University of Chicago Press.

CASTELLS, MANUEL (1997) *The Power of Identity (The Information Sage: Economy, Society and Culture)* Vol. II. London: Blackwell.

CLARKE, PAUL BARRY (1996) *Deep Citizenship*. London: Pluto.
CRUIKSHANK, BARBARA (1999) *The Will to Empower: Democratic Citizens and Other Subjects*. Ithaca, NY: Cornell University Press.
DAHL, ROBERT (1998) *On Democracy*. New Haven: Yale University Press.
DAHLGREN, PETER (1995) *Television and the Public Sphere*. London: Sage.
——, (1997) 'Enhancing the civic ideal in TV journalism' in Kees Brants *et al.*, eds, *The Media in Question*. London: Sage.
——, (2000) 'Communication and democracy in late modernity' in *New Media and Politics*, Barry Axford and R. Huggins, eds, London: Sage.
DAHLGREN, PETER and COLIN SPARKS, eds (1992) *Journalism and Popular Culture*. London: Sage.
DEAN, JODI, ed. (1997) *Feminism and the New Democracy*. London: Sage.
ELIASOPH, NINA (1998) *Avoiding Politics: How Americans Produce Apathy in Everyday Life*. Cambridge: University of Cambridge Press.
FALLOWS, JAMES (1997) *Breaking the News*. New York: Vintage Books.
FORNÄS, JOHAN (1995) *Cultural Theory and Late Modernity*. London: Sage.
FRANKLIN, BOB (1997) *Newzak and News Media*. London: Edward Arnold.
FULLINWIDER, ROBERT K., ed. (1998) *Civil Society, Democracy, and Civic Renewal*. Lanham: Rowman and Littlefield.
GANDY, OSCAR (2000) 'Dividing practices: segmentation and targeting in the emerging public sphere' in Bennett, Lance and Robert Entman, eds, *Mediated Politics: Communication in the Future of Democracy*. Cambridge: Cambridge University Press.
GELLNER, ERNEST (1994) *The Conditions of Liberty*. London: Allen Lane/The Penguin Press.
GIBBINS, JOHN and BO REIMER (1999) *The Politics of Postmodernity*. London: Sage.
GIDDENS, ANTHONY (1991) *Modernity and Self-identity*. Cambridge: Polity Press.
GRABER, DORIS (2000) 'Adapting political news to the needs of twenty-first century Americans' in Bennett, Lance and Robert Entman, eds, *Mediated Politics: Communication in the Future of Democracy*. Cambridge: Cambridge University Press.
GRODIN, DEBRA and THOMAS R. LINDLOF, eds (1996) *Constructing the Self in a Mediated World*. London: Sage.
HAGUE, BARRY N. and BRIAN D. LOADER, eds (1999) *Digital Democracy*. London: Routledge.
HERMAN, EDWARD and ROBERT MCCHESNEY (1997) *The Global Media*. London: Cassell.
HILL, KEVIN A. and JOHN E. HUGHES (1998) *Cyberpolitics: Citizen Activism in the Age of the Internet*. Lanham, MD: Rowman and Littlefield.
HOLMBERG, SÖREN (1999) 'Down and down we go: political trust in Sweden' in Norris, Pippa, ed. *Critical Citizens: Global Support for Democratic Governance*. Oxford: Oxford University Press.
HOLMES, DAVID, ed. (1997) *Virtual Politics: Identity and Community in Cyberspace*. London: Sage.
INGLEHART, RONALD (1997) *Modernization and Postmodernization: Cultural, Economic and Political Change in 43 Societies*. Princeton: Princeton University Press.
——, (1999) 'Postmodernization erodes respect for authority, but increases support for democracy' in Norris, Pippa, *Critical Citizens: Global Support for Democratic Governance*. Oxford: Oxford University Press.
INSTITUTE FOR THE STUDY OF CIVIC VALUES, http://www.libertynet.org/edcivic/iscvhome.html.
ISIN, ENGIN F. and PATRICIA K. WOOD (1999) *Citizenship and Identity*. London: Sage.
JANOSKI, THOMAS (1998) *Citizenship and Civil Society*. Cambridge: Cambridge University Press.
JONES, STEVEN G., ed. (1998) *Cybersociety 2.0*. London: Sage.
JORDAN, TIM (1999) *Cyberpower*. London: Routledge.
KITCHIN, ROB (1998) *Cyberspace: The World in the Wires*. Chichester: Wiley and Sons.
KYMLICKA, WILL (1995) *Multicultural Citizenship*. Oxford: Oxford University Press.

328 *Peter Dahlgren*

LIVINGSTONE, SONIA and PETER LUNT (1994) *Talk on Television*. London: Routledge.
LOADER, BRIAN D., ed. (1998) *Cyberspace Divide*. London: Routledge.
LULL, JAMES and STEPHEN HINERMAN, eds (1997) *Media Scandals*. Cambridge: Polity Press.
MARSHALL, T.H. (1950) *Citizenship and Social Class*. Cambridge: Cambridge University Press.
MELUCCI, ALBERTO (1996) *Challenging Codes: Collective Action in the Information Age*. Cambridge: Cambridge University Press.
MILES, STEVEN (1998) *Consumerism – as a Way of Life*. London: Sage.
MOUFFE, CHANTAL (1993) *The Return of the Political*. London: Verso.
MULGAN, GEOFF (1994) *Politics in an Antipolitical Age*. Cambridge: Polity Press.
MURDOCK, GRAHAM (1999) 'Rights and representations: public discourse and cultural citizenship' in Jostein Gripsrud, ed., *Television and Common Knowledge*. London: Routledge.
NORRIS, PIPPA (1999) *Critical Citizens: Global Support for Democratic Governance*. Oxford: Oxford University Press.
PETERSSON, OLOF, *et al.* (1998) *Demoktrati och medborgarskap*. Stockholm: SNS.
PRESTON. P.W. (1997) *Political/Cultural Identity*. London: Sage.
PUTNAM, ROBERT D. (1993) *Making Democracy Work: Civic Traditions in Modern Italy*. Princeton: Princeton University Press.
——, (1996) 'The Strange Disappearance of Civic America', *The American Prospect*, No. 24, winter.
RICHARDSON, KAY and ULRIKE H. MEINHOF (1999) *Worlds in Common? Television Discourse in a Changing Europe*. London: Routledge.
RIMMERMAN, CRAIG A. (1997) *The New Citizenship: Unconventional Activism, and Service*. Boulder, CO: Westview Press.
SANDEL, MICHAEL J. (1996) *Democracy's Discontent*. Cambridge, MA and London: The Belknap Press of Harvard University Press.
SCHUDSON, MICHAEL (1998) *The Good Citizen*. New York: Free Press.
SLATER, DON (1997) *Consumer Culture and Modernity*. Cambridge: Polity Press.
SLOAN, TOD (1996) *Damaged Life: The Crisis of the Modern Psyche*. London: Routledge.
SMITH, ANNA MARIE (1998) *Laclau and Mouffe*. London: Routledge.
SMITH, MARC A. and PETER KOLLOCK, eds (1999) *Communities in Cyberspace*. London: Routledge.
SPINNER, JEFF (1994) *The Boundaries of Citizenship*. Baltimore: Johns Hopkins University Press.
STEVENSON, NICK (1999) *The Transformation of the Media: Globalisation, Morality and Ethics*. London: Longman.
STREET, JOHN (1997) *Politics and Popular Culture*. Cambridge: Polity Press.
TREND, DAVID, ed. (1996) *Radical Democracy: Identity, Citizenship and the State*. London: Routledge.
TURNER, BRYAN, ed. (1993) *Citizenship and Social Theory*. London: Sage.
VAN STEENBERGEN, BART, ed. (1994) *The Condition of Citizenship*. London: Sage.
VAN ZOONEN, LIESBET (1998) 'A day at the zoo: political communication, pigs and popular culture', *Media, Culture and Society*, 20(2) April, 183–200.
VOET, RIAN (1998) *Feminism and Citizenship*. London: Sage.
WEINTRAUB, JEFF and KRISHAN KUMAR, eds (1997) *Public and Private in Thought and Practice: Perspectives on a Grand Dichotomy*. Chicago: University of Chicago Press.

16

Globalization and Cultural Identities

Keith Negus and Patria Román-Velázquez

Like many of the keywords used in the human and social sciences, globalization is a concept that has been discussed in different ways and continues to be the subject of considerable debate and disagreement. For some commentators, often enthusiastic advocates of greater international business and trade, the word globalization is descriptive of real changes occurring in the world, visible and audible on the streets of major metropolises and small villages, as ever more people, images and things seem to be moving across borders, creating new 'markets', breaking down barriers, and disrupting previous routines and a settled sense of the distance between different peoples and places. For other writers it is an idea that should be approached more cautiously and critically. In direct opposition to the view of its advocates, it is rejected as an ideological myth that conceals the continuing dominance of international capital and the endurance of unequal or imperial relations between states. Still critical, but less dismissive of the term, other writers use globalization to refer to processes and practices that are clearly crossing geographical borders, and to indicate a growing interconnectedness across the planet. However, such occurrences are judged to be far less 'global' than suggested by the 'one world' connotations that the idea carries with it.[1] In this chapter we will be aligning ourselves, more broadly, with the critical camp, suggesting that debates about globalization are centrally concerned with changing time–space relations and their consequences for how people understand themselves and their relationship to specific collectivities and territories.[2]

If globalization is a contested concept, so too is identity. Over recent years many questions have been raised about the permanence of any characteristic qualities attributed to and maintained by individuals, groups of people and places. As individual subjects, do we have a core personality or 'nature' that remains unchanged over time or do we acquire, or make up and adopt, new characteristics throughout our lives? As people are labelled and socially categorized, do terms such as man, woman, English, Asian, lesbian, African and working class capture the qualities and shared experiences that bind people to a common identity? Or, are these merely arbitrarily imposed labels based on the most superficial of indices (physical features, place of birth or social position), in turn obscuring a diversity of activities and values? When we refer to the identity of locations, whether a Scottish town, Jewish settlement or Latin barrio, do we point to some essential enduring qualities? Or are the identities of countries, cities, towns and neighbourhoods filtered through socially encoded meanings that are historically contingent, and continually open to change and transformation?

Central to these questions about individuals, groups and places have been discussions of the nation and nation-state. As Benedict Anderson (1983) once suggested, the nation depends for its existence upon a sense of social-psychological affiliation to an 'imagined community'. Anderson argued that the modern idea of the nation was facilitated by the emergence of the mechanical printing press and a form of print capitalism. This enabled a sense of collectivity, through standardized patterns of literacy mediated via the printed word, formed amongst people who would never be able to meet all the other members of their particular national grouping. Drawing on similar ideas about how media technologies and their modes of production, dissemination and reception shape our sense of belonging, a number of writers have suggested that the modern communication media, increasingly reaching us via satellites and the internet, are eroding such a sense of national identity. In the process, the media are challenging the ability of the nation-state to regulate its borders, and contributing to new transnational forms of attachment to a more 'global' community and 'cosmopolitan' polity.[3] Hence, debates about globalization have become intricately bound up with discussions about identities and culture.

There are two specific ways in which the dynamics of globalization are judged to be impacting upon our cultural lives. First, there is the common observation that commodified cultural forms, such as television programmes, films, sound recordings, magazines, news and documentaries, are moving ever more rapidly across the world or are being simultaneously transmitted or manufactured in a range of locations. This, it is argued, is creating lifestyles, experiences, events, fashions and daily practices that are shared by numerous people outside of their immediate vicinities. Second, and related, is a repeatedly stated anxiety about the consequences of this for the cultural practices and ways of life of different groups of people across the world. For a number of years, there has been concern that variously labelled 'traditional', 'folk' or 'indigenous' cultural practices are declining or being forced out of existence. Many of the debates about these two points feed into and draw from discussions about the power and influence of large media corporations, and connect with debates about patterns of media or cultural imperialism (hence, our argument in this chapter should connect with the other discussions of these issues that appear elsewhere in this volume).

In the following pages we intend to dwell in more detail on some of the issues that we have alluded to briefly in this introduction and to focus on some of the key dimensions through which processes referred to as globalization are judged to have an impact on cultural identities. We will stress globalization as involving changing time–space processes, and will highlight the significance of nation-state regulations, the commodification of culture and practices occurring within particular localities. These are by no means the only ways of focusing on globalization and cultural identities, but these themes provide an insight into some of the significant power relations through which a sense of identity can be realized. One of the points we will emphasize is that 'identities' cannot simply be interpreted, assumed or 'read' from the most obvious visual images or audible codes: television forms, dramatic genres, new musical styles that draw from a variety of sources, clothing that combines 'eastern' and 'western' forms of dress or displaced mixed cuisine. Such obvious manifestations do not in any straight-forward way indicate a change of identity, nor a movement towards 'hybrid' or 'cosmopolitan' identities. Our point is that cultural identities are established by people in relation to quite specific times and places; powerful social forces enable or allow certain practices and not others. Hence, to understand the conse-quences of globalization for cultural identity we need to do more than interpret the signs on the streets or codes being beamed into homes. We need to ask ques-tions about the presence and absence of people and things, and the practices that enable or constrain the endurance or transformation of identities.

Time–space processes and the link between territory and identity

The importance of the concepts of time–space and place, and their significance for the ordering of social life and understanding of cultural identities, has been recognized since the latter part of the nineteenth century. This has been the case in a number of disciplines and discourses, from art and literature to the physi-cal sciences. More recently, discussions of time–space processes have been an integral part of the elaboration and critique of theories of globalization.

Many of the key cultural forms and social practices that contribute to a sense of identity are profoundly territorial: we locate ourselves with reference to a nation, region, city, neighbourhood; we use concepts of class, race or ethnicity that imply certain correspondences between the members of groups and locali-ties or points of origin. Even such apparently universal categories as man and woman have been recognized as socially and culturally specific, and the codes and conventions of being masculine or feminine are bound up with behaviours formed in specific social and cultural settings.[4]

For a number of writers the dynamics of modernity and the processes of modernization (the two not necessarily coinciding) have led to the disruption and dislocation, but also to the reaffirmation, of such place-based identities. Nestor García Canclini (1990) has evoked a sense of this through the terms 'deterritorialization' and 'reterritorialization'. The former refers to 'the loss of any "natural" relationship between culture and geographical and social territo-ries'. This has been accompanied by a process of reterritorialization which involves the relocalization 'of old and new symbolic productions' (García Canclini, 1990: 288). Similar concepts have been employed by Anthony Giddens (1990) who has used the terms 'disembedding' and 're-embedding', linking these to the notion of 'time–space distanciation' and his argument, again similar to García Canclini's, that globalization is a 'consequence' of modernity – that is, an effect of the spread of those modern/modernizing institutions that were initially identifiable with 'the West', such as capitalism, industrialism, class relations and the nation-state (see Giddens, 1990).

Similar ideas can be found in writings that use the distinction between the global and the local, and point to the stretching and collapsing of social rela-tionships across time–space so that 'local happenings are shaped by events occurring many miles away and vice versa' (Giddens, 1990: 64). In practical terms, this means that the job of a worker in a manufacturing plant in northern Europe can be affected by pricing decisions, management changes or industrial disputes occurring in related businesses in South Africa, Central America or South East Asia. In terms of our sense of self, it highlights how we are increasingly drawn into, or actively develop, social relationships with distant others. This may be as superficial as fleetingly recognizing others through a shared lifestyle or habit of consumption, or it could entail an engagement in new forms of political identity, with solidarity based on shared concern about the environment, animal welfare or human rights abuses (rather than a politics based on a shared sense of belonging to a grounded ethnic group, nation, class or continent). The general idea here is that certain cultural practices have become deterritorialized or disembedded, lifted out of their association with a specific geographical place.

At the same time, reterritorialization or re-embedding involves the reaffirmation of the relationship between places and identities. This could involve renewed claims for the authenticity of artefacts or customs faced with perceived threats from globalization and under the rubric of national cultural heritage or ethnic exclusivity. It could also refer to how people who move and are 'displaced' simultaneously seek a sense of permanence in their new location. García Canclini (1990) notes how immigrants in new locations establish their permanence by distinguishing themselves from tourists and short-term visitors. Cultural forms and practices also move and are deterritorialized (for instance, rock, jazz or the blues are on the move and no longer synonymous with a particular region in the United States alone). Cultural practices are reterritorialized through such labels as 'Brazilian death metal' or national-ethnic categories such as 'African-American'. The key point here is that identities are continually understood in relation to places; people and things are continually being tied down and are not simply detached and free-floating postmodern signifiers without a referent.

Doreen Massey (1994) is just one writer who has contributed further to this discussion by arguing that quite clear power relations are involved in the tying of identities to places and their transcendence or detachment. In Massey's terms, we need to be aware of the 'power geometry', a phrase she introduced when critiquing those theorists (notably Giddens and Harvey) who explain changes according to the generalized dynamics of modernity or capitalism. Massey argues for a 'power-geometry' through which we can understand, in a more specific way, how people are placed and assume a position in relation to the politics of mobility, access, international migration, transportation, ethnicity and gender:

> [D]ifferent social groups and different individuals are placed in very distinct ways in relation to these flows and interconnections. This point concerns not merely the issue of who moves and who doesn't, although that is an important element of it; it is also about power in relation *to* the flows and the movement. Different social groups have distinct relationships to this anyway-differentiated mobility: some are more in charge of it than others; some initiate flows and movements, others don't; some are more on the receiving end of it than others; some are effectively imprisoned by it.
>
> (Massey, 1993: 61)

Massey's critique, highlighting the specific lived experiences and particular relationships that lurk within claims about globalization and time–space stretching and collapsing, is supported by other writers who stress the specific conditions within which prejudice, social divisions and affirmative identities based around race, ethnicity, class and gender are negotiated.[5] Hence a number of writers point to a similar set of issues, even if they conceive of them in slightly different ways, and emphasize a range of aspects in their arguments: globalization points to changing time–space processes and these are crucially connected to a sense of place, simultaneously producing contrasting dynamics; schematically thought of as involving social practices and cultural identities that are both deterritorialized/disembedded/dislocated and reterritorialized/re-embedded/relocated. In this chapter we follow Massey, in stressing that these dynamics are occurring within quite specific circumstances and relations of power.

The nation-state and the regulation of mobility and citizenship

The nation-state has been described as a 'bordered power container' (Giddens, 1985). For a number of writers one of the key questions at the hub of debates about globalization and cultural identities concerns the ability of the state to maintain control of its borders in the face of the movements of capital and culture. Both academic articles and popular journalism regularly present us with a world of people, images, things, words and sounds 'flowing' across the now permeable and breaking borders of this container; disrupting ways of life and transforming cultural conventions within, whilst spreading a range of influences outwards from particular states. At the same time, the globalization of capital and increasing use of electronic commerce is perceived (whether welcomed or feared) as an ineluctable force that is making it impossible for nations to manage their own economies. This in turn becomes an excuse for embracing neo-liberal principles according to which the public become markets, goods and services are allocated according to 'free' trade and citizenship is realized through consumer 'choice'.

Whilst this view of the-way-things-are is grounded in particular perceptions of reality and specific social experiences, it can be challenged in a number of ways. The economic argument rests on the assumption that national economies are breaking down, in a dramatically new way, due to outside influences, the imperatives of external trade and international commercial pressures. Whilst new patterns of international economic relations are certainly evident (see Held *et al.*, 1999), it should be remembered that national economies were formed in relation to international patterns of commerce and trade in the first place. The nation – as a political, economic and cultural institution – was crucially shaped during the 'Age of Empire' (Hobsbawm, 1989) when the economies of nations such as France, Holland, Britain, Belgium, Japan, Spain and the United States were produced and reproduced in direct relation to the subordination, annexation and/or material exploitation of colonies and other parts of the world. Space does not permit an extended discussion of this issue here,[6] but in terms of our focus on questions of identity the point we wish to stress is that the social-psychological and institutional sense of the nation was formed, not in isolation but in relation to other nation-states and in contradistinction to 'other' parts of the world that were different from the nation. The idea of the English nation, for example, was not only produced in relation to (and in contrast from) that of the Scottish, Irish, Welsh and French, but also in relation to those parts of the world that constituted 'the Empire'. The identity of the nation was formed as an economic and cultural entity in relation to other parts of the world (that is, in a 'global' context).[7]

A further, more concrete, issue here concerns the fact that, over the past 40 years (the epoch of apparently increasing global mobility), states have been tightening (rather than relaxing) their laws regulating the movement of people across borders. This poses a challenge for globalization theories which assume that culture 'flows' – as if people, images and things can just move across the world without any constraints or regulations influencing how such movements might occur. For example, certain types of food, books, electronic devices, clothes, cigarettes and liquors still have to comply with customs and duty regulations; and people still have to depart and arrive at seaports and airports and be subject to immigration controls.

Space is politically regulated and the movement of people across the world is directly related to the attempts to classify, order and control the exit and entrance of people out of and into different territories. The relations of power established by the nation-state through the use of immigration and later by policing immigrants within particular territories have a direct impact on the identity of places and the visibility of people at any given moment. Immigration controls are one of the means through which nation-states establish a distinction between those who belong to a nation and those who do not. Legislation to control territorial borders contributes to the construction of a national identity and a sense of belonging, whilst reinforcing forms of exclusion. This has clear implications for the relationship between cultural identities, people and places.

Research on the relationship between nation and migration has substantially sustained the argument that immigration legislation operates along the lines of racial, sexual and class discrimination.[8] Visas are granted to some people and not others. A cursory glance through the entry regulations for various countries will reveal a set of hierarchical criteria by which people are judged according to their nationality, social status, occupation or amount of capital they have available for investment. Such regulations are continually changed as states assess who they wish to allow within or exclude from their borders. For example, the history of British immigration law has been a narrative of changing regulations which attempted to restrict the entry of peoples from ex-colonial territories (whether the focus of legislation was India, the Caribbean or Hong Kong).

As education increasingly becomes subject to the pressures of globalization – or as universities seek the higher fees that can be obtained from non-nationals – so governments have sought to scrutinize the movements informing such recruitment. To cite just one example, in the summer of 1999 the Australian Government decided that foreign students were using enrolments at educational institutions as a means of illegally remaining in the country. As a result, the Government drew up lists of 'gazetted' countries from which students could enjoy 'streamlined processing'. As the *Times Higher Education Supplement* reported:

> Students from 'non-gazetted' countries have to undergo a 'genuineness assessment'. This involves an investigation by immigration officials. The gazetted countries cover

almost all those in Europe and North America, as well as a significant number in Asia, including Hong Kong, Indonesia, Japan, Malaysia, Korea, Singapore, Taiwan and Thailand. China and India are conspicuously classed as non-gazetted.

(Maslen, 1999: 12)

Likewise, around the world, those seeking asylum or fleeing persecution, disaster or conflict and claiming refugee status are judged and categorized according to a range of political, economic and cultural criteria. Being admitted as a refugee is not a straightforward humanitarian process but is dependent upon state classifications. Gaining entrance, receiving permission to stay for short or long periods, acquiring the papers to work or obtain benefits, being labelled as refugee, resident, alien or citizen – all are granted in relation to territorial origins, political and economic relations between states, family ties, occupation and, probably most cynically, the amount of capital an individual might bring into a country.[9] In the next section we will explain in more detail how this discussion of nation and migration is important for the realization of the cultural identities of both people and places.

Making and remaking the identities of places

Our first and most obvious point, following the section above, is that certain people are moving more freely than others and are thus able to participate in the making of identities across borders. Some individuals and groups are able to establish a presence in other places and to contribute to those very noticeable signs of cultural identity that are interpreted from what is so visible, audible and aromatic on the streets. Numerous cities contain multiple representations of cultural identities, ranging from distinct neighbourhoods, which may be locally known as Afro-Caribbean, Irish, Jewish or Chinese, to themed bars, clubs and restaurants offering a variety of 'ethnic cuisine'. It is sometimes assumed that the peculiar character of distinct parts of different neighbourhoods has been formed due to the way immigrant groups have brought 'their' culture with 'them'. 'People move with their cultures', as Held *et al.* (1999: 285) observe, implying that culture is an entity that is simply carried across borders, suggesting no process of transformation. Yet, culture as a whole way of life, as discursive practices and even as commodified artefacts or advertising images, is far more than a static thing that is carried or that flows unchangeable throughout history. Cultures are lived and cultural identities established, made and remade constantly, to return to an earlier point; identities are reterritorialized in new locations, given a specific grounding in a particular place.

Although there is no necessary relationship between places and identities, a social relationship develops through the particular ways in which places are transformed by usage and by the practices that occur in these places. One of the most obvious ways that places are given an identity is through the design and construction of buildings. Yet, this is no straightforward process. The form, content and texture of architecture is often a consequence of a series of struggles between architects, planning authorities, builders, material suppliers, various technical experts and engineers, community pressure groups, local political or commercial interests, and public and private investing institutions. As a result, completed buildings are often very different to the image presented in their initial plans or design.

A second obvious way that a sense of place-identity and identification develops is by people appropriating, transforming and using particular areas of the city for specific cultural practices. This not only involves interactions between people and buildings, but numerous cultural practices and interactions between different groups of people, and not just identities made exclusively within or amongst the specific groups of people in question (Irish, Brazilians, gay men . . .). As Gustavo Leclerc and Michael Dear write in their account of Latin life in Los Angeles:

> By sifting through the narratives of buildings, streets, and neighbourhoods, it is possible to glimpse a complex set of histories and geographies that can lead to new understanding of the formation of urban identity. . . . Taken together, the collective experiences of countless individuals define identity and meaning in a particular place, along lines of (for instance) class, gender, and ethnicity. In a reciprocal manner, the qualities of place act to condition and constrain the mechanisms of identity formation; thus, the neighbourhood protects us, at the same time as it holds us back, keeps us down.
>
> (Leclerc and Dear, 1999: 4–5)

Implied in this way of thinking about identities as built, constructed, facilitating and constraining is the possibility of further transformations of the existing character of places. In this sense, places are provided with identities that are not static but open to contestation and transformation.

It is with this sort of perspective that we should approach the 'global' movement of different groups of migrants and the formation of neighbourhoods with distinct identities (whether known as Chinatown, or Italian quarter or as a Latin or Hispanic neighbourhood). In addition, we should recognize that as certain cultural forms become popular or fashionable, so other groups and particular commercial interests become involved in constructing identities. This can produce a complex, contradictory and potentially tense environment. For example, as salsa music and various types of Latin dancing and food have become popular in London, so there has been a growth of commercially run clubs, bars and restaurants, and a concomitant increase in fiestas, concerts and cultural events sponsored by local governments and community organizations. Some of these events have produced sites for the meeting and mixing of musicians, dancers and DJs and the sharing of experiences between Latin and non-Latin people, and the potential for the forging of new cultural identities.

Yet, at the same time, other places constructed with a Latin identity have been contributing to divisions and social exclusion; providing a contrived environment invoking a mythical ambience of pre-Revolutionary Cuba or stereotypical images of beaches, palm trees, sunny holidays and hot Latin lovers, and deliberately seeking to attract wealthy, middle-class Londoners with disposable incomes. Meanwhile, often more concealed, are the many working-class cafés and clubs run by Latin Americans, who have been struggling to establish a presence and be recognized in the City since the 1970s.[10] Here, Latin Americans in London, like immigrant groups in other cities around the world, confront a contrast between self-supporting attempts to maintain a sense of continuous, yet changing, identity and the often exotic constructions of their own identities that can be found in many of the capital's bars, clubs and restaurants.

A further issue here concerns an individual's ability to participate in such places. Again this is still related to immigration regulations, and the internal surveillance and policing of different groups of people. Being admitted or being excluded, and being labelled in a certain way, has consequences for an individual's subjective sense of personal identity. Whilst we feel our sense of self to be 'internal', it is related to external circumstances and the way we have to continually deal with the labels that have been made up for us – labels that we have to confront, assume and conform to, or resist and negotiate.[11] This in turn has consequences for our ability to establish solidarity and a shared sense of belonging with others and the opportunity to participate in the making of places. Those who manage to enter another nation illegally or those who have entered legally but who choose to stay after their visa has expired ('overstayers') have to negotiate their spatio-temporal routes in quite distinct ways to the patterns adopted by other immigrants whose legal status is clearly defined. Immigrants who are categorized as overstayers or illegal cannot visibly express their identity nor move through a country or city without anxiety about their status being recognized and the fear of being discovered and deported. This encourages the development of alternative spatial patterns and routes across cities and countries. Many people in numerous places have to create alternative routes, in a similar manner to that adopted by Rubén Cárdenas who narrated the spatial patterns he developed in London when travelling from his workplace to his home once his visa had expired:

> When the visa ran out and I had to leave work at midnight, every time I came across a policeman on my way home I began to shiver and shake, but I learned to calm down and worked out a way home through the back streets of Pimlico. Before that I used to get off in Victoria tube station, but you encounter many police in that area, so now I get off at Pimlico which is a longer walk but with less chance of coming across policemen.
>
> (Cited in Castrillón, 1984: 39)

Being defined as an illegal immigrant or an overstayer requires people to give careful thought to their spatio-temporal movements and it also means operating socially at different spans of time and space. This not only has clear consequences for a sense of self-understanding and participation in collective demonstrations of identity, it also has consequences for meeting, mixing or integrating with other people.

This is an important issue, as a number of discussions of globalization and cultural identity have been informed by the notion of 'contact zones', an idea introduced by Mary Louise Pratt when discussing 'colonial encounters' within very specific relations of power. Pratt proposed the idea of a 'contact zone' as 'an attempt to invoke the spatial and temporal copresence of subjects previously separated by geographic and historical disjunctures, and whose trajectories now intersect' (1992: 7). A similar notion of meeting has been used in celebrations of new hybrid identities created as a consequence of transculturation, and was hinted at in our reference to the meeting of British and Latin musicians above. For example, Ulf Hannerz has written of the 'generative cultural process' that results from the 'coming together of distinct flows of meaning' (1996: 61), when boundaries are broken, when meanings (of sounds, words, images, people, things) that were previously separate are brought together, creating in the process a new synthesis or hybrid. In making this point he quotes Salman Rushdie's often repeated remark, made when discussing the book that caused him so much trouble:

> *The Satanic Verses* celebrates hybridity, impurity, intermingling, the transformation that comes of new and unexpected combinations of human beings, cultures, ideas,

politics, movies, songs. It rejoices in mongrelization and fears the absolutism of the pure. Mélange, hotchpotch, a bit of this and a bit of that is how newness enters the world.

(Cited in Hannerz, 1996: 65)

Whilst many diasporic identities and new art forms are created in this way, the mention of Rushdie should alert us to the political and social circumstances within which such meetings might or might not occur. To put it in Massey's terms, we should consider the 'power-geometry' and positions occupied by different people, and how this shapes the possibilities for interacting or coming together and creating newness in such contact zones. Not only do people move in particular ways, so too do the commodities that are often used for asserting or reinventing a sense of identity in a new location.

Identities and the commodification of culture

Numerous writers seem to agree that the distribution of commodified cultural forms are integrally linked to changing cultural identities. In broad terms, those who favour the 'homogenization of culture' thesis suggest that the international distribution of 'global brands', consumer products, advertising images, music, films, clothing styles and so on is leading to sameness, repetition, standardization and a 'global culture' lacking uniqueness and the potential for originality. This is an argument that can be found in popular journalism and in academic writings, and often appears when politicians evoke terms such as 'McDonaldization' or 'Cocacolonization' and, more generally, the spectres of Americanization or westernization. This type of reasoning can be traced back through critiques of the standardization of cultural production, to claims about the impact of 'mass production' on the public (who become 'masses') and to anxieties about the social consequences of the spread of capitalist industrialization in the nineteenth century.[12]

In contrast, the local resistance argument claims that such messages, media forms, commodities and social practices are appropriated in various ways, redefined and recontextualized and given a different meaning and alternative use. Again, this argument has a history and can be traced back via claims about active audiences and media 'uses and gratifications' research to a distinct strand of phenomenological social theory which places an emphasis on human 'actors' as the source of social meaning.

Both sides in the more recent debate assume that the use of commodities is integral to understanding an individual's sense of self and identity. They assume that we express some key aspects of our social identity through consumption patterns and preferences for food or art forms, through choice of media and music, and that these can be directly interpreted as a sign of individual and collective identities (hence ethnography and 'mass' observation, along with semiotics, have been the most popular methods used for interpreting such identities).[13] Whilst the homogenization of culture thesis often owes a debt to a crude form of political economy in stressing the direct impact of commodities on rather passive subjects, the local resistance argument tends to treat the commodities that are observed as given, without asking too many questions about how and why some and not other products, services, practices and forms are made available. In short, writers who favour this position remain fairly uncritical of the logic of consumerism and how this drives the dynamics through which goods or commodities are distributed around the world.

Whilst we agree that commodities are one possible means through which an individual can perhaps affirm or express a sense of subjective self, and are certainly a perpetual pressure against which a sense of public citizenship must be negotiated, it is important to understand how certain commodities and cultural forms come to be present and absent in different places around the world. Just as people move in particular ways, so do commodities, media forms and technologies; they become available to some people but not to others. If aspects of individual and collective identities are worked out in relation to cultural commodities then it becomes important to understand how this occurs. Not only should we be aware of the unequal power relations between producers and consumers, we should pay attention to the issue of distribution and how people gain access to the things that might or might not result in any change to a sense of identity. In short, we need to be aware of the influence of the corporations involved in moving and making available these commodities.

On this point, a number of writers have stressed the importance of the influence exerted by multinational corporations (MNCs). As David Held, Anthony McGrew, David Goldblatt and Jonathan Perraton point out:

> A small number of MNCs dominate world markets for oil, minerals, food and other agricultural products, while a hundred or so play a leading role in the globalization of manufacturing production and services. . . . MNCs play a major role in the generation and international diffusion of technology, accounting for around 80 per cent of world trade in technology and the majority of private research and development (R&D). Their huge capital demands and periodic large cash surpluses have made them key players in international financial markets. They play a significant role in the globalization of trade, finance, technology and (through output and media ownership) culture, as well as in the diffusion of military technology.
>
> (Held, McGrew, Goldblatt and Perraton, 1999: 236)

Whilst multinationals do not simply impose their will, and can be challenged in various ways, the fates and fortunes of entrepreneurs and small and medium-sized enterprises have to be realized *in relation* to the operations of the big conglomerates. This is apparent if we consider media ownership and cultural production. As has been well documented, a few large corporations (such as BMG, Sony, Disney, Universal, News International) account for the distribution of a huge proportion of the top-selling books, films, magazines and musical recordings (the products that generate the most revenue). Although many small companies also produce novels, films and music, these do not usually sell in such vast quantities. If such products receive critical acclaim, social recognition and, most significantly, go on to become commercially successful, then the small operator will usually be courted by the multinational. Indeed, for many years, the dynamics of cultural production have been characterized by a continual process of acquisitions financing and deal-making between small and large companies, and this has usually resulted in the small company becoming an operating unit of the large corporation (or key personnel moving over to the large corporation).[14]

Yet, the MNCs do not simply 'dominate' markets. As a number of researchers have found, in many parts of the world there are, quantitatively, far more locally produced films, musical recordings and television programmes being made, circulated and broadcast. However, these are not usually generating the same amount of revenue as the products distributed by the MNCs. Nor are these local producers able to exert the same influence over viewing and listening habits, buying patterns and the professional judgements of production and marketing executives. Rather than directly manipulating consumers, the influence of MNCs is often felt more strongly within the local offices of the corporation and its affiliates, and experienced in terms of the pressure to conform to a series of aesthetic and commercial agendas, working practices, production routines and working codes.

None of the major culture producing and media corporations have limitless sources of funds, so they allocate resources by establishing a series of commercial criteria and aesthetic hierarchies and use these to allocate greater investment to some genres, authors, film projects, performing artists, publications and not others.[15] Whether involved in finding and financing the production of films, books, recorded music, television programmes, musicals, magazines or academic textbooks, greater investment will be accorded to those products judged to produce the greatest return on investment. When these decisions are made, what is euphemistically called the 'international potential' of any new film, singer, novel or recording is of paramount importance, and will influence who and what is acquired.

Selling to an 'international market' appeals to Hollywood film producers as much as it influences deal-making at the Frankfurt Book Fair and the commercial assessment of a rock band or DJ entertaining a crowd in a small club in Sydney. International sales can provide the corporation (and musicians, directors and novelists) with extra income for proportionately less additional investment in production costs. Once initial investment has been recovered the cost of reproducing and distributing additional copies of films, novels or CDs is relatively low compared to the extra revenue that can be generated.

However, in making decisions about international promotion, the world outside is *imagined* in a very particular way. Despite numerous references to the term within business more generally, there are not simply 'global markets' waiting out there on the planet or spontaneously forming as members of the public gravitate towards certain artefacts and not others. The 'global market' is an idea that is constructed in a specific way by the entertainment industry, and made up in a contrasting but similar manner by other industries. Senior executives in the major corporations have adopted a particular way of understanding what global markets are and use a limited range of specific criteria when making assessments about the world. These include aesthetic judgements about the instruments, tempos, rhythms, voices and melodies or narratives, plots and story themes that are able to 'travel well'. It incorporates semiotic judgements about the types of image – faces, bodies, clothing styles – that are thought to be more suitable for an 'international audience'. It includes political judgements about areas of the world considered to be 'unstable' or where some music styles, novels and films are banned for moral or religious reasons. It includes economic judgements about the number of potential consumers who can be reached and assessments about parts of the world where the corporation may have difficulty collecting revenue. It includes marketing judgements about the availability of radio stations, retail outlets, television broadcasting systems and the social distribution of tape machines, CD players and television sets. Finally, it includes financial-legal judgements about the existence of copyright law that will ensure that television programmes and music recordings broadcast by the media, films shown in public or circulated for purchase on video, will generate rights revenue that will accrue to the corporation.

In this way the 'global' is given a specific identity. It is constructed in terms of a series of very particular criteria, and the world is divided up accordingly. One consequence is that greater attention is paid to those parts of the world (richer countries) and groups of people (high-spending elites within capital cities) that can be categorized as a viable 'market' and source of profits. Other people and places are considered to be of secondary importance or are simply ignored. On this point it is worth noting that in many parts of the world, people do not have access to the equipment for listening to recorded music or watching television in the home, or viewing films on video.

Consumer products and media forms and technologies are not distributed equally throughout the world. An insight into this issue can be gained by considering a small sample of some of the statistics produced by UNESCO. For example, recent (1996) figures for the number of television receivers per 1000 inhabitants show huge differences between countries, with Chad having 1.4, Pakistan 21, Kenya 25 and Senegal 41 in comparison to the 181 in Jamaica, and the figures of 510 for Kuwait, 516 for the United Kingdom and 684 for Japan. Grouped figures for the distribution of radio receivers indicate that there are 141 receivers per 1000 inhabitants in Africa, 802 for America and 514 for Europe.[16] In some slightly earlier research, Cees Hamelink used UNESCO figures from 1989 to draw attention to the stark contrast in the distribution of telephones:

> Of the world's 700 million telephones, 75 per cent can be found in the 9 richest countries. The poor countries possess less than 10 per cent, and in the most rural areas there is less than 1 telephone for every 1,000 people. There are more telephones in Japan alone (with a 1988 population of 121 million) than in the 50 nations of Africa combined (with a 1988 population 4 times that of Japan and a land mass more than 80 times greater).
>
> (Hamelink, 1995: 296)

Not only does this pattern of commodity circulation contribute to significant 'information imbalances' (Hamelink, 1995) across the world, the distribution of radios, televisions, telecommunications and musical equipment tends to reinforce existing patterns of social and economic inequality (Golding, 1994). The absence of certain technologies and lack of their cultural contents in some places is as significant as their abundance in other locations.

It is important to bear in mind these patterns and processes when thinking about how the public may establish bonds of identification with the sounds and images of celebrity figures that reach us through the audio-visual media. It is also important to take account of these circumstances when thinking about how anyone might express, affirm or refute particular identities through patterns of media consumption or appropriation. Such commodity-mediated aspects of our cultural identities can only be constructed or expressed out of what is made available through this process. No doubt numerous singers, musicians, actresses, films, books, products, clothes have the potential to criss-cross a globalizing world and to provide material for expressions of identity or to help us understand who we are or might be. Yet, only very few do.

Despite these corporate constraints, promotional pressures, social inequalities and cultural hierarchies there is a large amount of music and numerous films, novels and art forms moving across the world, many travelling in ways that are neither directed, controlled nor understood by the major entertainment companies. There is not simply one corporate dynamic driving the 'global' movement of cultural forms and influencing how these connect with a local sense of the self and collective belonging. Many films, books, musical recordings and artefacts are moved across the world despite being ignored by the major corporations, facilitated by the activity of enthusiasts whose actions contribute to media cultures and social and subjective identities that are far from institutionalized. Such dynamism is not sustained by an identifiable corporate 'culture industry' but instead by the cultural *industry* of enthusiasts, fans and cultural producers in the broadest sense of the term. As Raymond Williams once pointed out, whilst the term 'industry' has come to mean the 'institutions for production or trade', it can also be used to refer to 'the human quality of sustained application and effort' (1983: 165). This is industry as an effort of will, as a dynamic human quality rather than as a bureaucratized institution. This point is important, and is usually neglected by those writers who present overtly mechanistic or deterministic models of the culture industries and who neglect the idea that human industry is part of organizational industry. This point is also neglected by those who assume that the human effort involved in constructing a sense of individual and collective identity occurs in the act of consumption and creative appropriation.

Many people are actively involved in seeking out recordings, films, videos and novels, and engaged in assisting musicians, actors, directors, authors, poets to move across borders for a variety of non-commercial reasons. Numerous people are engaging daily in cultural dialogues and connecting with other enthusiasts. Such activities suggest a quite different link between time–space processes (or globalization), commodities and cultural identities. This is neither about a standardized identity imposed by powerful multinational media merchants, nor about the free appropriation of these products by a resistant creative audience. It is more complicated and unstable. Whilst more research would be needed to understand the intricate patterns that may be involved here, our general point is that many cultural identities are being realized through an engagement with practices and things that are not so visible or audible as stable commodities.

Conclusion

A focus on the link between globalization and cultural identities raises a number of issues of central importance in the study of the media and social life. Inevitably, we have not presented a comprehensive account but have chosen to highlight what we consider to be some of the key issues that cut across the ongoing debates preoccupying researchers in many disciplines. In particular, we have concentrated on three major themes: that of nation and migration; the transformation of places; and the circulation of commodities. We have suggested that when thinking about globalization and cultural identities, it is important to consider how these topics provide an insight into the power relations involved.

First, we focused on the nation-state to stress how space is politically regulated, borders controlled and how movement occurs in relation to particular attempts to allow or restrict the 'flow' of people and things. Second, we highlighted how places do not have intrinsic, unchanging identities but are made and given meaning through often complex processes that involve people interacting with and transforming their environment. Our third point concerned the movement of commodities and the way that goods, services, media and cultural forms do not reach everyone equally and are circulated in different ways.

In focusing on these issues and their consequences we have referred to three distinct but related notions of identity. First, the subjective sense of the individual self which is formed, framed and influenced by and within specific social circumstances, but which cannot be reduced to or explained solely as a 'social construction'. Second, we have referred to a collective sense of identity; our sense of who 'we' are, who or what we belong to, identify with and how we establish a sense of belonging and bonds of solidarity. Third, we have referred to the identity of places, from the abstract 'imagined' nation to the here and now of the local neighbourhood. Many assumptions about all of these types of identity have been called into question by theories of globalization (and in discussing this, we have pointed out that 'the global' has also been given a particular identity).

Whilst the term globalization has become an over-used buzzword and a rhetorical device used by business people and politicians of all persuasions, we cannot simply wish the word out of our vocabularies. Hence, there is a need to engage with this issue and to critically explore and research, with attention to empirical details and lived realities, the dynamics through which cultural identities are being altered or maintained, integrating this with an understanding of the different power relations involved. Questions about who and what is made absent and obscured by the processes that go by the name of globalization, are as important as understanding those signs of identity that are present and readily accessible.

Notes

1. For an overview of the different positions adopted towards globalization see Held, McGrew, Goldblatt and Perraton (1999). Further references drawn from the vast literature on this subject and relevant to discussions of globalization and cultural identity include Featherstone, 1990; Braman and Sreberny-Mohammadi, 1996; and Tomlinson, 1999.

2. For a more extended discussion of this issue see Román-Velázquez, 1999.

3. For discussions of the possibilities for cosmopolitan forms of solidarity and politics see Hannerz, 1996; Archibugi and Held (eds), 1995; and Cheah and Robbins (eds) 1998.

4. For discussions of debates about identities, specifically referring to issues of class, race, ethnicity, gender and sexuality (and again a selection from a vast literature) see Hall, 1992; Appadurai, 1996; Butler, 1990; and Negrón-Muntaner and Grosfoguel (eds), 1997.

5. See, for further discussions of this and related issues, Gilroy, 1993; Miles, 1993; and Waterman, 1996.

6. For further discussion of this point see Curran and Park, 2000; and Panitch and Leys (eds), 1999.

7. For further discussion of this point see Giddens, 1985.

8.   See Miles, 1993; and Jackson and Penrose, 1993.
9.   For example, in May 1994 the British Home Office announced that it was relaxing its immigration laws for those willing to enter the United Kingdom as investors, specifically if they were intending to invest £750,000.
10.   For further discussion of this issue see Román-Velázquez, 1999.
11.   We are drawing here on Ian Hacking's (1999) discussion of the 'fit' between people and social categories.
12.   See, for example, Adorno and Horkheimer, 1979; and Williams, 1963.
13.   This influence can be found in subcultural theory (Hebdige, 1979, for example) and also in Bourdieu's (1986) writings on distinction, taste and class differentiation.
14.   So, for example, A&M and Island became critically acclaimed 'independent' record labels acquired by PolyGram in the late 1980s which was in turn purchased by Universal ten years later; Miramax became a recognized 'independent' film producer owned by Disney. For further discussion of this issue in relation to the music industry see Negus, 1999; in relation to the film industry see Neale and Smith (eds), 1998; and in relation to the book industry see Coser, Kadushin and Powell, 1982. For a more general discussion see Mosco, 1996.
15.   For a more detailed discussion of the prioritising of artists in the music industry see Negus, 1992 and 1999.
16.   These figures are from UNESCO Statistics: radio receivers – total and number per 1000 inhabitants; television receivers – total and number per 1000 inhabitants; and the table on selected indicators (see http://unescostat.unesco.org).

References

ADORNO, T. and HORKHEIMER, M. (1979): *Dialectic of Enlightenment*, London: Verso.
ANDERSON, B. (1983): *Imagined Communities*, London: Verso.
APPADURAI, A. (1996): *Modernity at Large, Cultural Dimensions of Globalization*, Minneapolis: University of Minnesota Press.
ARCHIBUGI, D. and HELD, D. (1995): *Cosmopolitan Democracy*, Cambridge: Polity.
BOURDIEU, P. (1986): *Distinction: A Social Critique of the Judgement of Taste*, London: Routledge.
BRAMAN, S. and SREBERNY-MOHAMMADI, A. (eds) (1996): *Globalization, Communication and Transnational Civil Society*, Cresskill New Jersey: Hampton Press.
BUTLER, J. (1990): *Gender Trouble: Feminism and the Subversion of Identity*, London: Routledge.
CASTRILLÓN, S. (1984): 'Latin Americans in London', *Ten 8,* Vol. 16, 38–41.
CHEAH, P. and ROBBINS, B. (eds) (1998): *Cosmopolitics, Thinking and Feeling Beyond the Nation*, Minneapolis: University of Minnesota Press.
COSER, L., KADUSHIN, C. and POWELL, W. (1982): *Books, The Culture and Commerce of Publishing*, New York: Basic Books.
CURRAN, J. and PARK, M. (2000): 'Beyond Globalisation Theory' in Curran, J. and Park, M. (eds.) *De-Westernizing Media Studies,* London: Routledge.
GARCÍA CANCLINI, N. (1990): *Culturas Híbridas, Estrategias para Entrar y Salir de la Modernidad*, Mexico: Grijalbo.
GIDDENS, A. (1985): *The Nation State and Violence*, Cambridge: Polity Press.
——, (1990): *The Consequences of Modernity*, Stanford: CA: Stanford University Press.
GILROY, (1993): *Small Acts*, London: Serpents Tail.
GOLDING, P. (1994): 'The Communications Paradox: Inequality at the national and international levels', *Media Development*, Vol. 41 No. 4, 7–9.
HACKING, I. (1999): *The Social Construction of What?,* Harvard: Harvard University Press.

HALL, S. (1992): 'The Question of Cultural Identity' in S. Hall, D. Held and A. McGrew (eds), *Modernity and its Futures,* Cambridge: Polity Press.

HAMELINK, C. (1995): 'Information Imbalances Across the World' in J. Downing, A. Mohammadi and A. Sreberny-Mohammadi (eds), *Questioning the Media,* 2nd edn, Thousand Oaks, London: Sage.

HANNERZ, U. (1996): *Transnational Connections, Culture, People, Places,* London: Routledge.

HEBDIGE, D. (1979): *Subculture, The Meaning of Style,* London: Methuen.

HELD, D. MCGREW, A., GOLDBLATT, D. and PERRATON, J. (1999): *Global Transformations.* Cambridge: Polity.

HOBSBAWM, E. (1989): *The Age of Empire,* London: Sphere.

JACKSON, P. and PENROSE, J. (1993): *Construction of Race, Place and Nation,* London: University College of London Press.

LECLERC, G. and DEAR, M. (1999): 'Introduction: La vida Latina en LA' in G. Leclerc, R. Villa and M. Dear (eds), *La Vida Latina en LA Urban Latino Cultures,* Thousand Oaks, London: Sage.

MASLEN, G. (1999): 'Oz Gets Tough on Visa Abuse', *Times Higher Education Supplement,* 30 July, 12.

MASSEY, D. (1993): 'Power-geometry and a Progressive Sense of Place' in J. Bird, B. Curtis, T. Putnam, G. Robertson and L. Tikcner (eds), *Mapping the Futures, Local Cultures, Global Changes,* London: Routledge.

——, (1994): *Space, Place and Gender,* Cambridge: Polity.

MILES, R. (1993): *Racism after 'Race Relations',* London: Routledge.

MOSCO, V. (1996): *The Political Economy of Communication,* Thousand Oaks, London: Sage.

NEALE, S. and SMITH, M. (eds) (1998): *Contemporary Hollywood Cinema,* London: Routledge.

NEGRÓN-MUNTANER, F. and GROSFOGUEL, R. (eds) (1997): *Puerto Rican Jam, Essays on Culture and Politics,* Minneapolis: University of Minnesota.

NEGUS, K. (1992): *Producing Pop, Culture and Conflict in the Popular Music Industry,* London: Arnold.

——, (1999): *Music Genres and Corporate Cultures,* London: Routledge.

PANITCH, L. and LEYS, C. (eds) (1999): *Global Capitalism Versus Democracy,* Rendlesham: Merlin.

PRATT, M. (1992): *Imperial Eyes,* London: Routledge.

ROMÁN-VELÁZQUEZ, P. (1999): *The Making of Latin London: Salsa music, place and identity,* Aldershot: Ashgate.

TOMLINSON, J. (1999): *Globalization and Culture,* Cambridge: Polity.

WATERMAN, P. (1996): 'A New World View' in Braman, S. and Sreberny-Mohammadi, A. (eds), *Globalization, Communication and Transnational Civil Society,* Cresskill New Jersey: Hampton Press.

WILLIAMS, R. (1963): *Culture and Society,* Harmondsworth: Penguin.

——, (1983): *Keywords.* London: Fontana.

17

No Gain, No Game? Media and Sport

David Rowe

Introduction: a media take-over of sport?

It is not unusual, in a bar or lounge room anywhere in the capitalist West, to hear sports fans, especially when they are male and middle-aged, complain that the media (by which they usually mean television) have taken over their favourite sport. Television, they will protest, has changed sport for the worse – it, the litany goes, has altered the rules and times of the game for its convenience; deprived it of any administrative independence; become a rich man's indulgence and plaything; and has so pampered and flattered athletes that they have turned into 'superbrats'. All the while, they will probably have one eye on the sports action on screen, using the scheduled and unscheduled breaks to discuss the latest sporting controversy generated on radio and in the press. If a major sporting event is not covered on free-to-air television, they will be outraged, and if it is 'siphoned' on to pay television, they will grumble before losing resolve and paying the pay-per-view or subscription fees, the latter ensuring them access to at least one 24-hour sports channel.

The above scenario reveals several features about turn-of-the-twenty-first-century sport, media and audiences, but the most important is that, irrespective of levels of happiness or uneasiness about current circumstances, the media are central to the conduct and destiny of contemporary sport – and sport is crucial to the present health and future of the media. It is almost commonplace now for analysts of sport and media to observe that much of the most dramatic and absorbing action is taking place off the field of play. As media moguls battle over securing team franchises and broadcast rights, free-to-air television duels with its 'pay' counterpart over the best TV sports properties, and broadsheet newspapers poach each others' celebrity sports journalists, it becomes clear that a large media sports audience is a very precious commodity indeed.

This chapter will discuss the underlying reasons for the extraordinarily intense fight for the sports viewer, listener and reader, and the extent to which the media may now be said to have colonized – or, more graphically, cannibalized – the sporting cultural formation. It reviews the condition of media sport, analysing recent organizational developments and the research that has been applied to them (with 'cameo' case studies of television's relationship with the Olympics and with association football, and using the Rupert Murdoch-controlled News Corporation as a prime example of the business of media sport). If it is accepted that mass media and sport can no longer be seen as separate socio-cultural entities, it may also be suggested that the media have reshaped sport to the extent that they have inadvertently undermined its economic, social and cultural integrity. This chapter will also, therefore, appraise the overall cultural and ideological impact of the provision of such extravagant media space and resources for sport, arguing that the condition of media sport is a useful index of shifts within advanced cultural capitalism in its postmodern phase. Before exploring the deeper resonances of the growth of the media–sport nexus, however, it is necessary to appreciate the sheer size and scope of what I call the 'media sports cultural complex' (Rowe, 1999).

Meeting the media sports cultural complex

A cursory glance through contemporary print and electronic media reveals the extent to which they are deeply reliant on sport to supply large wedges of regular content. When media and sport are discussed, it is usually television that comes to the fore, but long before sport became pivotal to the economics of free-to-air and pay television it was a staple of both print and radio. Descriptions of sports events and the presentation of results have been features of the Anglophone press for centuries (Goldlust, 1987; Harris, 1998), and sports photography has provided visual stimulus in newspapers since the invention of the medium (Cashman, 1995). But the sheer density of contemporary sports coverage in newspapers (not to mention specialist and generalist magazines) is astonishing. For example, a popular broadsheet newspaper like *USA Today* has a sports section running to sixteen pages, while tabloids like the (London) *Sun* and the *Daily Mirror* regularly have sports sections of over twenty pages. This is clearly not just a 'popular' phenomenon – an august broadsheet like *The New York Times*, for example, carries a daily 'tear-out' sports section of at least eight pages, while Britain's *Guardian Sport* section (in a newspaper that greatly prizes its seriousness) is at least twelve pages.

The designated sports sites of newspapers do not exclusively contain information and discussion of sport and sport-related matters. These can frequently be found in general news (not uncommonly as front-page lead stories) and in the features, business, lifestyle and other sections of the newspaper. In such spaces, the latest Olympic corruption or drugs scandal, celebrity sports profile or takeover bid for a major football club appear with alarming frequency. As will be discussed below, such changes suggest that sport, with its history of bourgeois and aristocratic support for certain forms (like racing, 'the sport of kings', or rugby union, 'the game they play in heaven', as their catch-cries go), has never fitted entirely comfortably into the classification 'popular culture', and that its current massive presence across 'high' and 'low' media (whether ascribed as causal or symptomatic) reveals that it cannot easily be labelled (and dismissed) as the cultural fare of the working and other subordinate classes (Elias and Dunning, 1986). Nobody, for example, who has witnessed the association football (known as soccer in those countries where the code is not hegemonic) boom in Britain over the last decade can fail to notice how football-watching has spread across what was once regarded (even if somewhat mythologically) as a substantial class-cultural divide.

The press does still exercise the kind of cultural leadership in sport that is evident in other disciplines of journalism, with multiple columns of newsprint devoted to everything from the detailed recording of results, to ghosted commentaries by sports celebrities in the tabloids, to in-depth profiles and features in the broadsheets. Yet it is the electronic media that occupy the key positions of power in the communication of sport to dispersed publics. Radio, the more flexible and user-friendly of the two key electronic media, brought immediacy and atmosphere to sports commentary, but it is television, with its priceless capacity to turn 'seeing at a distance' (Weber, 1996) into a sense of 'having been there' (Barthes, 1977), that dominates the discourse of mass media and sport. This is because television, more comprehensively than any other medium, has turned sport into an essential component of its organizational infrastructure and textual product, and has succeeded in transforming major sports events (and the remote viewers that they attract) into a pivotal commodity whose value can be realized and exploited in myriad ways.

Before examining these more conventional features of mass media sport, however, we must also acknowledge the scope and density of the complex of institutions, social groups, forms, practices, myths, values and meanings in which it is located. While other theorists have used the concept of the complex to demonstrate the tight interdependency of media and sport – Sut Jhally (1989) traces the contours of the 'sports/media complex' and Joseph Maguire (1993) provides a more strictly productivist model of the 'media/sport production complex' – they do not quite do justice to the sprawling and undisciplined nature of the media–sport relationship. In numerous sites and moments in everyday life, sport has insinuated itself throughout the media, as they may most broadly be conceived, in constituting a highly diffuse media sports cultural complex. This dynamic entity includes the more obvious media genres and texts like the specialist sports magazines *Sports Illustrated* and *Total Sport*; (auto)biographies of prominent sports people like Michael Jordan, Martina Navratilova and Linford Christie; numerous manuals and videos devoted to improving one's golf swing or tennis serve; self-consciously literary anthologies like *The Faber Book of Soccer* (Hamilton, 1992), *The Picador Book of Sportswriting* (Coleman and Hornby, 1996) and such annual collections as *The Best American Sports Writing*; and feature films that draw heavily on the high levels of affect generated by sport (like *Chariots of Fire*, the *Rocky* series, *Raging Bull*, *Field of Dreams*, *Jerry Maguire* and *Space Jam*).

Beyond such overtly sports and sports-related media texts the media sports cultural complex also embraces the advertising slogans (like 'Just Do It', 'Whatever it Takes' and 'I Can') for the sports leisurewear of companies such as *Nike*, *Reebok* and *Adidas*, the advertisements that festoon our streetscapes and 'mediascapes' (Appadurai, 1990), and our own roles as 'walking billboards' whose clothing and footwear carry the corporate logos denoting and connoting positive messages about sport. It also incorporates the use of sports metaphor in political discourse (such as the ubiquitous 'level playing field'), in business journalism ('the race for profits') and in advertising (from celebrity endorsements to grand metaphors and similes about companies, customers and even whole nations as being 'on the team' – see Rowe, 1995). The media sports cultural complex also incorporates – directly and by evocation – the scandal and gossip that is disseminated because of the celebrity status of sports stars (McKay and Smith, 1995; Rowe, 1997).

At a reasonably lofty level of public discourse (although still involving a good deal of personal and private detail), sports governance scandals such as those involving corruption in the International Olympic Committee (over the receptiveness of some individual members to inducements and rewards from bidding cities and their allies) and in world soccer's governing body FIFA (where it has been alleged that votes for the current presidency were 'bought'), and the taking of performance-enhancing drugs in competitive cycling, weight-lifting, athletics, rugby league, swimming and other sports, can easily become major (if the pun can be forgiven) running news stories.

Alongside, and often intersecting with, such matters of public import are media coverage of the everyday lives, public arraignments and private peccadilloes of those who are or have been involved in some capacity with elite sport. A random content analysis of (at least the western) media and everyday conversation over the last few years would log multiple (sometimes staggeringly cumulative) references to former gridiron player O.J. Simpson's trial for murder; footballer David Beckham's marriage to Victoria ('Posh' Spice) Adams; the marital break-up of tennis player Andre Agassi and actress Brooke Shields; the various transgressions of footballers Paul Gascoigne and Diego Maradona; iceskater Tonya Harding's conspiracy to assault team-mate Nancy Kerrigan; rugby union player Will Carling's reported relationship with the late Diana, Princess of Wales and his sundry other romantic liaisons; the 'sex, drug and maul' confessions of former British rugby captain Lawrence Dallaglio; the sex life, sexuality and/or sex appeal of retired sprinter Carl Lewis, tennis players Anna Kournikova and Amelie Mauresmo, diver Greg Louganis, rugby league player Ian Roberts, ex-Major League baseballer Billy Bean, footballers Ryan Giggs and (the late) Justin Fashanu, basketballers 'Magic' Johnson and Dennis Rodman, and on and on.

In briefly recording these matters it can be noted that I have slipped, inevitably, into the kind of 'tabloidese' that forms the principal sub-language of media treatments of the extra-sporting activities of elite sports people. What I have tried to show is that the mass media's relationship with sport is not one that can be easily isolated within the 'appropriate' media divisions – the sports reports on television and radio, the sports pages of newspapers, and the specialist sports magazines. The formidable, multifunctional efficiency of the media has ensured that sport is an inescapable aspect of contemporary life. Yet within the chaotic, polyvalent media sports cultural complex there are also highly rationalized forces at work seeking to make (material and cultural) capital from sport. Indeed, there is an inherent tension between the drive to stimulate and sustain interest in sport by whatever means with the need to carefully manage its media image and to exercise control over the distribution of the intellectual property rights that pertain to individual sports, organizations and personnel. Nowhere are such contradictory sensitivities and motives more apparent than in the area of television broadcast rights.

Eyes on the prize: exclusive broadcast rights

As in other culture industries where corporate capitalism has taken strong root, the economics of media sport are dependent on the widespread promotion of cultural forms, and the expensive acquisition and fierce defence of their associated intellectual property rights. The continually expanding scale of the economic value of broadcast sport is exemplified by the various 'telephone number' contracts related to TV broadcast rights. The exponential growth in the value of media sport properties is exemplified by the escalating amounts paid by NBC for US TV rights to the summer Olympic Games. In 1980 the broadcasting world was shocked by NBC's extravagance in paying out over US$72 million for the rights to televise the boycott-afflicted (in protest against the invasion of Afghanistan by the then Soviet Union) Moscow Olympics. By 1995 the same network had pledged US$894 million for the US TV broadcast rights to the 2008 Olympics, the venue of which had not even been decided at that time. The escalating cost of the US TV rights to the Olympics can be seen as a response to the somewhat belated recognition by the increasingly hard-nosed rights sellers, the International Olympic Committee (IOC), of their global commercial value, paralleled by the heightened competition between media corporations for the Olympics property. Among these, Rupert Murdoch's News Corporation has been the most conspicuous force, offering the IOC a rumoured US$1 billion for worldwide rights and even threatening to set up a rival competition if the bid failed (Rowe and McKay, 1999). That Murdoch did not succeed in securing the broadcast rights to the Games probably reflects the IOC's concern over the potential loss of authority to, in a suitable sporting metaphor, such a 'hard ball'-playing media proprietor. That he has not, to date, set up a competing (presumably entitled) 'Murdoch Super Olympics' is testimony to the power of the Olympic 'brand', albeit one with a somewhat diminished commercial allure since the belated recognition in 1999 of endemic corrupt practice and high-handed organizational secrecy in the IOC detailed by Simson and Jennings (1992).

The figure of Murdoch looms regularly and intimidatingly on the landscape of media sport, securing broadcast rights (such as those to American 'gridiron' and to British Premier League soccer) and even sports clubs ownership (like that of the LA Dodgers) in some instances and failing in others (as in the respective cases of the Olympics and Manchester United Football Club, to be discussed more fully below), but always to inflationary effect. It is useful to examine Murdoch as a case study in media sport entrepreneurship, not least to demonstrate how sheer monopoly and commodity logic is not yet totally hegemonic in the media sports cultural complex. For example, in the European market the European Broadcasting Union consortium of mostly public broadcasters has managed to persuade the IOC to accept an inferior rights bid package (for Olympic Games well into the twenty-first century) to that of a Murdoch-led consortium of commercial free-to-air and pay TV operators. The concern, it seems, is that the reach of Games' viewing would be reduced by siphoning some events on to pay and subscription television (Wilson, 1998), a development that would not only negatively affect the 'cultural citizenship' rights attached to Olympic viewing, but also the long-term gross commercial value to advertisers and sponsors of the IOC's claim – in a broadcast analysis summary ironically echoing the American civil rights movement of the 1960s – that 'The Whole World Watches the Olympics' (Tomlinson, 1996).

To the chagrin of individual media proprietors like Murdoch who have assiduously cultivated sports industry personnel and national political leaders (the latter most notably, in Murdoch's case, Ronald Reagan, Margaret Thatcher, Jiang Zemin and Tony Blair), supra-state, neo-feudal sports organizations like the IOC and popular, fan-based movements can prove obstructive to ambitions to capitalize fully on the possibilities of broadcast sport. But the direct and indirect economic benefits in terms of network exposure and status, audience size and loyalty, heavy concentration of content, advertising rates, cross-marketing, subscription and pay-per-view payments, sale of ancillary electronic services and so on bestowed by ownership of TV sport are so considerable that the competition for prime media sports properties is, despite some setbacks – like the failure by Murdoch as discussed below to purchase Manchester United, or the hugely expensive 'Super League War' against Kerry Packer and the Australian Rugby League (see Rowe, 1999) – becoming ever more intense. It is for this reason that in 1998 American television networks spent over US$15 billion on the broadcast rights for American football games for the next eight years. For commentators such as Paul Sheehan, this did not mark the high point of the media sport market:

> This stratospheric number is a foretaste of the revolution that is about to engulf television, and Rupert Murdoch's global sporting empire is playing a central role in that revolution. The revolution will occur on several fronts, all at the same time.
>
> (Sheehan, 1998: 4)

The involvement of Murdoch in this sport – as well as in golf, cricket, rugby union, rugby league, boxing, athletics and many others – is reflective of a lesson well learnt in 1992, when a single TV sport acquisition (English Premier League soccer) at a stroke turned his failing BSkyB satellite service in Britain (in which News Corporation is the largest – 40 per cent – shareholder) into a highly profitable enterprise with a rapidly expanding subscriber base and many broadcast hours of globally desirable content that could be disseminated into other emerging pay TV markets (Goodwin, 1998). In publicly acknowledging its importance to his global operations, Murdoch subsequently described sport as the 'cornerstone of our worldwide broadcasting' (cited in Bellamy, 1998: 77) and, at the 1996 annual meeting of News Corporation, stated that:

> ... sport, and football in particular, 'absolutely overpowers' film and all other forms of entertainment in drawing viewers to pay television. 'We have the long-term rights in most countries to major sporting events and we will be doing in Asia what we intend to do elsewhere in the world – that is, use sports as a battering ram and a lead offering in all our pay television operations.'
>
> (Quoted in Millar, 1998: 3)

Developing the logic of this metaphor of media capital laying siege to the (often residually medieval) citadel of sport, it is apparent that having breached its walls and become well installed, another antiquarian metaphor comes into play – that of the Trojan Horse. Rather than be forced to pay more and more for broadcast rights in a bull market, media proprietors see it as preferable to own the whole operation 'lock, stock and barrel'. For this reason media companies are investing more heavily not just in the representation of sport's product, but in its manufacture from ground level by means of ownership and control of individual sport's companies. Such enhanced vertical and horizontal integration has a tendency towards monopoly and the reduction of competition (described by the participants in more anodyne terms as 'corporate synergies' and 'strategic alliances'), but is attractive to those sports enterprises (which sports fans persist in calling their clubs and teams) that have already moved a long way along the path of capital accumulation by becoming publicly listed companies. The promise of injections of media capital and instant stock market 'killings' through the higher share prices driven by attempted take-overs can prove tempting for the boards of listed companies that are also sports teams. The brief case study below, conducted into the Murdoch/BSkyB 1998 bid for Manchester United Football Club (which was first floated on the stock market in 1991), the world's wealthiest and perhaps best known sport's 'brand', illuminates well the contending forces at work in the construction and commercial exploitation of media sports texts and properties.

Media and sport convergence: television goes team shopping

In September 1998, front-page and lead-item news in Britain was dominated by the announcement that Rupert Murdoch had made a substantial bid to buy Manchester United Football Club. After brief negotiations, the United Board agreed to recommend acceptance of a raised bid of £623 million. The debates surrounding the Murdoch bid are informative in two respects: first, although not the primary focus of this chapter, in regard to how rival news media cover each others' affairs; and second, and more importantly, concerning the attractions and dangers of a full integration of media and sport.

Unsurprisingly (except for those who naively believe that the news media report their own and their rivals' financial affairs fairly and honestly), the Murdoch press strongly supported the move, with the tabloid *Sun* excitedly declaring (through a front-page title pun on the name of the team's home ground, Old Trafford) the coming of 'Gold Trafford', declaring that 'Fans and shareholders will [also] benefit with a ticket-price freeze and a stock market windfall', and quoting its News Corporation 'stablemate' Sky in assuring club supporters that 'The deal is good for you, your club, and football' (Kay, Thompson and Fitton, 1998: 1, 6). In the inside pages the newspaper judged, with the liberal use of favourable vox pops, that both celebrity and rank-and-file Manchester United supporters were 'Skyly Delighted' (Griffin, Scott and Patrick, 1998: 5–6). The Murdoch-owned establishment broadsheet *The Times* was rather more understated and even-handed, but its main comment on the sports pages was entitled 'A marriage made in heaven for United followers' (Holt, 1998: 28). The rival broadsheet *Guardian*, however, saw the pre-nuptial contract between BSkyB and Manchester United differently: 'Courtship ends as soccer and TV are united'. After observing that the 'Sky deal follows a path well trodden on the Continent' by media proprietors like Silvio Berlusconi (owner of AC Milan), Murdoch's ownership of US basketball, baseball and ice hockey teams, and the likelihood of other listed soccer clubs like Newcastle United, Tottenham Hotspur and Aston Villa coming under the control of other large media companies like Granada and Carlton (Millar, 1998: 3), the *Guardian* editorial (1998: 15) declared that 'This deal is riddled with conflicts of interest' and that 'Sky must be resisted'.

The *Sun's* direct tabloid competitor, the *Mirror*, in appropriately contrasting style, offered a front-page, digitally enhanced photographic image of a demonically reddened Rupert Murdoch, complete with horns and pointed ears in a visual pun on the team's nickname (the Red Devils). Punning further on the Murdoch picture, in which he is making a point with a finger to which satanically sharp nails had been attached, the question is posed in large type 'Will the only man in Britain who thinks that Rupert Murdoch should own Manchester United please raise his right index finger now . . . [?]'. The story proper then opened with the uncompromising observation (and yet another pun, this time on a popular book and film about soccer fandom)[1] that 'FURY at tycoon Rupert Murdoch's plan to buy Manchester United reached fever pitch last night' (Corless, 1998: 1).

But commercial competitors were not the only opponents of the bid, with Labour Government politicians like Sports Minister Tony Banks publicly stating their misgivings, and fans' groups like the Independent Manchester United Supporters Association vocally opposing the take-over. Some 6 months later, after an inquiry by the (then) Monopolies and Mergers Commission (MMC), the take-over was blocked, with the Industry and Trade Secretary, Stephen Byers, stating:

> The MMC's findings are based mainly on competition grounds, where they concluded that the merger would adversely affect competition between broadcasters. . . . They also examined wider public interest issues, concluding that the merger would damage the quality of British football . . . by reinforcing the trend towards growing inequalities between the larger, richer clubs and the smaller, poorer ones.
>
> (quoted in *Sydney Morning Herald*, 1999: 34)

The difficult political decision that the Blair 'New' Labour Government had to take in thwarting a powerful but fickle media ally demanded a low-key presentation of its decision. However, the celebrations on the day of the announcement in an independent Manchester United supporter's website delicately entitled 'You Can Stick Yer **cking Murdoch Up Yer Arse', were unconstrained:

> Today has been a great day for United fans, and a great day for football fans in general . . . BSkyB's £623m bid to buy Manchester United has been rejected by the Monopolies and Mergers Commission. And all I can say is . . . thank God. And thank IMUSA [the Independent Manchester United Supporters Association] too . . .
>
> A Murdoch take-over would have been the worst possible thing for United. It would have well and truly taken the heart and soul out of what Manchester United stands for – and whilst over the last few years there's no doubt that corporate interests have eroded some of that, we can at least rest assured that the world's most powerful media baron and high profile promise-breaker won't get his hands on our club.
>
> (DC Rants: 1999)

It would be misleading, however, to see such highly charged expressions of soccer fan sentiment – one newspaper headline (*Sun Herald*, 1999: 38) read 'United fans 1, Murdoch 0' – as having a determining effect on economic ownership and control trends in media sport. While, clearly, matters of public interest did have some bearing on the decision, as noted above it could be argued on strictly commercial grounds that the overall health of a relatively even and widespread competition (both financially and in terms of performance on the field) is more likely to be secured and to make for compelling spectacles for TV audiences than highly predictable sports events, given that unpredictability is a key component of the attraction of live TV sport (see, for example, Wenner and Gantz, 1998).

A counter-argument by the proponents of media-inspired sports (post)modernization is that such defences of the *status quo* merely prop up unviable clubs and disadvantage individual sports within the total sports market and entertainment sector (so that media capital will flow to other sports, like basketball or golf, or to other leisure industries such as film or fast food). From such a position, sport is a component of the overall entertainment industry in which absolute or comparative advantage must be maximized, and where familiar organizing principles (like those based on the local or the national) are being superseded by new ones (like the elite and the global). Hence, it is argued, because TV viewers vastly outnumber those who can attend a sporting event in real time and space, and with their economic value to the sport commensurately larger, the logic of the market-place demands unimpeded development. Both inter-state political and economic 'harmonization' and globalizing pressures under the 'new economic division of cultural labour' (Miller *et al.*, 2001) have had undeniably pronounced, reconfiguring effects on soccer and on other sports.

The 1995 'Bosman ruling' (see Redhead, 1997: 27–28) affirming mobility of labour within the European community (and precipitating a possible global deregulation of the football labour market), coupled with the lucrative TV rights agreement for the small number of Premier League teams and the consequent public listing of clubs like Leicester City and Leeds United, precipitated a 'boom' in English soccer (albeit, as Lee (1998) notes, substantially debt-fuelled), making the Premier League the most highly capitalized in the world, and also one in which the notion of the 'nation' has been progressively de-centred, such that a leading team like Chelsea can field few or no English players at any given match. By 1998, a serious attempt (also, for the moment at least, stymied) was made by Murdoch and fellow media proprietors including Berlusconi to introduce a European Super League in the belief that a regular competition between leading clubs from countries including England, France, Italy, Spain and Holland would create an even higher-quality televisual 'product'. Finally, full economic integration of media and sport has been, as noted above, permitted in other European countries (such as France, where the leading club Paris St Germain is owned by the major TV company Canal Plus), leading BSkyB Chief Executive Mark Booth to complain that:

> This is a bad ruling for British football clubs who will have to compete in Europe against clubs who are backed by successful media companies.
>
> (Quoted in the *Sun Herald*, 1999: 38)

Such arguments did not win the day in this instance, but the pressure from television companies to take more direct control over one of their prime commodities, especially with the arrival of digital broadcasting and the much-heralded convergence of telecommunications, broadcasting and computing, is intense. The rhetoric chiefly deployed in offering this media sport abundance is the advantaging of the sports fan, who will be 'liberated' from the tyrannical rationing system imposed by free-to-air television and released into a world of 24-hour specialist sports channels in which the viewer can use the new technology to become their own TV producer and researcher (Rowe, 1999). The degree to which sports fans are persuaded by this promise is questionable, given the above-recorded events surrounding the Murdoch ownership of Manchester United and the resistance to his aforementioned move on the pay TV coverage of rugby league (the most popular winter sport in New South Wales and Queensland) in Australia despite the opposition of fellow media entrepreneur Kerry Packer, rival pay TV operator Optus and many 'dyed in the wool' fans (where a 'Stop Murdoch Committee' predated its equivalent in Manchester United: see Rowe and McKay, 1999). In considering these issues, it is necessary to go beyond political economic analysis to consider more precisely the benefits and attractions that TV sport offers to its actual and potential viewers.

Sport appeal

In order to understand how central sport is to the economics, content and schedule structure of television, it is important to appreciate the deep imbrication of contemporary sport and the electronic media as demonstrated in the previous section. But the possession of this knowledge does not, in any developed theoretical sense, explain the desirability of sport as a media commodity. In order to come to terms with the dialectic of economics and culture in the production of the contemporary sports media, it is necessary to understand why sport is popular in the first place, and how the media – especially television – can sustain and promote its popular appeal. For example, it is perfectly possible for television companies to expend vast sums on acquiring the exclusive broadcast rights to reasonably (and, for some, unfathomably) popular pursuits like trainspotting or loud mobile phone usage in public spaces. These activities could be the recipients of saturation media promotion and there would, no doubt, be no shortage of practitioners willing and able to sell the rights to the public viewing of their practice for a handsome reward. However, it is probable that such broadcasts would be an abject failure, although it is important to allow for the occasional 'off-the-wall', improbable success – for example, the runaway ratings success of televised sheepdog trials in New Zealand – that may turn out to have some 'organic' appeal in their local context.

There are, first, certain intrinsic aspects of sport that fit it well for television and for other media. These include sport's astonishing flexibility as an element of media and everyday discourse able to straddle, effortlessly, different 'disciplines' – the 'nowness' of breaking news and the 'liveness' of current events, as well as its availability for analysis in many forms (anticipatory, current, *post mortem*, nostalgic). Umberto Eco's (1986: 162) throwaway comments on this point have probably been excessively cited, but they merit a quick reprise in this chapter in pithily revealing the proliferating nature of 'sports chatter', the 'sport cubed' which is 'a discourse on a discourse about watching others' sport as discourse'.

In structural terms, sports events do lend themselves easily to media formats. They are usually strictly timetabled (and increasingly disciplined by the demands of global – yet still western-dominated – television, which helps explain why marathon runners in various Olympic Games have been forced to run in murderously hot conditions so that US television audiences can watch at a convenient time). They are governed by formal rules whose framing and implementation can be endlessly debated and disputed (and, once again, are increasingly subject to media control, with TV-encouraged rule 'innovations' like tie breaks in tennis and penalty shoot-outs in soccer, not to mention whole new game forms like one-day cricket and 'skins' golf, ensuring schedule- and ratings-friendly sports TV forms). Sports events also, in most cases, have unequivocal (even, paradoxically, in the case of a draw) results – available, again, for celebration, bemoaning or disputation – which find a solid basis on which to build a massive discursive edifice. The formal unpredictability of live sports contests also means that viewers can feel that they are watching 'history in the making' a point made memorably in Don DeLillo's (1997) novel *Underworld*, in part a meditation on the symbolic resonances of a 'home run' in a 1951 New York baseball game being hailed as 'The Shot Heard Round the World' at the dawn of the Cold War.

But all these formal properties and possibilities for media sport could never be realized unless large numbers of people in many different countries actually cared deeply about what, at face value, often look like pointless and absurd physical manoeuvres. The media, therefore, are crucial to the health of contemporary sport because they have the capacity to convey and relay often intensely local events to vast audiences – and not infrequently to bring 'alien' or 'placeless' sports events to local sites – and to enhance the intensity of the sporting experience. This power is never more obvious than when the media sporting nation combines diverse affective elements in an orgy of imaginary mutual reinforcement.

The nation constituted around its sporting representatives and communicated internally and externally by means of the media apparatus is the key cultural symbol linking media and sport at deep levels of human emotion. The nation – which when stripped of all its formal symbols of identity and belonging is a rather abstract legal entity relating to formally recognized spatial sovereignty – is brought to active life when its internal fractures and fissures are temporarily occluded. There are few spectacular opportunities for conjuring up the nation as an agentic force. Regular grand rituals like national holidays offer spectacles which, while highly expressive, generally lack tension and uncertainty. Even great nation-building (Whannel, 1992) sporting (in this case horse-racing) rituals like the Derby and the Grand National in Britain, Australia's Melbourne Cup, the Kentucky Derby in the USA, and France's Prix de L'Arc de Triomphe lack a certain competitive *frisson* because, while foreign horses, trainers and jockeys do take part, the outcome is constructed around betting on individual competitors of often common or mixed national lineage.

As George Orwell (1992) among others has famously noted, there is little that stimulates the nationalist urge more than military combat, but warfare is immensely tragic and debilitating. For Orwell, international competitive sport offers a much tidier way of promoting jingoism – sport is 'war minus the shooting'. This statement is often misunderstood as approving of sport as a manifestation of the 'civilizing process' which has seen a resort to physical violence to resolve disputes, as well as unruly and often cruel popular leisure pursuits like 'folk' football and bare-knuckle fighting, succumb to the logic of 'sportization' (Elias and Dunning, 1986). Irrespective of Orwell's disdain for the proto-militaristic dimensions of sport (a quality that the founder of the modern Olympics, Baron Pierre de Coubertin, somewhat ambivalently saw as enhancing the combat-readiness of young people while improving the levels of international understanding that would make precipitate warfare less likely: see Hill, 1992), it is only through the modern media that international sport can be carried to geographically dispersed (inter)national audiences. At the same time, it is sport – especially when the nation's international, even global, reputation is 'on the line' – that supplies the media with an almost unprecedented opportunity (give or take the occasional funeral of a princess, and other such rare and unpredictable mega-media events) to persuade vast swathes of the population to be voluntarily and simultaneously captured.

As this chapter was being prepared for publication several mega-media sports spectacles occurred or were imminent. From the 1998 soccer World Cup in France (with an estimated cumulative television audience of '37 billion people worldwide', Austin, 1998: 4) through the 1999 cricket and rugby World Cups in Britain and athletics in Spain, to the 2000 Sydney Olympic Games (which can be relied upon to produce record single-event (for the Opening Ceremony) and cumulative viewing figures: see Gordon and Sibson, 1998; Real, 1996; Wilson, 1998) spliced by many other massive TV events like Wimbledon and the Super Bowl, audiences have presented themselves in staggering numbers before the screen. They have not been coerced into such disciplined behaviour, but instead have participated in the name of viewing pleasure, sporting affiliation and national identity. By encouraging a sense of collective purpose between sport and nation in this way, the media can promote public viewing of its programmes as a patriotic practice in which nationally constituted media, through their own commentators, the viewing public and sporting representatives, are engaged in an 'organic' process of national celebration which brings these disparate elements together as a 'team'. In other words, the global sports media seek to re-instantiate the idea of nation just as they work assiduously to bypass it.

To return to our case study of (especially British) soccer, several writers have analysed the Euro 96 tournament held in Britain as a classic instance where the sports media invoked and remoulded notions of the (sporting) nation. Jon Garland and Mike Rowe's (1999) neo-Orwellian analysis of the English press's symbolic resurrection of imperial glory records how readily the media can feed off, circulate and promote popular imagery and sentiment about national destiny, projecting historically derived ambitions and resentments on to sporting contests, and extrapolating from their outcomes moral lessons about 'the state of the nation' (see also Blain and O'Donnell, 1998; Harris, 1999). Much was made in the electronic and print media of 'football coming home' for Euro 96, with this birthplace return also a nostalgic recreation of the better times that seemed to stretch from the British Empire's zenith to England's sole World Cup victory at 'home' in 1966 (Miller *et al.*, 2001). For example, when the English national team played Germany in the semi-final, the *Sun* and *Mirror* unashamedly played on heroic memories of the two World Wars with stories like 'Let's Blitz Fritz' and 'Achtung! Surrender' (Garland and Rowe, 1999: 85). At such moments, when there is often confused debate about Britain's standing within Europe and about England's position within the United Kingdom (Boyle and Haynes, 1996), the highly intense, saturation coverage of sport in the media creates opportunities not only for both the positive re-affirmation of national cohesion (as in the prominent role of Nelson Mandela in the celebration of South Africa's 1995 victory in the rugby union World Cup in the only just post-apartheid South Africa) and for the resurrection of ugly racial stereotypes that are patently anachronistic in a multiracial, multicultural nation (Carrington, 1998).

While the nation is unquestionably one of the most powerful symbolic entities through which sport and its attendant mythologies can elicit, by means of the media, high levels of popular affect, it is by no means the only locus of identification. The media sports cultural complex operates freely as a vehicle for the enunciation and articulation of many modes of identity. Local and provincial newspaper, radio and television stations servicing the delimited space of suburbs, cities and regions can, through sport, encourage strong place-based identities, especially in times of crisis. For example, when in 1997 the de-industrializing provincial Australian city of Newcastle won a major rugby league competition only 5 months after its once largest employer, the multinational resource corporation BHP, announced the closure of its steelworks, the local media routinely deployed the sporting victory as a metaphor for class-based group cohesion and collective determination to 'overcome the odds' (Rowe and M^{C}Guirk, 1999).

In ideological terms, as we have seen, such deployments of sports mythologies always entail a series of exclusions and co-optations. Hence, for example, the place-based celebration of (usually male and often predominantly working-class) sport also generally entails the neglect and marginalization of women's sport, whereby women have to struggle in most cases (intermittent mega-sports spectacles like the Olympics excepted) for more than proportionally single-digit television and newspaper coverage (Creedon, 1994). Furthermore, even where there is demonstrable success for some members of subaltern groups through sport – as in the instances of African-American athletes of the 'superstar' variety (both pre- and post-retirement) like the basketballers Michael Jordan and Shaquille O'Neal, and athletes Carl Lewis and Michael Johnson – there are clear dangers that the media's projection of attractive images of black athletes and concentration on their financial success imply a generalizable solution to the 'race problem' (McKay, 1995). Such considerations return us, finally, to the social significance of the media–sport nexus.

Conclusion: the sports watching brief

In this chapter I have sought to demonstrate the depth and scope of media investment in contemporary sport – and of sport's involvement with the contemporary media. This relationship is now so intimate and enduring that it may be necessary to create ugly neologisms to describe the new phenomenon – 'spodia', perhaps, or 'medort' (which could be appropriately contracted by Francophone sporting romantics to 'mort'). It would be unrealistic to attempt to turn back the tide and demand an immediate withdrawal of the media from sport. Not only would this cause great economic dislocation for both institutions, but sports fans who have come to rely on 'armchair' live action, super-slow-motion replays, striking still sports photographic images, in-depth game analysis in the press and regular radio and TV sports news bulletins (not to mention the proliferating sports websites) would be mightily disgruntled. In any case, if the media did completely dominate sports organizations today, the cost of broadcast rights, sponsorship and endorsement would be nominal rather than, as in the instances discussed above, exorbitant. Sport, therefore, still has the power of its own popular appeal that it can strategically wield over the media to sometimes substantial advantage.

The analytical task, then, is not to deplore the media involvement in sport, but to monitor and regulate those sensitive areas where full integration is likely to damage the interests of sport and of sports followers – such as in the 'siphoning' of quality sport from free-to-air to pay television; the marginalization of locally based supporters by media organizations that give priority to remote living-room audiences; the damaging of sports competitions and of minority sports and smaller clubs by the media-instigated monopolization of capital by the elite few, and so on. Beyond the strict confines of competitive sport, it is also important to analyse critically how sport and its mythologies are used by and in the media through metaphor and as ideology. Just as the media sports cultural complex has its manifest pleasures and uses, those same characteristics are open to various abuses and damaging deployments. It is the simultaneous appreciation of these factors, alongside a working understanding of the profound and ever-deepening intrication of media and sport within globalizing culture industries in the context of even more extensive social transformations, that can now properly be called a 'key competency' in contemporary media studies.

Notes

1. Hornby (1992) and *Fever Pitch* (1997).

References

APPADURAI, A. (1990) 'Disjuncture and difference in the global cultural economy', *Public Culture*, 2(2): 1–24.

AUSTIN, K. (1998) 'The main game', *The Sydney Morning Herald – The Guide*, 8–14 June: 4.

BARTHES, R. (1977) 'The rhetoric of the image' in *Image-Music-Text*, London: Fontana.

BELLAMY, R.V. (1998) 'The evolving television sports marketplace' in L. Wenner (ed.) *MediaSport*, London: Routledge.

BLAIN, N. and O'DONNELL, H. (1998) 'European sports journalism and its readers during Euro 96: 'Living without the Sun' in M. Roche (ed.) *Sport, Popular Culture and Identity*, Aachen: Meyer and Meyer Verlag.

BOYLE, R. and HAYNES, R. (1996) 'The Grand Old Game: Football, media and identity in Scotland', *Media, Culture & Society*, 18(4): 549–64.

CARRINGTON, B. (1998) '"Football's Coming Home", but whose home? And do we want it? Nation, football and the politics of exclusion' in A. Brown (ed.) *Fanatics! Power, Identity and Fandom in Football*, London: Routledge.

CASHMAN, R. (1995) *Paradise of Sport: The Rise of Organised Sport in Australia*, Melbourne: Oxford University Press.

COLEMAN, N. and HORNBY, N. (eds) (1996) *The Picador Book of Sportswriting*, London: Picador.

CORLESS, F. (1998) 'Red devil', *Mirror*, 8 September: 1.

CREEDON, P.J. (1994) (ed.) *Women, Media and Sport: Challenging Gender Values*. Thousand Oaks, California: Sage.

DC RANTS (1999) *You Can Stick Yer **cking Murdoch Up Yer Arse, http://www.dcus.demon.co.uk/ manu/dcrants/dcomment16.html*, 9 April.

DeLILLO, D. (1997) *Underworld*, New York: Scribner.

ECO, U. (1986) Sports chatter, in *Travels in Hyperreality*, New York: Harcourt Brace Jovanovich: 159–65.

ELIAS, N. and DUNNING, E. (1986) *Quest for Excitement: Sport and Leisure in the Civilizing Process*, Oxford: Basil Blackwell.

Fever Pitch (1997) Channel Four Films.

GARLAND, J. AND ROWE, M. (1999) 'War Minus the Shooting? Jingoism, the English Press, and Euro 96', *Journal of Sport & Social Issues*, 23(1): 80–95.

GOLDLUST, J. (1987) *Playing for Keeps: Sport, the Media and Society*, Melbourne: Longman Cheshire.

GOODWIN, P. (1998) *Television under the Tories: Broadcasting Policy 1979–1997*, London: British Film Institute.

GORDON, S. and SIBSON, R. (1998), 'Global television: The Atlanta Olympics opening ceremony' in D. Rowe and G. Lawrence (eds), *Tourism, Leisure, Sport: Critical Perspectives*, Melbourne: Cambridge University Press: 204–15.

GRIFFIN, P., SCOTT, S. and PATRICK, G. (1998) 'Skyly delighted: Stars and fans unite to hail Man U super-deal', *Sun*, 7 September: 5–6.

Guardian (1998) 'Murchester United? Sky must be resisted', 7 September: 15.

HAMILTON, I. (ed.) (1992) *The Faber Book of Soccer*, London: Faber & Faber.

HARRIS, J. (1999) 'Lie Back and Think of England: The Women of Euro 96', *Journal of Sport & Social Issues*, 23(1): 96–110.

HARRIS, M. (1998) 'Sport in the newspapers before 1750: Representations of cricket, class and commerce in the London press', *Media History*, 4(1): 19–28.

HILL, C. (1992) *Olympic Politics*, Manchester: Manchester University Press.

HOLT, O. (1998) 'A marriage made in heaven for United followers', *The Times*, 7 September: 28.

HORNBY, N. (1992) *Fever Pitch*, London: Victor Gollancz.

JHALLY, S. (1989) 'Cultural studies and the sports/media complex', in L. Wenner (ed.) *Media, Sports and Society*, Newbury Park, California: Sage.

KAY, J., THOMPSON, P. and FITTON, P. (1998) 'Gold Trafford: £565m Sky deal makes Utd most valuable team in the world', *Sun*, 7 September: 1, 6.

LEE, S. (1998) 'Grey shirts to grey suits: the political economy of English football in the 1990s' in A. Brown (ed.) *Fanatics! Power, Identity and Fandom in Football*, London: Routledge.

MCKAY, J. (1995) '"Just Do It": Corporate sports slogans and the political economy of enlightened racism', *Discourse: Studies in the Cultural Politics of Education*, 16(2): 191–201.

MCKAY, J. and SMITH, P. (1995) 'Exonerating the hero: Frames and narratives in media coverage of the O.J. Simpson story', *Media Information Australia*, 75: 57–66.

MAGUIRE, J. (1993) 'Globalization, sport development, and the media/sport production complex', *Sport Science Review*, 2(1): 29–47.

MILLAR, S. (1998) 'Courtship ends as soccer and TV are united', *Guardian*, 7 September: 3.

MILLER, T., LAWRENCE, G., MCKAY, J. and ROWE, D. (2001) *Playing the World: Globalised Sport and the New International Division of Cultural Labour*, London: Sage (in press).

ORWELL, G. (1992) 'The sporting spirit' in Hamilton, I. (ed.) *The Faber Book of Soccer*, London: Faber & Faber: 37–40.

REAL, M. (1996) *Exploring Media Culture: A Guide*, Thousand Oaks, CA: Sage.

REDHEAD, S. (1997) *Post-Fandom and the Millennial Blues: The Transformation of Soccer Culture*, London: Routledge.

ROWE, D. (1995) *Popular Cultures: Rock Music, Sport and the Politics of Pleasure*, London: Sage.

——, (1997) 'Apollo undone: the sports scandal' in J. Lull and S. Hinerman (eds), *Media Scandals: Morality and Desire in the Popular Culture Marketplace*, New York: Columbia University Press.

——, (1999) *Sport, Culture and the Media: The Unruly Trinity*, Buckingham, UK: Open University Press.

ROWE, D. and MCGUIRK P. (1999) '"Drunk for Three Weeks": Sporting success and city image', *International Review for the Sociology of Sport*, 34, 2: 125–41.

ROWE, D. and MCKAY, J. (1999) 'Field of soaps: Rupert v. Kerry as masculine melodrama' in R. Martin and T. Miller (eds) *Sportcult*, Minneapolis, MN: University of Minnesota Press.

SHEEHAN, P. (1998) 'Game, set and match: Murdoch, the champion of world sports', *Sydney Morning Herald – The Guide*, 23 February–1 March: 4–5.

SIMSON, V. and JENNINGS, A. (1992) *The Lords of the Rings: Power, Money and Drugs in the Modern Olympics*, London: Simon and Schuster.

Sun Herald (1999) 'United fans 1, Murdoch 0', 11 April: 38.

Sydney Morning Herald (1999) 'Britain says no to Murdoch's Manchester bid', 12 April: 34.

TOMLINSON, A. (1996) 'Olympic spectacle: Opening ceremonies and some paradoxes of globalization', *Media, Culture & Society*, 18(4): 583–602.

WEBER, S. (1996) 'Television: Set and screen' in A. Cholodenko (ed.) *Mass Mediauras: Form, Technics, Media*, Sydney: Power Publications.

WENNER, L.A. and GANTZ, W. (1998) 'Watching sports on television: Audience experience, gender, fanship, and marriage' in L. Wenner (ed.) *MediaSport*, London: Routledge: 233–51.

WHANNEL, G. (1992) *Fields in Vision: Television Sport and Cultural Transformation*, London: Routledge.

WILSON, H. (1998) 'Television's *tour de force*: The nation watches the Olympic Games' in D. Rowe and G. Lawrence (eds), *Tourism, Leisure, Sport: Critical Perspectives*, Melbourne: Cambridge University Press.

18

Representation and Popular Culture: Semiotics and the Construction of Meaning

Christine Geraghty

The involvement of mass audiences in the representations proposed by popular culture has been one of the main areas of debate in work on the mass media. How far can the mass media produce culture that speaks of popular concerns rather than the interests of ownership? How do audiences engage with cultural texts as varied as, for example, photographs, television series and best-selling novels? To what extent do the values of the popular press or television, as expressed in the way they use words and pictures, dominate or control the way in which we think about the world? Such questions are crucial to our understanding of the media and in this chapter I want to outline not answers, but frameworks for understanding the implications of such questions in relation to media texts.

There are, of course, many ways of looking at such questions, a number of which are explored in other chapters in this volume. My focus will be specifically on representation and the media text. It can be argued that the way in which we engage with the media depends more on the habits and practices of our daily life – buying the newspapers on the way to work, reading a women's magazine in the bath, turning on the television to keep the children amused – than on the specific pleasures of the cultural product. It may also be argued that understanding of the media depends on knowledge about media ownership, and economic and technological developments. In both cases, I would suggest that the particularities of cultural texts are important both to the pleasure we take in them and the use we make of them. While work on texts cannot give all the answers, it should form part of the equation. In this chapter, then, I will look at particular examples of textual analysis and use them to explore issues of representation, a concept that has been crucial to the development of theoretical work on the media.

To re-present, to mediate, to image . . . if we make into active verbs the nouns we use so commonly in communications and media studies – representation, media, image – we can see how powerfully the language we have at our disposal frames our understanding. What it suggests is a process whereby a pre-existing given, whether it be a physical object or philosophical abstraction, is translated so that it can be comprehended and experienced by a recipient, an observer, an audience. In the process, the mediation may be presented as reflection, with the implication that the original is relatively unchanged by the process; or there may be questions of bias, distortion, re-framing so that somehow the purity of the original is lost. A particular relationship is established by this vocabulary in which the reader or viewer is involved in recognizing, checking, reconstructing the original from the media production – the photograph, the television series, the newspaper article – or else is taken in or absorbed by it. I intend to focus on some of the implications of using the term 'representation' in relation to the mass media by analysing specific examples from television and the press so as to demonstrate what is at stake in the process of transmission we so readily associate with the media.

Work on representation in the media is crucially marked by the development of semiotics in linguistics and the application of its techniques to communications systems that also involve images. Accounts of the work on language systems developed through semiotics can be found in more detail elsewhere,[1] but it is important to note certain principles. Semiotics was significant in work on the media because it attempted to break the notion of mediation and to show that the key relationship within a language system was not between a word and its referent, a pre-existing object to which the word referred; instead it was argued that a word's meaning was established through its relationship with other words and that it was recognized because it was different from other words – 'cat' was 'cat' because it was not 'mat' or 'cot'; further, what it signified or referred to was not a particular cat but the concept of a cat. This had important consequences for how language systems, and by extension other communications systems, might be conceived. It created a structure in which the key relationships were inside the language system rather than between language and something conceived of as being outside language, in the 'real world'; indeed the 'real world' did not pre-exist language but was constructed through it. Semiotics also emphasized the abstraction of language systems in which a word referred to a concept rather than a particular object; it proposed that language did not spring naturally from a relationship between word and object but was based on conventions that the users of a language had to learn.

Abstraction, convention, construction – these were all concepts which were to have important consequences in the development of studies of the media, particularly in studies of photography, film, television and the press, all of which involved representation based on visual images as well as spoken or written language. By bringing these concepts to bear, it was possible to see, for instance, that a photograph was composed not just in the usual sense by the photographer but by conventions of colour, lighting and subject which helped to fix meaning; that films were understood through the way in which they referred to each other in generic systems such as 'The Western'; that newspaper layout and the composition of headlines were not determined by what happened 'out there' but by the conventions internal to the press. Most importantly, semiotics challenged the notion of transparency in mediation – the media as a window through which we see the world or a mirror in which society is reflected. The notion that the language of the image was 'rhetoric' (Barthes, 1977), was based on construction not reflection, undermined some key value judgements in the area. If language was not a process of reflection, why were the mimetic claims of realism so highly valued as compared to the non-realist forms of, for example, melodrama? If media texts were a construction, what was the significance for audiences of their claims to represent reality?

I will come back to some of these questions in looking at particular examples, but it is important at this stage to note that the prevalence of visual images in the media posed particular problems for the use of semiotics. For, in visual representation relying on photography, it could be argued that the relationship between the image and the object imaged was not abstract or arbitrary. A photograph of a cat might signify the concept of a cat but it also relied on the concept of resemblance by referring to this cat, at this moment, in this place. Barthes in 'Rhetoric of the image' reflects on the way in which the photograph's capacity to record 'reinforces the myth of photographic "naturalness"' and generates 'an awareness of its having-been-there' (1977: 44). For Bill Nichols, writing about documentary film, the link between the visual sign and the particular object it refers to 'anchors the image in the specificity of the given moment' (1990: 108) and 'refers us back to the historical' (111). Even in fiction, the visual image can generate a sense of something beyond the initial construction – John Wayne, constructed as a star through his films and publicity material, plays a dying man in *The Shootist*, but part of the meaning of his fictional character is generated by the visible signs of his own final illness. Thus the double reference of the visually recorded image, to the particular as well as the general, to the local as well as the abstract, remained a problem to those who wanted to adapt the insights of semiotics to the study of media texts.

Semiology has been criticized for promoting too narrow a focus on texts and for being too hermetically sealed in its own systems to allow for analysis of the processes of historical change. In addition, concern has been expressed within communications studies at the adoption of semiotic approaches for visual languages which lack 'anything equivalent' to the stable vocabulary, syntax and grammar of 'natural language' (Corner, 1986: 53). As Ellen Seiter put it, in a statement on television which could be applied to other media forms, 'because television is based on weaker codes than those that govern verbal languages, it is, as a system of communication, unstable; it is constantly undergoing modification and operates by conventions rather than by hard-and-fast rules' (1992: 49). Accepting these limitations, I nevertheless want to look at three media representations in the context provided by semiotics' emphasis on language as a construction in order to tease out the possibilities and limitations of this approach.

Understanding a photograph

The first example I want to recall and use is that of a photograph, or rather a series of photographs, taken and used in the press when Charles and Diana, then the British Prince and Princess of Wales, were on an official visit to South Korea in November 1992. The photographs showed us two people, one male one female, formally dressed, unsmiling, as they turned away from each other to gaze abstractly out of the frame. The images are a professional construction, taken by the many photographers accompanying the royal tour, cropped to focus attention on the two figures – isolated from each other, the two heads, looking away – and thus framed and laid out on the front pages of the British press they enter into the international circulation of images.

In understanding such images we bring a number of frameworks to bear, a number of discourses that help to organize meaning. We draw on different kinds of knowledge and a study of that process suggests that the meaning of a photograph is not hidden or immanent in the picture but is constructed through a range of different signifying practices. During the process of recognition and understanding, we relate what we see in a photograph, the visual signs, to a wider set of understandings. Some of these may be signified directly from what is in the photograph, others depend on the cultural knowledge that can be activated by the photograph.

Take Diana's hat, for instance. The photographs tell us which particular hat Diana was wearing that day and avid royal watchers may be able to recognize it as one she has or has not worn before. But the hat also, if we understand what certain kinds of dress signify, tells us that this is a formal occasion with all that that implies in terms of being on 'best behaviour'. It may also be a sign of how royalty are marked as different from 'ordinary' women who do not in modern Europe wear hats very often. And if we have experience of the way in which Diana is perceived to operate as a fashion leader we may also be drawn to judge her physical appearance: does the hat suit her? Thus, in understanding the photograph, we are called on to use our understanding of codes of dress, which operate both inside and outside photography, in order to understand some of its meaning.

The photographs depict two people, a man and a woman. These need to be identified through cultural knowledge as members of the British Royal Family. The capacity to identify and name the people may be accompanied by a set of associations with hierarchy, history and tradition which surround royalty in Britain. In this context, the pair may be understood to be participating in a particular kind of formal occasion at which they have themselves a representative function. But, set against that understanding of the formal roles and traditions of British royalty, may be a more scurrilous discourse of gossip and speculation about the behaviour of some members of the royal family, including these two. Thus, the photograph can be understood through the associations that invoke the privileged position and private stresses of the modern royal family.

The photographs, therefore, may be placed in these kinds of general contexts and for some press photographs this may be enough. The British press and magazines like *Hello* frequently featured photographs of Diana which could be understood almost entirely in the context of royalty, fashion and glamour – this is what she was wearing, isn't she dazzling? But press photographs often need to be understood in the context of news – this photograph is important at this point because it tells us something new. The meaning of the photograph then has to be established more clearly so that the viewer is guided to the appropriate response.

One way of doing this is, to use Barthes' term, to 'anchor' the meaning through the written text that accompanies it. The written text then rules out as inappropriate certain meanings and underlines others as being correct; the viewer does not necessarily have to follow this guidance but other readings run the risk of being deemed irrelevant or deviant. In this example, the written text warned us that it was not enough to understand the photograph through discourses of fashion or the royal family. To do so would be to miss the point of the unsmiling faces turned away from each other. The meaning of this is

underlined by articles such as that in the *Daily Mail* which was headlined
'Charles and Diana face new crisis' and began 'This is the picture that reveals
the rift between the Prince and Princess of Wales. The physical and emotional
distance between them is clear' (3/11/92). The written text thus focuses attention
on one specific aspect of the photograph, the demeanour of the couple, and suggests, quite forcibly, that this is where the photograph's meaning must be found.

A number of professional practices allow this anchoring to take place: it is
conventional in newspapers to accompany photographs with headlines and cap-
tions in order to make their meaning more stable; it also conventional that photographs are used to support written text and to provide evidence that backs up
journalists' stories. But the practice is also supported by other discourses that
encourage us to understand the photograph in this way. By reading the photograph as 'the break-up of the marriage' we place it in the context of a narrative,
the story of the marriage which has been told through the media – in the press,
on television, in books. Narrative organization encourages us to make sense of
a story by looking for the way in which one event causes or has an effect on the
next and by associating individual participants with particular character traits.
At this point in the Charles and Diana story, the overarching narrative has
moved from the bachelor prince choosing a suitable bride through the fairytale
wedding and the birth of two sons to the estranged couple trapped in marriage
and the subsequent separation. This narrative is not the invention of any one
journalist or indeed the media as a whole. It is a structure that draws on different kinds of story – fairy tales, family sagas, the movement from adolescence to
adulthood – and provides the means of making sense of a mass of information,
selecting what is significant and giving it meaning. Thus a photograph of
Charles and Diana can be understood through where it is placed in that story.
The narrative encourages a reading which emphasizes the turned-away heads,
the gazes out of the frame, the sense that being trapped in the official car is the
physical equivalent of the trap of their marriage. But could the South Korean
photographs have been used in the early years of the marriage to signify the way
in which the happy couple took their formal duties seriously and performed
them well, not daring to look at each other in case personal happiness distracted
them from serious affairs of state?

Charles and Diana are, of course, public figures. Most of us have no personal
knowledge of them and it would seem that we cannot therefore call on direct
knowledge to understand their photographs in the way we might with our own
photos. But in some senses our direct experience is called on to create meaning
– not our experience of Charles and Diana but of our own personal lives. The
story of the royal couple straddles the public and the personal spheres, spheres
that we are used to thinking of as separate. On the public side are placed issues
of economics, employment, the law, the constitution; on the personal side, are
falling in love, getting married, having children. The two spheres are actually
inseparable but in general the public sphere is conceived of as the place for
experts – politicians, economists, judges – while we are all deemed to have varying degrees of experience of the private sphere. It is that expertise we bring to
bear on the photograph of Charles and Diana. We are not asked to scrutinize
the faces of politicians at a summit meeting for signs of likes and dislikes – the
formal photographs used suppress that kind of enquiry – but to understand how
the South Korean photographs speak of the break-up of this marriage we can

call on our own experience. We use our particular experiences of relationships to create a generality (this how such couples look) to apply to a particular couple (yes, Charles and Diana are in trouble).

And so we are back with the photograph and the way in which it seems to offer a particular access to reality, the sense that it offers evidence of the truth if we can bring to it the right keys. The more general discourses I have been describing are locked back into a discourse specific to photography – that of impassively recording private emotions, of catching and exposing moments whose significance might otherwise be lost and of searching out that which the participants might wish to conceal. The discourses I have described above – of dress, of royalty, of the personal sphere – can be used to make meaning because they are channelled through the photograph's promise to make the particular instance, the independent event, the secret relationship available to our gaze.

In analysing a photograph in this way, I want to stress two points in particular. First, our understanding of the photograph is based on a play between the particular and the general, between the specifics of the image and the general discourses of photography, social structures and personal behaviour. These more general associations are what Barthes called connotations or 'a body of "attitudes"' (1977: 47) which are used to fix the meaning of a particular image. This process is not a game of 'free association' but almost its opposite, of ruling out a range of possibilities in favour of those that make sense in terms of our more general social experience. The associations, though they will vary from reader to reader, also provide the common basis for discussing the photograph; the less the common ground is shared – Who is Princess Di? Why aren't they speaking? – the less there is a basis for communication. Second, Barthes suggests that it is through connotations that an individual image is connected with the ideological formations of the society that produces it; Barthes speaks of 'a body of "attitudes"' because the knowledges we bring to bear on the photograph are also positions – on romance, on royalty, on the ability of a photograph to tell us the truth. These positions are not monolithic but, again, unless we can place ourselves within a range of attitudes to, for instance, the British royal family the photograph will lack significance in that discourse. And, indeed, in discussing the photographs of the royal visit, it is important to note that meanings based on an understanding of South Korean mores are likely to be lost on British audiences. Thus an active role is given to the audience in this process of understanding since meaning depends not on the photograph itself but on the resources of the viewer. This does not mean we can be content with the lazy cliché that 'everyone sees things differently'; instead what are offered are ways of thinking about how those differences are structured and can in their turn be understood. The viewer may be active but is not free.

The story of Diana of course had a tragic ending which was itself subject to many interpretations and which is now something that we bring to bear in reading the photographs of her married life. But it is worth pointing to the way in which, before her death, she had tried to provide 'the anchor' to her own image, to wrest the meaning of her photographs away from the commentators. Significantly, she used television to do this through the 1995 *Panorama* interview. Television has the added dimension of sound, and frequently on the news, for instance, there is a disjuncture between sound and image as the commentators tell the viewers how to interpret what they are seeing, doing the task performed by written copy in the newspapers. In her television interview, Diana was trying to get over that disjuncture by speaking for herself about what her image meant. The attempt was the more audacious since it meant redefining what the language of royalty might signify. Thus, she claimed the title of queen but used the language of romance to do so, suggesting that she wanted to be thought of as the 'Queen of Hearts'. The reception of this language in the interview, of which women were much more supportive than were men, underlined the importance of considering gender in seeking to understand representation.[2]

Representation and gender

We make sense of a news photograph in the context of its claim to represent reality, its evidential or documentary status. But questions about representation and the mediation of reality also arise with fictional material. I want in this section to consider how the question of women's representation in soaps led on to more general issues of the relationship between soap opera and women viewers.

Much of the impetus for early work on the representation of women came from the feeling that the available 'images of women' were not adequate, generating the common complaint, 'We're not really like that.' It is a complaint that can be made by any group which feels itself to have an identity that is misrepresented by the media and is most consistently made by those who feel themselves to have little power within media institutions and little control over what they do. The complaint 'women are not really like that' – rests on a number of assumptions which need to be unpicked. First, it suggests that an important function of the media is to make realistic representations, an assumption which, as we saw earlier, depends on the concept of mediation between the audience and what is being represented. Second, it asserts the importance of the representation at least getting closer to what 'we are really like'. This is not necessarily a naive position but one that rests on an understanding of the way in which the typical is used in media representations to highlight certain common characteristics that are deemed important. Representation, then, takes on the representative function of showing what a particular group is like to others and therefore has a public function. Third, there is in the complaint a sense that a more accurate representation is important to those being represented because it affects how they see themselves and limits their own sense of possibilities. The question of realistic representations is thus a complex one in which their power in public and private constructions of identity is at stake.

In this context we need to consider what is meant by 'real'. Julie D'Acci in her account of the US programme *Cagney and Lacey* quotes some comments from fans of the programme which provide a useful starting point. One writes 'When I watch these two women working together being friends, fighting, loving and surviving it's so believable . . . I can think of no other show I've ever seen that's had real women, ordinary, living, breathing women as its stars' (1994: 179). And another: 'I know I speak for all women when I say it's about time there has been a television show which portrays two real and human women who are successful as police detectives. . . . We prefer to watch a show which has as its stars people like ourselves living probable and possible lives' (178). In both these examples, we get a sense of the importance of the representative quality of the two characters who seem real because they are ordinary, recognizable because they are 'like us'. But these responses indicate the demand for a particular kind of reality in which the women characters also embody positive characteristics – they work, they survive, they are friends. So what is being welcomed by these viewers is a representation which it is felt will be positively helpful to women trying to live such a life and educational to those who are dismissive about what women can do. D'Acci quotes another letter which is quite specific about this. 'Most importantly, though, it is the only show on television today that is an honest and thorough example of the roles which women . . . play in our society today' (180).

This demand by women viewers for a more positive representation of women characters can be seen in some feminist television theory of the late 1970s/early 1980s. Although the case of *Cagney and Lacey* is in some ways exceptional, a similar concern for positive representation, if not for quite such explicit models, can be found in feminist writing on soap opera. Terry Lovell commented on the presence of 'strong independent women' in *Coronation Street* and welcomed 'an important extension of the range of imagery which is offered to women within popular forms' (1981: 52), and in *Women and Soap Opera* (Geraghty, 1991), I pointed to the way in which female friendship and a shared understanding between women is an important factor in British and US prime-time soaps.

Feminist theorists have, however, been cautious about the progressive model of which *Cagney and Lacey* is an example. For such writers, the intervention of semiotics and its subsequent developments had made the double call for realism and role models problematic. An emphasis on realism seemed to depend on a failure to recognize the constructed nature of all such representation and to be rooted in a belief that a perfect transparency could be achieved. Griselda Pollock, for instance, argued in 1977 that it was 'a common misconception to see images merely as a reflection, good or bad, and compare "bad" images of women (glossy magazine photographs, fashion advertisements etc.) to "good" images of women ("realist" photographs, of women working, housewives, older women, etc.)'. Instead Pollock argued that 'one needs to study the meanings *signified* by women in images' (my emphasis, 1977: 26) but in doing so she recognized a gap growing between the call for more realistic representation of women within feminism generally and the work on signification being undertaken by feminists working on representation.[3] In a rather separate but related development, there was concern that the desire for a positive role model seemed to privilege one type of woman over others and involved rejecting 'more "feminine" traditional roles' in a way that seemed to collude with male denigration of them. Instead, feminist critics in media and cultural studies turned to the programmes such as soap operas and prime-time melodramas which were for many women a source of pleasure with a view to examining the way in which they constructed femininity and represented women's lives.

One important recognition was that realism should not necessarily be equated with the surface detail of everyday life. Ien Ang's *Watching Dallas* suggested that, despite the programme's surface glamour and its apparent distance from the day-to-day lives of its international audiences, viewers found a psychological believability, particularly in the character of Sue Ellen, which enabled them to recognize and identify with her emotional problems and difficulties. Indeed, Ang argued (1985) that the melodramatic format of *Dallas* allowed for the expression of these emotions in a more direct and forceful way than the restrictions of realism allowed. Experiences were represented in such as way that they could be felt rather than merely observed.

This notion of the personal sphere of emotion, elaborated by critics such as Charlotte Brunsdon (1981 and 1991) was of crucial importance in developing work on how women were represented and what they signified. The separation of the public and private spheres, which we saw in play in potential readings of the royal photographs, was identified as a key device in both defining femininity and denigrating it. The domestic space of the home and the problems of personal relationships, particularly in the family, are constructed as being female concerns; the work needed to keep the home and family going is not given the same recognition or status (let alone pay) as that performed in the public sphere. Soap opera, it was argued, was one of the few formats on television that both acknowledged the nature of women's work in the private sphere and endorsed it. Soap operas may represent women in the traditional roles (the mother, the bitch) that so outraged the fans of *Cagney and Lacey* but did not identify them as 'lesser'. The women in soaps were portrayed as wives, mothers, daughters, girlfriends, and many of the stories revolved around the emotional problems generated by these relationships. What was important, however, and what gave women viewers pleasure was the care and intensity with which the problems in these relationships were played out and the value given to women's role in maintaining them.

In endorsing soap operas and the relationship they establish with women viewers, feminist media theorists, including myself, found themselves in a somewhat paradoxical position. Awareness of the processes of signification meant that such writers distanced themselves from complaints about the misrepresentation of women on television while at the same time the re-evaluation of soap opera meant that, in media theory, feminism was strongly associated with programmes that privileged the traditionally feminine associations between women and emotions. Carrying this further, some writers have seen in the relationship created between soap operas and their female audiences the potential for women to defy dominant understandings of femininity and the appropriate position of women. This possibility centred on the creation of a separate 'gendered, oppositional space' in which women may 'produce their own meanings and strategies' (Seiter *et al.*, 1991: 244). Women's recognition of and identification with the world represented by soaps combined with the discussion and gossip that marks soap opera viewing to create a space in which women might express the inexpressible. In this space, it is argued, what Mary Ellen Brown calls 'a feminine discourse' (1990: 190) can be established in which emotional relationships can be discussed in terms of power and the subordinated position of women in their social roles can be acknowledged by women viewers. In this analysis, the viewer is not merely active in the process of understanding media products, as we saw in the previous section, but also resistant. In the gendered space of soap watching, women viewers may recognize the constraints under which women operate and acknowledge the pain they cause or mockingly defy them. Soaps allow them to recognize not so much real women but the reality of their position and put them in a position, potentially, to resist more dominant and oppressive modes of representation.

Work on soap opera has been extremely fruitful in opening up work on representation and it has gone well beyond the textual analysis associated with semiotic work on representation. It has drawn attention to the constructions of femininity and masculinity that frame our understanding and has demanded that attention be paid to the intimate detail of the audience's relationship with particular modes of representation. Two more general processes should be noted in this work. First, it is rooted in the notion that soap operas can be understood not so much as a mass media product imposing a particular kind of representation on women from above but as a product of popular culture, claimed from below because it can support women's resistance to male domination. Thus, while production issues are important (particularly when as in the case of *Cagney and Lacey* they can change or stop the programme), the meaning and importance of the representations lie with the audience. Second, the emphasis in this work has been on how meaning is established within the context of domestic viewing and often in talk between women viewers. The call for greater realism in the images of women seemed to indicate a need for a public acknowledgement of the importance of representation and a change in how such representations are produced. Work on soaps, on the other hand, gives greater value to consumption and the possibilities of resistance in consumption. In this shift, the argument has moved on to more private and hidden terrain, the space of the feminine. How far the resistances of 'feminine discourse' can translate into change and activity outside the 'gendered space' remains for me an unanswered question.

Representation and emergency shows

Programmes such as soaps, with the exception of some British programmes, make little claim to the realist project of reflecting the world; for other programmes, however, engagement with events and issues of debate in the public world is crucial to their success. In this final section, I want to turn to this type of television programming and take as an example those programmes that deal with crimes and emergencies, and dramatize events that have happened to 'real people'. In looking at such programmes, I want raise further questions about representation, focusing in particular on the increasingly blurred lines between factual and fictional presentation of material in this area, and ask how far the tools provided by semiotics are adequate for their analysis.

Television has a strong tradition of using the drama of emergency work by the police or medical staff, in particular, as the basis for programmes. The documentaries in this field follow John Corner's dictum that most documentary work is premised on the 'powerful way in which recording apparatus can certify the independent existence of that which is recorded' (1990: viii). This emphasis on accurate reflection is present also in fictional representations of the police such as the US series *NYPD* and the British *The Bill*, and in other programmes featuring the emergency services, such as *Casualty* (hospital and ambulance services) and *London's Burning* (the fire service). *The Bill*, for instance, employs 'resident experts on police procedure' who are involved in plot development at an early stage to 'ensure fiction stays in step with reality' (broadcast, 14 October 1994: 23).

Semiotics, as we have seen, challenged the notion that meaning was transparent, was imminent in some world outside and could thus be communicated through an accurate reflection of it. In their analysis, media theorists have used semiotics to contest not only this notion of reflection but also to query the traditional dividing lines between fact and fiction which were based on it. In looking at documentary or actuality material, such critics noted the importance of fictional constructions in shaping the audience's understanding. An early example of work in this area is provided in an article by Cary Bazelgette and Richard Paterson (1981) on British television's coverage of the siege of the Iranian Embassy in London in 1980. The article focused on the ending of the siege when the SAS (the Special Air Services regiment) stormed the building and rescued the hostages while killing five of the six men who had been holding them; this outcome was shown 'live' on television (with some use of time lapses) and the BBC's Editor of Television News declared that the broadcast was 'a definitive example of just how high standards of broadcast journalism really are in this country' (Schlesinger, 1981: 29). Bazelgette and Paterson, however, refused this discourse of journalism with its emphasis on the reporting and recording of events and emphasized also 'the conventions and codings involved in the construction of the story' (55). What was offered to the television viewers was, they suggested, a representation that could best be understood through fictional codes; 'it was the convention and myth of thrillers that spilled out of fiction into the Bank Holiday's evening's viewing' (59). In this reading, particular emphasis was placed on the conventions of narrative as a chain of events connected by cause and effect and leading to closure. Far from raising troubling questions about the use of military force by the state, the violence of the ending was acceptable in part because it was narratively appropriate; 'the existence of a narrative structure . . . enabled the thriller ending, the storming of the embassy by the SAS appearing magically as if from nowhere, in disguise, to be accommodated' (60). The constructed nature of the event and its creation of meaning through fictional devices is revealed through the act of criticism and was not evident to the makers nor, presumably, the participants.

A recent development in television programming has been the integration of documentary and fiction formats into the emergency show in which real events are used either through video and/or reconstruction as the basis for the programme. Sarah Kozloff describes the US programme *Rescue 911* as blending 'reenactments and documentary footage, actors and "real people", to recreate the "true stories" of victims of life-threatening situations, victims who were saved by the assistance of emergency personnel' (1992: 73). British versions of such programmes feature the police, ambulance personnel, the fire service, and even, in *Police Stop*, video recordings of vehicle accidents and incidents on motorways.

In most cases, programmes such as this use the notion of public service as a guarantee of their good intent. Typical in this is the BBC's *Crimewatch UK*, produced with the active co-operation of the police, which seeks to involve the public by using reconstructions of crimes to prompt viewers to ring in with information that might help to solve them; or *Rescue 911* which frames each story with suggestions on how accidents might be avoided or ameliorated by the actions of ordinary people as well as those of the emergency personnel; or *Police Stop*, which provides a stern commentary on the perils of bad driving to accompany the bumps and crashes featured in the official video.

Alongside these moral purposes, however, the programmes also employ and place a value on devices that are more usually the property of fiction. The stories of *Rescue 911* are as Kozloff indicates 'excruciatingly suspenseful' (73), relying on fast cutting, action hidden from the protagonists but not the viewer, and a piling up of incident. The compressed nature of the story means that characters are flat rather than rounded and are used to stand for positions and emotions (victim, fearful mother). This together with the exemplary nature of the stories gives them a melodramatic tone not normally associated with the narrative devices of documentary practice. Programmes, like *Crimewatch UK* which reconstruct murder or violent attacks inevitably show women or the elderly in the vulnerable positions made familiar by crime fiction, in the dark streets or hearing suspicious noises within the fragile home. The attraction of *Police Stop* is to allow a voyeuristic viewing of the crashes and spills made familiar in feature film car chases, sometimes using music or humorous comment to accompany the less serious episodes. These programmes do not try to present themselves merely as reports or to disguise their construction, their use of narrative and other devices more commonly associated with fiction; instead they make construction overt, presenting re-construction as part of their attraction, inviting the audience to be engaged in the emotional pull of the drama as well as to play the part of concerned public citizens.

These programmes, therefore, pose a particular kind of problem with regard to representation and the use of semiotics to understand images that are based on people who have an existence outside the programmes' images. Bill Nichols has suggested limitations to the semiotic approach when it comes to documentary generally. He comments on the way in which such an approach takes images of people as signifiers with meaning dependent on their relation to other elements in the signifying chain. 'Useful as this approach may be to the refutation of the notion of transparency between image and reality,' he goes on, 'it does not quell the disturbances semiosis sets up in the bodies of those who have their image "taken". Legal principles of privacy, libel and slander attest to some of the dimensions of conflict' (1991: 271). While semiotics has been helpful in thinking through the implications of the visual image for the viewer's understanding, he suggests that it does not provide a framework for addressing the political, moral and ethical questions that arise over the position of the viewed.

This seems particularly pertinent in the case of the emergency shows where it is precisely the fact of their basis in real people's lives that lends urgency and immediacy to the programmes. The programmes do not need to resort to the fictional accuracy of *The Bill* or *NYPD* because their stake in real events is of a different order. Kozloff suggests that the suspense of *Rescue 911* is based in part on our sense that the stories have 'the unpredictability, the unforeseeable "messiness", of "real life"' and that 'the show capitalizes on a certain "reality effect" – knowing that the action really transpired along these lines makes the peril and the stakes much higher than they would be in an overtly fictional text' (1992: 74). *Crimewatch UK* reiterates the reality of the events it deals with by its use of surveillance video recordings, the interviews with relatives or survivors and the emphasis on dates and times which, quite apart from their value to the detecting process, give a particular sense of being there. The blurred video images of *Police Stop*, far from detracting from the programme, reinforce its sense of being fleetingly captured from another source that had different purposes – reality literally as it moves.

The unease engendered in this combination of fictional display and documentary appeal seems to be present in the punctuation which Kozloff uses in her description of *Rescue 911*; the inverted commas around "real people", "real life" and "reality effect" indicate an understandable uncertainty about the status of the concepts being referred to by these television images. For if these images are signifiers like any other why should they be marked as different except that our entertainment relies precisely on them being different? This distinctive emphasis on a reality base has extended in the 1990s to a wide range of programmes including docu-soaps such as *Hotel* (1997) on British television and US daytime talk shows such as *Ricki Lake* (1993). The talk shows, in particular, draw attention to their construction and theatricality (Shattuc, 1998) but the allegation that the shows actually make up, rather than provoke, the emotional displays on which they rely calls into question their status. It is not just their integrity but their value as entertainment that is diminished if they are revealed as only construction.

Conclusion

In looking at issues of representation through these three case studies, I have tried to show the ways in which semiotic methods, with their emphasis on construction and convention, have been helpful in analysing how images are understood in the mass media. Through such analysis, media theory has begun to describe the complex process of understanding that we bring to a newspaper photograph, a television fiction or a piece of news footage and has challenged the notion, so deeply embedded in our common-sense responses, that visual images rely on revelation rather than construction and process. In addition, semiotics drew attention to the possibilities of an active role for the audience in understanding such constructions and paved the way for work on the relationship between text and viewer which characterizes feminist writing on soaps. But I have marked also points where it seems to me that semiotics led to something of an impasse. Such a moment occurred when, as Pollock described, feminists tried to make a bridge between 'images of women' and 'real women'. In writing on soap opera and women's fiction, it was possible to move out of that dilemma by working with the grain of feminine/female representations and to find the possibilities of resistance within them. The emergency shows, too, which use reality as entertainment also raise questions about representation that are difficult to think through in a framework bound by semiotics. As with soaps it would be possible to focus on the potential of audience resistance, as Shattuc (1998) does, by stressing the way in which audience members are translated into performers and given partial access to the telling of their own story. Nevertheless, questions still remain about who has the power to control and organize meaning and how those meanings are understood and used. To answer these questions, we need political and ethical frameworks and audience research methods that go beyond the vocabulary of representation.

Notes

1. Helpful general accounts can be found in Culler (1976), Turner (1990) and Seiter (1992), among others.
2. Useful studies of the Diana phenomenon written immediately after her death can be found in *Screen* (spring 1998) and in *Planet Diana* (Re:Public, 1997).
3. The article was mainly concerned with photography but similar arguments were made about images on film and television.

References

ANG, I., 1985: *Watching Dallas*, London: Methuen.
BARTHES, R., 1977: *Image – Music – Text*, Heath, S. (trans.), London: Fontana.
——, 1993: *Camera Lucida*, London: Vintage.
BAZALGETTE C. and PATTERSON R., 1981: 'Real entertainment: the Iranian embassy siege', *Screen Education*, winter 1980/1, No. 37.
BROWN, M.E., 1990: 'Motley moments: soap opera, carnival, gossip and the power of utterance' in M.E. Brown (ed.), *Television and Women's Culture,* London: Sage.
BRUNSDON, C., 1981: 'Crossroads: Notes on soap opera', *Screen*, Vol. 22, No. 4.
——, 1991: 'Pedagogies of the feminine: feminist teaching and women's genres', *Screen*, Vol. 32, No. 4.
CORNER, J., 1986: 'Codes and cultural analysis' in Collin R. *et al.* (eds) *Media, Culture and Society*, London: Sage.
——, 1990: 'Preface.' in Corner, J. (ed.), *Documentary and the Mass Media*, London: Edward Arnold.
CULLER, J., 1976: *Saussure*, London: Fontana.
D'ACCI, J., 1994: *Defining Women: Television and the case of Cagney and Lacey*, Chapel Hill: University of North Carolina Press.
GERAGHTY, C., 1991: *Women and Soap Opera*, Oxford: Polity Press.
KOZLOFF, S., 1992: 'Narrative theory and television' in R. Allen (ed.), *Channels of Discourse*, London: Routledge.
LOVELL, T., 1981: 'Ideology and *Coronation Street*' in R Dyer (ed.), *Coronation Street,* London: British Film Institute.
NICHOLS, B., 1990: 'Questions of magnitude' in Corner, J. (ed.), *Documentary and the Mass Media*, London: Edward Arnold.
——, 1991: *Representing Reality*, Bloomington and Indianapolis: Indiana University Press.
POLLOCK, G., 1977: 'What's wrong with images of women?', *Screen Education*, autumn, No. 24.
Re:Public, 1997: *Planet Diana Cultural Studies and Global Mourning*, Kingswood: Research Centre in Intercommunal Studies, University of Western Sydney Nepean.
SCHLESINGER, P., 1981: 'Princes Gate 1980: the media politics of siege management', *Screen Education*, winter 1980/1, No. 37.
SCREEN, 1998: 'Flowers and tears: the death of Diana, Princess of Wales', spring, Vol. 39, No. 1.
SEITER, E., 1992: 'Semiotics, structuralism and television' in R. Allen (ed.), *Channels of Discourse*, London: Routledge.
SEITER, E., BORCHERS, H., KREUTZNER, G. and WARTH, E., 1991: '"Don't treat us like we're so stupid and naive": towards an ethnography of soap opera viewers' in Seiter, E., Borchers, H., Kreutzner, G. and Warth, E. (eds), *Remote Control*, London: Routledge.
SHATTUC, J., 1998: '"Go, Ricki": politics, perversion and pleasure in the 1990s' in C. Geraghty and Lusted, D. (eds), *The Television Studies Book,* London: Arnold.
TURNER, G., 1990: *British Cultural Studies*, London: Routledge.

19

'Influence': The Contested Core of Media Research

John Corner

The idea of the media as agencies of influence was the central idea in the earliest studies of mass communication and it retains its centrality in the expanded and intellectually more diverse sphere of current international media research. Indeed, there can be few more provocative questions to ask a media researcher anywhere in the world, no matter what their sub-specialism, than 'How do notions of media influence inform your enquiries?' There would be many wary responses to this question, including some that would wish to deconstruct its terms, but the answers would rarely lack interest. Even 'not at all' would open up some illuminating further dialogue.

In many studies, influence is an implicit premise. Much enquiry into policy, for instance, or into the production of news or changes in media formats and styles, although it may not raise the question of influence directly, is given its significance by ideas about the political, social and cultural consequences media processes carry. In other studies, however, 'influence', variously defined, becomes the primary focus of investigation by the use of a number of concepts and methods which are often the cause of dispute. Across the history of media research, the various strands of enquiry into 'influence' constitute the largest body of theoretical and empirical scholarship, and also the one that has attracted the greatest amount of funding from both public and corporate sponsors.

This may be contrasted with literary study or even the majority of studies of cinema, where a sense of the intrinsic aesthetic interest of texts themselves prevails, and where an interest in the 'social' is more likely to be a matter of the contexts of production and of thematic and formal resources than anything to do with what follows socially from a book being read or a film being screened – although questions of this kind are, on occasion, the source of broader public alarm, particularly in relation to violent or sexually explicit cinema.

Such an emphasis, implicit or explicit, on questions of influence, can be related to two features of media systems worldwide, whatever its other origins. First of all, the modern media are primary producers and distributors of popular knowledge, most routinely, though by no means exclusively, in the form of news. This is still regarded as one of their core functions, and consideration of it immediately raises questions about the relationship between the circulation of public knowledge and the nature of the political and social order. These questions are of profound historical importance in the development of ideas about democracy, about the interplay between state or corporate publicity and public opinion, and about the proper role of journalism and the criteria for judging this role. The continuing pertinence of such issues is well attested by other chapters in this book. Then there is the sheer *scale* of mediation in modern societies, the routine permeation of everyday life by the products and systems of major sectors of international as well as national industry. Although it is many years since the arrival of radio and then television reshaped the contours both of the everyday and 'the public', a sense of the possible power of the media follows partly from the magnitude and intensity of their operations as well as from their privileged role in knowledge circulation.

Yet, given all this, there has been in the recent academic literature both a growing dissatisfaction with the way in which 'influence' has been studied and suggestions that we may need to move beyond the very idea itself to other ways of investigating how the media are implicated in modern life. This dissatisfaction has been expressed from within the social scientific strand of enquiry, where the long history of experimental and fieldwork studies appears to provide little to sustain a clear narrative of 'progress' (see Cumberbatch and Howitt, 1989; Gauntlett, 1995). It has also been expressed from within the newer strands of cultural studies work; here, the steady displacement of 'ideology' as a primary term of analysis (a term very much to do with kinds of influence) by a newer focus on reception and interpretation, and by an often 'postmodern' framing of questions of pleasure, choice and identity, has changed the character of the field and its ways of thinking about power (Curran, 1990, picked up on aspects of this change; see also McGuigan, 1992; and the more recent critical treatment in Philo and Miller, 2000).

In this chapter, I want to consider aspects of the past, present and future of 'influence' in media research. Although I shall refer to some of the many available reviews of the influence literature, my concern will not be with offering another overview of decades of study but with setting influence in a more developed social theoretical context than is routinely provided for it. I want to provide a framework for thinking critically about the idea of influence and the ways it has been, and can be, put to work in enquiry. Some reviews of 'influence and effects' have essentially been exercises in bibliography with a thin connecting thread of descriptive commentary. My intentions are different, but I recognize the need for any reader new to the area quite quickly to refer what I say to specific studies, historical and current, perhaps first of all in the digest forms variously available in the literature and then selectively in closer detail. For readers who wish to gain a broader overview of particular methodological developments I can do no better than refer them, in the first instance, to the two previous editions of this book, in which McLeod *et al.* (1991) and Livingstone (1996) offer detailed and clear accounts. In particular, I have found Livingstone's review, and her attempt at assessing recent re-orientation, extremely useful in my own teaching and in preparing this present chapter.

The core of my account will explore some of the different ways in which 'influence' has been perceived as a research goal and the more important arguments that surround it. There have been arguments at the level of theories and concepts, often showing their awareness of broader public anxieties, and others that have been focused primarily at the level of methodology. Perhaps more than in any other area of media research, debates about influence and effects have tended to be 'method driven' – they have been about procedures of measurement – in a way which I think has finally had unfortunate consequences for the address to more general questions concerning *what* precisely is being researched. Nordenstreng (1968) brings this out well in a review which retains its pertinence across a 30-year gap, noting that 'the field is full of technicians, but the engineers and idea-men are not numerous' (211).

'Influence' is not, of course, a term used solely about the consequences of the media. This is a point worth taking a little further.

Influence, society and individuals

In common usage, 'influence' is a term premised on the implicit conventions of individual self-determination on the one hand, and interpersonal and social existence on the other; conventions which are always in tension in modern societies. We talk of being 'influenced' when we can discern a significant causal link between external factors and a view we have formed or perhaps an action we have undertaken, where *other* possibilities practically existed (i.e. there was no direct constraint on outcomes either through objective circumstances or human coercion).

In many spheres of life, we freely admit to being 'influenced' – by parents, by educational institutions, by friends, colleagues and partners. We can boast of this influence, and be proud of it as a positive formative feature in making us who we are. Celebrities are fond of doing this, in newspaper or broadcast interviews. Or we can regret it, as an unwelcome contribution which perhaps has had to be countered. Certainly, to be 'easily influenced' is not seen to be a good thing, indicating too little firmness in the boundaries separating the inner us from the outer world. And, in social exchange, we may sometimes wish to affirm our self-determinative powers against suggestions, explicit or otherwise, that our actions or opinions can be directly attributed to external causes in a way that seems to demean our own strength of identity and our ability to regulate ourselves as persons-in-the-world.

All this suggests a level of anxiety about 'influences' in social life at the same time as it points to a widespread acceptance of them as routine phenomena ranging in scale and kind from the marginal influence of a schoolfriend in the forming of a taste for a kind of music to the sustained and perhaps calculated influence of a parent in the development of general social attitudes. Perhaps we might need to distinguish, too, between those routine relations of influence where the subject of influence *uses* external guides, including the judgements of others, as a factor in determining opinion or action (and therefore as a factor in some form of *deliberation*) and those where an intentional, persuasive effect is *exerted upon* the subject. The former can be seen as instances of *circumstantial influence*, the latter as instances of *directed influence*, although a real distinction between the two will in many cases be hard to achieve. We can also note how the first category is so broad as to involve, in varying degrees, most spheres of social action. This sort of influence is a necessary and continuous part of being an individual in society – we are registering a steady flow of influential 'messages' every day. The second sort is open to ethical dispute of a kind that has been at the centre of the debate about advertising's impact upon social identity and modes of living and which, at the political level, becomes the long-running debate about the right use of 'persuasion' and 'publicity' within democratic societies, where the free exercise of popular judgement is a founding principle (see Mayhew, 1997, for a review).

Perspectives on media influence

One of the reasons why questions continue to be posed so sharply about media influence is that 'the media' are still a relatively recent phenomenon in their electronic, mass-systemic form. Although they have, in most modern societies, become naturalized as a part of everyday existence, in a paradoxical way they can still often be thought of as a set of institutions and processes somehow distinct from the core identity of social and individual life. So, for instance, there is 'American life' and then the 'American media'. If this view is held too rigidly, the question of the 'impact' of media upon politics, society and culture can be asked in a way that posits the action of one discrete entity upon another and thereby perhaps adds a sense of alien intrusion to anxieties about the processes of influence.

If we pose the rather unhelpfully general question 'Are the media influential or not?', then it is hard to imagine any intelligent person saying 'No'. That is to say, there is a widespread assumption that, at this very general level, the media can be seen to exert various discernible influences upon the nature and direction of social life. It is useful here to distinguish between their influence upon *institutionalized processes* (upon the 'system level' as some sociological work describes it, see for instance McLeod *et al.*, 1991) and their influence upon *individual consciousness* (and, indeed, upon the individual subconscious too).

Taking the former, the spheres of political organization and processes, the funding and organization of sport and the styles, tastes and values of youth culture would be just three examples of areas where the media have exerted a profound shaping influence internationally. Evidence for this is richly manifest in the economic and institutional documentation of these areas – for instance in the changing character of electoral campaigns, in the way in which football in Britain has developed over the last decade and in the marketing pattern of the commodities (clothing, music and leisure activities) that underpin youth culture.

If we turn to the individual level, documentation may be far less easily to hand. However, if we admit the idea of 'circumstantial influence' outlined above, then it is commonly accepted that every day, in a variety of ways, people are 'influenced' by what they read in newspapers, hear on radio and see on television. A holiday programme may convince them to visit Greece in summer, a feature on cancer prevention may finally persuade them towards a healthier diet, a series of news reports on child abductions may lead them, at least temporarily, to become more concerned about their children's trip to school. As I write, there is little doubt that images on television are playing some part in the formation of their perceptions (and also mine) about the justness of NATO actions in Kosovo. Some of these ways of using the media as a resource may not strike them as being 'influence' but it would be my view, to which I shall return, that there is no good reason for discounting these myriad and mundane ways in which mediation carries implications for the formation of understanding, judgement and the conduct of life. We must note that media influence is very unlikely to be the *sole causal factor* at work here and that in many cases an *intention to persuade* (leading to what I termed earlier 'directed influence') may not be present. To make assumptions of this kind begs large questions and goes many steps beyond the recognition that a relation of influence exists.

In considering both these levels of media influence, the argument starts in earnest when we try to calculate the precise scale and nature of the influence which areas or items of media output have had on specific actions and behaviours. Although, as I have noted, we may find that much influence upon institutionalized processes can be evidenced through existing documentation (e.g. official reports, policy documents, marketing surveys, social statistics), this aid to enquiry will neither preclude the need for more detailed investigation nor prevent dispute. Assessing precisely how the media have contributed to the decisions and actions of individuals will, however, present a very distinctive challenge both of data collection and measurement. In both cases, establishing the *social origins* of influencing elements (as, for example, in specific intentions, corporate goals or structures of production) will be very difficult to do, although it might seem very important to attempt.

The above view of influence, unexceptionable though it might seem, is in fact at odds with one strand of media influence enquiry. This strand works with the idea that the finding of influence *per se* is of significance. It also assumes that where influence is found, in whatever sphere, then its presence is likely to be a bad thing. One reason for this is that many researchers have worked with a quite specific model of what is involved in media influence. They have often either seen it exclusively within the terms of the 'persuasion paradigm', as the result of propagandistic and manipulative design, intended somehow to 'trick' or bypass the rational processes of the audience (as, for instance, in much political communication and in advertising) or they have seen media portrayals to be a stimulus strong enough to generate emotional states which in turn induce bad behaviour (as, classically, in a long-running strand of research into screen violence). In both cases, there has been a tendency to ignore or at least to underestimate the way in which the media are *symbolic processes*, working through the production of meaning. Allowing for the ways in which social circumstances act as 'variables' in the influence the media have is one thing – the research tradition has been alert to the need for differentiation here – but recognizing what is involved in making *cultural sense* of media output opens up a further, and vital, dimension to the study of how the output of the media bears on perception, attitude and action.

We can say, then, that some research into influence has had a tendency to make two mistakes. It has closed down the definition of 'influence' in a way that does not take full account of the consequential character of the range of media–social and media–individual relationships routinely occurring in modern societies. And it has ignored, or at least underestimated, the complexities of cultural interpretation and evaluation that come into play when media products, their images, speech and writing, are attended to by diverse audiences. The term 'effects' has often been used in this narrower tradition of work and, whilst it might be considered in many contexts to be a synonym for 'influence', I think it can also be seen as a term even more vulnerable to simplistic usage in respect both of the kind and strength of the causality implied. We certainly need to be concerned about the various processes of calculated public persuasion within a society. We need to ask questions about the use of the media as instruments of power (for a fine discussion of the way ideas about 'power' often relate confusingly to those about 'influence' see Wrong, 1998). But seeing the influence of the media entirely within the framework of this concern is a mistake which will work to limit argument and enquiry.

Research into influence: a broad typology

Classifications of research by period or by conceptual and methodological orientation are extensively present in the review literature, to varying degrees of detail. Here, I simply want to suggest four broad strands of work on media 'influences and effects' in order to support my own commentary. Simplification and foreshortening are very high risks and I refer the reader to more detailed schemes for anything like an adequate historical account or for proper differentiation between strands and sub-strands (Gauntlett, 1995, is a recent overview as well as a critique). McQuail (1977 and 1994) offers a broad itemization which I have found useful, but there are many more specialized attempts at imposing schematic order (for instance, that of Blumler and Gurevitch, 1982; McLeod et al., 1994, concerning political effects studies; and Vine, 1997, on studies of violence).

The early 'mass society' perspective

This is largely a speculative, philosophical engagement with the possibilities of media influence, occasioned by the arrival of modern media systems (particularly radio) into society. American writers such as Lippmann and Dewey wrote in the 1920s about some of the risks that new forms of mediated knowledge introduced into the established political and social system, radically changing, and perhaps distorting, the existing character and flow of information as a resource of citizenship (Lippmann, 1922; Dewey, 1927). The experience of Fascism in Europe directed a number of social theorists, including the notable Frankfurt School scholar Theodor Adorno, towards the analysis of mass psychology and the new techniques of 'persuasion' (see the collection of work in Adorno, 1991). Adorno, along with several other cultural intellectuals, emigrated to America in the 1930s and therefore helped to bring to bear this tradition of critical anxiety on the distinctive commercial profile of radio and then television in the United States. The tenor of much writing is that the mass media are potentially both powerful and negative agencies of 'control'. Their rapid growth and its impact are seen as just cause for cultural and political concern, if not alarm.

'Effects' as a focus for empirical social science

There is a rich, highly differentiated, multi-stranded body of work which develops in the 1930s and, under steady revision, runs through to current study, although I will suggest the value of regarding work since the 1980s within the terms of a separate classification. A number of distinguished scholars make their mark on this broad phase of study – Paul Lazarsfeld and Elihu Katz notable among them (see, for instance, the classically defining work on media and opinion formation in Lazarsfeld *et al.*, 1944, and Katz and Lazarsfeld, 1955). There is an emphasis here on inventively applying the tools of sociology and social psychology to the measurement of various kinds of influence. Sociological models are used in creating new approaches to survey analysis and to the conceptualization of influence as working within a diversified social system, whilst social psychology informs work on the mechanisms of influence and devises 'experimental' methods for reproducing influence processes in controlled conditions allowing closer observation than data collection by survey or fieldwork. There is a concern with questions of *duration* – the spans of time over which lines of influence can be plotted – and a growing belief that a registering of slow, long-term consequences may be more important than a focus on relatively rapid change. There is also an increasing awareness of different *outcomes* of influence, including the difference between change of opinion and reinforcement of opinion and a recognition of the complex nature of the relationship between mental changes and behavioural action (such as voting).

To attempt to characterize any common findings across a classification so stretched is extremely hazardous, given the sheer range of work undertaken over a considerable period of time. However, by framing enquiries within an increased awareness of the social and psychological variables intervening between 'message' and 'influence' (Katz and Lazarsfeld, 1955, for instance, brought out strongly the way in which forms of social interaction modified any 'straight' media–audience relationship) accounts were produced that were far less dramatic in their assessment of media impact than the earlier, more speculative commentaries. The idea of a 'limited effects' model gained ground, producing a revised and cooler climate of discussion (if not at times a complacency) about the media's functions in society. Work on violence tended to be something of an exception, perhaps due partly to the highly charged nature of public feeling on this topic and to the continuing popular salience of the idea that media depictions are one important cause of violent behaviour.

Although it might best be regarded as a separate development from influence studies and indeed a reaction to them, the approach of 'Uses and Gratifications' research, which developed in the 1940s, and was redeveloped in the 1960s and 1970s on both sides of the Atlantic (see Blumler and Katz, 1974), is strongly related to the intellectual perspectives of this body of research. In the innovative work gathered together under the label, an 'audience-end' focus is introduced, the question now being, in a classic phrasing, 'what audiences do *with* the media' rather than 'what the media do *to* audiences'. In placing the emphasis on audience use rather than media impact, 'Uses and Gratifications' can be seen as having much in common with the later development of 'reception studies' from within cultural studies (see below).

Neo-Marxist perspectives on ideology

Marxist theories of ideology, theories about the strategic circulation of forms of 'common sense' which work to the benefit of dominant economic groups, only minimally informed studies in the social science tradition, but their impact on

European (including British) work in the developing area of cultural studies was formative in the 1970s and 1980s. Drawing on the writings of the French social philosopher Louis Althusser (particularly 1971) and the pioneer British cultural analyst Stuart Hall, accounts of ideological reproduction as, in part, a consequence of the media, put far more emphasis on the linguistic/symbolic character of mediation than had most work in the social sciences. They also mixed a strongly pessimistic vein about the power of the media (comparable in some instances with the early mass society theorists) with a slightly contradictory sense of the complexities and internal tensions of perception and of consciousness underlying such categories as 'attitude' and 'opinion' (the widely influential study of television – Fiske and Hartley, 1978 – shows both these characteristics). 'Ideology' was essentially a term of theoretical critique rather than of empirical investigation. However, the application of it within substantive audience research produced (most notably in Morley, 1980) what has become one of the most marked new emphases in the international media research of the last two decades – a reception analysis grounded in the plotting of audience interpretation (see, for instance, the reviews in Lewis, 1991; Morley, 1992; Moores, 1993; Corner, 1991 and 1996; Livingstone, 1998a). It is a rather ironic twist in research history that an attempt to produce a strong account of media influence in new terms ended up by discovering so much intervening complexity that it gave (unintended) encouragement to a perspective often seen as inimical to the whole idea of 'influence and effects'. I shall comment further on this in a later section.

Revised and interdisciplinary perspectives

This final category is more impressionistic than the others and, like 'Effects' (above), it holds together diverse studies. What connects them is their formation within a changed intellectual climate. Although earlier scholars were often alert self-critics and although the value of spanning disciplinary boundaries is not a new perception, few areas of media research have remained immune from the energetic disputes about conceptualization and method that have swept across both the arts and the social sciences in recent years. Perhaps studies of influence and effects have been the focus of more sceptical, and sometimes openly hostile, attention than any other sub-field.

Yet, internationally, the empirical investigation of influence continues and, although it does so with considerable variation, some mutual ignorance and a good deal of mutual suspicion, there is more awareness of symbolic form and interpretation, of the complexities of consciousness and action, and of the contingencies of culture, than at any previous period. (The essays in three collections – Bryant and Zillman, 1994; Hay et al., 1996; and Dickinson et al., 1998 – show this well at the level both of debate and of substantive study.) There is now a broader sense of the range, variety and complexity of the media's involvement in resourcing consciousness and informing social organization. A 'cognitivist' approach, stressing the conditions and mechanisms of understanding, has become dominant across many sectors of enquiry, together with a judgement that many earlier 'limited effects' findings were at least partly the consequence of the limitations in research design. This has to be seen in perspective. The very idea of 'limited effects' was in part a cautious, empirical response to earlier tendencies towards alarmist speculation about 'unlimited effects' and it therefore cannot be understood properly without the previous history of commentary. But a more refined, elaborated and qualified engagement with the notions of 'agenda-setting' (how the media might *help* to define the terms of public debate), 'priming' (how certain themes might be made prominent by their media coverage), and 'framing' (how media accounts draw on and implicitly reproduce given social and political assumptions, marginalizing others) has given further subtlety to enquiry. Iyengar and Kinder (1987) is a classic experimental study here (into the consequences of political news on TV for popular knowledge and judgement), making good use of a range of research approaches of the kind I discuss below and reflecting critically on previous attempts at plotting media power. Scheufele (1999) offers a recent and valuable account of how the concept of 'framing' (again, a strongly cognitivist idea, to do with the media as constructors of knowledge) has been variously used in theories of media influence.

At the same time, investigations into the conditions of public and popular knowledge have drawn extensively from the recorded speech of interviews and group discussions, often displaying a concern for interpretative variables similar to that of reception analysis (Neuman, Just and Crigler, 1992, is one influential example). The kinds of bearing media have on the practices by which people sustain their general sense of cultural membership and attendant values have received attention from a number of perspectives, among them the 'cultural indicators' project devised by the eminent American scholar, George Gerbner. Here, the idea of 'cultivation' replaces the idea of 'effects' in order to suggest better the cultural centrality and depth of the processes under investigation (see, for instance, Gerbner *et al.*, 1994; Shanahan and Morgan, 1999).

Each approach has, within the new climate, been subject to critical debate and, as I noted earlier, it would be wrong to emphasize mutuality in a situation where disciplinary division and firm disagreement (about, for instance, the importance of statistical indicators) is still apparent. But a greater cross-disciplinary engagement and more imaginative and reflexive research designs are nevertheless establishing themselves, with results now evident at conferences and in journals.

Measurement, evidence and proof

In studies of media influence, the requirement for measurement, and particularly for quantitative indicators, follows both from the grounding protocols of social scientific research and, often too, from the desirability of funding agencies having a clear, statistical basis for the corporate and/or public changes of policy that 'findings' might suggest. Research had needed to produce indicators as independent as possible from speculative opinion, given the sensitivity of many of the questions at issue and the controversiality of the practical options of research-using bodies (including tougher forms of regulation).

Behaviour is clearly a stronger indicator to find than 'opinion' or 'attitude', which in turn are stronger than a 'perception' or a 'feeling'. As one moves further away from the media-dependent action (the purchase, the vote, the violent act) towards the various constituents of mental life, not only do questions of identification and quantification become increasingly a challenge, but the significance level of the influence, and therefore the value of the research, are at risk of being diminished.

It is interesting in this respect how often commentaries refer back to Cantril *et al.*'s (1940) study of the widespread public panic produced by the US radio broadcast of H.G. Wells's fiction *War of the Worlds* in 1938. The dramatization involved simulated news bulletins in which the reporter gave a 'live' account of a Martian invasion. Many listeners had tuned in to the programme only after it had begun and, failing to realize its fictitious status, their responses included not only alarm but physical action (leaving their homes and taking to the streets on foot and in cars in order to escape the attack). The Cantril study valuably documents media–social relations at a particular phase in the development of radio practices and radio use but what it says about media power is less clear. For the primary factor in the 'Martian invasion' scare was surely that a widespread public trust in radio journalism was unwittingly extended to a realistic simulation. At one level, what the incident tells us is that if you give an audience alarming knowledge using the format of factual information, and if a significant part of that audience fails to note that mimicry is being performed, then it is likely to become distressed. What is chiefly pointed to here, the background to the freakish drama of the event itself, is precisely that steady, routine influence of the media upon our everyday knowledge (often 'circumstantial') which I discussed in the opening part of this chapter. Certainly, no startling power of *persuasion*, as is sometimes suggested, seems evidenced, despite the pertinence of what happened to our broader social understanding of trust, interpretation, suggestibility and the psycho-social character of panic.

The *War of the Worlds* case is distinctive in so far as it shows quite marked and short-term behavioural changes in relation to one single item of media output. It is not therefore surprising that it is often referred to rather uncritically. It seems to represent the 'perfect case' of media influence, the one which researchers have so often set out either to simulate by experiments or discover by fieldwork, two lines of enquiry I now want briefly to consider as modes both of measurement and argument.

The experimental model

The experimental model for conducting research has a strong lineage in social psychology and has formed one major strand of research into influence. In experimental approaches, the researchers classically seek to measure the patterns and mechanisms of media impact by setting up controlled 'events' in which small selected audiences are exposed to media items and their responses assessed with a degree of detail only made possible by the 'laboratory conditions' prevailing. So, for instance, in the more physiological approaches, a whole range of bodily reactions can be monitored (e.g. heartbeat, eye movement, breathing and perspiration). Control of the media exposure itself allows close attention to thematic and formal features and to selectivity, for instance, in perception and recall (many reception studies can be considered 'soft' forms of experimentalism). Various 'before' and 'after' models can be applied, with questionnaires, interviews, group discussion and perhaps even practical tasks being used to indicate the parameters of change (Cumberbatch and Howitt, 1989; the excellent essays in Bryant and Zillman, 1994; Gauntlett, 1995; and Livingstone, 1996, all offer detailed commentary on the range of applications, together with examples).

The experimental model has obvious drawbacks, many of which follow from the gap between the arranged conditions and the normally obtaining social circumstances for attention and response to media materials. The researcher has to make interventions (sometimes radical) in the mediation process precisely in order to gather the data required. The real indicativeness of the results then becomes contentious as the 'distortions' introduced into the process by the structure, management and guiding terms of the research design become the focus of critical debate, particularly by those who wish to emphasize the embeddedness of the media's identity and function in everyday routine.

Within research on violence, for example, the work of Bandura *et al.* (1963) has been often cited (Livingstone, 1996, comments on it helpfully in her discussion of methodology and so does Cumberbatch, 1998). In this research, children were shown one of three short films each of which involved a different depiction of boys at play, two of the films involving violence with different outcomes for the 'attacker': victory and reward in one case, defeat and punishment in the other. When observed in a playroom through a one-way mirror, the children's subsequent behaviour was seen to show a far greater level of imitative aggression (hitting a doll) among the group that had seen the film in which violence was rewarded. The results can been as suggestive for real-life, domestic contexts but they can also be viewed as so strongly a 'construct' of the experimental situation (for instance, implicitly cueing the children into their behaviours by the setting and by the very short interval between viewing and 'play') as to have no significance whatsoever. Arguments here finally connect with central debates about the nature of the social sciences, what they can claim to 'know' and how far their techniques of enquiry can parallel those to be found in the natural sciences (see, again, Cumberbatch and Howitt 1989; Gauntlett, 1995; Cumberbatch, 1998).

Although researchers themselves have clearly recognized the special terms of their experimental settings, I think it is true that perception of the qualifications these might place on the general validity of conclusions has sometimes been displaced by an emphasis on the technical excellence of the measuring devices or the sheer statistical clarity and precision of the data pattern emerging (the point made by Nordenstreng, cited earlier). A failure of the 'sociological imagination' has occurred at these points, but I would want to suggest that to move from this judgement to a dismissal of experimentalism *per se* is to beg several questions about the aims and practical options for media enquiry which deserve a more cautious, and tolerantly inter-disciplinary, appraisal.

The field study model

The second broad approach to influence research has been through varieties of field study. Field studies cover a wide range of techniques, including surveys based on questionnaires but by no means restricted to these. Among the advantages of such techniques over 'experimental' designs are the engagement with a much broader and internally diverse sampling of population, the opportunity to connect with naturally occurring rather than experimenter-induced exposures to media material, and the chance of tracking long-term changes by longitudinal programmes of enquiry. A whole range of social setting and viewer variables can be introduced into work of this kind (e.g. of household type, of given pattern of media use, of given relation to preferred genres or to content classifications) which elude experimental research design. The recognition of these kind of variables as factors in the nature and direction of media influence has played a major part in the conceptual development of the area, moving it a long way from those ideas about vulnerable masses and suggestible minds that underpinned some of the first writings on the topic.

The disadvantages include, importantly, the real difficulties of getting close to the interface between media materials and the actual practices of reading, listening and viewing. Outside of the 'experimental' setting, a tracking of specific media discourses and the responses they produce becomes harder to achieve and tends to give way to the establishing of a broader, more abstract, and possibly more diffuse, pattern of indicators and perceived correlations. The identification of potentially significant variations in media exposure also becomes more problematic outside of a design in which 'input' is managed by the researcher. Questions about *how* the media may exert particular influences tend to be exchanged for questions about overall levels and directions of influence. Without the issue of 'How?' firmly on the agenda, correlative data and argument can often either become unhelpfully dispersed in their implications or, conversely, encourage simplistic assumptions about the actual processes at work 'behind the figures'.

As I noted above, there are indications that a more developed mutual awareness and dialogue across the different strands of work on influence and on audiences is emerging. I think this is likely to encourage a more comprehensive and connected sense of what is at issue and where present understanding is deficient. In particular, the relationship between qualitative and quantitative data and the possibilities for complementary, combined use of different kinds of evidence, are certain to provide a focus for future debate and development (see the useful discussions of this in Gavin, 1998, and Morrison, 1998). There are also signs that journalists are at least beginning to recognize that the so-called 'inconclusiveness' of influence studies (particularly in sum) is often a function of the real complexity of the processes under investigation rather than an inadequacy or unworldly naivety on the part of researchers. Less simplistic expectations here would certainly encourage a better climate for public debate.

Terms of critique and renewal

In this section, I want to consider in closer detail some aspects of the work of the last decade. I want first to look more closely at the way in which the notion of *interpretation* has become central to debate and then to consider how questions of generic difference, questions about the 'influence profiles' of distinct areas of output, have begun to figure in study.

Influence and interpretation

Taking seriously the practices of interpretation as productive of meaning can be seen to have posed three different kinds of challenge to ideas about influence. First of all, for those approaches (once dominant within cultural studies) which predicted kinds of potential influence from analysis of form and content, the demonstration of a real interpretative variety showed just how hazardous such

prediction was. The foreclosure of 'reading' by 'text', as in versions of structuralist semiotics (Fiske and Hartley, 1978, might be an example, despite its illuminating suggestiveness about form), could no longer provide a basis for
research. Second, for a wider range of studies, the extent of interpretative variation raised more general questions about the efficacy of media as agencies of
'transmission'. These were useful questions to raise, but there was sometimes a
tendency to ignore or underplay the degree of convergence and commonality of
meaning identified in reception studies in favour of an emphasis upon *difference*.
In fact, very few empirical studies (certainly not Morley, 1980) demonstrated a
scale of variation sufficient to pose an obstacle to the idea that the media were
able to perform an initiating role in the circulation of public meaning, providing
definitions, framings and 'telling' images, albeit within a complex patterning of
interpretation and value, which needed to be taken into account in any enquiry.
Homogeneity of meaning was definitely ruled out but heterogeneity was qualified by strong strands of common understanding (Curran and Sparks, 1991,
bring out this issue well in their study of the impact of the popular press). Third,
there was a stressing of audience 'resistance', drawing on the newer recognition
of interpretative activity and perceiving this activity, either in fact or in potential (the difference not always made clear), as *critical*, often following Fiske,
1987, in this emphasis. In such a view, media meanings were 'received' within
quite radically transforming terms of socially situated viewing and reading.
Viewers and readers were able routinely to apply a self-conscious scepticism that
substantially modified and even rejected that which did not fit with situated
experience and values. Within the strongest versions of this view, the problem of
media power could seem virtually to disappear altogether since, whatever the
shortcomings of media production, audiences had acquired their own internal
'immunity system' against the possibility of the media contributing negatively to
perception and to consciousness.

The extremity of this position, and its blurring of assertion, aspiration and
evidence, is well identified in Miller and Philo's excellent polemic (1996) about
the various ways in which certain strands of media research became nervous of
talking about influence. The fact that audiences drew on personal and social
frameworks of understanding and judgement in making sense and attributing
significance really provided grounds for revising, not abandoning, an enquiry
into media power. Empirical evidence of 'resistance' was at best sketchy. As
Morley himself has pointed out (see Morley, 1992, for a fine, retrospective commentary), the stronger highlighting of interpretative frameworks suggested the
need to broaden the question of the media and social power to include attention
to the cultural and discursive conditions of different audiences and readerships,
not to shift to an entirely separate agenda.

The most common initial consequence of the new emphasis on reception was
a nervous stand-off between 'interpretation' and 'influence' as key terms in the
exploration of the relationship between media and public consciousness. This
was reflected both in media studies research and in teaching. Only more recently
has there been an attempt to incorporate both terms in theory and research
design and in my concluding paragraphs I want to look at some examples of
this. First, however, following these comments on interpretation, I want to raise
the related issue of how genre and generic function are factors newly recognized
as significant.

Genre and 'influence profile'

The way in which media representations resource and guide consciousness and understanding, and therefore exert influence thorough interpretation, can be seen to vary according to generic forms and purposes (again, a point Morley has noted in assessment of his own study – see Morley, 1992 – and which has been brought out more fully in Livingstone, 1998a). This variation is not a matter of clear and firm distinctions, since the generic recipes of the media overlap and develop, with 'hybridization' a strong element in recent television formats, across both fictional and factual models. But failure to attend to questions of genre, and the way in which generic conventions cue specific kinds of viewing relation (affecting credibility, imaginative investment and interpretative approach) and not others, has been a problem in some modes of influence research, particularly in those studies of violence that have moved across generic boundaries with little sense of the implications they might carry for the viewing experience (a point brought out in Barker and Petley, 1997, particularly with respect to the controversial Newsom report on the effect of screen violence upon British children: see Newsom, 1994).

Although risking over-simplification, it is instructive to note how questions of knowledge and pleasure variously relate to genericity, taking television as an example. For instance, advertising often brings us both, but the knowledge we get from it is, in most cases, framed by our broader, generic understanding that it is advertising's job, as professional and commercial 'directed influence', to persuade us of product quality by the most effective, legal means. Routine attention to advertising is likely to involve a 'discounting effect', precisely because of the established generic function of promotion and its attendant devices of exaggeration and selectivity. As I have suggested elsewhere (Corner, 1995), advertising often involves a form of 'play' with its audiences and it has to seek its influence through the terms of this play, which may involve the use of a self-conscious appeal to fantasy.

We can contrast this with news and current affairs programming, where a well-defined knowledge effect can be exerted through a strongly projected expositional discourse combined with pictures (the specific function of images within persuasion processes across all visual genres could usefully be given more attention). There may a general 'discounting' frame at work here too, in relation to the overall credibility of TV news, but in most countries, although it may be on the increase, this is not likely to be as strong as that applied to advertising. In relation to specific news stories, however, different social and biographical factors will produce different terms of viewer engagement. A given news story will pass into audience consciousness and use within a range of interpretative possibilities, perhaps initiating diverse emotional states (e.g. indignation, disgust, delight, positive and negative affective alignments with given groups and individuals depicted). The generic function of news to define, classify and visually instantiate is not over-ridden by such item-specific and audience-sensitive variations, but we can only fully understand the exercising of this function if we take the fact of these variations into account (see Dahlgren, 1988, and Lewis, 1985, for a more developed argument on this point).

Depictions of violence occur across a number of genres. In news and documentary programmes they are likely to be communicated within terms of a journalistic knowledge-effect (as shocking *information*), however much the character and 'look' of this now varies across different news outlets. In drama, they can be used both to disgust us by the way they relate to negative kinds of human and social behaviour or please us in their appeal to fantasy and/or in their projection of strong kinetic and character values. In the former case, a social knowledge-effect is involved, since we are being invited to become involved in a degree of moral deliberation. In the latter case, whilst we may 'learn' something about the contexts and procedures of violent acts, this is secondary to the kinds of imaginative play we make with what we see and the satisfactions we draw from this. These satisfactions are likely to include fantasies of agency in which we enjoy something of the experience of being violent (again, of course, dramatic fictions vary greatly in the way their formal organization encourages this effect).

In some countries, depending on the legal controls placed upon the public circulation of images, another good example would be erotic or pornographic representation, itself taking a number of different sub-generic forms (discussed well in McNair, 1996). Here is a hugely profitable area of media representation which, in some ways like advertising, has distinct designs on its audience (most definitely, 'directed influence', even if also a function of consumer choice). It is intended both to increase sexual appetite and, for some viewers, to act as a focus for a subsequent sexual experience. The extent to which it is used as 'recipe knowledge' in sexual encounters will depend in part on the way in which the fantasy frames used in its viewing interact with the frames governing real behaviour. This, in turn, will partly be a matter of how the specific representations which might inform (and influence) behaviour relate to the broader range of cultural codes for audio-visual portrayal, how the specific acts portrayed relate to the social and cultural rules informing a given viewer's normative scheme, and then possibly how these acts are defined and perceived within a specific legal system and its sanctions. Clearly, a difference emerges when a comparison is made with most depictions of violence. I have remarked how these, too, often appeal to fantasies of 'agency' but their social acceptability (frequently a matter of public contention) depends on the retention of a firm fantasy/reality division, since their encouragement of parallel real behaviours would immediately be subject to firm social and legal sanctions. Indeed, their legitimate use is seen entirely to lie in the imagination because, unlike pornography, they do not have any outlet of acceptable activity as a point of 'conclusion' (a short-term *end* for exerted influence).

The generic dimension of media–audience relations, together with the different framings of attention and audience investment they bring, could usefully figure more strongly in future discussion of media influence and in approaches to researching it.

It is perhaps worth noting here how the study of children and the media constitutes a distinctive sub-field of research, particularly with respect to work on violent depiction and on advertising. That this is so is not surprising given the 'vulnerability' it is assumed children have as a result both of being more impressionable and less experienced than adults (an assumption that needs to be questioned in the way it directs research but that clearly carries cogency as a general observation). There is classic work in this area (Himmelweit *et al.,* 1958, connects with the strengths and empirical scope of the broader social science tradition) but some of the more recent studies (see, for instance, Hodge and Tripp,

1986; Buckingham, 1996; and Livingstone, 1998b) have shown a conceptual imagination and a methodological enterprise which often surpasses that shown in mainstream projects. They have identified processes of influence by drawing on both social science and 'cultural' perspectives and they have attempted to open a genuine cross-disciplinary debate that can both inform, *and be informed by*, teachers and parents among others. More recognition of this work and the need to develop it is now being shown by researchers in other areas, with consequent benefits for the broader conduct of enquiry.

New developments in 'public issue' research

Given much of the above, it is not perhaps surprising that some of the most interesting developments in researching influence have come from studies that look at particular public issues, thereby framing the analysis within specific thematic and temporal limits, and allowing for the fact that the consequences of mediation are likely to vary greatly with topic and with topical context. In Britain, studies from the University of Glasgow Media Research Group have been notable here for a number of reasons, constituting one mode of what Jenny Kitzinger has called the 'new effects research' (see the critical reviews in Kitzinger, 1998 and 1999). A first strong characteristic is that they have worked with the idea of viewer interpretation, and potential variation, as a primary element of research design. Second, they have incorporated close attention to viewers' and readers' own accounts within study frameworks also able to offer quantitative analysis. Third, their focus has been on knowledge, and the diverse and sometimes contradictory resourcing of knowledge, so they have not felt the pull of those more direct, linear models of impact which, in much research on depicted violence as well as on the effectiveness of political campaigning, have proved so hard to resist, despite claims to have done so. Fourth, they have developed an awareness of generic difference, recognizing that, for instance, soap operas may even be more important than news in the public circulation of knowledge about certain social themes.

The studies undertaken include, among other topics, work on public perceptions of industrial conflict (Philo, 1990), AIDS (Miller *et al.*, 1998), children and TV violence (Philo, 1999), mental illness (Philo, 1996), the BSE beef crisis (Reilly, 1999) and child sex abuse (reported concisely in Eldridge *et al.*, 1997).

A methodological feature of this work is the use, mostly alongside other techniques, of 'script writing exercises' in which sampled viewers are asked to put together a news report using a sequence of still photographs and their own commentary script. These exercises were used in the study by Philo (1990) of the 1980s coal miners' strike and have since been developed both in their design and application. As a means of assessing how far a public vocabulary for engaging with issues and problems is derived from the media and how this derivation is mixed, in different confirmatory or questioning combinations, with other sources of knowledge, the approach is productive. Like all experimental methods, it courts the risk of introducing an 'experimental effect' (here, in terms of respondent briefing and perhaps in the provision of items for the exercise) which can skew what follows. The researchers are aware of this, as they are also aware of the special challenge of adequately differentiating respondent practice which appears uncritically to replicate conventional news treatments from that which works more self-consciously as imitation, and that which articulates a criticism and, perhaps, partial alternatives. The approach nevertheless has the further broad advantage that, rather than being dispersed into a matter of discrete elements of knowledge in public circulation, the bearing of media upon consciousness is seen as significantly a matter of the *kind of stories being told* and the values that specific sets of images, phrases and descriptions exert on the way in which people perceive, and feel about, public matters. It therefore has an interest in the *narrative* aspects of knowledge – the way in which story structures project relations of value, entailment and causality – also found elsewhere in recent studies (see, for instance, Shanahan and Morgan, 1999). The account of the reporting of child abuse in Eldridge *et al.* (1997), in which Kitzinger was the principal researcher, is illuminating here in identifying the terms of interlinkage between differently sourced knowledge. It also connects its findings to some of the wider questions about influence I have attempted to explore in this chapter.

Research at Liverpool University has also pursued questions of 'influence' in work focused primarily on questions of perception and comprehension in respect of the television depiction of unemployment, nuclear energy and the economy (see Richardson and Corner, 1986; Corner *et al.*, 1990; Gavin, 1998). One feature of the Liverpool work has been its attempt to make progress with an enquiry into specific reportorial uses of imagery and language, and viewer understandings of these, while at the same time relating this to questions about the broader interpretation of a public issue as documented in viewer accounts. Understanding of the television reports and understanding of the topics themselves (both, again, raising issues concerning the narrative organization of knowledge as well as issues of informational content) converge in a way that poses a challenge for the research focus, but that also reflects the real dynamics of membership of a mediated society.

Although he has been a strong critic of social science enquiry into 'effects', David Gauntlett's approach to examining the role of television in the perception of environmental matters among children (Gauntlett, 1996) has much in common with the Glasgow studies. This includes the use of practical exercises (here, video production) to engage with questions concerning children's attitudes towards both the issue itself and media representations of it (some aspects of the general methodology are explained more fully by Gauntlett's colleagues in MacGregor and Morrison, 1995). Gauntlett argues as follows:

> ... for a subject where the audience have received most of their input on the subject from the mass media, as it was established was the case with the environment and children in this study, then the videos which they produce can be assumed to reflect their understanding of which issues and angles are the most pertinent and pressing; and this can be presumed to have been influenced by the media.
>
> (Gauntlett, 1996: 85)

Clearly, these assumptions indicate that the approach is not without interpretative hazards, but, like the Glasgow work, it represents a merging of 'reception' and 'influence' agendas in a manner that is able to go some way towards locating the force and direction of media accounts within the broader constituents and contours of public meaning.

Ellen Seiter's (1999) study of cultures of viewing and attitudes towards television in different social settings – including preschool, a parents' support group and a fundamentalist Christian community – makes its original contribution by sensitively exploring the terms of everyday concern about television, particularly the concern of parents about children's viewing (to an extent complementing that work I noted earlier which focuses on the children's own experience). Seiter offers a well-documented account of how 'lay theories' of media influence work to inform family and community life and to make many of those she talks with critical and fearful. Whilst not sharing the majority of her respondents' fears, and wanting always to locate them within specific conditions of social and domestic living, Seiter develops a kind of 'ethnography of anxiety' which adds a valuable new dimension to academic ideas about television's cultural identity and about popular apprehensions of its power.

I suggested earlier that it is hard for research on violence to work with an agenda directly to do with the conditions and terms of knowledge (rather than of emotional reaction). In an excellent study, Schlesinger *et al.* (1992) attempted to do this by centrally placing in their respondent data the accounts of women who had been the victims of violence themselves and assessing these alongside the accounts of women who had not. The research findings offer a detailed survey of the range of memories and understandings, as well as emotions, that screened depictions can generate, as 'television' is read against 'reality' and sometimes *vice versa*. No one who has read the study could doubt the potentially powerful consequentiality of dramatic portrayal in our society, even allowing for the special interest of the research in the more sensitized viewer.

In fact, since most concern about violent depictions is focused on forms of dramatic entertainment which aim to *please*, a real absence in the research literature has been an engagement with viewing *pleasures*. There is much to be done here, partly in developing a revised version of the influence agenda and partly in pursuit of a new dimension to reception studies. Hill's highly original approach (1997) to the kinds of cultural pleasure audiences get from viewing violent films suggests one way forward, which would entail getting to know far more about the satisfactions given by enacted violence and some of the factors of theme and treatment which play a part in encouraging regular viewing. For instance, a better sense of the present 'limits of taste' as perceived by different audience groupings and further enquiry into viewers' moral framings of their own viewing (an illuminating aspect of Hill's study, comparable in some respects to the explorations of Seiter, discussed above) would be valuable. This is particularly the case in view of the widespread hypocrisy and cultural naivety that continue to accompany the 'media violence' issue and that, while they may not be directly reproduced in academic enquiry, continue to exert strong pressures on press and public reception of findings (a point well brought out in Barker and Petley, 1997).

Conclusions: the future of 'influence'

The search for the direct consequences of media upon individual consciousness and behaviour in the form of 'message x was the determinate and traceable cause of thought or action y' is largely futile, given the degree of interpenetration between media, culture and everyday life. Researchers of the early period often recognized this, at least partially, and attempted to respond to it by a conceptual and technical refinement of their study designs in order to cope with the degrees of indirectness and variability they judged to be at work. Since then, reception studies have emphasized the nature of mediation as a symbolic inter- action in which the interpretative activity of audiences, drawing on varying cul- tural resources, is a constitutive factor. But all this should not stop us from being interested in, and investigating as closely as we can, the kinds of consequence media systems have for the terms of public life and private consciousness, even if there is a relationship of mutuality connecting all three. They produce these consequences routinely as they variously and selectively respond to elements in the 'life of society' (indeed, the 'life of the world') and initiate others, within dif- ferent generic recipes. They provide the defining *context* for the modern public and are primary institutional *sources* for the ways in which modern experience is themed, classified and imaged. Research always needs to locate its specific enquiries, its theories and its hypotheses, within this setting of continuous, mun- dane influence which is both routinely 'directed' (e.g. advertising, party political broadcasts) and routinely 'circumstantial' (as in our selective deployment of all kinds of materials), with the interplay between the two modes being itself a mat- ter of routine, sometimes self-consciously and perhaps anxiously monitored, sometimes not. If research loses sight of this setting, it is in danger of working with what is finally a naive and limited sense of the significant and with an unhelpful tendency to think about the media's impact *upon* society rather than media's consequentiality *within* society.

I have used the term 'resource' at several points in this chapter, but to see the media's influential functions simply as being a matter of 'resourcing knowledge' is to work with too passive a general sense of how media operate, as the raw material for interpretative design and purposive use. It is the opposite error to seeing them as autonomous agencies which directly determine the nature of society according to a malign plan. For, embedded though they are within the intricate contours of culture, media systems have an economically and socially privileged role in the organization of popular knowledge and of pleasure. It therefore makes perfectly good sense for people, quite apart from any suspicions they may entertain about 'intentions', to be alert to the volume, character, ori- entation and symbolic usage of what is in circulation, to its various official and corporate sources and to how it is regulated.

If the risk for many pioneer studies was a notion of influence too 'hard' and precise in its presumed lines of causality, too conclusively plottable across the pattern of variables, the risk for new studies is that of dispersal into a 'soft' com- plex of interacting tendencies, defeating any programme of systematic investi- gation wishing to go beyond the merely suggestive. I hope to have shown that in recent work study can find several pointers towards a focused and disciplined engagement and I have wanted to suggest that the methodological quest, across different traditions, is more astute and less quixotic than is sometimes por- trayed, even if it has sometimes been hampered by the grandness of its aspira- tions. (And also perhaps by the expectations of those funding it!) Once again, I recommend the consulting of more detailed overviews than mine and selective readings across the full diversity of primary work.

'Influence' has a history of confusion as well as of dispute – progress towards greater clarity and differentiations of kind and scale are certainly needed, together with a more explicit recognition in research of this troubled conceptual heritage. But it continues to indicate an indispensable point of reference in media research, as I suggested at the start of this chapter. Once we stop asking questions about it, struggling to answer them with research tools that seem best to fit our various partial and selective agendas, a great deal of purpose disappears from whatever other questions we choose to ask about the media, especially those about interpretation.

References

ADORNO, T., 1991: *The Culture Industry: Selected Essays on Mass Culture*. London: Routledge.

ALTHUSSER, L., 1971: *Lenin and Philosophy and Other Essays*. London: New Left Books.

BANDURA, A., ROSS, D. and ROSS, S.A., 1963: 'Imitation of film-mediated aggressive models', *Journal of Personality and Social Psychology 66*: 3–11.

BARKER, M. and PETLEY, J. (eds), 1997: *Ill Effects: The Media/Violence Debate*. London: Routledge.

BLUMLER, J. and GUREVITCH, M., 1982: 'The political effects of mass communication' in M. Gurevitch, T. Bennett, J. Curran and J. Woollacott (eds), *Culture, Society and the Media*. London: Methuen: 236–67

BLUMLER, J. AND KATZ, E., 1974: *The Uses of Mass Communication*. London and Beverly Hills: Sage.

BRYANT, J. and ZILLMAN, D. (eds), 1994: *Media Effects: Advances in Theory and Research*. Hillsdale, NJ: Lawrence Erlbaum.

BUCKINGHAM, D., 1996: *Moving Images: Understanding Children's Emotional Responses to TV*. Manchester: Manchester University Press.

CANTRIL, H., GAUDET, H. and HERZOG. H. 1940: *The Invasion From Mars: A Study in the Psychology of Panic*. Princeton, NJ: Princeton University Press.

CORNER, J., 1991: 'Meaning, genre and context: the problematics of knowledge in the new audience studies' in J. Curran and M. Gurevitch (eds), *Mass Media and Society*. London: Edward Arnold: 267–84.

——, 1995: *Television Form and Public Address*. London: Edward Arnold.

——, 1996: 'Reappraising reception: aims, concepts and methods' in J. Curran and M. Gurevitch (eds), *Mass Media and Society*, 2nd edn, London: Edward Arnold: 280–304.

CORNER, J., RICHARDSON, K. and FENTON, N., 1990: *Nuclear Reactions: Form and Response in Public Issue Television*. London: John Libbey.

CUMBERBATCH, G. and HOWITT, D., 1989: *A Measure of Uncertainty: The Effects of the Mass Media*. London: John Libbey.

CUMBERBATCH, G., 1998: 'Effects' in A. Briggs and P. Cobley (eds), *The Media: An Introduction*. London: Longman: 262–74.

CURRAN, J. and SPARKS, C., 1991: 'Press and popular culture', *Media, Culture and Society* 13(2): 215–37.

CURRAN, J., 1990: 'The new revisionism in mass communication research: a reappraisal' in *European Journal of Communication* 5(2/3): 135–64.

DAHLGREN, P., 1998: 'What's the meaning of this?', *Media, Culture and Society*. 10(3): 285–301.

DEWEY, J., 1927: *The Public and its Problems*. New York: Henry Holt and Co.

DICKINSON, R., Harindranath, R. and Linné, O. (eds), 1998: *Approaches to Audiences: A Reader*. London: Arnold.

ELDRIDGE, J., Kitzinger, J. and Williams, K., 1997: *The Mass Media and Power in Modern Britain*. Oxford: Oxford University Press.

FISKE, J. and HARTLEY, J., 1978: *Reading Television*. London: Methuen.

FISKE, J., 1987: *Television Culture*. London: Methuen.

GAUNTLETT, D., 1995: *Moving Experiences: Understanding Television's Influences and Effects*. London: John Libbey.

——, 1996: *Video Critical: Children, the Environment and Media Power*. Luton: John Libbey.

GAVIN, N. (ed.), 1998: *The Economy, Media and Public Knowledge*. London: Leicester University Press.

GERBNER, G., GROSS, L., MORGAN, M. and SIGNORIELLI, N., 1994: 'Growing up with Television: The Cultivation Perspective' in Bryant, J. and Zillman, D. (eds), *Media Effects: Advances in Theory and Research*. Hillsdale, NJ: Lawrence Erlbaum.

HAY, J, GROSSBERG, L. and WARTELLA, E. (eds), 1996: *The Audience and its Landscape*. Boulder, Colorado: Westview.

HILL, A., 1997: *Shocking Entertainment*. Luton: John Libbey.

HIMMELWEIT, H.T., OPPENHEIM, A.N. and VINCE, P., 1958: *Television and the Child*. Oxford: Oxford University Press.

HODGE, R. and TRIPP, D., 1986: *Children and Television: A Semiotic Approach*. Cambridge: Polity.

IYENGAR, S. and KINDER, D.R., 1987: *News That Matters: Television and American Opinion*. Chicago: University of Chicago Press.

KATZ, E. and LAZARSFELD, P., 1955: *Personal Influence: The Part Played by People in the Flow of Mass Communication*. Glencoe: Free Press.

KITZINGER, J., 1998: 'Resisting the message: the extent and limits of media influence' in Miller *et al.*, *The Circuit of Mass Communication*. London: Sage: 192–212.

——, 1999: 'A sociology of media power: key issues in audience reception research' in G. Philo (ed.), *Message Received*. London: Addison Wesley Longman.

LAZARSFELD, P., BERELSON, B. and GAUDET, H., 1944: *The People's Choice*. New York: Duell, Pearce and Sloan.

LEWIS, J., 1985 'Decoding television news' in P. Drummond and R. Paterson (eds), *Television in Transition*. London: British Film Institute: 205–34.

——, 1991: *The Ideological Octopus: Explorations into the Television Audience*. New York and London: Routledge.

LIPPMANN, W., 1922: *Public Opinion*. New York: Macmillan.

LIVINGSTONE, S., 1996: 'On the continuing problems of media effects' in J. Curran and M. Gurevitch (eds), *Mass Media and Society*, 2nd edn, 305–24.

——, 1998a: *Making Sense of Television*, 2nd edn, London: Routledge.

——, 1998b: 'Mediated childhoods' in *European Journal of Communication* 13(4): 435–56.

MACGREGOR B. and MORRISON, D., 1995: 'From focus groups to editing groups: a new method of reception analysis', *Media, Culture and Society* 17(1): 141–50.

MCGUIGAN, J., 1992: *Cultural Populism*. London: Routledge.

MCLEOD, J., KOSICKI, G.M. and MCLEOD, D.M., 1994: 'The expanding boundaries of political communication effects' in B. Jennings and D. Zillman (eds), *Media Effects: Advances in Theory and Research*. Hillsdale, NJ: Lawrence Erlbaum: 123–62.

MCLEOD, J., KOSICKI, G.M. and PAN, Z., 1991: 'On understanding and misunderstanding media effects' in J. Curran and M. Gurevitch (eds), *Mass Media and Society*. London: Arnold: 235–66.

MCNAIR, B., 1996: *Mediated Sex*. London: Arnold.

MCQUAIL, D., 1977: 'The influence and effects of mass media' in J. Curran, M. Gurevitch and J. Woollacott (eds), *Mass Communication and Society*. London: Arnold: 70–94.

——, 1994: *Mass Communication Theory: An Introduction*, 3rd edn, London: Sage.

MAYHEW, L., 1997: *The New Public*. Cambridge: Cambridge University Press.

MILLER, D. and PHILO, G., 1996: 'The media do influence us', *Sight and Sound*. December: 18–20.

MILLER, D., KITZINGER, J., WILLIAMS, K. and BEHARRELL, P., 1998: *The Circuit of Mass Communication*. London: Sage.

MOORES, S., 1993: *Interpreting Audiences*. London: Sage.

MORLEY, D., 1980: *The 'Nationwide' Audience*. London: British Film Institute.

——, 1992: *Television Audiences and Cultural Studies*. London: Routledge.

MORRISON, D., 1998: *The Search For a Method*. Luton: University of Luton Press.

NEUMAN, W., JUST, M. and CRIGLER, A., 1992: *Common Knowledge: News and the Construction of Political Meaning*. Chicago: Chicago University Press.

NEWSOM, E., 1994: 'Video violence and the protection of children', Memorandum 13 in House of Commons Home Affairs Committee, *Video Violence and Young Offenders*, Session 1993–4, Fourth Report, London: HMSO: 45–59.

NORDENSTRENG, K., 1968: 'Communication research in the United States: a critical perspective' in *Gazette XIV* (3): 207–16.

PHILO, G. (ed.), 1996: *Media and Mental Distress*. London: Longman.

——, (ed.), 1999: *Message Received*. London: Addison Wesley Longman.

PHILO, G. and MILLER, D. (eds), 2000: *Market Killings*. London: Longman.

PHILO, G., 1990: *Seeing and Believing*. London: Routledge.

——, 1999: 'Children and film/tv/video violence' in Philo (ed.), *Message Received*. London: Addison Wesley Longman: 35–53.

REILLY, J., 1999: '"Just another food scare": public understanding and the BSE crisis' in Philo, G. (ed.), *Message Received*. London: Addison Wesley Longman: 128–45.

RICHARDSON, K. and CORNER, J., 1986: 'Reading reception: mediation and transparency in viewers' accounts of a TV programme', *Media, Culture and Society* 8(4): 485–508.

SCHEUFELE, D., 1999: 'Framing as a theory of media effects', *Journal of Communication* 49(1): 103–22.

SCHLESINGER, P., DOBASH, R.E., DOBASH, R.P. and WEAVER, C., 1992: *Women Viewing Violence*. London: British Film Institute.

SEITER, E., 1999: *Television and New Media Audiences*: Oxford: Clarendon Press.

SHANAHAN, J. and MORGAN, M., 1999: *Television and its Viewers*. Cambridge: Cambridge University Press.

VINE, I., 1997: 'The dangerous psycho-logics of media "effects"' in Barker, M. and Petley, J. (eds), *Ill Effects: The Media/Violence Debate*. London: Routledge.

WRONG, D., 1998: 'The concept of power: boundless or delimited?' Ch. 4 of *The Modern Condition*, Stanford: Stanford University Press: 36–46.

Index